THE ROUGH GUIDE TO
CAMBODIA

ROUGH
GUIDES

This sixth edition updated by
Meera Dattani and Gavin Thomas

Contents

Introduction to
Cambodia

Cambodia is a small country with a big history. Now a modest player on the world stage, this was once the seat of one of Asia's most magnificent early civilizations, the mighty Khmer Empire of Angkor, whose legendary temples continue to provide a touchstone of national identity – as well as attracting millions of visitors every year. Away from the temples, much of the country remains refreshingly untouristed and, in many places, largely unexplored.

Cambodia's sleepy **towns** and cities are a delight, with their faded colonial architecture and old-fashioned charm, while in the countryside a host of memorable **landscapes** await, from the mighty Mekong River and great Tonle Sap lake to the remote forested highlands of Rattanakiri, Mondulkiri and the Cardamom Mountains. Down south, in complete contrast, the coast serves up a beguiling cocktail of nonstop-party hedonism, idyllic beaches and magical islands.

Much of Cambodia's appeal derives from its slightly anachronistic, faintly time-warped character. Compared to the far more populous and economically developed countries of Thailand and Vietnam that hem it in on either side, Cambodia remains an essentially **rural** society, and something of a regional backwater. The country's provincial hinterlands appear to have changed little in generations, offering a refreshing throwback to an older and simpler era (from the outside at least), with beautiful stilted wooden houses set amid a patchwork of rice paddies and sugar palms. And although living standards for most of the population are basic in the extreme, Cambodians as a whole remain among Asia's friendliest and most welcoming people.

It's perhaps this warmth and hospitality which most impresses many visitors to Cambodia – and which is all the more astonishing given the country's tragic recent past. For many, Cambodia remains synonymous with the bloody excesses of the murderous **Khmer Rouge** regime, whose delusional leaders succeeded in killing or causing the deaths of perhaps two million or more of their fellow citizens – around twenty percent of the population. Not until 1998 were the Khmer Rouge driven from their final strongholds,

ABOVE FRIEZE OF DANCERS, PREAH KHAN TEMPLE

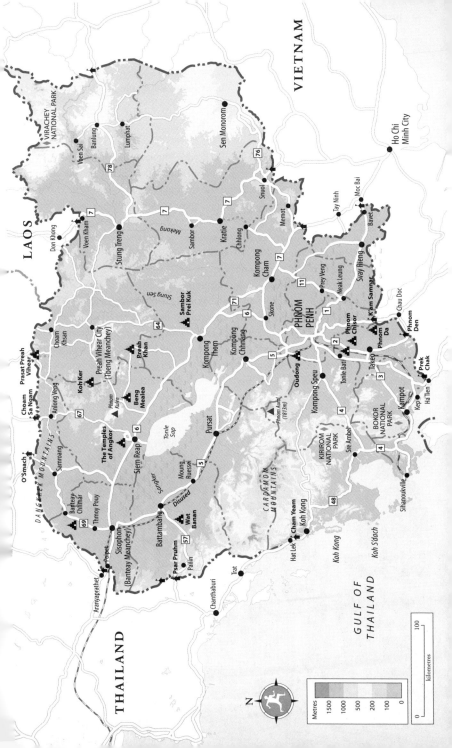

THAILAND

LAOS

VIETNAM

VIRACHEY
NATIONAL PARK

Veen Sai
Banlung
Lumphat
78
Sen Monorom
76
Ho Chi
Minh City

Don Khong
Voen Kham
7
Stung Treng
7
Sambor
Kratie
7
Chhlong
Snuol
Memot
Tay Ninh
Moc Bai
Bavet

Mekong
Kompong
Cham
7
11
Prey Veng
Neak Leung
Svay Rieng
Chau Doc

Stung Sen
Sambor
Prei Kuk
71
Skone
6
PHNOM
PENH
1
K'ham Samnar
Phnom
Chisor
Phnom
Den

Choam
Khsan
Preah Vihear City
(Tbeng Meanchey)
Preah
Khan
64
Kompong
Thom
Kompong
Chhnang
5
2
Phnom
Da
Phnom Den

Prasat Preah
Vihear
Koh Ker
Beng
Mealea
Phnom
Kulen
Oudong
Takeo
Prek
Chak
Ha Tien

Choam
Sa Ngam
Anlong Veng
67
The Temples
of Angkor
6
Siem Reap
Tonle Sap
Pursat
Phnom Aural
(1813m)
Kompong Speu
3
Kampot
Kep

O'Smach
Samroang
Sangker
Moung
Ruessei
5
KIRIROM
NATIONAL
PARK
Sre Ambel
BOKOR
NATIONAL
PARK
Sihanoukville

Banteay
Chhmar
Thmoy Pouy
69
Battambang
Disused
Wat
Banan
57
48
Cham Yeam
Koh Kong
Koh Kong
Koh Sdach

DANGRÊK MOUNTAINS
Sisophon
(Banteay Meanchey)
Psar Pruhm
Pailin
Hat Lek

Aranyaprathet
Poipet
CARDAMOM
MOUNTAINS

Trat
Chanthaburi

GULF OF
THAILAND

N

Metres
1500
1000
500
200
100
0

0   100
kilometres

and even now many of their former cadres occupy positions of power and responsibility, not least premier Hun Sen, the nation's leader since 1985. Unsurprisingly, emotional scars from this period run deep and through every layer of Cambodian society – the memory of a nightmare from which the country is only slowly and painfully awakening.

Where to go

Dubbed the "Pearl of Asia" during its colonial heydey, **Phnom Penh** remains one of Southeast Asia's most engaging capitals: big enough (and with sufficient anarchic traffic and urban edge) to get the pulse racing, but still retaining a distinct small-town charm, its tree-lined streets fringed with ramshackle old French-colonial buildings and dotted with rustic temples and bustling markets. The heart of the city is the beautiful riverfront, backdropped by the magnificent Royal Palace and Silver Pagoda's colourful stupas, while further afield, the contrastingly sombre Toul Sleng Genocide Museum provides harrowing reminders of the country's tragic recent past.

The main reason that most people come to Cambodia, however, is to visit the world-famous **temples of Angkor**. Dozens of magnificent monuments dot the countryside here, rising out of the enveloping forest like the archetypal lost-in-the-jungle ancient ruins of every Hollywood film-maker's wildest dreams. Top of most visitors' lists are the unforgettable **Angkor Wat**, with its five soaring corncob towers; the surreal **Bayon**, plastered with hundreds of superhuman faces; and the jungle temple of **Ta Prohm**, its crumbling ruins clamped in the grip of giant kapok trees. It's also well worth heading further afield to escape the crowds and visit other Angkorian monuments, including beautiful **Banteay Srei**, covered in an

extravagent flourish of carvings; the jungle-smothered ruins of **Beng Mealea**; the sprawling city-temple complex of **Koh Ker**; and, especially, the magnificent **Prasat Preah Vihear**, dramatically situated on top of a mountain above the Thai border. Gateway to the temples is vibrant **Siem Reap** – Cambodia's principal tourist town, but retaining plenty of idiosyncratic charm, and well worth a visit in its own right. From Siem Reap, looping around the great **Tonle Sap lake** – an attraction in itself, home to dozens of remarkable floating villages – brings you to **Battambang**, one of the country's most engaging cities.

Cambodia's **east** retains something of a frontier atmosphere, with the majestic Mekong River bounding one side of the region and the remote highlands of Rattanakiri and Mondulkiri to the west. All routes into the region pass through the atmospheric colonial-era Mekong-side town of **Kompong Cham**, beyond which the road continues north along the river to **Kratie**, where there's a similarly languid riverside ambience and a small population of rare Irrawaddy dolphins just upstream. Getting out to the remote northeastern provincial capitals of **Banlung** and **Sen Monorom** takes more time and effort but is worth it for a sight of Cambodia's remote forested uplands, which (despite rampant logging) remain home to abundant wildlife and the nation's diminishing indigenous chunchiet communities.

A world away in scenery and atmosphere from pretty much everywhere else in the country, Cambodia's rapidly developing **coast** offers an increasingly upbeat and hedonistic taste of tropical beach life. The biggest and busiest town here is **Sihanoukville**, looking increasingly like a miniature slice of Thailand, with beaches and bars aplenty. Just offshore lies a string of more tranquil (though also rapidly developing) islands, while just outside Sihanoukville are the idyllic bays, beaches and mangrove forests of the lush **Ream National Park**.

LEFT BANTEAY SREI TEMPLE

FACT FILE

• Cambodia is about one and a half times the **size** of England – roughly the same area as the US state of Oklahoma.

• Cambodia's population is around **16 million**, of which 98 percent is Khmer. The remainder consists of ethnic Chinese and Vietnamese (together just over one percent), the Cham and the chunchiet.

• **Theravada Buddhism** is practised by 96 percent of the population, alongside some animism and ancestor worship; the Cham are Muslim.

• Cambodia is a **constitutional monarchy**, with an elected government comprising two houses of parliament, the National Assembly and the Senate.

• Average **annual income** is just $1200 per capita, making Cambodia the second-poorest country in Southeast Asia (after Myanmar – and compared to a per capita income of $5800 in neighbouring Thailand). Average life expectancy, though improving, is just 64 years.

• Cambodia has one of the world's highest rates of **deforestation**. Logging increased by almost 15 percent between 2001 and 2014 – a loss of over 5500 square miles of forest.

• Cambodia has changed its **name** more frequently than almost any other country in the world. Within the past half-century it's been known variously as the Khmer Republic (1970–75), Democratic Kampuchea (under the Khmer Rouge, 1976–79) and the People's Republic of Kampuchea (1979–89). It's now officially called the Kingdom of Cambodia.

• The **Cambodian flag** is embellished with an image of Angkor Wat – one of only two national flags in the world (along with Afghanistan) with a picture of a building on it.

AVERAGE MAXIMUM DAILY TEMPERATURES (°C) AND AVERAGE MONTHLY RAINFALL (MM)

	Jan	Feb	Mar	Apr	May	Jun	Jul	Aug	Sep	Oct	Nov	Dec
PHNOM PENH												
°C	31	32	34	35	34	33	32	32	31	30	30	30
Rainfall (mm)	10	10	45	80	120	150	165	160	215	240	135	55

Quieter coastal destinations include attractive **Kampot**, with its mixed French and Chinese influences, and the beguiling resort of **Kep**, with a minuscule beach and atmosphere of faded gentility. Backdropping the heavily touristed coast, the contrastingly remote and difficult-to-reach **Cardamom Mountains**, best accessed from the southwestern province of **Koh Kong**, provide unspoilt upland scenery and pockets of remarkable biodiversity.

When to go

Cambodia is warm all year round, though there are several distinct seasons. There is little rain between November and May, the so-called **dry season**, which itself divides into two distinct phases. The **cool season** (Nov–Feb) is the peak time for tourism – mild enough to explore the temples in comfort but warm enough to sunbathe by the coast. Humidity and temperatures rise slightly during the **hot season** (March–May), with Phnom Penh and Battambang seeing peak daytime temperatures of 33–35°C. This is the time to hit the coast, although Angkor is usually bakingly hot. Visiting during the **rainy season** (roughly June–Oct) can present certain practical challenges, but it is also a fascinating time to see the country as it transforms into a waterlogged expanse of tropical green under the daily monsoon deluges (the rains fall mainly in the afternoons; mornings are generally dry). Getting around (particularly in September and October) isn't always easy: dirt roads turn to mud and flooding is commonplace. Not surprisingly it's also the quietest time for tourism (even Angkor is relatively quiet) and the countryside is at its lushest.

Author picks

Our authors spent months researching this latest edition of the *Rough Guide to Cambodia*, travelling extensively in their attempts to unearth the best the country has to offer. Here are a few of their favourite experiences.

Running amok The national dish, *amok* (p.29) offers a quintessential taste of Cambodia. Although no two recipes are the same, the best *amoks* are soothingly mild, with intense lemongrass flavours, seasoned with coconut and galangal and a hint of spice. Try one at *Le Tonle Tourism Centre* (p.224), *Sugar Palm* (p.152) or *Frizz* (p.84).

Shopping for kramas Hunting for *kramas* (p.38) is a great way to explore Cambodia's markets. Kompong Cham market (p.215), the Angkor Night Market in Siem Reap (p.155) and Phnom Penh's Russian Market (p.92) offer fertile *krama*-hunting territory – or visit Phnom Srok (p.127) to see them being produced.

Lesser-known temples Some of the finest temples are relatively free from crowds. The magnificent Pre Rup (p.182) and Bakong (p.187) see only a fraction of the visitors who overrun Angkor Wat and the Bayon. And for a real Indiana Jones experience, head for the remote temples of Banteay Chhmar (p.128) and Preah Khan (Kompong Thom) (p.195).

Taking to the water Lakes and rivers are writ large on the map of Cambodia. Be sure to see the Tonle Sap floating villages (p.109, p.112 & p.158), go dolphin-watching or kayaking on the Mekong (p.221 & p.224) or the Tatai River (p.267), or relax on a sunset river cruise in Kampot (p.276) and Phnom Penh (p.59).

Desert island paradise It doesn't take much effort to find your own strip of pure white sand on one of Cambodia's idyllic islands. Scene-stealers include Long Set Beach on Koh Rong (p.260), Lazy Beach on Koh Rong Samloem (p.260), the beaches of Ream National Park (p.264) and Koh Totang's pretty shores (p.265).

> Our author recommendations don't end here. We've flagged up our favourite places – a perfectly sited hotel, an atmospheric café, a special restaurant – throughout the guide, highlighted with the ★ symbol.

LEFT TRADITIONAL WEAVING IN MONDULKIRI **RIGHT FROM TOP** KOH RONG SAMLOEM; CHICKEN AMOK; PREAH KHAN TEMPLE

18

things not to miss

It's not possible to see everything that Cambodia has to offer in one trip – and we don't suggest you try. What follows is a selective and subjective taste of the country's highlights: natural attractions and cultural treasures, serene beaches and vibrant towns, and – of course – the finest of the temples at Angkor and elsewhere. Each highlight has a page reference to take you straight into the Guide, where you can find out more. Coloured numbers refer to chapters in the Guide section.

1

1 ROYAL PALACE AND SILVER PAGODA
Page 59
The extravagant Royal Palace and Silver Pagoda, in the heart of Phnom Penh, are home to fabulous murals and a treasure-trove of Khmer sculpture.

2 KAMPOT
Page 274
Blissfully unhurried southern backwater with a plethora of idyllic guesthouses and restaurants beside the Kampot River.

3 BANTEAY SREI
Page 188
One of the smallest but most perfect of all Angkor's temples, constructed from delicate rose-pink sandstone and covered in a positive riot of intricate carvings.

4 ANGKOR WAT
Page 164
This unforgettable temple, crowned with soaring towers and embellished with intricate bas-reliefs, represents the zenith of Khmer architecture.

5 OTRES BEACH
Page 250
Sihanoukville's furthest flung beach is mellower (and prettier) than its sandy in-town siblings; perfect for a few days of idle beachcombing.

6 IRRAWADDY DOLPHINS
Page 221

These rare mammals live in small groups along a stretch of the Mekong in the northeast.

7 TOUL SLENG AND CHOEUNG EK
Pages 69 & 100

Harrowing monuments to Cambodia's grisly past during the Khmer Rouge's murderous rule.

8 ANGKOR THOM
Page 170

Angkor's greatest walled city, entered through magnificent gateways and housing some of the country's finest monuments, including the haunting Bayon.

9 SEN MONOROM
Page 238

Trek through the jungle with elephants and visit remote ethnic-minority villages from this laidback town in the remote highlands of eastern Cambodia.

10 APSARA DANCING
Page 154

Khmer classical dance at its most elegantly stylized, with beautifully costumed performers evoking the legendary apsaras of Hindu mythology.

11 TONLE SAP LAKE
Page 157

The watery heart of rural Cambodia, this miniature inland sea is dotted with dozens of traditional floating and stilted villages, many inhabited by the country's ethnic Vietnamese.

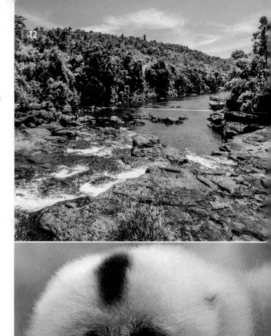

12 TATAI RIVER
Pages 267 & 269

Kayak, trek or enjoy sunset cruises along the mangrove-lined Tatai River in the Cardamom Mountains.

13 WILDLIFE AND BIRDWATCHING
Pages 233, 239 & 160

Walking with the elephants in Mondulkiri, gibbon-spotting in Rattanakiri, birdwatching around the Tonle Sap – Cambodia offers a wealth of natural attractions.

14 CAMBODIAN CUISINE
Page 26

Cambodia's cuisine offers plenty of surprises – and there are numerous courses available to help you unravel the secrets of Khmer cooking.

15 PSAR TOUL TOM POUNG
Page 92

Wonderful Phnom Penh city market, packed with vibrant silks and curios.

16 REAM NATIONAL PARK
Page 264

Abundant wildlife, secluded beaches and bays, and the beautiful mangrove-fringed Prek Touek Sap River.

17 TREKKING IN RATTANAKIRI
Page 233

Trek into the forested highlands of Rattanakiri, home to tall trees, rare wildlife and the indigenous chunchiet.

18 BANTEAY CHHMAR
Page 128

One of Cambodia's largest but least-touristed temples, with majestic jungle-covered ruins and extraordinary arrays of carvings.

Itineraries

Cambodia is a small country by Asian standards, but you'll still need at least a month to really see everything it has to offer. The rapidly improving road network means that it has never been easier to explore, making many formerly remote destinations much more accessible. That said, getting from A to B can still be time-consuming, and the country is best taken at a leisurely pace.

THE GRAND TOUR

Two weeks suffice to get a taste of the best that Cambodia has to offer, from the great temples of Angkor to the hedonistic beaches of the south.

❶ **Phnom Penh** Acclimatize in the vibrant but endearingly small-scale capital. **See p.50**

❷ **Kratie** Head to the engagingly somnolent French-colonial town of Kratie for a taste of riverside life next to the magical Mekong, with rare Irrawaddy dolphins, floating villages, river islands and flooded forests aplenty. **See p.219**

❸ **Siem Reap and Angkor** Settle down to a few days (or more) in lively Siem Reap, exploring the magnificent Angkor temples and the floating villages of the Tonle Sap. **See p.138**

❹ **Preah Vihear and further flung temples** Venture out to the stunning mountaintop temple of Preah Vihear, perhaps with a side trip to the jungle temple of Beng Mealea and the vast ruined citadel of Koh Ker. **See p.197**

❺ **Battambang** Colonial riverside town with laidback nightlife and the quaint bamboo railway. **See p.113**

❻ **Sihanoukville and the islands** Venture south to Cambodia's coastal party town, a good base for some lovely offshore islands. **See p.247**

❼ **Kep's offshore islands** Use Kep as a jump-off point for sleepy Rabbit Island (Koh Tonsay), among others. **See p.286**

❽ **Kampot** Chill out in this pretty, laidback riverside town, a good base for the picturesque surrounding province. **See p.274**

WILD CAMBODIA

Cambodia boasts an outstanding array of natural attractions, from the great Mekong River to remote upland forests.

❶ **Kratie** Go dolphin-spotting at nearby Kampie, then take to a kayak or bike to explore the marvellous river islands, flooded forests and floating villages of the Mekong. **See p.219**

❷ **Banlung** Trek into the forests of Virachey National Park and explore the waterfalls and volcanic lake of Yeak Laom. **See p.230**

❸ **Sen Monorom** Walk with elephants at the Elephant Valley Project and go birdwatching or gibbon-spotting in the pristine tracts of forest surrounding Sen Monorom. **See p.238**

❹ **Beng Mealea** Visit the jungle-smothered ruins of Beng Mealea temple – looking much as it must have done when the first Western explorers stumbled upon it a century ago. **See p.192**

❺ **Phnom Kulen** Discover where the great Angkorian empire began at the remote mountain shrine of Phnom Kulen. **See p.191**

ABOVE RABBIT ISLAND

❻ Tonle Sap Take the ferry from Siem Reap to Battambang across the great Tonle Sap lake, which during the rains becomes the largest freshwater lake in Southeast Asia. **See p.157**

❼ Chi Phat Head to this village in the southern Cardamoms for organized hikes through upland forests to waterfalls and ancient sites. **See p.270**

❽ Ream Spy shore birds and dolphins as you explore the lush mangroves and beaches of this beautiful national park by boat. **See p.264**

UNDISCOVERED CAMBODIA

There might be some two million visitors a year clambering over the ruins of Angkor, but much of Cambodia remains undiscovered.

❶ Stung Treng Rewarding, little-visited stretch of the Cambodian Mekong, complete with dolphins, flooded forests, ancient ruins and spectacular waterfalls. **See p.225**

❷ Preah Vihear City Take the cross-country highway through Cambodia's northern backcountry to this remote provincial capital. **See p.195**

❸ Anlong Veng Notorious for its associations with the infamous Pol Pot, the dusty town of Anlong Veng and the nearby Dangrek

Mountains provide fascinating glimpses of the final days of the Khmer Rouge. **See p.201**

❹ Banteay Chhmar For a truly authentic lost-in-the-jungle temple experience, ride the bumpy road from Sisophon to the vast temple complex of Banteay Chhmar, buried in the forests of Cambodia's far northwest. **See p.128**

❺ Kompong Chhnang For an alternative to the increasingly touristed floating villages of Siem Reap, make for the floating villages just outside Kompong Chhnang. **See p.106**

❻ Angkor Borei Stuffed with statues, ceramics and photographs of the excavations, Angkor Borei's fascinating museum makes the trip to the remains of this Funan-era city highly worthwhile. **See p.289**

❼ Koh S'dach archipelago These picturesque islands offer a truly authentic taste of coastal Cambodia. **See p.265**

❽ Koh Kong: the Areng Valley The biodiverse Areng Valley, deep in the Cardamoms, is home to the endangered Siamese crocodile and prime territory for trekking, kayaking and mountain biking. It's accessible on tours from Koh Kong but you'll need at least four days – better still a week – to do it justice. **See p.268**

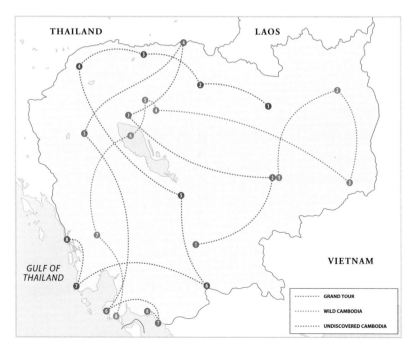

A TUK-TUK DRIVER IN PHNOM PENH

Basics

Getting there

There are no direct flights to Cambodia from Europe, North America, Australasia or South Africa, so if you plan to fly into the country you'll need to get a connecting flight from elsewhere in Southeast or East Asia.

There are direct flights to **Phnom Penh** from an increasing number of cities in the region including Kuala Lumpur, Singapore, Seoul, Bangkok, Vientiane, Ho Chi Minh City, and several cities in China (including frequent connections with Hong Kong). Alternatively, it's also possible to fly direct to **Siem Reap** from Singapore, Bangkok, Ho Chi Minh City, Kuala Lumpur and a number of other Asian destinations.

Flights from the UK and Ireland

There are plenty of daily flights, many nonstop, from **London Heathrow** to Southeast Asian cities, with some airlines offering connections to Phnom Penh. The most direct routes are currently via Bangkok with Thai Airways (around 11–12hr from London, plus another 1hr on to Phnom Penh), and via Dubai and Yangon with Emirates. There are also slightly more circuitous one- or two-stop connections via Kuala Lumpur and Ho Chi Minh City (Saigon), plus a growing number of two-stop connections via the Gulf. From **Ireland**, it's a matter of either getting a cheap connection to London Heathrow or flying to Cambodia via a different European (or possibly Gulf) hub.

Thai Airways (Ⓦthaiairways.com), Singapore Airlines (Ⓦsingaporeair.com) and Malaysia Airlines (Ⓦmalaysia-airlines.com) offer some of the most competitive fares to Cambodia, with return fares to Phnom Penh starting at around £530.

Flights from the US and Canada

Flying from the **east coast** of North America generally involves a stop in either Europe or the Gulf, followed by another change of plane in Asia.

There are also currently a few one-stop options from New York travelling via Shanghai, Guangzhou, Tapei or Seoul, although these aren't generally any quicker than more direct two-stop options. From the **west coast**, it's quicker and cheaper to fly westward via an Asian city – there are currently one-stop options from Los Angeles via Hong Kong, Guangzhou, Shanghai, Seoul and Taipei. Return fares from both the east and west coasts start at around US$1100. Total journey times from the east coast are from around 24hr upwards, and from the west coast from around 20hr, depending on connections.

From Canada, there are one-stop flights from Toronto and Vancouver via Taipei, Seoul and Shanghai (and also via Guangzhou from Vancouver), taking from around 24hr upwards from the east coast, and from around 20hr from the west coast, depending on connections. Return fares from Toronto start at around Can$1500, and from Can$1000 from Vancouver.

Flights from Australia, New Zealand and South Africa

There's a wide selection of flights from **Australia and New Zealand** to Bangkok, Kuala Lumpur, Singapore and Ho Chi Minh City, with onward connections to Phnom Penh and Siem Reap. Return fares from Australia to Phnom Penh start at around Aus$1200; from Auckland, Christchurch and Wellington flights start from roughly NZ$2000.

Travelling from **South Africa** to Cambodia via an Asian hub city, fares start at around ZAR12,000 return.

Round-The-World flights

If Cambodia is only one stop on a longer journey, you might want to consider buying a **Round-The-World (RTW)** ticket. Cambodia can be added to itineraries offered by airline consortium Star Alliance (Ⓦstaralliance.com), for example. Bangkok or Singapore are more common ports of call for many RTW tickets; from the UK, prices start at

---

A BETTER KIND OF TRAVEL

At Rough Guides we are passionately committed to travel. We believe it helps us understand the world we live in and the people we share it with – and of course tourism is vital to many developing economies. But the scale of modern tourism has also damaged some places irreparably, and climate change is accelerated by most forms of transport, especially flying. All Rough Guides' flights are carbon-offset, and every year we donate money to a variety of environmental charities.

around £1250 for an RTW ticket including either of these destinations.

Getting there from neighbouring countries

There are numerous land borders into Cambodia open to foreigners from neighbouring Thailand, Vietnam and Laos. **Visas** (see p.46) are issued on arrival at all of these.

From Thailand

There are currently six border crossings between Cambodia and **Thailand** open to foreigners. All are open daily (7am–8pm) with visas being issued on arrival at all points; **e-visas** (see p.46) are currently only accepted at Poipet and Koh Kong. Travelling into Thailand, citizens of most western countries can get a visa on arrival.

Far and away the most popular of the six crossings is the mildly infamous crossing at **Poipet**, on the main highway between Bangkok and Siem Reap (see p.130). The Trat/**Koh Kong** crossing further south (see p.267) is good for Sihanoukville and Phnom Penh. There are two further crossings in the east at Ban Pakard/**Pailin (Psar Pruhm)** (see p.125), an hour by road to Battambang, and at Ban Leam/**Daun Lem** (although this crossing is basically a casino development in the middle of nowhere, and of little practical use). Finally, there are two remote and little-used (by foreigners at least) crossing points in northern Cambodia at Chong Sa Ngam/**Anlong Veng** and Surin/**O'Smach**. The Anlong Veng crossing (see p.202 is relatively straightforward to reach. Getting to O'Smach is decidedly tricky, however – you'll need to find a bus or shared taxi from Siem Reap or Sisophon to the town of Samroang, and then another one on to the border. On the Thai side of the border, songthaews and motorbike taxis ferry travellers from the check-point to the minibus stop, from where a/c minivans run to Prasat and on to Surin, 70km north of the border (every 30min 6am–5.30pm; 2hr; 45 baht).

From Vietnam

There are currently seven border crossings open to foreigners travelling overland from **Vietnam** (daily 7am–5pm). For entering Cambodia, note that e-visas are valid only at the Bavet crossing. Visa requirements for those heading into Vietnam are currently in a state of flux and you may need to arrange a visa before arrival – check the latest situation before you travel. The busiest crossing is at Moc Bai/**Bavet** (see p.103), 200km southeast of

Phnom Penh on the main road to Ho Chi Minh City. Also popular is the crossing at Chau Doc/**K'am Samnar** (see p.103) on the Bassac River. There are two further border crossings in the south at Tinh Bien/**Phnom Den** near Takeo, and at Hat Tien/**Prek Chak** east of Kep, plus three little-used crossings in eastern Cambodia (see p.213) at Xa Mat/**Trapeang Phlong** east of Kompong Cham; Loc Ninh/**Trapeang Sre**, southeast of Snuol, and Le Tanh/**O Yadow**, east of Banlung.

From Laos

There's just one border crossing with **Laos**, at Nong Nok Khiene/**Trapeang Kriel** (see p.226) in the far north of Cambodia, 57km beyond Stung Treng. The border is open daily (7am–5pm) and both Cambodian and Lao visas are available on arrival.

Tour operators

If you want to avoid the hassle of making your own arrangements you might consider travelling with a **specialist tour operator**. However, although Cambodia is well covered, many tour companies still include it only as part of a visit to another Southeast Asian country. Tour prices start at around £500 for land-only options; those that include international flights tend to be £1200 to £1500, while choosing luxury accommodation and specialist activities, such as golfing, can set you back more than £4000.

Agents and operators

AGENTS

North South Travel UK ☎ 01245 608 291, ⓦ northsouthtravel .co.uk. Friendly, competitive travel agency, offering discounted fares worldwide. Profits are used to support projects in the developing world, especially the promotion of sustainable tourism.

On the Go Tours UK ☎ 020 7371 1113, ⓦ onthegotours.com. Runs group and tailor-made tours throughout the world, including Cambodia, Vietnam and Thailand.

STA Travel UK ☎ 0333 321 0099, US ☎ 1800 781 4040, Australia ☎ 134 782, New Zealand ☎ 0800 474 400, South Africa ☎ 0861 781 781, ⓦ statravel.co.uk. Worldwide specialists in independent travel; also student IDs, travel insurance, car rental, rail passes, and more. Good discounts for students and under-26s.

Trailfinders UK ☎ 0207 368 1200, Ireland ☎ 016777888 ⓦ trailfinders.com. One of the best-informed and most efficient agents for independent travellers.

Travel CUTS Canada ☎ 1800 667 2887 ⓦ travelcuts.com. Canadian youth and student travel firm.

USIT Ireland ☎ 01 602 1906, Australia ☎ 1800 092 499 ⓦ usit.ie. Ireland's main student and youth travel specialists.

TOUR OPERATORS

About Asia Charming City, Charles De Gaulle Avenue, Siem Reap
☎ 092 121059, Ⓦ aboutasiatravel.com. One of the country's leading
travel specialists, offering upmarket private tours from their home base in
Siem Reap. All their Angkor tours have been customized using scientific
footfall studies and clever crowd-avoidance techniques which enable you
to see the temples at their best. They also offer a range of other
countrywide tours including a "Temples and Jungles Escape" featuring
three nights in a tented floating lodge on the Tatai River, and an ingenious
"Great Lake Circuit" combining Siem Reap, Battambang and Phnom Penh
with boat trips around and across the Tonle Sap. All profits are used to
support local schools.

Backyard Travel ☎ 800 2225 9273, Ⓦ backyardtravel.com.
Specialist Asia operator offering cross-country biking, trekking,
community development projects and luxury trips.

Cambodia Holiday Architects ☎ 01242 253 073, Ⓦ cambodia
holidayarchitects.net. Dedicated Cambodian specialists offering
tailor-made, very reasonably priced holidays designed by a team of
destination experts.

Cambodian Pride Tours ☎ 088 836 4758, Ⓦ cambodian
pridetours.com. Kratie-based tour operators (see p.224) offering a good
range of countrywide tours including an excellent selection of trips along
the Mekong and up into the hills of the northeast.

Exotissimo Travel Cambodia SSN Center no. 66, Norodom Blvd,
Phnom Penh ☎ 023 218948, Ⓦ exotravel.com. Huge range of
Cambodia itineraries including culinary, photographic, family, wildlife and
responsible travel tours.

Explore! UK ☎ 01252 883946, US ☎ 1 800 715 1746, Canada
☎ 1 888 216 3401, Australia ☎ 1300 439 756, New Zealand ☎ 0800
269 263, Ⓦ explore.co.uk. Small-group operator offering a good selection
of tours, with soft adventure trips that include walking and cycling.

Geographic Expeditions US ☎ 888 570 7108, Ⓦ geoex.com.
Luxury customized and small-group tours including Angkor jaunts
alongside more off-the-beaten-track offerings, including Cardamom
Mountains village homestays.

Grasshopper Adventures Vicious Cycles, 23 Street 144, Phnom
Penh ☎ 012 462165, Ⓦ grasshopperadventures.com. Half-day to
15-day cycling tours, such as "Angkor at Twilight" and one that combines
yoga and eco-stays.

Hanuman 310 St 12, Phnom Penh ☎ 023 218396, Ⓦ hanuman
.travel. Phnom Penh-based Mekong region specialists since 1990,
offering a huge range of tailor-made tours – mainstream itineraries
alongside motorbiking, wildlife, birdwatching and cycling.

Inside Asia ☎ 0117 370 9758, Ⓦ insideasiatours.com. Small-group
and tailor-made tours by a leading Asian specialist that cover destinations
across the country. Both mainstream and alternative experiences are
offered, such as Phnom Kulen hikes, Pre Rup sunrise visits, Tonle Sap
birdwatching and others.

Intrepid Travel UK ☎ 0808 274 5111, US ☎ 1 800 970 7299,
Australia ☎ 1300 3797 010, Ⓦ intrepidtravel.com. Solid range of
Cambodia offerings including cycling and culinary tours, and an emphasis
on low-impact tourism.

Journeys Within UK ☎ 0776 796 7211, US ☎ 877 454 3672,
Ⓦ journeys-within.com. Southeast Asia specialists offering a varied

selection of Cambodian offerings including luxury tours, family and
responsible travel/volunteering itineraries, and a special "Green Season"
(monsoon) trip – while foodies will love the 15-day "culinary immersion"
tour (with Thailand and Laos).

Noble Caledonia UK ☎ 020 7752 0000, Ⓦ noble-caledonia.co.uk.
Pricey boat tours boarding in the Vietnamese Delta, cruising the Mekong
to Phnom Penh and Kompong Cham, exploring the Tonle Sap and finally
disembarking at Siem Reap for the temples of Angkor.

Responsibletravel.com UK ☎ 01273 823 700, Ⓦ responsible
travel.com. Online travel agent offering a huge range of Cambodia tours
run by various companies, all with an ethical emphasis.

See Cambodia Differently Siem Reap ☎ 0208 1505150,
Ⓦ seecambodiadifferently.com. Siem Reap-based Cambodian
specialists offering an extremely varied selection of tours ranging from
birding and photography through to beach and golfing holidays. Their
"Secret Temple" tour offers a brilliant way of getting to all the major
off-the-beaten track sites in a single trip.

Spice Roads 296, Krous Village, Siem Reap ☎ 063 964323,
Ⓦ spiceroads.com. Interesting cycling tours around Cambodia and
Southeast Asia, including visits to Kampot's pepper farms and the
Cardamom Mountains.

Terre Cambodge Siem Reap ☎ 077 448255, Ⓦ terrecambodge
.com. Countrywide trekking and mountain-bike expeditions (up to two
weeks) with village accommodation or camping around Siem Reap.
Around $90/person/day on longer tours.

Trans Indus UK ☎ 0844 879 3960, US 1 866 615 1815,
Ⓦ transindus.co.uk. Leading Asia specialists with a small range of
private and group tours, including interesting river trips and Mekong
cruises.

Getting around

**Getting around Cambodia is all part of
the adventure. Massive improvements
to the national highway network in the
past few years have made travel much
easier than it once was, with many
formerly dirt roads now surfaced and
new highways built. Even so, getting
from A to B remains time-consuming:
roads are still narrow and bumpy, while
regular wet-season inundations play
havoc with transport (and often wash
away large sections of tarmac in their
wake).**

Note that travel can be difficult over **public
holidays**, especially the Khmer New Year (see p.37).
On New Year's Eve everyone heads for their home
village and all available transport heads out of town
– even more packed than usual. Phnom Penh in
particular becomes very quiet, with hardly a moto
or tuk-tuk available, and the few that remain make a
killing by doubling their fares.

By plane

Cambodia Angkor Air (Ⓦcambodiaangkorair.com) is the nearest thing Cambodia currently has to a national airline, plus international flights to Beijing, Guangzhou and Shanghai. Further flights are provided by a handful of (even) smaller operators. **Cambodia Bayon Airlines** (Ⓦbayonairlines.com) also has flights between Phnom Penh, Sihanoukville and Siem Reap, plus Ho Chi Minh City, while **Sky Angkor** (Ⓦskyangkorair.com) and **Bassaka Air** (Ⓦbassakaair.com) fly between Siem Reap and Sihanoukville. Fares on all airlines are broadly similar, with flights between Phnom Penh, Siem Reap and Sihanoukville for around $60–80 one-way.

By bus

Buses (*laan tom*) are the cheapest – and also usually the most convenient – way to get around Cambodia, connecting all major cities and towns (although some smaller places aren't yet on the bus network, and others, such as Banlung, Sen Monorom and Pailin, have only a few services a day). **Fares** are very reasonable, starting from around $6 from Phnom Penh to Sihanoukville and $8 to Siem Reap.

All buses are **privately run**, operated by a growing number of companies. Phnom Penh Sorya is the biggest; others include Rith Mony, GST, Paramount Angkor and Capitol Tours. Most vehicles are well past their best, but perfectly comfortable, although the majority carry on-board videos meaning that most journeys are made to an accompaniment of relentlessly crooning Cambodian pop singers and Chinese gangster flicks. A couple of companies such as Giant Ibis and Mekong Express operate **luxury express buses** on the most popular routes with modern vehicles, complimentary snacks and even on-board wi-fi.

Buses generally arrive and depart from their respective **company offices**. Unfortunately, this means that there are no bus stations or suchlike in

---

which to get centralized information about **timetables** and fares. Some guesthouses or tour operators can provide this information; otherwise you'll have to visit all the individual offices until you find the right bus at the right time.

By minibus

Minibuses, which leave from local transport stops, provide the main alternative to buses, at a similar (or sometimes slightly higher) price. These generally serve the same routes as buses, and also run some routes and go to some destinations not served by bus (between Sen Monorom and Banlung, for example). They also tend to be slightly faster. On the downside, most usually get absolutely packed and can be seriously uncomfortable, especially for taller travellers (there's little legroom at the best of times, unlike on the buses, which are relatively luxurious in comparison). There are also a few **deluxe minibus** services on the main intercity and international routes (Mekong Express is the main operator). Fares are relatively high although you should at least be guaranteed a reasonably comfortable seat and a vehicle not stuffed full of people, sacks of rice, used car parts and the occasional chicken.

By shared taxi

Shared taxis are the third main option when it comes to travelling by road. These are generally slightly more expensive but also somewhat faster than buses and minibuses, although the driving can often be hair-raising, especially if you're sat in the front. They also serve local destinations off the bus and minibus network. On the downside, like minibuses they get absurdly packed: three people on the front passenger seat is the norm (with the driver sharing his seat as well), and four in the back. You can pay double the standard fare to have the whole front seat to yourself, and you can hire the entire taxi for around five or six times the individual fare. Shared taxis usually leave from the local transport stop. There are no fixed schedules, although most run in the morning, leaving when (very) full.

By boat

For years, Cambodia's appalling roads meant that travelling **by boat** was the principal means of getting between Phnom Penh and Siem Reap, but these days it's easier and quicker to travel by road. Even so, boats (seating about thirty people) still run daily between Phnom Penh (see p.76) and Siem Reap (see p.144), as

---

well as Siem Reap and Battambang (see p.117). The trip to or from Phnom Penh isn't particularly scenic, as the Tonle Sap lake is so vast it's more like being at sea. The trip to or from Battambang is more interesting, combining a trip across the Tonle Sap with a journey down the Sangker River. Neither journey is particularly comfortable: space and movement are restricted, and a cushion, plenty of water, food and a hat will make things more bearable. Be aware that in rough weather the Tonle Sap can whip up some fierce waves.

Boats run daily south along the Mekong between Phnom Penh and the Vietnamese border at **Chau Doc** – this can be arranged via local guesthouses, travel agents or directly at the tourist dock. From **Sihanoukville** in the south, regular ferries and speedboats depart several times a day to Koh Rong and Koh Rong Samloem.

By train

Cambodia's colonial-era **railway network** was largely destroyed during the Khmer Rouge period but is now being slowly restored and reopened. The line between **Phnom Penh and Sihanoukville** reopened in 2016, with stops at Takeo and Kampot and comfortable modern carriages. Trains currently run once a day from Phnom Penh to Sihanoukville on Fri, Sat and Sun, and on Sat and Sun (twice) in the opposite direction; the full route takes around 7hr and costs $7. As yet, tickets are only sold at the stations (☏078 888582, ⓦ royal-railway.com).

The second part of the network, between **Phnom Penh and Poipet** on the Thai border, is still under renovation. Latest reports suggest that the first section of line from Poipet may open during 2017, connecting with the line in Thailand, although it appears unlikely that this will get further than Sisophon, if it even reaches that far. The reopening of the entire line through to Battambang and Phnom Penh – and, beyond that, the ultimate dream of a railway linking Bangkok, Phnom Penh and Ho Chi Minh City – most likely remains years from completion. In the meantime, if you want to ride the rails in this part of the country your only option is to take a trip on the quirky **bamboo railway** (see p.115) in Battambang.

By car

It's virtually impossible to rent a **self-drive car** in Cambodia, and even if you do, driving yourself entails numerous headaches. **Problems** include finding appropriate documentation (your driving licence from home may or may not be considered sufficient – some companies will ask for a Cambodian driving licence, for which you'll need to take a driving test), haphazard driving by other road users, and insufficient insurance – any loss or damage to the vehicle is your responsibility. Lack of designated car parks is another real problem. Given all this, it's far less hassle, and probably cheaper, to hire a **car and driver** (see p.25).

By motorbike

Motorbikes offer a great way off exploring rural Cambodia, especially if you want to get off the beaten track, and most roads are relatively empty and make for enjoyable and stress-free riding. Motorbiking in major cities, however, is hazardous, given the unruly and unpredictable traffic, and best avoided, while scams involving the theft of rented motorbikes (see p.35) have also been reported. Motorbikes can be **rented** from numerous guesthouses and other places, with vehicles ranging from bog-standard automatic scooters (usually around $6–8 per day) up to more serious touring bikes and dirt bikes. We've listed useful places throughout the guide.

Always check the condition of the bike before heading off on a long trip – if it breaks down, it's your responsibility to get it repaired or returned to the owner. Motorbike **theft**, in Sihanoukville and the south in particular, is a real issue. The bike's security is your responsibility, so look to rent from a company that provides installed wheel locks and always make sure you leave it somewhere secure when you stop; guesthouses will often bring it inside for you at night. Note also that foreigners aren't allowed to hire motorbikes in Siem Reap – at least in theory (see p.145).

Away from the main highways take advice on local road conditions, as often even relatively short distances can take a long time. Motorcycle **helmets** are compulsory for both driver and any passengers: you risk being stopped by the police and issued with a fine (15,000 riel) if you're not wearing one – even premier Hun Sen was forced to cough up (to great popular amusement) when nabbed riding helmetless in 2016. Note that road checks are particularly prevalent just before holidays and the weekend.

By bicycle

Cycling in Cambodia can be a rewarding experience, at least away from the big cities – just remember that all motorized traffic takes precedence over bicycles, and you may find that you have to veer onto the verge to get out of the way of speeding cars and trucks. Bicycles are available for rent at many guesthouses and elsewhere. Many are gearless antiques, usually costing $1–2 per day, although some places have good mountain bikes for rent (from around $5 per day and upwards). A good way of getting in the saddle either for a day or a longer trip is to arrange a **tour** with one of the operators listed on p.21.

City transport

Getting around most Cambodian towns and cities generally involves the use of either a **moto** or a **tuk-tuk** (*romorque*). With both tuk-tuks and motos make sure you always **agree the fare beforehand**. Short journeys around town typically cost $1, or $2 and upwards for longer journeys, with fares generally a bit higher in Phnom Penh and Siem Reap. Longer journeys should be a slightly cheaper by moto than by tuk-tuk.

Motos and tuk-tuks are also useful for short **tours** and trips out of many towns. Tuk-tuks are the most popular form of transport around the temples of Angkor, while motos are sometimes the only way of visiting sites not accessible by sealed roads. Fares for longer hire periods will vary depending on what sort of mileage you'll be doing and the state of the roads you'll be travelling along.

City taxis are available in Phnom Penh and Siem Reap. Uber is not yet available, although a local taxi-booking app, Exnet (for Android phones only), was launched in 2016 for Phnom Penh.

Motos

Motorbike taxis, or **motos**, are the staple means of travelling short (and sometimes long) distances in Cambodia, although riding on the back of a moto in the middle of anarchic traffic isn't everybody's

> ## ADDRESSES
> Finding your way around towns in Cambodia is generally easy as most of them are laid out on a **grid plan**. Nearly all towns have street signs; usually a few main streets have names, with the majority being numbered. Despite that, most Cambodians have little idea of street numbers, so to locate a specific address you're best off heading for a nearby landmark and asking from there.

idea of fun. Passengers ride pillion behind the driver – Cambodians typically squeeze on as many passengers as possible (three is common), although it's sensible to stick to just one passenger per bike (in Siem Reap, motos are forbidden from taking more than one foreigner at a time). Although you'll see Cambodian women sitting side-saddle, it's safer if you sit astride and, if necessary, hang onto the driver.

Moto drivers tend to congregate around transport stops, major local landmarks and road junctions – expect to be touted for custom on a fairly regular basis. Note that recently introduced laws now require passengers on a moto to wear a **helmet** – if your moto driver can't give you one, don't get on. If you have **bags**, the driver will squeeze them into the space between his knees and the handlebars – moto drivers are adept at balancing baggage, from rice sacks to backpacks, between their legs while negotiating chaotic traffic.

Motos can be taken on quite long trips **out of town** – indeed it's the only way to get to some places, although it's not particularly comfortable.

Tuk-tuks

Pricier than motos, **tuk-tuks** (sometimes referred to by their French name, *remorques*) were only introduced to Cambodia in 2001 but have since caught on in a big way and are now found in most provincial towns – although in more remote areas they're still fairly few and far between. A unique local variant on the vehicles found in Thailand and Vietnam, the Cambodia tuk-tuk consists of a covered passenger carriage seating up to four people pulled by a motorbike – a fun and secure way of getting around. The motorbikes that pull them, however, are the same ones used as motos, and so are woefully underpowered, which makes for a slow trip, especially if you've got three or four people on board – even with just one or two passengers they can struggle to go much faster than your average bicycle.

Cyclos

A dying breed, found only in Phnom Penh, and decreasingly so there, the **cyclo** (pronounced *see-klo*, from the French – *cyclopousse*) is much slower than a moto or tuk-tuk. They are good for leisurely rides and views of the street but more or less useless for longer journeys or if you want to get anywhere in a hurry. Cyclos take one passenger (or two at a squash) in a seat at the front, with the driver perched on a seat behind over the rear wheel.

Car and driver

If you want to cover long distances at reasonable speed and without the discomfort of a moto your only option is to hire a **car and driver**, although these are often difficult to come by except in major tourist centres and expensive compared to other means of transport. Count on around $50–100 per day, depending on how far you want to go.

Accommodation

Finding accommodation is seldom a problem, standards are generally good and prices are still among the lowest in Asia. Phnom Penh, Siem Reap and Sihanoukville all have plenty of accommodation in all categories, and even smaller towns usually have a reasonable choice of guesthouses and a couple of modest hotels.

Budget accommodation

Budget accommodation in Cambodia is generally excellent value, available in a range of guesthouses and hotels (note that many places which call themselves guesthouses are actually more like small hotels). Most places are functional concrete boxes, although there's a growing range of more characterful accommodation, particularly on the coast and islands and up in the hills of the northeast, where you'll find rustic wooden cottages, stilted cabanas and even the occasional treehouse. Most places have a mix of **fan and a/c** rooms or give you the option of taking a room with or without the a/c turned on – which can often save you $5/night or more if you go without. Fan rooms typically go for around $7–8/night, a/c for $13–15 (or a bit more in Phnom Penh and Siem Reap). Virtually all rooms are **en-suite** with shower, sink and Western-style toilets,

although some places have cold water only. **Wi-fi** is available pretty much everywhere (and is virtually always free) apart from village homestays, and there might also be a TV, although it won't always have any channels on it worth watching. Some but not all places have **mosquito nets** – mozzies aren't usually a major problem, although it's still worth bringing your own net. Note that you might also be able to bargain down your room rate if you're going to be staying in one guesthouse/hotel for a few nights or longer, especially in more downmarket places.

There's also a burgeoning number of **hostels** in Siem Reap, Phnom Penh, Kampot and Sihanoukville. Fancier places offer a/c dorms and beds fitted with individual plugs and reading lights although if you're travelling in a couple the price of two dorm beds (often around $8 per person) may not work out any cheaper than taking a double room somewhere else. On the islands a number of establishments offer **hammocks** for a few dollars, and **tents**.

Mid-range and luxury

Mid-range (roughly $25–75 per night) and luxury ($75 and upwards per night) accommodation is found only in major towns and tourist hotspots. **Mid-range** accommodation includes smart business-style hotels along with lower-end boutique hotels and resorts. Facilities are often not significantly different from those in more expensive rooms in budget hotels and guesthouses (with a/c, hot water, minibar and perhaps tea- and coffee-making

Accommodation **prices** throughout the guide are based on the cost of the cheapest **double room** or **dorm bed** available at each particular establishment in high season (Nov–Feb). Prices tend to fall during the rainy season (June–Oct), particularly at more upmarket places, where rates can drop by up to a third – although note that rates (especially in more expensive places) can fluctuate widely from month to month, or even week by week, according to season and demand. Prices given in this book should be treated as a guideline only. **Single rates** are usually around two-thirds the price of a double room, but are only available in a minority of places. Rates in some places (particularly more upmarket establishments) may include **breakfast** (indicated by **BB** in reviews). The majority of places can now be **booked online** via their own websites (which sometimes offer discounts) or via the usual booking websites, although this generally adds a small surcharge to the price.

VILLAGE HOMESTAYS AND OTHER OPTIONS

An increasing number of off-the-beaten-track destinations in Cambodia are now organizing **village homestays,** offering visitors the chance to experience traditional rural life at first hand. Homestays typically provide simple but comfortable accommodation in a local house, with home-cooked meals included and the option of taking various add-ons which might include village tours, ox-cart rides, boat trips and the chance to visit local workshops or farms. Rewarding homestays include a range of places in the northeast (see box, p.216); at the magnificent Banteay Chhmar temple (see p.130); in the countryside outside Takeo (see p.288); and at Chi Phat in the southern Cardamom Mountains (see p.271).

   Airbnb (W airbnb.com) offers an increasing number of places to stay in Phnom Penh, Siem Reap and on the coast, while **Homestay.com** also has a growing selection of places, mainly in the Siem Reap area.

facilities), although rooms are likely to be more comfortably and stylishly furnished, and you'll probably also get a pool plus in-house restaurant and perhaps other facilities including a gym or spa. Breakfast may also be included in the price.

   Luxury accommodation is widely available in Phnom Penh, Siem Reap, Sihanoukville and a few places elsewhere – reserve in advance and check online for special deals. Accommodation in this price bracket ranges from international five-star chain hotels through to chic boutique hotels and idyllic resorts constructed in traditional Khmer style. Many top-end establishments offer memorable style and luxury at far lower prices than you might pay in other Asian countries, although rates at the very best places still run into hundreds of dollars per night.

   At more expensive places be sure to check whether **government tax and service** are included in the quoted price, as these can add as much as twenty percent to the bill.

Food and drink

Cambodia's distinctive, delicious and surprisingly little-known cuisine has drawn on numerous sources, but remains recognizably its own. Many of the country's classic dishes are local riffs on dishes from either neighbouring Thailand (although more delicately spiced, and with considerably less chilli and sugar) or Vietnam. Chinese influences are also strong, as is the legacy of the French, from whom the Khmers inherited their enduring love of baguettes, coffee and beer.

   Food is traditionally cooked in a single pot or wok over a charcoal stove; although gas burners are being introduced in the cities, many people prize the smoky flavour that food acquires when it's cooked over charcoal. A lot of dishes are fried in palm oil and aren't drained before serving, so can be quite greasy.

   As in many countries where **rice** is the staple food, the most common way to refer to eating in Cambodia is **nyam bai**, literally "eat rice".

Where to eat

The cheapest food in Cambodia is available from **street hawkers,** who ply the streets with their handcarts and portable stoves and BBQs dishing up offerings ranging from fried noodles and baguettes through to fresh fruit and ice cream. The country's **markets** are another good source of cheap food, open both day and night (though often in separate locations) and at prices only slightly higher than those charged by street hawkers. Each stall usually has its own speciality, and you can order from any stall in the market irrespective of where you're sitting. When you've finished, you pay the stall closest to you for the whole lot and they'll sort out the money among themselves.

   Khmer restaurants come in various shapes and sizes. More upmarket places have extensive menus (although usually in Khmer only) featuring all the usual Cambodian staples. Cheaper places (usually most numerous around transport stops) will just have whatever's available in a row of pots set at the front. Lift the lids and point at what you want; your chosen dishes will be served in separate bowls along with a plate of rice. Prices at the cheapest places are similar to those at market stalls; fancier establishments are often on a par with cheaper tourist restaurants.

   Tourist restaurants with English-language menus and Western cuisine are found only in larger towns and traveller hubs, usually serving up a mix of mainstream Khmer dishes and Western standards. Phnom Penh and Siem Reap also have a decent range of more upmarket restaurants specializing in French, Italian, Indian, Thai, Japanese and other leading international cuisines.

Khmers tend to eat early by Western standards. In the provinces, especially, don't expect to find anywhere open after 9pm, and some places close even earlier. You won't usually need to **book in advance** except in the most popular restaurants in larger cities.

What to eat

Chicken and pork are the staple meats. **Beef** is rarer (and more expensive) as cows are prized as work animals, while the meat itself is often tough. **Fish** is plentiful and the main source of protein for most Cambodians. Near the Tonle Sap lake there's a particularly good choice of **freshwater** varieties, and **sea fish** is plentiful along the coast, though inland it's only readily available in the specialist (and inevitably expensive) restaurants of Phnom Penh. Cambodia's markets offer up a wide range of **vegetables**, some of which will be unfamiliar, all delivered fresh daily – although few of them find their way onto restaurant menus.

Flavourings and accompaniments

The starting point of many Khmer recipes, **kroeung** comprises a paste of freshly ground spices and leaves. All cooks have their own versions, although commonly used spices include lemongrass, ginger, galangal, turmeric, garlic, shallots and dried red chillies.

Cambodia's signature flavour, **prahok** is a fermented fish paste with a pâté-like consistency used as a base ingredient in many Khmer recipes and also served as an accompaniment to be mixed into food, although the intensely salty, anchovy-like flavour is something of an acquired taste. The classic **prahok ktis**, consisting of *prahok* combined with pork and coconut milk in a richly flavoured curry-like concoction, is usually served with assorted vegetables for dipping.

Other accompaniments include **dips** of chilli sauce and soy sauce – to which you can add chopped chillies and garlic – which are either left in pots on the table or served in individual saucers.

Breakfast

A popular breakfast dish, **kuy teav** is a nourishing noodle soup made with clear pork broth and including a mix of greens and meat. Exact recipes vary widely, both in terms of the meat they include

MARKET DELICACIES

Cambodians eat just about everything, including **insects**. In the markets you'll see big trays of grasshoppers, beetles and crickets, usually fried, sold by the bag and eaten like sweets; **snails** are also a popular market-stall snack. **Spiders** are a speciality of Skuon (see box, p.28) but can increasingly be found in major tourist spots elsewhere, while fried **snakes** are also a common sight, as are tiny sparrows (*jarb jeyan*), and other small **birds**, deep-fried and served whole, complete with tiny shrivelled head and claws. **Frogs**, meanwhile, are commonly used in stir-fries both in local markets and upmarket restaurants.

(some versions may feature pork offal, as well as shrimp or squid), garnishings and accompanying sauces. The broth may also sometimes be served separately so that the diner can decide how wet to make the dish.

A meat-free alternative to *kuy teav* is **nom banh chok** (often referred to simply as "Khmer noodles"). Another popular breakfast dish (although it's available throughout the day), *nom banh chok* is typically sold by female street hawkers who carry the ingredients in baskets hanging from a pole balanced on their shoulders. Thin rice noodles (cold) are extracted from one basket and topped with assorted greens, after which a fish-based, lemongrass- and kaffir-flavoured broth is ladled over them to create a soup.

Another staple breakfast dish, the simple but delicious **bai sach chrouk** consists of marinated pork grilled slowly over charcoals to a meaty sweetness, after which it's sliced thinly and served with rice and pickled vegetables.

Another perennial favourite, **borbor** (rice porridge) is usually available at market stalls, night markets and in some cheap restaurants, either as breakfast or an evening dish. *Borbor* can either be left unseasoned and used as a base to which you add your own ingredients – dried fish, pickles, salted egg or fried vegetables – or cooked in stock, with pieces of chicken, fish or pork and bean sprouts added before serving.

Soups and hotpots

Soups (*somlar*) are a mainstay of Khmer cuisine, and often a meal in themselves rather than simply an appetizer. Common examples include the refreshingly tart **somlar ngam ngau**, a clear lemon broth flavoured with herbs, pickled limes and winter melon (ash gourd), and the warming chicken soup, **sgnor sach moan**. The sour and tangy **machu kroeung** features a rich combination of meat and fried peanuts in chicken broth with greens, saffron and lemongrass, all spiced with *kroeung*, while the rich and warming **samlor kako** (or *korko*) comprises a rich mix of vegetables plus meat (traditionally pork), flavoured with *prahok* and *kroeung*.

Another variant on the Cambodian soup is the **hotpot** (known as *yao hon* or *chhang pleung*, meaning "fire pot"). Like phnom pleung (see p.29) this is a DIY meal, a bit like a fondu, with a burner plus pot of broth brought to your table in which you cook your own meat, noodles and vegetables.

Salads

As in Thailand, spicy salads (although never as fiery as their Thai equivalents) feature largely on many Khmer menus. **Green mango salad** (*svay nhom pakea kiem*) is one classic dish, made from shredded green mango, dried shrimp and fish paste topped with crushed peanut. Also popular is **banana flower salad** (aka banana blossom salad; *nhom tro yong chek*) combining finely sliced pieces of banana flower (faintly reminiscent of artichoke) with mixed greens and chicken, with the large but inedible outer shell of the flower sometimes serving as a kind of bowl in which the whole thing is served. **Lap Khmer** (aka *plear sach ko*) is another favourite, comprising thin slices of beef in a spicy mix of greens, lime and plenty of red chilli. In restaurants the beef is generally flash-fried, although the traditional version of the recipe uses raw beef cured, ceviche-style, in the lime dressing.

Stir-fries and noodles

Stir-fries (*cha*) are China's major contribution to Khmer cuisine, originally introduced (it's said) by immigrants from Hokkien, but since given their own uniquely Cambodian twist. Just about anything can be (and is) stir-fried, ranging from chicken and seafood through to frog's legs and red ants, cooked with ingredients like ginger, lemongrass, garlic and basil, and served with either rice or noodles. "Curried" stir-fries (*cha kroeung*), cooked with *kroeung*, have a particularly Cambodian flavour. Down on the coast, **fresh crab** (*kdam cha*) stir-fried with green Kampot pepper is deservedly popular. Many stir-fries also feature the surprisingly tasty **morning glory** (*trokuon*, often called "water spinach"), a water plant with a thick, hollow stem and a taste vaguely reminiscent of Chinese *bok choy*.

A popular street snack, the tasty, meat-free **lort cha** consists of very short, very fat (yes, they do look like worms) rice noodles stir-fried with greens and soy sauce then mixed with bean sprouts, chilli and soy sauce and topped with a fried egg. Another popular dish is **beef lok lak**, a local variant of the Vietnamese *bo luc lac*, or "shaking beef" (referring to the rapid shaking of the beef in the pan during frying). This comprises a meaty portion of cubed beef pieces in oyster sauce and palm sugar, served with rice (or, sometimes, french fries), sliced tomatoes and cucumbers and lettuce. You may also get a (rather incongruous-looking) fried egg on top. Tasty when good, although the beef can often be pretty tough.

SPIDERVILLE

Most visitors to Cambodia pass through the nondescript little town of **Skuon** at some point in their travels. Located at the junction of NR6 and NR7 between Phnom Penh, Siem Reap and Kompong Cham, it's one of the most important crossroads towns in Cambodia. What it's really famous for, however, is its **edible spiders** – more precisely, a type of Asian tarantula, around 5cm across, known locally as *ah pieng* and considered something of a delicacy when deep-fried with a hint of salt and garlic. According to local gourmands they taste a bit like crunchy fried prawns and are best tackled as though eating a crab: pull off the legs and you can suck the flesh which comes away with them, though be wary of the body, as it can be unappetizingly slushy and bitter. Spiders also crop up around the country **pickled in wine**, a tonic especially favoured by pregnant women.

Quite how the practice of eating spiders began is something of a mystery. One theory suggests that it dates from the starvation years of Khmer Rouge rule, when desperate villagers began foraging for eight-legged snacks in the jungles of Kompong Thom province. Nowadays you'll likely see platters piled high with spiders at restaurants in and around Skuon – a lot of buses stop here for a comfort break – giving you the chance to see, and perhaps even try, this unusual delicacy.

Curries and amok

Often referred to as Cambodia's national dish, **amok** is traditionally made with fish (*amok trei*), although most restaurants also now offer versions with chicken or (less successfully) beef. Fish or meat are wrapped up inside a parcel of banana leaves (or a coconut shell) with *kroeung*-spiced coconut milk and then slowly steamed. Exact preparations vary quite wildly – properly made, the coconut milk should congeal to an almost custard-like consistency, although many *amoks* come out looking rather like a Thai-style curry.

Cambodia's own take on the classic Thai red curry (although usually significantly less spicy), the **Khmer red curry** is another coconut-based recipe with meat, fish or seafood cooked in *kroeung*-flavoured coconut milk. A slightly feistier variant is the **beef saraman curry** (aka Khmer Muslim beer curry) beloved of Cambodia's Cham Muslim minority, somewhat reminiscent of Thai massaman curry, with beef, vegetables and peanuts cooked in coconut milk or dry roasted coconut.

Grilled meat and seafood

Cambodians love a BBQ, with smoky, **charcoal-grilled** meats, fish and seafood widely available from street hawkers and at market stalls, served with mango dipping sauces or pickled vegetables. Particularly popular on the coast and in Phnom Penh is **grilled squid** (*ang dtray-meuk*), with squid grilled on wooden skewers and served with a garlic and chilli sauce.

A number of restaurants around the country (particularly in Siem Reap) specialize in the so-called "Cambodian BBQ", or **phnom pleung** (literally "hill of fire") – a lot like the better-known Korean BBQ, with tables equipped with small burners on which you cook your own selection of meat and/or seafood, accompanied by dipping sauces, vegetables and noodles, which you boil in the small "moat" surrounding the burner.

Snacks

Cambodian **snack foods** are legion, the range varying with the time of day. Eaten with breakfast or as an afternoon snack, available from street vendors and at restaurants, **noam bpaow** are steamed dumplings, originating from Chinese cuisine, made from white dough filled with a mix of minced pork, turnip, egg and chives. **Cooked bananas** are also widely eaten as snacks, seasoned with salt and grilled over charcoal braziers, or wok-fried in a batter containing sesame seeds.

> ### TOP 5 FINE DINING
> **Chanrey Tree, Siem Reap** See p.151
> **Cuisine Wat Damnak, Siem Reap** See p.152
> **Jaan Bai, Battambang** See p.119
> **Malis, Phnom Penh** See p.85
> **Van's, Phnom Penh** See p.84

Steamed or grilled eggs are incredibly popular and are available everywhere. The black "thousand-year eggs" that you see at markets and food stalls are duck eggs that have been stored in jars of salt until the shells turn black; by that time the whites and the yolks have turned into a jelly, not dissimilar in texture to soft-boiled eggs.

A particular speciality of the Kratie area, **krolan** are bamboo tubes containing a delicious mix of sticky rice, coconut milk and black beans, cooked over charcoal and sold bundled together by hawkers (usually in the provinces). The woody outer layer of the bamboo is removed after cooking, leaving a thin shell that you peel down to get at the contents.

Seasonally available are **chook**, the large circular fruit of the lotus flower, sold in bundles of three or five heads. Each contains around 25 seeds: pop them out of the green rubbery pod, peel off their outer skins and consume the insides, which taste a bit like garden peas.

Another classically Southeast Asian curiosity, found at night markets or served up with beer, is **balut** (known as *pong tia koun* in Cambodia, literally ducks' eggs with duckling). Said to give strength and good health, it really does contain an unhatched duckling, boiled and served with herbs and a pepper and lemon sauce.

Desserts and sweets

Specialist stalls, opening around lunchtime in the markets or in the late afternoon and evening along the street, serve Cambodian **desserts** in a vast range of colours and textures. Small custards, jellies and sticky-rice confections are displayed in large flat trays and cut or shaped into bite-sized pieces to be served in bowls, topped with grated ice and a slug of condensed milk; mixes of dried and crystallized fruits, beans and nuts are also on offer, served with ice and syrup. Larger towns generally have a bakery or two producing a variety of vaguely Western-style **cakes**.

Fruit

Colourful **fruit** stalls can be found every-where in Cambodia, and the selection is

VEGETARIANS AND VEGANS

There's an increasing number of proper **vegetarian** (and even vegan) cafés and restaurants in the main tourist centres. Elsewhere, restaurants generally serve a few vegetable stir-fries, soups, salads and so on, although the concept of vegetarianism isn't widely understood and in local restaurants you can't always be sure that bits of meat or fish won't be added. If in doubt, ask for your order to be cooked without meat (*ot dak sait*) or fish (*ot dak trei*) – although even then you can't always be sure that it won't be prepared using meat stock or fish sauce, while pans aren't necessarily washed out between cooking meat and vegetable dishes. **Vegans** will need to make sure that no eggs are included (*ot yoh pong mowan*) as these are widely used.

enormous – stallholders will always let you try before you buy if you don't know what you're looking at. Imported apples, pears and grapes are also available, though comparatively expensive.

Bananas come in several varieties. Commonest are *jayk oumvong*, which is slender and stays green when ripe; *jayk numvar*, a medium-sized, plump, yellow banana, said to cool the body; and the finger-sized, very sweet *jayk pong mowan*, said to be warming, which is a little pricier than the other kinds. Relatively rare are the large, dry and fibrous red or green bananas, generally used for cooking.

The **durian** (*tooren*) is a rugby-ball-sized fruit with a hard, spiky exterior. Much sought after by Khmers, it's an acquired taste for most Westerners thanks to its fetid smell (often compared to that of a blocked drain). Inside are several segments, each containing two or three stones surrounded by pale yellow, creamy textured flesh, which can be quite addictive once you've got over the odour.

Longans (*meeyan*) have a long season and are often sold still on the twig. The cherry-sized fruit have a hard brown skin; the flesh inside is similar to that of lychees in texture and flavour. Bright green and prickly skinned, **soursops** (*tee-ab barang*) are pure white inside and have a tart but sweet taste. Hard, round and a bit like a bright-green cricket ball, **guavas** (*troubike*) have a crunchy, dry texture a bit like a hard pear. The flat brown pods of **tamarind** (*umpbel*) are simple to eat: split open the pods and discard the fibrous thread inside, then suck off the rich brown tangy flesh, minding the hard seeds. The most picturesque of Khmer fruits, though, has to be the rosy pink **dragon fruit** (*pelai sroegar ne-yak*), grown on a climbing cactus-like vine. Inside its waxy skin, the moist, pure-white flesh is dotted with black seeds and has quite a subtle taste, verging on bland.

Drinks

Cambodian **tap water** in larger cities is technically safe to drink but probably best avoided, lest the unfamiliar microbes and high levels of chlorination produce a stomach upset. Cheap bottled water is available everywhere. Be aware that **ice** may not be hygienic except in Western restaurants, although the ice-factory-produced cylindrical cubes with holes in the middle are usually OK.

Tea and coffee

Cambodians drink plenty of Chinese-style **green or jasmine tea**, which is readily available in coffee shops and from market stalls; it's normally served free of charge with food in local restaurants. **Western-style tea** (usually a Lipton's teabag) is only usually available in tourist cafés and restaurants.

Local restaurants and market stalls serve **coffee** from early morning to late afternoon, but in the evenings it can be difficult to find except at restaurants geared up for foreigners. Many Cambodians drink their coffee iced – if you want yours hot, ask for it to be served without ice (*ot dak tuk kork*). Beans are traditionally roasted with butter and sugar, plus various other ingredients that might include anything from rum to pork fat – something of an acquired taste. Note that if you order white coffee (*kafei tuk duh gow*) the milk will most likely be super-sweet condensed milk rather than fresh (or powdered) milk – another acquired taste. Black coffee (*kafei kmaow*) is frequently served with sugar unless you specify otherwise.

Coffee often comes (and generally tastes better) **iced** (*kafei kmaow tuk kork*). Iced milk coffee is particularly nice, with flavoured beans and sweet condensed milk combining to produce an intense, almost chocolately beverage – although the ice itself may not always be one hundred percent hygienic.

Soft drinks

For a drink on the hoof, iced **sugar-cane juice** (*tuk umpow*) is very refreshing and not actually that sweet. It's sold everywhere from yellow carts equipped with a mangle through which the peeled canes are passed, sometimes with a piece of orange added for extra taste. Equally refreshing is the juice of a **green coconut** (*tuk dhowng*): the top is hacked

SUGAR PALMS

Crowned with distinctive mops of spiky leaves, **sugar palms** are of great importance to the rural Cambodian economy, with every part of the tree being put to good use. The sweet **juice** extracted from the palm's flower-bearing stalk is either drunk fresh or fermented to produce **palm beer**, traditionally sold by hawkers, although nowadays also available in tourist centres and local supermarkets. **Palm sugar**, much used in Khmer cooking, is made by thickening the juice in a cauldron and then pouring it into cylindrical tubes to set, after which it resembles grainy honey-coloured fudge. Palm **fruits**, slightly larger than a cricket ball, have a tough, fibrous black coating containing juicy, delicately flavoured kernels, which are translucent white and have the consistency of jelly; they're eaten either fresh or with syrup as a dessert.

Further sugar-palm products include the **leaves**, traditionally used as a form of paper and still used in thatch and to make wall panels, woven matting, baskets, fans and even packaging. The **root** of the tree is used in traditional medicine as a cure for stomach ache and other ailments. Perhaps because the trees furnish so many other products, they are seldom cut for their **wood**, which is extremely durable. However, palm-wood souvenirs can be found in Phnom Penh and Siem Reap, easily identifiable by their distinctive light-and-dark striped grain, and palm-wood furniture has become fashionable in some of the country's boutique hotels.

off and you drink the juice before getting it cut in half so you can eat the soft, jelly-like flesh.

Fruit shakes (*tuk krolok*) are an important part of an evening's consumption: juice stalls, recognizable by their fruit displays and blenders, set up in towns all over the country from the late afternoon. You can order a mixture of fruits to be juiced or just one or two; coconut milk, sugar syrup, condensed milk and shaved ice are also added, as is a raw egg (unless you specify otherwise – *ot yoh pong mowan*).

When not added to coffee or tea, **milk** (*tuk duh*) is sometimes drunk iced, perhaps with a bright red or green cordial added. Freshly made **soya milk** (*tuk sun dike*) is sold in the morning by street vendors; the green version is sweetened and thicker than the unsweetened white. Soya milk is also available canned, as is **winter-melon tea**, a juice made from the field melon that has a distinctive sweet, almost earthy taste.

Alcohol

Virtually all restaurants and most night-market stalls serve **beer** (*sraa bier*). There's a wide range of identikit lagers on sale, with Angkor and Cambodia the most widely available brands, sold in cans, small and large bottles and sometimes on draught. Prices range from around $1 for a glass of draught to around $2.50 for a large bottle. For something a bit different, look out for the various craft beers produced by the Kingdom Brewery in Phnom Penh.

Spirits are generally only found in larger restaurants and Western bars. Imported **wines** are available in smarter restaurants and Western-oriented places. When not downing beer, Cambodians themselves usually prefer to stick to local, medicinal **rice wines**, which are available at stalls and shops where glasses of the stuff are ladled from large jars containing various plant or animal parts. Another local brew is **sugar-palm beer**, sold in villages straight from the bamboo tubes in which the juice is collected and fermented.

Health

Health care in Cambodia is poor. Even the best hospitals have inadequate facilities, low standards of cleanliness and appalling patient care, and should be used only in a dire emergency. For anything serious, if you are able to travel then get to Bangkok. Should you have no option but to go to a Cambodian hospital, try to get a Khmer-speaker to accompany you.

In Phnom Penh and Siem Reap a couple of private Western-oriented **clinics** offer slightly better care than the hospitals, at a higher cost. Wherever you seek medical attention, you will be expected to pay up front for treatment, medication and food.

All towns have a number of **pharmacies** (typically daily 7am–8pm) stocking an extensive range of medications, although staff aren't required to have a dispensing qualification – and check expiry dates before you buy anything. Fake medicines also abound and there's no easy way to determine if what you're buying is the real thing. Whenever possible buy only in Phnom Penh (see p.94) or Siem Reap (see p.157), which have a couple of reputable pharmacies employing qualified personnel who can help with diagnosis and remedies for simple health problems.

Consider getting a pre-trip **dental check-up** if you're travelling for an extended period, as the only places to get reliable dental treatment in Cambodia are in Phnom Penh and Siem Reap. If you wear **glasses**, it's worth taking along a copy of your prescription (or a spare pair of glasses); you can get replacements made quite cheaply in Phnom Penh and Siem Reap.

Vaccinations and immunizations

It's worth checking before you leave that you are up to date with **routine** immunizations, such as tetanus and diphtheria. For Cambodia, you should consider immunizing yourself against hepatitis A, tuberculosis and typhoid; inoculations against hepatitis B, rabies and Japanese encephalitis are recommended if you are going to be at a particular risk (for example if you're working in a remote area). You'll need to produce proof that you've been vaccinated against yellow fever in the event of arriving from an infected area (West and Central Africa, or South America).

It is as well to consult your doctor or travel clinic as early as possible since it can take anything up to eight weeks to complete a full course of immunizations. All inoculations should be recorded on an **international travel vaccination card**, which is worth carrying with you in case you get sick.

Hepatitis

Hepatitis A, a viral infection of the liver, can be contracted from contaminated food and water – shellfish sold by hawkers and untreated water are particular risks in Cambodia – or by contact with an infected person. Symptoms include dark-coloured urine, aches and pains, nausea, general malaise and tiredness, with jaundice following after a few days. A blood test is needed for diagnosis, and rest, plenty of nonalcoholic fluids and a high-carbohydrate diet are recommended for convalescence. A single shot of immunoglobulin offers short-term protection against hepatitis A.

Far more serious is **hepatitis B**, passed via contaminated body fluids; it can be contracted through non-sterile needles (including those used in tattooing and acupuncture), sexual contact or from a blood transfusion that hasn't been properly screened. Symptoms include nonspecific abdominal pain, vomiting, loss of appetite, dark-coloured urine and jaundice. Immunization may be recommended if you are staying in Asia for longer than six months. If you think you have contracted hepatitis B, it's especially important to seek medical attention.

A **combined vaccine** is available offering ten years' protection against hepatitis A and five years' against hepatitis B; your doctor will be able to advise on its suitability.

Tuberculosis, rabies and tetanus

Tuberculosis, contracted from droplets coughed up by infected persons, is widespread in Cambodia and is a major cause of death in children. You may have been inoculated against the disease in childhood, but if you're unsure, consider a skin (Heaf) test, which will determine if you already have immunity.

Rabies is contracted from the bite or saliva of an infected animal. Vaccinations are recommended if you're going to be spending a long time in rural areas; but even if you've been vaccinated, if you are bitten (or licked on an open wound) you will need to get two booster injections as quickly as possible, preferably within 24 to 48 hours.

Tetanus, a bacterial infection that causes muscular cramps and spasms, comes from spores in the earth and can enter the blood circulatory system through wounds and grazes. If left untreated it can cause breathing problems and sometimes death. It's worth checking if you've been vaccinated against tetanus in the last ten years and getting a booster if necessary.

Typhoid and cholera

Typhoid and cholera, bacterial infections that affect the digestive system, are spread by contaminated food and water, and outbreaks are thus usually associated with particularly unsanitary conditions.

Symptoms of **typhoid** include tiredness, dull headaches and spasmodic fevers, with spots appearing on the abdomen after about a week. Vaccination is suggested if you plan to stay in rural areas of Cambodia, but it doesn't confer complete immunity, so it remains important to maintain good standards of hygiene. Outbreaks of **cholera** are a regularly occurrence in Cambodia. Symptoms including sudden, watery diarrhoea and rapid dehydration, and medical advice is essential to treat the infection with antibiotics. There is no effective vaccine.

General precautions

Cambodia is a hot and humid country, and **dehydration** is a potential problem, its onset indicated by headaches, dizziness, nausea and dark urine. **Cuts** and raw blisters can rapidly become infected and should be promptly treated by cleaning and disinfecting the wound and then applying an air-permeable dressing.

Bites and stings

Insects are legion in Cambodia and are at their worst around November, at the start of the dry season, when there are stagnant pockets of water left from the rains. Even during the hot season (March–May) they come out in the evenings, swarming around light bulbs and warm flesh – they're annoying rather than harmful, with the exception of mosquitoes (see below).

If you're heading to the coast, it's a good idea to take an insect repellent. **Sand flies** can be an issue, delivering bites that may become red and itchy, and which you should avoid scratching.

Sun and heat

Even when the sky is overcast the Cambodian sun is fierce, and you should take precautions against sunburn and heat stroke wherever you are. Cover up, use a high-protection-factor **sunscreen**, wear a hat and drink plenty of fluids throughout the day.

Hygiene and stomach complaints

Though catering facilities at many restaurants and food stalls can appear basic, the **food** you'll be served is usually absolutely fresh; all ingredients are bought daily and are mostly cooked to order. A good rule of thumb when selecting a place to eat is to pick one that is popular with locals. Food from street hawkers is usually fine if it's cooked in front of you. Tap water isn't drinkable, but bottled water is available everywhere – stick to that and be cautious with ice, which is often cut up in the street from large blocks and handled by several people before it gets to your glass (though in Western restaurants it will probably come from an ice-maker).

Stomach complaints

The most common travellers' ailment is **upset tummy**. Travellers' **diarrhoea** often occurs in the early days of a trip as a result of a simple change in diet, though stomach cramps and vomiting may mean it's food poisoning. If symptoms persist for more than a couple of days, seek medical help as you may need antibiotics to clear up the problem.

Most diarrhoea is short-lived and can be handled by drinking plenty of fluids and avoiding rich or spicy food. Activated charcoal tablets help by absorbing the bad bugs in your gut and usually speed recovery; they're sold across the counter

at pharmacies, but consider bringing some with you from home. It's often a good idea to rest up for a day or two if your schedule allows. In the event of persistent diarrhoea or vomiting, it's worth taking **oral rehydration salts**, available at most pharmacies (or make your own from half a teaspoon of salt and eight teaspoons of sugar per litre of bottled water).

Unless you're going on a long journey, avoid taking Imodium and Lomotil. These bung you up by stopping gut movements and can extend the problem by preventing your body expelling the bugs that gave rise to the diarrhoea in the first place.

Dysentery and giardiasis

If there is blood or mucus in your faeces and you experience severe stomach cramps, you may have dysentery, which requires immediate medical attention. There are two forms of the disease, the more serious of which is **amoebic dysentery**. Even though the symptoms may well recede over a few days, the amoebae will remain in the gut and can go on to attack the liver; treatment with an antibiotic, metronidazole (Flagyl) is thus essential. Equally unpleasant is **bacillary dysentery**, also treated with antibiotics.

Giardiasis is caused by protozoa usually found in streams and rivers. Symptoms, typically watery diarrhoea and bad-smelling wind, appear around two weeks after the organism has entered the system and can last for up to two weeks. Giardiasis can be diagnosed from microscope analysis of stool samples, and is treated with metronidazole.

Mosquito-borne diseases

Given the prevalence in Cambodia of serious diseases spread by mosquitoes, including multi-resistant **malaria**, it is important to **avoid being bitten**. Mosquito nets often aren't provided in guesthouses and hotels, so it's worth bringing your own.

Wearing long trousers, socks and a long-sleeved top will reduce the chances of being bitten. **Insect repellents** containing DEET are the most effective, although you may want to consider a natural alternative such as those based on citronella.

Malaria

Malaria is prevalent year-round and can be found throughout the country with the exception of Phnom Penh, Siem Reap and the area immediately around the Tonle Sap lake. There's a high risk of malaria in northeastern Cambodia and in the central northern section of the country north of Kompong Thom between Stung Treng and Anlong

Veng – if you're travelling to these areas anti-malarial pills are usually recommended. Malaria risks in the remainder of the country are relatively low, and anti-malarials aren't usually advised except for those with medical conditions or those spending a long time in rural areas – although it's important to check the latest situation and seek professional medical advice before making a decision.

Malaria is contracted from the night-biting female anopheles mosquito, which injects a parasite into the bloodstream. Chills, fevers and sweating ensue after an incubation period of around twelve days, often along with aching joints, a cough and vomiting, and the symptoms repeat after a couple of days. In Cambodia the dangerous **falciparum** strain of the disease predominates; if untreated, it can be fatal.

Anti-malarial medication needs to be started in advance of arriving in a risk area. **Malarone** (atovaquone/proguanil) and **doxycycline** are the two most frequently prescribed anti-malarials for Cambodia. **Mefloquine** (aka Larium) is also sometimes recommended, but has the drawback of well-publicized side effects and may not be effective in northern provinces close to the Thai border thanks to the presence of mefloquine-resistant malaria in these areas. Note that taking anti-malarials doesn't guarantee that you won't contract the disease, a fact that reinforces the need to avoid being bitten.

Dengue fever

Outbreaks of **dengue fever** occur annually in Cambodia. Spread by the day-biting female aedes mosquito, this is a viral disease that takes about a week to develop following a bite. It resembles a bad case of flu; symptoms include high fever, aches and pains, headache and backache. After a couple of days a red rash appears on the torso, gradually spreading to the limbs. There may also be abnormal bleeding, which requires medical attention.

No vaccine is available and there is no effective treatment, although paracetamol can be taken to relieve the symptoms (*not* aspirin, which can increase the potential for bleeding); you should also drink plenty of fluids and get lots of rest. Although the symptoms should improve after five or six days, lethargy and depression can last for a month or more – consult a doctor if symptoms persist. Anyone who has previously contracted dengue fever is at particular risk if they subsequently contract a different virus strain, which can result in **dengue haemorrhagic fever**. In this condition the usual symptoms of dengue fever are accompanied by abdominal pain and vomiting; immediate medical help should be sought, as it can be fatal.

Zika

The **Zika virus** is also transmitted by the *aedes* mosquito. Occasional cases have been reported in Cambodia, while the presence of the disease in nearby countries including Thailand and Vietnam creates the potential for future outbreaks in the country – in late 2016 the US Center for Disease Control advised pregnant women planning to visit Cambodia to consider postponing their trips given the perceived risks.

Japanese encephalitis

Japanese encephalitis is a serious viral disease carried by night-biting mosquitoes that breed in the rice fields. The risk is highest between May and October. It's worth considering vaccination if you're going to be in rural areas of Cambodia for an extended time or are visiting during the high-risk period. Symptoms, which appear five to fifteen days after being bitten, include headaches, a stiff neck, flu-like aches and chills; there's no specific treatment, but it's wise to seek medical advice and take paracetamol or aspirin to ease the symptoms.

Sexually transmitted diseases

Cambodia has one of Asia's highest levels of **HIV/AIDS** infection, much of it the result of the country's burgeoning sex trade. An estimated 0.6 percent of the adult population aged 15–49 carries the disease, although rates are slowly falling from a high of 2 percent at the beginning of the millennium thanks to vigorous intervention by health services. **Syphilis** and **gonorrhoea** are also rife. **Condoms** are widely available, although it's best to stick to Western brands wherever possible.

MEDICAL RESOURCES

Canadian Society for International Health ☎ 613 241 5785, ⓦ csih.org. Extensive list of travel health centres.
CDC ☎ 1800 232 4636, ⓦ cdc.gov/travel. Official US government travel health site.
Hospital for Tropical Diseases Travel Clinic UK ⓦ www.thehtd .org/TravelClinic.aspx
International Society for Travel Medicine US ☎ 1404 373 8282, ⓦ istm.org. Has a full list of travel health clinics.
MASTA (Medical Advisory Service for Travellers Abroad) UK ⓦ masta-travel-health.com
Tropical Medical Bureau Ireland ☎ 01 2715 200, ⓦ tmb.ie
The Travel Doctor ⓦ traveldoctor.com.au. Lists travel clinics in Australia, New Zealand and South Africa.

Crime and personal safety

Despite its turbulent recent history, Cambodia is now a generally safe country in which to travel. It's important to be mindful, however, of the fact that Cambodia is one of the most heavily mined countries in the world, and also has significant quantities of unexploded ordnance (UXO) lying around – always stick to well-trodden paths in the countryside.

Crime

While there have been incidents of armed robbery against locals and tourists, violent crime is rare. Bag-snatching from tuk-tuks and motos is the most common crime affecting visitors, reaching a peak at festival times, most notably Khmer New Year, when finances become stretched. There's no need to be overly suspicious, but, equally, be aware that a small but significant number of visitors continue to be mugged at gunpoint, even in busy tourist areas. If you are unfortunate enough to find yourself being robbed, on no account resist.

With the above in mind, it's a very good idea to keep all valuables well out of sight. Never leave your bags lying around unprotected when sitting around in cafés, transport stops and so on, and be careful when using pricey and easily snatchable phones, cameras or similar, including wallets and purses. It's also worth making sure that all bags are hidden between your legs if travelling by moto – **snatch-and-grab** robberies have also been reported, with victims occasionally being pulled off the back of motos by the straps of their bags during attempted grabs.

There have also been reports of **drink spiking**, especially in Sihanoukville, so it's worth being aware of this when out on the town. Don't leave your drink unattended and don't accept the offer of a drink from anyone you don't know well.

All incidents should be reported to the **police** as soon as possible – you'll need a signed, dated report from them to claim on your travel insurance – and, if you lose your passport, to your embassy as well. In Phnom Penh, Siem Reap and Sihanoukville, English-speaking **tourist police** will help, but in the provinces you'll have to deal with the local police,

SCAMS

Scams are, by their very nature, constantly changing – here are a few of Cambodia's most popular:

Motorbike theft Particularly prevalent in Siem Reap and Phnom Penh, this involves you hiring a motorbike which is then stolen, forcing you to pay the full cost for a replacement. Many thefts are allegedly committed by the rental agencies themselves, who steal the bikes they've just hired out in order to claim the replacement value. Try to get your own lock to secure the bike, and don't put the name of your hotel on the rental agreement if you can help it lest you (and the bike) be followed back there. And be sure to record any pre-existing damage to the bike before you rent it as well.

Orphanage tourism Visiting an orphanage, spending some time interacting with local kids and perhaps making a donation to help keep things running might seem like a good thing to do. Unfortunately, many Cambodian "orphanages" have been set up purely for the sake of squeezing donations out of foreigners, either casual visitors or longer-term volunteers. Most of the children aren't actually orphans at all, but have been handed over by their parents in return for money or some other inducement (perhaps, ironically, the promise of a better future for their kids). The children, meanwhile, have not only been plucked from their homes but are also denied proper schooling (the responsibility for which is often placed in the hands of well-meaning but unqualified short-term volunteers), while there is also widespread evidence that many suffer systematic abuse in their new "homes".

Baby milk Popular in Siem Reap, this scam sees you approached by a young girl carrying a baby (not necessarily her own) and asking you plaintively for your help in buying some powdered milk (or other essential) for her child. You pay an inflated price for the milk, which is then returned clandestinely to the shop, with "mother" and shopkeeper splitting the loot.

Fake monks Another mainly Siem Reap scam during which a "monk" approaches you attempting to sell you some kind of good-luck charm for a not-inconsiderable sum. Any self-styled monk who attempts to sell you stuff or asks for money is – patently – not what they seem.

who are unlikely to have more than a smattering of English, so if possible take a Khmer-speaker with you. Though the vast majority of Cambodian police will do their best to help in an emergency, a small minority are not averse to trying to elicit money from foreigners. If you're riding a motorbike or driving a motor vehicle, they may well deem that you've committed an offence. You can argue the "fine" down to a few dollars and may as well pay up, although if you can stand the hassle and don't mind wasting a lot more time you may feel it worth reporting such incidents to the police commissioner.

Road accidents usually attract vast crowds of curious onlookers, and if any damage to property or injury to a person or domestic animal has occurred, then you'll have to stay at the scene until the police arrive. It's the driver's responsibility to come to a financial arrangement with the other parties involved. In spite of their general amiability, it's not unknown for locals to try to coerce foreigners into coughing up money, even if they are the innocent party or merely a passenger.

Drugs

As you'd expect given its proximity to some of the world's major drug-producing regions, drugs both soft and hard are common in Cambodia. **Marijuana** is widely available, especially around the southern beaches, and you'll be approached by peddlers on a fairly regular basis in all major tourist spots. Possession is of course illegal, and although prosecutions are rare, purchasing and consuming dope always carries a risk of falling foul of the police – and most likely having to pay some sort of backhander in order to avoid having charges pressed. **Hard drugs** including opium, cocaine and so on are also available. Needless to say the authorities take a much dimmer view of these than of dope, and possession may well earn you a term in the nearest Cambodian prison – and, given the suspect quality of a lot of the drugs sold on the street, could even be fatal. There have been cases of

travellers dying after buying what they believed to be cocaine but which turned out to be pure heroin.

Note that in the case of any medical complications the nearest properly equipped hospital is in Bangkok.

Land mines and unexploded ordnance

The UN estimates that between four and six million **land mines** were laid in Cambodia between 1979 and 1991, but no one really knows. The Vietnamese and the government laid them as protection against Khmer Rouge guerrillas, who in turn laid them to intimidate local populations; neither side recorded the locations of the minefields. To date more than two thousand minefields have been identified (usually through members of the local population being blown up), and new locations are regularly being reported – 111 people were killed or injured by mines in 2015 alone, with the highest proportion (28) in Battambang province around the Thai border. Several organizations are actively working at de-mining the countryside, and at the number of casualties is decreasing; but given the scale of the problem, it will be many years before the mines are cleared completely (see p.305). In rural areas, take care not to leave well-used paths and never take short-cuts across rice fields without a local guide. Areas known to be badly contaminated are signed with a red skull and the words "Beware Mines".

As if this problem weren't enough, in the 1970s the United States dropped more than half a million tonnes of **bombs** on Cambodia. This began as part of a secret and illicit plan to expose the Ho Chi Minh Trail used by communist North Vietnamese troops, and ended up in a massive countrywide bombing campaign to support the pro-American Lon Nol government against the Khmer Rouge. **Unexploded ordnance** (UXO), or explosive remnants of war (ERW), remains a risk in rural areas, with the southeast, centre and northeast of the country particularly affected; in the countryside don't pick up or kick any unidentified metal objects.

CHILDREN AT RISK

Cambodia has an unfortunate reputation as a destination for paedophiles, and child sex tourism has grown here as a result of crackdowns on child prostitution in other Southeast Asian countries. The Ministry of the Interior (National Police) asks that anyone witnessing child prostitution in Cambodia immediately report it to the police on their national **hotline** (1288 or 023 997919). You might also register your concerns with ChildSafe (012 311112 in Phnom Penh, 017 358758 in Siem Reap, 012 478100 in Sihanoukville; thinkchildsafe.org/hotline). Child Helpline Cambodia (1280) provides further information and counselling to affected children.

The media

Much of Cambodia's media is sponsored by the country's political parties and continues to be subject to government whims – in 2016 the country ranked 128 out of the 180 countries measured in terms of press freedom by Reporters Without Borders, a relatively lowly position, although still ahead of Thailand, Laos and Vietnam.

Newspapers and magazines

Cambodia has around ten daily **Khmer-language newspapers**. The two main dailies are *Rasmei Kampuchea* (*Light of Cambodia*) and *Koh Santepheap*, both of which are pro-government. Cambodia's three **English-language newspapers** – the *Cambodia Daily* (Ⓦcambodiadaily.com; published daily except Sun), the *Phnom Penh Post* (Ⓦphnompenhpost.com; Mon–Fri) and the *Khmer Times* (Ⓦkhmertimeskh.com; Mon–Fri) – can be found at newsstands in larger cities. It's also worth looking out for the several English-language **magazines**. *Asia Life* (Ⓦasialifemagazine.com; free from cafés and restaurants) is the *Time Out* of Phnom Penh, with news about all the latest happenings in the capital.

Television and radio

Cambodia's fifteen-odd **Khmer TV stations** broadcast a mix of political coverage, game shows, concerts, cartoons and sport. Guesthouses and hotels usually offer **cable** and, increasingly, **satellite TV** stations, including BBC World, CNN, CNBC, HBO, National Geographic and Star Sport.

Among the many **Khmer radio stations**, just a couple carry English programmes. Love FM on **97.5 FM** features a mix of Western pop, news stories and phone-ins.

Festivals

Cambodians are always celebrating a festival of some sort, heading out to the temple with family and friends or taking off for the provinces; unsurprisingly, festivals are the busiest times for shopping and travelling. For details of public holidays, see "Travel essentials" (see p.43).

The most significant **festival** of the year is **Choul Chhnam** (Khmer New Year; April 13 or 14), when families get together, homes are spring-cleaned and people flock to the temples with elaborate offerings. **Pchum Ben** (late Sept/early Oct), or "Ancestors' Day", is another key date on the festive calendar. Families make offerings to their ancestors in the fifteen days leading up to it, and celebrations take place in temples on the day itself.

Marking the start of the planting season in May, the ceremony of **Bon Chroat Preah Nongkoal** (Royal Ploughing Ceremony), held at Lean Preah Sre park in Phnom Penh, combines animism, Buddhism and plenty of pomp. It begins with chanting monks asking the earth spirits for permission to plough. Then ceremonial furrows are drawn, rice is scattered and offerings are made to the divinities. The most important part of the ceremony, however, is what the Royal Bulls choose when offered rice, grain, grass, water and wine. Rice or grain augur well; water signifies rain; grass is a sign that crops will be devastated by insects; and wine, that there will be drought.

The **Bon Om Toeuk** water festival (early Nov; see p.58) celebrates the moment when the current of the Tonle Sap River, which swells so much during the rainy season that it actually pushes water upstream, reverses and flows back into the Mekong. The centre of festivities is Phnom Penh's riverbank, where everyone gathers to watch boat racing, an illuminated boat parade and fireworks.

Buddhist **offering days** (exact dates vary according to the lunar calendar) are also colourful occasions: stalls do a roaring trade in bunches of flowers that are taken to temples and used to decorate shrines at home. Lotus buds – the traditional offering flower to the Buddha – are artistically folded to expose their pale-pink inner petals, while jasmine buds are threaded onto sticks and strings as fragrant tokens.

Culture and etiquette

These days the handshake has become quite common in Cambodia, and is used between Cambodian men or when Cambodian men greet foreigners; generally, however, women still greet foreigners using the traditional Cambodian form of greeting, the sompeyar.

The **sompeyar** is a gesture of politeness and a sign of respect. Typically, it is performed with hands placed palms together, fingers pointing up, in front of the body at chest level, and the head is inclined slightly forward as if about to bow. When greeting monks, however, the hands should be placed in front of the face, and when paying respects to Buddha (or the king), the hands are put in front of the forehead. The *sompeyar* is always used towards those older than yourself, and is taught to children at an early age.

Cambodians are reserved people and most find **public displays of affection** offensive. Holding hands or linking arms in public, though quite a common sign of friendship between two men or two women, is considered unacceptable if it involves a member of the opposite sex; even married couples won't touch each other in public. Traditionally, Cambodian women would not have gone out drinking or have been seen with a man who was not her fiancé or husband, although younger people in the larger cities are gradually adopting more westernized ways.

Everywhere in Cambodia, travellers will gain more respect if they are **well dressed**. Cambodians themselves dress modestly, men usually wearing long trousers and a shirt. Many women wear blouses rather than T-shirts, and *sampots* (sarongs) or knee-length skirts, but many also wear trousers or jeans, and younger girls in larger cities can increasingly be seen in the kind of short skirts and strappy tops favoured by their Western counterparts. Even so, as a general rule it's best to avoid skimpy clothes and shorts unless you're at the beach.

When **visiting temples** it's important to wear clothes that keep your shoulders and legs covered. Hats should be removed when passing through the temple gate and shoes taken off before you go into any of the buildings (shoes are also removed before entering a Cambodian home). If you sit down on the floor inside a shrine, avoid pointing the soles of your feet towards any Buddha images (in fact, you should observe the same rule towards people generally, in any location). **Monks** are not allowed to touch women, so women should take care when walking near monks, and avoid sitting next to them on public transport.

Cambodians are often intrigued at the **appearance of foreigners**, and it is not considered rude to stare quite intently at visitors. Local people may also giggle at men with earrings – in Cambodia boys are given an earring in the belief that it will help an undescended testicle. It's worth bearing in mind that **displaying anger** won't get you far, as the Khmers simply find this embarrassing.

Shopping

Cambodia has a great range of souvenirs – colourful cotton and silk fabrics, wood and stone carvings, lacquerware, jewellery and much more. Local handicrafts have also been given a boost thanks to various local and NGO schemes set up to give Cambodia's large disabled population and other disadvantaged members of society a new source of income by training them in various traditional crafts.

Local **markets** are often the best place to hunt for collectibles. In the capital, Central Market and Psar Toul Tom Poung (Russian Market) are the places to buy souvenirs, and there are also several excellent markets in Siem Reap. In both towns you'll also find plenty of specialist **shops**, galleries and hotel boutiques – usually more expensive, though quality is generally significantly higher.

As a general rule, when shopping for souvenirs it's a good idea to buy it when you see it. Something unusual you chance upon in the provinces may not be available elsewhere.

Textiles

The ubiquitous chequered scarf, the **krama**, worn by all Cambodians, is arguably the country's most popular tourist souvenir, and there are plenty to buy in markets everywhere. Many *krama*s are woven from mixed synthetic threads; although the cloth feels soft, a *krama* of this sort is hot to wear and doesn't dry very well if you want to use it as a towel. The very best *krama*s come from Kompong Cham and Phnom Sarok and are made from cotton (*umbok*). Those from Kompong Cham are often to be had from female peddlers in the markets – a large one costs around $3.

Though cotton *krama*s feel stiff and thin at first, a few good scrubs in cold water will soften them up and increase the density of texture. They last for years and actually improve with wear, making a cool, dust-proof and absorbent fabric.

Silk

The weaving of **silk** in Cambodia can be traced back to the Angkor era, when the Khmer started to imitate imported cloth from India. Weaving skills learned over generations were lost with the Khmer Rouge, but the 1990s saw a resurgence of silk weaving in many Cambodian villages.

Silk is produced in fixed widths – nearly always 800mm – and sold in two lengths: a **kabun** (3.6m),

BARGAINING

Prices are fixed in shops and malls, but you're expected to **bargain** in markets and when buying from hawkers. Bargaining is seen as an amicable game and social exchange. The seller usually starts at a moderately inflated price: for cheapish items, with a starting price below $10, expect to be able to knock around a third off; with pricier items you might be lucky to get a reduction of ten percent. To keep a sense of perspective while bargaining, it's worth remembering that on items like a T-shirt or *krama*, the vendor's margin is often as little as a thousand riel.

sufficient for a long straight skirt and short-sleeved top; and a **sampot** (half a *kabun*), which is enough for a long skirt. Sometimes the silk will have been washed, which makes it softer in both texture and hue – and slightly more expensive. **Silk scarves** are inexpensive (around $5–6) and readily available.

There are several different styles of fabric, with villages specializing in particular types of weaving. **Hol** is a time-honoured cloth decorated with small patterns symbolizing flowers, butterflies and diamonds, and traditionally produced with threads of five basic colours – yellow, red, black, green and blue (modern variations use pastel shades). The vibrant, shimmering hues change depending on the direction from which they are viewed. **Parmoong** is a lustrous ceremonial fabric, made by weaving a motif or border of gold or silver thread onto plain silk. Some *parmoong* is woven exclusively for men in checks or stripes of cream, green or red, to be worn in sarongs. Traditional wall-hangings, **pedan**, come in classical designs often featuring stylized temples and animals such as elephants and lions; they're inexpensive ($5–10) and easily transportable.

Other fabrics

Clothes made out of **Bamboo fabric** are also increasingly available (Bambou Indochine in Phnom Penh and Siem Reap is the main retailer) – expensive but marvellously soft, and also much more environmentally friendly to produce than cotton. Cheap "**pashmina**" scarves are sold in huge quantities in many tourist markets but are unlikely to contain much, if any, genuine pashmina wool.

Wood and stone carvings

Wood and stone carvings are available in a wide range of sizes, from small heads of Jayavarman VII, costing just a couple of dollars, to almost life-sized dancing apsaras costing hundreds or thousands of dollars. In Phnom Penh you'll find a good selection along Street 178 near the National Museum, or in Psar Toul Tom Poung. Quality varies from shop to shop, with the more mass-produced items

inevitably lacking finesse. To find something really fine you're better off at the workshop of the Artisans d'Angkor in Siem Reap (see p.14) or a traditional stone-carving village such as Santok (see p.207) or Choob (see p.127).

Antiques and curios

Antiques and **curios** can be found at specialist stalls in and around Psar Toul Tom Poung in Phnom Penh, and at the Siem Reap Night Market. Look out for the partitioned **wooden boxes** used to store betel-chewing equipment, as well as elegant silver boxes for the betel nuts, phials for the leaves and paste, and cutters for slicing the nuts. There are plenty of **religious artefacts** available too, from wooden Buddha images and other carvings to brass bowls and offering plates.

You may occasionally find antique traditional **musical instruments**, such as the *chapei*, a stringed instrument with a long neck and a round sound-box; and the *chhing*, in which the two small brass plates, similar to castanets in appearance, are played by being brushed against each other.

Compasses used in the ancient Chinese art of feng shui can be bought for just a few dollars; they indicate compass directions related to the five elements – wood, fire, earth, metal and water. You might also be able to search out **opium weights**, used to weigh out the drug and often formed in the shape of small human figures or animals.

Cambodia's ancient temples have suffered massively from looting, and although it's unlikely that you'll be offered ancient figurines (most of the trade goes to Bangkok or Singapore), many other stolen artefacts – such as chunchiet funerary statues from Rattanakiri – are finding their way onto the market. To export anything purporting to be an antique you'll need the correct paperwork, so check that the dealer can provide this before agreeing a deal. Also be aware that Cambodians are expert at artificially ageing their wares and be sure that you want the item for its own sake rather than because of its alleged antiquity.

Silver and gold

Most **silverware** in Cambodia is sold in Phnom Penh and produced in villages nearby, particularly Kompong Luong. The price will give you an indication of whether an item is solid silver or silver-plated copper – a few dollars for the silver-plated items; more than double that for a comparable item in solid silver. Silver necklaces, bracelets and earrings, mostly imported from Indonesia, are sold only for the tourist market (Khmers don't rate the metal for jewellery) and go for just a few dollars in the markets.

There's nothing sentimental or romantic about the Khmer obsession with **gold jewellery**. This is considered a means of investment and explains the hundreds of gold dealers in and around markets all over the country. Gold is good value and items can be made up quickly and quite cheaply to your own design, and even set with gems from Pailin and Rattanakiri.

Other collectibles and consumables

Items made from **recycled materials** are among Cambodia's most interesting souvenirs. **Bags**, wallets and purses created from recycled packaging (Elephant Concrete Cement sacks are particularly popular) can be found in many places, while in Phnom Penh and Siem Reap you'll also find more unusual creations like **jewellery** made from recycled bullets and shell casings, or out of beads made from recycled paper.

Local **spices** and other foodstuff are also widely available – often offered in fancy packaging in touristy markets, although you'll find identical stuff at half the price in local supermarkets, including local coffees and spices, particularly packets of the prized **Kampot pepper**. Cambodian-made spirits including rice wines and rums are also increasingly available. **Basketry items** are another cheap and lightweight (if bulky) souvenir, generally woven in villages by women and including a wide range of baskets, bowls and plates.

Travel essentials

Climate

Cambodia remains consistently hot year-round – seasons are defined principally by rainfall rather than temperature (see box, p.8). The **dry season** runs from November to May, subdivided into the so-called **cool season** (Nov–Feb), the peak tourist period, and the slightly warmer and more humid **hot season** (March–May). The **rainy season** (roughly June–Oct) is when the country receives most of its annual rainfall, although occasional downpours can occur at pretty much any time of year.

Costs

Cambodia is one of the cheapest Asian countries to visit, and although prices are starting to creep up, the country still offers outstanding value.

Good budget **rooms** are available for around $7–8 in most parts of the country (slightly more in Phnom Penh and Siem Reap). **Eating** is also cheap. A meal at a local market or Khmer restaurant can be had for $2 or even less, while main courses in tourist restaurants start from as little as $3 (although upscale places can cost considerably more). A small bottle of mineral water costs just 1000 riel, while draught beer usually sells for $1 a glass. **Transport** is similarly inexpensive – $1 per hour of travel suffices as a rough rule of thumb, although you'll pay a bit more on certain routes or when travelling with more upmarket bus companies. **Entrance fees** are also generally modest – tickets to visit the temples at Angkor are excellent value, although a few museums and other sights are disproportionately expensive.

Transport and **tours** are the two things most likely to blow your budget. Hiring a car and driver to explore remote temples like Banteay Chhmar, Koh Ker, Preah Khan (Kompong Thom) and Preah Vihear can easily set you back something in the region of $60–100 per day. Tours are also pricey. Visiting the temples of Angkor by tuk-tuk is relatively inexpensive, but more unusual tours – birdwatching and boat trips, quad-biking, horseriding, and so on – will generally set you back at least $60 a day, and often much more.

All of which means that by staying in budget guesthouses, eating at local restaurants and markets and travelling on public transport you could conceivably get by on as little as $10 per person a day if travelling in a couple and cutting out all extras. Eating in tourist restaurants, indulging in a few beers and taking the occasional tour by tuk-tuk will push this up to $15–20 a day. For $50 a day you can live very comfortably, staying in nice hotels and eating well, while $100 a day allows you to stay in luxurious accommodation – although it's also possible to spend a lot more than this.

Sales tax of ten percent and various levels of service charge are sometimes added to the bill in more upmarket hotels – always check whether quoted rates include all taxes or not. Tax is also sometimes added to food at fancier restaurants – in which case this should be clearly stated on the menu.

Electricity

The electrical supply is 220 volts AC, 50Hz. Most Cambodian sockets take two-pin, round-pronged plugs (although you'll also find some which take two-pin, flat-pronged plugs). The electricity supply is pretty reliable, although power cuts are not unknown and some places (particularly island resorts in the south) may rely on solar power, while electricity in village homestays may only be available after dark.

Gay and lesbian Cambodia

Cambodia is one of Asia's most gay-friendly destinations. Same-sex activity is not illegal, and homosexuality and other alternative lifestyles and sexual behaviours are a recognized (if not always completely accepted) aspect of national culture, as evidenced by the regular drag and ladyboy shows of Phnom Penh, Siem Reap and Sihanoukville (for some interesting background see Ⓦen.wikipedia .org/wiki/LGBT_rights_in_Cambodia). As you'd expect, the gay scene (Ⓦcambodia-gay.com) is liveliest in the big cities: Siem Reap, Sihanoukville and, especially, Phnom Penh. Gay-friendly hotels include the Arthur & Paul Hotel (Ⓦarthurandpaul .com) and Rambutan Resort (Ⓦrambutanresort .com) in Phnom Penh and the Men's Resort and Spa

in Siem Reap (Ⓦmens-resort.com). Tours are run by Ⓦtravelgayasia.com, whose website also has lots of useful information about gay-friendly bars and other venues.

Insurance

Before travelling to Cambodia you'd do well to take out an insurance policy to cover against theft, loss of personal items and documentation, illness and injury. However, before you pay for a new policy, it's worth checking whether you are already covered: some all-risks home insurance policies may cover your possessions when overseas, and many private medical schemes include cover when abroad – check that they cover Cambodia. Students will often find that their student health coverage extends during the vacations and for one term beyond the date of last enrolment.

A typical **travel insurance policy** usually provides cover for the loss of baggage, tickets and – up to a certain limit – cash or cheques, as well as cancellation or curtailment of your journey. Most of them exclude so-called "dangerous" activities unless an extra premium is paid: in Cambodia this can mean scuba diving, riding a motorbike and trekking.

Internet

Getting online in Cambodia is relatively easy, with virtually all hotels and guesthouses offering **free wi-fi** (as do many restaurants and bars). Internet cafés are fairly thin on the ground, although there are usually one or two in most towns of any size. Rates are generally cheap (2000–4000 riel/hr), although connections may be slow.

Laundry

You can get laundry done practically everywhere, at hotels and guesthouses or at private laundries in all towns. Prices are pretty uniform, at 500–1000 riel

---

ROUGH GUIDES TRAVEL INSURANCE

Rough Guides has teamed up with WorldNomads.com to offer great **travel insurance deals**. Policies are available to residents of more than 150 countries, with cover for a wide range of adventure sports, 24hr emergency assistance, high levels of medical and evacuation cover and a stream of travel safety information. Roughguides.com users can take advantage of their policies online 24/7, from anywhere in the world – even if you're already travelling. And since plans often change when you're on the road, you can extend your policy and even claim online. Roughguides.com users who buy travel insurance with WorldNomads.com can also leave a positive footprint and donate to a community development project. For more information, go to Ⓦroughguides.com/travel-insurance.

per item or $1–2 per kilogram. In Phnom Penh and Siem Reap there are a number of places with driers, giving a speedy turnaround (3hr).

Mail

Mail to Europe, Australasia and North America takes between five and ten days. Stamps for **postcards** cost around 2000 riel to Europe/North America.

Airmail parcels to Europe and North America cost more than $25 per kilo, so if you're heading to Thailand it's worth waiting until you get there, where postage is cheaper. You'll be charged 3000 riel for the obligatory customs form, detailing the contents and their value, but it isn't necessary to leave the package open for checking. Post offices also sell cardboard boxes for mailing items.

Poste restante mail can be received at the main post offices in Phnom Penh, Sihanoukville and Siem Reap, for 500 riel per item. When collecting mail, bring your passport and ask them to check under both your first name and your family name.

Maps

Most maps of Cambodia are horribly inaccurate and/or out of date. Far and away the best is Reise Know-How's *Kambodscha* map (that's "Cambodia" in German), beautifully drawn on un-rippable waterproof paper, and as detailed and up to date as you could hope, given Cambodia's ever-developing road network.

Money

Cambodia uses a **dual-currency system**, with local currency, the riel, used alongside (and interchange-ably with) the US dollar, converted at the almost universally recognized rate of 4000 riel to US$1 (an exchange rate which has remained stable for several years now), although fractionally different conversion rates of $1 to 4100 or 4200 riel are occasionally applied. **Riel notes** (there are no riel coins, nor is US coinage used in Cambodia) are available in denominations of 50, 100, 500, 1000, 2000, 5000, 10,000, 20,000, 50,000 and 100,000. You can **pay** for most things – and will receive change – either in dollars, in riel, or even in a mixture of the two; there's no need to change dollars into riel. Larger sums are usually quoted in dollars and smaller amounts in riel. Torn or badly soiled dollar bills may be rejected.

Things get a bit more confused near the Thai border, where Thai **baht** are generally preferred to riel, or at Bavet, the Vietnamese border crossing, where you may be quoted prices in Vietnamese **dong**. If you don't have baht you can generally pay in US dollars or riel, though you might end up paying fractionally more.

There are ATMs at both Phnom Penh and Siem Reap international airports and in the border areas at Poipet, Bavet and Koh Kong, so you can get US$ cash as soon as you **arrive in Cambodia**. Note also that unless you have obtained a **Cambodian visa** in advance, you'll need $35 in cash to buy one on arrival.

Bargaining

Prices at upmarket hotels, shops, food stalls, cafés and restaurants are fixed, as are fares for bus journeys and boat trips. However, when shopping in markets, taking motos, tuk-tuks or cyclos, **bargaining** is expected. Prices in cheaper hotels can sometimes be negotiated, particularly if you're staying for a few nights or longer.

Accessing your money

All large (and an increasing number of smaller) Cambodian towns now have **ATMs** accepting foreign cards and dispensing US dollars. The two main networks are those belonging to **Canadia Bank** and **Acleda Bank** (pronounced *A-See-Lay-Dah*), both of which accept Visa and MasterCard. Virtually all banks generally charge a $4–5 withdrawal fee on top of whatever fees are levied by your card provider.

An increasing number of places accept **credit cards**, typically mid- and upper-range hotels and Western-oriented restaurants and shops in bigger towns and cities. You may be charged a surcharge (around five percent) if paying by card, however.

Most banks also change **travellers' cheques** (although few use them these days), usually for a two-percent commission; travellers' cheques in currencies other than dollars are sometimes viewed with suspicion and may be rejected. You can also get **cash advances** on Visa and MasterCard at some banks and exchange bureaux (including the Canadia, ANZ and Acleda banks). It's also possible to have money **wired from home**. The Acleda Bank handles Western Union transfers, while the Canadia Bank is the agent for Moneygram. Fees, needless to say, can be steep.

If you need to **change foreign currency** it's easiest to head to a bank – there are foreign

EXCHANGE RATES

Exchange rates are currently $1=4000 riel, £1=4900 riel, E1=4220.

exchange facilities at all branches of Canadia Bank. Alternatively, there are also usually one or two **money changers** around most markets in the country (look for the big stacks of banknotes piled up in front of their stalls). Thai baht, pounds sterling and euros are all widely accepted for exchange, although other currencies may not be, especially outside larger cities and tourist centres. Check your money carefully before leaving and feel free to reject any notes in poor condition, especially larger-denomination dollar bills with tears or blemishes.

Banking hours are generally Monday to Friday 8/8.30am to 3.30pm (often also Sat 8.30–11.30am).

Opening hours and public holidays

Key **tourist sights**, such as the National Museum, the Royal Palace, Silver Pagoda and Toul Sleng Genocide Museum in Phnom Penh, are open every day including most public holidays. The temples at Angkor, Tonle Bati and Sambor Prei Kuk and the country's national parks are open daily from 7.30am to 5.30pm (while a few are open from dawn to dusk). **Markets** open daily from around 6am until 5pm, **shops** between 7am and 7pm (or until 9/10pm in tourist areas). The main **post office** in Phnom Penh is open from 7.30am to 5.30pm Monday to Friday. In the provinces, post office hours tend to be 8am to 11am and 2pm to 5.30pm (earlier on Saturday), with some, in Siem Reap, for example, open on Sunday. **Banks** tend to open Monday to Friday from 8.30am to 3.30pm, and sometimes on Saturday as well, between 8.30am and 11.30am. Pretty much everywhere apart from Phnom Penh, Siem Reap and Sihanoukville is fairly dead after around 9pm at night, or indeed earlier.

Public holidays

Dates for Buddhist religious **holidays** are variable, changing each year with the lunar calendar. Any public holidays that fall on a Saturday or Sunday are taken the following Monday.

Note that public holidays are often "stretched" by a day or so, particularly at Khmer New Year, Pchum Ben and for the Water Festival.

CALENDAR OF PUBLIC HOLIDAYS

January 1 International New Year's Day
January 7 Victory Day, celebrating the liberation of Phnom Penh from the Khmer Rouge in 1979
February (variable) Meak Bochea, celebrating Buddhist teachings and precepts
March 8 International Women's Day

April 13/14 (variable) Bon Chaul Chhnam (Khmer New Year)
April/May (variable) Visaka Bochea, celebrating the birth, enlightenment and passing into nirvana of the Buddha
May 1 Labour Day
May (variable) Bon Chroat Preah Nongkoal, the "Royal Ploughing Ceremony"
May 13–15 (variable) King Sihamoni's Birthday
June 1 International Children's Day
June 18 The Queen Mother's Birthday
September 24 Constitution Day
Late September/early October (variable) Pchum Ben, "Ancestors' Day"
October 15 King Father's Commemoration Day, celebrating the memory of Norodom Sihanouk
October 23 Anniversary of the Paris Peace Accords
October 29–November 1 (variable) King's Coronation Day
November 9 Independence Day
Early November Bon Om Toeuk, "Water Festival"
December 10 UN Human Rights Day

Outdoor activities

Cambodia's vast potential for **outdoor and adventure activities** is slowly being tapped, with myriad tour operators offering an ever-expanding spread of one-day trips and more extended tours. The main appeal of most outdoor activities is the chance to get off the beaten track and out into the countryside for a glimpse of traditional Cambodian rural lifestyles, with numerous trekking opportunities, along with trips by bike, kayak and boat.

Trekking, ranging from one-day to week-long hikes, is the major draw in the upland forests of eastern Cambodia. Banlung is the main trekking centre, while there are also a growing range of hiking opportunities at Sen Monorom, including the chance to walk through the forest with elephants at the innovative Elephant Valley Project and other local sanctuaries (see p.239). Hiking trips around Siem Reap can be arranged through Hidden Cambodia and Beyond Unique (see p.145). In the south, you can hike into the southern Cardamoms from the community-based ecotourism project Chi Phat (see p.270) – they arrange trekking and cycling trips that last from just a morning to a few days. The Wild KK Project in Koh Kong (see p.268) offers multi-day adventures into the Areng Valley (deep in the Cardamoms), including hiking, cycling and kayaking.

Cycling tours are another popular option, ideally suited to Cambodia's predominantly flat terrain and extensive network of relatively traffic-free rural backroads. Tours in Siem Reap are run by Camouflage, Grasshopper Adventures and several other operators (see p.145), in Phnom Penh by

SEY

Walk around any Cambodian town towards dusk and you'll see groups of young men stood in circles in parks, on pavements, or any other available space playing the uniquely Cambodian game of **sey**. The aim of the game is simple, with a kind of large, heavily weighted shuttlecock being kicked from player to player around the circle, the goal being to keep the shuttlecock in the air for as long as possible. It's a kind of collaborative keepy-uppy rather than a competitive sport, although players typically attempt to outdo one another in the flamboyance of their footwork. Simple side-footed kicks keep the shuttlecock moving; cheeky back heels gain extra marks for artistic merit; and for maximum kudos players attempt spectacular behind-the-back overhead kicks, before the shuttlecock falls to the ground, and the game begins again.

Grasshopper Adventures (see p.77), in Battambang by various operators (see box, p.118), and in the south by Spice Roads (see p.268). There are also loads of cycling possibilities around the Mekong, with tours run by Xplore Asia in Stung Treng (see p.227) and by a couple of operators in Kratie (see box, p.224). The country's rough backcountry dirt tracks are also a magnet for **off-road motorbike** enthusiasts; in Siem Reap, Hidden Cambodia and Siem Reap Dirt Bikes (see p.145) organize a range of group dirt-biking tours. **Quad-biking** excursions can also be arranged in Siem Reap through Quad Adventures Cambodia (see p.145), in Sihanoukville through Woody's All-Terrain Adventures (see p.254), and around Phnom Penh through Quad Bike Trails (see p.77).

Cambodia's majestic lakes and rivers are another major draw. **Kayaking** trips are run by Sorya Kayaking Adventures in Kratie (see p.224), Green Orange Kayak in Battambang (see p.118), Indo Chine EX in Siem Reap (see p.145) and Xplore Asia (see p.227) in Stung Treng. There are also plenty of **boat trips** on the Mekong available at Kompong Cham, Kratie and Stung Treng; around the various floating villages on the Tonle Sap at Siem Reap, Kompong Chhnang and Pursat; and around Ream National Park, Koh S'dach and the islands near Kep in the south. **Watersports**, snorkelling and island-hopping trips are all available from Sihanoukville, and **diving** at Sihanoukville and Koh S'dach (see p.253).

Horseriding excursions are available through The Happy Ranch in Siem Reap (see p.146). There's some outstanding **birdwatching** around the Tonle Sap lake at the Prek Toal Biosphere Reserve and at Ang Trapeang Thmor Crane Sanctuary between Siem Reap and Sisophon and at other locations. Excellent tours are run by the Sam Veasna Centre in Siem Reap (see p.146) to twitching hotspots countrywide.

There are **balloon**, **helicopter** and **microlight** flights above the temples of Angkor, while real adrenaline junkies should make for Flight of the Gibbon in Siem Reap (see p.145), which offers treetop **ziplining** adventures through the forest canopy, or the Mayura Zipline across Bou Sraa waterfall (see p.241) in Sen Monorom. There's also **rock climbing**, **caving** and **Via Ferrata** in Kampot (see p.277).

Phones

If you're going to be spending long in Cambodia or making a lot of calls it's well worth buying a local **Sim card**, which will get you rates for both domestic and international calls far below what you're likely to pay using your home provider (although obviously you'll need to make sure that your handset is unlocked first – or buy one locally). Sim cards can be bought for a few dollars at most mobile phone shops; you'll need to show your passport as proof of identity. International calls can cost as little as US$0.25 per minute, while domestic calls will cost about 300–500 riel per minute.

Cambodia's three main **mobile phone service providers** are Cellcard (Ⓦcellcard.com.kh), Smart (Ⓦsmart.com.kh), and Metfone (Ⓦmetfone.com.kh), all of which offer reliable countrywide coverage, with Cellcard perhaps being the best. If you want to use your home mobile phone, you'll need to check with your phone service provider whether it will work abroad, and what the call charges are to use it in Cambodia. Most mobiles in the UK, Australia and New Zealand use GSM, which works well in Southeast Asia, although not all North American cellphones will (for example the CDMA-type phones used on the Verizon and Sprint networks).

You can make **domestic** and **international phone calls** at the post offices and telecom offices in most towns. These services are invariably run by the government telecommunications network, Camintel (Ⓦcamintel.com). Some internet cafés also allow you to make calls via **Skype**; better places have headphones with a microphone so that you can talk in reasonable privacy.

EMERGENCY NUMBERS

There are no nationwide **emergency numbers** in Cambodia. If you need medical or police assistance, ask staff at your accommodation to dial local emergency services on your behalf. There are English-speaking tourist police in Phnom Penh (p.94), Siem Reap (p.157) and Sihanoukville (p.259). In Phnom Penh you can call the following numbers: ☎ 117 (police), ☎ 118 (fire) and ☎ 119 (ambulance), although the person answering won't necessarily speak English. Your embassy (see p.94) and travel insurance provider should also have an emergency number in the event that you require urgent medical attention, are the victim of a serious crime, or manage to get yourself arrested.

To **call Cambodia from abroad**, dial your international access code, followed by ☎ 855, then the local area code (minus the initial 0), then the number.

Photography

Cambodians generally love being photographed – although it is common courtesy to ask first; they also take a lot of photos themselves and may well ask you to stand in theirs. It's best to avoid taking photographs of anything with a military connotation, just in case. You can get your digital shots transferred to CD or printed at most photo shops in Phnom Penh and Siem Reap, although the quality of the prints may not be as good as you'd get at home.

Time

Cambodia is 7hr ahead of GMT; 12hr ahead of New York and Montréal; 15hr ahead of Los Angeles and Vancouver; 1hr behind Perth; 4hr behind Sydney and 5hr behind Auckland; 5hr ahead of South Africa. There is no daylight saving time.

Tipping

Tipping is not generally expected, but a few hundred riel extra for a meal or a tuk-tuk or moto ride is always appreciated.

Toilets

Finding a toilet (*bong-kun*) if you get caught short can be tricky. There are no public conveniences apart from a few places set up by enterprising individuals that you can use for a few hundred riel – they'll almost certainly be Asian-style squat toilets, rather than western thrones. In a big town your best bet is to dive into the nearest large hotel or restaurant. Out in the sticks there are (smelly) toilets at the back of most restaurants or find a convenient guesthouse. And don't expect to find any toilet paper except in smart urban establishments. Out in

the country you may have to do as locals do and find the nearest available bush.

Tourist information

There are **tourist offices** in many larger towns, but most are chronically underfunded, totally lacking in English-speaking staff, and often closed. The best source of local information on the ground is likely to be your hotel or guesthouse, or a local tour operator or travel agent. There are no Cambodian tourist offices abroad, and Cambodian embassies aren't equipped to handle tourist enquiries.

Travellers with disabilities

Cambodia has the unhappy distinction of having one of the world's highest proportions of disabled people per capita (around 1 in 250 people) – due to land mines and the incidence of polio and other wasting diseases. That said, there is no special provision for the disabled, so travellers with disabilities will need to be self-reliant. Stock up on any medication, get any essential equipment serviced and take a selection of spares and accoutrements. Ask about hotel facilities when booking, as lifts are still not as common in Cambodia as you might hope.

Getting around temples can be a problem, as even at relatively lowly pagodas there are flights of steps and entrance kerbs to negotiate. The temples at Angkor are particularly difficult, with steps up most entrance pavilions and the central sanctuaries. However, negotiating at least the most accessible parts of the temples is possible with assistance, while some tour operators may also be able to arrange customized visits including all required assistance – try Cambodia specialists About Asia (ⓦ aboutasiatravel.com).

Travelling with children

Travelling through Cambodia with children in tow is not for the nervous or over-protective parent,

EIGHT FUN THINGS FOR KIDS

Ballooning above Angkor See p.169
The bamboo railway See p.115
A trip to the circus See p.155 & p.118
Walking with elephants at Sen Monorom See p239
Kayaking in Kratie See p.224
River trampoline in Kampot See p.277
Fun buggies in Sihanoukville See p.254

although many families find it a rewarding experience, especially with slightly older kids. Cambodians love children, although the protectiveness of the West is nonexistent and there are no special facilities or particular concessions made for kids. On **public transport**, children travel free if they share your seat; otherwise expect to pay the adult fare. It's worth considering hiring a car and driver, although child car seats aren't available. Many **hotels** and guesthouses have family rooms, while extra beds can usually be arranged. Note that under-12's are admitted free to the Angkor Archaeological Park (passport required as proof, or they'll be charged the adult fee).

If you're travelling with a baby or toddler, you'll be able to buy disposable nappies, formula milk and tins or jars of baby food at supermarkets and minimarkets in the major cities, but elsewhere you need to take your own supplies.

Visas

Visas for Cambodia are required by everyone apart from nationals of Laos, Malaysia, the Philippines, Singapore, Vietnam, Thailand and Indonesia. Visas are issued **on arrival** at all international airports and international land borders; alternatively you can apply in advance either for an **e-visa**, or for a traditional visa through your nearest embassy or consulate.

A single-entry **tourist visa** obtained on arrival ($35; one passport photograph required, or pay $2 to have your passport photo scanned) is valid for thirty days, including the day of issue; it is valid only for a single entry into the country and can be extended once only ($50), for a further month. **Business visas** ($40) are also valid for 30 days but can be extended as many times as you want and allow for multiple entries into Cambodia. Note that Cambodian officials at border crossings may attempt to squeeze a bit of extra money out of you in various ways – for instance by making you pay for your visa in baht at a punitively bad exchange rate. Having an e-visa (see below) avoids this hassle.

Single-entry, thirty-day tourist **e-visas** are available online at ⓦevisa.gov.kh ($30 plus a $7 processing charge), although they are only valid if you enter through the airports at Phnom Penh or Siem Reap, or overland at Koh Kong, Bavet and Poipet. They're particularly useful if you're entering overland via Poipet and wish to avoid the traditional hassles and scams associated with this crossing (see p.130).

Tourist and business visas can only be **extended** in Phnom Penh at the Department for Immigration (Mon–Fri 8–11am & 2–4pm; ☎017 812763, ⓦimmigration.gov.kh), 8km out of the centre opposite the airport at 332 Russian Blvd. Given the serious amounts of red tape involved and the inconvenient location of the office, however, it's far

CAMBODIA ONLINE

GENERAL INFORMATION

Beauty and Darkness ⓦ mekong.net/cambodia. Documents the dark side of Cambodia's recent history, and contains a photo gallery and biographies of some of those who survived the Khmer Rouge atrocities; also some travelogues.

Cambodia Daily ⓦ cambodiadaily.com. Selected features and supplements from recent editions of the newspaper.

Cambodian Information Centre ⓦ cambodia.org. Varied

site offering information on everything from clubs and organizations to the legal system.

Cambodia Tribunal Monitor ⓦ cambodiatribunal.org. Up-to-the-minute information on the Genocide Tribunal.

Phnom Penh Post ⓦ phnompenhpost.com. Website of Cambodia's leading daily English-language newspaper.

TRAVEL AND TOURISM

Andy Brouwer ⓦ andybrouwer.co.uk. This Cambodiaphile's site is full of travelogues, interviews with eminent Cambodian experts and links to associated sites.

Cambodian Ministry of Tourism ⓦ mot.gov.kh. Features the country's highlights, province by province, plus information on accommodation, history and Khmer culture.

Canby Publications ⓦ canbypublications.com. Convenient online extracts from Cambodian city guides.

Tourism Concern ⓦ tourismconcern.org.uk/asia/cambodia. Essential information on human, animal and environmental issues relating to tourism in Cambodia.

BEER GIRLS AND TAXI GIRLS

Cambodia's **beer girls**, mostly mostly working in local restaurants and bars, will approach you almost before you've sat down. Each representing a brand of beer, they rely on commissions based on the amount they manage to sell, and will keep opening bottles or cans and topping up your glass, hoping to get you to drink more. Some beer girls may drink and chat with men to up their consumption, but that's as far as it goes.

While beer girls are somewhat looked down upon, the **taxi girls** who frequent the karaoke parlours and nightclubs are beyond the pale. Usually from very poor families, they have a role akin to that of hostess, dance partner and sometimes call girl rolled into one. If you invite them to join you at your table or dance with you, the charge will be added to your bill at the end of the evening, as will the cost of their drinks.

The **abuse** that taxi girls receive is a serious issue, and a number of NGOs in Cambodia – ⓦ daughtersofcambodia.org, for example – have been set up to offer women alternative incomes in the form of spa and beautician training, handicrafts and the like.

preferable to use one of the **visa-extension services** offered by travel agents and guesthouses in town, who will do all the running around for a commission of around $5–10. If you **overstay** your visa you'll be charged $5 per day. There is no **departure tax**.

CAMBODIAN EMBASSIES AND CONSULATES OVERSEAS

Australia 5 Canterbury Crescent, Deakin, ACT 2600 ☎ 02 6273 5867, ⓦ embassyofcambodia.org.nz.

Canada Contact the Cambodian embassy in the US (see below).

Ireland Contact the Cambodian embassy in the UK (see below).

Laos Thadeua Rd, KM2 Vientiane, BP 34 ☎ 021 314950, ⓦ camemb.lao .mfa.gov.kh.

New Zealand Contact the Cambodian embassy in Australia (see above).

Thailand 518 / 4 Pracha Uthit Rd (Soi Ramkamhaeng 39), Wangtonglang, Bangkok ☎ 02 957 5851, ⓔ camemb.tha@mfa.gov.kh.

South Africa Contact the Cambodian embassy in the UK (see below).

UK 64 Brondesbury Park, Willesden Green, London NW6 7AT ☎ 020 8451 7850, ⓦ cambodianembassy.org.uk.

USA 4530 16th St, Washington DC 20011 ☎ 202 726 7742, ⓦ embassyofcambodia.org.

Vietnam 71A Tran Hung Dao St, Hanoi ☎ 04 942 4788, ⓔ camemb .vnm@mfa.gov.kh; 41 Phung Khac Khoan, Ho Chi Minh City ☎ 08 829 2751, ⓔ camcg.hcm@mfa.gov.kh.

Volunteering

There are plenty of opportunities to do **voluntary work** in Cambodia – although in almost all cases you'll actually have to pay to do it. It's worth bearing in mind that although volunteering in Cambodia might appear an entirely altruistic way of putting something back into the country, many schemes (particularly short-term placements and one-day projects) are not without their ethical complications. Any work connected with orphanages (or indeed any organization which charges you money to work with children) should be treated with caution (see p.35). In addition, short-term unskilled volunteer programmes may actually take jobs away from locals, while some projects are specifically designed with overseas volunteers in mind, rather than the needs of local communities. The longer you can volunteer for, the more likely you are to do some real good. Look online to see what's currently available, and research thoroughly before commiting to make sure that any project you volunteer for has demonstrable and sustainable long-term benefits for local communities – spending a day painting a local school, for example, may seem like a good and useful thing to do, but may actually be a waste of money, and simply leave the local village with a hastily and badly decorated building plus a pile of empty paint cans.

Women travellers

Travelling around Cambodia shouldn't pose any problems for foreign women. All the same, you may feel more comfortable dressing reasonably modestly in towns, cities and rural areas, particularly during the day when many sights, such as temples and Phnom Penh's Royal Palace, require shoulders and knees to be covered anyway. In Sihanoukville, on the islands, and to some degree in Kampot and Kep, things are certainly more relaxed. Keeping an eye on your drink and not walking in unlit areas at night are your best precautions, but there is certainly no need to be paranoid.

If you do find yourself in a situation where someone oversteps the mark, a firm "no" is usually enough. If this doesn't work, then kick up a huge fuss so that everyone in the vicinity knows that you're being harassed, which should shame the man into backing off.

Phnom Penh and around

WAT PHNOM BAS-RELIEF, PHNOM PENH

1

Phnom Penh and around

"A city of white buildings, where spires of gold and stupas of stone rocket out of the greenery into the vivid blue sky." Such was American visitor Robert Casey's description of Phnom Penh in 1929, in which he also noted the shady, wide streets and pretty parks. The image bears a remarkable resemblance to the Phnom Penh of today, with its open-fronted shops and shophouses bustling with haggling traders, and roadsides teeming with food vendors and colourful, busy markets. But make no mistake; the biggest changes are still to come. Along with a flourishing food scene, lively café culture and entrepreneurial spirit, Phnom Penh is thriving and while it hasn't, as yet, been overwhelmed by the towering high-rises that blight the capitals of neighbouring Southeast Asian countries, it is experiencing rapid development amid a huge building boom. Situated in a virtually flat area at the confluence of the Tonle Sap, Bassac and Mekong rivers, the capital of Cambodia and the heart of government is a captivating city of great charm and vitality, crisscrossed by broad tree-lined boulevards and dotted with colonial villas, modern architecture and some of the country's best boutique hotels, hostels and restaurants.

Such is the city's enterprise and energy it's difficult to believe that a generation ago it was forcibly evacuated and left to ruin by the **Khmer Rouge**. Inevitably, and in spite of many improvements, some of the scars are still evident: side roads are pot-holed and strewn with rubble, some of the elegant villas are ruined beyond repair, and when it rains the antiquated drainage system backs up, flooding the roads.

It is testimony to the unflappable good nature and stoicism of the city's inhabitants that, despite past adversity, they remain upbeat. Many people do two jobs to get by, keeping government offices ticking over for a few hours each day then moonlighting as moto drivers or tutors; furthermore, the Cambodian belief in **education** is particularly strong here, and anyone who can afford to sends their children to supplementary classes outside school hours. This dynamism constantly attracts people from the provinces – newcomers soon discover, though, that it's tougher being poor in the city than in the country, and are often forced to rent tiny rooms in one of the many **shanties** on the city's outskirts, ripped off for the privilege by affluent landlords.

Most of the city's **sights** are between the Tonle Sap River and Monivong Boulevard, in an area bordered by Sihanouk Boulevard in the south and Wat Phnom in the north.

NATIONAL MUSEUM, PHNOM PENH

Highlights

❶ Mekong boat trips Cruise the river as the sun sinks behind the Royal Palace. **See p.59**

❷ Royal Palace The soaring golden spires of the Throne Room are Phnom Penh's most memorable sight. **See p.59**

❸ Silver Pagoda Home to a sacred emerald Buddha and a vast mural. **See p.62**

❹ National Museum A superb collection of sculptures from Cambodia's temples. See p.65

❺ Toul Sleng Genocide Museum Former S-21 prison and torture centre, now a grim museum to Khmer Rouge atrocities. **See p.69**

❻ Wat Phnom See the city from the summit-top temple of Wat Phnom. **See p.71**

❼ Cyclo rides Enjoy a spin through the old French quarter and its colonial villas. **See p.79**

❽ Food and drink The capital – especially around Street 308 – has some of Cambodia's finest restaurants and bars. **See p.82**

❾ Psar Toul Tom Poung (Russian Market) Bargain for fine silks, antiques and curios at one of Phnom Penh's most enjoyable markets. **See p.92**

❿ Choeung Ek The "killing fields", where a stupa containing thousands of human skulls honours victims of the Khmer Rouge. **See p.100**

HIGHLIGHTS ARE MARKED ON THE MAPS ON P.52 & PP.56–57

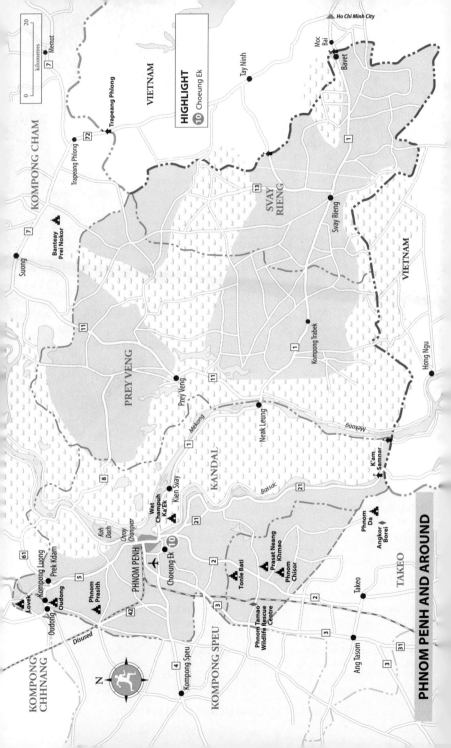

PHNOM PENH AND AROUND

HIGHLIGHT
10 Choeung Ek

VIETNAM

Ho Chi Minh City

Moc Bai
Bavet

Tay Ninh

KOMPONG CHAM

Memot

Trapeang Phlong

Trapeang Phlong

SVAY RIENG

Suong

Banteay
Prei Nokor

Svay Rieng

VIETNAM

PREY VENG

Kompong Trabek

Prey Veng

Hong Ngu

Mekong

Neak Leung

Mekong

KANDAL

K'am
Samnar

Wat
Champuh
Ka'Ek

Kien Svay

Bassac

Koh
Dach

Chroy
Changvar

TAKEO

Angkor
Borei

Phnom
Da

PHNOM PENH

Choeung Ek
10

Prasat Neang
Khmao

Kompong Luong

Prek Kdam

Oudong

Phnom
Prasith

Tonle Bati

Phnom
Chisor

Lovek

Oudong

Phnom Tamao
Wildlife Rescue
Centre

Takeo

KOMPONG
CHHNANG

Disused

KOMPONG SPEU

Kompong Speu

Ang Tasom

N

kilometres
0   20

For tourists and locals alike, the lively **riverfront** – a wide promenade that runs beside the Tonle Sap for nearly 2km – is the city's focal point. In the evenings, residents come here to take the air, snack on hawker food and enjoy the impromptu waterside entertainment; the strip also shows the city at its most cosmopolitan, lined with Western restaurants, cafés and bars. Three key tourist sights lie close by. Arguably the most impressive of the city's attractions is the elegant complex housing the **Royal Palace** and **Silver Pagoda** that dominate the southern riverfront. The palace's distinctive four-faced spire towers above the pitched golden roofs of its Throne Hall, while the adjacent Silver Pagoda is home to a stunning collection of Buddha statues. A block north of the palace is the **National Museum**, a dramatic, hybrid building in leafy surroundings housing a fabulous collection of ancient Khmer sculpture dating back to as early as the sixth century. Also near the river are **Wat Ounalom** – whose austere grey stupa houses the ashes of many prominent Khmers – and bustling hilltop **Wat Phnom**, whose foundation is said to predate that of the city. The old French administrative area, often referred to as the **French quarter**, surrounds the hill on which Wat Phnom sits, home to fine **colonial buildings**, while to the southwest the Art Deco **Central Market** sits close to the city's business district. To the south, the jam-packed **Russian Market** is a popular souvenir-sourcing spot while another much-visited sight, though for completely different reasons, is the **Toul Sleng Genocide Museum**: a school that became a centre for the torture of men, women and children who fell foul of Pol Pot's regime.

Many visitors stay just a couple of days before hopping on to Siem Reap and Angkor, Sihanoukville and the southern beaches or to the Vietnamese border crossings at Bavet and Chau Doc. However, there are plenty of reasons to linger. The capital has the best **shopping** in the country, with a vast selection of souvenirs and crafts, and an excellent range of **cuisines** in its many restaurants. There are also several rewarding **day-trips** from the city out into the surrounding countryside.

Brief history

Cambodian legend – passed down through so many generations that the Khmers regard it as fact – has it that in 1372 a wealthy widow, **Daun Penh** (Grandmother Penh), was strolling along the Chrap Chheam River (now the Tonle Sap) when she came across the hollow trunk of a koki tree washed up on the banks. Inside it she discovered five Buddha statues, four cast in bronze and one carved in stone. As a mark of respect, she created a sanctuary for the statues on the top of a low mound, which became known as **Phnom Penh**, literally "the hill of Penh" and in due course, the hill gave its name to the city that grew up around it.

The founding of the city

Phnom Penh began its first stint as a **capital** in 1432, when King **Ponhea Yat** fled south from Angkor and the invading Siamese. He set up a royal palace, increased the height of Daun Penh's hill and founded five **monasteries** – Wat Botum, Wat Koh, Wat Langka, Wat Ounalom and Wat Phnom – all of which survive today. When he died, his sons variously took succession, but in the sixteenth century, for reasons that remain unclear, the court had moved out to Lovek, and later Oudong, and Phnom Penh reverted to being a fishing village.

SAFETY IN PHNOM PENH

While Phnom Penh is no longer the Wild West town it once was, **robberies** are not unknown, and there have been instances of bags being snatched from tourists walking around key tourist areas. Moto passengers, too, are increasingly the target of bag-snatchers, so you should exercise caution when taking **motos** at night. It's certainly not worth being paranoid, but taking a tuk-tuk at night may be a safer option – and always keep your bags and valuables well out of sight of passing motorbikes.

1

Little is known of the subsequent three hundred years, though records left by missionaries indicate that by the seventeenth century a multicultural community of Asian and European traders had grown up along the banks of the Tonle Sap, and that Phnom Penh, with easy access by river to the ocean, had developed into a prosperous **port**. Gold, silk and incense were traded, along with hides, bones, ivory and horn from elephants, rhinoceros and buffalo. Phnom Penh's prosperity declined in the latter part of the century, when the Vietnamese invaded the Mekong Delta and cut off the city's access to the sea. The eighteenth century was a period of **dynastic squabbles** between pro-Thai and pro-Vietnamese factions of the royal family, and in 1770, Phnom Penh was actually burnt down by the Siamese, who proceeded to install a new king and take control of the country.

As the nineteenth century dawned, the Vietnamese assumed control over Cambodia's foreign policy but by 1812 Phnom Penh became the capital once again, though the court retreated to Oudong twice over the next fifty years amid continuing power struggles between the Thais and the Vietnamese.

Phnom Penh under the French

In 1863, King Norodom (great-great-grandfather of the current king, Norodom Sihamoni), fearful of another Vietnamese invasion, signed a treaty for Cambodia to become a **French protectorate**. At the request of the French, he uprooted the court from Oudong and the role of capital returned decisively to Phnom Penh, a place which the recently arrived French described as "an unsophisticated settlement made up of a string of thatched huts clustered along a single muddy track, the riverbanks crowded with the houseboats of fisher-folk". In fact, population estimates at the time put it at around 25,000. Despite Phnom Penh regaining its access to the sea, with the Mekong Delta now under French control, it remained very much an outpost, with the French far more concerned with the development of Saigon, now Ho Chi Minh City.

In 1889, a new Senior Resident, **Hyun de Verneville**, was appointed to the protectorate. Wanting to make Phnom Penh a place fit to be the French administrative centre in Cambodia, he created a chic colonial town. By 1900, roads had been laid out on a grid plan, a law court, public works and telegraph offices were set up, and banks and schools built. A **French quarter** grew up in the area north of Wat Phnom, where imposing villas were built for the city's French administrators and traders; Wat Phnom itself gained landscaped gardens and a zoo.

Towards independence

In the 1920s and 1930s, Phnom Penh grew prosperous. The road network was extended, facilitated by the infilling of drainage canals; the Mekong was dredged, making the city accessible to seagoing vessels; parks were created and communications improved. In 1932, the city's **train station** was built and the railway line linking the capital to Battambang was completed. Foreign travellers were lured to Cambodia by exotic tales of hidden cities in the jungle.

In 1963, the country's first **secondary school**, Lycée Sisowath, opened in Phnom Penh, and slowly an educated elite developed, laying the foundations for later political changes. During **World War II**, the occupying Japanese allowed the French to continue running things and their impact on the city was relatively benign; in October 1941, after the Japanese had arrived, the coronation of Norodom Sihanouk went ahead pretty much as normal in Phnom Penh.

With **independence** from the French in 1953, Phnom Penh at last became a true seat of government. An educated middle class began to gain prominence, café society began to blossom, cinemas and theatres thrived, and motorbikes and cars took to the boulevards. In the mid-1960s a national sports venue, the Olympic Stadium, was built and international celebrities, such as Jackie Kennedy, began to visit.

The civil war and the Khmer Rouge

The period of optimism was short-lived. Phnom Penh started to feel the effects of the Vietnam War in the late 1960s, when refugees began to flee the heavily bombed border areas for the capital, and Cambodia's own **civil war** of the early 1970s turned this exodus into a flood. **Lon Nol**'s forces fought a losing battle against the **Khmer Rouge** and, as the city came under siege, food became scarce despite US efforts to fly in supplies.

On **April 17, 1975**, the Khmer Rouge entered Phnom Penh. Initially welcomed as harbingers of peace, within hours the soldiers had ordered the population out of the capital. Reassurances that it was "just for a few days" were soon discredited, and as the people – the elderly, infirm and the dying among them – left laden with armfuls of possessions, the Khmer Rouge set about destroying the city. Buildings were ransacked, roofs blown off; even the National Bank was blown up. For three years, eight months and twenty days, Phnom Penh was a ghost town while the country suffered under the Khmer Rouge's murderous regime.

Vietnamese and UN control

With the **Vietnamese entry** into Phnom Penh on January 7, 1979, both returnees and new settlers began to arrive, although many former inhabitants either could not or would not return, having lost everything and everyone. Those arriving in the city took up residence in the vacant buildings, and to this day, many live in these same properties. During the Vietnamese era, the capital remained impoverished and decrepit, with much of the incoming aid from the Soviet Union and India finding its way into the pockets of senior officials. By 1987, Vietnamese interest was waning, and by 1989 they had **withdrawn** from Cambodia.

The United Nations subsequently took charge, and by 1992 the country was flooded with highly paid **UNTAC** forces (UN Transitional Authority in Cambodia). The atmosphere in Phnom Penh became surreal: its infrastructure was still in tatters, electricity and water were spasmodic, telecommunications nonexistent and evening curfews in force, yet the city boomed as hotels, restaurants and bars sprang up to keep the troops entertained. Many Phnom Penh residents got rich quick on the back of this – supplying prostitutes and drugs played a part – and the capital gained a reputation for being a free-rolling, lawless city, a reputation it has now more or less shaken off.

Modern Phnom Penh

The city of today is slowly **repairing** the dereliction caused nearly four decades ago; roads are much improved, electricity is reliable and many of the charming colonial buildings are being restored. Alongside, an increasing number of skyscrapers, high-rise apartment blocks and shopping malls are steadily peppering the horizon, particularly along Monivong and Sihanouk boulevards, and there are ambitious plans for the area near Independence Boulevard and Koh Pich. The revival of Cambodia's railway network in 2016 with trains running between Phnom Penh and Sihanoukville, via

PHNOM PENH ORIENTATION

The city of Phnom Penh extends roughly from the **Chroy Changvar Bridge** in the north to the **Yothapol Khemarak Phoumin Boulevard** in the south. There's no fixed "centre", although some refer to the area around the yellow-domed **Psar Thmei** (literally New Market, better known as Central Market) or around the Royal Palace as such.

There are two major north–south routes, **Norodom** and **Monivong** boulevards (and to a lesser extent, the easterly **Sothearos Boulevard** that snakes north towards **Sisowath Quay**), both intersected by the two great arcs of **Sihanouk/Nehru** and **Mao Tse Toung** boulevards, which act as ring roads. Together, these four thoroughfares cut the city into segments and can be useful points of reference for specifying locations to taxi, tuk-tuk and moto drivers.

1

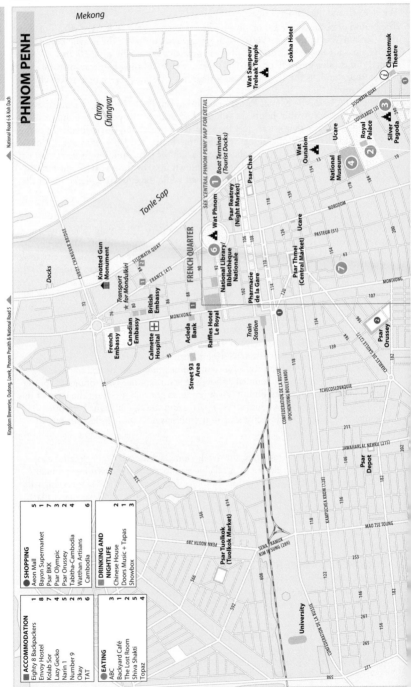

PHNOM PENH

Mekong

Chroy Changvar

Tonle Sap

Docks

CHROY CHANGVAR BRIDGE

SISOWATH QUAY

FRANCE (47)

FRENCH QUARTER

MONIVONG

SISOWATH QUAY

SOTHEAROS (3)

NORODOM

PASTEUR (51)

MONIVONG

CONFEDERATION DE LA RUSSIE (POCHENTONG BOULEVARD)

CHARLES DE GAULLE (217)

TCHECOSLOVAQUIE

JAWAHARLAL NEHRU (215)

KAMPUCHEA KROM (128)

PENN NOUTH 289

SENA PRAMUK KIM IL SUNG (289)

MAO TSE TOUNG

CONFEDERATION DE LA RUSSIE

National Road 6 & Koh Dach

Kingdom Breweries, Oudong, Lovek, Phnom Prasith & National Road 5

Grand Phnom Penh Water Park, National Road 4, Royal Phnom Penh Hospital & Airport

Wat Sampeuv Treleak Temple

Sokha Hotel

Chaktomuk Theatre

Royal Palace

Silver Pagoda

Wat Ounalom

National Museum

Boat Terminal (Tourist Docks)

Psar Chas

Wat Phnom

Psar Reatrey (Night Market)

SEE 'CENTRAL PHNOM PENH' MAP FOR DETAIL

National Library/ Bibliothèque Nationale

Pharmacie de la Gare

Psar Thmei (Central Market)

Psar Orussey

Knotted Gun Monument

Transport for Mondulkiri

British Embassy

French Embassy

Canadian Embassy

Calmette Hospital

Acleda Bank

Raffles Hotel Le Royal

Street 93 Area

Train Station

Psar Depot

Psar Tuolkok (Tuolkok Market)

University

Ucare

Ucare

ACCOMMODATION	
Eighty 8 Backpackers	1
Envoy Hostel	8
Kolab Sor	7
Lazy Gecko	4
Narin 1	5
Number 9	2
Okay	3
TAT	6

SHOPPING	
Aeon Mall	5
Bayon Supermarket	1
Psar BKK	7
Psar Olympic	3
Psar Orussey	2
Tabitha-Cambodia	4
Watthan Artisans Cambodia	6

EATING	
ABC	3
Backyard Café	2
The Lost Room	1
Shiva Shakti	5
Topaz	4

DRINKING AND NIGHTLIFE	
Chinese House	2
Doors Music + Tapas	1
Showbox	3

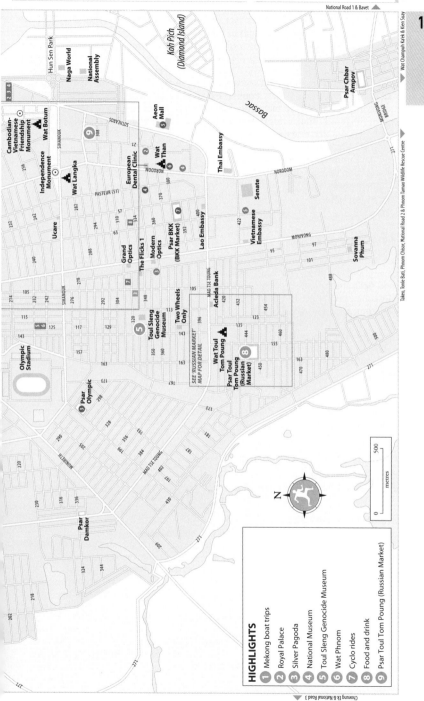

National Road 1 & Bavet

Koh Pich (Diamond Island)

Basac

Wat Champuh Karek & Kien Svay

Takeo, Tonle Bati, Phnom Chisor, National Road 2 & Phnom Tamao Wildlife Rescue Centre

Choeung Ek & National Road 3

1

Hun Sen Park

Naga World

National Assembly

Psar Chbar Ampov

MONIVONG BRIDGE

271

Cambodian-Vietnamese Friendship Monument

Wat Botum

Aeon Mall

Independence Monument

Wat Langka

SIHANOUK

SOTHEAROS

Wat Than

European Dental Clinic

NORODOM

Thai Embassy

308

PASTEUR (51)

221

242

240

232

Ucare

282

294

310

334

63

Senate

Lao Embassy

Vietnamese Embassy

Psar BKK (BKK Market)

Grand Optics

The Flicks 1

Modern Optics

NORODOM

370

380

392

400

422

MONIVONG

95

97

101

488

Sovanna Phum

ACLEDA Bank

420

432

454

460

480

500

271

Toul Sleng Genocide Museum

Two Wheels Only

105

113

123

135

143

SEE 'RUSSIAN MARKET' MAP FOR DETAIL

MAO TSE TUNG

396

Wat Toul Tom Poung

Psar Toul Tom Poung (Russian Market)

444

155

163

650

470

Olympic Stadium

Psar Olympic

208

328

356

193

199

384

MONIRETH

290

302

220

230

316

336

Psar Damkor

MAO TSE TUNG

402

187

181

173

167

163

157

129

117

115

143

125

105

348

304

292

276

278

214

324

344

218

202

271

209

602

438

197

N

0   500
metres

1

Takeo and Kampot, plus Emirates' new flights between Dubai and Phnom Penh (via Yangon) are further promising signs of the city's renaissance.

With tourism firmly in its sights, the municipal government has set out elaborate plans to continue smartening up the city, ranging from dictating the colour in which buildings will be painted (creamy yellow) to evicting squatters, makeshift shops and legitimate inhabitants from areas designated for development. **Boeung Kak Lake**, for example, once a popular backpacker area, has been filled in, against a backdrop of protests to make way for a vast private development. On the eastern end of Sihanouk Boulevard, **Hun Sen Park** and **Naga World** – a sprawling casino and hotel complex heavily invested in by Cambodia's prime minister, Hun Sen – dominate the waterfront. Heritage experts fear for the city's rapidly diminishing colonial buildings. A recent report put the number at just over 500, with only 34 retaining enough original features and grandeur to be designated "first class". It remains to be seen how many other changes this dynamic city will face, but for now at least, the feeling is broadly optimistic.

The riverfront

Sisowath Quay, hugging the river for nearly 4km from the Chroy Changvar Bridge to Chaktomuk Theatre, is the heart of Phnom Penh's tourist scene, with a **night market, food stalls** and a plethora of **bars and restaurants** near the Royal Palace and National Museum. From Street 106, midway along, the quay forms a broad promenade extending almost 2km south.

Every autumn, the riverside is thronged with crowds flocking to the boat races and festivities of the water festival **Bon Om Toeuk** (see below). For the rest of the year, the riverfront is one of the most pleasant places to walk in Phnom Penh, becoming busier in the late afternoon when the locals come out to **dah'leng** or "promenade" along the bank. At about 5pm, the pavements around the public garden by the Royal Palace turn into a huge picnic ground as mats are spread out, food and drink vendors appear and impromptu entertainment begins. At its southern end is Chaktomuk Theatre, one of several structures in the city designed by **Vann Molyvann**, the godfather of **New Khmer architecture** in the 1950s and 1960s.

Preah Ang Dong Kar shrine

Home to a statue of a four-armed Buddha, the small **Preah Ang Dong Kar shrine**, opposite the Royal Palace, draws big crowds. The story goes that a crocodile-shaped flag

---

THE BON OM TOEUK TRAGEDY

The most important festival in the Cambodian calendar, **Bon Om Toeuk**, known as the Water Festival, attracts over two million provincial visitors each year to celebrate the reversing of the flow of the Tonle Sap River (variable, late Oct to mid-Nov). Many come to support their teams during the three days of boat racing, but most soak up the atmosphere with their families, eat copiously from the myriad street vendors and scoop up bargains from sellers who lay their wares out along the riverfront. After dark, the town remains just as animated, with free concerts and fireworks.

The sheer volume of people weaving a fragile dance along the riverfront is a spectacle in itself, but in 2010, the volatile mixture of millions of exuberant people and zero crowd control led to a tragedy. During the extravagant closing ceremony, panic broke out as the several-thousand-strong crowd poured onto a narrow footbridge, causing a stampede in which 351 died. In subsequent years the festival was cancelled as a mark of respect and it was only fully reinstated in 2016.

1

MEKONG CRUISES

At the top end of Sisowath Quay opposite the night market, tourist boats leave for late-afternoon **cruises** along the Tonle Sap and Mekong rivers, with many also heading to Silk Island and even Oudong. Numerous companies ply the route: **Crocodile Cruises** (☎012 981559, ⍟crocodilecruise.com; sunset tour $15/person for 2hr, Silk Island $35/4hr; private hire $15/hr), offers free pick-up and more style (and comfort) than some other boats, with cushioned armchairs and loungers. Likewise, **Kanika** has an extra-spacious boat, moored further south by the *Himawari Hotel* (☎017 915812, ⍟kanika-boat.com; sunset tour $7/person/$15/person with wine/tapas; 80min; dinner cruise $20/person for 1hr 45minr). **Tara Prince**, a former royal boat, provides free pick-up and return ($26/person for 2hr incl finger food and all drinks). You can also hire boats privately (around $15/hr, depending on the number of passengers).

appeared in the river, and on Buddhist holidays it would miraculously appear on a flagpole. Now, the spirit of the flag, Preah Ang Dong Kar, has a permanent home here and people – including students nearing their exams – buy flower and incense from the vendors nearby before making offerings asking for wealth, luck and happiness.

Wat Ounalom

Sothearos Blvd, between streets 172 and 156 • Daily 6am–6pm

The rather sombre concrete stupa that fronts Sisowath Quay belies the fact that **Wat Ounalom** is one of Phnom Penh's oldest (and most pleasant) pagodas, dating back to the reign of King Ponhea Yat in the fifteenth century. It is also one of the most important, as the headquarters of Cambodian Buddhism, and in the early 1970s over five hundred monks lived here. It also housed the library of the Institute Bouddhique, subsequently destroyed, along with many of the buildings, by the Khmer Rouge, but has since been re-established at a new location near Sihanouk Boulevard.

The pagoda itself gets its name by virtue of being home to an *ounalom*, a hair from the **Buddha's eyebrow**, which is contained in the large stupa behind the **vihara** (assembly hall); if anyone is around at the small bookshop, ask to gain access. Within the stupa are four sanctuaries, the most revered being the one facing east, where there's a fine bronze Buddha.

The monks use the vihara, which dates from 1952, in the early morning, after which time visitors can enter. Unusually, it's built on three floors, and houses a commemorative statue of Samdech Huot Tat, the venerable fourth patriarch of Cambodian Buddhism, murdered by the Khmer Rouge. Despite its unappealing exterior, the dark-grey stupa is worth a quick look for its **crypt**, in which hundreds of small cubicles hold the funerary urns of Cambodian notables, most of which are adorned with bright plastic flowers and a photograph of the deceased.

Royal Palace and Silver Pagoda

The **Royal Palace** and **Silver Pagoda** are Phnom Penh's most iconic buildings, their roofs adorned with soaring golden nagas and spires that glint enticingly against the sky. Built in traditional Khmer style, the wall which encases this complex of royal buildings, manicured gardens and relic-stuffed temples is painted pale yellow and white, the two colours representing, respectively, the Buddhist and Hindu faiths. Nothing exists of King Ponhea Yat's palace, built here in 1434, and very little of the wooden palace of King Norodom, great-great-grandfather of the current king, who moved the capital here from Oudong in 1866. Indeed, the current Royal Palace, official residence of **King Sihamoni**, dates back less than a hundred years, with most of the buildings

1

reconstructed in concrete in the early twentieth century. However, the complex is well worth a visit for its classic Khmer architecture, ornate gilding and tranquil French-style landscaped gardens. The Silver Pagoda, ringed by a mythological muralled wall, is a particular highlight for its elaborate silver-tiled floor and priceless Buddha statues.

ESSENTIALS

Location The entrance to the complex is on Sothearos Blvd, between streets 240 & 184.

Opening hours Daily 8–11am & 2–5pm; to do the complex justice, allow at least 2hr, but note that staff start to close up 30min before the actual closing time.

Entry fee $10.

Route From the palace entrance, you're routed in an anti-clockwise direction, visiting first the royal buildings then the Silver Pagoda.

Restrictions The royal residence itself is always closed to the public. On occasions, the Throne Hall is closed for royal receptions and when the king has a meeting with his ministers.

Dress code Knees and shoulders must be covered. You are not allowed to carry a full-size backpack. Hats and shoes should be removed before entering certain buildings.

Guides English-speaking guides can be hired at the ticket office for $10. They provide a wealth of information, not just on the palace and pagoda, but also on Buddhist and Khmer culture.

Photography Not permitted inside the Throne Hall or the Silver Pagoda.

Eating and drinking There are a couple of refreshment stalls at the end of the route.

Shopping A shop on the site sells expensive silk, postcards and silver pieces.

Royal Palace

When visiting the **Royal Palace**, you may find that one or two of the royal buildings are either cordoned off or are no longer on display. At the time of writing, the **Pavilion of Napoleon III** is closed, with no conclusive reopening date. There's still plenty to see, but if there's something you're particularly interested in, check with the guides at the entrance.

The Victory Gate

Entering the pristine outer gardens, dotted with topiary trees and an ancient bodhi tree, takes you towards the **Victory Gate**, which opens onto Sothearos Boulevard and faces the entrance steps to the Throne Hall. Traditionally only used by the king and queen, it's now used to admit visiting dignitaries. Just to the north of the gate, the **Moonlight or Dancing Pavilion** (Preah Thineang Chan Chhaya) was built for twilight performances of classical Cambodian dance, as a dais for the king to address the crowds and as a venue for state and royal banquets.

KING SIHAMONI

Dancer, teacher, artistic director and United Nations representative, **Norodom Sihamoni** (born 1953) is the son of the late **Norodom Sihanouk** and his seventh wife Monineath – his name is made from the first four letters of each of their names. Elected king by the Throne Council in October 2004, on the surprise abdication of his father, most of his life was spent outside Cambodia. From the age of 9, he was educated in Prague where he learned dance, music and theatre; he later studied cinematography in Korea.

Other than his early childhood, the three years **in prison** with his family in Phnom Penh during the Khmer Rouge years was the longest time spent in his homeland until becoming king. On the arrival of the Vietnamese, the royal family went into **exile** and for a year Sihamoni acted as private secretary to his father, but from 1980 he was in Paris where he spent the next twenty years as a professor of classical dance. From 1992, Sihamoni was Cambodia's permanent representative at the UN, and in 1993 he became its **UNESCO ambassador** – resigning both positions on becoming king. Sharing his father's love of cinema, Sihamoni was also director-general of a production company, Khemara Pictures, and has a couple of ballet films to his credit. He is a bachelor and keeps a lower profile than his late father, leading a quiet life of reading and meditating. He does nothing to excite the media but seems generally well regarded by Cambodians.

The Throne Hall

The present **Throne Hall** (Preah Tineang Tevea Vinicchay), still used for meetings and formal receptions, was inaugurated by King Bat Sisowath in 1917 as a faithful reproduction of Norodom's wooden palace, demolished in 1915. As befits a building used for coronations and ceremonies, it's the most impressive building in the royal compound, topped by a much-photographed four-faced tower. The roof has seven tiers (counted from the lowest level up to the base of the spire) tiled in orange, sapphire and green, representing, respectively, prosperity, nature and freedom. Golden nagas at the corners of each level protect against evil spirits.

The hall's broad entrance staircase – its banisters formed by seven-headed nagas – leads up to a colonnaded veranda, where each column is topped by a garuda with outstretched wings, appearing to support the overhanging roof. Peering into the **Throne Room** from the east door, you'll find a ceiling painted with finely detailed scenes from the *Reamker* (see box, p.63) in muted colours, and walls stencilled with pastel leaf motifs and images of celestial beings, hands together in the traditional Cambodian *sompeyar*

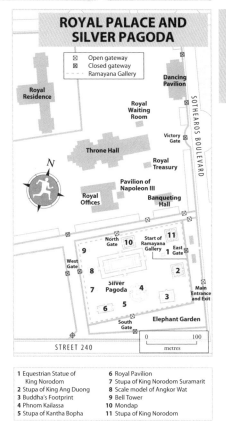

ROYAL PALACE AND SILVER PAGODA

⊠ Open gateway
⊠ Closed gateway
--- Ramayana Gallery

Royal Residence

Dancing Pavilion

Royal Waiting Room

Victory Gate

Throne Hall

Royal Treasury

Pavilion of Napoleon III

Royal Offices

Banqueting Hall

North Gate **10**
Start of Ramayana Gallery **11**

9
East Gate **1**

West Gate **8**

2

7 Silver Pagoda **4**

3

Main Entrance and Exit

6 **5**

South Gate

Elephant Garden

STREET 240

0   100
metres

1 Equestrian Statue of King Norodom
2 Stupa of King Ang Duong
3 Buddha's Footprint
4 Phnom Kailassa
5 Stupa of Kantha Bopha
6 Royal Pavilion
7 Stupa of King Norodom Suramarit
8 Scale model of Angkor Wat
9 Bell Tower
10 Mondap
11 Stupa of King Norodom

gesture (palms together, head slightly bowed). Down the centre of the hall runs a 35m-long, deep-pile carpet, its pattern and colours matching the surrounding tiles, and flanked by rows of gilt standard **lamps**, each supported by ceremonial nagas.

The north and south entrance doors are protected by large mirrors, believed to deflect bad spirits. Unfortunately, since access to the Throne Room is forbidden, it is almost impossible to get a proper view of the two elaborate golden **coronation thrones** ahead. They occupy a dais in the centre of the hall, above which a nine-tiered white and gold parasol, symbolizing peacefulness, heaven and ambition, is suspended; two large garudas on the ceiling guard the thrones.

At the rear of the hall is an area where the king holds audiences with visiting VIPs and where the busts of seven royal ancestors are displayed. **Anterooms** off the hall are used for different purposes: there are separate bedrooms for the king and the queen for the seven nights after the coronation when the royal couple have to sleep apart; a prayer room for the king; and a room to store the king's ashes after his death, while his stupa is being built.

The Royal Waiting Room

The imposing **Royal Waiting Room** (Hor Samranphirum), to the north of the Throne Room, is used on coronation days. In previous years, the king and queen would mount ceremonial elephants from the platform on the east side of the building for the

1

coronation procession but this tradition ended in 1962. A room at ground level stores royal musical instruments and coronation paraphernalia, and the pavilion currently houses a collection of artefacts gifted to the monarch by foreign heads of state.

The Royal Treasury

Just south of the Throne Hall is the **Royal Treasury** (Hor Samritvimean) or the 'Bronze Palace', which houses coronation regalia, including the opulent bodyguard uniforms, the Great Crown of Victory, the Sacred Sword and the Victory Spear. It also contains some of the items previously displayed in the Pavilion of Napoleon III (see below).

The Pavilion of Napoleon III

Currently closed for refurbishment, the incongruous grey cast-iron building with a domed clock tower and observation gallery is the **Pavilion of Napoleon III**, used by Empress Eugénie during the inauguration of the Suez Canal in 1869. Presented to King Norodom by Napoleon III in 1876, the pavilion was re-erected here and became a museum of **royal memorabilia**. Downstairs, glass cases contain royal silver and china tableware. There's also an anteroom with paintings on subjects ranging from Venetian canals to Chinese landscapes, and a room glinting with gleaming medals. At the top of the stairs, the austerity of the building is relieved by a collection of silk costumes elaborately embroidered in gold thread, made by Queen Kossomak (the present king's grandmother) for the royal dancers. Royal portraits upstairs include pictures of King Sihanouk as a dashing young man.

Preah Tineang Phochani

The rather plain building to the east of the Napoleon pavilion is **Preah Tineang Phochani**, a classical dance hall once used to host royal receptions and meetings. Adjacent is the royal complex's south gate; pass through it and cross the alleyway to enter the courtyard of the Silver Pagoda by its north gate.

Silver Pagoda

Constructed in 1962 by King Sihanouk to replace the wooden pagoda built by his grandfather in 1902, the **Silver Pagoda** is so called for its 5329 silver floor tiles (only a few of which are visible), each around 20cm square and weighing more than 1kg. It's also known as **Wat Preah Keo Morokot**, the Temple of the Emerald Buddha, after the green Baccarat crystal **Buddha** within. The pagoda itself is clearly influenced by Bangkok's Wat Phra Kaeo, also home to a precious crystal. Although more than half its contents were stolen during the Khmer Rouge years, the pagoda itself survived pretty much unscathed; it was even used to demonstrate to the few international visitors that the regime was caring for Cambodia's cultural history. A rich collection of artefacts and **Buddha images** remains, making the pagoda more a museum than a place of worship.

The pagoda

The vihara or hall is approached by a stairway of imported Italian grey marble; to enter, you'll need to leave your **shoes** in the racks. The silver tiles inside are almost entirely covered with a tatty protective carpet, though a roped-off section by the entrance affords glimpses of their delicately hand-engraved leaf motifs. Atop a five-tiered dais in the centre of the room is the **Emerald Buddha**, seated in meditation. Some sources say this is a modern reproduction; others date it from the seventeenth century; whatever the case, at just 50cm in height, it's put in the shade by the magnificence of the images surrounding it. One of the most dazzling is the life-sized **solid gold Buddha** at ground level, in the centre of the dais. Produced in Phnom Penh in 1904 for King Sisowath, it weighs 90kg and is encrusted with 2086 diamonds and precious stones. To its right, a silver seated Buddha is perched on top of a display case, while to the left is a case containing delightful gold **statuettes** depicting key events from the Buddha's life. The tiny, highly detailed representations show him taking his first steps as a child on seven lotus pads, meditating under a bodhi tree and reclining on reaching nirvana.

Tucked away behind the dais is a serene, life-sized standing Buddha from Burma, the elegance of its aged, cream marble undiminished by the brash red of the wooden pedestal. A haphazard, though interesting, collection of Buddhas and other artefacts lines the back wall. The weighty gilded-wood **ceremonial litter**, over two metres long and complete with a throne, was used to transport the king on coronation day and required twelve men to carry it.

Display cases containing a diverse collection of objects, such as daggers, cigarette cases, headdresses and masks, used for Royal Ballet performances of the *Reamker* (see box below) line the walls. However, recent years have seen many of the most impressive and precious exhibits replaced by a motley selection of frankly not very exciting items. It's not known if they being restored or have been removed permanently. Before leaving, check out the unusual **stained-glass windows**, one of which shows Hanuman (see box below) astride a winged tiger.

The courtyard

Quiet and verdant, the pagoda courtyard is full of monuments. Just east of the Silver Pagoda is the monument of a **horseman**. Now bearing a head of Norodom, it began life as an equestrian statue of Napoleon III, a typically megalomaniac gift from the French emperor. On either side are heavily embellished twin **stupas** – Norodom's to the north, Ang Duong's to the south (the latter also has a stupa at Oudong). In the east corner of the compound, a small plain pavilion contains a huge **footprint of the Buddha** (Buddhapada), a representation of the Buddha dating from the time before images

---

THE RAMAYANA

The famous Hindu epic poem, the **Ramayana**, addresses the moral themes of good versus evil, duty, suffering and karma through the story of **Rama**, the seventh avatar of **Vishnu** (see p.310). A popular theme in Cambodian art and culture, its many episodes are depicted in temple carvings, pagoda art, classical dance and shadow puppetry. A simplified Cambodian version, the **Reamker**, also exists, and is more often portrayed in dance than in visual art.

The story begins with the ten-headed, twenty-armed **Ravana**, king of the *rakasa* demons, terrorizing the world. As only a human can kill him, Vishnu agrees to appear on earth in human form to re-establish peace, and is duly born as Rama, one of the sons of Emperor Dasaratha. In due course, a sage teaches Rama mystical skills, which come in handy in defeating the demons that crop up in the tale and in stringing Shiva's bow, by which feat Rama wins the hand of a princess, **Sita**.

The emperor plans to name Rama as his heir, but the mother of one of Rama's half-brothers tricks her husband into **banishing** Rama to the forest where he is accompanied by Sita and another of his half-brothers, the loyal **Lakshmana**. After Rama cuts off the ears and nose of a witch who attacks Sita, Ravana gets his revenge by luring Rama away to hunt, using a demon disguised as a golden deer. Lakshmana is despatched to find Rama, whereupon Ravana abducts Sita and takes her to his island kingdom of **Lanka**. While Rama enlists the help of Sugriva, the monkey king, Sita's whereabouts are discovered by **Hanuman**, monkey son of the wind god. Rama and the monkey army rush to Lanka, where a mighty battle ensues, ending when Rama shoots the golden arrow of Brahma at Ravana who, pierced in the heart, dies ignominiously.

Although the tale as told in Cambodia often ends here, there are two standard denouements. In one, Sita steps into fire and emerges unscathed, proving she has not been "defiled" by Ravana, after which the couple return home to a joyous welcome and Rama is crowned king. In the alternative, sad, ending, Sita is exiled back to the forest where she gives birth to twins. When they are 12, the twins are taken to court and Rama is persuaded that he is their father. He begs forgiveness from Sita and she calls on Mother Earth to bear witness to her good faith. In that moment the earth swallows Sita up, leaving Rama to mourn for 11,000 years.

1

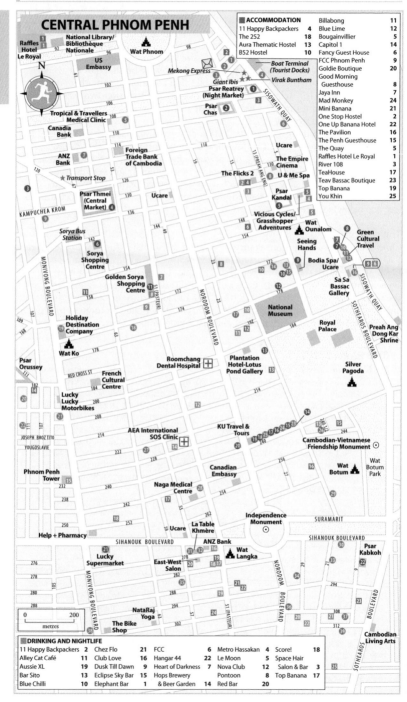

CENTRAL PHNOM PENH

ACCOMMODATION		Billabong	11
11 Happy Backpackers	4	Blue Lime	12
The 252	18	Bougainvillier	5
Aura Thematic Hostel	13	Capitol 1	14
B52 Hostel	10	Fancy Guest House	6
		FCC Phnom Penh	9
		Goldie Boutique	20
		Good Morning Guesthouse	8
		Jaya Inn	7
		Mad Monkey	24
		Mini Banana	21
		One Stop Hostel	2
		One Up Banana Hotel	22
		The Pavilion	16
		The Penh Guesthouse	15
		The Quay	5
		Raffles Hotel Le Royal	1
		River 108	3
		TeaHouse	17
		Teav Bassac Boutique	23
		Top Banana	19
		You Khin	25

DRINKING AND NIGHTLIFE							
11 Happy Backpackers	2	Chez Flo	21	FCC	6	Metro Hassakan	4	Score!	18
Alley Cat Café		Club Love	16	Hangar 44	22	Le Moon	5	Space Hair
Aussie XL	19	Dusk Till Dawn	9	Heart of Darkness	7	Nova Club	12	Salon & Bar	3
Bar Sito	13	Eclipse Sky Bar	15	Hops Brewery		Pontoon	8	Top Banana	17
Blue Chilli	10	Elephant Bar	1	& Beer Garden	14	Red Bar	20

1

were permitted to be made, along with ancient manuscripts written on palm leaves – rare survivors of Cambodia's humid climate. Another stylized Buddha's footprint, this one a gift from Sri Lanka, can be found nearby in the pavilion atop the artificial hill, **Phnom Mondap**.

Southwest of Phnom Mondap is the open-sided stupa of the daughter of King Norodom Sihanouk, Kantha Bopha, who died of leukaemia as an infant in 1952, and whose name has been given to children's hospitals in Phnom Penh and Siem Reap. Behind the Silver Pagoda is a **scale model** of Angkor Wat, an odd sight amid the religious and funerary relics. In the west corner is a **bell tower**, its pealing used to signal the opening and closing of the compound's gates. By the north gate is the **Mondap**, once housing palm-leaf texts, now containing a statue of Nandin, the bull ridden by Shiva.

The Ramayana mural

Around the courtyard runs a fabulous 642m-long **mural**. Telling the epic tale of the *Ramayana* in minute detail, the mythical scenes were painted in vibrant colours by forty artisans working in 1903–04. The gallery cover has not protected the panels from water damage and despite a partial restoration in 1985, work is ongoing to preserve what remains. Running **clockwise** from the east entrance gate, the depiction begins with the **birth of Rama** and covers his marriage to **Sita**, her abduction and her rescue by the **monkey army**. Two of the most delightful scenes, both in good condition, show the monkey army setting out for Lanka (south gallery) and crossing to the island (north gallery).

Outside the south gate

Leaving the courtyard by the south gate leads to a jumble of buildings and a small garden where, until 1962, **elephants** were tied up when not at work: look out for the elephant-shaped boxes and a pavilion of howdahs and cow carts. Another building houses an exhibition related to the coronation of King Sihamoni.

National Museum

Street 13, cnr street 178, north of the Royal Palace • Daily 8am–5pm, last admission 4.30pm • $5, $10 with audio guide, camera/video (courtyard only) $1/$3; English-speaking guides can be hired at the entrance ($6)

Cambodia's impressive dark-red sandstone **National Museum** houses a rich collection of sculpture, relics and artefacts dating from prehistoric times to the present. The collection had to be abandoned in 1975 when the city was emptied by the Khmer Rouge; it was subsequently looted and the museum's director murdered. By 1979, when the population returned, the roof had collapsed and the galleries and courtyard gone to ruin – for a time, the museum had to battle to protect its exhibits from the guano (bat faeces) produced by the millions of **bats** that had colonized the roof; these were finally driven out in 2002.

1

Designed by the French archaeologist, architect and all-round polymath, George Groslier, the museum first opened in 1918 and comprises four linked **galleries** forming a rectangle around a leafy courtyard, its roof topped with protective nagas. **Entrance** to the museum is via the central flight of steps leading to the East Gallery. The massive wooden doors, dating from 1918 and each weighing over a tonne, have carvings reminiscent of those at Banteay Srei (see p.188). The galleries are arranged broadly chronologically, moving clockwise from the southeast corner; allow at least an hour for the visit. Take time to enjoy the peaceful courtyard or have a drink and some surprisingly good food in the museum's café. Traditional dance performances take place here in the evenings.

East Gallery

The most striking piece in the **East Gallery** is a massive sandstone **garuda** – more than 2m tall, its wings outstretched – which dates from the tenth-century Koh Ker period. Displays in this collection comprise mainly sculpture, including an interesting combination of Buddhist and Hindu images; some from the fifteenth to seventeenth centuries are of gilded copper and lacquer. The case to the left, closest to the gallery entrance, houses a fine statuette of Shiva and Uma on Nandin, while another contains an intricate Buddha atop a naga, framed within a separate arcature; just beyond is a miscellaneous collection of hands and feet from long-disintegrated statues.

The gallery also has a number of bronze artefacts, some dating back to the Funan period (first to sixth century). These include an assortment of elaborate candleholders, heavy elephant bells, religious water vessels and paraphernalia for **betel-nut** preparation, including betel-nut containers in the shape of peacocks.

The far corner chamber has an interesting collection of **wooden Buddha statues** in various states of gentle decay, all post-Angkor and showing signs of the paints with which they were once decorated.

South Gallery

The gracious head and shoulders of a vast, hollow reclining **Shiva**, with two of his four arms remaining, takes pride of place in the **South Gallery**. Also on display are a small but intricate collection of **Sanskrit inscriptions** on stones dating back to the fifth and sixth centuries, many from the southern province of Takeo, supporting evidence of the province's political and religious importance during the pre-Angkor period.

Pre-Angkor

Further into the South Gallery, the focus remains on the **pre-Angkor** period (pre-ninth century), with slim, shapely sixth-century Buddhas in relaxed postures, their hair piled on top of their heads in tight ringlets. These early sculptors, though skilled – the carved garments give an impression of the contours of the bodies underneath – had yet to master carving in the round, so the statues are carved in **high relief**.

Occupying pride of place is a 3m-tall, eight-armed image of **Vishnu** dating from the Phnom Da era (sixth century). The figure wears a plain, pleated loincloth low at the front and pulled up between the legs; the hands hold a flame, a conch and a thunderbolt, all symbols of Vishnu. A stone arc supports the figure, but in a step towards carving in the round, it has been chipped away between the arc and the limbs. Close by is a sixth-century high relief of **Krishna**, standing left arm aloft, holding up Mount Govardhara.

Tucked under the roof in the central courtyard are Sanskrit-inscripted stones, and a series of voluptuous female statues of Durga and female divinities, wearing elegantly draped *sampots* (Cambodian traditional dress), line the wall. Facing the statues inside the museum is a fine and varied collection of **linga** in excellent condition.

Angkor period

A ninth-century, Kulen-style **Vishnu** in the portico of the South Gallery marks the shift to the more formal **Angkor period** (ninth to thirteenth centuries). You can see how sculptors stabilized the statue's bulk, carving the right leg slightly forward of the body and supporting the arms with a staff and sword. The late ninth-century **Preah Ko period** is characterized by comely figures, epitomized by the shapely statue of Queen Rajendradevi.

Passing between a pair of delicately carved sandstone columns, you enter the west section of the South Gallery and move into the **Bakheng period** (late ninth to early tenth century), exemplified by a 2m-tall Shiva from Phnom Krom.

During the **Koh Ker period** (early to mid-tenth century), sculpture became more dynamic, as illustrated by the athletic torsos of two wrestlers entwined in a throw (in the courtyard window). It's worth stepping outside here to see some of the original heads of the divinities from the causeway to Angkor Thom, and also an unusual ablutions bowl made from polished schist rock, the spout in the shape of a buffalo head.

This section also contains some fine statues from the tenth-century temple of **Banteay Srei**, regarded by many scholars as one of the high points of Khmer art. On a central plinth, a smiling **Shiva** and his (sadly headless) wife Uma face the south. He is unadorned save for a carved necklace, but in situ they would have been draped with precious jewellery.

West Gallery

Dating from the late tenth century on, the sculpture in the **West Gallery** is more formal than in earlier periods. An elegant example of a graceful female statue of the eleventh-century **Baphuon period** is the slender, small-breasted Lakshmi, consort of Vishnu; her *sampot* dips at the front to reveal her navel and rises above the waist at the back. By this time, Buddhism was gaining influence, illustrated here by the Baphuon-era seated Buddhas, some showing a faint smile and sheltered by the seven-headed naga.

The **Angkor period** is lightly represented, freestanding sculptures having been largely replaced by the mighty bas-reliefs carved in situ at the temples. One of the few noteworthy examples is a pediment from the west entrance of Angkor Wat, depicting part of the *Jataka*, the stories describing the previous incarnations of the Buddha. On the wall, a striking pediment from Banteay Srei illustrates a scene from the *Mahabharata*, the Hindu epic of two warring families, showing two cousins, Bhima and Duryodhana, in mortal combat.

Towards the far end of the gallery is the museum's most famous statue, the image of **Jayavarman VII** from the **Bayon period** (late twelfth and early thirteenth centuries). Sitting cross-legged in meditation, the king is portrayed as a clean-shaven, slightly rotund middle-aged man, his expression peaceful. The head may well be familiar – it's much reproduced as a tourist souvenir. The Buddhist theme resumes in the Bayon-period exhibits at the north end of the gallery, where a thirteenth-century pediment from Prah Palilay shows a seated Buddha in the earth-witnessing mudra.

North Gallery

Leaving the stone statuary behind, you skip forward a few centuries to the miscellany of the **North Gallery** whose most impressive exhibit is the cabin of a nineteenth-century **royal boat**, made of elaborately carved koki wood. Inside, the floorboards are smooth and polished, while leaves, flowers and dragons decorate the exterior. The cabin would have been lavishly furnished, ensuring that the king could travel in relative comfort.

1

The massive funerary **urn** in the centre of the gallery, nearly 3m tall and made of wood, silver and copper overlaid with gilt, was used for the ashes of King Sisowath in 1927 and again in 1960 for those of King Norodom Suramarit, the grandfather of the present king.

Not to be missed is a magnificent **wall panel**, one of a pair looted from Banteay Chhmar temple in 1998 by the military personnel who were supposed to be guarding it. The blocks were cut out from the enclosing wall using machinery, loaded onto lorries and smuggled across the Thai border en route for sale in Bangkok, but were seized by Thai police on the way. Both were returned to Cambodia in 2000. Another panel reassembled here depicts a larger-than-life, multi-armed image of Lokesvara; there are also paintings of scenes from the *Reamker*, royal parade paraphernalia and a weaving loom.

Wat Botum Park and around

South of the Royal Palace complex, flanking Sothearos Boulevard, peaceful **Wat Botum Park** gets its name from the adjacent temple. Within the park is a golden stupa commemorating the sixteen people killed outside the old National Assembly (corner of Street 240 and Sothearos Blvd) building on March 30, 1997, when grenades were thrown into a rally led by the Sam Rainsey party. Further south, the **Cambodian-Vietnamese Friendship Monument** – massive sandstone figures of a Khmer woman holding a baby, flanked by two armed Vietnamese liberation soldiers – commemorates the Vietnamese liberation of Phnom Penh from the Khmer Rouge in January 1979.

The park is a lovely place to stroll just before sunset, when a handful of fitness trainers set up boom boxes and Cambodians pay 1000 riel to join them in a rigorously choreographed, unofficial **aerobics** class. You will see others taking a gentler, but equally serious, approach to exercise by walking determined laps around the park.

Wat Botum

Sothearos Blvd

Wat Botum is one of the five original monasteries founded by Ponhea Yat in 1442 (see p.53). Situated west of the Wat Botum Park, the present structure was built by King Sisowath Monivong and dates from 1937; fortunately, it escaped damage by the Khmer Rouge. The grounds are crammed with elaborate and picturesque chedis – notably the tall white gold-tipped Buddha's Relic Pagoda – many of which hold the ashes of rich politicians and important monks; enormous, gaudy statues of giants, lions and tigers pepper the grounds. It's a wonderful place to escape the heat and noise, with several places to sit and enjoy the quiet.

Hun Sen Park complex

Hun Sen Park, now home to **Naga World**, a gaudy casino, hotel and restaurant complex, lies east of Sothearos Boulevard, and spills into adjacent **Koh Pich**, or Diamond Island. It's hard to imagine that this was once a quaint offshore farming village – the area now hosts a children's park, ornamental gardens, golf course, water park and vast exhibition centre. It was on the footbridge linking Koh Pich to the mainland that the **stampede** occurred during the water festival in November 2010 (see box, p.58). To the south lies the **Buddhist Institute** and the enormous **National Assembly** building.

SPIRIT HOUSES

The alleys around Wat Prayuvong, around 300m south of the Independence Monument, are the city's centre for the manufacture of **spirit houses** (see p.313) and religious statuary – you can't miss the brightly painted displays on the roadside. Although everything is now made in concrete, the artistry remains elaborate and the variety is fascinating; a number of artists here also do religious paintings, some on an impressive scale.

Independence Monument

Intersection of Sihanouk and Norodom blvds

Sitting amid an elongated strip of grassy park stretching west from Hun Sen Park and Naga World, the **Independence Monument** (aka Victory Monument) was built to commemorate independence from the French in 1953 but now also serves as a cenotaph to the country's war dead. The distinctive, dark-red sandstone tower was designed by **Vann Molyvann**, renowned for his style of **New Khmer architecture** in the 1950s and 1960s. Completed in 1958, it is reminiscent of an Angkorian sanctuary tower, its multi-tiered roofs embellished with over a hundred nagas. It's a dramatic sight at night when the fountains are floodlit in red, blue and white, the primary colours of the national flag.

Wat Langka

Cnr Sihanouk Blvd & Street 51 · Public meditation classes four times a week (see p.77)

Sprawling **Wat Langka**, one of the five pagodas founded in the city by King Ponhea Yat in 1442, gets its name from its historic ties with monks in Sri Lanka. The pagoda vies with Wat Ounalom for importance, and many of the monks here are highly regarded teachers. Within the vihara, scenes from the Buddha's life feature an idiosyncratic local touch – one shows Angkor Wat, while another depicts tourists climbing Wat Phnom.

Toul Sleng Genocide Museum

Entrance off Street 113 · Daily 7am–5.30pm; docudrama screened at 10am & 3pm · $3; $6 with audio guide; English-speaking guide $6 · A short moto ride from the centre

Originally the Toul Svay High School, from 1975 to 1979 the disturbing **Toul Sleng Genocide Museum** was the notorious Khmer Rouge prison known as **S-21**, through whose gates more than thirteen thousand people (up to twenty thousand according to some estimates) passed to their deaths. S-21 was an interrogation centre designed for the educated and elite: doctors, teachers, military personnel and government officials. The regime was indiscriminate in its choice of victims; even babies and children were among those detained, and subsequently slaughtered, to eliminate the possibility of them one day seeking to avenge their parents' deaths.

Beyond the gates, still surrounded by high walls and ringed by barbed wire, an eerie silence descends on the complex of four buildings, which are juxtaposed harshly against the palm and frangipani trees in the former school playground. Up to 1500 prisoners were housed here at any time, either confined in tiny cells or chained to the floor or each other in the former classrooms. Changing exhibitions also take place on the upper floors of the blocks.

At the time of writing, the only two living survivors of the prison, mechanic Chum Mey and artist Bou Meng, have taken up an informal residency near the museum entrance where they are allowed to sell their memoirs and, in Bou Meng's case, his

1

artwork. Their respective skills kept them alive at S-21 and their mission is to ensure that Cambodia's genocide is never forgotten.

A visit to S-21 is a shocking and harrowing experience (make use of the excellent audio guide which is both informative and poignant). Many visitors prefer to head here after first going to Choeung Ek (see p.100).

Block A

The southernmost block, **Block A** (to the left of the ticket booth), comprises three floors of cells that still contain **iron bedsteads** and the shackles used to chain the prisoners to the beds. Chilling, grainy photos in each room depict the unrecognizable corpse of the bed's final inhabitant. When the Vietnamese army entered the prison in January 1979, they found just seven prisoners alive; the corpses of fourteen prisoners who had died shortly before were discovered in the cells and buried in graves in the courtyard.

Block B

Walking across the garden past school gym apparatus used by the Khmer Rouge as a grotesque torture device, you come to **Block B**. On the ground floor, you can see hundreds of black-and-white **photographs** of the victims, their eyes expressing a variety of emotions, from fear through defiance to emptiness. Each one holds a number; the Khmer Rouge officials were meticulous in documenting prisoners and sometimes photographed victims following torture (also on display). The guides can tell you stories of some of the photographed victims and the audio guide also offers detailed insights. The five rooms also contain victims' clothing, photographs of forced labour camps and portraits of Khmer Rouge leaders.

Block C

The terrace and upper-storey **balconies** of **Block C** are still enclosed with the barbed-wire mesh that prevented the prisoners attempting escape or jumping to a premature death. The partition cells on each floor, of wood or brick, are so small that there is hardly room to lie down. Although the majority murdered here were Cambodian, including scores of Khmer Rouge cadres detained by the paranoid regime, foreigners, both Western and Asian, were also interrogated and tortured. At the end is a room where visitors can offload emotions, comments and wishes with a "graffiti area" provided on plastic panels.

Block D

Things get no easier emotionally as you progress into **Block D**. Here methods of **torture** are outlined, some of them unflinchingly depicted in paintings by the artist Van Nath, one of the survivors. Prominent is a **water chamber** where prisoners were systematically held under water until they confessed. Worth reading are the sombre extracts in the exhibition area from forced "confessions", and the exchanges of letters between the

---

VISITING S-21 AND THE KILLING FIELDS

Many people visit **Tuol Sleng Genocide Museum** (S-21) and the "killing fields" of **Choeung Ek** (see p.100) in one trip, either on organized guided tours or independently. Logically, the museum should be visited first, as prisoners were taken from S-21 for execution in the open fields, 12km away. However, many visitors do the opposite because, as the day goes on, crowds and heat increase at Choeung Ek. Regardless of order, visiting both on the same day provides a fuller – if more distressing – understanding of the prisoners' experience and journey.

1

cadrcs, who continued to victimize prisoners until their declarations conformed to the guards' own version of the truth. Newer exhibitions focus on other aspects, such as international visits during the time and how the regime covered up the atrocities.

Upstairs is the White Lotus Room, a calm space with water, mats and cushions, where visitors are invited to rest or reflect. In another room, the Documentation Centre of Cambodia, documentaries are screened twice daily. At the time of writing, it was Red Wedding, which looks at forced marriages under the Khmer Rouge regime.

On the way out, past the memorial in the courtyard, there's a glass panel which details the ongoing, if limited, criminal tribunals against the surviving Khmer Rouge leaders.

The French quarter

During the colonial era, **Wat Phnom** was at the heart of the **French quarter**, its leafy boulevards graced by several delightful **colonial buildings**, including the main post office, the National Library, *Raffles Hotel Le Royal* and the rather grand train station. Many of these survive today and the area is worth exploring, on foot or by cyclo, to get a taste of their historic grandeur.

Wat Phnom

Northern end of Norodom Blvd • Daily 6am–6.30pm • Foreigners $1

In the northeast of the city, set back just a few hundred metres from the riverfront, the imposing white stupa of **Wat Phnom** sits atop the hill that gave the city its name. This is one of the principal pleasure spots for the inhabitants of Phnom Penh, drawing the crowds especially at weekends and on public holidays. Before climbing the hill (which is just 27m high), you can either buy your **ticket** from the payment booth or a roving guard will inevitably approach you for cash once you reach the top. The nicest way up the hill is by the **staircase** flanked by nagas on the east side, passing bronze friezes (depicting scenes of battle) and dancing apsaras (reproductions of bas-reliefs at Angkor Wat) on the way.

The sanctuary on the summit has been rebuilt many times, most recently in 1926, and nothing remains of the original structures. The surrounding **gardens** were originally landscaped in the late nineteenth century by the French, who also installed a zoo (of which nothing remains) and a giant lawn clock on the south side of the hill – a new one, a gift from the Chinese, took its place for the millennium – with a dial that glows in fluorescent colours at dusk.

The vihara

Inside the **vihara** (remove shoes before entering) is a sitting Buddha, visible through the haze of burning incense, encircled by wall paintings evoking depictions of the *Jataka* stories, which describe previous incarnations of the Buddha. A constant stream of Khmer pass through the pagoda, paying their respects and trying to discover their fortunes by holding a palm-leaf book above their head and, without looking, inserting a small pointer between the pages; the page contains the prediction, although sometimes it takes three attempts to get an acceptable fortune.

Behind the vihara is a small shrine to **Daun Penh**, the woman credited with founding the sanctuary here (see p.53). The shrine contains her much-revered genial image, while the large white stupa contains the ashes of King Ponhea Yat.

Preah Chao shrine

On the north side of the hill just below the summit is a busy shrine to **Preah Chao**, a Tao goddess whom people come to ask for good luck, health or success with their

1

business; her helpers, Thien Ly Than (who can see for 1000 miles) and Thuan Phong Nhi (who can hear sounds 1000 miles away), stand close by. Judging by the elaborate **offerings** on the altar, it seems that many requests are granted – it's not unusual to see whole cooked chickens, surrounded by their cooked innards and unlaid eggs, offered on plates. Resident **monkeys** frequently steal the offerings; feeding them is said to be a good way of acquiring merit for the next life, as is releasing the tiny "merit" birds that hawkers sell from cages all around the hill – you may spot a Cambodian buying up an entire cage – although it is rumoured that the birds are trained to fly back to their cages once released and many birds die from the stress of their captivity.

The post office

Street 13, cnr Street 102, one block east of Wat Phnom • Mon–Fri 7.30am–5.30pm

Phnom Penh's main **post office** is housed in a fine colonial building east of Wat Phnom. Dating from the early twentieth century, it occupies one side of a colonial square just off the river which in pre-Khmer Rouge years bustled with cafés and restaurants; an attempt is being made to resurrect the area, but there's a way to go yet. The post office itself was restored in 2001; an old photograph of the interior hangs on the wall inside, the counters shown still recognizable today.

The National Library (Bibliothèque Nationale)

Street 92, between Wat Phnom and Raffles Le Royal • Mon–Fri 7.30–11.30am & 2–5pm

Set well back from the road, the **National Library** is a fine colonial building dating from 1924. During Pol Pot's regime, the books were either destroyed or tossed out onto the pavement, and the building was turned into a stable. In the 1980s, the Vietnamese filled up the shelves with their own books, though barely a decade later, these were bound with string and sold by the kilo. It's now the French who are helping to gradually restock the library's eclectic collection (with Francophone titles). A room off the ground-floor reading room contains a collection of rare, century-old palm-leaf manuscripts, the colour of parchment.

Raffles Hotel Le Royal

Western end of Street 92

The **Raffles Hotel Le Royal**, established in 1929 and set in lush tropical gardens, is a fabulous blend of colonial, Khmer and Art Deco styles. Even if you're not staying (see p.81), you should take a look at the grand teak staircase and the *Writers' Bar*, head to the *Elephant Bar* to check out its collection of vintage photos and have a cocktail (see p.88), or simply drop into the conservatory – a delightful spot for morning coffee or afternoon tea.

The train station

Western end of Street 106

The **train station** occupies a commanding position, facing the grassy avenue that runs between streets 106 and 108 to the river. Built in the early 1930s, it has an impressive Art Deco facade and was a hive of activity until the network was decimated during the Khmer Rouge years of the mid-1970s. It saw little activity after that, other than the freight trains running to and from Kampot, but in 2016, services resumed between Phnom Penh and Sihanoukville (see box, p.76).

The unmistakeable blue stupa in front of the station, **Preah Sakyamoni**, used to contain a relic of the Buddha (the relic was removed to the more tranquil Oudong in

CLOCKWISE FROM TOP LEFT PSAR THMEI (P.74); STREET 104; SISOWATH QUAY (P.58) >

1

HORROR IN THE EMBASSY

Screened by high white walls, the **French Embassy** sits on the western side of Monivong Boulevard, just south of the traffic island. In April 1975, eight hundred foreigners and six hundred Cambodians took refuge here from the Khmer Rouge, whereupon they were held hostage and denied diplomatic privileges. Eventually, foreigners and Cambodian women married to foreign men were released and escorted to the airport. Cambodian men married to foreign women had to remain, never to be seen again.

2002, from where it was stolen in 2013), while behind the station, an old 1929 steam train has been restored and put on permanent display. Outside are refreshment stalls where you can pick up cold drinks and basic snacks.

Boeung Kak Lake
North of the French quarter, around St 93

While the lake itself no longer exists – it was sold to a developer, Shukaku Inc., who filled it in 2010 – this area, once home to four thousand families, is currently the site of an **urban art** project. Develop Boeung Kak (ⓦdbk-art.com), based around Street 93, has street murals, an annual street art festival and the occasional pop-up shop or café. How long it will last is anyone's guess, as the development is still scheduled to go ahead.

Psar Thmei (Central Market)

Daily 7am–6pm

Edged on four sides by busy traffic-clogged streets, the much-photographed **Psar Thmei** (literally "New Market" but better known as **Central Market**) was designed by the French in 1937 and hailed at the time as Asia's largest. The original Art Deco design, highlighted by the enormous central dome and unusual cruciform shape, has made it a central, if unlikely, landmark. Reopened in 2011 after extensive renovations, its bustling domed central hall is laid out with stalls selling jewellery, spectacles and watches while its four enormous wings house low-grade electronics, household items, clothing and fabrics along with fresh produce, souvenirs and flowers. While there may be better bargains to be had at atmospheric but cramped **Psar Toul Tom Poung** (Russian Market), Central Market's airy open feel makes it far more pleasant to explore. To stroll around the food stalls is an eye-opening, if smelly, experience, with every type of meat, fish, fruit and vegetable on display. It's a good place for a cheap feed, too; fringing the market to the south are **food stands** selling local dishes for a few thousand riel.

Chroy Changvar Bridge and around

As you travel north towards the **Chroy Changvar (Japanese) Bridge**, the city becomes less attractive, albeit interesting for its history. The bridge, spanning the Tonle Sap, was blown up in 1973 either by (depending on who you believe) Lon Nol forces attempting to hold off the Khmer Rouge from entering the city, or by the advancing Khmer Rouge forces. Known from then on as *spean bak*, "broken bridge", it is now often referred to as *chuowa chuoul hauwy*, "not broken anymore". To others it is the "Japanese Bridge", as it was rebuilt with funds from Japan in 1993.

The roundabout at the northern end of Monivong Boulevard, just before the bridge, contains the curious **Knotted Gun Monument**. In 1999 after the last of the Khmer Rouge had surrendered, the government, concerned about the proliferation of firearms, seized all the guns it could lay its hands on and, amid great political

1

fanfare, had them crushed. The remains were melted down and a sculpture of a **revolver** with a knot tied in its barrel was cast. However, cynics say that only the broken guns were smashed and that the good ones were handed out to the police and military.

ARRIVAL AND DEPARTURE   PHNOM PENH

If you're travelling to Phnom Penh by **road** or **boat**, you'll most likely arrive at one of several terminals that lie within 1.5km of Central Market. **Flights** arrive 8km west of town. Wherever and whenever you arrive, there are always tuk-tuks or motos available. Most towns and cities in Cambodia can be reached directly from Phnom Penh. **Siem Reap** is particularly easy to get to, served by a daily boat up the Tonle Sap, plentiful road transport along NR6 and regular, if expensive, flights.

BY PLANE

Pochentong International Airport The compact airport is 9km west of the city on NR4, a 30–60min drive from the centre, depending on traffic. Facilities in the international arrivals hall include several 24hr ATMs, money exchange, phones, a post office, a tourist information desk (see p.77), shops, cafés and an efficient tuk-tuk and taxi booth operating a fixed-price ($9 tuk-tuk; $12 taxi) service to the city. Motos are not allowed inside the terminal, but there are always plenty waiting on the main road, about 200m across the car park; the fare into town is $3–5.

Airlines Bangkok Airways, 61 Street 214 (☎023 971771, ⓦbangkokair.com); Cambodia Angkor Air, 206 Preah Norodom Blvd (☎023 6666786, ⓦcambodiaangkorair .com); Cathay Dragon formerly Dragon Air, Regency Complex, 168 Monireth Blvd (☎1800 209783 toll-free, ⓦdragonair .com); China Southern Airlines, 53 Monivong Blvd (☎023 430877, ⓦcs-air.com); EVA Air, Suite 11, 79 Street 205 (☎023 219911, ⓦevaair.com); Jet Star Asia Airlines, 333B Monivong Blvd (☎023 220909, ⓦjetstar.com); Lao Airlines, 58B Sihanouk Blvd (☎023 222956, ⓦlaoairlines.com); Malaysia Airlines, 35–37 Street 214 (☎052 3962508, ⓦmalaysiaairlines.com); Qatar Airways, Vattanac Capital Tower, 66 Monivong Blvd (☎023 963800, ⓦqatar.airways .com); SilkAir, Unit 2–4a, Monireth Blvd/St 217 (☎023 988629, ⓦsilkair.com); Thai Airways, 298 Mao Tse Toung Blvd (☎023 214359, ⓦthaiair.com); Vietnam Airlines, 41 Street 214 (☎023 215998, ⓦvietnamairlines.com). Destinations: international Bangkok (10 daily; 1hr 10min); Doha via Ho Chi Minh City (daily; 10hr 30min);

Dubai via Yangon (daily; 9hr); Ho Chi Minh City (4–5 daily; 45min); Hong Kong (1–2 daily; 2hr 25min); Kuala Lumpur (4 daily; 1hr 50min); Shanghai (daily; 3hr 40min); Singapore (4 daily; 2hr); Taipei (1–2 daily; 3hr 15min); Vientiane (1–2 daily; 1hr 20min). Destinations: domestic Siem Reap (5–6 daily; 45min). Note domestic carriers in Cambodia come and go with alarming frequency and schedules change regularly, so it's best to check with a travel agent for the latest timetable. At time of writing, Cambodia Angkor Air was the only scheduled carrier operating (expensive) services to Siem Reap from Phnom Penh (Cambodia Bayon Airlines and Sky Angkor Airlines operate charter services between Sihanoukville and Phnom Penh).

BY BUS

Bus companies There is no central bus station. Buses depart from their own offices or depots, many of which are in the vicinity of Central Market or near the night market and Street 104 at the northern end of Sisowath Quay. In addition, an increasing number offer free pick-up from city-centre hotels and guesthouses. Phnom Penh Sorya (southwest of Psar Thmei) has the largest depot in the city and serves all provincial towns, sometimes using smaller twenty- to thirty-seat coaches for the more distant or less popular destinations,. They also run daily a/c coaches to Bangkok, Vientiane and Ho Chi Minh City (HCMC). Giant Ibis and Mekong Express offer the most comfortable services to Siem Reap, Battambang, Sihanoukville, Kampot and HCMC. Virak Buntham's night buses (some with flat beds) travel to Siem Reap, Sihanoukville, Battambang, Bangkok

---

KINGDOM BREWERIES

Cambodian beer might not be world famous but a brewery tour offers a fun diversion from Phnom Penh's more conventional sights. **Kingdom Breweries**, 1748 NR5, 1km north of the Chroy Changvar Bridge (tours Mon–Fri 1–5pm or by arrangement; $6; ☎023 430180, ⓦkingdombreweries.com), was established in 2009 as a boutique label. The 30-minute tour gives you an insight into the brewing process – interesting if you've never witnessed this sort of thing before – and includes a tasting at the end in the atmospheric Tap Room or riverview terrace. The beer's not bad either. On the first Friday of the month, they host TGIF with all-you-can-drink draught beer, burgers and fries for $12/person (6–11pm).

1

via Poi Pet, and Koh Kong (Cham Yeam border). Most operators schedule long-distance departures for the morning, although those for the most popular destinations, including Siem Reap and Sihanoukville, leave throughout the day. As at all bus stations and depots, it's a good idea to keep a close eye on your bags, whichever company you travel with.

To HCMC Journeys to HCMC, which is still often referred to as Saigon, can be made without joining a new bus across the border, and any official dealings are done with the assistance of the bus operators. You still have to get your visa at least 24 hours in advance from your guesthouse although some nationalities are eligible for a 15-day visa exemption (no return within 30 days of departure).

To Bangkok Getting to Bangkok from Phnom Penh usually involves a change of vehicle after crossing the border.

To Laos If you're not heading direct to Vientiane, check if your ticket is just to the border or through to Don Det, 4000 Islands.

Destinations Bangkok via Poipet (6 daily; 12–15hr); Battambang via Pursat (10–12 daily; 6hr); Ho Chi Minh City via Bavet (16 daily; around 6hr); Kampot (5 daily; 4–5hr); Kep (5 daily; 4–5 hr); Kompong Cham (2–4 daily; 2–3hr); Koh Kong (3 daily; 6–7hr); Kratie (2–3 daily; 6–7hr); Siem Reap (hourly; 6–7hr); Sihanoukville (hourly; 4–5hr); Stung Treng (daily; 9hr); Vientiane (daily; 24hr).

BY SHARED TAXI AND MINIBUS

With decent buses from Phnom Penh to all but the most remote locations in Cambodia, shared taxis are less necessary nowadays, at least for travellers. Minibuses, however, remain popular and, thanks to significant road improvements, they now run to Kratie, Stung Treng, Rattanakiri and Mondulkiri as well as all the key destinations, with most companies offering hotel pick-up.

Transport stops for shared taxis If you're keen on experiencing a shared taxi, you can find shared vehicles reasonably easily. For destinations north of the city, including Kompong Thom, Siem Reap, Kompong Cham, Battambang and Poipet, shared taxis and minibuses use the transport stop (and the streets around it) 100m northwest of Central Market. For Takeo, Kampot, Kep or

Sihanoukville or the border town of Bavet (commonly called Moc Bai) pick up a shared vehicle by Central Market or Psar Olympic. If you're going a long way, it's worth getting to your preferred transport stop by 6am or 7am. Later, when fewer people travel, you may have a long wait while the drivers gather up enough customers to make the trip worthwhile. For destinations closer to town, such as Takeo, you'll be able to get a shared taxi until mid-afternoon – after that, departures become less frequent. Note that the frequencies listed below are rough estimates – there are no fixed schedules. If you're arriving in Phnom Penh via shared taxi, you'll find that transport stops are inundated with moto and tuk-tuk drivers, although they often won't speak much English so it's wise to carry a map.

Destinations Bangkok via Poipet (4–5 daily; 12hr); Battambang via Pursat (5–6 daily; 6hr); Ho Chi Minh City via Bavet (several daily; 6–7hr); Kampot (8 daily; 3hr); Koh Kong (2–3 daily; 6hr); Kompong Chhnang (2 daily; 2hr 30min); Kompong Thom (8 daily; 3hr); Sen Monorom (4–5 daily; 6–7 hr); Siem Reap (hourly; 6–8hr); Sihanoukville (6 daily; 4hr); Sisophon (6 daily; 7hr).

BY TRAIN

A new route (see box below) launched in 2016 operates between Sihanoukville and Phnom Penh via Takeo and Kampot leaving Fri, Sat, Sun, and public holidays. Sihanoukville (7hr), Kampot (4hr 40min–5hr), Takeo (1hr 30min); tickets $4–7 available at station (☎078 888582, ⊛royal-railway.com).

BY BOAT

Since travelling by bus has become cheaper and faster, taking the boat to Siem Reap is less popular, although for many the experience is worth the price and time. There is just one service a day. A handful of express boats also depart daily for Chau Doc in Vietnam. Note that there are no longer boat services to Battambang, Kompong Cham or Kratie.

Departures Boats for Siem Reap ($28–35) and Chau Doc ($25–29) leave from the passenger boat terminal (also known as the Tourist Docks) on the river near the main post office and Street 104. Companies take it in turns to depart

---

RETURN OF THE RAILWAY

In April 2016, Cambodia's Royal Railway reinstated its first railway route in over six years. Many hope that this marks the beginning of a Cambodian railway revival, following the ravages to the system under the Khmer Rouge regime. Two trains operate between Phnom Penh and Sihanoukville, stopping in Takeo and Kampot. At the time of writing, services were running on Friday, Saturday and Sunday, with extra services during Khmer holidays. One train also carries cargo and vehicles. Trains are reasonably punctual although it's worth factoring in some extra time. As yet, tickets aren't sold in town, so advance purchase is at the station only (☎078 888582, ⊛royal-railway.com).

for Siem Reap daily. Seating is reserved; you can buy your ticket in advance from most hostels and guesthouses or at the docks. Hang Chau (w hangchautourist.vn) and Blue Cruiser (w bluecruiser.com) both operate daily departures

to Chau Doc while Mekong Explore (w bookmebus.com /en/mekong-explore) sails to Siem Reap and Vietnam.
Destinations Chau Doc (3 daily; 4–5hr); Siem Reap (1 daily; 7hr).

INFORMATION

Tourist information At the airport's international arrivals hall (Mon–Fri 8am–5pm). There is also a tourist information office near the Chaktomuk Theatre, although it mainly touts city tours.

Visitor guides and listings Phnom Penh Visitors Guide is a free quarterly English-language booklet with details of places to stay, restaurants and sights, a map and a bit of history. You'll find copies in most guesthouses, restaurants and Western cafés; extracts are available online at w canbypublications.com. Pocket Guide Phnom Penh is produced every four months (w cambodiapocketguide .com). For film screenings, theatre performances and other entertainment, the Cambodia Daily (w cambodiadaily .com) has a "What's On" section on Fri, with classified ads for restaurants and bars on Tues and Thurs; the daily Phnom

Penh Post (w phnompenhpost.com) is another useful source of information. Asia Life (w asialifemagazine.com /cambodia) has features on new openings and exhibitions.

Travel agents The following well-established firms employ English-speaking staff and act as both travel agents and domestic tour operators: KU Travel & Tours, 77 Street 240 (☎ 023 723456, w kucambodia.com); Holiday Destination Company, 262D Monivong Blvd (☎ 023 218585, w holidaydestination.asia) and Green Cultural Travel, 339E0 Sisowath Quay (☎ 023 900534, w greenculturaltravel.com). Mango Cambodia (☎ 023 998657, w mangocambodia.com) and Backyard Travel (☎ 023 998657, w backyardtravel.com) also do good day-trips and ones further afield.

TOURS

Culinary tours Ducky, a passionate foodie, offers excellent local food experiences with trips that include an evening market and barbecue tour ($25), and roving dinners ($70) where you eat each course in a different restaurant (w urbanforage.co).

City tours Numerous companies offer tours around Phnom Penh, Silk Island and Oudong, including Urban Adventures (☎ 012 391780, w urbanadventures.com), Capitol Tours (☎ 023 7241040, w capitoltourscambodia .com) and Cambodia Walkers (☎ 010 908316, w cambodiawalkers.com). Asian Trails have a good selection to Phnom Chisor, Tonle Bati and Ta Prohm (☎ 023 216555, w asiantrails.travel).

Cycling tours Grasshopper Adventures at Vicious Cycles, 23 Street 144 (☎ 012 462165, w grasshopperadventures .com) organizes excellent half-day guided tours of Koh Dach's quiet backwaters by day and night ($45) and one-day trips for experienced riders up to Oudong ($89) on quality mountain bikes. Bicycle rental ($4 a day), e-bike ($12 a day) hire, repairs and accessories also available.

Cyclo and walking tours Khmer Architecture Tours (e contact@ka-tours.org, w ka-tours.org) run cyclo (and walking) tours for $15 around key post-1953 architectural sights. You can also download a self-guided walking map.

Photography tours Nathan Horton (☎ 095 891965, w nathanhortonphotography.com) and Cambodia Photo Tours (☎ 060 873847, w cambodiaphototours.asia) both offer tours run by professional photographers.

Quad biking Village Quad Bike Trails (☎ 099 952225, w villagequadbiketrails.com) organize tours (daily 7.30am & 12.30pm; 1hr/$35 and at 4pm; 90min/$40) to the Killing Fields and through the Cambodian countryside, plus a full-day tour which also includes Tonle Bati and Phnom Tamao Wildlife Rescue Centre ($155).

Vespa tours Hop on the back of a moto, driver included, for a city spin with Vespa Adventures (☎ 078 995455, w vespaadventures.com). Insider's Phnom Penh costs $59 including entry fees; the night-time experience at $69 includes food and drink.

ACTIVITIES

Cookery courses Learn to prepare traditional Khmer food including vegetarian at La Table Khmère, 11E Street 278; morning classes include a visit to a local market (☎ 012 238068, w cambodia-cooking-class .com; $20). Feel Good Café, 79 Street 136 also offers cookery courses Tues–Sat (☎ 017 497538, w bit.ly /feelgoodcookery).

Meditation and yoga One-hour silent meditation sessions are held at Wat Langka (Mon, Thurs & Sat 6pm,

Sun 8.30am; free), supervised by English-speaking monks. Some wats have more yoga-orientated meditation classes, and NataRaj Yoga, 52 Street 302 (☎ 012 250817, w yoga cambodia.com), has yoga and Pilates classes for $9/ session.

Running The Hash House Harriers organize a run around the city most Sundays ($5). Meet 2pm outside the train station (☎ 099 353325, e apphhh1@gmail.com, w p2h3.com).

1

TIME TO RELAX

Phnom Penh is full of **massage parlours and spas** and while some do double up as brothels, there are countless reputable ones where you can get a massage, aromatherapy, body scrubs and other beauty treatments for a fraction of the cost at home. Most will offer a traditional (dry) Khmer body massage as well as oil, head and foot massages; others will extend to aromatherapy and beauty treatments. Spas are found all over town, including along the riverfront. Foot massages are often carried out on reclining chairs while body massages take place on partitioned beds or in private rooms.

SPAS

Bodia Spa Cnr Street 178 & Sothearos Blvd ☎023 226199, ⊚bodia-spa.com. Bodia's indulgent massages, facials, wraps and beauty treatments in a beautiful setting are worth the extra price (from $24/hr). Book in advance. Daily 10am–midnight.

Bliss Spa, 29 Street 240 ☎012 613386, ⊚blissspacambodia.com. Lives up to its name, with rooms set around a quiet inner courtyard and a tempting menu of massages, scrubs and beauty treatments (from $23/hr). Daily 9am–9pm.

Daughters of Cambodia 321 Sisowath Quay ☎023 727158, ⊚daughtersofcambodia.org. This riverside shop and café, run by an organization which helps victims of trafficking, has a first-floor spa offering massages, manicures and pedicures. Daily 9am–5.30pm.

East West Salon, 16 Street 278 ☎023 727158, ⊚eastwest-hairsalon.com. This hair and beauty salon in popular Boeung Keng Kang also offers waxing, facials and massage. Tues–Fri noon–8pm, Sat 9am–5pm (salon); Daily 10am–10pm (massage).

Friends'n'Stuff 215 Street 13 ☎016 737456, ⊚bit.ly/friendsnailspa. Part of the Friends initiative which offers hospitality training to vulnerable children, their Phnom Penh gift store has a nail bar attached. Daily 9am–5.30pm.

Seeing Hands 12 Street 13, near the National Museum ☎012 234519. Feel good and do good at this ethically minded massage parlour, set up with the help of an NGO which works with the blind in Cambodia. Khmer, Thai and shiatsu massage and reflexology on offer (from $8/hr). Daily 8am–10pm.

U&Me Spa 229 Sisowath Quay ☎023 986822 ⊚unme-spa.com. Excellent, affordable massages (from $8/hr) and beauty treatments in a relaxed riverside setting. Two other branches in BKK (216B St 63 and 18 St 306) also have a hair salon. Daily 9am–10pm.

Swimming The *Blue Lime* (adults only) *Patio* and *252* hotels, and *Eighty8* hostel, all have pools open to non-residents as long as they purchase food and drink. Phnom Penh Sports Club, St 271 corner of St 464 (☎023 6368809; ⊚ppsportsclub.com) is excellent value; $5 for use of pool, gym, steam, sauna, jacuzzi, aerobics and table tennis plus well-priced hair and massage treatments too. The Grand Phnom Penh Water Park (☎023 997882, ⊚bit.ly/ppwater park) north of the centre has water slides and swimming pools (daily 9am–6pm; Mon–Fri $5, weekends $7).

GETTING AROUND

Although it's possible to see many of Phnom Penh's sights on foot, the heat and humidity, allied with the city's traffic and dust, don't make **walking** a particularly pleasant experience. Pedestrians *never* have the right of way in Cambodia, and Phnom Penh is a place to exercise 360-degree vision, even at traffic lights and the striped, so-called "pedestrian" crossings. **Motos**, **tuk-tuks** and to a lesser extent **cyclos** are the workhorses of local transport, readily available all over town, picking you up from the kerb and dropping you outside your destination.

BY MOTO

Fares Around $1–2 per trip, more if you're travelling out of the centre, in the rain, or after dark, when you might pay $3–4. It may be safer to take a tuk-tuk at night.

Drivers Some moto drivers speak a little English, especially those who hang out around the riverfront and other places where foreigners congregate. Elsewhere, you'll find English-speaking drivers few and far between, so it's useful to learn some landmarks, such as markets and monuments, and have a map handy.

BY TUK-TUK

Tuk-tuks are more comfortable than motos, especially when two or more people are travelling together, or in the rain, as they have roll-down side-curtains. Don't expect a speedy trip though as they are powered by titchy motorbikes and progress can be painfully slow, particularly if there are a few people and their bags aboard.

Fares Journeys around town cost $2–4 or about $15–20 for a half day. There is talk of introducing metered tuk-tuks but for now, negotiate the fee before you set off.

1

BY CYCLO

Unique to the capital and increasingly rare, cyclos provide a leisurely way to get around, although they do cost slightly more than motos. You'll find a few along Street 158 near Billabong Hotel near Sorya Mall, and around Central Market.

BY TAXI

Taxis don't cruise for fares, although a few enterprising drivers meet incoming boats along the riverfront. Hotels and guesthouses can organize taxis or call one of the recommended firms; expect to pay $4–5 for a single daytime journey within the city, or $6–8 at night. Most vehicles are unmarked, but a few now use a meter system and have illuminated signs on their roofs.

Day hire Taxis for hire by the day can often be found lined up on the east side of Monivong Blvd, near Central Market. The going rate is $25–35/day around the city, and $40–70/day out of town, depending where you're going.

Taxi firms Taxi DCP Phnom Penh (☎010 900150, ⓦtaxidcpphnompenh.com) is a 24hr taxi service with reliable English-speaking, and female, drivers. Global (☎011 311888, ⓦbit.ly/globalpp) provides a 24/7, metered service (call to book), while Exnet Cambodia Taxi (☎092 333740, ⓦbit.ly/exnetpp) offers an experience similar to Uber and Grab; download the app to see nearby drivers.

BY CAR OR MOTORBIKE

Due to the chaotic driving, the shameless speed traps and the police checks, the vast majority of visitors to Phnom Penh opt for car with driver rather than driving themselves (bookable through a travel agent or your hotel/guesthouse), although motorbikes are a great way of exploring the surrounding countryside. If you do intend to rent a car or a motorcycle, be aware that even by the impatient standards of Cambodian driving, Phnom Penh motorists take the biscuit. It's best not to insist on claiming your right of way or to be too heavy on the horn – incidents of road rage here can be violent. More an annoyance than a danger are the policemen who stop foreigners and blatantly demand a $5 "fine" (ie bribe). It's unlikely you'll get away without paying, so it's easier to simply pay up rather than protesting your innocence; you can usually bargain them down to a dollar or two.

Car rental firms If you decide to go it alone try Avis, 62 Monireth Blvd (☎023 884744, ⓦavis.com.kh).

Motorbike rental firms French-run outfit The Bike Shop, 31 Street 302 (☎012 851776; ⓦmotorcycle cambodia.com), has 110cc city runabouts for $6/day or off-road bikes from $30/day. They offer 24/7 support and organize tours, too. Lucky! Lucky!, 413 Monivong Blvd (☎012 212788), has been going for years, and charges $7/day for a 110cc moped and $15/day for a 250cc off-road bike, with discounts on longer rentals. Helmets are provided, but no insurance. Two Cambodia, 34C Street 376 (☎012 200513; ⓦtwocambodia .com) rents semi-automatics for $7/day and bicycles from $2/day.

ACCOMMODATION

Phnom Penh has an increasing number of guesthouses and hotels catering for all pockets and tastes, from basic rooms and designer dorms to boutique hotels and opulent colonial-era suites. No matter when you arrive, you should have no difficulty **finding a room** – though the very cheapest places fill quickly. If you intend to stay for more than a couple of nights, it's worth asking for a **discount** at guesthouses and mid-range places. With luxury accommodation, you'll often get a better deal by booking online or as part of a package. Free **wi-fi** is almost always included.

ESSENTIALS

Budget hotels The former backpacker area around Boeung Kak Lake has all but disappeared – along with the water. Most of the budget accommodation is now in little clusters, along Street 258 and Street 172 in the centre of town, around Central Market and, increasingly, around Street 278 in trendy Boeung Keng Kang (known as BKK) near the NGO residential area. Riverfront properties are generally pricier, but there are a handful of cheap places either right on or near the riverfront.

Mid-range hotels Recent years have seen increased competition in the mid-range bracket, particularly boutique hotels, with plenty of options along the riverfront, around the National Museum and in BKK. Along with café- and shop-lined Street 240, BKK is one of the hottest locations in town, with cosmopolitan restaurants, cafés, spas and boutiques springing up all around. Next on the watch list is Tonle Bassac between Street 51 and the river, including the Street 308 strip, and the Russian Market neighbourhood (BKK3).

Luxury hotels Phnom Penh has some wonderful upmarket options, many of them proving excellent value, with the pride of place going to *Raffles Hotel Le Royal*.

Serviced apartments If you are staying for a month or more, you could consider the serviced rooms/apartments offered by several hotels such as *Colina* and *Bougainvillier*. These go for around for $700–1000/month. You can also find good-value options on Airbnb.

THE RIVERFRONT

Bougainvillier 277C Sisowath Quay ☎023 220528, ⓦbougainvillierhotel.com; map p.64. This boutique

1

PHNOM PENH ADDRESSES

Thanks to the French, who laid out the city on a **grid system**, Phnom Penh is remarkably easy to navigate. The **major streets** all have little-used official names, which have been changed periodically to honour particular regimes or sponsoring countries, although the current names have been around since the mid-1990s. The rest of the streets are **numbered** and generally pretty easy to find. North–south streets have the odd numbers, with the low numbers nearest the river; even-numbered streets run east–west, with the low numbers in the north of the city. Signage is improving, and areas of town are even acquiring district names that are posted above the road.

Individual **buildings** are numbered, but are almost without exception difficult to locate, as the numbering doesn't run consecutively and the same number is often used more than once on the same street. Cruising until you spot your destination is often the only option unless you can call ahead for directions. It must be said that buying a local SIM card for your phone can be invaluable in Cambodia.

hotel has a terrific location and spacious rooms with Cambodian textiles and furnishings in muted tones. Fantastic rooftop Sky Bar (happy hour 4–7pm) and French and Khmer dishes at its Ibiza Lounge restaurant. Breakfast included. Monthly rates available too. $50

FCC Phnom Penh (formerly Foreign Correspondents Club of Cambodia) 363 Sisowath Quay ☎023 992284, ⓦfcccambodia.com; map p.64. Booking is recommended to secure one of the seven en-suite rooms, all named after Angkorian temples. Rooms aren't as atmospheric as you might expect of a hotel that's linked to the *FCC*'s legendary bar (see p.87), but they're comfortable and modern, and some have great river views. Breakfast included. $75

Jaya Inn 319 Sisowath Quay ☎081 567281, ⓦjaya-inn.com; map p.64. This ten-room boutique hotel with an urban design feel is a stand-out option right on the river. Comfortable beds and the rainfall shower are highlights. Breakfast included. $60

★**Lazy Gecko Guesthouse** 1D Street 258 ☎078 786025, ⓦlazygecko.asia; map pp.56–57. Recently revamped, this long-standing backpacker guesthouse has mixed and female-only dorms with king-sized beds, en-suite hot water bathrooms, plus private fan and a/c rooms. Lively café serves gastro pub food and has DJ nights and barbecues. A nano-brewery is planned. Dorms $5, doubles $12

Number 9 Hotel 7C Street 258 ☎ 023 984999, ⓦnumber9hotel.com; map pp.56–57. One of Phnom Penh's first "boutique" backpackers' hotel has a sleek, modern bar-restaurant, a/c rooms plus a rooftop hot tub and pool table on the first floor. $20

Okay Guesthouse 3BE Street 258 ☎012 300804, ⓦokay-guesthouse.com; map pp.56–57. Welcoming, family-run hostel with a lively backpacker-friendly restaurant. Rooms are basic, a little faded, but clean, and they run a useful travel desk. The place next-door has similar prices, with a cosy communal area but far less appealing rooms. $12

One Stop Hostel 85 Sisowath Quay ☎098 991184, ⓦonederz.com/phnom-penh; map p.64. Scrupulously clean, friendly hostel facing the Tonle Sap river with a variety of a/c dorms, with and without windows, and two female dorms. All have large lockers and comfy beds with personal socket and lamp. Free tea and coffee in the lounge. $7

The Quay 277 Sisowath Quay ☎023 224894, ⓦthequayhotel.com; map p.64. This boutique hotel – all soft cushions, plush carpets and cutting-edge design – has an excellent street-level restaurant as well as a revamped roof terrace with bar and jacuzzi; perfect for happy-hour drinks overlooking the river. Staff are delightful. Book direct for better discounts. $65

River 108 2 Street 108 ☎023 218785, ⓦriver108.com; map p.64. A luxurious Art Deco-styled boutique hotel, in shades of muted silver and gold with tinkling fountains, just a stone's throw from the river. Book direct for a slightly lower rate. $85

AROUND THE NATIONAL MUSEUM AND ROYAL PALACE

Aura Thematic Hostel 205A Street 19 ☎023 986211, ⓦaurahostel.com; map p.64. Behind the Royal Palace, this immaculate hostel has en-suite, a/c male, female and mixed dorms, each one individually designed, with single or double pod-style beds; there's a private four-bed VIP room too and breakfast from $1. The Eluvium Rooftop Lounge (daily events and happy hour 5–8pm) is also open to non-guests. Dorm $5

★**B52 Hostel** 52 Street 172 ☎070 323285, ✉lb52 .phnompenh@gmail.com; map p.64. A newcomer on a busy street, this backpacker hostel has two spotless ten-bed dorms (one with a balcony), a six-bed female dorm and a handful of private rooms. Everything is en-suite with hot-water showers. There's a sociable bar-restaurant plus friendly owner and travel services. Dorms $5; doubles $18

Blue Lime 42 Street 19Z, off Street 19 ☎023 222260, ⓦbluelime.asia; map p.64. This adults-only (over 16s) boutique hotel, tucked down a little alley behind the National Museum, has an understated, contemporary style and is a lovely little haven in the middle of the action. Rooms are minimalist and fresh, with all mod cons, and some have their own private plunge-pool and terrace. The day-beds around the main pool are the perfect place to unwind, and the restaurant serves Western food. Breakfast included. $50

Good Morning Guesthouse 42 Street 23 ☎093 866999, ⒲goodmorningguesthouse.com; map p.64. Family-run guesthouse in a quiet spot near the palace, with lovely gardens and private rooms, some with a/c. The cheapest have shared bathrooms (hot-water showers) and a good-value quad room ($20). Delicious Western and Cambodian food, home-made rice wine and free drinks with meals at happy hour (4–7pm). Free pick-up for bus arrivals; airport pick-up $7 (official price $9). Fan $7; a/c $13

★**The Pavilion** 227 Street 19, behind Wat Botum ☎023 222280, ⒲thepavilion.asia; map p.64. Boutique guesthouse in two impeccably converted colonial mansions. Rooms (all a/c) are beautifully presented; garden bungalows are tiny, but some come with private pools. With its swimming pool (guests and members only, no kids allowed), sunbeds, verdant gardens, poolside restaurant, bar and small spa, this place is almost impossible to leave. $60

The Penh Guesthouse 70B Street 244 ☎023 211376, ⒲the-penh-guesthouse.com; map p.64. Lovely twelve-room guesthouse on a tiny street near the palace. The a/c rooms are smart with fridge and safe, and there's a lovely balcony where you can order breakfast and drinks. $26

AROUND CENTRAL MARKET (PSAR THMEI) AND TOWARDS THE RIVERFRONT

11 Happy Backpackers 87–89 Street 136 ☎088 7777421, ⒲11happybackpackers.com; map p.64. Large and friendly hostel with a mix of no-bunk, a/c dorms and simple en-suite fan and a/c rooms (some without windows). There's a spacious, leafy rooftop restaurant-bar complete with pool table, comfy chairs and lots of nooks for hiding away. It also houses the community-run Flicks 2 cinema and the tour desk can organize visas and tickets. Dorms $5; doubles (fan) $10

Capitol 1 14 Street 182 ☎023 548409, ⒲capitoltourscambodia.com; map p.64. A backpacking institution, travellers come here (entrance on Street 107) for the great-value accommodation, food and inexpensive tours. Rooms are a bit cell-like but plentiful, and it's a handy overnighter for buses leaving Central Market. Fan $5; a/c $10

★**The Billabong Hotel** 5 Street 158 ☎023 223703 ⒲thebillabonghotel.com; map p.64. This hybrid hotel-hostel has a fantastic pool, an assortment of private rooms (breakfast included) plus spotless, spacious dorms (including female-only) – all en-suite with a/c, balcony,

lockers and free towels. The poolside bar-restaurant serves good Western and local food (breakfast from $2, fried rice $3.50). Dorms $6; doubles $35

Fancy Guest House 169B Street 15 ☎023 211829, ⒲fancyguesthouse.com; map p.64. In a great location near the riverfront, this family-run hotel ticks all the boxes, with sparkling rooms all with a/c and hot showers. The cheapest rooms have no windows; the more expensive have balconies. $18

AROUND WAT PHNOM

Eighty8 Backpackers Street 88, just off Monivong Blvd ☎023 5002440 ⒲88backpackers.com; map pp.56–57. In a slightly out-of-the-way location, but still within walking distance of Wat Phnom and the riverside, this boutique backpacker favourite has a pool, a stylish open bar and a restaurant with an extensive menu. There are five dorm rooms – one with pod-style beds with sliding doors, offering a completely private sleeping space – a female dorm, and cheaper beds in the "above bar" mixed dorm. Double and family rooms all have a/c and hot water, some with balconies. Dorms $6.40; doubles $24

★**Raffles Hotel Le Royal** Street 92, off Monivong Blvd ☎023 981888, ⒲raffles.com; map p.64. Dating from 1929, this impressive Art Deco hotel, set in lovely gardens, was restored in 1997 to its original understated elegance, and still offers every modern convenience. Engravings of old Cambodia grace the corridors, and the luxurious rooms are individually decorated with specially commissioned prints and Cambodian artefacts. The main restaurant is the epitome of elegance, and there are bars, a patisserie, shops, spa and pool. Afternoon tea or a happy-hour cocktail (daily 4–9pm; half-price) in the *Elephant Bar* is a must. $240

BETWEEN CENTRAL MARKET (PSAR THMEI) AND THE OLYMPIC STADIUM

Narin 50 Street 125 ☎023 991955 or ☎099 881133, Ⓔntouchnarin@hotmail.com; map pp.56–57. One of Phnom Penh's earliest guesthouses, this old wooden house has decent, cosy rooms (some with a/c, all with hot water), friendly English-speaking staff, cheap food in a balcony restaurant and traveller services. Fan $10; a/c $15

TAT 52 Street 125 ☎012 921211, ⒲tattooguesthouse.com; map pp.56–57. This cheerful family-run guesthouse is another long-timer, with basic rooms, communal TV, and a rooftop restaurant serving Cambodian and Chinese food. Sister guesthouse *TATTOO*, to the south, is similarly priced (fan $10; a/c $14). Fan $8; a/c $12

BOEUNG KENG KANG (BKK) AND AROUND THE INDEPENDENCE MONUMENT

★**The 252** 19 Street 252 ☎023 998252, ⒲the-252.com; map p.64. This superb Swiss-run, boutique hotel

1

stands out for its stylish well-appointed rooms – some with fab balconies – helpful, smiling staff and lovely 13m pool with lounging pavilions. The food and cocktails are pretty good too. $\overline{\underline{55}}$

Envoy Hostel 32 Street 322 ☎ 023 220840, ⓦ envoy hostel.com/phnompenh; pp.56–57. A converted villa in a popular neighbourhood with spotless a/c dorms, private bunk/double rooms, modern bathrooms and a rooftop terrace. A large communal area by the kitchen and lots of chill-out areas helps the sociable and relaxed buzz as do the helpful staff. Dorm $\overline{\underline{7}}$; doubles $\overline{\underline{24}}$

Goldie Boutique Guest House 6 Street 57, btw streets 282 & 278 ☎ 099 986222, ⓦ goldieguesthouse .com; map p.64. Split across three buildings, the fifteen a/c rooms in this little hotel are well equipped and brightly decorated, some with a balcony ($25). Staff can help with travel queries and there's a spa, bar and restaurant. $\overline{\underline{20}}$

Mad Monkey 26 Street 302 ☎ 023 987091, ⓦ madmonkeyhostels.com; map p.64. Occupying two buildings across from each other, this flashpacker hostel has gained a reputation for its party pool, chill-out areas and lively bar and restaurant. The a/c en-suite dorms have extra-large bunk beds and the private rooms are smart. Dorms $\overline{\underline{7}}$; doubles $\overline{\underline{18}}$

Mini Banana 135 Street 51 ☎ 023 726854, ⓦ mini -banana.asia; map p.64. Tucked away off Street 51, the restaurant here is the highlight, with its French chef rustling up gourmet burgers and more. The new sixteen-bed a/c dorm has three bathrooms, and seven private rooms include two with a/c. Dorms $\overline{\underline{7}}$; doubles $\overline{\underline{13}}$

One Up Banana Hotel Cnr street 51 & 288 ☎ 023 211344, ⓦ 1uphotelcambodia.com; map p.64. A secure, well-organized hotel with tidy a/c rooms with desks, kitchenettes, TVs and safes. The upper rooms are a bit quieter. Long-term rates available. $\overline{\underline{30}}$

TeaHouse 32 Street 242 ☎ 023 212789, ⓦ maads.asia /teahouse; map p.64. Creatively designed boutique hotel mixing Chinese decor and urban design; the smart a/c rooms have excellent showers, TV and minibar. There's an atmospheric Tea Lounge, shaded pool, spa and fusion dining in the open-sided restaurant. $\overline{\underline{45}}$

Top Banana 9E0 Street 278 ☎ 012 885572, ⓦ topbanana.biz; map p.64. An original Phnom Penh party haunt, *Top Banana* remains a backpacker favourite. Rooms and dorms have been upgraded, and the newly designed bar and lounge area continues to attract non-guests. Dorms $\overline{\underline{6}}$; doubles $\overline{\underline{14}}$

TONLE BASSAC (AROUND STREET 308 AND BASSAC LANE)

Teav Bassac 30 Street 9 ☎ 023 982828, ⓦ teavbassac hotel.com; map p.64. Nineteen-room boutique hotel with a pool, tropical gardens and beautiful spa. There's an excellent restaurant and great city views from the rooftop bar. Rooms are contemporary and use local artwork. $\overline{\underline{60}}$

★ **You Khin** 13A Street 830 ☎ 023 224843, ⓦ youkhin house.com; map p.64. Calm, welcoming guesthouse, a few blocks from lively Street 308 that has seven smart a/c rooms off an airy central staircase, with enclosed shower cubicles (as opposed to the usual wet rooms) and four rooms in the new block. The open-air restaurant serves delicious local food and there are guitars for guests to strum on. On the first floor is a beauty spa and above it a library with TV and pool table. Profits go towards local education projects. $\overline{\underline{39}}$

TOUL TOM PONG (RUSSIAN MARKET) AND TOUL SLENG (S-21)

Colina Boutique Hotel Cnr streets 123 & 440, near Russian Market ☎ 023 221088, ⓦ colinaboutiquehotel .com; map p.86. One of only a handful of hotels in this area with comfortable and beautifully designed rooms – some with balconies and all with city views. Gorgeous rooftop pool, bar and restaurant overlook the Russian Market area, and there's a spa, café and Khmer restaurant. Breakfast included. $\overline{\underline{45}}$

Kolab Sor 436 Street 310, near Tuol Sleng Genocide Museum ☎ 023 979797, ⓦ kolabsorhotel.com; map pp.56–57. There are just a few decent hotels in the neighbourhood developing around Toul Sleng (S-21 Museum). This one has lovely, cosy rooms, plus a restaurant and tenth-floor Sky Bar (5pm–midnight) with great views. Breakfast included. $\overline{\underline{40}}$

EATING

Phnom Penh has a vast range of places to eat, from cheap noodle shops and market stalls to Khmer fine-dining, late-night bistros and pricier Western places. Many guesthouses also have small, sometimes middling, sometimes surprisingly decent, restaurants. On the whole, food in the city is both good and fairly priced. The bustling **riverfront and Sisowath Quay** are lined with cafés, restaurants and bars serving cuisine from all over the world; the attractive location means that the cheapest single-course meals go for $4–5. For a cheaper choice of backpacker-friendly restaurants and bars, head to nearby neon-lit **Street 172** or to the classy cafés and gastro-spots along **Street 240** between streets 7 and 19. A little more upmarket (but much more laidback than the riverfront) is **Boeung Keng Kang (BKK)** – broadly the area between Streets 51 and 63, from Street 278 and extending south to Street 306 – packed with swish cafés, refined but reasonably priced restaurants and bars. On the other side of Street 51, east of Norodom Blvd, **Street 308** and **Bassac Lane** are packed with atmospheric places, while the area around the **Russian Market** is fast becoming one of the city's go-to spots.

ESSENTIALS

Prices You can easily eat for well below $5 if you stick to market stalls, unfussy Cambodian restaurants and some of the Indian and Chinese places. In backpacker guesthouses, you'll be able to eat for around $4, but once you venture into tourist-centred and Western-oriented establishments, prices rise and you'll be looking at around $4–7 for a simple main course. In slightly plusher places, and those with a prestigious location, expect to pay upwards of $6–10 for a main, maybe slightly more. The most expensive places to eat are in the restaurants of the premier hotels and in a few independent establishments (many of them French), where you could easily pay $15–20 and above for a main course (especially if it involves imported meat), with extra for vegetables and accompaniments.

Markets The markets are great places to fill up on traditional Khmer dishes: try the Central Market (see p.74), Psar Kabkoh, a few blocks southeast of Independence Monument, where dozens of sellers cook into the early evening, and the night market (see p.92).

Street food Stalls and roadside vendors sell simple takeaway noodle and rice dishes for roughly $1, while fresh baguettes and rolls are sold in the markets in the morning and are available all day around the city from hawkers with handcarts.

Self-catering and picnics It's easy to buy fresh produce and tinned goods from the markets; to buy Western provisions such as cheese, yoghurt, chocolate and brown bread, you'll have to go to one of the supermarkets (see p.93). Fresh fruit can be bought everywhere, from markets, local stores and street vendors.

RESTAURANTS

Street 136, west of Central Market, is home to a cluster of inexpensive – and roaringly popular – Chinese places, and for a slap-up meal, some luxury hotels have excellent Chinese restaurants. Similarly, there's a cluster of Japanese restaurants along Street 63, between streets 422 and 462, in BKK1. There are also plenty of Indian, Pakistani and Bangladeshi restaurants, especially popular with the expat community, and a staggering variety of Western establishments – you could eat something different every night for a month, from pizza and pasta to grilled steaks, fresh sushi and crunchy salads. For fine dining on imported meat and wine, there are some noteworthy French restaurants as well as some fancy fusion places – expensive by Cambodian terms, but a fraction of what you would pay in the West. Near Psar Kabkoh, south of Independence Monument, are a few barbecue restaurants, beloved of the Cambodians, where you can eat at small plastic stools, while along Monivong and Sihanouk blvds are plenty of places where you cook meat and vegetables in a pot of stock at your table.

THE RIVERFRONT AREA

Bopha Phnom Penh (Titanic) Sisowath Quay, just south of the Tourist Docks ☎023 427209, ☻bopha -phnompenh.com; map p.64. A huge, decadent restaurant and lounge bar with an open front looking over the Tonle Sap. Gilt furnishings, wide wicker chairs and ornamental water features abound, and the food is perfectly good if on the pricier side with mains from $9. The main draw is the nightly apsara performance between 7.30 and 9.30pm. Daily 5.30am–11pm.

Happy Herb Pizza 345 Sisowath Quay ☎097 994 3225, ☻happyherbpizza.com; map p.64. This long-running joint still serves up a decent pizza (and some good vegetarian choices). Pizzas start at $4 and can be made "happy" – with a marijuana-infused butter base – for $1 more. It also does tasty pasta, plus burgers, sandwiches and Cambodian dishes from $1.50–5.50. Call for free delivery. Daily 8am–11pm.

Mekong River Sisowath Quay, cnr Street 118 ☎092 415761; map p.64. It's not the finest food, but this restaurant is the place for late-night munchies with burgers, breakfasts and cheap beer served all through the day and night. Daily 24hr.

★**Pop Café da Giorgio** 371 Sisowath Quay, next to the FCC ☎012 562892; map p.64. This tiny long-running Italian restaurant is where the expats come to eat authentic pasta (from $6.50), pizza (from $7.50) and gnocchi ($7.50). What it lacks in size, it more than makes up for in atmosphere and the quality of its food. Daily 11.30am–2pm & 6–10pm.

River Crown 1 Street 178 ☎023 5552599, ☻bit.ly /rivercrown; map p.64. Stylish second-floor restaurant and bar with views of the river and the FCC. Staff are friendly and food well priced (Khmer curries from $5.50, chilli crab penne $7.50). It's also a good spot for a sunset drink, with a 4.30–7.30pm happy hour offering $1 draught beer and half-price cocktails. Daily 8am–midnight.

AROUND THE NATIONAL MUSEUM AND ROYAL PALACE

David's Homemade Noodle House Street 13, cnr Street 172 ☎012 351890; map p.64. Order noodles and dumplings here and see them hand-rolled and cooked from scratch in the streetside kitchen. Textures, flavours and dipping sauces are delicious. There's a second restaurant across the road at 168 Street 13. Daily 9am–10pm.

Fresh Chilli 4 Street 172 ☎077 787864; map p.64. Cambodian food only at this locally run restaurant, whose tagline is "We support Khmer food". From fried tarantulas to delicious stir-fried fish with ginger ($4.75), it's a welcome addition to this busy street. Daily 9am–11pm.

★**Friends Creative Tapas** 215 Street 13, near the National Museum ☎012 802072, ☻friends-restaurant .org; map p.64. Run by an NGO, Mith Samlanh, that works with street youths, training some of them in the restaurant

1

EATING WITH A CONSCIENCE

Several cafés and restaurants in Phnom Penh either offer training in the catering trade to the disadvantaged or donate profits to help those in need. All are atmospheric places to grab a bite or a coffee.

Café Yejj See p.86.
Connecting Hands See p.86.
Friends Creative Tapas See p.83.

Restore One Café See p.87.
Romdeng See p.85.
Sugar 'n Spice Café See p.87.

and catering business. Famed for its Western and Asian fusion tapas, coffees and cocktails, dishes include mini falafel burgers, braised pork quesadillas ($5.75) and Burmese chicken curry ($6.25). Daily 11am–11pm. Kitchen closes 10pm.

Frizz 67 Street 240 ☎ 023 220953, ⓦ frizz-restaurant .com; map p.64. The menu at this small but excellent and moderately priced restaurant helpfully includes an accurate English translation of Cambodian dishes. Try the fish amok ($5) or the Khmer barbecue *chhnang phnom pleung* ("volcano pot") – a tabletop charcoal brazier, on which you can cook your own meat and vegetables ($6.50, min 2 people). Daily 7am–10pm.

Tamarind 31 Street 240 ☎ 012 830139, ⓦ tamarindpp; map p.64. Find the world on a plate at this breezy three-storey restaurant serving Middle Eastern, Khmer, Thai and Mediterranean food. There are excellent tagines, tapas, Lebanese meze and small Asian dishes; the set lunch for $6.95 is good-value and baklava with the rum-and-raisin ice cream is heaven. Try to get a table on the upper terrace and enjoy a cocktail looking over the street. Daily 9am–midnight.

The Vegetarian 158 Street 19 ☎ 012 905766; map p.64. This veggie restaurant with a pretty garden terrace serves super-cheap food – most mains, such as creamy lotus root with cashew nut curry and soy meat *lok lak*, are $3 or less. Juices cost from $1.75 and they do snacks such as tofu puffs ($2). Daily 10.30am–8.30pm.

AROUND PSAR THMEI (CENTRAL MARKET) AND TOWARDS THE RIVERFRONT

Mamak's 17 Street 114 ☎ 012 777990; map p.64. Since opening in 1992, this inexpensive halal Malaysian restaurant has become a Phnom Penh institution. *Roti canai*, a paper-thin bread cooked on a griddle and eaten with curry sauce ($1.20), is a popular breakfast dish, washed down with *teh tarek*, a sweet, milky red tea, or *teh thomada*, the same minus the sweet milk. Other dishes include spicy fish steaks, crispy fried chicken, vegetable curries and a tasty chicken *nasi lemak* ($3.50). Daily 7am–8pm.

La Marmite 80 Street 108 ☎ 012 391746; map p.64. One of Phnom Penh's longest-running French restaurants, this laidback little corner bistro (not far

from the night market) has a mostly French menu (croque monsieur $7, beef bordelaise $8.50, snails $6.50), a good wine list and the best crème brûlée in town. Daily 11am–10pm.

Restaurant 26 Cnr streets 13 & 136; map p.64. Come here for a filling *bai sach chrouk* (pork and rice) breakfast ($1.25) or try the fried chicken rice ($2.25); its early hours make it a good place to fuel up before catching a morning bus. Daily 4am–5.30pm.

★**Sam Doo** 56–58 Kampuchea Krom Blvd ☎ 017 427688; map p.64. The a/c scarlet-hued surroundings of this popular Chinese restaurant are a welcome respite from the busy market; standouts include the juicy Sichuan pepper shrimps ($7.20), roast duck ($7) and renowned dim sum (from $2.20). Daily 7am–2am.

AROUND WAT PHNOM

Hummus House 95 Sisowath Quay, near the night market ☎ 092 483759, ⓦ bit.ly/hummushouse; map p.64. This popular Lebanese joint is the go-to place for kebabs, meaty shawarmas, hummus wraps ($3) and delicious home-made bread. Daily 10.30am–10.30pm.

Van's 5 Place de la Poste, Street 102 ☎ 023 722067, ⓦ vans-restaurant.com; map p.64. A beautiful, restored colonial building (formerly the Indochina Bank) opposite the post office is where you'll find some of Phnom Penh's best French cuisine (with a price tag to match). Service has the kind of flair you'd expect in Paris, and the food is traditional, rich and extravagant; just peek at the foie gras and wagyu beef menus. It's not cheap (rack of lamb $30) but the two-course business lunch ($15) is good value. Daily 11.30am–2.30pm & 5–10.30pm.

La Volpaia Place de la Poste, 20–22 Street 13 ☎ 023 992739, ⓦ lavolpaia.com; map p.64. Opposite the post office and *Van's*, this no-frills family Italian keeps it simple and delicious, and boasts a great French and Italian wine list to accompany the pasta and pizza dishes (margherita pizza/risotto ai funghi $8). Mon–Fri noon–2.30pm & 5.30–10.30pm, Sat & Sun noon–10.30pm.

SOUTH OF PSAR THMEI (CENTRAL MARKET)

Beef Soup Restaurant Favour Hotel, 429 Monivong Blvd ☎ 023 219336; map p.64. Locals reckon this is the best place in town for tabletop cooking. The beef version is the house speciality – you'll pay around $10/person for a serving of thinly sliced meat, several plates of vegetables, including mushrooms and tofu, noodles and a bubbling pot of stock. The waitresses will help you with the protocol, or you can just copy the locals. Daily 6–9.30pm.

Mama 10 Street 111 ☎ 011 424766; map p.64. Opposite *Capitol 3* guesthouse, *Mama* has become a bit of an institution – the Cambodian landlady dishes up cheap traditional Khmer and French-inspired food from $1.50. Great place for breakfast (from 1500 riel) before the early bus. Daily 7am–9pm.

Nouveau Pho de Paris 258 Monivong Blvd ☎ 012 844833; map p.64. An enduring favourite, this popular Chinese, Cambodian and Vietnamese restaurant serves huge steaming bowls of tasty *pho* (beef and noodle soup $3.50), spring rolls with chilli and peanut dipping sauce, succulent crispy duck and the like (around $4–6 each) from a picture menu. Daily 6.30am–10pm.

★**Romdeng** 74 Street 174, near Monivong Blvd ☎ 092 219565, ⓦ romdeng-restaurant.org; map p.64. This non-profit training school for former street youths serves excellent regional Cambodian food in a colonial villa with a leafy terrace. Try the beef and banana flower salad ($5.75), pumpkin and courgette amok ($6) or, if you dare, the crispy fried tarantulas in black pepper and lime ($5.25). Daily 11am–11pm. Kitchen closes 10pm.

Royal India 21 Street 111, just south of Capitol Guesthouse ☎ 012 855651; map p.64. This simple, friendly restaurant dishes up consistently good and reasonably priced North Indian food. The halal menu is comprehensive and includes chicken and mutton curries from $3, dahl for $2 and refreshing sweet and salty lassi. Daily 9.30am–9.30pm.

BOEUNG KENG KANG (BKK) AND AROUND THE INDEPENDENCE MONUMENT

Anise 2C Street 278, off Street 57 ☎ 023 222522, ⓦ anisehotel.com.kh; map p.64. Rooms are a little drab at this mid-range hotel but the wraparound terrace café is a lovely spot for a fruit smoothie, ice coffee or some food. Dishes include fusion amok ravioli ($5.95), green mango salad ($4.75) and quesadillas ($4.95) plus inventive desserts and freshly baked pastries. Daily 6–11pm.

Chinese Noodle House 553 Monivong Blvd ☎ 012 937805; map p.64. This tiny place is always, justifiably, packed – the fresh pulled noodles, made at the front of the restaurant, are delicious whether sunk into soups or fried, ($2), as are the speciality pork-and-chive dumplings ($1.80). Daily 10am–10pm.

Magnolia 55 Street 51, cnr street 242 ☎ 012 529977, ⓦ magnoliarestaurants.com; map p.64. This breezy courtyard restaurant – with a mouth-watering menu of Vietnamese and Thai delicacies – offers real value for money. The *pho* soup ($3.50) is excellent and it's great for

breakfast with Vietnamese *banh mi* sandwiches and pancakes from $3. Daily 6am–11pm.

Sovanna 2C Street 21 ☎ 011 840055, ⓦ bit.ly/sovanna bbq; map p.64. This authentic Cambodian BBQ restaurant is beloved by Khmers for its charcoaled meats and ice-cold beers. Barbecued dishes come with a zesty dipping sauce that you mix yourself and raw veggies. The vast menu includes grilled pork ribs ($3), beef *lok lak* ($4.50) and fried rice with crab ($3). Its livelier sister restaurant, *Sovanna II*, is a few doors along. Daily 6–11am, 4–11pm.

Yakitori Jidaiya 17 Street 278 ☎ 023 6302254; map p.64. Don't be surprised if staff shout "*sama sama!*" (welcome) as you enter this small but lively Japanese BBQ restaurant that serves up *teppanyaki* from $3, spicy fried chicken ($4) and a tasty Khmer-style spaghetti bolognese ($3.50). Daily 11am–2pm & 5pm–midnight.

TONLE BASSAC (AROUND STREET 308 AND BASSAC LANE)

The Italian House Street 312, end of Street 9 ☎ 092 230207, ⓦ bit.ly/italianhousepp; map p.64. The owner of this relatively new pizzeria is both a pizza pro and builder, hence the impressive wood-fired oven and fine Neapolitan pizzas (from $8). Daily 5–10pm.

★**The Lost Room** 43 Street 21 ☎ 078 700001, ⓦ thelostroom.asia; map pp.56–57. It's worth hunting down this exposed brick bistro with small back bar – home to some of the city's best fusion food. Dishes, designed for sharing, include a moreish crispy pork belly in dark ale ($8.50), a Moroccan spiced crispy duck ($9.50) and pear and blue cheese parcels ($5.50). Book ahead, and if you're not good with maps, ask them to send a tuk-tuk to pick you up. Daily 5–10pm.

Malis 136 Norodom Blvd ☎ 023 221022, ⓦ malis -restaurant.com; map p.64. A trendy, upmarket Cambodian restaurant in a stylish modern building with tables around a raised pond in the courtyard. Popular with wealthier Khmers and the city's expat business and NGO workers, it serves traditional and modern Khmer food, such as pork and banana blossom salad ($7) and chicken/beef curry in lotus leaf ($10). With some dishes over $15, it's not the cheapest but you can get a breakfast of noodle soup and coffee for around $5. Daily 6am–10pm.

★**Mama Wong's** 41 Street 308 ☎ 097 8508383, ⓦ mamawongs.com; map p.64. Excellent dumpling and noodle house on bustling Street 308 with a near-faultless menu. Top picks include the spring onion pancakes ($2) and prawn and chive dumplings ($4.50). Most mains $5. Daily 11am–11pm.

SOUTH OF THE CENTRE

Shiva Shakti 17 Street 63, off Mao Tse Toung Blvd ☎ 012 813817; map pp.56–57. Classical Indian-Moghul cuisine in an upmarket setting, with specialities including

1

tender kebabs, paneer and tandoori dishes. Expect to pay upwards of $8 for a single dish with rice and chapati or naan bread. Daily 10am–10pm.

Topaz 162 Norodom Blvd, near Wat Than ☎ 015 821888, ⊛ topaz-restaurant.com; map pp.56–57. Arguably the best French food in town, served in a startlingly modern building, with fine wines and exceptional succulent steaks. You can fork out up to $99 for a top-of-the-range steak, but most mains are under $30 and pasta from $10. The best option is the $25 three-course set lunch that includes wine. Daily 11.30am–2pm & 6–10.30pm.

TOUL SLENG (S-21) AND TOUL TOM PONG (RUSSIAN MARKET/BKK3)

ABC Street 360, near Tuol Sleng Genocide Museum ☎ 015 909898; map pp.56–57. Choose which vegetables, noodles and meat (from $1.50) you want, and cook them yourself at tabletop barbecues. Great fun and a local favourite. Daily 4–11pm.

★**Alma Café** 59c Street 155, cnr Street 468 ☎ 092 424903, ⊛ bit.ly/almacafe; map below. Charming, authentic Mexican place near the Russian Market. Breakfast tacos and burritos ($4.50) and a daily changing lunch menu (posted nightly on their Facebook page) includes pulled pork quesadillas and tortilla soup ($5.50), home-made guacamole and desserts such as tequila lime cake ($2). A real find. Wed–Mon 8am–2pm & 5.30–9.30pm.

PHNOM PENH: RUSSIAN MARKET

● EATING			■ DRINKING AND NIGHTLIFE	
Alma Café	6		Alchemy	2
Banh Mi & Bros	4		Long After Dark	1
Café Yejj	3		● SHOPPING	
Khmer-Thai			Peace Handicrafts	3
Restaurant	1		Psar Toul Tom Poung	
Lot 369	5		(Russian Market)	1
Restore One	2		Rajana	2

■ ACCOMMODATION	
Colina Boutique Hotel	1

Banh Mi & Bros 78 Street 450 ☎ 085 400880, ⊛ banhmiandbros.com; map below. Fill up on *banh mi* (Vietnamese sandwiches); bacon and egg ($2.20) and veggie roll ($3.50). Money-saving "combos" with drink and dessert for $2 extra. There's another branch in BKK1 at 173 Street 63. Daily 10am–10pm.

Café Yejj 170 Street 450, cnr of Russian Market ☎ 092 600750, ⊛ bit.ly/cafeyejj; map below. Social enterprise café, training vulnerable young people and women and serving everything from breakfast ($2.75) to green curry ($5.25) and a tempting menu of Middle Eastern dishes (falafel $4.50). Daily 8am–9pm.

Khmer-Thai Restaurant 26 Street 135, near Wat Toul Tom Poung ☎ 012 321616; map below. Slightly outside the main Russian Market area, this classy restaurant doesn't advertise, but is still packed every night by locals in the know. Inexpensive Khmer and Thai food is served in good-sized portions; try the tasty pickled cabbage with pork $4. Daily 11am–2pm & 4.30–9pm.

CAFÉS AND COFFEE SHOPS

Though Phnom Penh's busy café society of the 1950s and 1960s vanished during the war, there has been a massive revival recently, with many places attached to galleries or shops, and new ones opening frequently. *Browns* is the country's very own, upmarket chain of coffee shops.

ARTillery Street 240½, near Street 19 ☎ 078 985530, ⊛ artillerycafe.com; map p.64. A creative little café that's one of the best spots for healthy, organic, vegan, gluten- and sugar-free food. Try the hummus heaven sandwich ($4), super-foods salad ($5) or the vitamin vitalizer power juice ($2.50). Daily 7.30am–9pm.

Backyard Café 11B Street 246 ☎ 078 751715, ⊛ backyardeats.com; map p.64. Backyard also specializes in organic, vegan, gluten- and sugar-free food. Try the chia pudding ($4) for breakfast, pesto chicken salad ($6.50) and no-pasta lasagne ($7.50). Tues–Sun 7.30am–8pm, Mon 7.30am–4pm.

Bloom Café 40 Street 222 ☎ 077 757500, ⊛ bit.ly /bloomcafe; map p.64. A training café for Cambodian women that serves the most irresistible cupcakes, Fairtrade tea and coffee amid relaxed surroundings. Tues–Sun 7.30am–8pm, Mon 7.30am–4pm.

Connecting Hands 42H Street 278 ☎ 078 588810, ⊛ bit.ly/connectinghands; map p.64. Another one of Phnom Penh's training cafés, this is a lovely quiet spot with a varied menu – breakfast burritos ($5.95) fried rice ($4.50) and coconut calm smoothie ($3) are all recommended. Mon–Sat 9am–6pm.

Delishop (Comme à la Maison) 13–15 Street 57 ☎ 023 360801, ⊛ bit.ly/delipp; map p.64. Adored by expats and visitors alike, this café is set off the road in a quiet garden and does a roaring trade in fresh bread and pastries (coffee éclair $2.50). Perfect for coffee and a croissant while you read the paper. Daily 6am–10.30pm.

★**Feel Good II** 11B St 29 ⓣ017 497538, ⓦfeelgoodcoffee.com.kh; map p.64. One of only a handful of cafés where they roast, grind and brew the coffee (flat white $2.50) on site – the smell of roasting beans will entice you through the front door. On the menu are wraps, sandwiches, burgers and bagels. The original *Feel Good*, on Street 136 near the river, is a little busier (open 7.30am–6pm) and has a gallery upstairs. Daily 7.30am–4.30pm.

★**Java Café** 56 Sihanouk Blvd ⓣ023 987420 ⓦjavacambodia.com; map p.64. Fill up on soups, salads and home-made muffins ($2) or unwind on a balcony overlooking the Independence Monument; the upper level also has a gallery with changing exhibitions. Daily 7am–10pm.

Lot 369 313C Street 454, Russian Market ⓣ012 345541, ⓦfacebook.com/lot369; map opposite. This courtyard café, run by Australian expats, not only offers great coffee (from the *Feel Good* roastery) and great food, but also prides itself on offering fair working conditions. The Facebook page posts daily deals. Daily 7.30am–6pm.

Restore One 23 Street 123, Russian Market ⓣ016 302727, ⓦbit.ly/restoreone; map opposite. Avocado with poached eggs, hearty soups and some of the tastiest burgers around, this café also doubles up as a training centre, with profits helping to set up educational facilities in poor villages. Daily 7am–5pm.

The Shop 39 Street 240 ⓣ092 955963, ⓦtheshop-cambodia.com; map p.64. Not only does *The Shop* offer a fantastic café atmosphere, but has great deli sandwiches and pastries (from $1) and coffee too. Their *Chocolate Shop* is a few doors along on the same street. Daily 6.30am–7pm.

Sugar 'n Spice Café 321 Sisowath Quay ⓣ077 657678 527028, ⓦdaughtersofcambodia.org/visitor-center; map p.64. This first-floor café is run by Daughters of Cambodia, an NGO offering sex workers and victims of trafficking support and employment. Snack on gooey chocolate brownies or opt for healthy salads, soups and sandwiches. There's a nail spa upstairs and a gift store downstairs. Daily 9am–5.30pm.

DRINKING

There's no shortage of **drinking** venues in Cambodia's capital. While some visitors flock to the seedy, smoky girlie bars that proliferate off Sisowath Quay and along Street 51, there's a lot more to Phnom Penh's bar scene, from the sophisticated, trendy cocktail bars in **BKK** (see p.89), and around the **Russian Market** and **Street 308/Bassac Lane**, to the rooftop bars overlooking the river and a growing craft beer scene. There are a number of lower-key hangouts too, often with live music though some may double up as pick-up joints. Most bars and restaurants promote daily **happy hours** from late afternoon to well after sunset (although many start much earlier) when you can sink 50c glasses of draught beer, $1.50 G&Ts or $2 cocktails. Phnom Penh also has an emerging **gay scene**, with a few great venues and more popping up every year.

BARS AND PUBS

THE RIVERFRONT AREA

Chinese House 45 Sisowath Quay ⓣ087 237893, ⓦchinesehouse.asia; map pp.56–57. A drink inside this beautiful restored colonial villa is a real treat, with a dedicated sommelier on hand to recommend French and other wines. The Pan-Asian and Khmer-inspired menu is on the pricey side (seafood laksa $16.75, coriander miso tofu $14.95) but the circular bar, murals and furnishings are really special. Mon–Thurs 11am–1am, Fri & Sat 11am–2am, Sun 11am–midnight.

★**FCC Phnom Penh** (formerly Foreign Correspondents Club of Cambodia) 363 Sisowath Quay ⓣ069 253222, ⓦfcccambodia.com; map p.64. Possibly the most atmospheric bar in the region (imagine a Southeast Asian version of the bar in *Casablanca)*. The balmy air, whirring ceiling fans and spacious armchairs invite you to spend a hot afternoon getting slowly smashed. Relatively pricey; the drinks are worth it (happy hour 5–7pm) but the food is not. Daily 6am–midnight.

Metro Hassakan Cnr Sisowath Quay & St 148 ⓣ023 222275, ⓦbit.ly/hassakan; map p.64. Formerly *Café Metro*, this stylish a/c cocktail bar serves delicious food (green curry with chicken $7), plus small plates from $3 and creative cocktails – try the lychee martini $5.80. Daily 9.30am–1am.

Le Moon Amanjaya Pancam Hotel, 1 Street 154 ⓣ023 214747, ⓦbit.ly/lemoon; map p.64. A swanky rooftop bar with comfy sofas and enviable views of the river, Wat Ounalom and the glinting spires of the palace. The excellent cocktail list (from $5) is complemented by nibbles such as salmon blinis. Daily 5pm–1am.

AROUND THE NATIONAL MUSEUM AND ROYAL PALACE

Alley Cat Café 43 Street 19Z, off Street 19 ⓣ012 306845, ⓦalleycatcafe.biz; map p.64. This rocking restaurant-bar dishes up enormous breakfasts and Mexican dishes, with nightly specials including Tues and Sat ribs ($6 for a half-kilo). There's live music on Fri (7–10pm) and open-mic nights Sun (5–8pm). A great place to hang out for a few happy-hour beers. Tues–Sun 10am–10pm.

★**Bar Sito** 3 Street 240½ (opposite ARTillery Café) ⓣ077 252732, ⓦbit.ly/barsito; map p.64. A small,

1

seductive speakeasy located up an easy-to-miss alleyway just off Street 240 that serves amazing cocktails (try the lychee *caipiroska* $5) in low-lit a/c surroundings with connecting rooms via swinging bookcase doors. Food is available from the *Townhouse Supper Club* opposite. Tues–Sat 8pm–2am.

Blue Chilli 395 Street 178 ☎012 566353, ⓦbit.ly /bluechillibar; map p.64. Expect extravagant decor and handsome barmen at this all-welcoming gay bar near the National Museum. Artistic, and very funny, drag shows on Fri and Sat nights. Daily 5pm–2am.

Hops Brewery and Beer Garden 17 Street 228 ☎023 217039, ⓦbit.ly/hopsbrewery; map p.64. The city's first German-style "biergarten" with an on-site microbrewery, garden, art lounge and sports bar. Their Facebook page lists regular events such as barbecue nights. Daily 11am–midnight.

AROUND PSAR THMEI (CENTRAL MARKET) AND TOWARDS THE RIVERFRONT

11 Happy Backpackers 87–89 Street 136 ☎088 7777421, ⓦ11happybackpackers.com; map p.64. The rooftop bar and restaurant of this huge backpacker hostel is a fun place to start the evening. There's a pool table, comfy chairs and great city views. Happy hour 7–9pm. Daily noon–late.

Dusk Till Dawn Bar 46–48 Street 172 ☎017 839546, ⓦbit.ly/reggaebar; map p.64. Also known as the Reggae Bar, this upbeat, Kenyan-owned rooftop reggae bar doles out plenty of rum and cokes and fruit punches high above Street 51's throbbing nightclub district. Daily 4pm–4am.

AROUND WAT PHNOM

★**Elephant Bar** Raffles Hotel Le Royal, Street 92 ☎023 981888, ⓦraffles.com; map p.64. Splash out on a cocktail (there are over thirty gins to choose from) and soak up the 1930s elegance, with ambience and service to match, including live music from the resident pianist. Two-for-one happy hour 4–9pm. Daily noon–midnight.

SOUTH OF CENTRAL MARKET (PSAR THMEI) AND TOWARDS THE OLYMPIC STADIUM

Eclipse Sky Bar Phnom Penh Tower, Monivong Blvd ☎023 964171, ⓦbit.ly/skybarpp; map p.64. This upscale open-air rooftop bar isn't cheap but is easily the best place for sunset cocktails (from $5; 30 percent discount 5–7pm), live music and a dazzling 360-degree panorama of the city, river and distant hills. The D22 restaurant-bar below is also excellent. Daily 5pm–2am.

BOEUNG KENG KANG (BKK) AND AROUND INDEPENDENCE MONUMENT

Aussie XL 205A Street 51 (near Street 288) ☎023 301001, ⓦaussiexl.com; map p.64. Popular spot near

Street 278 whose cheap drinks and food (including home-made pies, burgers, spit-roasted pork and wood-fired pizza) attract a lively mix of backpackers, travellers and expats. Also shows Aussie sports matches. Daily 9am–10.30pm.

Score! 5 Street 282 ☎023 221357, ⓦscorekh.com; map p.64. Cavernous sports bar with a 5m x 5m screen, a handful of slate pool tables and loungers, plus sneaker-clad staff. Food includes stodgy favourites such as poutine, nachos, burgers and pies (around $5–7) and a mean weekend lunchtime roast. Sun–Thurs 8am–midnight, Fri & Sat 8am–2am.

Top Banana Bar 9E Street 278 ☎012 885572, ⓦtopbanana.biz; map p.64. The rooftop bar of this sociable backpacker hostel is a great place to meet travellers. Live music, beer pong, 4–8pm happy hour and dancing on the furniture until the early hours are standard behaviour. Act like a regular and order the house speciality cocktail, "wingman" (dark rum and lemonade), for $2.75. Daily 8am–3am.

TONLE BASSAC (AROUND STREET 308 AND BASSAC LANE)

Chez Flo 37 Street 308 ☎012 986270, ⓦbit.ly/chez flobar; map p.64. Friendly French owner Flo can usually be found behind the bar at this inviting spot. As well as a good selection of wines and cocktails, Flo also prepares home-made nibbles including delicious terrines, cold cuts and cheeses. Daily 11am–2pm, 5–11pm.

Hangar 44 Bassac Lane, off Street 308 ☎085 232137, ⓦbit.ly/hangar44; map p.64. One of several atmospheric bars in an alleyway off Street 308, this is one of the most eye-catching – both a bar and showroom for Moto Cambodge's motorbikes. Great cocktails, food from a "Bassac Lane nibbles menu" and regular rock bands. Daily 5pm–midnight.

Red Bar Cnr streets 29 & 308 ☎010 729655; map p.64. There's always a good atmosphere at this lively spot, with $1 draught beer, and $2.50 mixers during the 5–8pm happy hour. Daily 5pm–1am.

TOUL SLENG (S-21) AND TOUL TOM PONG (RUSSIAN MARKET)

Alchemy 36 Street 123, two blocks east of Russian Mkt ☎077 749686, ⓦbit.ly/alchemypp; map p.86. An industrial-design gastropub with courtyard garden, which offers inventive cocktails from $5 from the resident mixologists plus craft beers. Events include live music, DJ nights, quizzes and comedy. Daily 5pm–midnight, Fri & Sat 5pm–1am.

★**Long After Dark** 86 Street 450 ☎017 275824 ⓦbit .ly/longafterdark; map p.86. This retro-inspired drinking den plays great music and has a fantastic menu of cocktails, craft beers and over 55 whiskies. The delicious food includes toasties ($2.75), fish and chips ($6.75) and Sunday roasts. Daily noon–late.

Showbox 11 Street 330, near Tuol Sleng Genocide Museum ☎017 275824 ⓦbit.ly/showboxpp; map pp.56–57. Great bar in slowly developing Toul Sleng neighbourhood, 1km from the Russian Market, with live music, open-mic and comedy nights. Buy a beer before 6.30pm and enjoy a free beer over the following hour. Good-value food too; toasties and fried rice from $2.50, or get a sausage roll and pie fix from $5. Daily 11am–12pm.

NIGHTLIFE

Phnom Penh is a great little party town, with late-night bars and a smattering of clubs along the riverfront, while **Street 51** has a couple of haunts open till dawn. High-end options are springing up along Street 214, a few blocks back from the Royal Palace, and there are three clubs at the Nagaworld complex by Hun Sen Park. A sizeable chunk of Phnom Penh's nightlife is geared towards Khmer men, and revolves around girlie bars, karaoke, dance halls and local discos which play a deafening mix of Thai, Filipino and Western pop as well as traditional Khmer music and songs. Ask locals for the most popular spots of the moment; **nightclubs** usually don't get going until 10pm and beer girls (see box, p.47) are usually on hand to pour the drinks. Keep your wits about you and don't get too drunk or obnoxious. There can be a thuggish element in those places frequented by the rich, bored sons of the Cambodian nouveau riche; and while it's not something to be nervous about, if you step on their feet on the dancefloor or stare at their female companions you may have a real incident on your hands.

LIVE MUSIC AND NIGHTCLUBS
THE RIVERFRONT/WAT PHNOM AREA

★ **Doors Music + Tapas** Cnr streets 47 & 84 ☎023 986114, ⓦdoorspp.com; map pp.56–57. This awesome urban venue hosts a diverse variety of musical acts ranging from classical Spanish guitarists, opera singers and pianists to international DJs, salsa nights and local funk bands. Decor is distinctive, with the murals of street artist Sheryo adorning the walls. Drinks are brilliantly inventive and fried squid ($5) and home-made Spanish sausage ($9) are the tapas highlights.

Space Hair Salon & Bar Street 136 ☎089 963066, ⓦspacehairpp.com; map p.64. This innovative venue is a hair and beauty salon by day before transforming into a lively gay bar at night. Daily 9pm–late.

AROUND THE NATIONAL MUSEUM AND ROYAL PALACE

Nova Club Street 214 ☎097 7165000, ⓦbit.ly/nova clubpp; map p.64. You need to dress up to get into this swanky club, one of several on rapidly developing Street 214. Playing host to local and international DJs, its extensive cocktail menu will keep you busy at the bar. Daily 9pm–4am.

AROUND PSAR THMEI (CENTRAL MARKET) AND TOWARDS THE RIVERFRONT

Heart of Darkness 38 Street 51, ☎023 222415; map p.64. It's definitely over-rated, but this gothy club has been here for an age and is one of those places every visitor should visit once. Be warned, it can get almost unbearably loud inside. Daily 8pm–sunrise.

Pontoon Cnr streets 172 & 51 ☎0101 300400, ⓦpontoonclub.com.com; map p.64. Phnom Penh's largest club is a perennial favourite with the local and expat crowd; attractions include visiting DJs (Goldie once played here), a beautiful amber bar, an intriguing range of cocktails and some comfy couches to lose yourself in. They also host a popular drag show, *Shameless*, every Wed. Daily 10pm–sunrise.

BOEUNG KENG KANG (BKK) AND AROUND INDEPENDENCE MONUMENT

Club Love Street 278 ⓦbit.ly/clublovepp; map p.64. A late-night, handily air-conditioned club with guest DJs, special events and cheap drinks (happy hour 11pm–midnight) including free shots. Daily 11pm–4am.

ENTERTAINMENT AND ARTS

After being virtually obliterated by the Khmer Rouge, Cambodia's **artistic and cultural traditions** are gradually seeing a revival, thanks largely to the few performers and instructors who survived the regime. **Cinema** is taking off too; after the years of repression, 2010 saw the launch of the first annual **Cambodian International Film Festival** (ⓦcambodia-iff .com). **Galleries**, meanwhile, hosting changing exhibitions of art and sculpture, proliferate; check ⓦasialifemagazine .com, the *Phnom Penh Post* and Friday's *Cambodia Daily* for listings.

ARTS AND CULTURE

Cambodian Living Arts ☎017 998570, ⓔbookings @cambodianlivingarts.org ⓦcambodianlivingarts .org. The CLA aims to revive and encourage traditional cultural expression in communities across Cambodia by hosting living arts classes and supporting performing arts (classical and folk dance) productions. They perform traditional dance shows nightly at the National Museum $15 (7pm; Mon–Sat Oct–March).

Chaktomuk Theatre On the riverfront next to the

1

tourist office ☎023 725119, ⓦbit.ly/chaktomuk; map p.64. The theatre occasionally hosts Khmer plays and musical shows but performances are fairly infrequent – check the listings in the Friday edition of the *Cambodia Daily*.

Meta House 37 Sothearos Blvd, south of Sihanouk Blvd ☎023 224140, ⓦmeta-house.com. A centre for Cambodian contemporary art, the German Cambodian Cultural Centre offers free afternoon Cambodian documentary screenings (4pm) and more mainstream nightly films (7pm; $2), as well as live music, visual poetry and regular art exhibitions.

Kickboxing Reproduced on the bas-reliefs of Angkor Wat, the ancient tradition of kickboxing is now enjoying a revival. Bouts start with loud music and much posturing by the contestants – though watching the animated antics of the crowd, for whom betting on the outcome is the main attraction, can be as fascinating as the fights. Ask at your hotel or guesthouse for details of forthcoming bouts, which often take place at a TV studio a few kilometres out of town.

Sovanna Phum Cnr streets 99 & 484 ☎023 987564, ⓔsovannaarts@yahoo.com. Cultural shows at a performing arts society a little way out of town, with performances of classical and folk dance, and shadow puppetry at 7.30pm on Fri and Sat nights ($10).

CINEMA

The Flicks 1 39b Street 95, near Tuol Sleng Genocide Museum ⓦtheflicks.asia. This volunteer-staffed community movie house screens mainstream, arthouse and Cambodian films ($3.50/person) in intimate sofa-filled a/c rooms with food to order. Film schedules can be found online. There's a second cinema, Flicks 2, at 90 Street 136, inside *11 Happy Backpackers*.

Institut Français 218 Street 184 ☎023 213124, ⓦinstitutfrancais-cambodge.com. Regular screenings of French films, usually subtitled in English, shown during the week ($2).

The Empire 34 Street 130 ☎023 224140, ⓦthe -empire.org. Small, 22-seat, a/c movie theatre screening mostly mainstream films; *The Killing Fields* is screened every day and a new schedule is announced each Tuesday. An all-day pass costs $3.50 and there's a downstairs restaurant and bar.

GALLERIES

Lotus Pond Gallery Plantation Hotel, 28 Street 184 ☎023 215151, ⓦbit.ly/lotuspondgallery. It's worth wandering into the glorious courtyard of this boutique hotel to check out the latest exhibition around the lotus pond.

Java Café 56 Sihanouk Blvd ☎023 987420, ⓦjava cambodia.com; map p.64. Set in a colonial villa overlooking the Independence Monument, this is one of the city's first "culture cafés", mounting regular art exhibitions. Daily 7am–10pm.

Sa Sa Bassac 18 Sothearos Blvd ☎017 774864, ⓦsasabassac.com; map p.64. A gallery and resource centre with a reading room, this collaborative project curates and archives Cambodian contemporary visual culture. Tues–Sat 10am–6pm.

SHOPPING

Phnom Penh is the best place to shop in Cambodia, with **traditional markets** selling everything from traditional cotton *kramas* (Cambodian scarf) and beautiful silk *sampots* – the word for both the traditional Khmer skirt and a sufficient length of fabric to make one – which a **tailor** can then make up into garments of your own design, to myriad hand-crafted wooden, stone and silver trinkets. Contemporary wood carvings and marble statues make bulky souvenirs, but are so evocative of Cambodia that it's hard not to pick up one or two. You will also see hundreds of intricate (usually low-grade) silver pots in the shape of animals, which tuck more neatly into backpacks or suitcases. **Jewellery** is sold in abundance too, gold and silver, set with stones and gems in all imaginable designs and colours, and there are wonderful **antiques and curios**, both originals and replicas of old wooden pagoda statues and a huge assortment of decorative boxes and trunks. **Haggling** is an essential part of market shopping, with prices starting ludicrously high – check around a few stalls before buying, as they will often sell identical pieces.

MARKETS

Psar BKK South of Street 380; map pp.56–57. Very few visitors venture to this market, which is a shame as it's clean and authentic. The fresh food stalls are particularly appealing and many sellers at the market have been cooking the same dishes, such as *ban hoi* (rice noodle salad; $1.25), for years. Uniquely, Psar BKK also has a few stalls selling secondhand and vintage clothes and bags from across Asia. Daily 6.30am–5pm.

Psar Chas Cnr Street 13 & Ang Duong; map p.64.

Otherwise known as the Old Market, and located at the southern end of the French quarter, this is one of the city's more traditional markets. Although it's not the cleanest it's easy to get to and its fruit and vegetable stalls are particularly photogenic. Daily 7am–6pm.

Psar Kabkoh Street 9, south of Sihanouk Blvd; map p.64. A small market geared around fresh produce, with a number of good food vendors. Daily 6am–10pm.

Psar Kandal Street 13, near Wat Ounalom; map p.64. A genuine and easily accessible low-slung market close to

1

the riverfront, where you can browse the usual displays of clothing, jewellery, electronics, fruit, meat and vegetables and get a cheap meal at one of the noodle vendors. You can also get a scalp massage, hair wash and blow-dry for under $3 at one of the many hair salons inside. Daily 7am–6pm.

Psar Olympic Off Street 199 southwest of the Olympic Stadium; map pp.56–57. A top spot for fabrics, visited by people from all over the country who buy wholesale for resale, plus the usual clothes and bags stalls. Daily 8am–5pm.

Psar Orussey Street 182; map pp.56–57. Vendors from all over Cambodia, selling just about anything from dried fish to TVs to clothing, trade at this sprawling place over two floors. The stalls are crammed together and it can be confusing, but the merchandise is a good bit cheaper than elsewhere. The adjacent Street 166 is big on traditional Khmer and Chinese medicine shops where leaves, tree bark and various animal parts, usually boiled in water or soaked in wine, are sold as tonics. Daily 7am–5pm.

Psar Reatrey (Night Market) Along the riverfront between streets 106 & 108; map p.64. A night market that's popular mainly with tourists and local youngsters, selling clothes, mobile phones and a good range of souvenirs, art and curios. It's a good place to go native and enjoy a meal on the mats laid out by street hawkers at the western end as the sun goes down. Daily 5.30–11.30pm.

Psar Thmei (Central Market) See p.74.

Psar Toul Tom Poung (Russian Market) Cnr streets 163 & 444; map p.86. It gets its name because all its goods used to come from Russia, one of the few countries to provide aid to Cambodia during the Vietnamese occupation. The collapse of the USSR put paid to cheap imports but – ramshackle and tremendous – this market retains its reputation as *the* place to buy textiles, antiques and silver, not to mention motorbike parts. At the south end of the market you'll find stalls selling bootleg DVDs, fake designer bags, silver jewellery, Chinese-style furniture, photocopied books, handicrafts and piles of multicoloured silks; book sellers colonize the west, and the north is taken over with hardware stalls, a small food quarter and mechanics workshops. It is charming in its dilapidation, though a high fire risk with narrow exit routes – it's also meltingly hot. Daily 8am–5pm.

SHOPS AND MALLS

A growing number of classy boutiques sell clothes, jewellery and soft furnishings, particularly in BKK (see p.82) and swanky Street 240. Sihanouk Blvd, near Lucky Supermarket, has several designer stores, including Lacoste and a branch of the high-street store Mango.

BOOKSHOPS

Bohr's Books 3 Sothearos Blvd, near Wat Ounalom ☎ 012 929148, ⊛ bit.ly/bohrsbooks; map p.64. New and used titles, and a decent selection of Cambodian and Southeast Asia-related guides. Daily 8am–8pm.

D's Books 79 Street 240 ☎ 092 527028, ⊛ bit.ly/ds bookshop; map p.64. An excellent place to stock up on secondhand books (both fiction and non-fiction) in many languages. Daily 9am–9pm.

Monument Books 111 Norodom Blvd nr St 240 ☎ 023 223622, ⊛ monument-books.com; map p.64. Huge stock of English books, papers and magazines, with additional branches at the airport and Aeon Mall. Daily 8.30am–8.30pm.

BOUTIQUES

★**A.N.D. Boutique** 52 Street 240 ☎ 023 224713, ✉ artisandesigners@gmail.com; map p.64. Brilliant Fairtrade store selling cool, stylish tops, shorts and dresses, some from vintage and leftover fabrics, plus gorgeous bags, scarves and some jewellery. There's another store across the road and a third at 3 Street 178. Daily 8am–8pm.

Bliss 29 Street 240 ☎ 023 215754, ⊛ blisscambodia .com; map p.64. Well-known boutique specializing in stylish women's resort wear; the breezy lightweight cottons are perfect for the beach. It also sells scarves, purses, a kid's collection and homewares. Daily 9am–9pm (7pm Mon & Wed).

★**Trunkh** 180 Street 13 near National Museum ☎ 012 812476, ⊛ trunkh.com; map p.64. Cool new concept store selling loungewear, Khmer-influenced homewares, screen-printed tea towels, artwork and vintage-style signs. Tues–Sun 10am–7pm.

MALLS

Aeon Mall Sothearos Blvd ☎ 023 901091, ⊛ aeonmall phnompenh.com; map p.64. Phnom Penh's first mall is a slick affair with the usual mix of department stores, high-end stores, international labels such as Levi's and Mango, and air-conditioned cafés, plus cinema, bowling and a food court. Daily 9am–10pm.

Golden Sorya Shopping Centre Street 51 ☎ 070 888 079; map p.64. Aiming at the middle to lower end of the market, this low-rise mall sells clothes and electrical goods and has a couple of minimarts. Hours vary.

Sorya Center Point Street 63 ☎ 023 210018, ⊛ bit .ly/soryapp; map p.64. This eight-storey monolith, south of Central Market, feels more like a department store – you'll find fashion, branded make-up, sportswear, electrical equipment and a branch of Lucky Supermarket. There's also a food hall, cinema and roller rink. Daily 8am–9pm.

SOUVENIRS

"Art Street" Street 178; map p.64. Dozens of small warehouses selling an array of paintings and small sculptures created for the tourist market. Daily 8am–8pm.

SHOPPING WITH A CONSCIENCE

Numerous NGOs, other organizations and some private individuals have shops and outlets that directly help street children, women at risk and/or the disabled and other disadvantaged groups.

★**Daughters of Cambodia** 321 Sisowath Quay ☎089 910203, ⓦ daughtersofcambodia.org/visitor-center; map p.64. This little boutique, selling interesting jewellery, kids' clothes, gifts and accessories, is run by women who have been rescued from the sex trafficking industry, and profits go towards saving other victims. Lovely riverview café and nail salon on the first floor. Daily 9am–5.30pm.

Friends 'N Stuff 215 Street 13 ☎023 5552391, ⓦ friendsnstuff.org; map p.64. A branch of the *Friends* family (see p.78), the shop sells clothes, bags, jewellery and secondhand books, and has a nail salon. Can also be found at Stall 434 in the Russian Market and in Romdeng restaurant. Daily 11am–9pm.

Mekong Quilts 47–49 Street 240 ☎023 219607, ⓦ mekong-plus.com; map p.64. Brightly coloured quilts, cushions and throws in every pattern imaginable, plus bamboo accessories, scarves and purses made by impoverished women who receive the profits of their work. Mekong Plus, the NGO behind the outlet, provides scholarships and promotes health initiatives in remote villages in Cambodia and Vietnam. Daily 9am–7pm.

Peace Handicrafts 39C Street 155 ☎023 993331, ⓦ peacehandicraft.com; map p.86. Land-mine survivors and polio-disabled people produce carefully

crafted silk items for sale in their cooperative shop. Mon–Sat 8am–5pm.

Rajana Cnr streets 450 & 155 ☎023 993642, ⓦ rajanacrafts.org; map p.86. Sales of silk and bamboo crafts, scarves and bags from Khmer fabrics and jewellery from recycled bomb shells help to support the NGOs' Fairtrade training programmes. Mon–Sat 8am–5pm, Sun 10am–6pm.

Tabitha-Cambodia Cnr streets 51 & 360 ☎023 721038, ⓦ tabitha-cambodia.org; map pp.56–57. Non-profit NGO-run place selling silks made into garments and soft furnishings, cards, packed coffee and more. It operates by training disadvantaged women to sew; you can watch them at work outside and on the first floor. Daily 9am–8pm.

★**Watthan Artisans Cambodia (WAC)** Wat Than, 180 Norodom Blvd ☎023 216321 ⓦ wac.khmerproducts.com; map pp.56–57. A cooperative of disabled artisans, some as a result of land mines and polio, who produce a range of handicrafts on site: silk scarves, home furnishings, wood carvings and basketwork with sewing and woodwork. Also at the *White Mansion Hotel*, 26 Street 240; *Patio Hotel*, 134Z Street 51; and *River Home Hotel*, Street 258. Daily 8am–6pm.

Couleurs d'Asie 33 Street 240 ☎092 987572, ⓦ couleursdasie.net; map p.64. Lovely store selling carefully chosen home decoration, clothing and unusual gifts, with a sewing workshop for commissioned fabrics. Mon–Sat 8am–7pm, Sun 8am–5pm.

Estampe Vintage Store 197A Street 19 ☎012 826186, ⓦ bit.ly/estampevintage; map p.64. Fabulous vintage store selling original Cambodia and Southeast Asia maps, photographs and documents plus movie posters, trinkets and postcards. Mon–Fri 11am–7pm, Sat 9.30am–5.30pm.

Le Lezard Bleu 61 Street 240 ☎023 986978, ⓦ lelezardbleu.com; map p.64. A boutique gallery that focuses on contemporary art and design, including paintings and little brass Buddhas. Mon–Sat 8am–7pm, Sun 8am–5pm.

SUPERMARKETS

Bayon Supermarket 33–34 Street 114 ☎023 881266; map pp.56–57. A good selection of canned produce, cereals and other dry goods, as well as chilled items and cheese. Daily 8am–9pm.

Lucky Supermarket 160 Sihanouk Blvd ☎081 222028, ⓦ luckymarketgroup.com; map p.64. There's a vast choice of food items, from cheese to chorizo, at this popular chain store; there are several in the city but this one is the most central. Daily 8am–9.30pm.

Thai Huot 99–105 Monivong Blvd ☎023 724623, ⓦ thaihuot.com; map p.64. This large store on busy Monivong Blvd is one of the best for spices, and European products including cheese. There's a second store at 214 Street 63. Daily 7.30am–8.30pm

DIRECTORY

Dentists Roomchang Dental Hospital, 4 Street 184 (Mon–Sat 8am–5pm; ☎023 211338, emergency ☎011 811338, ⓦ roomchang.com) offers free consultations, is reasonably priced and has English-speaking staff. European Dental Clinic, 160A Norodom Blvd (Mon–Fri 8am–1pm &

2–7pm, Sat 8am–1pm, Sun emergency-only; ☎023 211363, ⓦ eurodentalcambodia.com), with English/French/Spanish/Khmer-speaking dentists.

Doctors For emergencies, travel-related illnesses, tests or vaccinations contact International SOS Clinic at 161 St 51

1

(Mon–Fri 8am–5.30pm, Sat 8am–noon ☎023 816911, ⓦbit.ly/sosclinic). Also, Tropical & Travellers' Medical Clinic, 88 Sreet 108 (Mon–Fri 9–11.30am, 2.30–5pm; Sat 9–11.30am, ☎023 306802, ⓦtravellers medicalclinic.com).

Embassies and consulates Australia, 16B National Assembly St (☎023 213470, ⓦcambodia.embassy.gov .au); Canada, 27–29 Street 75 (☎023 430813, ⓦbit.ly /canadapp; Laos, 15–17 Mao Tse Toung Blvd (☎023 997931); Thailand, 196 Norodom Blvd (☎023 726306, ⓦthaiembassy.org/phnompenh); UK, 27–29 Street 75 (☎023 427124, ⓦbit.ly/britishembassypp; US, 1 Street 96 (☎023 728000, ⓦkh.usembassy.gov) Vietnam, 436 Monivong Blvd (☎023 726274, ⓦvietnamem bassy-cambodia.org).

Emergencies Ambulance ☎119 (from an 023 phone) or ☎023 724891; fire ☎118 (from an 023 phone) or ☎023 723555; police ☎117 (from an 023 phone) or ☎023 366841; tourist police 023 942484; hotline to report child exploitation ☎012 311112, ⓦchildsafetourism.org – English is spoken on all these numbers.

Hospitals Calmette, north end of Monivong Blvd (☎023 426948, ⓦcalmette.gov.kh) or Royal Phnom Penh Hospital, 888 Russian Blvd (☎023 991000, ⓦroyalphnom penhhospital.comtal.com).

Internet With the wi-fi explosion, internet cafés are less common; you'll find a few places with computers along streets 172, 258 & 278; rates around $1/hr.

Money ATMs can be found everywhere, both at the airport and in town. ABA, ANZ and Canadia Bank all have branches along Sihanouk Blvd between Street 63 and the Olympic Stadium; at the time of writing, all charged a variable transaction fee for withdrawing cash. Exchange booths around town display their currency rates with some of the best to be had at Central Market. Western Union

(ⓦwesternunion.com) has branches all over town where you can exchange travellers' cheques, receive/make money transfers and get money on Visa and MasterCard (US$ only).

Opticians Several cluster along Sihanouk and Norodom Blvd with a handful near Lucky Supermarket, and in general offer a speedy, good service. Try Grand Optics, 337 Monivong Blvd (☎012 346748, ⓦgrand-optics.com), or EyeCare Optical, 166 Norodom Blvd (☎023 991148, ⓦeyecareoptic.biz); five other branches including Aeon Mall.

Pharmacies Trained English-speaking pharmacists are available at Pharmacie de la Gare, 124 Monivong Blvd (daily Mon–Sat 7am–7pm, Sun 7am–5pm ☎023 430205, ⓦpharmacie-delagare.com/en), which stocks a good selection of Western medicines. Alternatively, there are numerous branches of U-Care (Daily 8am–10pm ☎023 224199 ⓦu-carepharmacy.com) around town and Help+ Pharmacy at 322 Monivong Blvd is open 24 hours (☎023 210338, ⓦbit.ly/Pharmacy24).

Photography There are outlets all over town, with several of the better ones (where you'll find items such as digital memory cards) on Monivong Blvd, near Central Market.

Post The main post office is on Street 13, between streets 98 & 102 (Mon–Fri 7.30am–5pm, Sat 7am–noon). Cambodia Post doesn't have the best reputation; try TNT (☎023 430922, ⓦtnt.com) or DHL, 353 Street 110 (☎023 427726, ⓦdhl.com.kh).

Visas For visa extensions, it's easier to do it through a travel agent or your guesthouse, usually with no more than a $5 commission. The Department of Immigration (☎017 812763, ⓦimmigration.gov.kh) is out of town on Russian Blvd opposite the airport but is not worth the hassle or expense.

Around Phnom Penh

Just a short journey from Phnom Penh brings you to a landscape of rice paddies and sugar palms, scattered with small villages and isolated pagodas. The **Chroy Changvar peninsula**, the tip of land facing the city centre at the confluence of the Tonle Sap and Mekong rivers, is home to a collection of villages and feels very removed from the bustle of central Phnom Penh; its western side, facing the Royal Palace, is being transformed into a riverside park. The southernmost tip is now the property of the *Sokha Resort* group whose newest concrete monolith is rapidly growing. A short way further northeast, reached by a short ferry trip from Phnom Penh, lies **Koh Dach**, a lush green island in the Mekong, whose inhabitants weave silk and grow a wide variety of produce on the fertile alluvial soil.

A short moto ride southwest of the city, the "killing fields" and memorial at **Choeung Ek** make a logical, if macabre, progression from a visit to the Toul Sleng Genocide Museum. Also south of the city, off NR2, the compact Angkorian temple of **Tonle Bati** enjoys a riverside location, and is a good place for a picnic. Further south, there are spectacular views from the ancient hilltop temple of **Phnom Chisor**. Both sites could be

1

combined as a day-trip, along with **Phnom Tamau**, an excellent wildlife rescue centre run by the Wildlife Alliance.

Wat Champuh Ka'ek, east of town off NR1, has a remarkable collection of ten thousand Buddhas and can be tied in with a trip to **Kien Svay**, a popular riverside village about 15km from the city. **Phnom Brasat**, some 27km northwest of town off NR5, is home to a kitsch collection of pagodas, while further north rise the distinctive hills of the old capital **Oudong**, dotted with the stupas of various kings; nearby are the scant remains of **Lovek**, its predecessor as capital.

Chroy Changvar peninsula

At the confluence of the Tonle Sap and Mekong rivers, facing Phnom Penh city centre • Once across the Chroy Changvar Bridge, take the first right, which heads right around the headland (moto $2)

The 3km spit of land that makes up the **Chroy Changvar peninsula** was once a farming area – controversially, however, the Phnom Penh authorities cleared out the villagers from the western side and turned it into a riverside park, facing the promenade on the city side. Condominiums and other developments are also on the cards, amid talk of a "skyscraper city". For now, however, it remains a good spot to watch the sunset over the city, sipping a coconut at one of the refreshment stalls, and if you make your way northeast along the banks of the Mekong you'll pass through several friendly villages inhabited by the **Cham**, Cambodia's Muslim minority.

Koh Dach (Silk Island)

Some 6km from Phnom Penh • Ferries run regularly throughout the day, departing when full (moto and driver 1500 riel, foot passengers 1000 riel) from jetties signposted off NR6 across Chroy Changvar. Alternatively, guesthouses and travel companies organize group tours including by bike (from $10/person) and group and private cruises run from the tourist dock ($20/hr)

Set in the middle of the Mekong 6km from Phnom Penh is **Koh Dach.** Technically made up of two islands (one is tiny), and often referred to as the **Mekong Islands**, this is primarily an agricultural community – peanuts are an important cash crop. The 10km-long island is home to a number of stilt-house villages, and you'll see a good cross-section of rural life as you meander along its leafy tracks. The island is noted for its **weaving** of *sampots*, and in the dry season looms clack away beneath the houses, producing colourful reams of cotton and silk. As soon as you arrive you'll be invited into a home to watch the weavers in action, before being encouraged to browse and buy. As the river level falls after the rainy season, a wide sandy **beach** is exposed at the northern end of Koh Dach, where food stalls and picnic huts serve traditional dishes and tasty fried chicken.

Wat Champuh Ka'Ek

12km east of Phnom Penh, off NR1 • After the Monivong Bridge take the first right (Street 369) along the Bassac River – the pagoda is on the left after 7km (a moto/tuk-tuk should cost around $10/15 return)

The ten thousand Buddha statues at **Wat Champuh Ka'Ek**, fashioned in just about every possible shape, size and material, were donated by wealthy patrons, from whose gifts the pagoda derives its somewhat unsettling, conspicuous affluence. The monks here are much respected and well-connected – it's not unusual to find them performing elaborate ceremonies for well-heeled Cambodians and dignitaries, including the prime minister, who wish to gain merit in the next life or to receive blessings in this one.

The pagoda is entered through an avenue lined with devas (gods) on one side and asuras (demons) on the other, a favourite Cambodian theme; the Buddhas are arrayed in air-conditioned splendour in the modern-looking **hall** across the compound, ranged in floor-to-ceiling tiers and illustrating every one of the forty mudras along the way.

1

If the **vihara** is open, it's worth peeking inside to see the unusually decorated walls – by Cambodian standards these are stark, painted pale yellow and stencilled with golden Buddha images. The wat may have functioned as a prison during Khmer Rouge rule; a small white memorial stupa nearby, surrounded by a small lotus pond, contains skulls and bones found in the pagoda grounds.

Kien Svay (Koki Beach)

18km southeast of Phnom Penh, off NR1 • Follow NR1 for about 14km after the Monivong Bridge. The turning for the beach is on the left (Sokimex petrol station on the right), through an ornate portico that looks like a pagoda gateway with a sign for "Wat Kien Svay Tourism". Expect to pay around $10/15 for a return moto/tuk-tuk

Once optimistically hailed by some locals as "the new Kep" (see p.283), **KIEN SVAY** or **KOKI BEACH**, 18km southeast of Phnom Penh, is nothing like Kep, but it's a fun, local experience nonetheless. At weekends, it positively throngs with people venturing out from Phnom Penh to picnic at the rows of stilt-huts on the banks of the Mekong. Hawkers and food stalls sell all kinds of food, which you can eat while lazing around your hut (rented for $3–4) while small boats ply the river with fish and lobsters for sale, and will cook your chosen specimen for you on their on-board barbecues; a quick boat trip costs around $4.

The villages around Kien Svay are well known for their **weaving**, traditionally done by the women, though more men are joining in; silk and mixed-thread scarves and *kramas* are produced here for the markets in Phnom Penh.

Phnom Prasith

24km northwest of Phnom Penh • Take NR5 north for 11km to Prek Pneuv Market, then take a left onto an unsealed road and continue for 13km to the site (a moto should cost $15 return, tuk-tuk $22–25)

The complex of pagodas at **Phnom Prasith**, spread over a distance of about 5km, originally comprised just two hilltop sites (the "East Hill" and the "West Hill"), but now sprawls over several locations. The monks and nuns here hope to develop the site to Angkorian proportions and as the building of new sanctuaries is seen as gaining particular merit, it's not unusual for wealthy patrons to make sizeable financial contributions.

Wat Phnom Reap

The most popular of the sites is **Wat Phnom Reap or Prasat Vihear Sour**, reached through a Bayon-style gateway of enormous faces flanked by elephants. The track is lined with asuras and devas tugging on two nagas, there to protect the city's wealth in an impressive attempt at re-creating the southern gate of Angkor Thom in Siem Reap. Dominating the compound is the amazing carmine-red concrete reproduction of Angkor Wat, **Prasat Mahar Nokor Vitmean Sour**; it was completed in 1998, after just two years' work. A colonnaded gallery runs around the outside, sheltering elaborately decorated walls; apsaras nestle in niches, while bas-reliefs illustrate scenes from the life of Buddha and commemorate the construction of the temple by depicting the people who donated either money or labour. Next to it, the entrance to **Prasat Pik Vongkot Boreay Brom Mlop** is guarded by two imposing statues of Hanuman, each standing on one leg with sword raised.

East Hill Buddha

A few kilometres up the road beyond Wat Phnom Reap, on the first hill you come to, is the **East Hill Buddha**, a much-restored, 15m-long reclining Buddha carved out of the hillside. It's reputedly quite ancient and along with the overgrown Hindu temple (currently undergoing restoration) in the grounds below, may be the only surviving parts of the sixth- or seventh-century pre-Angkorian ruins known to have been here.

PREAH VESSANDAA

A popular theme at Cambodian pagodas is the tale of Preah Vessandaa – one of the previous **incarnations of the Buddha** – which is often told in tableaux, the figures usually life-sized and garishly coloured. According to the story, an old man, Chuchuk, was given a young woman, Amita, to be his wife in repayment of a debt. The couple were unable to have children, and Amita was snubbed by the other women. Knowing of King Vessandaa's generosity, Amita persuaded her husband to ask Vessandaa for two of his children. When depicted in temples, the story – usually told in a series of ten or so scenes – tells of Chuchuk's adventures on the way to the palace. One scene at Phnom Prasith shows Chuchuk dangling in a tree where he has been chased by the hunter Chetabut and his dogs; to escape, the old man lies that he is one of the king's messengers. As Chuchuk approaches the palace, the king's children run off, only to be discovered hiding under lily pads by the king, who grants them to the old man. After getting lost on his way home, Chuchuk ends up in the kingdom of the children's grandfather, who pays a ransom to buy them back. As told in Cambodia, the story ends when Chuchuk spends the money on a feast at which he gorges himself to death – a graphic injunction against the vice of gluttony.

Steep steps lead up to the summit (the road offers a gentler climb) and vihara, where a series of **tableaux** illustrate scenes from the story of **Preah Vessandaa** (see box above). The countryside views from the top are spectacular.

Kompong Luong

Heading north out of the capital, **NR5** follows the Tonle Sap River most of the way to Oudong, passing Cham villages and new mosques (most mosques having been destroyed – and Cham religious leaders murdered – by the Khmer Rouge). This area is important for the production of **prahok** (fermented fish paste), and in January and February the air is pungent with the odour of drying fish. Just beyond the new bridge at Prek K'dam, around 33km from Phnom Penh, is the village of **KOMPONG LUONG**. Once the royal port for Oudong, the village has for centuries been famous for its **silverwork**, and several generations of silversmiths, including an increasing number of women, still work together here to craft cups, bowls and all manner of small boxes in animal and fruit designs, shaping and decorating them by hand. Visitors are welcome to watch and buy; though there's not much difference in price from the markets of Phnom Penh.

Oudong and around

Oudong, 37km northwest of Phnom Penh, was the capital of Cambodia for 248 years, playing host to the crowning of several monarchs, including Norodom, great-great-grandfather of the current king. However, in 1866, King Norodom was persuaded by the French to relocate the capital from here to the more strategically positioned Phnom Penh; the court, totalling more than ten thousand people, moved en masse and Oudong was abandoned. The old wooden city has long since rotted away, but the **site**, with shrines and stupas scattered across two **hills**, remains important to pilgrims and has been designated a tourist spot The views from the top are quite spectacular. At the base, food stalls are in abundance as are the ubiquitous hammock-strung stilted huts beloved of the Cambodians who pile in here on weekends and national holidays.

Nearby **Lovek** was the capital of Cambodia during the reign of King Ang Chan in the sixteenth century, before being captured by the invading Thai. These days there's little to see other than two shrines, Wat Preah Kaew (Pagoda of the Emerald Buddha) and Wat Preah Ko (Pagoda of the Sacred Cow). However, the name of Lovek has been passed down through a well-known local legend (see box, p.98).

1

THE LEGEND OF LOVEK

When Lovek was the capital, it was said to house two statues of **Preah Ko** and **Preah Kaew** that contained sacred texts, written in gold, recording "all the knowledge and wisdom in the world". During one of the periodic conflicts between the Thai and Khmer, the Thai army was encamped outside Lovek, which it had repeatedly failed to capture, and was about to make its seasonal retreat in advance of the rains. The story goes that the Thai fired a cannon loaded with silver coins into the bamboo thickets that afforded the city some natural protection. During the rainy season, the Khmer gradually cleared the bamboo in their search for the coins, such that the Thai were easily able to capture the city in the following dry season. Removing the statues to Ayutthaya, the Thai were able to read the sacred texts and so became more knowledgeable than the Khmer. The legend has it that the statues are still hidden in Bangkok and that when they are returned to Cambodia the country will once again have ascendancy over Thailand.

Phnom Preah Reach Troap

While many visitors endure the steep slog up 509 steps to the new stupa atop this hill, there's a gentler ascent from Preah Atharas (see opposite), before descending the steeper staircase at the end. However, given that most tours still begin at the new stupa, the order below reflects that; simply reverse if starting at Preah Atharas

Visible from afar, the stupas on top of **Phnom Preah Reach Troap**, the larger of the two hills at Oudong, are something of a landmark. Approaching from NR5, you'll arrive at the foot of this hill – otherwise known as the Hill of Royal Fortune, as the royal treasure was hidden here during the war with the Thai in the sixteenth century. As you approach, before ascending the staircase, you'll pass a small structure on the left that contains human remains collected from a Khmer Rouge execution site nearby.

The new stupa

At the top of the staircase there's a gleaming marble terrace, behind which, and framed by the Buddhist and Cambodian flags, the spire of the modern grey, 42m-high **stupa** dominates the skyline. From here, the panoramic vistas across flooded rice fields, villages pricked by sugar palms and the Tonle Sap are stunning.

Built in 2002 to safeguard a sacred golden urn thought to contain the ashes of three small bones of the Buddha (which were originally interred in Phnom Penh), the stupa was broken into in 2013. Thieves stole the urn, along with other sacred relics, causing widespread outrage. The suspects were caught, and at the time of writing, remain in prison.

A short staircase leads up to the base of the stupa, adorned with nagas, elephants and lions, revealing memorable views of the western plains. Just to the northwest lies the sparkling, modern golden temple of the modern Vipassana Dhura Buddhist Centre complex (see opposite).

Damrei Sam Poan

South from the new stupa is a trio of funerary reliquaries. The oldest of these, **Damrei Sam Poan**, was built in 1623 by King Chey Cheta for the ashes of his uncle and predecessor, King Soriyopor, who founded Oudong. Surrounded by charmingly decayed elephant statues, this stupa is badly overgrown and the inner brick is starting to crumble. Until recently it had the tallest spire on the hill.

Tray Troeng

Beyond Damrei Sam Poan is the crumbling **Tray Troeng**, built in 1891 by King Norodom for the ashes of his father, King Ang Duong (though some think his ashes are in the Silver Pagoda in Phnom Penh). Some of the glazed ceramic flowers that once covered this distinctive stupa can still be seen, but since local children used to sell them to tourists when they "fell off", they've now been replaced with modern alternatives.

1

Chet Dey Mak Prohm

As you wander down the pathway to the southeast of Tray Troeng, you come across a fourth notable structure, known as **Chet Dey Mak Prohm**, easily recognizable by the four faces that cap its spire. The pale-yellow stupa contains the ashes of King Sisowath Monivong (r. 1927–41).

Preah Ko Keo and Preah Neak

Several of the older shrines southeast of Chet Dey Mak Prohm are worth seeking out. These include **Preah Ko**, featuring a particularly appealing statue of Nandin, the sacred mount of Shiva. Worshippers pour water over the bull's head, rendering the water holy, to then be taken home. Nearby, **Preah Neak** contains a Buddha seated on a coiled naga, its multiple heads curved over to afford him protection.

Preah Atharas

Just before you hit the hill's southeastern staircase, a huge temple comes into view. The once ruined columns and rotten roof beams of **Preah Atharas** (*atharas* being an ancient unit of measure equal to eighteen cubits) have been replaced and restoration work is ongoing. This pagoda was built by the Chinese in the thirteenth century to seal the cave – so legend has it – of a mythical sea monster, which had to be contained to stop the Chinese losing their dominance over the Khmer. The vihara was heavily damaged during fighting between Lon Nol and the Khmer Rouge and received further attacks from the Khmer Rouge post 1975. For many years only a shoulder and part of the right side of the 11m-high seated Buddha remained; it has now been resplendently restored.

Oudong's smaller hill

A separate stairway flanked by nagas leads up Oudong's **smaller hill**, 100m beyond the foot of the southeastern staircase of Phnom Preah Reach Troap. At the top is a small, damaged mosque, **Vihara Ta Sann**, built by the more open-minded King Ang Duong, and the ruins of a large reclining Buddha whose giant feet are all that can be seen rearing up from the pink bougainvillea. Just beyond is a stark, ageing stupa dating back to 1567 and built by King Bat Boromintho Reachea – but for whom, no one seems to know.

Vipassana Dhura Buddhist Centre

At the foot of Phnom Preah Reach Troap, the expansive **Vipassana Dhura Buddhist Centre** complex is worth a quick visit to marvel at its imposing jade Buddha and beautifully painted walls. Another vast reclining Buddha can be seen in the smaller shrine southeast of the complex, and in the centre of the large basin to the north stands a golden statue of **Preah Neang Kong Hing**, goddess of the Earth who draws water from the end of her long plaited hair. The small pavilion next to the temple once housed the glass-encased remains of an orange-robed mummified monk, the most venerable Sam Bunthoem, who was shot in Wat Langka in 2003 by assailants angry at his encouragement of monks to vote in the National Assembly elections. At the time of writing, his cremation and the building of a memorial stupa are scheduled for 2017.

ARRIVAL AND DEPARTURE **OUDONG**

By bus Oudong, 37km from Phnom Penh, can be reached by taking the Kompong Chhnang bus on NR5; tell the driver and he'll let you off by the orange archway. From there, take one of the waiting motos for the final 3km ($1–2).

By tuk-tuk For around $30, you can take in several rural villages en route to Oudong; for a few dollars more you could combine Oudong with Phnom Prasith.

By bicycle You can cycle to Oudong with Grasshopper Adventures (see p.77).

By organized tour Several companies (see p.77) offer organized and tailor-made tours around Phnom Penh. Alternatively, you can do a day-trip by boat (☎017 915 812, ⓦkanika-boat.com)

1

Choeung Ek

12km southwest of Phnom Penh • Daily 7am–5.30pm • $6 incl. audio guide • ☎ 023 211753 • Approx $10–15 return by moto/tuk-tuk • Also visited on excursions run by guesthouses and agents; you could even cycle if you're prepared to brave the traffic (and dust). To drive here, find Monireth Blvd, southwest of Central Market, and follow it south, forking left at the large petrol station after the Acleda and ANZ banks, from where it's about 5km to Choeung Ek

Just 12km from Phnom Penh is the notorious site of **Choeung Ek**, where prisoners from Toul Sleng/S-21 were brought for execution. As portrayed so graphically in the 1984 film *The Killing Fields*, certain sites around the country (this is the best known) became places of **mass murder**, where the Khmer Rouge disposed of its enemies: men, women and children – even babies – who had allegedly betrayed the state. Early on, the victims were shot; later, to save on valuable bullets, they were bludgeoned or stabbed to death, and babies killed by being savagely thrown against trees, as loud music blared in the background. As fuel became scarce, victims were dragged out of the city and killed en route, their bodies dumped in the rice paddies closer to town.

It's hard to believe, amid the peaceful fields and pleasant countryside, that the **Choeung Ek Memorial** contains the remains of 8985 bodies exhumed here in 1980, when 86 of the burial pits were excavated. Anecdotal estimates suggest that more than 17,000 people may have been slaughtered here, and a further 43 mass graves under the lake at the site remain untouched; there are no plans for these to be investigated since as yet there is nowhere sufficient to house the remains to Buddhist standards. Inside the memorial – a gleaming glass-fronted stupa – skulls and bones are piled on shelves, seventeen tiers high, arranged by age and gender, with victims' tattered clothes below.

An excellent **audio guide** leads you circuitously around the site, stopping at various key points and finishing up at the memorial stupa. It includes harrowing commentary from victims, including an unforgettable one from a former Khmer Rouge guard. Make sure to wander around the eerily beautiful lake.

Before you leave, drop into the museum, where you can cool off in the air-conditioned "theatre" by watching a dated but informative short video. A raw and emotional declaration close by states, "We are absolutely determined no [sic] to let this genocidal regime to reoccur in Kampuchea."

Tonle Bati

35km south of Phnom Penh, off NR2 • Daily • Picnic hut rental $2/day • Book a tour with any number of operators or you can do the return journey by moto ($15) and tuk-tuk ($20–25)

Peaceful **Tonle Bati** is set on the banks of the Bati River in a well-tended grove of coconut and mango trees, where you can swim, fish and picnic as well as seeing the two small but appealing **temples**. You will be met by young girls selling flowers who are likely to follow you around until you leave, even if you're adamant about not buying.

Some 300m northwest of the temples are dozens of **picnic huts** built on stilts over the river, rentable by the day. The owners provide floor mats and cushions, plus a tray of drinks and snacks, and even inflated inner tubes for swimming. Alternatively, head to Seametrey Leisure Centre across the lake where there's a pool, restaurant and picnic huts, with profits going to the Children's Village it sits in.

Ta Prohm

The first temple you come to on entering the site is the larger of the two, **Ta Prohm**. Constructed in the early thirteenth century by Jayavarman VII – creator of the magnificent Angkor Thom – on the site of a sixth-century shrine, it's dedicated to the Hindu god Shiva (though Jayavarman eventually adopted Theravada Buddhism). The main entrance is from the east along a short laterite causeway, edged by flowers and shrubs. Piled up to the side at the entrance are broken chunks of masonry, some elaborately carved with scenes from the Churning of the Ocean of Milk (see p.168) or the *Ramayana* (see box, p.63). It's not uncommon for women and children to request donations as you walk around the site.

The sanctuaries

At the centre of the inner enclosure are the temple's five **sanctuaries**, its antechambers built in a cruciform shape, with shrines to the cardinal directions. Above the entrance, a carved stone image of a reclining Buddha has been colourfully coated in paint. The **main sanctuary**, of sandstone, contains an upright Buddha image, while the antechambers house damaged stone linga. Another image of Buddha, over the north arm of the cruciform, has been superimposed with a carving of a six-armed Vishnu, a change probably made when the Angkorian kingdom reverted to Hinduism after the death of Jayavarman VII.

Well-preserved **carvings** decorate the outside of the sanctuary and several tell unusual tales. High up on the northeast corner is a scene of two women and a kneeling man: one woman carries a basket on her head, containing the afterbirth from her recent confinement; the midwife, shown standing, was not given sufficient respect during the birth and has condemned the new mother to carry the basket for the rest of her life; her husband is shown begging for forgiveness. The corresponding spot on the northwest corner shows a king sitting next to his wife, who is said to have been unfaithful; below she is put to death by being trampled by a horse.

The north gopura

The north gopura once contained a statue of **Preah Noreay**, a Hindu deity who is said to bestow fertility upon childless women. Although the statue is still undergoing restoration (the feet which remain are believed to belong to another statue), women continue to arrive here to seek his help.

Yeay Peau

Some 100m north of Ta Prohm in the grounds of the modern Wat Tonle Bati, lies the single, sandstone, twelfth-century, Bayon-style temple of **Yeay Peau**. Wat Tonle Bati was badly damaged by the Khmer Rouge and some pieces of gnarled metal behind the main Buddha are all that is left of the original headless statue. Beside the Buddha is a statue of Peau, while outside in the courtyard are five large seated Buddhas, each with their hands in a different mudra.

LEGENDS OF YEAY PEAU

Various legends surround the **Yeay Peau temple**. One tells how King Preah Ket Mealea fell in love with a young girl named Peau, who gave birth to his son, whom she named Prohm. The king returned to his court but left behind a ring and sacred dagger so that in years to come, Prohm would be able to prove his regal descent. Prohm duly went to his father's court and stayed many years, presumably forgetting his mother, for when he finally returned home he fell in love with her, refusing to believe her when she said he was her son. To resolve the matter, it was agreed that Peau and Prohm would each build a temple; if he finished first she would marry him, and if she finished first, he would acknowledge her as his mother. The contest took place at night with the women helping Peau and the men assisting Prohm. In the middle of the night, the women raised a lighted candle into the sky. The men, thinking this was the morning star, settled down to sleep in the belief that they could not be beaten, leaving the women to carry on working and complete their temple first. (This rivalry between women and men is a common theme in Cambodian pagodas, cropping up many times in different guises.)

1

Phnom Chisor

65km south of Phnom Penh, off NR2 • Daily 7am–6pm • Foreigners $2 (pay at the summit) • A return moto costs around $30. The site is best visited as part of an excursion together with Tonle Bati

Originally known as Suryadri ("Sun Mountain"), **Phnom Chisor** was built early in the eleventh century by Suryavarman I and was once a site of some significance, housing one of four sacred linga installed by the king in temples at the boundaries of his kingdom. The views are quite astounding too. A hot and tiring flight of 412 steps ascends the hill from the south, but there is an alternative, easier stairway on the other side. Either way, there are refreshment-sellers at the top and bottom and, at weekends, midway as well. There's a modern pagoda at the summit and a burgeoning number of sanctuaries scattered about.

The **villages** east of Phnom Chisor weave very fine traditional *hol*, a patterned silk **sampot** traditionally worn during ceremonies. It's worth buying a piece if you can, although this isn't easy as most is produced to order. UNESCO is helping the weavers here relearn the use of natural dyes, a skill that was lost during the Pol Pot years.

Prasat Boran

At the far, northern, end of the hill, the ancient atmospheric temple of **Prasat Boran** (also known as Phnom Chisor temple) still retains some well-preserved carved sandstone lintels and, with several inner sanctuaries, it's wonderful for exploring. The temple was built opening to the east, from which side you get a stunning view across the plains and paddies to Angkor Borei. From the eastern doorway, the old entrance road leads straight to the foot of the hill and still retains its two gatehouses. In the entrance, two stone **basins** are filled with water, which is ladled out for blessings using a couple of large seashells. Some say the basins used to fill naturally – presumably from a spring – but after a US bomb came through the roof of the central sanctuary in 1973 (thankfully, it didn't explode) this stopped; it was rebuilt but part of the roof remains covered with corrugated iron. The very fine internal doors to the central sanctuary are decorated with images of Shiva standing on the back of a pig – although no one knows why.

Prasat Preah Ko Preah Kaew

One of the more interesting pagodas at Phnom Chisor, **Prasat Preah Ko Preah Kaew** (turn right at the top of the staircase when you reach the summit) contains images of the cow and small boy from which it gets its name. According to one legend, a pregnant woman climbed a mango tree to eat some fruit, despite being warned not to, and fell; the shock induced labour, and from her womb emerged a baby boy and a cow.

Phnom Tamao Wildlife Rescue Centre (PTWRC)

50km south of Phnom Penh, off NR2 • Daily 8.30am–4.30pm • Foreigners $5, car 2000 riel, motorbike 1000riel • ☎ 095 970175, ⓦ wildlifealliance.org/wildlife-phnom-tamao • If arriving with your own transport, look out for the signposts and archway 10km beyond Tonle Bati, from where it's a further 5km up the side road to the zoo entrance. You can also visit on a guided tour. The centre's own are pricey but highly rated with animal-feeding and access to non-public enclosures such as the rehabilitation area and tigers' den ($150/ person; profits to the project). Betelnut Tours (ⓦ betelnuttours.com) depart from *Lazy Gecko Guesthouse* ($40/person) while Free the Bears (ⓦ freethebears.org.au) operate a Bear Keeper for the Day programme (price on request)

Operated by the respected Wildlife Alliance, the **Phnom Tamau Wildlife Rescue Centre** is set in an area of regenerating scrub forest between Tonle Bati and Phnom Chisor. Most animals here were rescued from desperate situations: some as they were taken out of the country to satisfy demand for exotic foods and medicine in China and Thailand, others from markets where they were kept in tiny cages as pets or destined for restaurant tables. A team of dedicated keepers work here, and the centre is gaining a reputation for the successful rehabilitation and release of many

VIETNAM BORDER CROSSINGS

The most common crossing between Phnom Penh and Vietnam is **Bavet–Moc Bai**, while **K'am Samnar–Chau Doc** is also used. At the time of writing, several European nationalities can enter Vietnam visa-free for 15 days, but there's no return within 30 days of departure and you cannot extend a visa once you are there. Alternatively, you can apply for a visa from the embassy in your home country or in Phnom Penh. If you're heading to Kep or Kampot and then on to Vietnam, use the **Prek Chak–Hat Tien** crossing east of Kep (see p.284). Always check relevant embassy websites for updates on visa requirements.

BAVET–MOC BAI

For direct services between Phnom Penh and Ho Chi Minh City ($10–12), and vice versa, you no longer have to change buses at the border crossing (daily 7am–8pm); the bus operator will handle immigration, customs forms etc (Giant Ibis is among the recommended companies), although as with all crossings into Vietnam you will need to get your visa beforehand in Phnom Penh unless you're exempt (see above). If you're going it alone and haven't booked through-transport to HCMC, jump on a bus to Bavet and once you've crossed the border, take a motorbike taxi or minibus the 10km from Moc Bai to Go Dau, where you can get direct onward transport to HCMC – from the border, the journey should take less than 2hr. If you're coming into Cambodia from Moi Bac, you can take a shared taxi or minibus from Bavet to Phnom Penh ($5–7) or a private ride for $50. If you get stuck, you could stay in one of Bavet's many casinos but avoid if you can.

K'AM SAMNAR–CHAU DOC

Many people heading for Chau Doc in Vietnam go on organized trips from Phnom Penh (around $10–12) in which case your guide will arrange any transfers at the border. You will need to organize your visa in advance (unless the 15-day visa exemption applies/suits, see above), or ask your guesthouse/travel agent to. If you're going about it independently, it's possible to take an express boat ($25–35) from Phnom Penh to Chau Doc direct (see p.76). From the central market at Chau Doc, you can hop aboard a minibus bound for HCMC ($4). Note that e-visas are not valid for entry here; a standard 30-day tourist visa, extendable once, costs $30.

animals. The centre relies on private donations and sponsorship, so your entrance fee is going to a good cause.

One of the star attractions are the **tigers**, which by day prowl around a purpose-built deluxe enclosure; at night they are secured indoors and protected by armed keepers – poachers are still a cause for concern and a dead tiger can net thousands of dollars. Other highlights include **Malayan sun bears**, **black bears** and **elephants**, and there are other indigenous species – pileated gibbons, Siamese crocodiles, macaques, pangolins and various wild cats and fairly tame cranes, among others.

Battambang and the northwest

FLOATING VILLAGE LIFE, TONLE SAP LAKE

2

Battambang and the northwest

Strike north from Phnom Penh along NR5, west of the Tonle Sap, and you'll be following the route along which the Khmer Rouge retreated from Phnom Penh in 1979, ahead of the liberating Vietnamese forces. This is also the route that the invading Thai armies used in the opposite direction, as they repeatedly headed south to sack and pillage. Much of the northwest still shows clear Thai influence – not surprising, given that the area has been under Thai control for much of its modern history, and was only finally returned to Cambodia in 1946. These days the road is a busy corridor linking the capital to the Thai border and a trade route along which rice is transported from the sparsely populated but fertile plains to the more populous south.

The first two towns of any size along NR5 out of Phnom Penh are Kompong Chhnang and Pursat. A busy river fishing port, **Kompong Chhnang** takes its name from the terracotta pots (*chhnang*) that are produced throughout the district, while the major cottage industry in workaday **Pursat** is marble carving. Both towns are interesting mainly for the chance to visit the remarkable **floating villages** on the Tonle Sap lake.

North of Pursat is laidback **Battambang**, Cambodia's second-largest city, with a lazy riverside ambience and some of the country's finest colonial architecture. The surrounding province once had more temples than Siem Reap, although none was on the scale of Angkor Wat and most have long since disappeared. The few that remain are worth a visit, however, especially the hilltop site of **Wat Banan**, while the nearby mountain and temple complex of **Phnom Sampeu** offers a fascinating, if chilling, reminder of the atrocities of the Khmer Rouge. North of here the crossroads town of **Sisophon (Banteay Meanchey)** is the jumping-off point for visits to the massive, jungle-smothered Angkorian temple of **Banteay Chhmar**.

Kompong Chhnang and around

The old colonial town of **KOMPONG CHHNANG**, 83km north of Phnom Penh on NR5, is a quiet place to stop over for a day. As its name – meaning "Pottery Port" – suggests, the area is a major centre for the production of traditional terracotta pots (*chhnang*), which are despatched countrywide via ox cart (a slow but smooth method of transport which reduces the risk of damage to the fragile cargo). Several **pottery-making villages** can be visited nearby.

Kompong Chhnang dates back to colonial times, and has a rather more solid and permanent air than many of Cambodia's other provincial capitals. NR5 runs right through the centre, forming a wide boulevard bounded at one end by the imposing **Independence Monument** (looking rather like a big red cake stand) and the more

BAMBOO RAILWAY

Highlights

❶ **Floating villages** Boat between the houses of the remarkable Tonle Sap floating villages near Pursat and Kompong Chhnang. See p.109 & p.112

❷ **Battambang** Cambodia's laidback second city, with the country's finest colonial architecture, a lazy riverside setting and a burgeoning Western bar and restaurant scene. **See p.113**

❸ **Bamboo railway** Take a ride aboard one of Asia's quirkiest railways, with improvised "trains" running along a short section of track just outside Battambang. **See p.115**

❹ **Phnom Sampeu** Sprawling hilltop temple complex, once used as a Khmer Rouge prison, dotted with colourful shrines and vast caves. See p.122

❺ **Wat Banan** Engaging little ancient hilltop pagoda, with five crumbling towers – like a pocket-sized Angkor Wat. **See p.123**

❻ **Ang Trapeang Thmor** Wonderful wetlands, home to the elegant, endangered Sarus crane. See p.127

❼ **Banteay Chhmar** The most remote and least visited of Cambodia's great ancient temple complexes, with fabulously carved ruins half enveloped in jungle. **See p.128**

HIGHLIGHTS ARE MARKED ON THE MAP ON P.108

BATTAMBANG AND THE NORTHWEST

HIGHLIGHTS

1. Floating villages
2. Battambang
3. Bamboo railway
4. Phnom Sampeu
5. Wat Banan
6. Ang Trapeang Thmor
7. Banteay Chhmar

0 ___ 20
kilometres

THAILAND

OTDAR MEANCHEY

Banteay Chhmar ⑦

Banteay Tuop

Samroang

Aranyaprathet

Poipet

5

56

56

68

Ang Trapeang Thmor

⑥

BANTEAY MEANCHEY

Sisophon (Banteay Meanchey)

6

Ang Trapeang Thmor Crane Sanctuary

Phnom Srok

Choob

Kralanh

68

Ream Chea

SIEM REAP

5

59

Disused

Sangker

Wat Ek Phnom

Puork

6

Kbal Spean
Banteay Srei

Angkor Thom

Phum Pradak

Phnom Kulen

Psar Pruhm

PAILIN
Pailin

Kampong Poy

Phnom Sampeu

④ ② Battambang ③

Prek Toal Biosphere Reserve

Phnom Krom

Siem Reap

Angkor Wat

Beng Mealea

Prasat Yeah Ten

57

Sneng

⑤ Wat Banan

5

Bamboo Railway

Sangker

63

Chong Khneas

Wat Bakong

Roluos

Dam Dek

57

BATTAMBANG

Battambang Boats

Kompong Phluk

6

Kouk Thlok Kraom

Moung Ruessei

Tonle Sap

Phnom Penh Boats

Kompong Khleang

Moung Ruessei

5

Reang Tit

KOMPONG THOM

Phnom Krapang

Tomb of Khleang Muong

Chong Kos

①

PURSAT

Pursat

Kompong Luong

Phoum Kandal

Phnom Sam Koh

Stung Pursat

Ou Dah

Kravanh

55

5

52

Tonle Sap

Phnom Knang Trapeang

CARDAMOM MOUNTAINS

Phnom Aural

Ondoung Rossey

Kompong Chhnang

Hat Lek

Cham Yeam
Koh Kong

48

PEAM KRASAOP WILDLIFE SANCTUARY

5

KOMPONG CHHNANG

KOH KONG

48

Chi Phat

BOTUM SAKOR NATIONAL PARK

48

Andoung Tuek

Disused

Lovek

Oudong

Kompong Luong

Oudong

Prek Kdam

5

KIRIROM NATIONAL PARK

Kirirom

46

Chambok

Kompong Speu

KOMPONG SPEU

4

42

Phnom Prasith

PHNOM PENH

THE ETHNIC VIETNAMESE

The first Vietnamese settlers in Cambodia were **rice farmers**, many of whose ancestors migrated across disputed borders as long ago as the late seventeenth century; over generations they moved north along the Mekong and today mostly farm in the southeast provinces. The educated, predominantly Christian Vietnamese population of Phnom Penh has its origins in the **civil servants** brought over during Vietnamese rule and the French protectorate. Indeed, records of the time suggest that Phnom Penh was more Vietnamese than Khmer. These days, the majority of Cambodia's commercial fishing is accounted for by impoverished ethnic Vietnamese **fishing families**; predominantly Buddhist, they live in floating villages on the Tonle Sap and Mekong rivers, moving around with the annual inundation. Government estimates put the number of ethnic Vietnamese living in Cambodia at around 100,000, but given the difficulty of monitoring the large number that live in floating villages, the true figure is thought to be much higher.

Historically, Cambodians have long entertained feelings of hostility towards the Vietnamese, who are all too often referred to using the derogatory Khmer term, **Yuan**. The roots of this resentment go back to the Vietnamese annexation of the Mekong Delta in the seventeenth century. Tensions were exacerbated during the brief period of Vietnamese rule over the whole country, during which time they tried to impose their language, names and mores on the Khmer. The situation was aggravated during the French protectorate, when Vietnamese clerks were installed in Cambodia's administration, and not helped when the French redrew the Cambodia–Vietnam border in favour of the Vietnamese after World War II.

You're unlikely to witness any overt racism today, despite the recent surge in anti-Vietnamese feeling stirred up by Sam Rainsy's Cambodian National Rescue Party, which accuses the Vietnamese of taking Cambodian jobs and lands. Even so, it's as well to note that no Cambodian would be seen dead in the pointed hats worn by Vietnamese rice farmers, and that the country's current leader, Hun Sen, is often accused by his opponents of being a "Vietnamese puppet".

modest **Vietnamese Friendship Monument** (resembling an overambitious bird table) at the other. Southeast of here stretches the sedate old **French quarter**, with rambling villas set amid spacious walled gardens, some of them still retaining old colonial touches – even the large Kompong Chhnang Prison, bang in the middle of the district, has a rustic air.

The opposite side of town, northwest from the centre and past the bustling **Psar Leu market** en route to the fishing port and Tonle Sap lake, is contrastingly lively and ramshackle. The 1.5km-long road to the lake is actually built on a causeway across the water, and although modern buildings block most views of the lake you can still see a few stilted houses with water lapping around their bases. At the end of the road the waterfront offers fine views over the lake to the pair of floating villages offshore, while the hectic **fishing harbour** is a photogenic chaos of boats, fishermen and hawkers.

The floating villages

On the Tonle Sap lake, 2km from Kompong Chhnang • Small rowing boats for exploring the floating villages can be rented from the waterfront (around $8–10/hr)

The **floating villages** on the Tonle Sap lake make for a rewarding half-day excursion from Kompong Chhnang. The town is the principal fishing port for Phnom Penh, and throughout the year supplies of fresh fish are packed with ice and loaded daily onto a fleet of trucks to drip their way towards the city. The fishing families, primarily ethnic Vietnamese, live on the lake on **Phoum Kandal**, almost within touching distance of the shore, and **Chong Kos**, further out over the waters to the northwest – both far less touristy than the floating villages around the north end of the lake near Siem Reap (see p.158). Locals offer village tours in tiny wooden boats, rowed standing up – quoted prices can be on the high side, but, with a little persistence, can usually be bargained down.

KOMPONG CHHNANG

ACCOMMODATION
Chantea Borint Hotel ... 1
Sovann Phum Hotel ... 2

EATING
Soksan Restaurant ... 1
Sovann Phum Restaurant ... 2

The villages themselves are a fascinating sight, with each house floating upon its own miniature pontoon fashioned out of lashed-together bamboo trunks and other wooden flotsam. Dwellings are arranged around a neat grid of miniature "streets" busy with small fishing vessels, rowing boats and other craft, while tiny children paddle themselves, seated in large cooking pots, between the buildings. Some of the houses are little better than floating sheds; others are surprisingly luxurious, with comfortably furnished interiors complete with TVs and generators, their roofs sprouting satellite dishes and their pontoons festooned in miniature gardens of potted plants.

Phnom Santuk

3km west of the centre • Moto $5 return

Phnom Santuk is a mound of huge boulders in the grounds of the wat of the same name; climb to the top for views over rice paddies dotted with sugar-palm trees and the Tonle Sap. It's worth hiring a moto for the trip as they can weave their way across the rice paddies to the pot-making villages afterwards – a route you'd never find on your own.

Ondoung Rossey

7km northwest of Kompong Chhang • Moto $8 return; follow the Battambang road about 5km north from Kompong Chhnang and look for a small sign for the village on the left

The best-known of the pottery villages surrounding Kompong Chhnang is **ONDOUNG ROSSEY**, where locals work at preparing clay and spinning potting wheels in the shade of their houses (a small **Cambodian Crafts Federation** shop here sells a range of pottery). Almost every house in the village is involved in the pottery business – smaller pieces are made on a wheel spun by foot; larger items are hammered into shape with a large wooden spatula. Most are unglazed and unpainted, although some are embellished with simple etchings or appliqué designs. Items might include simple plates indented with dimples (used to bake tiny coconut cakes over charcoal fires) through to more elaborate elephant-shaped money boxes – which you'd have to break open to get at your savings.

ARRIVAL AND DEPARTURE

KOMPONG CHHNANG

Plentiful **buses** and **shared taxis** shuttle between Kompong Chhnang and Phnom Penh, with slightly less frequent services in the other direction to Pursat and Battambang (and beyond). The proposed Phnom Penh–Poipet **railway** (see p.23) is also likely to stop here, when complete.

By bus Buses drop off and pick up passengers either at the transport stop close to the Vietnamese Friendship Monument in the centre (where you'll also find a couple of makeshift stalls selling bus tickets, including one for Phnom Penh Sorya buses) or along NR5 nearby. Leaving Kompong Chhnang, you may be able to flag down a passing bus on the main road, although it's very hit-and-miss.

Destinations Battambang (15 daily; 4hr); Phnom Penh (20 daily; 2hr 30min); Pursat (15 daily; 2hr).
By shared taxi Shared taxis to/from Phnom Penh use the transport stop. Taxis to/from Battambang use the stop on the road just north of Psar Leu (although it's worth checking at the transport stop as well).

GETTING AROUND

Central Kompong Chhnang is easily walkable, although you might want to catch a **moto** or **tuk-tuk** if heading down to the lake ($1–2 one-way). **Bikes** ($2/day) can be rented from the *Chantea Borint Hotel*.

INFORMATION

Money ATMs at the Canadia and Acleda banks accept foreign Visa and MasterCards.

Shop There's a well-stocked minimart at the Tela petrol station.

ACCOMMODATION

Chantea Borint Hotel Near the Independence Monument 012 762988. Easily the most characterful place to stay in town, with a range of neat tiled rooms and bungalows (with hot water for an extra $2, or hot water and a/c for $7) set in a lovely courtyard garden on a leafy backstreet. There's also a small restaurant,

although it's open for breakfast only. $\overline{\$8}$
Sovann Phum Hotel NR5, 200m south of the Independence Monument 026 989333, sovannphumhotel.com. This bright modern hotel is Kompong Chnnang's most upmarket option, with smart a/c rooms and the town's best restaurant (see below). $\overline{\$16}$

EATING

Soksan Restaurant Next to the transport stop. Friendly little place (with English menu) serving tasty Khmer dishes (around $3), but no Western food bar a humble omelette or two. Daily 7am–8pm.
Sovann Phum Restaurant Sovann Phum Hotel, NR5, 200m south of the Independence Monument

026 989333. Proud home to the largest – or at least the heaviest – menu in Cambodia, featuring a range of Khmer/Chinese-style dishes, with a dash of Thai. Prices are slightly above average (mains $4–5), although quality's good and portions are big. Daily 7am–9pm.

Pursat and around

Named after a tree that used to grow along its riverbanks, the sleepy provincial capital of **PURSAT** is pretty much the quintessence of humdrum. Within Cambodia, it's famous mainly for being the nation's main **marble carving** centre, using stone quarried from the rocky outcrops of the nearby Cardamom Mountains and carved in workshops around the town and the surrounding countryside.

For visitors, the main reason to come is to explore the floating village of **Kompong Luong**, a fascinating settlement of wooden rafted houses arranged around a grid of watery "streets" amid the tranquil waters of the Tonle Sap. The town also provides a possible starting point for expeditions into the rewarding, but little explored, northern **Cardamom Mountains** (although the mountains are more easily accessed from Koh Ker on the southern coast – see p.270 for details). The town itself is laid out for a couple of kilometres along NR5 and bisected by the **Stung Pursat**, which flows northeast into the Tonle Sap. Most of the town's modest cluster of hotels and restaurants are close to the bridge over the river, on (or just off) the main road.

2

THE LEGEND OF KHLEANG MUONG

Located in the village of **Banteay Chei**, a few kilometres west of Pursat off NR5, the small, well-tended tomb of **Khleang Muong** is an attraction for locals. The story goes that in 1605, the Khmer were losing the war against the Thais, when Khleang Muong ordered his soldiers to dig a pit and to cast their weapons into it; he then committed suicide by throwing himself into the pit. Seven days later the Khmer army defeated the Thais with help from the ghosts of Khleang Muong and his army of soldiers. The victory is marked by an offering ceremony here in April or May each year, at the start of the planting season and just before the rains. The pavilion at the tomb contains a life-size bronze statue of Khleang Muong, now a national hero, and a matching one of his wife, who, according to legend, also killed herself. The site is easily reached by moto from Pursat, but it's probably only worth a visit if you're at a completely loose end.

Koh Sampovmeas

500m north of the market

The main attraction in town (for what it's worth) is the faintly surreal **Koh Sampovmeas** island, in the middle of the Stung Pursat. Once an unspoilt sandbank, the island has now been encased in painted concrete walls, giving it the appearance of an enormous ship, with small shrines at prow and stern and the space between neatly paved and lawned. Come dusk, it's usually busy with games of football, shuttlecock and impromptu aerobics classes, with lines of Pursat housewives dancing energetically to the stridently amplified strains of the Cheeky Girls, or similar.

Kompong Luong floating village

35–40km east of Pursat • Motorized boat trips around the village cost $10/hr • Head east along NR5 for 30km, then turn north at Krakor to the Tonle Sap; it costs around $12 return from Pursat by moto, $15–20 by tuk-tuk

KOMPONG LUONG is the closest of the Tonle Sap's **floating villages** to Pursat, though its precise distance from town varies, depending upon whether it's wet or dry season. Populated by a mixed community of Cham and Vietnamese families, the surprisingly large village (actually more of a floating town) is similar in design to those at Kompong Chhnang (see p.109), with buildings bobbing upon wooden pontoons and an extensive range of amenities including its own police station, temple and Catholic church.

The northern Cardamom Mountains

Pursat serves as a possible starting point for tours into the **northern Cardamom Mountains** – you can also explore the southern part of the range (see p.270) – but you'll have to arrange trips in advance through a tour operator in Phnom Penh (see p.21). Still mostly inaccessible and unexplored, the Cardamom range is an area of outstanding natural beauty, its primary jungle rich in flora and fauna. A biodiversity study in 2000 established the presence of nearly four hundred different species of animal, including tigers, Asian elephants, gaur and a population of critically endangered Siamese crocodiles, previously considered extinct in the wild.

The road from Pursat up into the mountains climbs steeply through the forest, crossing tiny gorges and streams. **Ou Dah**, 56km from Pursat, is an attractive spot with rapids and a small waterfall in the jungle-clad hills. Alternatively, at **Chrok La Eing**, 73km southeast of Pursat, there's a cascade and river for a swim. Bear in mind that there's also a high risk of malaria in the mountains, so take precautions against mosquito bites.

ARRIVAL AND INFORMATION   PURSAT

By bus Buses stop on the NR5 west of the main bridge, at (or opposite) their respective offices.

Destinations Battambang (15 daily; 2hr); Kompong Chhnang (15 daily; 2hr); Phnom Penh (15 daily; 4hr 30min).

By shared taxi or minibus These usually arrive at/depart from the transport stop, about 1km west of the bridge on NR5. If possible, ask to be dropped by the main bridge (*spean thmor*), from where it's a just a couple of hundred metres to the hotels and guesthouse.

Money The ATMs at the Canadia and Acleda banks, next to one another on the main road, accept foreign Visa and MasterCards.

ACCOMMODATION

KM Hotel West bank of the river, 300m north of the bridge ☎052 952168, ⓦkmhotel.com.kh. Pursat's newest and smartest option, in a peaceful riverside setting with spacious, attractively furnished and well-equipped a/c rooms plus a passable in-house restaurant, big pool and small spa. BB $22

Phnom Pech Hotel West bank of the river, 200m north of the bridge ☎052 951515. Well-run hotel offering a mix of slightly dated but comfortable fan and a/c rooms (plus hot water in fan rooms for an extra $2). Fan $7; a/c $14

Pursat Century Hotel Main road ☎015 350278, ⓔpursatcenturyhotel@gmail.com. Solid mid-range option, offering spacious tiled rooms (either in the old wing, or in the smart new wing for an extra $5) with hot water and a foyer stuffed with chintzy wooden furniture and assorted pots, plus restaurant. Fan $8; a/c $15

EATING

Lam Siveng Restaurant Main road ☎012 826948. Pretty little restaurant full of wooden furniture and cabinets packed with marble carvings. There's an English menu and a good range of mostly Chinese food (mains around $2–3), plus a few Khmer and Vietnamese options. One of the few places in town where you can get a passable coffee (hot or iced). Daily 8am–9pm.

Tepmachha (aka The Magic Fish) Restaurant West bank of the river, 750m north of the market ☎012 921144. Friendly little place in an attractive setting right over the river, with simple Khmer and Chinese dishes (plus English menu) for $2.50–4. Daily 9am–9pm.

Battambang

Cambodia's second-largest city, laidback **BATTAMBANG** seems to have the best of various worlds: big enough to have all the energy and bustle you'd expect of a city of around 200,000 people, but still small enough to feel like a proper slice of Cambodia, and lacking both the hyperactive traffic and crowds of Phnom Penh and the tourist hordes and wall-to-wall touts of Siem Reap. Headline attractions may be slightly lacking, but there's still plenty to fill a few days in and around town, plus an increasingly large selection of restaurants and bars fuelled by the growing number of expats who now call the city home.

The main draw in Battambang (the last syllable is usually pronounced *bong* rather than *bang*) is the city's time-warped collection of **colonial architecture**, with some interesting day-trips around town – including fun countryside rides on the quirky **bamboo railway**.

Brief history

The history of Battambang, which was founded in the eleventh century, is quite separate from the rest of Cambodia – for much of its existence the town fell under **Thai** rather than Khmer jurisdiction. In 1795, a Cambodian named **Baen** became lord governor of **Battambang province** (which at the time incorporated territory as far away as Siem Reap), paying tribute to the king in Bangkok, which effectively moved Battambang from Cambodian to Thai rule. Throughout the **nineteenth century** the province, although nominally under Thai jurisdiction, was largely left to its own affairs under a succession of all-powerful governors from the Baen family – a self-sufficient fiefdom, isolated from both Thailand and Cambodia.

The province was returned to Cambodia in 1907, at which time Battambang town was little more than a collection of wooden houses on stilts. The French moved in, modernizing the town and constructing the colonial shophouses you see today – modern Battambang still has a decidedly Francophone flavour both architecturally and culturally, with a considerable number of Gallic expats calling the town home. Battambang fared relatively well during the **Khmer Rouge** years, although Khmer

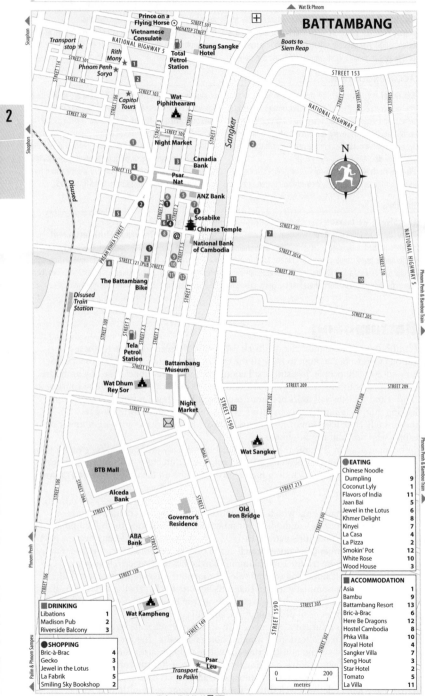

BATTAMBANG

Wat Ek Phnom

Prince on a Flying Horse
Vietnamese Consulate
MOHATEP STREET
STREET 501
Transport stop ★
NATIONAL HIGHWAY 5
STREET 101
Rith Mony ★
Phnom Penh Sorya ★
STREET 103
Total Petrol Station
Stung Sangke Hotel
Boats to Siem Reap
STREET 153
STREET 601
STREET 604
STREET 60h
Capitol Tours ★
STREET 106
STREET 109
STREET 103
Wat Piphitheam
STREET 2
NATIONAL HIGHWAY 5
STREET 3
STREET 109
STREET 2
Night Market
Canadia Bank
STREET 1
Disused
STREET 115
Psar Nat
ANZ Bank
Sosabike
Chinese Temple
National Bank of Cambodia
STREET 201
STREET 201A
STREET 203
STREET 205
PREAH VIHEA STREET
STREET 121 (PUB STREET)
The Battambang Bike
STREET 1
Disused Train Station
STREET 100
STREET 3
STREET 1.5
STREET 2
STREET 125
Tela Petrol Station
Battambang Museum
STREET 127
Wat Dhum Rey Sor
Night Market
STREET 159D
STREET 209
STREET 209
STREET 202
STREET 208
STREET 1
Wat Sangker
BTB Mall
Alceda Bank
ROAD 1A
STREET 213
STREET 300
STREET 106
STREET 104A
STREET 135
Governor's Residence
Old Iron Bridge
ABA Bank
STREET 3
STREET 1
STREET 139
STREET 305
STREET 159D
STREET 102
Wat Kampheng
STREET 149
Psar Leu
Transport to Pailin

Sangker
Siophon
Siophon
Disused
Phnom Penh
Pailin & Phnom Sampeu
Phnom Penh & Bamboo Train
Phnom Penh & Bamboo Train
Phnom Penh & Bamboo Train

N

2

Wat Banan, Wat Ko (5km) & 13

0   200
metres

Rouge forces launched repeated attacks throughout the province after they were driven west to Pailin and in 1994 even briefly captured Battambang itself. Ferocious battles occurred around Wat Banan and Phnom Sampeu until the amnesty of 1996.

Psar Nat and around

Marking the centre of town is the **Psar Nat** market building, a huge, rather mildewed orange pile dating from the 1930s, with functional modernist lines and, at either end, a pair of white clock towers, none of whose various faces ever seem to be telling the right time.

The shophouses

The streets immediately south of the Psar Nat market are where you'll find most of Battambang's old **shophouses** – perhaps the finest pocket of colonial-era architecture in the country, despite the damage wreaked by modern additions, rebuildings and renovations. Most buildings follow the traditional Asian shophouse plan, with an open-fronted shop downstairs and living quarters above – the ground-floor shop is typically set back under a wide colonnaded walkway created by the overhanging upper storey, typically embellished with elaborate wrought-iron balconies. The best-preserved shophouses are along the photogenic and increasingly gentrified **Street 2.5**, many of whose old buildings have now been restored and converted into touristy bars, restaurants, shops and so on. Those along **Street 1.5** are looking rather run-down, while many of the facades along **streets 1, 2 and 3** have been buried beneath big plastic signs and other gimcrack modern additions. Ongoing attempts to have the city listed as a UNESCO World Heritage Site may lead to major restorations being carried out over the next few years, including the removal of all commercial hoardings.

The railway station

A short detour off Street 3 brings you to Battambang's neat little 1920s **railway station**, complete with original ticket counters. The building has been cleaned up and is now in

THE BAMBOO RAILWAY

Following the destruction of Cambodia's railways during the Khmer Rouge era, enterprising locals in Battambang made good the deficiency with the ingenious **bamboo railway** (*norry*), which runs along a stretch of disused track just outside town. Originally used to transport people, livestock and goods, it's now mainly tourists who ride the rails. A couple of dozen "trains" run up and down the line, each just a couple of metres long, consisting of a simple four-wheeled metal undercarriage with a detachable wooden platform placed on top. Trains were formerly propelled using long poles in the manner of an Oxbridge punt but are now powered by small motorbike or tractor engines, reaching speeds of around 40km/hr. If two trains meet en route, the one with the fewest passengers cedes right of way and is dismantled on the spot (the work of less than a minute) and cleared from the line, allowing the other to pass.

The planned resumption of regular train services along the line (see p.23) has thrown the **future** of the bamboo railway into doubt. Locals are currently suggesting that it will cease running in 2017, although similar predictions have been doing the rounds for years and it's possible that the bamboo railway will continue to run at least a little longer.

PRACTICALITIES

The start of the line is about 7km from Battambang ($4 return by moto, $5 by tuk-tuk). The line itself runs for some 6km, with a fare of $5 per person (or $10 to hire an entire "train" irrespective of how many people are on it, although drivers may try for more). Trips up and down the line last around 30min, with trains departing as soon as sufficient passengers have climbed on board. You'll be set down for a quick walk around the village at the far end of the track, where numerous handicrafts stalls and persistent hawkers await your dollars.

reasonably good shape – which is more than can be said for the trio of overgrown platforms and the weed-choked tracks behind.

The riverfront

Battambang's sweeping **riverfront** with its wide grassy banks and paved walkway is a great place for a stroll. Originally the Sangker River was just 5m wide here, but when the Dambang River south of town was dammed, the Sangker gradually widened, and is now at least 30m wide (depending on water levels). In the late afternoon fruit-shake and food stalls set up near the post office while the park across the nearby bridge turns into a vast outdoor gym as the health-conscious housewives of Battambang come to exercise after work in the shadow of the eye-catching **Wat Sangker**, instantly recognizable thanks to its modern Bayon-style gateway, topped with four enormous faces.

Chinese temple

Street 1, one block south of Psar Nat

Easily missed during a walk along the riverfront is the sixteenth- or seventeenth-century **Chinese temple**, a diminutive one-storey structure (restored in 1921) wedged in tightly between the surrounding shops. The temple's dark-red doors and heavily ridged roof tiles edged with ceremonial dragons look quite incongruous amid the area's colonial architecture. Inside the temple, the rather ferocious-looking god, Kwan Tai, is worshipped at a small altar; despite his looks he's revered for his loyalty and integrity.

A few doors south of the Chinese temple, look out for the florid mansion housing the **National Bank of Cambodia** – one of Battambang's finest colonial buildings.

Battambang Museum

Street 1 • Mon–Fri 8–11am & 2–5pm • $1; no photography

The modest **Battambang Museum** comprises a gloomy hall full of statues and carvings dating from the seventh to the twentieth centuries – many are of considerable interest, despite the drab setting and lack of information. Exhibits include fine Buddhas along with various gods, nagas, yaksha (demons), lions, lingas and a number of intricate lintels, many of them featuring Indra riding his three-headed elephant Airavata, a common motif in Khmer art. Look out too for the thirteenth-century statue of a bodhisattva "tattooed" with a thousand Buddhas, and a well-worn depiction of Yama on a buffalo.

Wat Dhum Rey Sor

Street 3, behind Battambang Museum

One of the two oldest temples in Battambang, **Wat Dhum Rey Sor** has been restored several times since its construction in 1848. Its name means "Pagoda of the White Elephant" after the pairs of white elephant statues flanking the eastern and western

---

DAMBANG KROGNUING

While you're in Battambang you may see two distinctive **statues** relating to a bizarre legend surrounding the town's name, which literally translates as "lost stick". According to the tale, a man named **Dambang Krognuing** turned black after eating rice stirred with a black stick; he then deposed the king and assumed the throne. The erstwhile king's son subsequently defeated Dambang Krognuing with the aid of a magical flying horse, despite a vain attempt by the interloper to hurl his black stick at the prince's steed. A massive statue of Dambang Krognuing decorates the traffic circle on the way out of town towards the airport, while a statue of the prince on his flying horse sits at the north end of Street 3.

entrances to the vihara. The base of the vihara is decorated with a series of colourfully painted, low-relief carvings depicting scenes from the *Ramayana* – look out for Hanuman riding a steam engine on the east wall.

Wat Piphithearam

Street 3, one block north of Psar Nat market

Another ancient temple, the venerable **Wat Piphithearam** is best approached from the south, where the gates are guarded by two *yeaks* (giants). The temple's monks claim that these used to sport threatening expressions, though now they wear a benign look – a strange example of the Khmer belief in metamorphosis. Many of the monks speak English and will give you a tour of the vihara (in exchange for letting them practise their language skills), which features some elaborate modern murals illustrating the life of Buddha.

Governor's Residence

Street 1, around 1km south of the centre • No entrance to the building, but visitors are free to wander around the grounds

South of the centre, the flamboyant **Governor's Residence** adds a decidedly Gallic flourish to this part of town, with a grand entrance flanked by a pair of lions and two canons dated 1789. The pale-orange building itself could easily pass for a miniature château somewhere on the Loire, complete with blue-grey shuttered windows, elaborate floral stucco decoration and a big red tiled roof – only the carved elephant heads on either side of the portico spoil the otherwise perfect illusion of provincial France.

ARRIVAL AND INFORMATION   **BATTAMBANG**

The proposed Phnom Penh–Poipet **railway** (see p.23) will eventually run through Battambang, connecting directly to the capital in one direction and the Thai border and Bangkok in the other.

By bus Buses are operated by several companies including Phnom Penh Sorya, Capitol and Rith Mony. All have offices in town (clustered together north of the centre), although it's easiest to book tickets through your hotel or guesthouse. Arriving in Battambang, buses now terminate at the new bus station around 3km west of town, from where it's a $2 ride by tuk-tuk to the centre. Leaving Battambang, bus companies normally send a minibus around to pick up passengers from their hotels and take them out to the bus station.

Destinations Bangkok (3 daily; 9hr); Kampot (1 daily; 10hr); Kompong Chhnang (15 daily; 4hr); Pailin (2 daily; 2hr); Phnom Penh (15 daily; 6hr 30min); Poipet (4 daily; 3hr); Pursat (15 daily; 2hr); Siem Reap (8 daily; 4hr); Sihanoukville (1 daily; 11hr).

By minibus Private minibuses (operated by Mekong Express, Golden Bayon and others) are most easily booked through your hotel.

Destinations Bangkok (1 daily; 8hr); Kompong Chhnang (10 daily; 3hr 30min); Pailin (6 daily; 1hr 30min); Phnom Penh (10 daily; 6hr); Poipet (6 daily; 2hr 30min); Pursat (10 daily; 2hr); Siem Reap (6 daily; 3hr 30min); Sisophon (6 daily; 2hr).

By shared taxi Shared taxis arrive at/depart from the transport stop in the north of town, although some may drop you off at a hotel of your choice or at Psar Nat in the centre; transport from Pailin arrives at Psar Leu, 1km southwest of town.

By boat Battambang is connected to Siem Reap by a daily thirty-seater boat (departs 7.30am; 6hr in the wet season, up to 8hr or more during the dry; $25), a rewarding trip down the Sangker River and across the Tonle Sap. It is, of course, a lot quicker and cheaper to reach Siem Reap by bus, but the journey by water is far more memorable, although not particularly comfortable – take food, plenty of water and (ideally) a cushion. Boats arrive and depart from the pier on the east bank of the river just north of Spean Thmei, about 1km north of the centre, assuming water levels are high enough; at other times of the year you may have to take a minibus for part of the journey.

GETTING AROUND

By moto and tuk-tuk There are plenty of motos and tuk-tuks touting for custom. Short hops around town cost $1–2.

By bike and motorbike Bikes are available for hire at numerous places including Soksabike, The Battambang Bike and some guesthouses for around $1–2/day for a gearless "city bike" or $5–6/day for a mountain bike. Motorbikes are harder to come by – try the *Asia Hotel, Hostel Cambodia* or the Gecko shop, all of which have a few scooters for $7/day.

2

TOURS AND ACTIVITIES

Boats The Gecko shop runs river cruises on the Sangker river ($8 per person in a group of 1–2 people, $6 per person in a group of 3 or more).

Circus An offshoot of Siem Reap's Phare (see p.155), the Phare Ponleu Selpak circus (w phareps.org) puts on shows around four times a week at 7pm at its big top on NR5 towards Sisophon. Adults $14, children under 12 $7.

Cookery classes Several restaurants around town run

cooking classes (usually lasting around 3hr, with classes both morning and afternoon) including *Coconut Lyly*, the adjacent *Nary Kitchen* (☎ 012 763950, w narykitchen.com), and *Smokin' Pot*. Classes at all these places cost $10.

Kayaking Green Orange Kayak (☎ 017 736166, w fedacambodia.org) organize half-day kayaking trips ($12 plus $5 for a local guide) along the Sangker River between Battambang and Ksach Poy village.

ACCOMMODATION

Asia Hotel North of the market ☎ 053 953523, w asiahotelbattambang.com. Spotless modern hotel offering a wide variety of shiny, spotless and very comfortably furnished rooms at ultra-competitive prices, although the very cheapest lack windows and come with cold water only. A/c available for an extra $5. **$6**

Bambu East of the river ☎ 053 953900, w bambuhotel.com. This neat boutique resort is the swankiest option in town, with pretty little two-storey garden villas in pseudo-Khmer village style set behind a medium-sized pool. The cool and spacious tiled rooms come with mod cons including iPod dock, rain shower and minibar, and there's also a good in-house restaurant. Rates include breakfast. **$90**

★**Battambang Resort** Wat Ko Village, 5km south of the centre ☎ 012 510100, w battambangresort.com. Idyllic resort a short drive south of the city, with spacious rooms set among gorgeous gardens dotted with coconut palms and mango trees. Facilities include a big pool and an attractive pavilion-style restaurant, and there's a good range of tours on offer – or just lounge on a hammock or cruise the lake on a pedalo. **$60**

★**Bric-à-Brac** 2 St ☎ 077 531562, w bric-a-brac.asia. In a lovingly renovated old shophouse bang in the centre of town, this personable little boutique guesthouse offers a loving homage to the spirit of old Asia – like being dropped suddenly between the pages of a Somerset

Maugham novel. The three individually designed rooms are filled with an entertaining medley of vintage furnishings and curios, while cleverly distressed finishes make the whole place look like a rather upmarket opium den. Quality breakfasts, a free happy-hour drink, use of a nearby pool and Battambang's most comfortable beds round things out. BB **$125**

Here Be Dragons East of the river ☎ 089 264895, w herebedragonsbattambang.com. Inexpensive waterfront accommodation in a mix of bright and colourful fan rooms and comfortable dorms – choose between the six-bed dorm with fan ($3 per person) or the eight-bed dorm with a/c ($5). The lively programme of events includes yoga sessions, movie screenings, cocktail and BBQ nights, plus a popular quiz every Wed evening. **$10**

Hostel Cambodia Preah Vihea St ☎ 017 728038. Acceptable if uninspiring budget lodgings in a selection of functional but comfortable dorms (six-bed $4 per person; 14-bed $3.25), all with a/c and hot water, plus individual lockers and bed-sockets.

Phka Villa East of the river ☎ 053 953255, w phkavilla.com. Attractive little hotel with bijou bungalows arranged around pleasant gardens and a good-sized pool. The ten rooms are on the small side but nicely furnished in vaguely colonial style with four-poster beds, well-appointed bathrooms and little verandas for idle lounging. Rates include breakfast. **$55**

BIKING IN BATTAMBANG

Bike tours are a popular way to explore the countryside around Battambang, with several operators in town now offering tours.

The Battambang Bike 2.5 St ☎ 095 578878, w battambangbike.com. Half- and full-day countryside tours and trip to Phnom Sampeu and visits to a bat cave at Phnom Sampeu ($18/38). They also run an enjoyable half-day city tour combining cycling, walking and a boat trip, plus countryside and Wat Banam tours by jeep.

Butterfly Tour 309 St ☎ 089 290045, w butterflytours.asia. Further half- and full-day bike ($17/38) tours taking you to a range of rural settings

including paddy fields, villages and temples, plus half-day trips to Ek Phnom, sunset tuk-tuk trips to Phnom Sampeu and walking tours of Battambang city. Their office is some way out south of the centre so easiest to book by phone or email.

Soksabike 1.5 St ☎ 012 542019, w soksabike.com. Battambang's oldest and best bike-tour operator runs enjoyable half- and full-day bike tours ($27/50) through the Battambang countryside, with the chance to meet local families and visit cottage industries.

Royal Hotel 100m west of Psar Nat ☎053 952522, ⓦroyalhotelbattambang.com. Long-running travellers' favourite, set around an airy atrium and with accommodation ranging from small fan rooms with cold water to spacious a/c rooms with hot. It's not quite as smart as other places in the same price range, although the central location and helpful staff more than compensate, and it's a good place to sort out trips, tours and onward transport. Fan $8; a/c $13

Sangker Villa East of the river ☎097 7640017, ⓦsangkervilla.com. Homely, French-owned boutique bolthole in a pretty little villa at the end of a peaceful cul-de-sac. Accommodation is in eight neat little white rooms with a/c and cable TV, and there's also a pocket-sized saltwater pool in the neat little garden at the back.BB $45

Seng Hout 50m north of Psar Nat ☎053 952900, ⓦsenghouthotel.com. Comfortable and very competitively priced mid-range hotel in a pair of buildings just north of the market. Choose between comfortable rooms in the older building (where's you'll also find the hotel's pool and gym) and slightly smarter but more sterile rooms (some windowless) in the new wing (same price) to the south. A/c costs an extra $5. $10

Star Hotel Just north of the centre ☎053 953522, ⓦstarhotelbattambang.com. Similar to the nearby *Asia*, with a wide range of rooms of various shapes, sizes and prices, all comfortably furnished with big carved beds, desk, TV and fridge. A/c available for an extra $5. $10

Tomato West of Psar Nat ☎095 647766. The cheapest option in town is in an attractive shophouse-style building with a pretty ground-floor terrace shaded by enormous potted plants, and with a second building over the road. The rooms are not much more than spartan boxes but reasonably clean and quiet – and given the price you really can't complain. There's also a basic but very cheap dorm ($2 per person). $3

La Villa East of the river ☎053 730151, ⓦlavilla -battambang.com. Appealing seven-room boutique hotel in a renovated 1930s merchant's house, brimming with time-warped colonial character and a decidedly formal (verging on crusty) old-school Gallic atmosphere. Rooms are beautiful little period pieces (somewhat lacking in furniture) and there's a good restaurant in the former orangery serving quality French and Khmer food, plus a nice little bar and small pool in the attractive garden. Advance booking recommended. $75

EATING

Battambang is famed for its abundant **natural produce**, including its sweet green-skinned pomelos and oranges – have a look around Psar Nat to see what's fresh. There are also inexpensive **food stalls** around Psar Nat, while in late afternoons a busy **night market** sets up on the street south of Wat Piphithearam. More stalls set up at about 4pm on the riverfront near the post office.

Chinese Noodle Dumpling (Lan Chov Khorko Miteanh) Street 2 ☎ 092 589639. A local institution and a popular breakfast stop, serving up great noodles and the best dumplings (steamed or fried) in town at giveaway prices. Mains $2. Daily 9am–9pm.

Coconut Lyly Street 111 ☎016 399339, ⓦcoconutlyly .com. Short selection of Khmer mains ($4–4.50) of the sort you'd find on pretty much every other menu in the country, but beautifully cooked and the amok is superb. They also run cooking classes (see p.118). Daily 9am–10pm.

Flavors of India Street 121 ☎053 731553. Spacious restaurant serving up a decent selection of veg and non-veg North Indian standards (mains $3.50–7) including tandoori specialities and a reasonable vegetarian selection. Daily 10am–11pm.

★Jaan Bai Street 2, junction with Street 1.5 ☎097 398 7815. Battambang's most innovative restaurant (the menu supervised by Australian Thai-food guru David Thompson) serves top-notch Khmer, Thai and Vietnamese dishes in tapas-size portions (small plates $3–5, large plates $5–7) using seasonal organic produce. Try the signature slow-cooked beef rib with *prik nam pla* ($12), braised for six hours in coconut water. Daily 11am–9pm (last orders).

Jewel in the Lotus Street 2.5 ☎092 2600158. Charge your chakras at this attractive modern café offering a short selection of snacks and light meals ($4–7). These are served alongside a weird and wonderful beverage selection including hibiscus and mulberry leaf teas and coconut-flower cider vinegar smoothies; you can also concoct your own smoothie from such exotic ingredients as bee pollen, organic hemp, raw honey, spirulina and Ceylon cinnamon. Daily 8am–5pm.

Khmer Delight One block south of Psar Nat, between Street 2 & Street 2.5 ☎053 953195. One of the nicest-looking restaurants in town, with lots of cane furniture and romantic lighting after dark. Features all the usual Khmer dishes, some Indian and Asian classics and Western standards such as spag bol and fish and chips – a mite expensive (most mains around $5–6) but good quality and served in big portions. Daily 9.30am–10pm.

Kinyei Street 1.5 ☎069 734745. Tiny café on a quiet backstreet corner serving some of the best coffee in town, plus a good selection of breakfasts and light meals (around $5), plus home-cooked cakes. Daily 7am–4pm.

La Casa West of the market, opposite the Royal Hotel ☎081 610177. Italian-owned joint serving up delicious pizza ($6–7) along with good pastas and salads – although

2

the decor, seating and soundtrack could all do with a bit of TLC. Daily 11am–2.30 & 5–10.30pm.

La Pizza East of the river ☎ 096 3607417, ⓦ facebook La Pizza Battambang. Stylish new restaurant in lovely old balconied house next to the river serving good pizzas ($5.50–8.50) in a range of traditional and local flavours, plus crepes and salads. Sit either in the shady garden or grab a seat on the balcony upstairs. Daily except Wed 5–10pm.

Smokin' Pot Two blocks south of Psar Nat ☎ 012 821400. Best known for its long-running cookery classes (see p.118), this simple café-restaurant also serves reliable

and inexpensive Khmer food, plus a good Thai selection (mains $3–4) at bargain prices. Daily 7am–10pm.

White Rose Street 2 ☎ 012 691213. This long-running local restaurant attracts both tourists and locals, with a substantial menu of inexpensive Khmer and Chinese dishes (mains $2–3.50), plus a good selection of Western breakfasts and shakes. Daily 8am–10pm.

Wood House West of the market, opposite Royal Hotel ☎ 093 312685. Cosy little café with all the usual travellers' essentials ranging from breakfasts, salads and sandwiches alongside a simple selection of Khmer and Western mains ($3.50–5), plus good crepes and cocktails. Daily 7am–10pm.

DRINKING

Libations Bric-à-Brac, Street 2 ☎ 077 531562, ⓦ bric -a-brac.asia. This convivial pop-up pavement bar (part of the Bric-à-Brac shop and guesthouse) offers the perfect ringside seat from which to watch Battambang at night. The excellent selection of drinks include wines, cocktails, quality international beers and shots ranging from limoncello and absinthe to Pimm's and pink gin. Spectacular cheese and charcuterie platters accompany. Daily 5–9pm.

Madison Pub Street 2.5 ☎ 053 6502189. No-frills little corner bar, popular with the city's Francophone expat

crowd, offering one of the city's better selections of tipples plus ice cream, crepes and a good selection of breakfasts for the morning after. Daily 7am–midnight.

Riverside Balcony Riverfront, south of the centre ☎ 010 337862. Great place for a sundowner, occupying the upstairs terrace of a fine old wooden house in a lovely riverside setting, with soft lighting, good music and a great drinks list with plenty of cocktails on offer. Good pizzas, too ($4–8.50). Happy hour 5–7pm. Tues– Sun 4–11pm.

SHOPPING

Bric-à-Brac Street 2 ☎ 077 531562, ⓦ bric-à-brac.asia. A treasure-trove of artworks and collectibles – some of them freshly sprung from the in-shop loom of owner-designer Morrison Polkinghorne – including textiles, tassels and assorted antiques sourced from across Cambodia and other parts of Asia. Daily 9am–9pm.

Gecko Street 1 ☎ 092 719985. Accessorize Cambodian-style, or hunt for souvenirs, at this little shop stuffed with locally made jewellery, *kramas*, silk scarves and T-shirts. Daily 8am–9pm.

Jewel in the Lotus Street 2.5 ☎ 092 2600158. Tucked away in the back of the café of the same name, this place stocks an eclectic and entertaining selection of kitsch and

quirky bric-à-brac including postcards, old vinyl, retro posters, colourful cigarette tins, plus assorted jewellery and clothes. Daily 8am–5pm.

La Fabrik Street 2.5 ☎ 010 349639. A good selection of quality bric-à-brac and collectibles, which includes attractive jewellery and handmade cosmetics, miniature elephants, lacquered coconut-shell bowls and drink-me bottles of Kampot rum. Daily 9am–9pm.

Smiling Sky Bookshop Street 3, next to the Chaya hotel ☎ 099 447066. Well-stocked secondhand bookshop with plenty of fiction both pulp and literary, plus a few Cambodian-related titles. Daily 8am–7pm.

DIRECTORY

Consulate The Vietnamese consulate is north of Psar Nat on Street 2 (Mon–Fri 8–11am & 2–5pm).

Health Polyclinique Visal Sokh (☎ 012 843415), next to the Vietnamese Consulate north of the centre.

Internet World Net, between Street 2 & Street 1.5 (daily 7am–8pm; 2000 riel/hr).

Massage Seeing Hands (massage by the blind) is available at several places around town, including on the road running west from the Chinese temple just west of 2.5 St; on 115 St about 50m west of the Royal Hotel; and a few doors west of *Madison Pub*. Don't expect any frills though

– you might find yourself being massaged in full view of the street.

Money There are plenty of ATMs around including at the Canadia, ANZ and ABA banks (all of which accept both Visa and MasterCard).

Post office Street 1 in the south of town (Mon–Fri 7–11am & 2–5pm).

Swimming pools Some hotels allow non-residents to use their swimming pools for a small daily fee, including the *Stung Sangke* ($5) and *Seng Hout* ($2).

CLOCKWISE FROM TOP LEFT SHRINE, WAT BANAN (P.123); COLONIAL HOUSE, BATTAMBANG (P.113); BANTEAY CHHMAR (P.128) >

Around Battambang

Within easy striking distance of Battambang, the ruined temples of **Wat Banan**, **Wat Ek Phnom** and **Prasat Yeah** are decidedly small beer compared to the great Angkorian monuments, but have an ancient and understated charm all of their own, and few other visitors to disturb the peace. Close by, sobering mementos of the Khmer Rouge era can be seen at the hilltop pagoda of **Phnom Sampeu** and **Kamping Poy** reservoir. All these sites, except Wat Ek Phnom, lie west of town and can be combined in various ways. Pairing a visit to Wat Banan with Phnom Sampeu makes for a particularly rewarding (longish) half-day tour (around $15 by moto, $20 by tuk-tuk), which can be extended to a full day with visits to Wat Yeah Ten and/or Kamping Poy, or a ride on the bamboo railway.

Wat Ek Phnom

12km north of Battambang on the river road • $1 • Return by moto from Battambang around $8, by tuk-tuk around $15

The modest ruins of the eleventh-century **Wat Ek Phnom** are relatively underwhelming, although the site and surrounding countryside are attractive enough, offering fine views from the main sanctuary, with its line of sandstone buildings joined by an enclosed walkway. The temple would originally have been reached via a couple of 2m-high terraces, though these have collapsed, and you'll now have to scramble up a small hill and through a broken section of the laterite wall surrounding the main sanctuary, or walk round to the slightly better-preserved south side, where a crumbling doorway survives, along with some carvings. A modern pagoda stands in front of the ruins, with an impressively large seated white Buddha presiding serenely to one side.

Phnom Sampeu

15km southwest of Battambang on NR57 towards Pailin • $1

The craggy limestone mountain of **Phnom Sampeu** (Boat Mountain), topped with a colourful cluster of temples and shrines, makes an interesting excursion, though it's best known for its tragic associations with the Khmer Rouge, who turned the buildings here into a prison, many of whose inmates were executed.

On arrival, you'll be dropped at the foot of the **steps** leading steeply up the hill – a hard climb featuring well over five hundred steps. Alternatively walk (or catch a moto) up the **road** on your left – much less strenuous. Whichever route you take, **don't stray from clearly defined paths** as most of the hills hereabouts are thought to be mined.

The ascent

Assuming you head directly up the steps, it's a steep **climb** of twenty to thirty minutes to reach the top. The steps divide about halfway up: the left-hand fork heads directly to the top; the right-hand fork climbs more gently past a series of small shrines and temples and a large seated Buddha before reaching the road up the hill. From here you can either follow the road up to the summit, or return to the steps, which head up past

---

CROCODILE TEARS

According to local legend, the hill of **Phnom Sampeu** is the broken hull of a ship, sunk by a lovestruck crocodile suffering from unrequited passion for a young girl. When the woman in question and her fiancé took to sea, the croc attacked and sunk their ship, and the lovers were drowned.

Some distance away to the northwest, another quite separate small hill, **Phnom Kropeu** (Crocodile Mountain), continues the tale: the local population, scared of the crocodile, drained all the water from the area so that he couldn't swim away, leaving the crocodile to perish, after which it transformed into the hill you see today.

two abandoned Russian-built **anti-aircraft guns**, remnants of the 1994–95 conflict, when Phnom Sampeu was at the front line of fighting between government forces and the Pailin faction of the Khmer Rouge.

The summit
The **summit** is topped with a cluster of structures, including the **Preah Jan** vihara and, next to it, an eye-catching gilded stupa (although beware the sometimes aggressive macaque monkeys who – literally – hang around up here, waiting to swipe food and other desirables from unwary tourists). During the Khmer Rouge era, the mountain-top buildings were used as a prison, interrogation centre and place of execution – it's thought that as many as ten thousand victims were pushed to their deaths over the edge of the rocks here, falling into the cave below.

   From the summit, another steep staircase leads down through a rock arch into a kind of natural amphitheatre below a gigantic slab of overhanging rock from which bats dangle in a sinister manner, with a pair of stone deities keeping solemn watch. This is traditionally known as the Theatre Cave (*leahng lacaun*) on account of the theatrical performances that were once staged here, although nowadays it's more commonly referred to as the **Killing Cave** due to the number of people who were killed here. Some of the bones and skulls of bodies found scattered across the ground have been collected and placed inside a small glass memorial, while further down the hill is a large reclining Buddha and a second memorial, with more bones piled up inside a metal cage.

Prasat Yeah Ten
Sneng, about 25km west of Battambang (and 10km beyond Phnom Sampeu)

West of Phnom Sampeu along the road to Pailin, in the village of Sneng, are the remains of the tenth-century **Prasat Yeah Ten** temple. There's not much left of the temple itself, although three doorways have survived topped with beautifully carved lintels, one depicting the ubiquitous Churning of the Ocean of Milk (see p.168). A couple of hundred metres further down the road, in the grounds at the back of a modern wat, are three extremely old **brick sanctuaries**, perhaps also dating back to the tenth century.

Wat Banan
20km southwest of Battambang • $2

Wat Banan, the best preserved of the temples around Battambang, makes a rewarding half-day trip combined with Phnom Sampeu (if you don't mind the horribly bumpy 45min ride between the two, following a backcountry dirt track through the paddy fields); you could also include Prasat Yeah Ten (see above) in the same trip. The temple was consecrated as a Buddhist shrine, although scholars are uncertain who built it or exactly when it was completed, which could have been any time between the tenth and thirteenth centuries.

   From the car park at the base of the hill, it's a steep climb up some 360 steps to the temple, with five sturdy towers poking up out of the trees (which, alas, largely obscure the views). Numerous carvings survive – those on the central tower are the best – including a number of apsaras (most of them now headless), various figures bent in prayer and a couple of finely carved, if rather eroded, lintels.

Kamping Poy
Around 30km west of Battambang by road • $1 • Take NR57 west from Battambang, then turn off north at Phnom Sampeu

The prettiness of the lake at **Kamping Poy** belies the fact that it was created by the Pol Pot regime using slave labour – more than ten thousand people died of overwork, malnutrition and disease during the construction of the 8km **dam** that bounds the lake. Completed in 1977, the dam lay at the heart of an extensive irrigation system and still allows dry-season rice cultivation. At weekends and holidays the place is packed with Cambodians messing around in the water, but during the week you'll have the place to yourself. The rim of the dam is navigable by moto or on foot for several kilometres, so even at busy times you can get away for a quiet swim; there are also rowing boats ($1/hr) to rent.

2

Pailin

Ringed by hills near the border with Thailand, the sprawling frontier town of **PAILIN** was once the gem-mining centre of Cambodia, although it's now a downbeat sort of place with not a lot going for it. Pailin's history is quite separate from the rest of Cambodia. Although originally part of the Khmer Empire, the area was conquered by the Burmese in 1558 and subsequently ruled by the Thais until 1946, with a population mainly comprising Thai Kula and Shan Burmese. In recent times the town is best known for its role as one of the last strongholds of the **Khmer Rouge**, although most people come here to **cross the border** into Thailand, around 20km away. Other local attractions include the hill of **Phnom Yat** and a couple of **waterfalls** in the surrounding countryside – but on no account wander off well-marked tracks, since the area is still one of the most heavily **mined** in the country.

Phnom Yat

1km or so south of the centre, on the southern edge of town • Walk, or catch a moto for around $1 or $3 return

South of Pailin centre is the small but unmistakeable hill of **Phnom Yat**, its summit dominated by mobile-telephone masts and a large temple (built by Shan migrants from Myanmar in 1922, and with a distinctly Burmese-looking stupa) – a peaceful spot from which to watch the sun go down. The hill was named after Yeah Yat, a Buddhist pilgrim (or possibly a witch) who arrived in Pailin with her husband at the end of the nineteenth century and set up a meditation centre on the hill. Yat is said to have received a message from the mountain spirits asking local hunters to cease killing forest wildlife and to build a pagoda upon the mountain, in return for which they would be shown where to find many valuable gems. The superstitious miners

---

THE KHMER ROUGE IN PAILIN

After being ousted from power in 1979, the **Khmer Rouge** found a natural bolthole in remote Pailin, with Pol Pot himself establishing his headquarters in the town from 1979 until 1993, when he fled first to Phnom Chhat (north of Poipet) and thence on to Anlong Veng. From Pailin, the Khmer Rouge controlled an extensive arc of territory along the Thai border, from south of Pailin up to Preah Vihear in the north (around a fifth of Cambodia in total) and waged a disruptive guerrilla war against the government in Phnom Penh. Campaigns were supported by tapping into the area's rich natural resources including gemstones and untouched forests – gem-mining alone is reputed to have earned them a monthly revenue of $10 million. They held out until August 1996 when, in a move that marked the beginning of the end for the Khmer Rouge, **Ieng Sary**, the local commander, struck a deal with the Cambodian government, gaining immunity from prosecution for himself and taking around four thousand soldiers over to the government side. The Pailin area was henceforth under nominal government control, although Ieng Sary continued to rule it almost as a private fiefdom until his eventual arrest in 2007, supported by the numerous ex-Khmer Rouge fighters who can still be found living in the environs of Pailin to this day.

THE GEM MINES

Pailin has been a **gem-mining** centre for nearly a hundred years – it's said that sapphires, rubies and garnets once lay everywhere on the surface. Now much of the land is mined out, and fortune-seekers have to dig deep into the rocky ground in search of the stones. It's hard toil for the prospectors and, for most, hope turns to wistfulness as they sift painstakingly through mounds of red dirt, sorting earth from rocks. Piles of spoil scar the landscape, creating an almost lunar scene.

Most of the claims are now abandoned, and those prospectors still at work are pretty secretive about their diggings. If you're interested, ask at *Bamboo Guesthouse* for information about where the current workings are, but note that there's little to see other than a hole in the ground and a pile of earth. Typical finds today are small garnets and topazes; rubies and sapphires are now rare.

did as they were told and were rewarded as promised – for a time at least – although nowadays discoveries of precious stones on the formerly gem-rich hillsides are increasingly rare.

Gory **tableaux** at the temple illustrate the fate that befalls those destined for hell, including a man having his tongue pulled out and another being boiled in oil. Tucked away behind the modern vihara is all that's left of the previous pagoda – wall paintings, floor tiles and a cracked stupa – following its destruction by the Khmer Rouge. At the bottom of the hill, the wall enclosing **Wat Ratanasaoporn** is covered in impressive bas-reliefs depicting the Churning of the Ocean of Milk (see p.168).

ARRIVAL AND INFORMATION PAILIN

By bus or shared taxi Pailin can be reached by bus or shared taxi from Battambang, a smooth 80km trip along NR57. There are currently two daily services (2hr), continuing on to the Thai border. Shared taxis to Pailin depart from Psar Leu in the south of Battambang, while reasonably regular shared taxis head on from Pailin to the border.

Money Although dollars and riel are both accepted in town, the Thai baht is the currency of choice. There are branches of the Canadia and Acleda banks with ATMs accepting foreign cards on the main road near the traffic circle.

CROSSING TO THAILAND FROM PAILIN

Not many travellers use the border crossing into Thailand (daily 7am–8pm) between Psar Pruhm and Ban Pakard, 20km from Pailin, although it's a lot more peaceful and quicker to cross than the notorious Poipet border crossing further north (see p.130). From Pailin, the border can be reached by occasional shared taxi ($2) or moto (around $5). At the border itself there's a small market and a couple of casinos, which entertain an almost exclusively Thai clientele. Once in Thailand you can take a minibus to Chanthaburi, then another bus to Bangkok, or to Trat for Koh Chang. If you're entering Cambodia, note that **e-visas** are not valid for entrance at this crossing.

ACCOMMODATION AND EATING

Pailin offers no gastronomic delights, but there are plenty of stalls in the market and cheap **restaurants** nearby. Near the top of the ridge road is the *Phkay Proek*, which isn't bad, serving up Khmer and Thai staples.

Bamboo Guesthouse 4km out of town on the road towards the border ☎012 405818. A pleasant refuge from central Pailin with a range of wooden bungalows in an attractive garden, all with hot water and a/c. The restaurant is one of the best in town, serving Khmer and Thai food, plus a few Western options. $15

Memoria Palace and Resort 5km west of Pailin ☎015 430014, ✉memoriapalace.com. An unexpected find in dusty Pailin, the relatively upscale *Memoria* offers attractive lodgings in an unspoilt hilltop location west of town amid the fringes of the Cardamom Mountains.

Accommodation consists of bright, spacious and very comfortable bungalows, plus three rustic thatched "ecolodges" (fan only; $30), and there's also a big saltwater pool and good restaurant. $55

Pailin Ruby West of the traffic circle on the main road through town ☎055 636 3603. The best place to stay in town and the least unruly (Pailin attracts a lot of truckers). Rooms are clean and pleasant enough, with en-suite bathrooms, TV and chunky wood furniture; hot water and a/c are available for an extra $5. $7

Sisophon (Banteay Meanchey)

Midway between Siem Reap and the Thai border the workaday town of **SISOPHON** has something of an identity problem. The official name is Sisophon, although it's little used by Cambodians themselves, who tend to refer to the town as either Srey Sisophon, Sereysophon or **Banteay Meanchey**, after the province of which it's the capital – while locals, for reasons not entirely understood, call it Svay (mango).

Names aside, Sisophon is notable mainly for its location at the junction of the roads to Siem Reap and Battambang – from where there's a trio of interesting sights (see p.127) that can be visited on the way to Siem Reap – and as the jumping-off point for a day-trip to the massive Angkorian temple ruins of **Banteay Chhmar**, one of the country's least-visited and most memorable ancient monuments.

ARRIVAL AND DEPARTURE   SISOPHON

By bus Several bus companies run services to Sisophon, including Sorya Phnom Penh, Capital, GST and Virak Buntham. Arriving by bus you'll either be dropped off at one of the bus company offices just east of the market or on the main road by the *Nasa Hotel*, where you'll be instantly pounced upon by a posse of cheery moto drivers. Leaving Sisophon, services depart from the various offices, or you could try flagging down something on the main road by the *Nasa*.

By shared taxi arrive/depart from the transport stop.
By train The proposed Phnom Penh–Poipet railway (see p.23) will also connect Sisophon directly to Poipet and Thailand when complete (and eventually to Battambang and Phnom Penh as well).
Destinations: by bus Bangkok (2 daily; 7–8hr); Battambang (10 daily; 2hr); Phnom Penh (15 daily; 7–8hr); Poipet (10 daily; 1hr); Siem Reap (10 daily; 2hr).

GETTING AROUND

You can **walk** across pretty much the whole of Sisophon in around 15min. There are plenty of motos, though hardly any tuk-tuks. For transport to Banteay Chhmar or other destinations around town, try the *Botoum* or *Nasa* hotels.

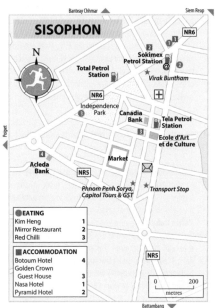

INFORMATION

Money The ATMs at the Canadia and Acleda banks accepts foreign Visa and MasterCards.
Shops There are well-stocked minimarts at the Total and Tela petrol stations.

ACCOMMODATION

Botoum Hotel Northwest side of town, just off the junction of NR5 & NR6 ☎012 687858, ✉botoum hotel@gmail.com. Simple hotel with friendly English-speaking owners and slightly grubby rooms with hot water and fan (plus optional a/c for $7 extra). Taller readers should beware the dangerously low-flying doors. $8
Golden Crown Guest House Town centre, just north of the market ☎012 969808. Simple, spacious tiled rooms with fan and cold water only or a/c and hot. Good value, although not much English spoken. Fan $7; a/c $12
Nasa Hotel Northern end of town, opposite the Sokimex petrol station ☎011 777702. The best hotel in town, offering big, bright and very comfortable a/c rooms with fancy carved wooden furniture, plus TV and fridge. Prices aren't astronomical, either. $15

Pyramid Hotel Northern end of town ☎054 668881, ⓦpyramid-hotel.com. Big, flouncy white wedding-cake of a hotel offering a variety of rooms (all a/c with hot water), from dark and faintly shabby-looking ground-floor doubles (not as nice as similarly priced rooms at the *Nasa*) to brighter and fancier deluxe rooms upstairs, plus a fifth-floor restaurant serving Western and Khmer dishes, and with switched-on service. **$15**

EATING

Food options in Sisophon are rudimentary. In the late afternoon and early evening, **food stalls** open on the south side of Independence Park.

Kim Heng Food Next door to the Nasa Hotel ☎012 503847. Proud possessor of Sisophon's only English-language menu, with a short selection of inexpensive Khmer and Chinese staples (mains $2–3). Daily 8am–9pm.

Mirror Restaurant Opposite the Sokimex petrol station. This bright little café is Sisophon's (modest) answer to a fast-food joint, with a big picture menu (Khmer only) promising a few simple Khmer dishes ($2–4)

plus ice cream, cold coffee and *KFC*-style chicken and chips. Daily 10am–8pm.

Red Chilli Poipet Rd. Respectable-looking local restaurant, with a big selection of classic Khmer dishes (mains $4–5) and enough wooden furniture to restock a rainforest. The menu is in Khmer only, so you'll have to either brush up your language skills or point at the pictures. Daily 8am–9pm.

Around Sisophon

A trio of local attractions – the stone-carving village of **Choob**, the traditional weaving village of **Phnom Sarok**, and the **Ang Trapeang Thmor Crane sanctuary** – can be combined into an interesting day-trip from Sisophon, or visited en route between Sisophon and Siem Reap.

Choob

NR6, 30km east of Sisophon • Around $10 return by moto

You'll know when you've arrived in the small village of **CHOOB** as soon as you see the roadside lined with sandstone carvings of Buddhas and apsaras – from the tiny to the enormous. The most prized (and pricey) types of sandstone have delicate veined markings, while some of the larger pieces take months to complete, with many commissioned by temples or government offices. For anyone prepared to lug a statue home, prices can be very reasonable after a bit of bargaining.

Phnom Srok

50km northeast of Sisophon • About $25 return by moto

Easily combined with a visit to Choob, **PHNOM SROK** is one of the few villages in the country where **sericulture** has been properly revived after the Khmer Rouge years and is also known throughout Cambodia for its thick cotton *kramas*, sold mainly in Siem Reap. Weaving looms clack away under the stilt-houses along the village's north street, and you'll see tree branches flecked with furry silkworm cocoons, looking like yellow balls. The families will be only too pleased to give you a little tour.

Ang Trapeang Thmor Crane Sanctuary

60km northeast of Sisophon • $10 • Visits can be arranged through Sam Veasna in Siem Reap (see p.146) or from Sisophon for around $25 by moto

North of Phnom Srok lies the **Ang Trapeang Thmor** reservoir, built by forced labour during the Khmer Rouge era. The reservoir and surrounding area now serve as a dry-season refuge for the globally endangered **Sarus crane** (*kriel*), one of Cambodia's largest birds – adults can grow to up to 1.3m – and instantly recognizable thanks to their distinctive red heads. Around 350 cranes visit the reserve between around January and March and the sanctuary is also home to many other rare waterbirds (about two hundred species have been spotted here) including the black-necked stork, greater spotted eagle and oriental plover. You might also be lucky enough to spot one of the sanctuary's Eld's deer, another highly threatened species.

2 Banteay Chhmar

The huge Angkorian-era temple of **Banteay Chhmar** is one of Cambodia's most memorable destinations, as fine as almost anything in Angkor itself but still attracting only a trickle of visitors and offering all the lost-in-the-jungle mystery and frisson which has long since vanished from other sites. Visiting the temple was formerly difficult and time-consuming, but the recent sealing of the road from Sisophon has made the site more accessible than ever, bringing it within a three-hour drive of Siem Reap. Visit now, before the coach parties arrive.

The temple, one of the prolific building works of the legendary **Jayavarman VII** (see p.294), was built in the late twelfth or early thirteenth century to serve as a memorial to four of his soldiers, killed while defending a royal prince in a battle against the Chams, and perhaps to the prince himself, who may also have died in the fighting. The prince is often identified as Jayavarman's son and successor, Indravarman, although it's more likely to have been a certain Srindrakumara, possibly the king's brother-in-law. The size of the settlement suggests that it played an important role in the overall structure of the Angkorian kingdom, and may – according to one theory – have served as the centre from which Khmer territories in Isaan (now part of northeast Thailand) were ruled.

The temple is best known for its magnificent **carvings**, once rivalling those at the Bayon and Angkor Wat, although many of these have been looted – most notoriously in 1998 when a group of rogue soldiers removed two massive panels and trucked them across the border for sale in Bangkok. Confiscated by the Thai police and returned to Cambodia, the panels are now in the National Museum in Phnom Penh. A massive programme run by the Global Heritage Fund and Heritage Watch is now slowly restoring the site, while efforts are also being made to have the temple listed as a UNESCO World Heritage Site.

The temple

The fourth-largest Angkor-era temple, Banteay Chhmar covers an area of around three square kilometres, surrounded by nine satellite temples and with a huge *baray* (reservoir), now dry, to the east. Four gateways at the cardinal points lead into the citadel, crossing the partly cleared moat via causeways flanked with Angkor Thom-style naga balustrades (although looters have now made off with all the nagas' heads). The temple's name literally means "Citadel of the Cat", probably a corruption of Banteay Chhmarl, meaning "small citadel" or "narrow fortress".

Most visitors approach via the **eastern entrance** next to the village (where you'll also find the ticket office), crossing the moat and passing a trio of well-preserved garudas before reaching the eastern gopura – now just a great mess of collapsed stone. As with many of Jayavarman's construction works across the empire, Banteay Chhmar appears to have been built quickly, with much of the temple lacking in proper foundations, which explains its present state of dramatic decay.

Left (south) of the gopura, the spectacular **eastern gallery** has been meticulously restored, stretching around a hundred metres and covered in a fabulous gallery of **bas-reliefs**. These rival the much more famous examples at Angkor Wat and the Bayon, and include memorable depictions of processions, state ceremonies, scenes of daily life, and the great naval battle between the Khmer and Cham on Tonle Sap (with the dead being devoured by crocodiles). Representations of a supersized Jayavarman dominate many of the scenes, accompanied by only slightly smaller images of the enigmatic prince, wearing a distinctive necklace.

Buildings originally stretched in an unbroken line all the way from the eastern to western gates, passing through three enclosures. The extraordinary masses of tumbled masonry now significantly obscure the original plan, although parts of the temple – a corridor here, a shrine there – survive intact. The inner enclosure is surrounded by a **gallery**, mostly filled in with accumulated rubble. Tiny Buddha images remain perched in some of the niches along the gallery roof, but many more have been crudely hacked out, either when the state religion switched from Buddhism back to Hinduism in the thirteenth century or as a result of looting.

The central section of the complex originally featured around fifty **face towers**, although many have now collapsed either partly or entirely, and the faces have vanished. Part of an eight-armed relief of Vishnu remains on the west face of the central tower, though sadly, like so many carvings here, it's missing its head.

Further **carvings** can still be seen on the exterior of the western wall of the second enclosure, including a spectacular 32-armed **Avalokitesvara** (there were originally eight similar carvings, although six have been removed by looters – you can still see the nearby breach in the wall from which they were taken). Immediately south, there's a panel showing scenes of daily life, while a little further north, past the western gateway, are carvings illustrating scenes from the *Ramayana*, including one warrior kickboxing a demon and (below) another monstrous-looking creature swallowing a horse. Further processions and battle scenes dot the southern wall.

Around the temple

Most of the nine satellite temples in the vicinity of the main temple are atmospherically ruined and you'll need to hire a guide (see below) to find them all. Just south of the temple, **Prasat Ta Prohm** is topped by an impressive Bayon-style face tower, while west of the temple **Prasat Samnang Tasok** remains picturesquely overgrown. East of the main temple lies the temple's original *baray*, originally more than 1.5km long but now dried up, with the remains of another temple, **Prasat Mebon** (accessible during the dry season only) at its centre.

Some 3km north of the main temple is another reservoir, the **Boeung Cheung Kru** (or "Pol Pot Baray"), built by forced labour during the Khmer Rouge era – now an important local water source and peaceful birdwatching site. Just across from the southwest corner of the moat enclosing the main temple is a French-run silk-weaving project, the **Soieries du Mékong** (ⓦ soieriesdumekong.com) where you can watch local women weaving silk and buy *kramas*.

Further afield, around 6km south of Banteay Chhmar, **Banteay Tuop** (or Top, meaning "Army Fortress") was probably constructed at the same time, possibly (as its name suggests) as a tribute to Jayavarman's victorious soldiers. Its four commandingly tall but decidedly precarious-looking towers are in such an advanced state of decay that it's a wonder they're still standing at all.

ARRIVAL AND INFORMATION   BANTEAY CHHMAR

From Sisophon It's about 60km from Sisophon to Banteay Chhmar, taking around 1hr. You may be able to arrange transport through the *Botoum*, *Pyramid* or *Nasa* hotels; alternatively, try the tuk-tuk or moto drivers hanging out by *Nasa* or ask around at the transport stop. The trip by moto costs roughly $25, by tuk-tuk around $30.

Opening hours Daily 6am–5.30pm.

Admission $5 (ticket also valid for Banteay Tuop).

Guides Guides ($10 per day) can be hired through the CBT office (see p.130) – useful for the main site, and essential if you want to properly explore the various outlying temples.

Tour packages Contact ⓦ visitbanteaychhmar.org, who arrange homestays in various houses around the village (see p.130) plus guides, transport, bike hire, boat trips and various village activities.

ACCOMMODATION

Homestays Banteay Chhmar village ☎ 012 435660, ⓦ visitbanteaychhmar.org. Although you can visit Banteay Chhmar on a day-trip from Sisophon, the local community also provides comfortable and well-run homestays in the village. It's best to arrange them in advance, although you may be able to set up something on the spot by visiting the Community Based Tourism (CBT) office just south of the temple on NR56A. Meals cost $2 for breakfast, and $4 each for lunch and dinner. $̲7̲ per person.

Poipet

Arriving from Bangkok at the dusty border town of **POIPET** provides the worst possible introduction to Cambodia – mainly thanks to the hassle-ridden border crossing, which has become mildly notorious thanks to the various low-grade scams practised upon new arrivals. The town itself has boomed massively in recent years thanks to the raft of **casinos** set up for Thai visitors (gambling is illegal in Thailand), and the glitzy duty-free casino zone next to the border is effectively a slice of foreign territory on Cambodian soil, with Thai the predominant language and baht the currency of choice. Away from the casinos the town remains a flyblown and faintly dismal sort of place, and one that most travellers choose to escape as rapidly as possible.

ARRIVAL AND DEPARTURE

FROM THAILAND
The border crossing The crossing at Poipet (daily 7am–8pm) is the main transit point between Cambodia and Thailand. Coming from Thailand, try to arrive as early as possible, since onward transport dries up significantly after noon, and if you cross after 5pm you may find yourself stuck in town for the night. The crossing is overused and undermanned at the best of times, but around midday

POIPET BORDER SCAMS

The following are just some of the most entrenched scams – which may well have evolved into new forms by the time you read this – so have your wits about you when entering Cambodia. Keep a beady eye on your possessions, too, as petty theft and pickpocketing is common. Also, there is no departure tax, whatever officials or anyone else tells you.

VISAS
It's best to buy an **e-visa** in advance (see p.46), which will speed your progress through immigration. If you don't have one already, you can get a visa on arrival at the border at a cost of $30 (bring one passport photo, or you may be charged an extra 100 baht in order to have your passport photo scanned; pay in dollars rather than baht, or again the fee may inflate). Ignore any touts or tuk-tuk drivers who might try to "help" you obtain your visa, no matter how legitimate they might look (including those posing as officials with fake ID badges and so on) – if pressed, just say you already have a visa. And avoid any attempts to lure you into the semi-spurious "Cambodian Consulate" on the Thai side of the border, where you'll pay double the official rate for a visa. All you actually have to do is wade your way through the various con artists, get yourself stamped out of Thailand and then walk over to the far side of the footbridge, where you can buy your visa at the official Visa Office at the clearly posted price, although even here you may be asked for an additional "processing fee", "stamping fee" or suchlike for an extra $1–3 – a bribe by any other name. A polite refusal to pay is perfectly in order, although it's probably worth coughing up the necessary lest you find that your visa is processed with excessive lethargy.

MONEY
Another regular scam involves money – you'll be told that **ATMs** in Cambodia charge inflated commission fees and/or that you should change all your baht at a bogus "government" exchange booth before crossing the border. All of which is nonsense – there are the usual ATMs in Poipet, and in any case baht are accepted throughout Poipet. That said, it's a good idea to bring some dollars with you just to be safe.

(when officials take their lunch breaks) is probably the worst time to cross – queues of an hour or longer are common. Try to avoid weekends and holidays if possible.

Onward transport When you arrive in Cambodia touts will attempt to herd you into the "Free Shuttle Bus Station" run by the Poipet Transport Association (for "Association" read "mafia"). Shuttle buses from here will take you to the **Poipet Tourist International Passenger Terminal**, 9km down the road, from where buses and shared taxis depart to Sisophon, Siem Reap, Battambang and Phnom Penh (most services depart in the morning, although buses to Siem Reap via Sisophon continue until around 5pm). Fares on services departing from here are roughly double the usual prices on these routes ($9 by bus to Siem Reap, for example, or $15 to Phnom Penh). If you want to avoid over-paying for your onward transport you'll need first of all to shake off the attentions of the possibly belligerent touts (you could say you're spending the night in Poipet itself and don't need transport) and possibly even local police (who may pursue you down the road, insisting – ludicrously – that it's illegal to take a place in a local bus or shared taxi) and make your way around 1.5km down the road by foot or moto to the area in front of the market, where various bus companies including Phnom Penh Sorya, Capitol Tours and GST have offices and buses. Most onward buses from here depart before noon, leaving for Siem Reap, Sisophon, Battambang and Phnom Penh. **Shared taxis** can also be picked up along the roadside here.
Destinations: by bus Battambang (8 daily; 3hr); Phnom Penh (15 daily; 8hr); Siem Reap (20 daily; 3hr); Sisophon (20 daily; 1hr).
Destinations: by shared taxi Battambang (4 daily; 3hr);

Phnom Penh (15 daily; 8hr); Siem Reap (25 daily; 3hr); Sisophon (10 daily; 1hr).

Pre-paid transport If you're on a pre-paid bus or minibus from Bangkok you'll have to locate your vehicle and then possibly hang around for an hour or more waiting for remaining passengers to come through, and possibly even longer if your driver decides to go hunting for further passengers to make the onward trip more lucrative.

TO THAILAND

By train The railway from Poipet to Sisophon, Battambang and – eventually – Phnom Penh (see p.23) may conceivably have entered service by the time you read this, although it's not likely to be of much use if you're heading to Siem Reap.

By bus Several companies (including Phnom Penh Sorya) run buses between Phnom Penh, Siem Reap and Bangkok. In theory this takes the headache out of arranging onward transport from the Thai side of the border, although in practice things might not work as smoothly as you'd hope thanks to cross-border bus company scams or simple inefficiency, and locating your bus on the far side of the border can sometimes turn into a major headache (companies generally use different vehicles on either side of the border) – meaning that it's a toss-up between buying a through ticket and trying to make your own way once over the border. If you do decide to travel independently, once across the border and into Thailand you'll need to make for Aranyaprathet – a 4km journey by tuk-tuk (around 80 baht) – from where buses depart regularly for Bangkok (throughout the day until around 6pm; 5hr); there are also a couple of trains, currently leaving at 6.40am and 1.55pm.

INFORMATION

Money It's a good idea to arrive with some dollars to buy your visa with and as a safety net to avoid possible money-changing scams. There are ATMs (Visa and MasterCard) at the Canadia, ANZ and Acleda banks in the town centre near

the market. Poipet operates on no fewer than three currencies: Thai baht, Cambodian riel and US dollars, although baht are generally preferred to riel. Try to get up to speed with latest exchange rates as quickly as you can.

ACCOMMODATION AND EATING

City Poipet Hotel Just off the north side of the main road, about 800m from the border ☎095 979893. Smartish modern hotel (wi-fi in the lobby only) with pleasant a/c rooms and friendly service, although not much English spoken. There's a decent restaurant attached but no English menu. $15

Good Luck Hotel and Restaurant 200m west of the market, about 1.2km from the border ☎011 722408. Located down a quiet side street and with simple, clean en-suite rooms with a/c and TV, plus a pleasant restaurant serving tasty Thai and Khmer food. $1

Siem Reap and the temples of Angkor

ANGKOR WAT

Siem Reap and the temples of Angkor

The main – and for some people the only – reason to visit Cambodia is to experience at first hand the world-famous temples of Angkor, a stupendous array of ancient religious monuments virtually unrivalled anywhere in Asia (only the temples of Bagan in Myanmar, built at around the same time, come close). The majestic temple of Angkor Wat, with its five iconic corncob towers rising high above the surrounding jungle, is the chief attraction, rivalled by the magical Bayon, which is embellished with superhuman images of the enigmatically half-smiling Lokesvara, and the jungle-smothered temple remains of Ta Prohm, whose crumbling ruins are squeezed between the roots of enormous trees and creepers. The sheer numbers of tourists descending on these sites may have eroded some of Angkor's prevailing mystery, although with judicious planning the worst of the crowds can still be avoided – and whenever you visit, the temples will leave an indelible impression.

Headline monuments aside, Angkor has an extraordinary wealth of attractions. Literally hundreds of major temple complexes dot the countryside hereabouts, spread over an area of some four hundred square kilometres, and for many visitors it's at these lesser-known destinations that the true spirit and magic of Angkor can still be found. Even a cursory tour of the outlying temples of **Roluos** gets you somewhat off the beaten track, while the intricately carved shrines of **Banteay Srei** are also within easy reach. Further afield the magnificent temple-citadels of **Beng Mealea** and **Koh Ker** can be conveniently combined in a single day-trip – perhaps with a visit to remote **Preah Khan** (Kompong Thom) added on. Further north stands the memorable temple of **Preah Vihear**, perched on a mountaintop overlooking Thailand and easily combined with a visit to the remote border town of **Anlong Veng**, famous for its Khmer Rouge associations and as the site of Pol Pot's death. Further east, the affable town of **Kompong Thom** provides a convenient jumping-off

THE BAYON, ANGKOR THOM

Highlights

❶ Siem Reap Cambodia's most tourist-friendly destination, packed with bustling pavement cafés, elegant restaurants and buzzing bars, but still with a healthy slice of old-fashioned, small-town charm. **See p.138**

❷ Apsara dance Laden with symbolism, this exquisitely stylized classical dance form was once performed exclusively for the king. **See p.154**

❸ Tonle Sap Ride a boat around the remarkable floating villages on Southeast Asia's largest freshwater lake. **See p.157**

❹ Angkor Wat Southeast Asia's most iconic building – the first glimpse of its soaring corncob towers is something you'll never forget. **See p.164**

❺ Angkor Thom Expansive ancient walled city enclosing lavish terraces, towers and temples, including the haunting Bayon with its forest of enigmatic faces. **See p.170**

❻ Ta Prohm Atmospheric temple, now half-consumed by the jungle, its crumbling buildings held in the clutch of giant trees. **See p.180**

❼ Banteay Srei Rosy-red sandstone temple with intricate carvings of female divinities. **See p.188**

❽ Prasat Preah Vihear Imposing temple poised in a spectacular position on a ridge above the Thai border. **See p.197**

HIGHLIGHTS ARE MARKED ON THE MAP ON PP.136–137

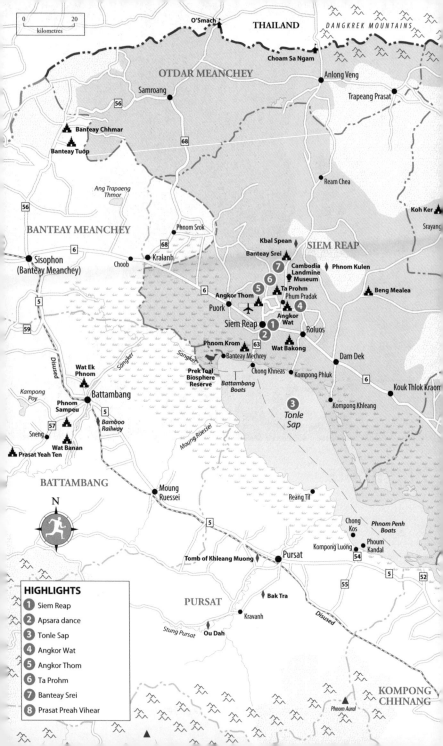

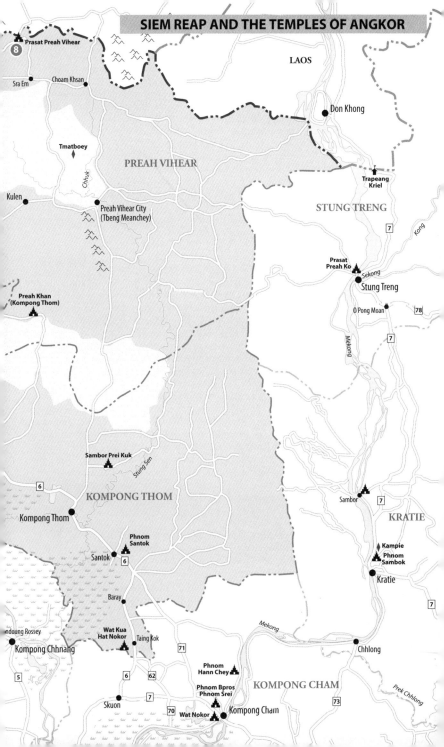

LAOS

Prasat Preah Vihear

Sra Em

Choam Khsan

Don Khong

Tmatboey

PREAH VIHEAR

Chhuk

Trapeang Kriel

Kulen

Preah Vihear City
(Tbeng Meanchey)

STUNG TRENG

7

Kong

Prasat Preah Ko

Sekong

Stung Treng

Preah Khan
(Kompong Thom)

O Pong Moan

78

7

Mekong

Sambor Prei Kuk

Stung Sen

6

KOMPONG THOM

Sambor

7

KRATIE

Kompong Thom

Phnom Santok

Kampie

Phnom Sambok

Santok

6

Kratie

Baray

7

ndoung Rossey

Wat Kua
Hat Nokor

Taing Kok

Chhlong

Kompong Chhnang

71

Mekong

5

6

62

Phnom Hann Chey

Prek Chhlong

73

KOMPONG CHAM

Phnom Bpros
Phnom Srei

Skuon

7

70

Wat Nokor

Kompong Cham

point for visits to the great pre-Angkorian temple complex at **Sambor Prei Kuk**, along with other nearby sites.

Gateway to the temples is **Siem Reap**, a former backwater town that has reinvented itself as Cambodia's tourist honeypot par excellence. It's crammed with tourists and touts, but remains one of the country's most enjoyable destinations – if you don't mind the fact that it bears increasingly little resemblance to anywhere else in the country. Siem Reap is also the starting point for visits to the remarkable **floating villages** on the great Tonle Sap lake and to wild **Phnom Kulen**, at the borders of the Kulen Mountains, which divide the lush lowlands from the barren north.

Three days is enough **time** to visit most of the major sites in the vicinity of Siem Reap, although adding a day or three allows time to visit one of the nearby floating villages and to take a more leisurely approach to the Angkor archaeological site itself – temple fatigue can set in surprisingly quickly if you go at the ancient monuments too quickly, and the slower you approach the vast treasury of Angkor, the more you'll gain from the experience. This is one of the world's great sights, and well worth lingering over.

Siem Reap

The once sleepy provincial capital of **SIEM REAP** (pronounced *See*-um *Ree*-up) is Cambodia's ultimate boomtown, its exponential growth super-fuelled by the vast number of global tourists who now descend on the place to visit the nearby temples of **Angkor**. The modern town is like nowhere else in Cambodia, packed with wall-to-wall hotels, restaurants, bars, boutiques, tour operators and massage parlours; its streets thronged day and night with tourists, touts and tuk-tuk drivers in a giddy bedlam of incessant activity, with endless quantities of hot food and cheap beer, and a nonstop party atmosphere.

It should be tourist hell, of course, but what's perhaps most surprising is that Siem Reap has somehow managed to retain much of its original small-town colonial charm. It's easy to spend much longer here than planned, wandering the city's lively markets, colourful wats and peaceful riverside walkways by day, and exploring its restaurants, bars and boutiques by dark. Major attractions in the town itself may be thin on the ground, but there's much to enjoy apart from the obligatory temple tours. The nearby **floating villages** on the Tonle Sap lake shouldn't be missed, while there are plenty of other **activities** and excursions to keep you busy, from horseriding and quad-biking through to cookery courses and apsara dance shows.

Brief history

Little is known about the **history** of Siem Reap, said to mean "Siam defeated" in commemoration of a battle that possibly never happened. Sprawling to east and west of the river of the same name, the town has only recently grown large enough to acquire its own identity. Visiting in 1935, Geoffrey Gorer described it as "a charming little village, hardly touched by European influence, built along a winding river; the native houses are insignificant little structures in wood, hidden behind the vegetation that grows so lushly… along the river banks." The only hotels at the time were the *Grand Hotel d'Angkor*, then "a mile out of town" according to Norman Lewis, who stayed here in 1951, although it's now long since been swallowed up by the ever-expanding city, and its sister establishment, the *Bungalow des Ruines*, opposite Angkor Wat. Siem Reap remained relatively undeveloped during the first **tourist rush** of the 1950s and 1960s, and much was destroyed when the town was emptied under the **Khmer Rouge**, although the *Grand*, the shophouses of the Old Market, Psar Chas, and the occasional colonial villa escaped unscathed.

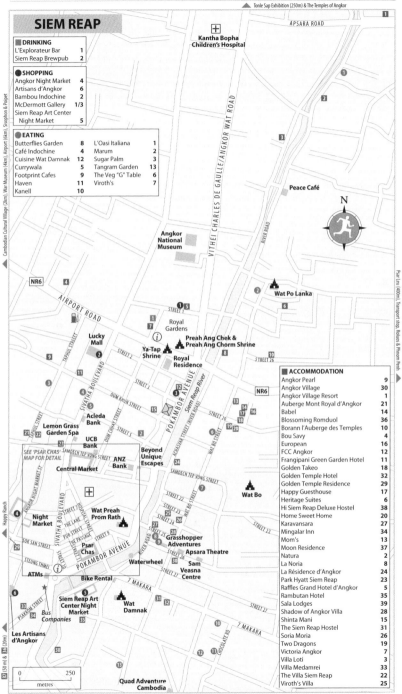

SIEM REAP

■ DRINKING
L'Explorateur Bar	1
Siem Reap Brewpub	2

● SHOPPING
Angkor Night Market	4
Artisans d'Angkor	6
Bambou Indochine	2
McDermott Gallery	1/3
Siem Reap Art Center Night Market	5

● EATING
Butterflies Garden	8	L'Oasi Italiana	1
Café Indochine	4	Marum	2
Cuisine Wat Damnak	12	Sugar Palm	3
Currywala	5	Tangram Garden	13
Footprint Cafes	9	The Veg "G" Table	6
Haven	11	Viroth's	7
Kanell	10		

■ ACCOMMODATION
Angkor Pearl	9
Angkor Village	30
Angkor Village Resort	1
Auberge Mont Royal d'Angkor	21
Babel	14
Blossoming Romduol	36
Borann l'Auberge des Temples	10
Bou Savy	4
European	16
FCC Angkor	12
Frangipani Green Garden Hotel	11
Golden Takeo	18
Golden Temple Hotel	32
Golden Temple Residence	29
Happy Guesthouse	17
Heritage Suites	6
Hi Siem Reap Deluxe Hostel	38
Home Sweet Home	20
Karavansara	27
Mingalar Inn	34
Mom's	13
Moon Residence	37
Natura	2
La Noria	8
La Résidence d'Angkor	24
Park Hyatt Siem Reap	23
Raffles Grand Hotel d'Angkor	5
Rambutan Hotel	35
Sala Lodges	39
Shadow of Angkor Villa	28
Shinta Mani	15
The Siem Reap Hostel	31
Soria Moria	26
Two Dragons	19
Victoria Angkor	7
Villa Loti	3
Villa Medamrei	33
The Villa Siem Reap	22
Viroth's Villa	25

Psar Chas and around

Bang in the centre of town is the bustling **Psar Chas** (Old Market), an enjoyably heterogeneous sort of place frequented both by locals (who come to stock up on fresh produce from the market's town-facing side) and tourists (who gravitate towards the souvenir-stacked stalls facing the river). It's not exactly your average authentic Cambodian market, of course, although the closely packed stalls and narrow alleyways offer a modest simulacrum of local life compared to the rest of the touristy city centre, and there's some good **shopping** to be had (see p.155).

The area around Psar Chas is the historic heart of Siem Reap, still boasting some original colonial-era **shophouses**, most of them now converted into vibrant restaurants and bars, with tables spilling out from shaded balconies onto the surrounding pavements.

The streets immediately north of Psar Chas are the epicentre of Siem Reap's tourist scene, nowhere more so than the riotous Street 8, popularly known as **Pub Street**, for obvious reasons, and filled until the early hours with raucous crowds of younger tourists from every corner of the globe. South and north of here, alleyways branch out

3

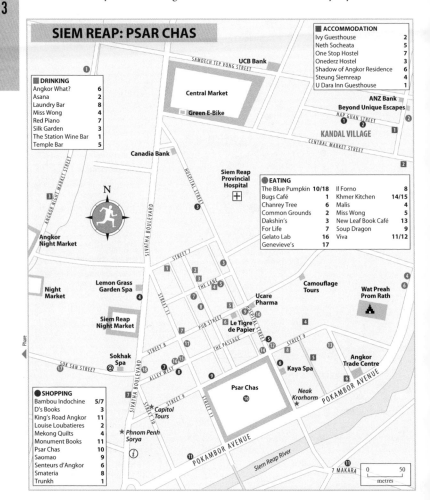

SIEM REAP: PSAR CHAS

ACCOMMODATION
Ivy Guesthouse	2
Neth Socheata	5
One Stop Hostel	7
Onederz Hostel	3
Shadow of Angkor Residence	6
Steung Siemreap	4
U Dara Inn Guesthouse	1

DRINKING
Angkor What?	6
Asana	2
Laundry Bar	8
Miss Wong	4
Red Piano	7
Silk Garden	3
The Station Wine Bar	1
Temple Bar	5

EATING
The Blue Pumpkin	10/18	Il Forno	8
Bugs Café	1	Khmer Kitchen	14/15
Chanrey Tree	6	Malis	4
Common Grounds	2	Miss Wong	5
Dakshin's	3	New Leaf Book Café	13
For Life	7	Soup Dragon	9
Gelato Lab	16	Viva	11/12
Genevieve's	17		

SHOPPING
Bambou Indochine	5/7
D's Books	3
King's Road Angkor	11
Louise Loubatieres	2
Mekong Quilts	4
Monument Books	11
Psar Chas	10
Saomao	9
Senteurs d'Angkor	6
Smateria	8
Trunkh	1

UCB Bank
SAMDECH TEP VONG STREET
Central Market
Green E-Bike
ANZ Bank
Beyond Unique Escapes
HAP GUAN STREET
KANDAL VILLAGE
CENTRAL MARKET STREET
Canadia Bank
HOSPITAL STREET
Siem Reap Provincial Hospital
ANGKOR NIGHT MARKET STREET
N
Angkor Night Market
SIVATHA BOULEVARD
STREET 7
Lemon Grass Garden Spa
THE LANE
Night Market
Ucare Pharma
Camouflage Tours
Wat Preah Prom Rath
Siem Reap Night Market
STREET 11
PUB STREET
Le Tigre de Papier
HOSPITAL STREET
STREET 9
THE PASSAGE
STREET 8
Angkor Trade Centre
Sokhak Spa
SOK SAN STREET
Kaya Spa
Phare
ALLEY WEST
Psar Chas
Neak Krorhorm
POKAMBOR AVENUE
SIVATHA BOULEVARD
STREET 9
Capitol Tours
STREET 10
STREET 11
Phnom Penh Sorya
POKAMBOR AVENUE
Siem Reap River
7 MAKARA
0   50
metres

MASSAGE, SPAS AND SWIMMING

You can hardly move in central Siem Reap without insistent calls of **"massage?"** following you down the street, particularly along Sihanouk Boulevard, Hospital Street and at the Angkor Night Market. While these are all bona fide establishments, the cheapest places, though usually clean, will probably give you your massage on a reclining chair or in a room with several massage couches, sometimes in full view of the street. Pay more and you'll get relaxing surroundings, a robe and a private room.

Most of the cheaper places offer traditional **Khmer-style massage** – neck, head, back, full massage and so on, with or without oil, while better places (see below) offer the full range of international massages, from Thai to Swedish, along with other spa treatments. A few places offer **"Seeing Hands" massage**, given by blind masseurs, while there are around a dozen **"fish massage"** places set up on pavements where you can sit with your feet in a tank for twenty minutes while shoals of little fish nibble the dead skin off your feet.

Many hotels and guesthouses have **swimming pools**, while some allow non-guests to use theirs for a fee (or if you take drinks or a meal). Unfortunately, the spectacular pools at the *Raffles Grand Hotel* and *Résidence d'Angkor* are out of bounds except for guests, although the lush pool at the *Victoria Angkor* runs them a close third and is sometimes open to non-guests, if the hotel isn't too full, although access costs a whopping $25. The *Angkor Village* hotel on 7 Makara is another option but is only open to guests in low season ($10). Cheaper pools include those at the *Stung Siemreap Hotel* ($5), the rather drab one at the *Siem Reap Hostel* ($6, including $5 bar credit), and the nicer garden pool at the *Kannell* restaurant ($5, or free with a meal). Alternatively, do as the Khmers do and head to the West Baray (see p.186) where you can swim, picnic and lounge about all day for nothing.

SPAS

Kaya Spa Hospital St, by Senteurs d'Angkor ❶063 966736, ⓦkaya-angkor.com. Traditional herbal and aromatherapy massages, plus scrubs, facials and wraps (from $21/hr).

Kong Kea Spa La Résidence d'Angkor ❶063 963390. Luxurious spa at one of the city's top hotels with signature Khmer and Indochina massages, Shirodhara, scrubs and facials (from $60/hr), plus small indoor pool.

Lemon Grass Garden Sivatha Boulevard, near the Park Hyatt hotel, plus a second branch further south on Sivatha Boulevard next to Khmer Touch restaurant ❶012 387385, ⓦlemongrassgarden.com. Excellent spa treatments at bargain prices including traditional

Khmer body, foot, head, shoulder and neck massages (most also available as "twin-touch" four-hand massages), facials, body scrubs along with manicures, pedicures and waxing (from $15/hr).

Pura Vida Citywide ❶081 357763, ⓦmassagesiem reap.com. Cut-price spa chain offering bargain, no-frills treatments at its seven branches (see the website for locations), including several dotted around Psar Chas (from $8/hr).

Sokhak Spa Sok San St ❶063 763797, ⓦsokkhakspa .com. Serene upmarket spa offering Khmer, Swedish, aromatherapy and four-hand massages along with reflexology, scrubs, wraps and facials (from $30/hr).

towards the parallel streets known as **The Passage** and **The Lane**, the entire area honeycombed with an incredible number of restaurants and bars and buzzing with tourists at pretty much any time of the day or night – a decidedly surreal experience if you've spent any time in the country's sleepier provinces.

Artisans d'Angkor

West off the southern end of Sivatha Blvd · Daily 7.30am–6.30pm · Free · ❶092 777462, ⓦartisansdangkor.com

A short walk west of Psar Chas, **Artisans d'Angkor** offers a fascinating snapshot of Cambodia's varied artisanal traditions collected under one roof in a single little crafts village. English-speaking guides meet visitors for a tour of the workshops where you can see students – selected from deprived local families – following intensive studies in skills including wood and stone carving, lacquer-work, gilding and silver-working. The gorgeous end products of all this work can be bought in the upmarket boutique attached to the centre (see p.155).

The centre has also revived local silk-weaving skills, lost during the Khmer Rouge era. Silk is produced at the **Angkor Silk Farm** (daily 8am–5pm; free) at Puok, 16km west of Siem Reap off NR6, where guides explain the intricacies of silk production and weaving. Free buses run from Artisans d'Angkor to the farm daily (9.30am & 1.30pm; returning 11.30am & 3.30pm).

Wat Damnak

East of the river opposite Psar Chas and behind the Siem Reap Art Center Night Market

Wat Damnak is one of the largest temples in Siem Reap, with dozens of colourful buildings scattered around extensive tree-shaded grounds – a pleasant respite from the heat and crowds. Originally a royal palace during the early-twentieth-century reign of King Sisowoth, the complex later served as a Khmer Rouge military depot and now doubles as the home of the Center for Khmer Studies, the largest library outside Phnom Penh.

The riverside and around

Siem Reap's nicest stroll is along the attractive **riverside walkway**, running along both sides of the Siem Reap River from Psar Chas north for 1km or so, passing a clutch of low-key sights en route before landing you at the Royal Gardens in front of the imposing *Raffles Grand Hotel d'Angkor*.

On the west side of the river just north of Psar Chas rise the spires of the imposing **Wat Preah Prom Rath**. The temple may date right back to the thirteenth century, although what you see now dates from after 1945 and features an impressively kitsch cluster of gaudy buildings festooned with Buddhist flags, and with a central vihara guarded by a pair of quaint, snow-white bulls.

North of Wat Preah Prom Rath, between the riverfront and Central Market, are the parallel Hup Guan and Central Market streets – now known collectively as **Kandal** ("middle") **Village** – which have recently been transformed into one of the city's most exclusive and artsy mini-neighbourhoods, with dozens of smart boutiques, restaurants and coffee shops crammed into the pretty colonial-style buildings.

Wat Bo

Around 200m east of the river along Street 22

The eighteenth-century **Wat Bo** is the oldest and most appealing of Siem Reap's Buddhist monasteries. The interior walls of the vihara, still in good condition, were decorated in the nineteenth century with scenes from the *Reamker* incorporating quaint scenes of everyday life – a Chinese merchant puffing on an opium pipe and French colonial soldiers watching a traditional dance performance among them. The pagoda is also home to a collection of old Buddha statues.

The Royal Gardens

At the northern end of the riverside walkway are the formal **Royal Gardens**, flanked by the venerable *Grand Hotel d'Angkor* to the north and the similarly time-warped *Victoria Angkor* to the west. On the south side of the gardens, a **shrine** to the sister deities Ang Chek and Ang Chom houses figurines of the two – thought to have been Angkorian princesses – in brass and bronze. Ang Chek is the taller of the two figures, both of which extend a hand in the characteristic "Have no fear" (*abhaya*) mudra. The statues, originally situated in the Gallery of a Thousand Buddhas at Angkor Wat, were later hidden from the eyes of invaders and treasure-hunters by successive generations of monks. Moved repeatedly, they finally arrived in their current shrine in 1990, where locals come to heap them with offerings daily.

Just to the west, now surrounded by a traffic circle and marked by a huge tree in the middle of the road, is a shrine to **Ya Tep**, a local spirit said to bring protection and luck to the Siem Reap area. The offerings left at the shrine are sometimes quite extravagant – whole cooked chickens are not unknown.

Angkor National Museum

Vithei Charles de Gaulle/Angkor Wat Rd, 1.5km north of the centre • Daily 8.30am–6.30pm • $12, children aged 6–11 $6, audio guide $5, discounts sometimes available for online reservations • ☎ 063 966601, ⓦ angkornationalmuseum.com

A visit to Siem Reap's **Angkor National Museum** is an essential adjunct to a visit to the temples themselves – the only downside is the rather hefty entrance fee. Choice pieces of ancient Khmer sculpture are beautifully exhibited in vast galleries, while multimedia presentations provide orientation, explain the wealth of statuary on display, and provide background on Cambodian history, heritage and religion. The fabulous gallery of 1000 Buddha images, in particular, should not be missed.

Kantha Bopha Children's Hospital

Vithei Charles de Gaulle/Angkor Wat Rd, 2.5km north of the centre • Concerts Thurs & Sat 7.15pm • Free • ⓦ beatocello.com

Dominated by a massive head of Jayavarman VII, the **Kantha Bopha Children's Hospital** is one of Cambodia's unsung wonders; here all treatment is free and charitable donations allow staff to be paid a living wage. Concerts are staged every Sat at 7.15pm by Dr Beat Richner – usually known as "Beatocello" – the Swiss doctor and cellist who oversees the hospital. Entrance is free, although donations, either of money, blood, or both, are warmly welcomed.

Cambodian Cultural Village

3.5km west of the centre along NR6 (Airport Rd) • Daily 8am–7pm • $15 • Around $5 from the centre by moto/tuk-tuk • ⓦ cambodianculturalvillage.com/en

West of the centre along the road to the airport, the **Cambodian Cultural Village** is one of those "see the whole country in an hour" theme parks that every country in Southeast Asia seems to have, with miniatures of many Cambodian temples and monuments alongside tableaux of wax figures portraying events from history. Given the spectacularly racked-up admission price, however, few overseas visitors bother.

War Museum

5km from the centre (4km west along NR6/Airport Rd, then 1km along a side road north) • Daily 8am–5.30pm • $5 (including guide) • ☎ 097 457 8666, ⓦ warmuseumcambodia.com • Around $5–6 from the centre by moto/tuk-tuk

Not far from the airport, Siem Reap's **War Museum** provides a salutary reminder of the three decades of fighting endured by Cambodia up until 1998. The collection includes significant quantities of military hardware including a MiG jet fighter along with various tanks and plenty of guns (some of them dating back to World War II). For many visitors, though, the museum's real highlight is the chance to talk with its guides, some of them war veterans and land-mine victims themselves, whose stories and reminiscences bring the Khmer Rouge era to life rather more vividly than the clunky piles of rusting weaponry.

ARRIVAL AND DEPARTURE   **SIEM REAP**

BY PLANE
For information about **flights** to Siem Reap, see p.22).
Airport transport Registered taxis ($8) and tuk-tuks ($6) for the 6km ride from the airport into town can be hired at a booth just outside the exit from the arrival

lounge. Minibuses from certain hotels meet planes, so look out for them if you've booked accommodation in advance, or intend to stay at one of them.
Airlines Air Asia, Siem Reap Airport (☎ 063 666333, ⓦ airasia.com); Bangkok Airways, Sivatha Boulevard

(☎063 965422); Cambodia Angkor Air, Sivatha Blvd, near Central Market (☎063 964488, ⚲cambodiaangkorair .com); Jetstar, Psar Chas (☎063 964388); Malaysia Airlines, Siem Reap Airport (☎063 964135); Vietnam Airlines, Angkor Shopping Arcade NR6/Airport Rd (☎063 964488).

BY BUS

Companies Siem Reap has a plethora of bus companies (including Capitol, Phnom Penh Sorya, Rith Mony), with most offices clustered southwest of Psar Chas around the junction of Sivatha Boulevard and Pokambor Avenue. Alternatively, tickets can be bought through most guesthouses and hotels. All run services along the popular Siem Reap–Phnom Penh route (including night buses) – the luxury buses run by Giant Ibis are the best (and priciest) of the bunch. There are significantly fewer services along the less-travelled routes to Battambang and Kompong Cham – try Phnom Penh Sorya, who have the widest network of services.

Stations and stops Buses terminating in Siem Reap pull into Chong Kov Sou bus station 3km east of town, a $4 tuk-tuk ride from the centre. A few through-buses may continue into town (or at least to the junction of NR6 and Pokambor Ave, north of the centre, a $2 tuk-tuk ride from the centre). Destinations Anlong Veng (2 daily; 2hr); Battambang (8 daily; 3hr 30min); Kompong Cham (5 daily; 6hr); Kompong Thom (20 daily; 3hr); Phnom Penh (20 daily; 6–8hr); Poipet (10 daily; 3hr); Sisophon (10 daily; 2hr).

BY SHARED TAXI AND MINIBUS

Arriving in Siem Reap Shared taxis stop at the transport stop 3km east of town, although most continue on into town.

Leaving Siem Reap Shared taxis to Phnom Penh and Kompong Thom, Sisophon (for Battambang), Poipet and Anlong Veng run from the roadside at the junction of NR6 and the turning to Siem Reap's Chong Kov Sou transport stop about 2km east of town. Destinations Anlong Veng (4 daily; 2hr); Kompong Cham (6 daily; 5hr); Kompong Thom (12 daily; 2hr 30min);

Phnom Penh (hourly; 5–6hr); Poipet (20 daily; 3hr); Sisophon (20 daily; 2hr).

BY BOAT

Arriving in Siem Reap Boats dock south of town at the port at Chong Khneas on the Tonle Sap about 15km from Siem Reap; the boat from Phnom Penh gets in between noon and early afternoon, while from Battambang it arrives mid- to late afternoon. Hotels will arrange for you to be collected from the port if you're staying with them; otherwise there's no shortage of tuk-tuks to take you into town ($6), not to mention guesthouse touts.

Leaving Siem Reap A boat leaves the Chong Khneas port daily at 7am for Phnom Penh ($35; 5–6hr) and at 8am for Battambang ($25; 6–8hr depending on water levels). You'll need to book your ticket at least a day ahead. If you buy through your guesthouse or hotel, a minibus will collect you from the door, which may mean setting out as early as 5.30am, as the vehicle will pick up passengers from various locations before heading down to the port; if you choose to make your own way to the port, allow 30min by tuk-tuk.

TO/FROM THAILAND VIA POIPET

Arriving from Thailand Many travellers arrive overland from Thailand via Poipet (see p.130), easily done in a single day, assuming you leave early enough.

Travelling to Thailand A number of Siem Reap bus companies run buses and minibuses from Siem Reap to Bangkok via Poipet, where they link up with onward transport operated by their Thai associates – although given the various scams and delays associated with buses/minibuses going in both directions, you might be better off travelling independently. Numerous buses run to the border at Poipet (3hr); alternatively, a shared taxi costs around $10 per seat, or $50 to hire the taxi outright. From the border at Poipet it's a further 4km to the Thai town of Aranyaprathet (around 60–80 baht by tuk-tuk). Getting to Aranyaprathet early will give you the option of choosing your onward transport in Thailand – either by bus, minibus or on the lunchtime train for the (approximately) 5hr trip to Bangkok.

INFORMATION

Tourist offices Government-licensed temple guides ($35/day) can be hired at any of the city's three tourist offices. These are located in the southwest corner of the Royal Gardens (daily 7.30am–5.30pm); on Sivatha Blvd near Psar Chas (Mon–Fri 8am–9pm, Sat & Sun 8am–5pm), and on Vithei Charles de Gaulle (Angkor Wat

Rd) on the way to the temples.

Siem Reap Angkor Visitors Guide This useful guide, published three times a year and available from some hotels, guesthouses and the tourist offices, contains detailed listings of places to stay, eat and drink. It's also available online at ⚲canbypublications.com.

GETTING AROUND

Information on getting to and around the **temples** is given in the Angkor section (see p.190).

By tuk-tuk or moto It's almost impossible to walk more than 10m in any direction in central Siem Reap without being

offered a tuk-tuk or moto – useful if you're staying somewhere out of the centre (count on $1/2 for journeys across town).

By motorbike Foreign tourists are technically banned from riding motorbikes around Siem Reap and the temples, ostensibly to safeguard them from having their bikes stolen by agents of the rental companies in order to elicit a replacement fee (see box, p.35), while it's also been claimed that tourists can't safely negotiate the chaotic traffic. In practice the ban is now widely flouted, with many places around town renting bikes out for around $12/day, but check the latest situation before you ride one to see whether you're likely to be pulled over by the police and fined – not to mention the serious risk of theft.

By e-bike E-bikes take the sweat out of cycling round the temples and also avoid the hassles associated with hiring a motorbike in Siem Reap. They're available from a number of places including Green E-Bike (☎ 095 700130, ✆ greene -bike.com), on St 6 on the south side of the Central Market ($10 a day). There are also a number of free recharge stations around Siem Reap and Angkor.

By bike Bicycles are available for rent in many places: for quality mountain bikes visit Camouflage (see below). For something cheaper, one option is the useful shop on the roundabout just east of the river at the junction of 7 Makara and River Rd, which has basic gearless bikes for $2/day, or fancier mountain bikes for around $4.

TOURS AND ACTIVITIES

There are tours aplenty in Siem Reap, although many budget outfits offer identikit temple or Tonle Sap itineraries, with rushed schedules and large group sizes – rather than booking the first tour proposed by your guesthouse or hotel it's well worth checking out the **operators** below. As a very general rule of thumb count on around $50 per person for a day, or $100/day for longer trips with overnight stays. For cookery classes, see p.151.

GENERAL TOURS

About Asia ☎ 092 121059, ✆ aboutasiatravel.com Upmarket one- and two-day guided tours of the temples by leading Siem Reap-based operator (see p.21) using innovative "crowd avoidance" itineraries to beat the rush.

Beyond Unique Escapes Kandal Village ☎ 063 969269, ✆ beyonduniqueescapes.com. This excellent operator is a good first port of call, with quality tours at surprisingly affordable prices, a maximum eight people per group and guaranteed departures irrespective of however many people do (or don't) turn up. Trips include a "day in the life" village tour, maybe helping with rice planting or harvesting; Tonle Sap tours to Kompong Khleang (depending on the season); and a good cookery class (see p.151). They can also customize private tours to suit, including hiking, cycling and photography trips. Full day tours $32–44/person.

Triple Adventures Cambodia ☎ 0888 366004, ✆ tripleacambodia.com. Enjoyable three-in-one day-trips combining a visit to Kompong Khleang floating village, lunch with the locals and a countryside bike ride. $39.

CYCLING AND ADVENTURE TOURS

As well as the cycling-tour operators listed below, a number of places offer **quad-biking**, including Quad Adventure Cambodia (✆ quad-adventure-cambodia.com), Siem Reap Quad Bike Adventure (✆ srquadbikeadventure .com) and Cambodia Quad Bike (✆ cambodiaquadbik .com). **Dirt-biking** can be arranged through Siem Reap Dirt Bikes (✆ siemreapdirtbikes.com), Cambodia Dirtbike Tours (✆ cambodiadirtbike.com), Kickstart Cambodia (✆ kickstartcambodia.com), Cambodia Trails (✆ cambodiatrails.com) and Hidden Cambodia (see below).

Cambodia Jeep Tours ☎ 012 908524, ✆ cambodia jeep.com. Tours in authentic American Army jeeps – you can even have a go driving one yourself. Itineraries include the usual temples, plus backcountry trips and tours to Phnom Kulen, Kbal Spean, Beng Mealea and elsewhere.

Camouflage Down the road opposite the northeast end of Pub St ☎ 012 884909, ✆ camouflagecambodia .com. Guided bike tours (20–65km) featuring a great range of temple and countryside itineraries, including a challenging Phnom Kulen itinerary. Trips $25–85.

Flight of the Gibbon 1km north of Ta Keo temple in Angkor Archaeological Park ☎ 096 999 9101, ✆ treetopasia.com. Get a monkey's-eye view of the forest canopy from ziplines and sky bridges weaving through the treetops, connected by high-level observation platforms – needless to say, you'll need a head for heights and a reasonable level of physical fitness. $59/person, and you'll also need an Angkor pass to reach the site.

Grasshopper Adventures Street 26 ☎ 012 462165, ✆ grasshopperadventures.com. Half- and full-day cycling tours of Angkor (including sunrise tours) and the local countryside on quality mountain bikes with expert guides and backup vehicle, plus fun (if pricey) combined cycling and kayaking tours. From $35/person.

Hidden Cambodia Adventure Tours Off Angkor Wat Rd, near Jayavarman VII Hospital ☎ 012 655201, ✆ hiddencambodia.com. Long-running operator specializing in multi-day adventure tours by dirt bike, as well as cycling, hiking, camping and 4WD trips off the beaten track to numerous destinations, including "humanitarian" tours with the focus on sustainable tourism. They also have their own lodge at Koh Ker.

Indo Chine EX ☎ 092 650096, ✆ indochineex.com. Kayaking trips on the Tonle Sap and around Prek Toal plus hikes and bike rides through the countryside around the temples and up to Phnom Kulen.

3

HORSERIDING

The Happy Ranch ✆ 012 920002, ⊛ thehappyranch .com. Enjoyable horseriding trips (1–4hr; from $20/hr) through the local countryside for everyone from complete beginners to experienced equestrians, plus horse-cart rides (1–2hr). Many of the horses are rescue horses – any visiting vets who can donate some time (even a few hours) are warmly welcomed.

YOGA AND MEDITATION

For drop-in yoga and meditation, the Peace Café (below) is a good option. There are also several rustic **yoga** and **meditation** retreats in the countryside around Siem Reap, including the Hariharalaya Meditation Retreat Centre (⊛ hariharalaya.com), Angkor Zen Gardens Retreat Center (⊛ angkorzen.com), and the Angkor Bodhi Tree Retreat and Yoga Centre (⊛ angkorbodhitree.com).

Peace Café River Rd ✆ 063 965210, ⊛ peacecafeangkor .org. Daily yoga sessions, plus private meditation classes and free "monk chat" sessions (Tues & Wed) offering the chance to talk to an English-speaking Cambodian monk.

NATURE AND WILDLIFE

Osmose Nature Tours ✆ 063 765506, ⊛ osmosetonlesap.net. Local NGO running ecotours to Tonle Sap and the bird sanctuary at Prek Toal (see p.160); can also organize local homestays.

Sam Veasna Centre Street 26 ✆ 063 963710, ⊛ samveasna.org. Cambodia's leading birdwatching specialist, with trips to major ornithological hotspots (including Prek Toal, Ang Trapeang Thmor, the "vulture restaurant" in Preah Vihear district and Seima Protected Forest in Mondulkiri) and exclusive access to Wildlife Conservation Society sites nationwide. Tours are well run and led by expert guides, although probably for keen twitchers and wildlife aficionados only, given the prices. Generally well over $100/person/day.

PHOTOGRAPHY

Angkor Wat Photography Tours ✆ 097 361 2648, ⊛ angkor-wat-photography.com. Rewarding photographic tours including day and night visits to Angkor Wat, plus trips around Phnom Kulen, Tonle Sap and after-dark Siem Reap.

Peace of Angkor Tours ✆ 092 874785, ⊛ peaceof angkor.com. Photography tours of Angkor and elsewhere, including trips to Prek Toal sanctuary and more remote temples including Preah Vihear.

ACCOMMODATION

Accommodation is scattered all over town. Many cheaper places can be found **around Psar Chas**, while there are further guesthouses **east of the river**, particularly in the little enclave around Street 20. Larger and more upmarket establishments tend to be located further north of the centre along **Airport** and **Angkor Wat roads**. If you fancy escaping the tourist hordes, note that ⊛ homestay.com have a number of **homestays** in the area.

AROUND PSAR CHAS

Blossoming Romduol Lodge Psakrom St ✆ 012 545811, ⊛ blossomingromduolsiemreap.com; map p.139. Efficient modern hotel with big bright tiled a/c rooms with balcony plus a good-sized pool and neat pavilion restaurant out the front – although a bit too much piped muzak. Excellent value at current rates. BB $18

Golden Temple Residence Sok San Rd ✆ 063 212222, ⊛ goldentempleresidence.com; map p.139. Stylish and enjoyable boutique hotel, full of colour and contemporary Cambodian style. The bright and spacious rooms come with smooth minimalist decor and all mod cons, and there's also a fine restaurant, spa, and a lovely pool complete with miniature waterwheel. Rates are on the high side, but include a 1hr complimentary massage, one free meal, airport pick-up and free apsara show. BB $200

Hi Siem Reap Deluxe Hostel River Rd ✆ 063 765569, ⊛ hisiemreap.com; map p.139. In a riverside house just south of the centre, this is more intimate and less institutional than most other hostels in town, with a mix of ten- and (for $1 extra) eight-bed dorms all with individual bed-sockets and reading lights. There's also a very comfortable four-bed female dorm and a few spacious, colourfully painted rooms, plus nice swimming pool and small bar, pool table, café, and free tea and coffee. Dorm $7; double BB $20

Ivy Guest House Kandal Village ✆ 012 380516, ⊛ ivy -guesthouse.com; map p.140. In an old, rustic, ivy-clad wooden house in cool Kandal Village, this is a Siem Reap guesthouse of the old school – basic, but with bags of character. Downstairs is a laidback café with bar and pool table, upstairs is a nice little veranda; accommodation is a mix of simple fan rooms (with cold water) and slightly posher a/c rooms (with hot water). Fan $8; a/c $15

Mingalar Inn (formerly the Mandalay Inn) Psakrom St ✆ 093 798079, ⊛ mingalarinn.com; map p.139. Long-running Siem Reap stalwart, and still one of the best cheapies in the city centre with a range of comfortable fan and a/c rooms (all with hot water), although some are beginning to look their age. The helpful staff can arrange all kinds of tours, and there's also a small gym and a good little restaurant. Excellent single rates, with rooms from just $8. Fan $15; a/c $20

Moon Residence Psakrom St ✆ 063 900085, ⊛ the moonresidence.com; map p.139. Beguiling little bolthole on busy Psakrom St, set around a serene courtyard pool, with restaurant and spa, and 18 well-equipped rooms in a cool minimalist style. A real haven just a few minutes' walk from the centre. BB $\overline{\underline{\$80}}$

Neth Socheata Off Pokambor Ave ✆063 963294, Ⓦnethsocheatahotel.com; map p.140. Central but very peaceful mid-range hotel on a pretty little pedestrianized alleyway just off the riverfront. Rooms (all with a/c and hot water) are nicely furnished and reasonably priced, although the cheapest lack windows. $\overline{\underline{\$30}}$

Onederz Hostel (formerly the One Stop Hostel @ Angkor Night Market) Next to Angkor Night Market ✆063 963525, Ⓔonestophostelsr2@gmail.com; map p.140. This large glass building in a very central location is one of Siem Reap's nicest hostels, with a spacious, light-filled downstairs lounge and café, rooftop pool and a mix of 12- and 6-bed dorms, all a/c and with individual bed-lights and sockets. Larger dorm $\overline{\underline{\$8}}$; smaller dorm $\overline{\underline{\$9}}$

One Stop Hostel Sivatha Boulevard ✆063 963625, Ⓔonestophostelsr@gmail.com; map p.140. One of the town's better and more modern hostels, with a selection of dorms, all a/c, with beds equipped with individual sockets and lights, plus hot water in all bathrooms. Choose between standard 10-bed dorms and smaller 4- or 6-bed dorms. There's also a ladies-only dorm. Larger dorm $\overline{\underline{\$7}}$; smaller dorm $\overline{\underline{\$8}}$

Shadow of Angkor Residence Pokambor Ave ✆063 964774, Ⓦshadowangkorresidence.com; map p.140. Recently renovated little hotel with smart modern rooms (all a/c with hot water) in an old colonial shophouse by the river – excellently located, and at competitive rates. $\overline{\underline{\$30}}$

Steung Siemreap Street 9 ✆063 965169, Ⓦsteung siemreaphotel.com; map p.140. Biggish mid-range hotel on a quiet street in the heart of town, offering big, attractively old-fashioned and nicely furnished wood-floored rooms plus swimming pool, gym, sauna and restaurant. Quoted prices are on the high side, although discounts are often available via online booking sites. $\overline{\underline{\$99}}$

Villa Medamrei Psakrom St ✆063 763636, Ⓦvillamedamrei.com; map p.139. Attractive and very affordable little boutique hotel in a central location and with exceptionally attentive staff. It's surprisingly stylish given the modest price, with stylish rooms (all with a/c, fridge and safe) clad in bright fabrics and colourful artworks covering every available surface. BB $\overline{\underline{\$30}}$

U-Dara Inn Guesthouse Kandal Village ✆063 760980, Ⓦu-darainn.com; map p.140. In a colonial-era shophouse in cool but quiet Kandal Village, this place has bags of old-fashioned character plus neat and cosy wood-pannelled rooms (all a/c with hot water). An enjoyably low-key throwback to earlier and less touristy times. $\overline{\underline{\$15}}$

EAST OF THE RIVER
SOUTH OF SAMDECH TEP VONG STREET

★**Angkor Village** Street 26, off Wat Bo St ✆063 963361, Ⓦangkorvillage.com; map p.139. Idyllic "village resort", much copied, but rarely bettered.

Accommodation is in Khmer-style wooden bungalows dotted around lush gardens and enveloped in greenery, like a miniature – but very luxurious – Cambodian village right in the heart of the city. Facilities include a nice pool and classy restaurant. BB $\overline{\underline{\$122}}$

Golden Temple Hotel 7 Makara ✆012 756655, Ⓦgoldentemplehotel.com; map p.139. Deservedly popular little resort hotel (part of the same group as the even more alluring *Golden Temple Residence* near Artisans d'Angkor) in a stylish building with traditional Khmer touches set around attractive gardens and bright, colourfully furnished rooms. There's also a spa, attractive restaurant and a good-sized pool complete with fancy fountain. Rates include a complimentary 1hr massage. BB $\overline{\underline{\$120}}$

Karavansara Street 25 ✆063 760678, Ⓦkaravansara .com; map p.139. Attractively renovated French colonial villa with a range of well-equipped rooms: choose between the slightly austere white Garden Courtyard Rooms and the fancier Colonial Heritage Suites. Facilities include a small rooftop pool, plus the upmarket *Taberu* restaurant which is set in a traditional Khmer wooden house in the garden. $\overline{\underline{\$47}}$

Rambutan Hotel (formerly the Golden Banana Boutique Resort) Phum Wat Damnak ✆063 766655, Ⓦrambutans.info; map p.139. Peaceful little hideaway (not to be confused with the adjacent *Golden Banana* or *Golden Banana Boutique Villa*), which is more boutique guesthouse than resort, with cool bungalows decorated in chic modern Asian style around an inviting pool. Their sister property, the *Rambutan Resort* (a few doors down the road) is very similar. BB $\overline{\underline{\$91}}$

★**Sala Lodges** South of the centre ✆063 766699, Ⓦsalalodges.com; map p.139. Stunning boutique resort with accommodation in eleven genuine Khmer wooden village houses, sourced from locations around the region and then dismantled, shipped to Siem Reap and painstakingly reassembled in situ. Each has been luxuriously renovated, offering a remarkable combination of bespoke luxury and authentic Khmer atmosphere. The result is unlike anything else in the country, like some fairy-tale rural village, surrounded by attractive gardens with a lovely infinity pool at its centre. Facilities include a bright café in the soaring reception building (a work of art in its own right), and rates include breakfast, free bikes and tuk-tuk. Pricey, but memorable – and rates fall significantly during low season. BB $\overline{\underline{\$330}}$

Shadow of Angkor Villa Wat Bo St ✆063 760363, Ⓦshadowangkorvilla.com; map p.139. Well-run and very competitively priced modern hotel with big, bright and well-equipped, if slightly bare, rooms (all with a/c and hot water), plus pool and restaurant. $\overline{\underline{\$30}}$

The Siem Reap Hostel 7 Makara ✆063 964660, Ⓦthesiemreaphostel.com; map p.139. The oldest hostel in town and still going strong, despite burgeoning competition. All dorms are a/c with individual bed-lights and sockets; choose between standard dorms with 8 or 10

3

3

beds and outside bathrooms or nicer six-bed deluxe dorms with in-dorm bathrooms and little balconies (but don't bother with the overpriced and unappealling rooms). There's also a small spa, pool table, yoga classes, tour desk, a rather drab little pool and a brilliant little a/c mini-cinema. Basic dorms $\underline{\$8}$; deluxe dorms $\underline{\$10}$; doubles $\underline{\$30}$

Soria Moria Wat Bo St ☎063 964768, ⓦthesoriamoria .com; map p.139. Siem Reap's most socially responsible hotel, established in 2007 by Norwegian expat Kristin Holdø Hansen and with majority-ownership now passed onto its staff, giving the local community a long-term stake in the success of the business. Rooms are bright and cheerful, with a hint of Scandinavian minimalist style (superior rooms for $10 extra are significantly larger), while the attractive *Fusion Kitchen* restaurant downstairs serves a good selection of Khmer classics and international tapas – all dishes cost just $1 on Wed. BB $\underline{\$40}$

Viroth's Villa Street 23 ☎063 761720, ⓦviroth-villa .com; map p.139. Super-cool boutique retreat sporting modern rooms with clean white decor and all mod cons, plus tranquil grounds with a spa and tiny swimming pool. BB $\underline{\$75}$

STREET 20 AND AROUND

Babel Off Street 20 ☎063 965474, ⓦbabelsiemreap .com; map p.139. Western-owned guesthouse in the little Wat Bo Rd backpacker enclave. The large, pristine white rooms come with a/c and hot water (some also have bathtubs), and there's a nice restaurant and bar, with seating in the verdant hotel garden. $\underline{\$25}$

European Off Street 20 ☎012 582237, ⓦeuropean -guesthouse.com; map p.139. Quiet guesthouse with large, spotless a/c rooms (all with hot water) set around an attractive, shady garden, plus a small but rather unappetizing-looking pool. Excellent value, if you don't mind the slightly moribund atmosphere. $\underline{\$12}$

Golden Takeo Off St 20 ☎012 785424, ⓦgoldentakeo guesthouse.com; map p.139. Another of the Wat Bo backpacker places offering comfortable accommodation at cut-throat prices. Rooms (with a/c and hot water for $4 extra) are nicely decorated with wall paintings and well equipped with TVs, desk and kettle. Excellent value, although the whole place is singularly lacking in atmosphere. $\underline{\$8}$

Happy Guest House Off St 20 ☎063 963815, ⓦhappy angkorguesthouse.com; map p.139. The liveliest of the Wat Bo backpacker places, centred on a sociable and shady pavilion restaurant out front. Rooms aren't quite as nice as in some other nearby places but are acceptable, and decent value – albeit a bit bare and past their best. Fan rooms come with cold water only, a/c with hot. Fan $\underline{\$9}$; a/c $\underline{\$12}$

Home Sweet Home Street 20 ☎063 760279; map p.139. This rather sterile place isn't nearly as homely as the name suggests, although rooms (with either fan and cold water or a/c and hot) are neat, clean and pretty good value at the price. Fan $\underline{\$8}$; a/c $\underline{\$13}$

Mom's Wat Bo St ☎012 630170, ⓦmomguesthouse .com; map p.139. Long-running establishment that is now more of a hotel than a guesthouse, but still owned by the same family and with super-friendly service. Rooms (all with hot water, a/c, safe and fridge) are spacious and spotless, and there's also a medium-sized saltwater pool out the back. $\underline{\$20}$

★ **La Résidence d'Angkor** Achasvar St ☎063 963390, ⓦresidencedangkor.com; map p.139. One of Siem Reap's top addresses, set in lush grounds and with oodles of cool contemporary Cambodian style, from the cavernous wood-framed entrance hall through to the stunning swimming pool fed by water bubbling from a lion and a linga. Rooms are luxuriously appointed with teak furniture, Khmer cotton and silk fabrics, and bamboo screens to mask the massive free-form bathtubs, and facilities include classy restaurant, airy pavilion bar, spa and gym. BB $\underline{\$430}$

★ **Two Dragons** Street 20 ☎063 965107, ⓦtwo dragons-asia.com; map p.139. There's a real home-from-home feel at this old Siem Reap stalwart, with friendly and efficient service, cosy and nicely furnished rooms (all with a/c, hot water and cable TV) and a small restaurant out front serving a good range of Thai, Khmer and Western food. $\underline{\$18}$

NORTH OF NR6

Angkor Village Resort Apsara Rd ☎063 963561, ⓦangkorvillage.com; map p.139. Luxurious, supersized version of the *Angkor Village* hotel (see p.147), with beautifully equipped cottages scattered around luxuriant gardens and a 200m-long, river-shaped swimming pool. $\underline{\$150}$

Borann l'Auberge des Temples North of NR6 ☎063 964740, ⓦborann.com; map p.139. Intimate and very peaceful lodge with just twenty rooms in five bungalows spread around extensive gardens stuffed with trees and shrubs. Rooms are beautifully designed with traditional Khmer styling (but no TVs – which adds to the general sense of peace), and there's a big pool and decent restaurant. BB $\underline{\$65}$

Heritage Suites Near Wat Po Lanka, 500m north of NR6 ☎063 969100, ⓦheritagesuiteshotel.com; map p.139. Secluded, luxurious Relais & Chateaux hotel with rooms and suites in a mix of colonial and contemporary styles (some with their own private gardens, including open-air shower or Jacuzzi). A traditional-style wooden hall houses the lounge, bar and an excellent gallery restaurant with Western/Khmer fusion food. Swimming pool and poolside bar, spa and airport pick-up by 1962 Mercedes. BB $\underline{\$150}$

Natura Riverside Rd ☎063 763980, ⓦnaturahotel resort.com; map p.139. As the name suggests, nature is very much to the fore at this seductive little riverside boutique resort. The minimalist white rooms (better on style than size and creature comforts) are set around a small garden and half-swallowed by the surrounding trees. There's also a saltwater pool and restaurant. BB $\underline{\$89}$

La Noria River Rd ☎063 964242, ⓦlanoriaangkor.com; map p.139. Suave boutique resort, with neat bungalows dotted around a lush garden and swimming pool. Rooms are decorated in a mix of cool whites and colourful Khmer fabrics, while regular shadow-puppet shows (see p.156) are held in the rustic garden restaurant. $50

★ **Pavillon d'Orient** Road 60 ☎ 098 655738, ⌨ pavillon-orient-hotel.com; map pp.162–163. Atmospheric setting that evokes the classic era of Cambodian travel in the 1920s and 1930s. Rooms are in four "mansions" scattered around a beautiful garden, decorated in a mix of colonial and Khmer style, with polished wooden floors and traditional fabrics. Facilities include two saltwater pools, spa and open-air restaurant. Rates include free use of a tuk-tuk throughout your stay. $95

Villa Loti 225 River Rd ☎ 063 963879, ⌨ resortla villaloti.com; map p.139. A real urban oasis, and a refreshing alternative to your usual concrete-box hotel, set in a lush little bamboo-walled garden with small pool and a surprisingly classy little restaurant. The eight stylish rooms occupy a traditional-style wooden house at the back, beautifully furnished with wooden fixtures and fittings in quasi-colonial style. BB $110

TAPHUL STREET AND AROUND

Angkor Pearl Off Taphul St ☎ 063 966202, ⌨ angkor pearl.com; map p.139. The ugly exterior conceals one of Siem Reap's better mid-range options, with very comfortable and surprisingly stylish rooms sporting wood-panelled walls and ceilings, and Khmer fabrics. Competitively priced, and with attentive service, plus a small restaurant and bar. BB $35

Auberge Mont Royal d'Angkor Taphul St ☎ 063 964044, ⌨ auberge-mont-royal.com/html; map p.139. Set in an attractive orange building, half hidden behind a lovely tree-smothered veranda, this appealing little hotel offers plenty of old-world Francophone atmosphere. The rooms are a little characterless, compared with the spacious lobby lounge, but perfectly comfortable and very affordable. BB $45

Frangipani Green Garden Hotel Oum Khun St ☎ 063 963342, ⌨ greengardenhome.com; map p.139. Intimate little mid-range hotel (more like an upmarket guesthouse, really) in an attractive veranda-fronted house set in a shady garden with swimming pool. The bright, white rooms all come with a/c and hot water, while colourful Cambodian fabrics provide a welcome splash of colour. $32

Park Hyatt Siem Reap Sivatha Blvd ☎ 063 966001, ⌨ siemreap.park.hyatt.com; map p.139. Landmark downtown establishment with 2m-tall apsaras welcoming you at each entrance and subtle hints of old French Indochina lurking in the architectural shadows. Inside there's a lovely sunken courtyard plus tree-studded pond and a skinny swimming pool beneath triumphal arches, while in-house amenities include *The Living Room* bar-café (with enjoyable faux-library decor) and the *Glasshouse* patisserie-cum-coffee-shop (with great ice cream). $300

The Villa Siem Reap Taphul St ☎ 063 761036, ⌨ thevillasiemreap.com; map p.139. Good-looking boutique guesthouse with neat a/c rooms (all with hot water, minibar and safe) decorated in minimalist whites and greys, plus three fancier bungalows ($45/55) in the lush gardens. Facilities include a decent-sized pool with plenty of loungers and a nice little patio restaurant. $30

THE ROYAL GARDENS AND AROUND

FCC Angkor Pokambor Ave ☎ 063 760280, ⌨ fccc ambodia.com; map p.139. Surrounded by trees in a picturesque riverfront location, this branch of Phnom Penh's *FCC* is more modern but still has plenty of character. Stylish rooms come with all the amenities you'd expect of a modern, boutique hotel, with a good restaurant, bar and spa. $80

Raffles Grand Hotel d'Angkor Royal Gardens ☎ 063 963888, ⌨ raffles.com/siemreap; map p.139. Siem Reap's most famous address, still sporting much of the colonial atmosphere it had when it opened back in 1932. Rooms, suites and villas are furnished in luxurious period style, decorated with Khmer artefacts and provided with all mod cons. Facilities include a stylish selection of restaurants and bars, bakery, boutiques, business centre, gym, tennis court, the sumptuous Amrita spa and a vast pool. $380

★ **Shinta Mani** Junction of Oum Khun & 14th St ☎ 063 761998, ⌨ shintamani.com; map p.139. Serene modern urban resort in a quiet side street a short walk from the centre. Run as part of the Shinta Mani Foundation, which supports a wide range of projects, with staff given a genuine stake in the success of the business – which accounts for the supremely friendly, attentive and efficient service found throughout the hotel. Rooms are spacious and superbly equipped, overlooking a central garden courtyard with big pool, and there's also an excellent restaurant and spa. $190

Victoria Angkor Central Park, west side of the Royal Gardens ☎ 063 760428, ⌨ victoriaangkorhotel.com; map p.139. Rivalling the *Raffles Grand Hotel d'Angkor* for period atmosphere, but at roughly half the price. The extensive facilities include a choice of restaurants, the lovely *L'Explorateur* bar (see p.153), spa, sauna, boutique and a gorgeous pool swathed in greenery. Angkor trips in the hotel's two vintage Citroens are also available, should you fancy splashing out $270 for a day's touring around the temples. BB $215

AIRPORT ROAD

★ **Bou Savy** Off Airport Rd ☎ 063 964967, ⌨ bousavy guesthouse.com; map p.139. Excellent family-run guesthouse, which, despite the inconvenient location, is particularly popular with volunteers and long-staying guests thanks to its homely atmosphere. There's a mix of rooms (all with hot water and fridge) spread over two buildings, so you might want to have a look at a few before you choose. The plant-strewn courtyard café is a nice place to hangout, and there's also a small but pretty pool.

Advance bookings recommended; rates include free pick-up. BB: Fan $\underline{\$18}$; a/c $\underline{\$25}$

AROUND SIEM REAP

Navutu Dreams 2.5km southeast of the centre ☎ 063 964864, ⓦ navutudreams.com; map pp.162–163. Luxurious "wellness retreat" arranged around a trio of pools and a giant thatched restaurant set amid rambling gardens. The 28 bright "eco-chic" rooms come with private garden (more expensive ones also have lap pools) while

activities include physical and mental detox programmes, yoga and cookery classes, and there's a fine spa. $\underline{\$90}$

Sojourn Treak Vilage Rd, Treak village, around 4km south of town ☎ 012 923437, ⓦ sojournsiemreap.com; map pp.162–163. Idyllic country resort set in peaceful countryside. The ten rooms, decorated in cool, modern Asian style, are in villas around a small pool and boast all mod cons (some have outdoor showers). Facilities include the cool Origins spa and attractive open-air thatched restaurant. Rates include breakfast and transfer to airport/port/bus station. $\underline{\$100}$

EATING

There's an astonishing number of **places to eat** in Siem Reap – you could stay a year and still not devour everything the city has to offer. Options range from cheap and cheerful backpacker cafés through to some of the best Khmer food you'll ever taste at places like *Cuisine Wat Damnak*, *Sugar Palm* and *Malis*, along with numerous socially responsible training cafés like *Haven* and *Marum*. There are also heaps of Western and international options, plus a burgeoning **coffee-house** scene. It's also a good place to challenge your tastebuds with some local **insect cuisine** at places like *Bugs Café*, or from various street hawkers around Psar Chas.

PSAR CHAS AND AROUND

The Blue Pumpkin Hospital St; map p.140. The original branch of this hugely popular café-cum-bakery, which now has outlets all round town. Construct your own snack or picnic from a wide selection of freshly baked breads, sandwiches, cakes, shakes and ice creams – and there's even a fair selection of alcoholic beverages, served in the "Cool Lounge" upstairs. There's a second branch nearby on Sivatha Blvd. Daily 6am–11pm.

Dakshin's Hospital St ☎ 063 964311; map p.140. This cool and spacious new outlet is a cut above the many other slightly ropey Indian establishments around town. The menu features a good range of North Indian meat ($7.50–8.50) and veg ($5–6.50) classics – tandooris, birianis, kormas and so on – plus a few South Indian dishes including thalis and dosas, all served in big portions, richly spiced. Pricey, but worth it. Daily 11am–2.30pm & 5–10.30pm.

For Life The Lane ☎ 012 545426, ⓦ forliferestaurant .com; map p.140. A local expat favourite, and usually a haven of calm amid the madness of Psar Char, serving excellent Khmer food (mains $4.50–5) including loads of authentic dishes such as *prahok ktis* (minced pork in fish sauce), *bobor* (porridge) plus all sorts of soups and salads. Daily 11am–11pm.

Gelato Lab Alley West ☎ 089 987469, ⓦ facebook .com/gelatolabsiemreap; map p.140. This shoebox-sized café does only two things and does them both very well. The superb gelatos and sorbets feature classic Italian flavours alongside more unusual creations including Cocco (with organic coconut from Koh Kong), chocolate with Kampot pepper, and dragonfruit sorbet, while the excellent selection of quality coffees warms the mouth nicely afterwards. Daily 9am–11.30pm.

Genevieve's Sok San Rd ☎ 081 410783, ⓦ facebook .com/GenevievesRestaurant; map p.140. Wildly popular

restaurant serving up a great selection of Khmer and international dishes, including good vegetarian options (mains $5–7). There's Western comfort food on offer, such as lasagne, but also fancier creations like pan-fried duck breast and slow-cooked pork belly, while the Khmer dishes are an explosion of Asian flavours – the chicken amok is a triumph. Reservations strongly advised, particularly for dinner. Mon–Sat noon to 2pm & 5.30–9.30pm.

Il Forno Between The Lane & Pub St ☎ 078 208174, ⓦ ilfornorestaurantsiemreap.com; map p.140. In the buzzing heart of the Psar Chas tourist zone, this stylish Italian restaurant feels like a busy corner of Milan, London or New York. The menu features superb pizzas straight from the Neapolitan wood-fired oven, excellent home-made pasta and top-notch mains using quality ingredients (black ink tagliolini with prawns and zucchini, for example, or porcini mushrooms with saffron). Pizza and pasta $5–10, mains $10–18. Daily noon–11pm.

Khmer Kitchen Corner of Hospital St and St 9 ☎ 012 763468, ⓦ khmerkitchens.com; map p.140. Excellent, inexpensive Khmer food (mains $4.50–5) in an atmospheric old shophouse, plus a few Thai dishes and cheap beer. There's also a second (smaller) branch at the corner of St 11 and Alley West (☎ 012 349501). Daily 9am–11pm

Miss Wong The Lane ☎ 092 428332, ⓦ misswong.net; map p.140. Elegant little venue, with opulent 1930s Shanghai-style decor – all moody lighting and rich-red walls. It bills itself as a cocktail bar (see p.153) but also has a short but excellent selection of classy contemporary Chinese food; mains ($7) include wine-flavoured chicken thigh and tea-smoked tofu pockets with mushroom stuffing, plus dumplings, hotpots, noodles and wonton. Daily 6pm–1am.

New Leaf Book Café Off Pokambor Ave ☎ 063 766016, ⓦ newleafbookcafe.org; map p.140. This handsome and sociable café is one of the centre's nicest places to hang out

COOKERY CLASSES

Taking a **cookery course** offers a great way to learn more about Cambodian cuisine. Classes typically last around three hours, starting with a visit to a local market to buy ingredients, after which you get into the kitchen and start cooking under the guidance of a trained chef, finishing off by eating the meal you've just prepared.

Beyond Unique Escapes Kandal Village ☎063 969269, ⓦ beyonduniqueescapes.com. Cooking classes (twice daily) with a difference, held just outside town and swapping the usual market visit for a walk through a rural village to see local food production at first hand and the chance to meet a village family and learn about Khmer cooking in a Cambodian home – after which you head to Beyond's purpose-built cooking pavilion in the village to have a go yourself. Vegetarian menus available. $24 half day, $40 full day.

Champey Cookery Cottage East of Pub St ☎077 566455; map p.140. Popular twice-daily classes with market visit plus cooking class, with your completed meal served in the attractive dining room out the back. A complimentary box of spices and recipe book are thrown in as part of the price. $25.

Cooks in Tuk Tuks The River Garden, River road, north of NR6, west of the river ☎063 965263, ⓦ therivergarden.info. Classes at this hotel start with the obligatory market visit, before cooking up a lunchtime feast with the produce you've purchased. $35.

Le Tigre de Papier Pub St, next to Angkor What? (see p.153) ☎012 265811. The original Siem Reap cooking class, running since 2003 at this Pub Street restaurant. Thrice-daily classes (10am, 1pm and 5pm) begin with the usual market visit to buy ingredients, followed by the preparation (and consumption) of a main course of your choice from the restaurant menu, plus starter and dessert. $15 (or $24 with two mains and two starters).

3

---

while browsing the extensive selection of secondhand books for sale. Good coffee and drinks, served in recycled jars with bamboo straws, plus snacks, sandwiches, all-day breakfasts and other comforting café fare. All profits go to support local causes. Daily 7.30am–9.30pm.

Soup Dragon Hospital St ☎012 731152; map p.140. Popular restaurant spread over three floors of a street-corner building, with great views of the crowds below. The food's not bad either, with a mainly Vietnamese menu (mains $6–8) featuring classics such as *bánh xèo* (rice pancakes), pho, hotpots, soups, stir-fries and spicy salads, plus a few Khmer and Western dishes. Daily 6am–midnight.

Viva Hospital St ☎092 209154, ⓦ vivasiemreap.com; map p.140. Wildly popular Mexican restaurant serving tasty cover versions of all the usual Tex-Mex classics (mains $5–7) including quesadillas, nachos, enchiladas, tacos and burritos galore. The restaurant's signature margaritas are cheap and go down fast – as do many of the punters come closing time. There's also a second branch on St 11. Daily 6.30am–midnight.

KANDAL VILLAGE AND AROUND

Chanrey Tree Pokombor Ave ☎063 767997, ⓦ chanreytree.com; map p.140. Stylish and romantic modern riverside restaurant serving up a short menu of authentic Khmer dishes (most mains around $10) given a fine-dining makeover. Choose from classic curries, stir-fries and salads or more unusual offerings including grilled stuffed frog or *prahok ktis*, a classic Cambodian combination of pork cooked with curry spices and fermented fish sauce. Daily 11am–2.30pm & 6–10.30pm.

Common Grounds Kandal Village ☎063 965687; map p.140. Smooth modern Kandal Village café serving good fresh cakes, sandwiches and light meals ($4–6), plus some of the best coffee in town. Profits go to support local charitable projects. Mon–Sat 7am–8pm.

Malis Pokambor Ave ☎015 824888, ⓦ malis-restaurant.com; map p.140. In a spectacular riverside Art Deco building with space for 300 diners, this new Siem Reap offshoot of the famous Phnom Penh restaurant (see p.85) serves up classy fine-dining renditions of traditional Khmer food (starters $8–10; mains $8–25). Begin with, say, Takeo sausages or beef skewers marinaded in *kroeung* and peppercorns then move on to fish head amok, Takeo pork chops or Kampot crab fried rice, all lovingly crafted and beautifully presented. Not cheap, but well worth it. Daily 11am–2pm & 6.30–10.30pm.

SIVATHA BOULEVARD AND AROUND

Bugs Café Angkor Night Market St ☎017 764560, ⓦ bugs-cafe.e-monsite.com; map p.140. The ultimate Cambodian challenge for have-a-go food heroes, serving up a largely insect-based menu, plus scorpion, snake and crocodile, all fashioned into neatly crafted tapas ($4–9). The fresh ants salad or cupcakes garnished with silkworms offer a (relatively) gentle introduction, after which you might brave an insect skewer (spiders, grasshoppers and waterbugs), a tarantula samosa or the signature "Bug Mac", perhaps rounded off with a slice of cricket cheesecake. Daily 5–11pm.

Cafe Indochine Sivatha Boulevard ☎012 964533, ⓦ cafe-indochine.com; map p.139. Elegant, slightly upmarket stalwart of the Siem Reap dining scene set in and around an old-style wooden Khmer house and serving up reliably good traditional Khmer food (mains $6.50–7.50) plus pasta and steaks. Choose between a seat al fresco on the ground-floor terrace or upstairs balcony, or in the a/c dining room inside. Daily 10am–3pm & 5–10pm.

Currywala Sivatha Boulevard ☎092 459723; map p.139. Looking a bit like a 1980s curry house in London's Brick Lane, this decor-impaired venue is a good spot for solid subcontinental food spiced with attitude and served in truly man-sized portions. The choice of North Indian classics (mains $5–8) ticks all the usual boxes and there's a good vegetarian selection (although weirdly many veg options are significantly more expensive than their meat counterparts). Daily 11am–10.30pm.

★**Sugar Palm** Taphul St ☎012 818143, ⓦthesugar palm.com; map p.139. This attractively rustic pavilion restaurant, located beneath a huge wooden house, is perfect for a romantic candlelit dinner. The menu focuses on authentic Khmer food with a short but inventive selection of dishes (mains $7–8) – frogs' legs with basil, for example, or squid with black Kampot pepper, plus flavoursome pomelo and green mango salads. Mon–Sat 11.30am–3pm & 5.30–10pm.

EAST OF THE RIVER

Butterflies Garden Street 25 ☎063 761211, ⓦbutterfliesofangkor.com; map p.139. Tranquil garden café with colourful butterflies (bought from local children) flitting between the tables. The menu features the usual Khmer ($5–6) and Western ($6–8) mains – the quality's pretty good, although service can be a bit hit-and-miss. Profits help support local community projects. Daily 6am–10pm.

★**Cuisine Wat Damnak** South of the centre ☎077 347762, ⓦcuisinewatdamnak.com; map p.139. Set in a traditional Cambodian house and garden, *Cuisine Wat Damnak* is regularly voted Siem Reap's top restaurant, with superb Khmer cuisine given a fine-dining makeover by French head chef Joannès Rivière, with five- and six-course tasting menus ($27/$31; vegetarian and vegan menus also available) featuring a regularly changing array of delicacies using the freshest seasonal produce. Reservations strongly advised. Tues–Sat 6.30–9.30pm.

Footprint Cafés St 26 ☎017 594644, ⓦfootprintcafes .org; map p.139. Chic little café with lots of books to browse and buy and a good selection of food including all-day breakfasts and loads of salads alongside inexpensive Western and Asian mains ($3–6.50) ranging from burgers and fish and chips to chicken satay. All profits support local community projects. Daily except Tues 6.30am–10pm.

★**Haven** Chocolate Rd ☎078 342404, ⓦhaven cambodia.com; map p.139. Peaceful expat-run training restaurant for local kids serving up well-prepared and nicely presented Khmer and Asian classics ($7–8), plus a small but judicious selection of Western dishes including good vegetarian and a couple of Swiss options. Seating is inside or in the lovely rambling garden. Booking is usually essential, although you might get lucky at lunch during the low season. Mon–Sat 11.30am–3pm & 5.30–10pm.

Kanell 7 Makara ☎063 966244, ⓦkanellrestaurant .com; map p.139. Chilled-out garden restaurant, with tables set out under thatched pavilions amid lush tropical greenery. There's a good selection of Khmer dishes (mains $7.50–9) and pricier Asian-influenced Western classics like fillet mignon in Kampot green pepper sauce. The small pool is free if you have a meal. Daily 10am–10pm.

Tangram Garden South of the centre ☎097 7261110, ⓦtangramgarden.com; map p.139. Relaxed garden restaurant serving up a regularly changing selection of Western meat dishes and vegetarian grilled and baked dishes (BBQ pork ribs, vegetable and tofu lasgne and so on; mains $4–7.50), backed up by a short but sweet drinks list, including good wines. Also home to the enjoyble Bambu Stage (see p.154). Mon–Sat 6–10pm.

The Veg "G" Table Café Wat Bo St ☎088 6423753, ⓦtheveggtablecafe.com; map p.139. Homely little café serving up excellent and inventive vegetarian dishes (some of which can also be adapted for vegans; mains $5.50) including veggie burgers, falafel, beetroot carpaccio, assorted salads and Siem Reap's most spectacular potato croquettes. Mon–Sat 11am–3pm & 6–9pm, Sun 11am–3pm.

Viroth's Wat Bo St ☎012 826346, ⓦviroth-restaurant .com; map p.139. Upmarket garden restaurant serving up inventive Khmer cuisine, including lots of pork, fish and seafood dishes, plus interesting salads and soups – banana blossom salad, sour squid soup and so on. The green papaya salad and the pork with lemongrass (*laab*) both come recommended. Mains $6–7. Daily 10am–2pm & 5–10pm.

NORTH OF THE CENTRE

L'Oasi Italiana (Da Roberto) River Rd, east of the river, 2km north of NR6 ☎092 418917, ⓦoasiitaliana .com; map p.139. Attractive garden restaurant – a slight schlep north of town but worth it for the excellent Italian cuisine including pizza and home-made pasta ($6–8), meats and fish mains ($7–12) and moreish breads and cheeses made in-house under the supervision of the resident Tuscan chef. Daily 11am–2pm & 6–10pm.

Marum Near Wat Po Lanka ☎017 363284; map p.139. Spacious outdoor restaurant set around a traditional-style wooden house, run as a training restaurant by Friends International. The excellent Asian-inspired fusion menu includes plenty of inventive and unusual creations like lotus, jackfruit and coriander hummus alongside locally inspired offerings including mini crocodile burger with banana crisps, or beef and red tree ants stir-fried with kaffir lime. Dishes ($4–6.50) are served in smallish, almost tapas-sized portions – you may want to order three or four between two people. Popular with tour parties so worth reserving, especially for dinner. Daily 11am–10.30pm.

AROUND SIEM REAP

Villa Chandara ☎089 663799, ⓦvillachandara.com; map pp.162–163. A memorable "experiential dining" experience quite unlike anything else on offer in Siem Reap. Start with a boat ride across the serene West Mebon reservoir at sunset then take a short stroll through an unspoilt village before reaching *Villa Chandara* itself, an idyllic outdoor dining space set among the paddy fields. Dinner comprises a fine-dining, five-course meal featuring eleven or so superb Khmer dishes with Prosecco on arrival and unlimited wine or other drinks throughout, all serenaded by local musicians after dark. $115 per person.

DRINKING

There's a hangover-inducing glut of **places to drink** in Siem Reap. Much of the city's drinking and nightlife is fairly down-at-heel – epitomized by the raucous, wall-to-wall drinking holes lined up along Pub Street, although more characterful and laidback bars can also be found here. Booze is cheap (and regular happy hours make things even cheaper) – draught beer (usually Angkor) is widely available at $0.75–1 a glass (sometimes even less) and cocktails usually go for just a few dollars. It's also worth trying some of the more unusual Asian-style cocktails available at places like *Asana* and *Miss Wong*, as well as *sombai* (rice wine infused with herbs and spices, available at *Asana* and elsewhere).

3

Angkor What? Pub St ☎012 731152; map p.140. "Promoting irresponsible drinking since 1998", *Angkor What?* is the dark heart of the raucous Pub Street scene – a grungy, graffiti-covered Black Hole of Siem Reap into which crazed punters insert themselves nightly in search of cheap beer, loud music and members of the opposite sex. Daily 4pm–3am.

★**Asana** Between St 7 & The Lane ☎092 987801, ⓦasana-cambodia.com; map p.140. Occupying the last surviving wooden house in central Siem Reap, *Asana* is what a traditional Cambodian village house would look like if you put a chic urban bar inside it. Piles of rice and flour sacks double as seats upstairs, while downstairs there's a swinging hammock-bed to lounge in. Slightly above-average prices, but well worth it, particularly for the moreish *sombai* and Asian-style cocktails ($4.50). Daily 11am–midnight.

L'Explorateur Bar Victoria Angkor hotel; map p.139. Siem Reap's most enjoyable colonial-style bar is the perfect place for cocktails or an after-dinner coffee or digestif, either in the period-style a/c interior or on the sultry terrace. Not as pricey as you might expect (beers and coffee $3, cocktails $8), especially during the two-for-one daily happy hour (5–7pm). Daily 6am–11.30pm.

Laundry Bar Northwest of Psar Chas ☎012 301743; map p.140. Lounge on a distressed leather sofa or shoot some pool at this long-running Siem Reap stalwart – usually pretty quiet, although things liven up considerably during the regular live-music sessions. Daily 4pm–2/3am.

★**Miss Wong** The Lane ☎092 428332, ⓦmisswong .net; map p.140. Alluring little retro-Shanghai-style bar and one of central Siem Reap's most enjoyable places to linger of an evening. The excellent cocktails (around $4.50) come with a pronounced Asian twist – Singapore slings, lemongrass Collins, apricot and kaffir lime martinis and so on – and there's excellent food too (see p.150). Daily 6pm–1am.

Red Piano Pub St ☎092 477730; map p.140. One of Pub Street's more civilized drinking spots, especially if you can bag one of the coveted streetside wicker armchairs. The excellent drinks list includes lots of Belgian beers (Duvel, Hoegaarden, Chimay and Leffe) and the signature "Tomb Raider" cocktail, still going strong after well over a decade. Daily 6.30am–midnight.

Siem Reap Brewpub Corner of St 5 and Shinta Mani ☎080 888555, ⓦsiemreapbrewpub.asia; map p.139. Stylish modern restaurant and microbrewery serving up quality beers by brewmaster Neo Say Wee, using German malts, Australian hops and craft yeast from New Zealand. There are six craft ales to choose from: blond, golden, dark and Indian pale ales, plus the more exotic Honey Weiss wheat beer and the lemongrass and pepper-scented Saison Ale. Daily 11am–11pm.

Silk Garden Off The Lane ☎088 3422900, ⓦsilkgarden bar.com; map p.140. "Siem Reap's Premier Gay Bar" (as it markets itself) is a good place for a drink irrespective of your sexual leanings – very central but spacious and pleasantly quiet most nights, and with a soothingly faux-rustic interior full of plants and multicoloured lanterns. Daily 2pm to midnight or later.

REFILL NOT LANDFILL

Launched in late 2016, Refill Not Landfill is an innovative project established by a group of Siem Reap expats to reduce the estimated 4.6 million plastic bottles consumed monthly by tourists in Cambodia. Visitors can buy a lightweight reusable aluminium bottle at one of the participating outlets and then refill it for free at dozens of water stations across the city. For locations and further details see ⓦfacebook.com/refillnotlandfillkh.

The Station Wine Bar (aka as KT Wine Bar) Street 7 ⊙086 988899, ⊛kt-winebar.com; map p.140. Sleepy wine bar offering a so-so selection of wines by the glass ($4) – usually a pretty relaxed and quiet place for a tipple, although it comes to life later in the evening during the regular Khmer comedy, ladyboy and music shows (Mon–Sat 10–11pm). Daily 5.30–11.30pm.

Temple Bar Pub St ⊙015 999922; map p.140. A grand-daddy of the Siem Reap nightlife scene, sprawling over three levels at the heart of the Pub St action. The middle floor is the nicest – and where the popular apsara show (see opposite) is also staged – with cheap beer, spangly red-and-gold Oriental decor and cushioned balcony perches for bird's-eye views of the mayhem below. Daily 7am–3.30am.

NIGHTLIFE AND ENTERTAINMENT

The city is a prime place to experience traditional Cambodian arts, including **shadow puppetry** and **apsara dancing**, while the stomach-churning acrobatics performed at the intimate Phare **circus** are also well worth a look.

CULTURAL AND SHADOW PUPPET SHOWS

A number of hotels around town offer traditional dance performances as part of a cultural show (dinner included). These usually feature several different styles including apsara dance, light-hearted items depicting popular folk tales, and choreographed enacted events from the *Reamker*, with dancers opulently attired in elaborate masks and costumes heavily embroidered and embellished with tails, epaulettes and wings. You will also have the opportunity to catch shadow puppetry (see box, p.156), a Cambodian folk art dating back to Angkorian times that was all but lost during the Khmer Rouge era but has since been revived.

Apsara Theatre Contact the Angkor Village hotel (see p.140) for information and reservations. Regular dance performances ($27, including dinner) at the a/c Apsara Theatre, opposite the *Angkor Village* hotel (Nov–March nightly; April–Oct Tues, Thurs & Sat).

Bambu Stage East of the river next to Tangram Garden restaurant (see p.152) ⊙097 7261110, ⊛bambustage .com. Angkor's history and culture comes to life in Bambu Stage's three enjoyable and innovative shows (6.45pm; $12.50, or $25 including dinner). "Angkor's Temples Decoded" (Tues) unravels the story of the great monuments using a mixture of lecture, colourful projections and live drawing and modelling, while "Snap!" (Fri) offers a historic photographic tour featuring 150 years of temple imagery and archive film footage. Bambu Puppets take the stage on Mon, Wed & Sat, with a riotous shadow-puppet show.

La Noria River Rd ⊙063 964242, ⊛lanoriaangko .com. Entertaining shadow-puppet shows by street children staged over dinner at this hotel (see p.148) every Wed evening. Only a few puppets are used at each performance, changes of character being affected by dressing them in different *kramas*. $7, plus whatever food you order from the restaurant's à la carte menu.

APSARA DANCE

No visit to Cambodia is complete without at least a quick glimpse of women performing the ancient art of **apsara dance**, as depicted on the walls of Angkor's temples. Wearing glittering silk tunics, sequinned tops (into which they are sewn before each performance to achieve the requisite tight fit) and elaborate golden headdresses, performers execute their movements with deftness and deliberation, knees bent in plié, heels touching the floor first at each step, coy smiles on their faces. Every position has its own particular **symbolism** – a finger pointing to the sky, for instance, indicates "today", while standing sideways to the audience with the sole of the foot facing upwards represents flying.

In the reign of Jayavarman VII there were more than three thousand apsara dancers at court – although dances were performed exclusively for the king, and so prized was their skill that when the Thais sacked Angkor in the fifteenth century, they took a troupe of dancers back home with them. Historically, the art form was taught only at the **royal court**, but so few exponents survived the ravages of the Khmer Rouge that the genre was very nearly extinguished. Subsequently, when Princess Boppha Devi – who had been a principal dancer with the royal troupe – wished to revive it, she found it helpful to study temple panels to establish the movements.

These days, the **Royal University of Fine Arts** in Phnom Penh takes much of the responsibility for training dancers, who are chosen not only for aptitude and youth (they start as young as 7), but also for the flexibility and elegance of their hands. It takes six years for students to learn the 1500 positions, and a further three to six years for them to attain the required level of artistic maturity. Also taught is the other principal Cambodian dance genre, *tontay*, in which the emphasis is on depicting folk tales and episodes from the *Reamker*. You'll be able to watch both styles of dance in the cultural performances put on by hotels and restaurants in Siem Reap and Phnom Penh.

Temple Bar Pub St ☏092 405760. Ever-popular and surprisingly good (considering they're free) apsara dance shows held on an upstairs stage in this long-running Pub Street bar (see opposite). Nightly 7.30–9.30pm; free.

CIRCUS

Phare Ring Road, south of intersection with Sok San Road ☏015 499480, ⓦpharecircus.org. Developed by the Phare Ponleu Selpak NGO (ⓦphareps.org) as part of their work with vulnerable Cambodian children and young adults, the Phare circus has proved a massive success both locally and internationally, with the troupe now touring regularly to destinations including Korea, Japan and India. Performances in the big-top tent feature regularly changing shows and casts, comprising a mixture of narrative theatre and spectacular feats of acrobatics. Advance reservations strongly recommended. Nightly 8pm; tickets $18–35, children aged 5–11 $10–18, under-5s free.

SHOPPING

Shopping in Siem Reap is second only to the capital for variety and quality, and in some ways it's much easier to shop here since the outlets are much closer together. The city abounds in inexpensive souvenir stalls selling all manner of goods, including T-shirts, silk tops and trousers, and traditional Khmer **sampots** in Western sizes (although note that many of the textiles here, such as the fabric used to make the cotton **sarongs** with elephant motifs, are imported from Indonesia).

3

MARKETS

Angkor Night Market Off Sivatha Blvd; map p.139. The most popular of Siem Reap's various after-dark markets, with hundreds of stalls selling vast quantities of just about every kind of craft and collectable produced in Cambodia, ranging from touristy tat to stylish souvenirs. More upmarket and unusual merchandise, including fine antiques and quality *kramas*, can be found in the market's older western section, with some of the best stuff at stalls hidden away towards the back. Most stalls 5 or 6–10pm.

King's Road Angkor/Made in Cambodia Market Junction of 7 Makara and River Rd ☏010 345643, ⓦkingsroadangkor.com; map p.139. Funky modern shopping and eating complex featuring a good range of unusual craft and fashion boutiques plus the daily Made in Cambodia Market, with stalls selling quality handicrafts, jewellery, *kramas*, bags, paintings and more. Check out the Claycult boutique, specializing in colourful, beautifully made (albeit pricey) ceramic-bead jewellery. Daily noon to 10pm.

Psar Chas (Old Market) By the river; map p.140. Siem Reap's main market for locals and, increasingly, tourists. The town-facing side of the market is geared more towards locals (including a big fresh produce section where you can pick up inexpensive spice packets). Things become increasingly touristy as you head towards the river, where you'll find dozens of little stalls heaped with huge piles of cheap (mainly factory-made) cotton and silk *kramas*, *sampots*, pashminas and other items of clothing (including the ubiquitous elephant-motif skirts and trousers), along with stalls selling silver, paintings, carvings and fun bags made from recycled rice sacks, food packaging and so on. Daily 10am–10pm.

Siem Reap Art Center Night Market East of the river opposite Psar Chas; map p.139. Smart night market filled with hundreds of handicrafts shops. Much of the stuff is similar to that found in Psar Chas and the Angkor Night Market, although there are also some more upmarket stalls selling superior carvings and jewellery.

CRAFT SHOPS AND GALLERIES

Artisans d'Angkor West off the southern end of Sivatha Blvd ☏092 777462, ⓦartisansdangkor.com; map p.139. The retail outlet of the Artisans d'Angkor (see p.141) sells an outstanding collection of premium-quality goods, including glossy lacquer-work, exquisite carvings, stunning fabrics and garments from their silk workshops at Puok. Prices are higher than anywhere else in the city, but the quality can't be beaten. Daily 7.30am–6.30pm.

Bambou Indochine Branches on Alley West and on Hospital St in Psar Chas, and at the Lucky Mall; ⓦbambouindochine.com; map p.139 & p.140. Countrywide boutique selling colourful original clothing for women, men and children in a range of cotton, silk, linen and (gorgeous but pricey) bamboo fabrics. Daily 9am–10pm.

Louise Loubatieres Hup Guam St, Kandal Village ☏012 902986, ⓦlouiseloubatieres.com; map p.140. Colourful little boutique selling upmarket crafts and collectibles made in Cambodia and Vietnam including ceramics, scarves, bric-a-brac and beautiful lacquered coconut shell bowls. Mon–Sat 10am–7pm.

McDermott Gallery FCC Complex, Pokambor Ave ☏012 274274, ⓦmcdermottgallery.com; map p.139. Upmarket gallery showcasing the work of acclaimed American photographer John McDermott, the so-called "Ansel Adams of Angkor", and his iconic pictures of the region's temples, people and landscapes, using infra-red film to create magically luminous and otherwordly effects. Many of the works on display cost thousands of dollars, although small unframed prints can be had for as little as $35. There is also a second (smaller) shop in the Raffles hotel. Daily 10am–10pm.

Mekong Quilts Sivatha Blvd ☏063 964498, ⓦmekong -quilts.org; map p.140. Colourful – albeit bulky – quilts, plus fun toys, bags, purses, pillowcases and so on, many in wacky, child-friendly designs. Shipping available. Daily 9am–10pm.

Saomao St 9, next to Psar Chas ☏012 818130, ⓦsaomao .com; map p.140. Exquisite, affordable jewellery with a twist, stocking a range of necklaces, bracelets and rings all made out

3

SHADOW PUPPETS

Shadow puppets are made of stretched, dried cowhide, the required outline drawn freehand onto the leather and pared out, after which holes are carefully punched in designated areas to allow back light (traditionally from a burning coconut shell) to shine through onto a plain screen. Once cut and punched, the figures are painstakingly **painted** using natural black and red dyes under the strict supervision of the puppet master. Two sorts of puppet are produced: *sbaek thom* and *sbaek toich* (literally "large skin" and "small skin"). The *sbaek thom*, used to tell stories from the *Reamker*, are the larger of the two, around 1–2m tall, and lack moving parts. By contrast, *sbaek toich* puppets have moveable arms and legs, and are commonly used to tell folk tales and stories of everyday life, usually humorous and with a moral ending. Both types are manipulated from below using sticks attached to strategic points.

of recycled bullets and shell-casings left over from Cambodia's war years, polished, patterned and sculpted into gorgeous designs mixing traditional motifs with contemporary style. Also sells locally made silk and cotton scarves, clothes and other quality bric-a-brac. Daily 9am–10pm.

Senteurs d'Angkor Hospital St ☎063 964801; map p.140. French chic is combined with the imaginative use of traditional Khmer materials to produce original (albeit pricey) products including *kramas*, candles, soaps, spices and flavoured coffees and teas. You can also visit their workshops (free), on the south side of NR6 about 1.5km from town. Daily 7.30am–10.30pm.

Smateria Alley West ☎012 647061, ⓦsmateria.com; map p.140. Beautiful selection of Italian-designed, Cambodian-made bags created from recycled plastic, fishing nets, leather offcuts and other bits and pieces, plus fun kids' rucksacks, pencil cases and wallets. Given the quality, prices are surprisingly modest. Daily 9am–11pm.

Trunkh Hup Guam St, Kandal Village ☎078 900932, ⓦtrunkh.com; map p.140. Fun shop selling quirky collectibles sourced from around Cambodia. Exact stock varies depending on what the owners have turned up on their latest road trip around the country but might include anything from handmade sarongs and ceramics through to old street signs and traditional furniture. Daily 10am–6pm.

BOOKS

As well as the places listed below, the *New Leaf Book Café* and *Footprints Cafés* (see p.150 & p.152) also have a fair selection of secondhand books for sale.

D's Books Hospital St ☎012 262404; map p.140. Extensive range of secondhand books – mainly fiction, plus a smattering of travel guides. You can also bring your own books to trade in for part exchange. Daily 10am–10pm.

Monument Books On the riverside south of Psar Chas ☎023 217617; map p.140. One of the city's best bookshops, including a superb selection of volumes on Angkor and the rest of Cambodia ranging from scholarly histories to glossy coffee-table tomes. Daily 8am–10pm.

MINIMARKETS AND SUPERMARKETS

Minimarkets For basic provisions, there are numerous minimarkets dotted around the centre (including a cluster of places along Sivatha Blvd, roughly opposite the western end of Pub St, which seem to cater exclusively to a clientele of intoxicated Western shoppers stocking up on beer and condoms).

Supermarkets There's a well-stocked supermarket in the Angkor Trade Centre on Pokambor Ave just north of Psar Chas, or try the similar Lucky Market supermarket in the Lucky Mall at the northern end of Sivatha Blvd.

DIRECTORY

Dentists International Dental Clinic, 545 NR6, just east of Royal Gardens (☎063 767618, ⓦimiclinic.com).

Golf There's an 18-hole course designed by Nick Faldo at the Angkor Golf Resort, 5km from town south off NR6 (☎63 767688, ⓦwww.angkor-golf.com).

Hospitals and clinics The Royal Angkor International Hospital, NR6, 2km from the airport (☎012 235888, ⓦroyalangkorhospital.com) is one of Cambodia's better hospitals, whereas the government-run Siem Reap Provincial Hospital, 500m north of Psar Chas (☎063 963111) should be used only as a last resort. For non-emergency treatments, your best bet may be the British Khmer Clinic, House A73, Charles De Gaulle Ave (☎069 630344, ⓦbritishkhmerclinic.com); they also do hotel call-outs.

Internet Try the big (but nameless) place on Sok San St, just west of Psar Chas (24hr; 3000 riel/hr).

Laundry Laundries can be found all over town, including several places around the junction of 7 Makara and River Rd just over the river southeast of Psar Chas, and along Psakrom St, southwest of Psar Chas. Most places charge $1/ kg of washing; some also offer quick turnaround, which includes tumble-drying (essential during the rainy season) for a bit extra. If you want to do your own washing (and have a coffee while you wait) the cute little self-service Missing Socks Laundry Café at the west end of Steung Thmei, just south of Angkor Night Market, is a great option.

Money There are plenty of banks and ATMs throughout Siem Reap, including loads of ATMs and a large Canadia

TOURS OF THE TONLE SAP

There are a number of options when it comes to touring the Tonle Sap.

TOUR OPERATORS

Beyond Unique Escapes Kandal Village ☎ 063 969269, ⓦ beyonduniqueescapes.com. Well-run and good-value tours to Kompong Kleang (see p.145), with guaranteed departures and small groups. Daily Nov–Feb; March–Oct Mon, Wed & Fri subject to water levels.

Ella ☎ 089 663799, ⓦ ellaboat.com. Travel in the grand style with luxurious tours of the Tonle Sap aboard this intimate and luxurious little wooden boat, complete with cocktails and canapés. From $335 for two people plus $50 per additional passenger.

Osmose Nature Tours ⓦ osmosetonlesap.net. Insightful lake trips run by this local NGO who specialize in the Prek Toal area of the Tonle (see p.160).

Tara River Boat ☎ 092 957765, ⓦ taraboat.com. The main tour operator for the lake, offering half-day tours ($29) on their big boat around Chong Khneas, plus sunset tours ($36) with free meal and unlimited drinks. They can also arrange trips to Kompong Phluk ($58), Kompong Kleang ($72) and Prek Toal ($165) using smaller boats. Tickets for most trips can be bought from hotels and tour operators in Siem Reap (see p.145).

Bank (with forex facilities) along Sivatha Boulevard near Psar Chas.

Pharmacies The best of the town's pharmacies is Ucare Pharma. Its main branch (daily 8am–midnight; ☎ 063 965396), with trained, English-speaking pharmacists, is on Hospital St near *The Blue Pumpkin*; branches also at the Lucky and Angkor National Museum malls. There are also plenty of pharmacies around Psar Chas and east of the river on NR6.

Phones You can make domestic calls from the booths around the markets and international calls at the main post office on Pokambor Ave (daily 7am–5.30pm).

Police The tourist police office is opposite the main entrance to the Angkor Archaeological Park (☎ 012 402424).

Post and couriers The post office is on Pokambor Ave (daily 7am–5.30pm). Local couriers include DHL, at 15A Sivatha Blvd near the Central Market (☎ 063 964949, ⓦ dhl.com).

Tonle Sap lake

Temples aside, you shouldn't leave Siem Reap without exploring the fascinating string of **lakeside villages** (both floating and stilted) on the nearby **Tonle Sap**, the massive freshwater lake that dominates the map of Cambodia. The majority of these lake's inhabitants are fishermen, mostly stateless ethnic **Vietnamese** who have been here for decades, despite being widely distrusted by the Khmer. Most live in extremely basic conditions, their livelihoods increasingly threatened by the government, which has awarded large fishing concessions to wealthy businessmen at the expense of local villagers and who now have to either practise their trade illegally or rent a share from a concessionaire.

The ever-increasing numbers of tourists visiting the Tonle Sap villages have provided an important new source of revenue, although the downside (at least from a visitor's point of view) is the steady erosion of traditional local life and the increasingly theme-park atmosphere, particularly at the coach-party honeypot of **Chong Khneas**, while even formerly quieter villages down the lake such as **Kompong Phluk** and **Kompong Kleang** are no longer wholly immune. For a more authentic view of the Tonle Sap, head to the floating villages near Pursat and Kompong Chhnang on the opposite side of the lake (see p.109 & p.112).

As well as the villages, twitchers are attracted to the lake to explore the **Prek Toal Biosphere Reserve**, home to numerous species of waterbird.

Phnom Krom

Access via the steep stairway that leads up from behind the petrol station in the village at the foot of the hill

If you're heading to the lake from Siem Reap, it's worth making a detour up the 137m-high hill of **Phnom Krom** to the grounds of a modern pagoda on the summit, which offers commanding **views** over the Tonle Sap from the top –particularly impressive at sunset. There's also a ruined tenth-century **temple** up here, built by Yasovarman I. The three crumbling sandstone sanctuary towers, dedicated to Vishnu (north), Shiva (centre) and Brahma (south), stand in a row on a low platform; a few carvings can still be made out, including an apsara on the north face of the north tower and a hamsa (sacred goose) on the south tower.

Chong Khneas

Around 18km south of Siem Reap (just offshore from the Siem Reap boat dock at Phnom Krom – arriving by boat from Phnom Penh or Battambang you'll pass the village as you pull in to the dock) • 90min boat trip $20/person plus $3 entrance fee for village (although you may be able to barter the boat price down)

The closest of the lakeside villages to Siem Reap (and the one that tuk-tuk drivers are talking about when they offer to take you to "the floating village"), **CHONG KHNEAS** now pulls in regular crowds of coach parties on whistle-stop tours looking for a quick taste of lakeside life after a morning at the temples – and is also popular with con-artists and main-chancers (including repeated demands from all and sundry for visitors to buy "charity rice" for a local school at up to $50 a bag). It's about as authentic as a plastic dodo although perhaps worth a look if you can't make it to any of the more peaceful villages further away around the lake. In the rainy season, when the lake floods right up to the foot of Phnom Krom, you can get a feel for the village just by walking along the causeway; during dryer parts of the year the village is moved further out onto the lake, and you'll have to get into a boat to see it properly.

Tourism notwithstanding, Chong Khneas remains a genuine **floating village** (see box below), and also the largest Vietnamese community on the lake, with houses (most of them little better than floating shacks) built on bamboo rafts, lashed together to keep them from drifting apart and arranged on an informal kind of grid-plan, with streets of water between.

Kompong Phluk

Around 35km from Siem Reap by road (turn south off the NR6 at Roluos) • Entrance to village plus boat trips $20/person

South of Chong Khneas on the lake is **KOMPONG PHLUK** – more authentic and, for now, more relaxed than Chong Khneas, although it is embracing tourism with a will. This is a **stilted** rather than a floating village (see box below), its buildings raised upon high wooden pillars, with the lake waters lapping around their bases. At the height of the **wet season** in September water levels can rise well above 10m, completely drowning the surrounding patches of forest and sometimes flooding the buildings of the village itself. During the **dry season**, lake levels fall progressively, and between March and May the waters usually vanish completely, receding around 500m from the village and leaving its houses stranded atop their huge stilts amid an expanse of mud.

FLOATS AND STILTS

The Tonle Sap villages are often generically described as the "floating villages", even though, in fact, not all of them are. Genuine **floating villages**, such as Chong Khneas – or those at Pursat and Kompong Chhnang (see p.109 & p.112) – are exactly that, with houses built on bamboo pontoons bobbing raftlike on the water, meaning that the entire village can be towed to a new location on the lake according to seasonally rising or falling water levels, and allowing its inhabitants convenient access to the best available supplies of fish. Conversely, other lakeside settlements, such as Kompong Phluk, are actually **stilted villages**, and float only in a metaphorical sense, their buildings being constructed on top of raised platforms perched above the water on high wooden stilts (like a supersized version of the traditional Khmer rural house). Needless to say, these villages occupy a fixed position, irrespective of prevailing water levels, and come the height of summer are generally left high and dry as the lake waters recede, stranding them amid lakeside mud.

For most of the year the village is wonderfully photogenic, its ramshackle wooden houses and the tops of surrounding half-drowned trees rising improbably out of the waters a kilometre or so offshore. Visiting at the height of the dry season, although less obviously picture-perfect, allows you to appreciate the buildings' remarkable architecture, with houses towering 10m or so overhead atop their platforms, like some miniature bamboo Manhattan. Living conditions are as basic as you'd imagine, although the village comes equipped with its own gendarmerie and school, perched in magnificent isolation amid the waters at the entrance to the village.

Villagers offer memorable rides in sampan-style boats between the trees of the surrounding flooded forest, while a marvellous raised wooden walkway between the trees has also been constructed; this is planned to connect to a big stilted restaurant further out over the lake. It is also possible to spend the night in a homestay in the village.

Banteay Mechrey

15km southwest of Siem Reap • Tours (2hr 30min to 3hr) run 7am to sunset • $15 per boat plus $2 per person • Canoe trips can be added to the boat trip for an extra $7 for 1–2 people

The smaller floating village of **Banteay Mechrey** (or Meachrey) is emerging as a popular and slightly quieter alternative to the increasingly over-touristed Kompong Phluk. The village is actually strung out along a small river just off the Tonle Sap itself, complete with an impressive pagoda. Fishing is, of course, the main local occupation, while there are also several small crocodile farms. The area is also rich in birdlife, similar to that at the nearby Prek Toal reserve (see p.160).

Kompong Khleang

About 50km southeast of Siem Reap by road (turn south off NR6 at Dam Dek) • Entrance to village $2 • Boats available for trips through village for around $20/hr

Around 20km further down the lake from Kompong Phluk is **KOMPONG KHLEANG**. This was a major centre of lake trade in the French colonial period and remains the most substantial settlement hereabouts, with around sixteen thousand inhabitants living in a mixture of stilted and floating houses (the latter mainly owned by members of the town's sizeable Vietnamese population). It's the largest but also the least touristed of the four main Tonle Sap villages, and also remains surrounded by water year-round, making it a good alternative to Kompong Phluk when the waters there have dried up.

CAMBODIA'S LARDER

The **Tonle Sap** is at once a reservoir, flood-relief system, communications route, home and larder to the people who live on and around it; even Cambodians who live nowhere near it depend on the lake as a rich food source.

At its lowest, in May, just before the rains, the lake covers an area of around 2500 square kilometres. Himalayan **meltwater** flows down the Mekong just as the monsoon rains arrive, causing the level of the river to rise so quickly that at Phnom Penh the pressure is sufficient to reverse the flow of the Tonle Sap River, which would normally drain the lake. As a result of this inflow, each year the lake inundates an area of more than **ten thousand square kilometres**, making it the largest freshwater lake in Southeast Asia. The flow of water reverts to its usual direction in late October or early November, the receding waters leaving behind fertile mud for the planting of rice, and nutrients for the fry that have spawned amid the flooded trees. February sees a bumper fish catch, much of it going to satisfy the insatiable Cambodian appetite for *prahok*.

The lake may not always be here; its fragile ecosystem is under threat, as upstream on the Mekong the Chinese continue with the controversial building of dams.

Prek Toal Biosphere Reserve

The Tonle Sap was designated a UNESCO Biosphere Reserve in 1997 – a status that reconciles sustainable use with conservation. One core area of the reserve, the **Prek Toal Biosphere Reserve** serves as a sanctuary for a wide range of waterbirds, including three endangered species – spot-billed pelicans, greater adjutant storks and white-winged ducks. Prek Toal lies on the northwest edge of the lake in the dry season and is easily reached from Siem Reap, though you'll have to take an organized tour – Osmose (see p.157) specialize in trips to the reserve.

The temples of Angkor: the Archaeological Park

3

Scattered over some four hundred square kilometres of countryside between the Tonle Sap lake and the Kulen Mountains, the **temples of Angkor** are one of the world's great architectural showpieces – an astonishing profusion of ancient monuments remarkable both for their size and number, not to mention their incredible levels of artistry. An idealized representation of the Hindu cosmos in stone, they range from great pyramidal

THE TEMPLES OF ANGKOR: STRUCTURE AND SYMBOLISM

First encounters with the temples of Angkor can be confusing, or worse. Myriad monuments survive, in varying states of ruin or otherwise, each with its own perplexing labyrinth of towers, enclosures, shrines, galleries, causeways and moats. Diverse and disorienting as they may initially appear, however – an effect exaggerated by the ravages of time – virtually all have numerous features in common, as well as a shared underlying structure and symbolism.

MODELS OF THE UNIVERSE

Most ancient Khmer temples follow a similar pattern, serving as a miniature symbolic representation of the **mythological Hindu cosmos**. At the heart of each temple, the central sanctuary tower or towers (most commonly five of them, arranged in the characteristic "quincunx" pattern, like the five dots on a dice) represents the mythical **Mount Meru**, considered the home of the gods and the heart of the physical and spiritual universe in both Hindu and Buddhist cosmology. These towers are typically enclosed by a sequence of concentric **enclosures**, stacked within each other like a sequence of Russian dolls, symbolizing the further mountain ranges around Mount Meru, with the whole contained within a **moat**, representing the enclosing earthly ocean. **Causeways** cross these moats, often flanked by "**naga balustrades**" showing gods and demons tugging on the body of an enormous serpent, alluding to the famous legend of the Churning of the Ocean of Milk (see p.168) and perhaps providing a symbolic crossing point between the secular spaces outside the temple and the abode of the gods within.

In all but one instance, temples were designed to be approached from the **east** to catch the rays of the rising sun, symbolizing life. Angkor Wat, however, faces **west**, the direction of the setting sun – and death.

STATE-TEMPLES AND THE CULT OF THE DEVARAJA

The majority of Angkor's most memorable and famous monuments – including Angkor Wat, the Bayon, Baphuon, Ta Keo, Pre Rup and Bakheng – are so-called **state-temples** – great pyramidal temple-mountains rising steeply through a series of sheer-sided storeys (equivalent to the enclosures of non-royal Khmer temples) towards a tower-topped summit. Each storey corresponds to one of the universes of Hindu cosmology, leading up to the topmost towers representing Mount Meru, the abode of the gods. All state-temples were constructed by a particular king for his own use. Temples built by one king were seldom used by the next, who would build in a new location – which accounts for the constantly shifting capitals of the Angkorian period. State-temples were not considered as a place of public worship but as the temple-mountains of Angkor Wat and Pre Rup through to the labyrinthine monasteries of Ta Prohm and Banteay Kdei, as well as more miniature and intimate sanctuaries such as Thommanon and Preah Ko.

Magnificent to begin with, the ravages of time and nature have added immeasurably to the temples' appeal, with individual monuments now stranded romantically amid great swathes of forest, often in various states of picturesque semi-ruin – a far cry from the great days of the Angkorian empire, when each temple would have formed the centrepiece of a string of once bustling (but now entirely vanished) villages, towns and miniature cities spread across the densely inhabited countryside. Some, like Angkor Wat and the Baphuon, have been meticulously restored; others, like Ta Prohm and Beng Mealea, remain half-choked by the encroaching jungle, their buildings smothered in a photogenic tangle of creepers and strangler figs.

The most famous of the temples is the legendary **Angkor Wat**, with its five magnificent corncob towers and vast complex of bas-relief galleries. Also on everyone's itinerary is the walled city of **Angkor Thom**, where you'll find the magical **Bayon** state-temple, topped with dozens of towers carved with enigmatic faces of the bodhisattva Lokesvara, one of ancient Cambodia's most iconic images. Nearby, the similarly iconic **Ta Prohm** also attracts crowds of visitors, its crumbling ruins shrines and statues held in the vice-like grip of giant tree roots.

3

---

private abode of each king's particular god – an aspect of the distinctively Khmer cult known as the **devaraja**, literally "god-king" (see p.293).

MONASTERIES AND SHRINES

The state-temples are just one aspect of Angkorian architecture, however, and smaller temples, monasteries and other structures abound. Most famous are the sprawling **monastic** complexes of Ta Prohm, Banteay Kdei and Preah Khan. These were public rather than private shrines, serving as monasteries, universities and places of worship for the hoi polloi. Very different in effect from the soaring state-temples, these "flat" temples (as they're sometimes described) nevertheless follow the same basic layout, with a cluster of central towers contained within concentric enclosures, the whole bounded by a moat.

LATERITE, BRICK AND SANDSTONE

The building materials used by the ancient Khmer changed over time. **Laterite** was the basic material, readily available and easy to quarry. This was used to construct walls and other functional structures, although its distinctively rough, pockmarked appearance made it unsuitable for fine decorative carving. Early Angkor-period temples were faced largely in **brick** (Sambor Prei Kuk and Prasat Kravan are two particularly notable examples), often carved with extraordinary finesse. Later on, the more valuable **sandstone** became the material of choice for the most important buildings, ranging from the delicate roseate sandstone used at Banteay Srei to the hard, slightly blackish stone at Ta Keo and the Baphuon. **Wooden** buildings would also have featured, although these have all long since vanished.

GODS AND GUARDIANS

Much of the beauty of Angkor can be found in the detail, with prodigious quantities of sculpture covering (in the finest temples) virtually every surface. **Doors** were the main focus, particularly **lintel** panels above entrances, often fantastically carved with gods or scenes from Hindu mythology and often featuring **mythical beasts** such as the *kala* and *makara*. In addition, many doors are flanked by guardian figures, known as **dvarapalas**. Heavenly **apsaras** are another favoured motif, while walls and door jambs are often decorated in the flamboyant **floral designs** so beloved of Khmer craftsmen. The famous narrative **bas-relief galleries** of the Bayon and (especially) Angkor Wat are among the most celebrated instances of Angkorian carving, although they're not found at any other temples. Perhaps most iconic of all, however, are the superhuman faces of the bodhisattva **Lokesvara** carved upon the towers of the Bayon, the gateways of Angkor Thom, and at various other locations around Angkor, smiling enigmatically in benign blessing over the lands beyond.

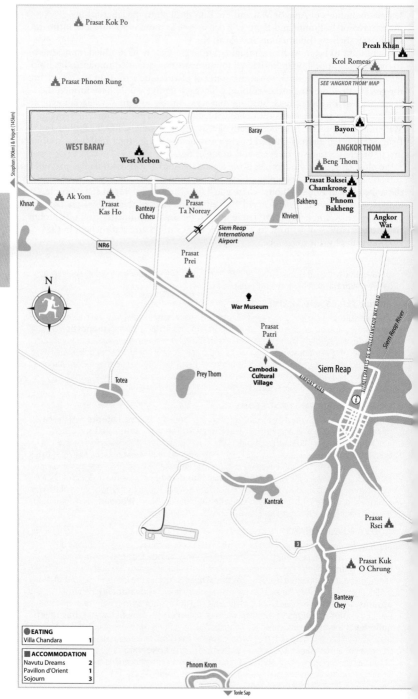

Siophon (90km) & Poipet (145km)

Prasat Kok Po

Preah Khan

Krol Romeas

Prasat Phnom Rung

SEE 'ANGKOR THOM' MAP

Baray

Bayon

WEST BARAY

West Mebon

ANGKOR THOM

Beng Thom

Prasat Baksei
Chamkrong

Ak Yom

Prasat
Kas Ho

Banteay
Chheu

Prasat
Ta Noreay

Bakheng

Phnom
Bakheng

Khnat

Khvien

Angkor
Wat

NR6

Siem Reap
International
Airport

Prasat
Prei

N

War Museum

Prasat
Patri

Totea

Prey Thom

Cambodia
Cultural
Village

Siem Reap River

Siem Reap

AIRPORT ROAD

Kantrak

Prasat
Rsei

Prasat Kuk
O Chrung

Banteay
Chey

Phnom Krom

Tonle Sap

EATING
Villa Chandara   1

ACCOMMODATION
Navutu Dreams   2
Pavillon d'Orient   1
Sojourn   3

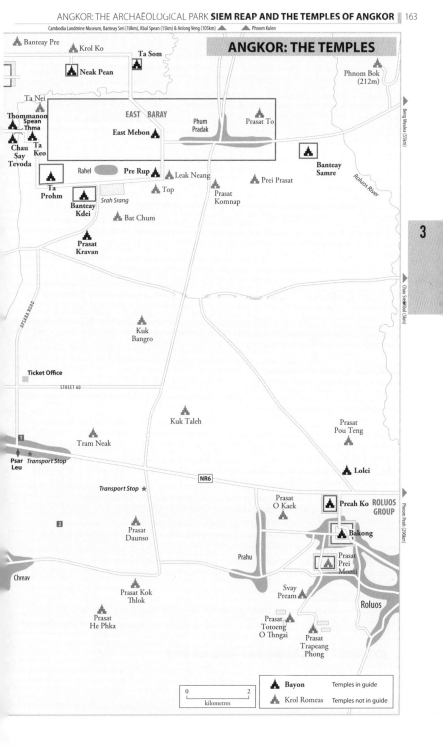

Cambodia Landmine Museum, Banteay Srei (10km), Kbal Spean (15km) & Anlong Veng (105km) ▲   ▲ Phnom Kulen

ANGKOR: THE TEMPLES

Banteay Pre
Krol Ko
Ta Som
Neak Pean
Phnom Bok (212m)

Ta Nei
EAST BARAY
Thommanon
Spean Thma
East Mebon
Phum Pradak
Prasat To
Chau Say Tevoda
Ta Keo
Banteay Samre
Rahel
Pre Rup
Leak Neang
Prei Prasat
Roluos River
Ta Prohm
Top
Banteay Kdei
Srah Srang
Prasat Komnap
Bat Chum
Prasat Kravan

Kuk Bangro

Ticket Office
STREET 60

Kuk Taleh
Prasat Pou Teng

Tram Neak
Psar Leu   Transport Stop ★
Lolei

Transport Stop ★
NR6
Prasat O Kaek
Preah Ko ROLUOS GROUP

Prasat Daunso
Bakong

Prahu
Prasat Prei Monti

Chreav
Svay Pream
Roluos

Prasat Kok Thlok
Prasat Totoeng O Thngai

Prasat He Phka
Prasat Trapeang Phong

Beng Mealea (55km) ▶
Chau Srei (Kol (5km) ▶
Phnom Penh (290km) ▶

3

0 ___ 2
kilometres

| ▲ **Bayon** | Temples in guide |
| ▲ Krol Romeas | Temples not in guide |

All the temples close to Siem Reap are contained within the so-called **Angkor Archaeological Park** and covered by a single entrance ticket (see p.190), as are a number of other headline attractions slightly further afield including **Banteay Srei**, a unique micro-temple of intricately carved reddish stone, and the **Roluos Group**, home to some of Angkor's oldest temples. Several other major Angkorian monuments can be found even further from Siem Reap, outside the Archaeological Park and covered by their own tickets. These include the jungle-smothered temple of **Beng Mealea** (see p.192), the great temple-towns of **Koh Ker** (see p.194) and **Preah Khan (Kompong Thom)** (see p.195), and the stunning **Preah Vihear** (see p.197) in the far north of the country, sitting high on a mountaintop above the Thai border.

Angkor Wat

However many times you've seen it on film or in photographs, nothing prepares you for the majesty of **ANGKOR WAT**. Dominated by five majestic, corncob towers, this masterpiece of Khmer architecture was built by Suryavarman II between around 1113 and 1150. Stunning from a distance, its intricacy becomes apparent as you approach, with every surface covered in fine detail. If time allows, it's worth visiting at different times of day to see how the colours of the stone change with the light.

Angkor Wat is unusual (although not unique) among ancient Southeast Asian temples in being oriented **towards the west**, rather than the east. One popular theory holds that the ancient Angkorians associated the west (direction of the setting sun) with death, and that the temple was also planned to serve as a grand funerary monument for Suryavarman after his death – although a rival explanation holds that Angkor Wat's orientation reflects the association between the west and the god Vishnu, to whom the temple is dedicated.

Moat and fourth enclosure

Entry to the complex is from the west, via an impressive laterite **causeway** built from massive blocks of stone and edged by the scant remains of a crumbling naga balustrade and with terraces guarded by lions.

The causeway crosses the 200m-wide **moat** to the western gopura of the **fourth enclosing wall**. The **western gopura** itself stretches for nearly 230m and has three towers, plus entrances large enough to allow elephants to pass through. Inside the southern section of the gopura is an eight-armed statue of **Vishnu**, more than 3m tall, while looking out from the gopura there's a panoramic view of the temple. The first of Angkor Wat's fabulous **apsaras** are carved into the sandstone on the eastern exterior of the gopura, their feet strangely foreshortened and skewed to the side.

From the gopura, a second **causeway** leads to the temple, 350m long and even more impressive than the one across the moat. The buildings partway along are libraries. In front of the temple is the cruciform-shaped **Terrace of Honour**, framed by a naga balustrade; apsara dances (see box, p.154) were once performed here and ceremonial processions received by the king. Beyond the terrace, a short flight of steps leads up to the third enclosing wall, whose western gopura is linked to a cruciform cloister and two galleries.

The third enclosure

Portraying events associated primarily with Vishnu, to whom the temple is dedicated, the famous Angkor Wat bas-reliefs, some 2m high on average, are carved into the wall

AVOIDING THE CROWDS AT ANGKOR WAT

As Angkor's headline attraction, Angkor Wat is filled with crowds of tourists virtually every hour of the day, although fortunately there's more space here to swallow up the visiting crowds than at places like the Bayon and Ta Prohm. The **best time** to visit is early morning from around 7am to 9am: after the sunrise-watchers have left and before the mass of coach parties arrives.

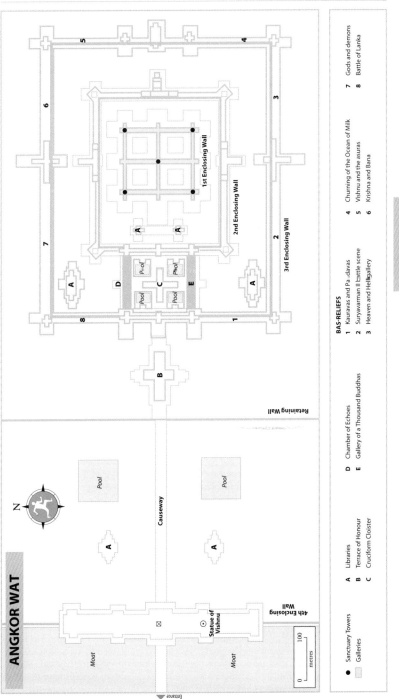

ANGKOR WAT

N

Entrance

Moat

Pool

Pool

Causeway

Moat

Statue of Vishnu

4th Enclosing Wall

0   100
metres

Retaining Wall

3rd Enclosing Wall

2nd Enclosing Wall

1st Enclosing Wall

● Sanctuary Towers

Galleries

A Libraries
B Terrace of Honour
C Cruciform Cloister

D Chamber of Echoes
E Gallery of a Thousand Buddhas

BAS-RELIEFS

1 Kauravas and Pandavas
2 Suryavarman II battle scene
3 Heaven and Hell gallery

4 Churning of the Ocean of Milk
5 Vishnu and the asuras
6 Krishna and Bana

7 Gods and demons
8 Battle of Lanka

3

of the magnificently colonnaded **gallery** that runs around the perimeter of the temple, forming the **third enclosure**. This was as far into the complex as the citizens of Angkor were allowed to get, and the scenes depicted were meant to impress them with their king's wealth and power, as well as contributing to their religious education.

Extending over 700m, the bas-reliefs are broken into sections by porches midway along each side, along with corner chambers. The older bas-reliefs are delicately carved with minute attention to detail, in contrast to the more roughly executed scenes added in the sixteenth century. In some areas you can still see evidence of the red and gold paint that once covered the reliefs, while other areas are black; one theory is that the pigments have been eroded and the stone polished by thousands of hands caressing the carvings over the years.

The account that follows assumes you progress around the gallery in an **anticlockwise** direction, in keeping with the ancient funerary practices.

West gallery: south section

The battle between the rival families of cousins, the **Kauravas** (marching from the left) and the **Pandavas** (from the right), as described in the *Mahabharata*, is in full swing in the first section of the gallery. Fighting to the death at Mount Kurukshetra, the two families are respectively backed by the supernatural powers of Kama, son of the sun god Surya, and Arjuna. Along the bottom of the panel, foot soldiers march towards the fray in the centre of the gallery; above them, generals ride in horse-drawn chariots or on elephants. Amid hand-to-hand combat, the Kaurava general, Bhisma, is shown shot through with arrows, while Arjuna can be seen on his chariot with Krishna serving as his charioteer.

Southwest corner

Despite erosion, some tales from the **Ramayana** (see box, p.63) and other Hindu legends can still be made out here. One panel shows Krishna holding up Mount Govardhan in one hand as a shelter for villagers against storms sent by Indra. Another depicts the duel between the monkey gods Valin and Sugriva, in which Valin dies in the arms of his wife after he is pierced by an arrow from Rama. Monkeys mourn Valin on the surrounding panels.

South gallery: west section

This gallery (running west to east on two levels) depicts a **battle scene**, beginning with a royal audience (upper level) and the palace ladies in procession (below). Further along, the Khmer commanders, mounted on elephants and shaded by parasols, muster the troops and march through the jungle. At the centre of the panel they surround Suryavarman II, who is of larger stature and has fifteen parasols around him. Beyond, the army – accompanied by musicians, standard-bearers and jesters – is joined by Cham mercenaries, identified by their moustaches and plumed headdresses. It's thought that the niches along the wall were used as hiding places for golden artefacts, though some say the chunks of stone were removed by devotees who believed they possessed magical properties.

South gallery: east section

Called the **Heaven and Hell gallery**, this panel, carved on three levels and nearly 60m long, shows the many-armed god Yama mounted on a buffalo and judging the dead. At the start of this section, a path is shown on the top level along which people ascend to heaven, while a corresponding route at the bottom leads to hell, the two paths being separated by a frieze of garudas. The people in heaven can be seen living a life of leisure in palaces, whereas sinners are pushed through a trapdoor into the underworld to have terrible punishments inflicted on them – gluttons are cut in two, vandals have their bones broken and rice stealers have red-hot irons thrust through their abdomens.

EXPLORING ANGKOR: TEMPLE ITINERARIES

There are around two dozen or so major temple sites at Angkor, scattered over a considerable area. Package tours tend to follow rigid routes around the sites, although with a little ingenuity you can tweak established itineraries and enhance your experience considerably. **Time** is very much of the essence. It's horribly easy to end up rushing around breathlessly, so that one site blends seamlessly into another and you end up templed-out and forgetting almost everything you've seen. All the major temples in the environs of Siem Reap can be seen **in three days** (see our recommended itinerary), although if you can spend longer than this – taking the temples at a more leisurely pace and visiting them during quieter periods of the day – you'll be richly rewarded (for details of the **best times to visit** the major sights, see the relevant accounts). Even if you can only spare three days it's well worth making space to revisit the major sites – Angkor Wat and Angkor Thom in particular – for a second or even third look at different times of the day, as well as taking a sunrise or sunset trip to one of the major monuments.

TRADITIONAL ITINERARIES

There are two traditional temple itineraries – the Small (or "Petit") Circuit and the Grand Circuit – each sold as off-the-peg day-tours just about everywhere in town.

3

Small Circuit Around 30km. Starts at Angkor Wat, heads north to the Bayon and the rest of Angkor Thom before continuing east to Thommanon, Chau Say Tevoda, Ta Keo, Ta Prohm, Banteay Kdei, Srah Srang and Prasat Kravan, traditionally concluding at sunset on Phnom Bakheng. The Small Circuit is usually done in just one day, but really contains too many major monuments to properly appreciate in this time – indeed you could easily spend a whole day exploring just Angkor Wat and Angkor Thom, perhaps rounded off by a sunset ascent of Phnom Bakheng. Given this, it's far better to break the circuit up and combine with the Grand Circuit over two, or even more, days.

Grand Circuit Around 36km, or 44km if you include Banteay Samre. Starts at Srah Srang then heads east, via Pre Rup, East Mebon (from where you can extend the circuit to Banteay Samre), Ta Som, Neak Pean and Preah Khan. The Grand Circuit can easily be explored in one day (even if you include outlying Banteay Samre), leaving you with a couple of hours to spare when you could visit one or two sights on the Small Circuit. **Roluos** The temples of Roluos – in a slightly outlying area west of Siem Reap – are generally covered in a separate day-trip. They could conceivably be combined with the Grand Circuit in a single, albeit long, day, although we wouldn't recommend it.

COMBINATIONS AND VARIATIONS

As they stand, the traditional Small and Grand Circuit itineraries are far from ideal. You could, however, mix and match to come up with something far more rewarding.

Small Circuit in reverse order You might consider doing the Small Circuit in anticlockwise order, starting at Banteay Kdei and finishing at Angkor Wat. This has the great advantage of seeing the sights in ever-increasing orders of magnificence, but also runs the risk that by the time you finish up at Angkor Wat you'll be so frazzled with myriad monuments that you won't be able to properly appreciate what you're seeing. **Small Circuit/Grand Circuit combo** It makes most sense to only tackle part of the

Small Circuit on one day, and then mop up the remaining Small Circuit sights during a tour of the Grand Circuit on a later visit, maybe by delaying a visit to the Small Circuit temple of Ta Prohm to the beginning or end of your Grand Circuit tour (which also allows you to visit the temple when it's less crowded), or doing the same with a couple of the temples within Angkor Thom (visiting the Bayon at the end of a Grand Circuit tour, for example, which again will land you at the temple when most of the coach parties have gone).

East gallery: south section

This gallery contains the most famous of Angkor Wat's bas-reliefs, depicting the **Churning of the Ocean of Milk** (see box, p.168). The bas-relief picks up the story just as the churning is about to yield results; in the central band of the panel, 92 bulbous-eyed

THE CHURNING OF THE OCEAN OF MILK

A popular theme in Khmer art is the **Churning of the Ocean of Milk**, a creation myth from the Hindu epic the *Bhagavata Purana*, which describes the various incarnations of Vishnu. At the beginning of this episode, the devas (gods) and asuras (demons) are lined up on opposite sides, trying to use **Mount Mandara** to churn the ocean in order to produce *amrita*, the elixir of immortality. They tug on the serpent **Vasuki**, who is coiled around the mountain, but to no effect. **Vishnu** arrives and instructs them to pull rhythmically, but the mountain begins to sink. Things get worse when Vasuki vomits a deadly venom, which threatens to destroy the devas and asuras; Brahma asks **Shiva** to drink up the venom, which he does, but it burns his throat, which is blue thereafter. Vishnu meanwhile, in his incarnation as the tortoise **Kurma**, supports Mount Mandara, allowing the churning to continue for another thousand years, after which the *amrita* is finally produced. Unfortunately, the elixir is seized by the asuras, but Vishnu again comes to the rescue as the apparition **Maya** and regains the cup of elixir. The churning also results in the manifestation of mythical beings, including the three-headed elephant, Airavata; the goddess of beauty, Lakshmi, who becomes Vishnu's wife; and the celestial dancers, the apsaras.

3

asuras with crested headdresses are shown holding the head of Vasuki and pulling from the left, while on the right, 88 devas, with almond eyes and conical headdresses, hold the tail. To the top, thousands of divine apsaras dance along the wall, and at the bottom, the ocean teems with finely detailed marine creatures.

The stupa just outside the east gopura was placed here in the early eighteenth century when the temple was a Buddhist monastery; its history is recorded on a wall inscription within the gopura itself.

East gallery: north section

The relief here was carved in the sixteenth century and the workmanship is rough and superficial. The scene records the asuras being defeated by Vishnu, who is shown with four heads and mounted on Garuda in the centre of the panel. The asuras approach from the south, their leaders riding chariots drawn by monsters; from the north, a group of warriors ride peacocks.

North gallery: east section

Also from the sixteenth century, the poorly rendered scenes here show the battle between **Krishna** and **Bana**, son of an asura who had come under Shiva's protection. Krishna, easily spotted with his eight arms and multiple heads, rides Garuda towards Bana, but is forced to halt by a fire surrounding a city wall, which Garuda quells with water from the Ganges. On the far west of the panel, a victorious Krishna is depicted on Mount Kailash, where Shiva entreats him to spare Bana's life. Also along this stretch of wall can be found an image of the elephant-headed god, Ganesh, his only appearance in the entire temple.

North gallery: west section

Better executed than the previous two sections, the panel here shows 21 gods from the Hindu pantheon in a terrific mêlée between **gods and demons**. Some of the easier ones to spot are (from left to right), the multi-headed and -armed Skanda, god of war, riding a peacock; Indra standing on the elephant Airavata; Vishnu mounted on Garuda and fighting with all four arms; Yama's chariot pulled by buffalo; and Shiva pulling his bow, while Brahma rides the sacred goose, Hamsa.

Northwest corner

More scenes from the **Ramayana** are to be found here, notably a depiction of Vishnu reclining on the serpent Anata. A bevy of apsaras float above him, while his wife, Lakshmi, sits near his feet. Below, a procession of gods comes to ask Vishnu to return to earth.

West gallery: north section

Turning the corner, you come to the superbly carved **Battle of Lanka**. In this action-packed sequence from the *Ramayana*, Rama is shown fighting the ten-headed, twenty-armed Ravana to free his wife, Sita, from captivity; bodies of the soldiers from the monkey army, Rama's allies, fall in all directions. The two adversaries are seen in the centre of the panel, Ravana in a chariot drawn by lions, Rama standing on the monkey king, Sugriva.

First level

From the top of the steps above the Terrace of Honour, further steps head up into the **third enclosure** (which is also the **first level** of the temple pyramid), bare save for two libraries in the northwest and southwest corners.

Linking the third and second enclosures is the so-called **Cruciform Cloister**, with four deep (but dry) pools in the centre and galleries to either side. That on the west side is known as the **Gallery of a Thousand Buddhas**, which once housed a vast collection of Buddhas collected over recent centuries when Angkor Wat was a Buddhist monastery; many were taken away for safe-keeping in 1970, while those that remained were later destroyed by the Khmer Rouge, though today a few modern images have taken their place. The gallery on the opposite side is the so-called **Chamber of Echoes**. Cambodians stand here with their backs to the wall and thump their chests with their fists, thrice, to bring good fortune. Surrounding the cloister is a gallery with a frieze of apsaras above and seated ascetics carved at the bases of the columns below. Many of the columns also bear Sanskrit and Khmer inscriptions.

Second and third levels

The **second level** of the pyramid is enclosed by a gallery with windows opening on the courtyard within, whose walls are carved with a remarkable collection of more than 1500 **apsaras**, each unique. Elegantly dressed, these beautiful creatures display exotic hairstyles and enigmatic expressions; even their jewellery is lovingly sculpted. These are the earliest depictions in Angkorian art of apsaras in groups, some posed in twos or threes, arms linked and hands touching.

During the time of Suryavarman II, only the high priest and the king were allowed to visit the **third level**, but now visitors can make the ascent – although there's usually a bit of a queue to climb the steep, ladder-like staircase to the top, and you'll need a decent head for heights.

ANGKOR FROM THE AIR

An exhilarating way to see Angkor is from the air. Although over-flying of the temples is not permitted, you can still get a wonderful overview by balloon, helicopter or microlight. Angkor passes are not required for any of these aerial excursions.

By balloon The cheapest option is from the gondola of a tethered helium balloon ($20, children $10; 15min) located between the airport and Angkor Wat. Weather permitting the balloon ascends to around 120m around thirty times a day, carrying up to thirty passengers at a time, offering a bird's-eye view of Angkor Wat and nearby temples. Traditional 30min sunset and sunrise balloon rides are run between Dec and mid-March by Angkor Ballooning (☎ 069 558888, ⓦ angkorballooning.com; $100) although depending on wind direction you may not see much of the temples, and reviews of the company's service and safety procedures are extremely mixed.

By helicopter and plane Helicopter trips around the Angkor Wat area are run by Helistar Cambodia (☎ 063 966072, ⓦ helistarcambodia.com) and Helicopters Cambodia (☎ 063 963316, ⓦ helicopters cambodia.com); prices at both start from around $95 per person for an 8min flight. The latter can also arrange longer flights to Beng Mealea, Koh Ker, Preah Vihear and Banteay Chhmar. MyFly runs flights in a two-seater plane (☎ 068 704601, ⓦ myfly.aero; from $69 for 15min).

By microlight Microlight Cambodia (☎ 096 6203676, ⓦ microlightcambodia.net) offers exhilarating early-morning and late-afternoon flights (20min–1hr; $120–280) around the temples and Tonle Sap.

Phnom Bakheng

The first state-temple to be built in the Angkor area, the temple-mountain of **PHNOM BAKHENG** was commissioned by Yasovarman I after he moved the capital here from nearby Roluos. Dedicated in 907, it originally lay at the heart of Yasovarman's new moated city of Yasodharapura, covering an area of some four square kilometres (parts of the moat are still visible along the road from Siem Reap, 600m before Angkor Wat). The temple itself isn't the most riveting monument in Angkor, despite its historical significance, but is worth a visit if only for the fine **view** from its summit, including a bird's-eye panorama of Angkor Wat.

The temple **pyramid** comprises five levels, built around a natural 67m-high hill, with steps and terraces hewn into the rock and then clad in sandstone (it takes around 15 minutes to walk to the top). Forty-four small towers are dotted around its base, with another sixty arranged around the terraces and lining the staircases above (twelve on each level), plus five principal towers at the top arranged, for the first time in Khmer architecture, in a quincunx to symbolize the five peaks of Mount Meru. The temple was consecrated to Shiva and the central tower would have contained a linga, now lost.

The temple is particularly popular towards **sunset**, when hundreds of tourists arrive to watch the sun go down over Angkor Wat.

Prasat Baksei Chamkrong

A few hundred metres north of Phnom Bakheng is the small, often ignored **PRASAT BAKSEI CHAMKRONG**, the sole monument built by Harshavarman I. Consecrated to Shiva and his consort, the temple wasn't finished in the king's lifetime and was re-consecrated by Rajendravarman I in 948. The simple structure comprises four square tiers of decreasing size, rising to a single brick sanctuary tower with decorated sandstone lintels and columns. A Sanskrit inscription on the door frame here records that the sanctuary contained a golden image of Paramenshavara, as Jayavarman II was known posthumously. If you want to head up to the top of the temple, take the northern staircase which is the best of a badly worn bunch.

Angkor Thom

The wall of the city is some five miles in circumference. It has five gates each with double portals… Outside the wall stretches a great moat, across which access to the city is given by massive causeways. Flanking the causeways on each side are fifty-four divinities resembling war-lords in stone, huge and terrifying…
Zhou Daguan, visited Angkor Thom 1296–97

Still recognizable from this description by the Chinese envoy Zhou Daguan, who visited the Khmer court at the end of the thirteenth century, the ruins of the great city of **ANGKOR THOM** form the physical and architectural centrepiece of Angkor, home to a trio of state-temples – **Baphuon**, **Phimeanakas** and the spectacular **Bayon** – as well as numerous other royal, religious and secular structures. The former city itself covers an area of three square kilometres, enclosed by a wide moat and an 8m-high wall

ELEPHANTS AT ANGKOR

Elephant rides are available both for the sunset ascent of Phnom Bakheng and at Angkor Thom, although we don't recommend them. In 2016 an elephant collapsed and died of a heart attack at Angkor after being forced to work in 40°C heat, and increasing numbers of people both locally and internationally are now calling for elephant rides at Angkor to be banned entirely.

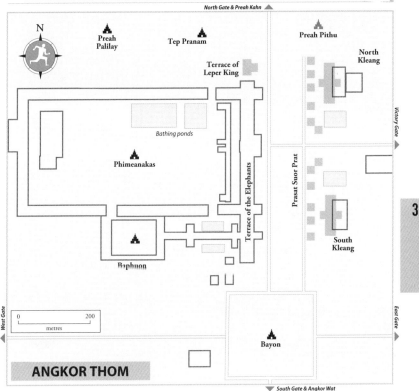

reinforced by a wide earth embankment (constructed by Jayavarman VII after the city had been sacked by the Cham in 1177). Sanctuary towers stand at each corner of the walls, which are pierced by five much-photographed **entry gates** – one per cardinal direction, plus an additional eastern portal, the Victory Gate. Each gate is topped by a tower carved with four huge faces looking out in the cardinal directions and approached via a causeway lined with huge naga balustrades. Nominally, these faces are said to represent the bodhisattva Lokesvara, although they also bear a certain similarity to carved images of Jayavarman VII himself, perhaps symbolizing the far-reaching gaze of the king over his lands and subjects.

The site is most usually approached from Angkor Wat through the 23m-high **south gate** and along a 100m-long **stone causeway** flanked by a massive naga balustrade, with 54 almond-eyed gods on one side, and 54 round-eyed demons on the other holding a pair of nine-headed nagas, which are said to protect the city's wealth. Most of the heads here are replicas, the originals having been either stolen or removed for safety to the Angkor National Museum. The base of the gateway itself is decorated with sculptures of **Indra** on a three-headed elephant; the elephant's trunks hold lotus blossoms that droop to the ground, doubling as improvised columns.

The Bayon

The state-temple of Jayavarman VII and his immediate successors, the **Bayon** is one of Angkor's most memorably mysterious and haunting sights, with its dozens of eroded towers carved with innumerable giant-sized images of the enigmatically

3

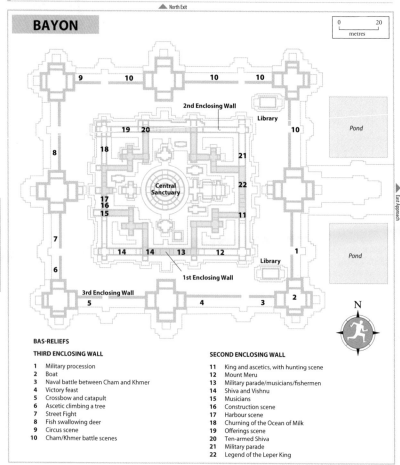

▲ North Exit

BAYON

0   20
metres

2nd Enclosing Wall

Library

Pond

Central Sanctuary

Library

1st Enclosing Wall

3rd Enclosing Wall

East Approach

N

BAS-RELIEFS

THIRD ENCLOSING WALL

1 Military procession
2 Boat
3 Naval battle between Cham and Khmer
4 Victory feast
5 Crossbow and catapult
6 Ascetic climbing a tree
7 Street Fight
8 Fish swallowing deer
9 Circus scene
10 Cham/Khmer battle scenes

SECOND ENCLOSING WALL

11 King and ascetics, with hunting scene
12 Mount Meru
13 Military parade/musicians/fishermen
14 Shiva and Vishnu
15 Musicians
16 Construction scene
17 Harbour scene
18 Churning of the Ocean of Milk
19 Offerings scene
20 Ten-armed Shiva
21 Military parade
22 Legend of the Leper King

half-smiling face of the bodhisattva Lokesvara. The **design** of the Bayon is unique among the state-temples of Angkor. Instead of a huge central pyramid, an impression of ascending height is created by a dense cluster of towers, with the main sanctuary towers rising out of the centre of the complex like a kind of Matterhorn carved in stone – the ultimate architectural representation of the mythical Mount Meru. Approaching the temple, all you can initially see is a mass of ill-defined stone, dark and imposing, looking from a distance like some kind of bizarre natural rock formation. It's only closer up that the intricacy of the design becomes apparent and you can begin to make out the 37 towers carved with massive faces. It is said that there are more than two hundred in all, although no one seems to know the exact number, and exactly why they are repeated so many times remains unclear.

Built in the late twelfth and/or early thirteenth century, the Bayon was intended to embrace all the religions of the kingdom, including the Islamic beliefs of the newly conquered Cham, but was consecrated as a Buddhist temple. When the state religion reverted to Hinduism, the Buddha in the central sanctuary was torn down and cast into the well below.

EXPLORING THE BAYON

Most coach parties descend on the Bayon from mid-morning to early afternoon, meaning that the **best time to visit** is either early in the morning (around 7–9am) or later in the afternoon. A good plan is to arrive at Angkor Thom in time for lunch, then spend the first part of the afternoon exploring the city's other sights (which will take at least a couple of hours) before heading to the Bayon at around 3/4pm, when the worst of the crowds have dispersed.

Drivers drop off passengers at various places at the beginning of visits to the Bayon and surrounding monuments. Make sure to know *exactly* where your driver is waiting to pick you up, as there's an awful lot of transport about, and several different parking areas.

3

Third enclosing wall bas-reliefs: east wall

Enclosing the central sanctuary is the **third enclosing wall** – actually a colonnaded gallery, though the roof has long since collapsed. Its outer walls are covered with extensive **bas-reliefs**, deeper and less fine than those at Angkor Wat (and some are unfinished). These were intended to be viewed **clockwise**, starting from the **midpoint of the eastern wall**, which is how they're described below.

Head south along the gallery from the east approach and on the **east wall** you'll see a **military procession** depicted on three levels; bareheaded soldiers with short hair march across the uppermost level, while the level just below depicts troops with goatee beards and elaborate hairstyles. Musicians and bareback cavalry accompany them, the commanders (with parasols) seated on elephants. Close to the next door into the courtyard are the army's camp followers, their covered carts much like those used today. At the lowest level are some fascinating scenes of everyday domestic and rural life, many of them still as true now as when they were first carved.

Third enclosing wall bas-reliefs: south wall

The **southeast corner tower** is unfinished, but its carving of a boat is remarkable for continuing all the way around the corner, where you'll discover the finest of the Bayon bas-reliefs, depicting the 1177 **naval battle** between the Khmer and the Cham on the Tonle Sap lake. The victorious Khmer, led by Jayavarman VII, are shown with bare heads, whereas the Cham wear vaguely floral-looking hats. At the start, the king is seen seated in the palace directing preparations for battle, as fish swim through the trees – as in a rainy-season flood. Along the bottom are more carvings drawn from everyday life on the banks of the Tonle Sap: fishing baskets – just like those used now – hang from the ceiling, skewers of food are cooked over a charcoal fire and women are seen picking lice out of one another's hair.

A bit further along, princesses are shown amusing themselves at the palace, while around them wrestlers spar and a boar fight takes place. Subsequently, battle commences. The Cham disembark from their boats to continue the fight on land against the Khmers, who, with short hair and rope tied around their bodies, are given the appearance of giants and are, of course, victorious. Back at the palace, **Jayavarman VII** himself looks on as the celebratory feast is prepared.

The western side of the south wall has carvings on its lower half only, including a panel showing arms, including a **crossbow** deployed from the back of an elephant and a **catapult** on wheels.

Third enclosing wall bas-reliefs: west wall

The first portion of the **western wall** is unfinished; look out here for an **ascetic climbing a tree** to escape from a hungry tiger, near the centre of the panel. Towards the centre of the panel, before the gopura, a **street fight** is in progress: people shake their arms in anger, while above, two severed heads are shown to the crowd.

Along the northern half of the west wall, look out for the scene showing men with sticks chasing other men with round shields, passing a pond in which a **large fish swallows a small deer**.

Third enclosing wall bas-reliefs: north wall

On the western side of the **north wall**, a light-hearted **circus** scene features jugglers, acrobats and wrestlers alongside a parade of animals including rhinos, rabbits and deer. The section beyond the north gopura is badly eroded, though you can just about make out the **fighting** between the Khmer and Cham resuming, with the Khmer running away towards the mountains. By the time you've turned the corner to the northern half of the east wall, the battle is in full swing, and even the elephants are taking part, one trying to rip out the tusk of another.

Second enclosing wall bas-reliefs

Inside the third enclosing wall, a passage on the middle of the south side of the central sanctuary leads up to the **bas-reliefs** of the **second enclosing wall**, raised up about 1.5m above the level of the third enclosure. These bas-reliefs aren't in great condition and are more difficult to follow than those of the third enclosing wall, being broken up by towers and antechambers into small panels. It is likely that these were only seen by the king and his priests, unlike the scenes in the third gallery, which would have been accessible to the hoi polloi. Interestingly, although the Bayon was dedicated as a Buddhist temple, there are plenty of depictions here of **Hindu gods**. As with the bas-reliefs on the third enclosing wall, these were intended to be viewed **clockwise**, starting from the **midpoint of the eastern wall**, which is how they're described below.

In the vestibule **south of the east gopura**, a **hunt** is shown in progress, below which the king is shown tarrying in the palace, surrounded by ascetics. The wall is a bit crumbled as you turn the corner into the south gallery, but it's possible to make out **Mount Meru** rising out of the ocean – here denoted by the fish. Beyond the tower, **warriors parade** from left to right, while a band of musicians leaves the palace. Below, a dead child is being placed in a coffin; close by, a fisherman casts his net from his boat, while apsaras hover above. **Shiva and Vishnu** appear in numerous, mostly worn scenes in the section **west of the south gopura**; towards the end of this section you'll see Shiva standing in a pool while ascetics and animals look on from the bank; in the same area people prostrate themselves around Vishnu, while a funeral is in progress.

In the **west gallery**, pop into the tower before the gopura and you'll find **musicians** playing celestial music while apsaras dance. Labourers hauling stones over rollers and lifting them into place can be seen in a curious **construction scene** (on the tiny section of gallery between the tower and the gopura) which oddly enough has had a depiction of Vishnu superimposed on it. Just before the gopura is a **harbour scene**, with chess players on board one of the boats, and a cockfight on another.

The first few sections of carvings beyond the west gopura are in poor condition, so head straight to the section of gallery **north of the tower**, where there's yet another depiction of the story of the **Churning of the Ocean of Milk** (see p.168). The reliefs around the corner in the **north gallery** are in better condition; in the first section servants are shown carrying offerings to a mountain sanctuary with elephants and other wildlife, while boats ferry in worshippers. **Beyond the western tower**, it's worth pausing to check out the pantheon of gods: a fine **ten-armed Shiva** is flanked by Vishnu on his right and Brahma on his left, and surrounded by apsaras.

Turning the corner, you're back in the **east gallery**, where there's a **military parade** featuring musicians accompanying cavalry, and a six-wheeled chariot drawn by Hamsa, the sacred goose and mount of Brahma. The final panel of note, in the gallery just before the gopura, pertains to the legend of the **Leper King**, in which the king contracts

FACE TOWERS

The face towers which gaze out over the Bayon and a number of other Angkorean monuments are enigmatic both in appearance and meaning. The most haunting and instantly recognizable symbol of Khmer architecture, face towers were first introduced during the reign of the great Buddhist monarch Jayavarman VII (see p.294), although exactly whose face they are meant to represent continues to be debated. Earlier archaeologists believed they might symbolize the Hindu deity Brahma, while another more recent interpretation suggests they represent a tantric Buddhist deity, perhaps Vajrasattva, Vajradhara or Hevaraja.

For the time being the most popular (or at least most widely repeated) explanation is that they symbolize Lokesvara (or Avalokitesvara, as he's more widely known outside Cambodia), the great bodhisattva of universal compassion. A twist is provided by the fact that the faces also bear a significant resemblance to carved portraits of Jayavarman himself – perhaps suggesting an attempt by the king to meld his own features with that of the god (whichever god it might have been) into a single all-seeing image of power both earthly and divine.

3

leprosy after being spattered with the venom of a serpent he fights. As women minister to the king, a cure is sought from ascetics.

The first enclosure and central sanctuary

Besides corner towers, the second enclosing wall appears to have a further three towers per side; these are actually part of the **first enclosing wall**, which takes the form of a toothed cross, the points of which merge into the second enclosing wall. The complexity of the construction is compounded in the first enclosure, where towers bearing four faces stand closely packed, at each angle of the cross and on the small sanctuaries.

Whichever route you take into the first enclosure, you'll be presented with a veritable forest of massive, four-faced towers, each face wearing an enigmatic expression with just a glimmer of a smile. Unusually in Khmer architecture, the low platform of the central sanctuary is more or less circular, with eight linked **meditation chambers** spaced around it.

Terrace of the Elephants

Laid out in alignment with the west wall of the Bayon, the **Terrace of the Elephants** originally served as the base for a now-vanished royal reception hall and viewing platform over the surrounding area. The terrace is named for the fabulous bas-reliefs frieze of elephants stretching some 300m along its eastern side, with hundreds of the beasts (and their mahouts) shown hunting and fighting with tigers, interspersed here and there with projecting statues of three-headed elephants, their trunks (entwined around lotus buds) forming impromptu columns. In other places the wall is decorated with lion- and garuda-headed creatures, their arms upraised as if supporting the weight of the terrace above.

Five elaborate sets of **staircases** lead up onto the terrace. On top of the terrace towards its northern end is a raised plaform, decorated with a frieze of hamsas, which would formerly have supported a royal building of some kind. Close by, at the northern end of the terrace, is a striking carving of a **five-headed horse**, hidden behind a later wall that was constructed to buttress the terrace.

Terrace of the Leper King

Adjoining the Terrace of the Elephants, the **Terrace of the Leper King** is believed to have been the site of royal cremations – appropriately, the headless statue on the terrace is that of Yama, god of the underworld, although the vandalized figure is in fact a reproduction. For many years, the statue was assumed to depict Jayavarman VII, who according to several legends contracted the disease himself.

The base of the terrace is covered with profuse **carvings** of gods and goddesses layered in tiers. On the south side at the base of the terrace a small gap leads into a narrow, trench-like walkway that loops around the terrace inside the exterior walls. Here you'll find the so-called "**hidden carvings**", similar to – but a little better preserved than – those outside, with tiers of deities above multi-headed nagas. The walkway was previously filled with rubble and covered over – the theory is that the original terrace (whose outer wall this was) had begun to collapse and so a new retaining wall was built around it.

Prasat Suor Prat

Rising on the opposite side of the road from the Terrace of the Elephants are the twelve distinctive laterite-and-sandstone towers now known fancifully as the **Prasat Suor Prat** ("Towers of the Tightrope Walkers"), although their purpose is unclear – and it certainly wasn't for supporting a tightrope. According to Zhou Daguan (although the story may be apocryphal) they were places for resolving disputes: the parties concerned were kept shut up in one of the towers for between one and four days, by the end of which time the guilty person would inevitably be struck down by some illness or affliction, while the innocent party would emerge as healthy as at the moment they went in.

3

The Kleangs

Behind Prasat Suor Prat are the **Kleangs**, comprising two sizeable rectangular buildings with 1.5m-thick walls filled with large balustraded windows – although exactly what they were built for remains unclear. The North Kleang is the older of the two and was erected towards the end of the tenth century, possibly by Jayavarman V or Jayaviravarman. The unfinished South Kleang is thought to have been constructed by Suryavarman I to balance the view from the royal palace.

Baphuon

Only recently reopened after fifty years of intermittent restoration (see box, p.178), the eleventh-century **Baphuon**, the state-temple of Udayadityavarman II, is one of the most brutally imposing of all Angkor's temples – a veritable mountain of stone, austere and faintly forbidding.

The principal approach is (as usual) from the east, along an impressive, 172m-long sandstone **causeway** raised on three sets of stone posts and with a ruined pavilion halfway (perhaps the base of what was originally a gopura), decorated with entertaining human and animal carvings.

At the end of the causeway rises the temple itself, centred on a mighty central **pyramid** (24m high) consisting of five steep tiers divided by galleries into three enclosures (and with steep wooden steps now replacing the hopelessly eroded original stone staircases). Each gallery has elaborate **gopuras** at the four cardinal points – the outermost of the three eastern gopuras is particularly impressive, topped by a lotus-petal motif and with engaging square carvings (on the inward-facing wall) depicting the animals of Chinese astrology. Further carvings can be found on the other gopuras depicting events from the *Ramayana* and *Mahabharata* and scenes from daily life, with intricate but shallow designs etched out of the blackish, hard-looking sandstone. Unlike the carvings at Angkor Wat and the Bayon, each event here is placed in its own individual panel, like a modern comic book, to be read from bottom to top.

The outermost (third) enclosure is also where you'll find Baphuon's most memorable and unusual feature. Rising above the enclosure, the entire west-facing wall at the base of the pyramid has been moulded into the form of a gigantic **reclining Buddha**. It's a remarkable sight, although the roughness of the stones from which the Buddha is formed means that it can be surprisingly difficult to make out the shape within the stones – at least until you've seen it, when it becomes suddenly obvious, like some clever optical illusion. If you can't immediately see it, try again from a vantage point somewhere right outside the temple, since it can actually be easier to perceive from a distance.

3

BAFFLING BAPHUON

Angkor's longest-running conservation saga, the **fifty-year restoration** of the **Baphuon** temple is a dramatic illustration of the pitfalls and perils of field archaeology in action. Work on the temple began in 1959 under the supervision of French architects, who decided that the only way to save Baphuon from collapse was to dismantle the vast structure piece by piece and then put it all back together again – a technique known as "anastylosis". The temple was therefore dismantled in preparation for its reconstruction, only for war to break out, after which work was abandoned in 1971.

All might have been well, even so, had the Khmer Rouge not decided, in a moment of whimsical iconoclasm, to destroy every last archaeological record relating to work on the temple, including plans showing how the hundreds of thousands of stones that had been taken apart were intended to fit back together again. So when restoration work finally restarted in 1995, conservators were faced (as Pascal Royère, who oversaw the project, put it) with "a three-dimensional, 300,000-piece puzzle to which we had lost the picture".

Progress, not surprisingly, was slow, and it wasn't until 2011 that restorations were finally concluded (at a total cost of $14m) and the temple restored to something approaching its former glory. Numerous unidentified stones can still be seen laid out around the complex, even so – unplaced pieces in a great archaeological jigsaw that will never entirely be solved.

Phimeanakas

The state-temple of Suryavarman I, **Phimeanakas** originally stood in the grounds of the royal palace. Subsequently used for many purposes, it was absorbed into Angkor Thom around two hundred years later. The temple is relatively small and simple in plan, with three, steep rectangular tiers, surrounded by a small moat and all the temple buildings crammed on the topmost level. Elephants (damaged) stand at the corners of each level, while lions flank the stairs.

The temple is designed to be approached from the east; the stairs up to the top are steep and narrow and don't allow you to step off onto the first two levels. Once at the top, you can walk around the surrounding gallery, at whose centre a single cruciform sanctuary tower is raised on a platform. Zhou Daguan recorded that the sanctuary was said to be home to a spirit that took the form of a nine-headed serpent by day and a beautiful lady after dark. The king was obliged to visit her every night before seeing his wife, or else disaster would follow.

To the north of the temple are two paved **bathing ponds**, the smaller for women and the larger for men.

Tep Pranam and Preah Palilay

Tep Pranam, a couple of hundred metres northeast from the Terrace of the Leper King, dates from the ninth-century reign of Yasovarman I, although not much survives of the temple except an impressive, 6m-high Buddha, seated in the bhumispara (earth-witnessing) mudra. The Buddha actually dates only from around the sixteenth century and appears to reuse stones from the original temple, while the head may be more recent than the body on which it sits.

Further west, set in an area of quiet woodland, is **Preah Palilay**. Of the former temple only the central sandstone sanctuary – dating from the first half of the twelfth century – survives more or less intact. It too has a large seated Buddha, of modern provenance.

Thommanon

Consecrated to Vishnu, the small but florid **THOMMANON** Hindu temple was built by Suryavarman II in the early twelfth century, probably at the beginning of his reign (and therefore roughly contemporaneous with Angkor Wat). The temple follows the standard layout of the time, with a cell-like sanctuary, topped with a tower and connected to a mandapa (antechamber). Gopuras stand to the east and west, although the planned north and south gopuras were apparently never built and the wall that originally enclosed the entire complex has now almost completely vanished.

The temple was restored in 1935 and is in good condition, as are its numerous **carvings**, with finely carved devatas (female deities) in jewellery and headdresses on the exterior walls of the sanctuary, while the smaller western gopura has pretty door columns with tiny praying figures enclosed in a swirl of foliage.

Chau Say Tevoda

The sister temple to Thommanon, just over the road, **CHAU SAY TEVODA** was another creation of Suryavarman II, although dating from the end of his reign rather than the beginning. Originally even more elaborate than its sibling across the road, the temple is now badly eroded, with ugly lumps of grey concrete used to patch together the old stonework.

The basic **layout** is similar to that at Thommanon, comprising a central sanctuary-plus-mandapa enclosed within a wall (now mostly disappeared) with four gopuras at the cardinal points; in addition, a pair of libraries stand on either side of the mandapa. Many of the temple's elaborate **carvings** survive in good condition, including some rich floral decorations on the mandapa and assorted devatas, although a few have had their faces bashed off.

Nowadays visitors approach from the road on the north side, although originally the main approach was from the east across the impressive raised **causeway** with octagonal columns that you can still see today, beyond which a pillar-lined pathway leads down to the nearby Siem Reap River.

Spean Thma

Just 200m east of Thommanon and Chau Say Tevoda is the ancient bridge of **Spean Thma**, built using carved sandstone from nearby temples. Once spanning the Siem Reap River, the bridge is now rather stranded, the river having shifted its course. If you step off the road you'll be able to spot mismatched carvings on some of the stones, which were probably recycled from elsewhere when the bridge was rebuilt in the sixteenth century.

Ta Keo

At the western end of the East Baray reservoir stands **TA KEO**, the imposing state-temple of Jayavarman V – an austere mountain of stone in the style of Baphuon and Pre Rup, topped with the usual quincunx of closely spaced towers. The temple was begun around 975 but never finished – legend has it that construction was abandoned after the temple was struck by lightning, an unlucky omen. Constructed entirely of sandstone, Ta Keo is practically undecorated; some sources say that the particular sandstone used is exceptionally hard and too difficult to carve, although fine (though weathered) floral carving around the base of the pyramid seems to contradict that.

Four sets of steep steps at the cardinal points climb up to the small **outer enclosure**, its eastern side almost completely filled by two long and narrow hallways decorated with baluster windows.

From here, further steps lead up into the slightly larger **inner enclosure**, enclosed by a narrow, cloister-like **gallery** (although only the base remains in places). This is the earliest example of what would subsequently become a recurrent feature of Khmer architecture, although unusually the gallery appears to be completely lacking in doors, suggesting that it served a purely decorative function. Two well-preserved **libraries** flank the steps on the enclosure's eastern side, their upper storeys decorated with false windows, and with a further pair of unidentified stone buildings next to them, tucked into the corners of the enclosure.

From here, you can climb one of the steep stairways that lead straight up the temple's three uppermost tiers to reach the **top of the pyramid**, more than 21m above the ground, and the five sanctuary towers, dedicated to Shiva.

Ta Prohm

The jungle-smothered ruins of **TA PROHM** are one of the most evocative of all Angkor's ancient monuments – its courtyards and terraces half-consumed by the encroaching forest, with shrines and pavilions engulfed by giant strangler figs and the massive roots of kapok trees clinging to walls, framing doorways and prising apart giant stones. The temple richly fulfils every Indiana Jones-cum-Tomb-Raider romantic cliché you could imagine – a uniquely serendipitous combination of human artifice and raw nature working together in accidental harmony, with impossibly picturesque results.

That, at least, is what the films and photographs suggest – the reality is slightly less romantic. Crowds are a serious problem, while massive ongoing restoration means that parts of the temple currently resemble an enormous building site as conservators attempt to walk the impossible tightrope between preserving Ta Prohm's original lost-in-the-jungle atmosphere while preventing it from being obliterated entirely by the surrounding forest. It's a magical place, even so, assuming you're not expecting to be left alone to commune with nature, and especially if you can time your visit to avoid the worst of the coach parties (see box below).

Brief history

Constructed by Jayavarman VII around 1186, Ta Prohm was a **Buddhist monastery** dedicated to Prajnaparamita, and would once have housed a statue of this deity in the image of the king's mother (inscriptions say that a further 260 holy images were installed in surrounding chambers and niches). The monastery accommodated twelve thousand people, who lived and worked within its grounds, while a further eighty thousand were employed locally to service and maintain the complex. Ta Prohm also supplied provisions and medicines to the 102 hospitals that Jayavarman instituted around the kingdom.

The site

As at other temple-monasteries such as the roughly contemporaneous Banteay Kdei and Preah Khan, Ta Prohm follows the archetypal pattern of the so-called Angkorian "flat" temple (see box, p.161) – although myriad collapsed walls and accumulated rubble have significantly blurred the neatness of the original plan.

The majority of visitors arrive **from Ta Keo** while on the Petit Circuit, approaching from the west, but if you use the track off the road northwest of Banteay Kdei, you can enter **from the east** as was originally intended, and which is how we describe it here.

Entering the site from the east, you pass through a collapsed gopura, from where a path heads some 500m through forest to reach the main **eastern gopura**, decorated

---

CROWDS AT TA PROHM

In tourist terms, **Ta Prohm** (along with Angkor Wat and the Bayon) is one of Angkor's three big sights, and as such gets overwhelmed with visiting coach parties on a regular basis throughout the day. Unfortunately, the relative smallness of the site means that negotiating your way through the ruins' narrow corridors and doorways in peak hours (roughly 10am–2pm) has all the charm of a visit to a major metropolitan subway station at the height of rush hour. The **best times to visit** are in the early morning (between 7.30am and 9am) or in the late afternoon (after 4pm), although even during these hours it's far from deserted.

CAN'T SEE THE TEMPLE FOR THE TREES

The great tropical trees of Ta Prohm, and many other temples, are an integral part of Angkor – literally so in many places. Tree seeds have germinated throughout Angkor in innumerable crevices in walls and buildings, their roots slowly pushing apart surrounding stones as they grow. These roots act both as agents of conservation and, eventually, destruction, sometimes helping support and even hold up buildings which might otherwise collapse, although once a tree has died and disintegrated the loosened, and by now unsupported, blocks are far more likely to fall apart.

There are two main species of trees at Ta Prohm and elsewhere. The silk-cotton (or kapok) tree, with thick brownish-grey roots, and the strangler fig, with a much finer but denser weave of greyish-white roots. The latter is actually a parisitic epiphyte, germinating in and growing out of the branches of a host tree and eventually enveloping and consuming it (hence the name) – although it seems equally happy to devour bits of temple, should nothing else be available.

---

with fine carvings depicting the life of the Buddha and topped with a huge kapok tree. Beyond here is the impressive terrace that formerly supported the buildings of the **Hall of Dancers** (similar to that at Banteay Kdei).

3

The main section

Walking across the terrace beyond the eastern gopura brings you to the main section of the temple – comprising a large third enclosure within which are the more tightly packed first and second enclosures, the entire edifice topped by a baffling profusion of small towers (39 in total) in various states of photogenic decay. Some of the most photographed **trees** in the world lie further in, scattered inside the second and first enclosures – usually complete with long queues of visitors waiting for their chance to have themselves snapped posing among the roots.

The remains of richly decorated walls and various apsaras survive within the **first enclosure**, almost as if nature has compensated for the overall destruction by preserving the details. At the heart of the temple is the surprisingly tiny **central sanctuary**, now bare inside, although small holes in the walls indicate that it was once clad in wood or metal panels.

From here it's worth continuing straight ahead and out onto the western side of the temple, then retracing your way back around the northern side of the third enclosure normally relatively peaceful even during peak times, where further giant kapok trees can be seen hugging the temple walls, with nothing but untouched forest beyond.

Banteay Kdei

BANTEAY KDEI (Citadel of the Cells) was built by Jayavarman VII as a Buddhist monastery over the site of an earlier tenth-century temple by Rajendravarman. The overall layout is similar to Ta Prohm, although the buildings here remained in fairly continual use until the 1960s and so lack the lost-in-the-jungle atmosphere that makes Ta Prohm so memorable – and, equally, the appalling crowds. That said, ongoing habitation failed to prevent some pretty major masonry collapses, perhaps due to a combination of low-quality sandstone and poor building techniques which characterize so many of the buildings from Jayavarman VII's reign – the most vulnerable sections are now propped up with permanent wooden struts and scaffolding.

Entrance is from the east, through the enclosing wall beneath a fine **gopura** topped with Lokesvara faces. A few minutes' walk brings you to the remains of a laterite causeway across a moat, connecting to the **Hall of the Dancers**, named for the reliefs of apsaras that decorate its pillars and exterior walls.

Immediately beyond the Hall of the Dancers is the temple proper, comprising a **central sanctuary** surrounded by two concentric **galleries** and topped by seven closely grouped **towers** – although the confusing jumble of tiny rooms and courtyards, and myriad collapsed walls, rather obscures the basic plan. Beautiful carvings survive here and there among the ruins, flecked in places with vivid splashes of green lichen and rust-red traces of their original paint, with elaborate leaf motifs on the walls and female divinities in niches – although many of the monastery's Buddha images have been crudely hacked out.

Srah Srang

East of Banteay Kdei, the royal bathing pool of **Srah Srang** was probably the work of Kavindramantha, an army-general-cum-architect who was also responsible for building the temples of East Mebon and Pre Rup. Excavated for Rajendravarman I, the pool once had simple earth embankments, and rules had to be issued to stop people allowing elephants to clamber over them to be bathed in the waters below. Two hundred years later, Jayavarman VII had the banks lined with sandstone and built a regal terrace offering views over the water. The remains of a paved causeway edged with naga balustrades, which once linked the pool with Banteay Kdei to the west, can also be seen here.

Prasat Kravan

South of Banteay Kdei is the simple little **PRASAT KRAVAN**, the Cardamom Sanctuary, consecrated around 921 during the reign of Harshavarman I and comprising a row of five brick towers sitting on a low platform – a 1960 restoration left them looking, if anything, a bit too neat and new, although the exceptional quality of the brickwork (precisely fitted, and held together using a kind of vegetable glue rather than mortar) might silence even the most hard-to-impress builder.

Male guardians in niches decorate the exterior of the **central tower**, although more interesting are the reliefs of Vishnu within – one shows him mounted on Garuda; another shows his dwarf incarnation, Vamana, bestriding the universe in three giant steps; while a third, a rather worn rendering of Vishnu with eight arms, was probably once covered in stucco and painted. The northernmost tower is dedicated to Lakshmi, wife of Vishnu and goddess of good fortune. Inside, an intricate relief shows her bare-breasted and wearing a pleated *sampot*, flanked by two kneeling worshippers and surrounded by swags of leaves and dangling pendant motifs.

Pre Rup

One of Angkor's most impressive monuments – and a highlight of the Grand Circuit – the great state-temple of **PRE RUP** (built by Rajendravarman and consecrated to Shiva in around 962) is the archetypal ancient Khmer temple-mountain. Access it from the eastern side, where five tall **brick towers** stand sentinel overlooking the road (space was left for a sixth tower, which never got built).

Entering the **first enclosure** you'll see a small stone "cistern" directly in front of you. Long assumed to be associated with cremations (the name Pre Rup means, literally, "turning the body"), it's now agreed that this probably formed the pedestal for a statue of Nandin. Flanking the cistern are a pair of brick libraries, their walls pierced with unusual slits to aid ventilation. Nearby, in the northeast corner of the enclosure, a small, square, laterite building – open on all sides – once housed a stele. The rest of the enclosure is largely filled with long halls, now mostly ruined.

Stairways guarded by lions lead up all four sides of the majestic **pyramid**. Twelve small, symmetrically arranged shrines stand around the lowest level. Five quincunx **towers** stand at the summit, soaring memorably above the surrounding forest canopy. The two towers on the western side (which once housed statues of Lakshmi and Uma)

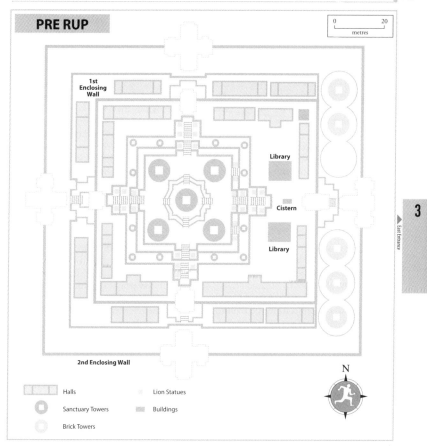

PRE RUP

0   20
metres

1st Enclosing Wall

Library

Cistern

Library

2nd Enclosing Wall

N

East Entrance

3

Halls

Sanctuary Towers

Brick Towers

Lion Statues

Buildings

feature carved reliefs of female divinities, including a four-headed Brahmi, a consort of Brahma, on the eastern side of the southwest tower (where you can also make out remnants of the gritty white-lime stucco that once coated the towers). Carvings of male deities adorn the central and two eastern towers, once home to statues of Vishnu and Shiva.

East Mebon

Erected in 953 for Rajendravarman, **EAST MEBON** (pronounced "*May*bon") once stood on an island surrounded by the waters of the (now dry) East Baray – the broad steps below each of the four gopuras were originally landing stages, as the temple would only have been accessible by boat. The temple was actually built by the king for his parents, although it's closer to the great state-temples in style, topped by a cluster of soaring, closely spaced towers – which would doubtless have looked even more memorable when seen rising from the waters of the East Baray. Impressive from a distance, the temple is relatively disappointing close up. Much of it would originally have been colourfully plastered and painted, although the general effect now is rather bare, the general austerity relieved only by the finely carved doorways and lintels that decorate the various gopuras and towers.

Access to the temple is via the eastern gopura, which brings you into the **outer enclosure**, lined with a series of ruined meditation halls. The western gopura, on the opposite side of the enclosure, features a reasonably preserved lintel carving of Vishnu in his incarnation as the man-lion Narasimha, ripping apart the king of the demons.

Above rise the two tiers of the central pyramid with almost life-sized **elephant statues** positioned at each corner, serving as guardians, and so facing outwards. Four sets of steps lead up to the **inner enclosure**, each flanked with a pair of towers, their doors finely decorated with carved foliage. Five rectangular, windowless laterite buildings (original function unknown) are arranged around the enclosure.

Further steps lead up to the topmost level and the five sanctuary **towers**, arranged in the customary quincunx pattern. These are made of brick but were originally covered in stucco – you can still see the numerous round holes cut into the brickwork to help the coating adhere. The **carvings** on the sandstone lintels are also worth a look: the central tower features Indra on his three-headed elephant Airavata (on its east side), Yama on a bullock (south) and Varuna on a swan-like hamsa (west).

Ta Som

The small, tumbledown Buddhist temple of **TA SOM** has been badly knocked about by time and the jungle but still has plenty of character, feeling a little like a miniature Ta Prohm without the crowds. The shrine was built by Jayavarman VII in the twelfth century and subsequently enlarged by his successor Indravarman II, which explains why the moat is, unusually, located inside the outer enclosure.

The usual approach is from the road to the west of the temple, passing through a gopura with face tower, over the small tree-filled moat and into the walled **central enclosure**. The sanctuary itself is nothing more than a single, crumbling cruciform tower. More interesting are the numerous niched **apsaras** decorating the walls around the enclosure, with unusual carvings including one (on the north side of the northern gate into the central enclosure) nestling a bird in her hand and others apparently wringing their hair out after a bath. Have a look, too, at the **gopura** on the eastern side of the central enclosure (next to the moat), with another face tower and a porch spectacularly engulfed in a giant strangler fig.

Neak Pean

The beautiful water temple of **NEAK PEAN** (literally "entwined serpents") is quite unlike anything else at Angkor, with a single tower sitting in the centre of a large pool, connected to four subsidiary pools at the cardinal points. It's really more of a symbolic water garden than a temple, although what it all originally meant remains unclear. The most popular theory holds that it represents Anavatapa, a mythical Himalayan lake whose waters had miraculous curative powers. Zhou Daguan describes it as "having a central square tower of gold with several dozen stone rooms", suggesting that the temple may even have been a kind of spa, with pilgrims coming to take the waters.

The temple stands on an island in the **northern baray**, which still fills up with considerable amounts of water after rain. Access to the temple is via a long wooden walkway across the water from the north; barriers prevent you from walking around the temple itself, although you can still get a good view of the complex. The sanctuary tower stands directly ahead, with carvings of Lokesvara on each of its four faces and two stone serpents curling around the base of the platform on which it stands (hence the temple's unusual name). The heads of the two serpents rise next to one another on the eastern side of the tower. Emerging from the waters of the pool close by is a large **statue** with tiny figures clinging to its sides: this is a depiction of Lokesvara in the form of a horse, Balaha, rescuing merchants from ogresses on an island off Sri Lanka.

Preah Khan

Built by Jayavarman VII on the site of an earlier palace, the massive complex of **PREAH KHAN** (not to be confused with the huge temple-citadel of Preah Khan in Kompong Thom province) served simultaneously as temple, monastery and university. As the last, it employed more than a thousand teachers and 97,840 ancillary staff – inscriptions found here reveal that ten tonnes of rice were delivered daily, enough to feed ten to fifteen thousand people. However, in 1191 Preah Khan was consecrated as a multi-faith temple, catering to worshippers of Buddha, Shiva and Vishnu, plus a further 282 gods, some made in the image of local dignitaries and national heroes. The main deity was Lokesvara, made in the likeness of the king's father, and placed in the central – Buddhist – sanctuary.

The site

The layout of the temple is similar to that of Banteay Kdei and Ta Prohm – indeed there's a distinct touch of Ta Prohm about the site as a whole, with tumbled heaps of greenish, lichen-coated sandstone half-smothered by the surrounding trees. Large portions of the structure have collapsed. As at Banteay Kdei, this may have been the result of faulty construction – the central area, closely packed with sanctuaries and passages, was extended on numerous occasions.

Most people now approach **from the west** (which is how we describe it below), although you can also enter in the traditional direction from the east, where the temple runs down to the waters of the northern *baray*. Even better, walk from one side to the other and arrange to be picked up by your driver on the opposite side to save backtracking.

The entire complex is surrounded by an enclosing wall and moat, with the usual gopuras and causeways in each cardinal direction. Approach from the west and you'll find the first section of the path lined with interesting **boundary stones**, their lower halves carved with cartoonish *kala*-like monsters – the niches at the top of each pillar once contained Buddha images, which were crudely cut out when the state religion reverted to Hinduism. Beyond here a **causeway** flanked by impressive naga balustrades and huge garuda carvings crosses the expansive moat to reach the forest-filled fourth enclosure.

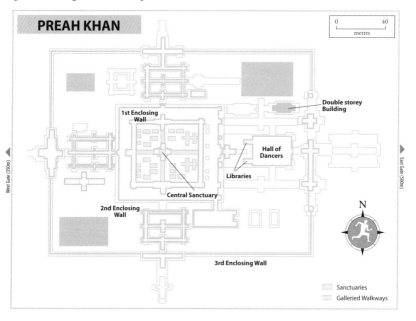

THE SACRED SWORD

The **sacred sword**, as Preah Khan translates, is said to have been a weapon ceremonially passed by Jayavarman II to his heir, and Cambodians still believe that whoever possesses this sword has the right to the country's throne – many believe a replica of the sword is kept under lock and key at the Royal Palace in Phnom Penh.

From here, it's a 250m walk through the trees to reach the main section of the temple. The relatively large **third enclosure** is decorated with beautifully carved apsaras in niches and on lintels. Beyond here lie the dense cluster of buildings within the tightly packed **second** and **first enclosures** (an intricate design further confused by large-scale masonry falls), with views of doors and windows framed within one another in receding, Escheresque perspectives. Patches of fine floral carving cover many of the walls and surfaces, as if in imitation of the natural vegetation consuming the buildings on all sides. Also dotted around here are more than twenty tiny sanctuaries that once contained holy images, while more would have been housed in the alcoves of the surrounding gallery.

At the heart of the temple, the **central sanctuary** contains a dome-shaped **stupa**, added in the sixteenth century. More tricky to find, in a collapsed section to the north, are two sublime carvings of the sisters **Indradevi** and **Jayadevi**, both wives of Jayavarman.

Continue through the temple to emerge back out on the eastern side of the third enclosure. In front of you is the **terrace of the Dancers' Hall** (similar to those at Banteay Kdei and Ta Prohm), dotted with columns carved with dancing apsaras, while to your left is an unusual two-storey building, its upper storey supported by a ring of round columns, which may have housed the **sacred sword** (see box above).

Continuing straight on from here brings you out at the **eastern gate** after another 500m or so. This side of the temple is almost a perfect mirror image of the western part (although slightly larger), with a forest path through the fourth enclosure leading to a gopura flanked by large garudas, another fine naga balustrade over the moat, and further boundary stones.

West Baray and West Mebon

Accessible only via the airport road from Siem Reap, Angkor's huge **West Baray** reservoir, 8km long and more than 2km wide, was excavated by Suryavarman I; it's been calculated that six thousand men would have needed more than three years to dig it out. The *baray* was restored in 1957 and, unlike the East Baray, contains water throughout the year, making it a popular local spot for **picnics and swimming**. Rest huts line the embankment at the leisure area to the south, which is also where you can rent a boat ($5) out to the island-temple, the **West Mebon**. This mid-eleventh-century temple, attributed to Udayadityavarman II, has practically disappeared; only the eastern towers, bearing small decorations of animals in square motifs, are in reasonable condition. The island on which it stands was once linked to the shore by a causeway, and surrounded by a wall with three pavilions per side and windows overlooking the *baray*.

Roluos Group

Off NR6, 12km east of Siem Reap, the temples now referred to as the **Roluos Group** – after the nearby village of that name – are spread out over the former site of the royal city of **Hariharalaya**, and encompass some of the earliest monuments of the Angkor period. Among those most easily visited are three brick-and-sandstone temples built by Indravarman I and his son, Yasovarman I, in the late ninth century, all featuring finely decorated columns and lintels. These are the **Bakong**, the first state-temple of the Angkor period; **Lolei**, which has particularly fine Sanskrit inscriptions; and **Preah Ko**, which preserves some elegant carvings.

Preah Ko

PREAH KO was the first temple to be built in Hariharalaya, constructed by Indravarman I in 879 to honour the spirits of his parents and grandparents, and also the original founder of Angkor, Jayavarman II. The temple sits right next to the road and is entered from the east through a ruined **gopura**, largely vanished but for a pair of impressive balustraded windows. Walking through the gopura you reach the temple's two inner enclosures, although the wall that originally divided them has all but disappeared. The eye-catching square brick structure (on your left as you enter) may have been a **library** or crematorium; ventilation holes have been cut into the top of the building, with eroded carvings of ascetics seated in niches between.

At the centre of the temple, on a low platform, stand six closely grouped brick-and-sandstone **towers**, arranged in two rows of three and still covered in places by the crumbling remains of the lime plaster which once covered them completely. The front three towers were dedicated to the king's paternal ancestors, watched over by a trio of sacred bulls (one headless) and with male guardians (*dvarapalas*) standing in niches at their corners. The three smaller rear towers were dedicated to maternal ancestors and have female guardians instead.

The towers are most notable for the fine **carvings** on their doorframes and lintels (a number of long inscriptions can also be seen on several doorjambs). Many feature a leering *kala* spewing out a floral arch, some with miniature horsemen galloping along the top of the arch and tiny figures riding three-headed snakes below, and with *makaras* at either end.

Bakong

The undoubted highlight of the Roluos circuit, **BAKONG** is the first of the great Angkor state-temples, prefiguring (if not quite rivalling) the huge temple-pyramids of Pre Rup and Baphuon. The temple was constructed by Indravarman I and consecrated to Shiva in 881, although surprisingly, the grand sanctuary **tower** at the very top wasn't added until some 250 years after the temple was first consecrated.

The entire complex is enclosed within a broad moat with a modern wat tucked into one corner – an unusually photogenic combination. From the parking area a **causeway** crosses the moat to the eastern gopura, beyond which stretches the temple's expansive **inner enclosure**, with the central pyramid rising out of its centre. As you enter the enclosure, the path is flanked by a pair of well-preserved hallways with ornate balustraded windows, along with two square buildings with ventilation holes in their walls, probably crematoria. Eight large brick towers in various states of decay are arranged around the base of the pyramid, two per side, their sandstone doors displaying some fine carvings.

The central **pyramid** is arranged over no fewer than five tiers, the overall design notably larger but less steep than later state-temples. Lions flank the staircase up the pyramid, while guardian elephants stand in each corner, similar to those at East Mebon. Spaced out around the fourth tier are twelve small sandstone shrines, now empty, though they would once have housed linga.

At the summit of the pyramid stands the solitary tower – a fine structure, although it looks rather lonely up there on its own, proving, perhaps, how much more visually satisfying is the traditional quincunx arrangement of towers at the summit of other state-temples.

Lolei

Now situated within the grounds of a modern pagoda, **LOLEI** originally stood on an artificial island in the centre of the **Indratataka Baray**, though the reservoir is now dry. Dedicated to the parents and maternal grandparents of Yasovarman I and consecrated to Shiva, the temple consists of four brick towers (six were originally planned), although one has now partially collapsed and the others are crumbling. Well-preserved Sanskrit inscriptions can be seen on the doorways of the rear towers, detailing the work rotas of temple servants, and there's also a particularly fine lintel on the rear northern tower.

Banteay Samre

Part of the Grand Circuit (although slightly remote from the other temples on that itinerary, and often omitted), **BANTEAY SAMRE** lies east of **Phum Pradak** village, 12km northeast of Siem Reap. No inscriptions have been found to date the temple, which was named after the Samres, a tribe that lived in the vicinity of Phnom Kulen. However, its style of architecture places its construction in the middle of the twelfth century, around the same time as Angkor Wat. It was superbly restored by French archaeologist Maurice Glaize – one of the most notable figures in the early history of Angkor conservation – in the 1940s.

Banteay Samre is unique among the Angkor temples in having **two moats** within the complex itself. The temple, enclosed by a high laterite wall with cruciform gopuras at each of the cardinal points, is approached via a 200m-long paved causeway. Entering through the east gopura, you arrive in an open gallery whose rows of sandstone columns were once part of a roofed gallery that would have run the full perimeter of the enclosure. The paved sunken area ahead was once the first of the moats, forming the second enclosure. Tales from the *Ramayana* are depicted on various **carvings** here – the siege of Lanka is shown on the gopura pediments, the fight between Rama and Ravana on the east tower, and Rama carried by Hanuman on the north tower.

Crossing the moat, you pass through another gopura, with double vestibules to the north and south, the passages of which connect to a raised gallery separating the two moats. Rising out of the inner moat like islands are the **central sanctuary**, connected to the walkway via a gopura to the east, and two **libraries**, which would only have been reachable by boat when the moats were filled.

Cambodia Landmine Museum

7km south of Banteay Srei on the main road to Siem Reap • Daily 7.30am–5.30pm • $5 • ☎ 015 674163, ⓦ cambodialandminemuseum.org

South of Banteay Srei temple, the **Cambodia Landmine Museum** is the creation of Aki Ra, a self-taught de-miner who was once forced to lay mines as a Vietnamese conscript. Crammed full of rusting mines and other military paraphernalia, the museum offers a stark reminder of the ongoing devastation caused by mines both in Cambodia and elsewhere (see p.305), describing some of the historical background and human stories behind these deadly explosives. Museum profits go to support local mine victims.

Banteay Srei

Even if you're feeling pretty templed-out, you'll be captivated by **BANTEAY SREI**, 35km northeast of Siem Reap. Built of fine-grained rose-pink sandstone, it's the most elaborately decorated of all Angkor's monuments, its walls, false doors, lintels and exotic soaring pediments all richly embellished with floral motifs and *Ramayana* scenes.

Banteay Srei is also unusual in having been built not by a king, but by two local **dignitaries**: Yajnavaraha, who was a trusted guru to the monarch, and his brother. It was Rajendravarman who granted them the land and permission for a temple to be built, but although the sanctuary was consecrated in 967 to Shiva, it wasn't actually completed until the reign of Jayavarman V.

The site

The temple **layout** is relatively simple, with three enclosing walls, an inner moat and a row of three sanctuary towers at its centre. If the **eastern gopura** by which you enter the temple seems oddly stranded, that's because there was never an enclosing wall here. Note the very fine carving above the exterior of the gopura's east door, showing the god **Indra** squatting on his three-headed elephant Airavata.

From the eastern gopura, a paved **processional way** leads 75m west to the main temple complex. Around the midway point, a pavilion to the north boasts a particularly detailed engraved pediment showing Vishnu in his incarnation as the man-lion Narasimha. Just before you reach the gopura in the third enclosing wall, you'll find a carved pediment (lying upright on the ground to the right of the doorway) showing Sita swooning as she is abducted by Ravana. The **gopura** itself is one of the most dramatic at the site, with soaring finials and the carved scrolls of fine leaf decorations and floral motifs.

In the rainy season, there are marvellous reflections of the temple when the moat within the third enclosure fills. The narrow **second enclosure** is jammed with six long galleries, each subdivided into rooms that might have been meditation halls.

First enclosure

Virtually no surface within the **first enclosure** remains unadorned, although unfortunately you're no longer allowed inside the sanctuary towers, and the platform on which they stand is roped off to protect the carvings.

The carvings on the **sanctuary towers** are almost fussy in their profusion. The niches around the central sanctuary shelter male **guardians**, while those on the other towers house serene female **divinities**, complete with elegant *sampots* and elaborate jewellery. Crouched near the temple steps are more guardians, mythical figures with animal heads and human bodies (although these are actually reproductions, the originals having been removed, like many of the best sculptures here, during the French colonial period and taken to the Guimet museum of Asian art in Paris, where they remain, despite attempts to have them returned to Cambodia). The *Ramayana* scenes carved on the lintels of the central tower are particularly fine, featuring, to the west, another depiction of Sita being carried off by Ravana; and, to the north, the fight between the monkey gods Valin and Sugriva. The multi-tiered roofs of the towers are decorated with tiny replicas of the temple towers – meant to be homes for the temple gods.

There are more fine carvings on the east pediment of the **south library**, where Ravana is shown shaking Mount Kailash; Shiva sits on the mountain's summit with his wife Parvati, while the forest animals run away in fear. On the west pediment, Parvati can be seen asking for the aid of Kama, the god of love, after Shiva ignores her offering of a rosary; she finally wins Shiva's attention and his hand in marriage after Kama obligingly shoots him with an arrow.

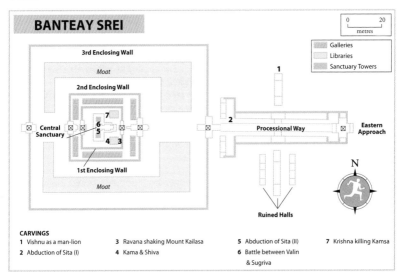

BANTEAY SREI

0   20

metres

Galleries

Libraries

Sanctuary Towers

3rd Enclosing Wall

Moat

2nd Enclosing Wall

Central Sanctuary

1st Enclosing Wall

Moat

Processional Way

Eastern Approach

N

Ruined Halls

CARVINGS

1 Vishnu as a man-lion

2 Abduction of Sita (I)

3 Ravana shaking Mount Kailasa

4 Kama & Shiva

5 Abduction of Sita (II)

6 Battle between Valin & Sugriva

7 Krishna killing Kamsa

The **north library** is dedicated to Vishnu and, accordingly, the carvings focus on him. The close parallel streaks on the east pediment represent rain pouring down on the forest, through which Krishna – Vishnu's human incarnation – and his brother make their way, surrounded by wild animals. Krishna is seen taking revenge on his cruel uncle, King Kamsa, on the west pediment, with the palace in uproar as Krishna seizes him by the hair and prepares to kill him.

Kbal Spean

Daily 5am–3pm; allow at least 90min for the visit – it takes around 45min to climb the hill

In a magical area of jungle on the western side of the Kulen Mountains, **Kbal Spean** was used by the Khmer as a hill retreat in the mid-eleventh century, during which period they carved sacred linga and Hindu gods into the bedrock of the river – the water flowing down the river would thus be blessed by the carvings before coursing on to Angkor. The scenes depicting Vishnu are of marvellous ingenuity, not only for their skilful execution but also for the way they are tailored to the contours of the riverbed. Although looters have crudely hacked out some sections of bedrock, the scenes are almost as remarkable today as they were when first carved.

The path follows the east bank of the river and has a couple of steep stretches; you'll come to the top of the hill, a natural bridge, after about forty-five minutes' walk, which is a good place to start. Upstream, lingas are carved into the riverbed–two reclining Vishnus and a carving of Uma and Shiva on the bull, Nandin. On the way down, stop to admire the veritable cobble of lingas, which including more reclining Vishnus and associated pantheon.

ARRIVAL AND DEPARTURE   TEMPLES OF ANGKOR: THE ARCHAEOLOGICAL PARK

There's no public transport to the temples, which are spread out over a fair area, so – unless you fancy **cycling** – you'll need to rent your own transport. **Tuk-tuks** are the most popular option – cheaper and more fun than a car, but more comfortable (and only slightly more expensive) than a **moto**. For **motorbike** hire, see p.145. There are also various ways to see the temples **from the air** (see p.169).

By tuk-tuk or moto Siem Reap is awash with tuk-tuks and motos, although it's probably best to rent one through your guesthouse or hotel; pretty much all drivers speak at least a little English. Approximate prices are $15/$12/$25 (tuk-tuk/moto/car) each for the Small Circuit, the Grand Circuit, and the Roluos Group. Add around $3/$2/$5 if you want to start in time for sunrise, and $10/$8/$12 if you want to add Banteay Srei. Going off-menu and combining temples from the various groups (see p.167) will mean bargaining a fare in advance.

By bike Cycling is in many ways the perfect way to experience the temples, although the distances involved are not inconsiderable: the Small Circuit is around 30km long, and the Grand Circuit a little over 35km. This might not sound like that

much in itself, but bear in mind that exploring the temples can be physically tiring on its own, even before you've started pedalling. If you do cycle, you might plan on visiting slightly fewer temples than if taking a vehicle. There are bike rental options in Siem Reap (see p.145), while some operators such as Grasshopper Adventures (see p.145) run guided bike rides around the temples. A less strenuous alternative is to rent an **e-bike** (see p.145).

By car A car and driver can be hired from most Siem Reap guesthouses and hotels, or from the tourist office (from $25). Costs are around $25/day around Angkor, $37 to Banteay Srei, $55 to Beng Mealea, $85 to Beng Mealea and Koh Ker, and $75 to Phnom Kulen.

INFORMATION

Opening hours Most of the temples are open 7.30am–5.30pm. Angkor Wat and Sra Srang open for sunrise at 5am, while Pre Rup and Phnom Bakheng are open sunrise to sunset (5am–7pm).

Entry passes You must buy a pass to enter the Angkor Archaeological Park, and you will need to show it at the various temples – prices were raised significantly (and with some controversy) in February 2017, with the cost of a

one-day ticket almost doubling overnight. Three categories of pass are available at the main ticket office: one day ($37; this can also be purchased after 5pm, allowing entry for sunset on the day of purchase and all the following day); three days, valid for three days during the following week ($62); and seven days ($72), valid for one month. Children under 12 are admitted free, but you must show their passport as proof of age; children aged 12 and over are charged the full entrance fee. One-day passes only can be bought at the ticket office between the airport and Angkor Wat, at Roluos Group and at Banteay Srei. Note that payment is by cash only. There is no need to provide a photo as these are now taken digitally at the ticket office. Separate tickets are required to visit Phnom Kulen (see below), Koh Ker (see p.194) and Beng Mealea (see p.192), with tickets issued at each temple.

Tour guides Highly trained, government-licensed guides to the Angkor temples can be booked through any of the various tourist offices in Siem Reap (see p.144), or sometimes at the ticket office, costing $35/day for an English-speaking guide. Note that guides do not drive tuk-tuks and tuk-tuk drivers do not guide.

Books There are several detailed and highly illustrated book-length guides to Angkor (see p.315), all widely available in Siem Reap (secondhand or pirated copies can be picked up for as little as $6 or so).

Safety If you plan to visit outlying temples we've not covered, you should seek advice from registered guides regarding the safety situation, as some sites have not been fully de-mined.

EATING AND DRINKING

There are a few **refreshment stalls** at most of the larger temple complexes, and restaurants at various places including Angkor Wat, the Terrace of the Leper King, Neak Pean and along the north side of Srah Srang – all sell fairly ordinary food at slightly inflated prices, most with English-language menus. Alternatively, bring a picnic; many Siem Reap hotels now offer a picnic basket, or make your own from one of the local supermarkets (see p.156) or the excellent *Blue Pumpkin* bakery (see p.150).

3

Phnom Kulen

50km north of Siem Reap • $20

It was at **PHNOM KULEN**, then known as Mahendrapura, that Jayavarman II had himself consecrated supreme ruler in 802 (a date that is regarded as marking the start of the Angkorian period), instigating the cult of the devaraja (see p.293). Although ancient temples are scattered here and elsewhere in the Kulen Mountains, none of these can be visited due to the lack of roads and the danger of land mines. Instead, the main reason to visit Phnom Kulen, 50km north of Siem Reap, is to gawp at the massive **reclining Buddha** carved out of a huge rock in the sixteenth century – and once you're here you may find yourself very taken with the piety of the Buddhist devotees who come to worship at a chain of shrines. Unfortunately, the Angkor pass isn't valid at Phnom Kulen, and the high entrance charge coupled with the cost of getting here keeps all but the most dedicated explorers from visiting. Note too that the area was heavily **mined** by the Khmer Rouge and is yet to be fully cleared. Don't wander off to locations other than those described here unless you have an experienced local guide.

The hill

From the ticket office at the foot of the hill the road climbs steadily through forest to a sandstone plateau. On the left a track leads to a parking area from where you can walk down to the river where you may be able to make out some of the **linga** for which the river is famed, but as they're only 25cm square, they're hard to spot on the riverbed if the waters are high or turbid. It's a further 1km or so to the top of the hill, which is packed with stalls selling refreshments and Khmer medicine, from where there are good views over the surrounding Kulen Mountains. A short climb brings you to a busy pagoda, Preah Ang Thom, which features a much-revered and impressive **reclining Buddha**, carved into a massive boulder, usually busy with Cambodians making offerings. A simple but impressive frieze of Buddha heads is carved around the base of the rock.

There are further forest **shrines** behind the pagoda – follow the locals, who come armed with huge bundles of incense to ensure they have enough to make offerings at all the shrines on the circuit. Nearly every boulder has a legend attached to it – one with holes that look like claw marks is said to be where Hanuman crash-landed. At the end of the track, Cambodians come to wash their faces in water from a **holy spring** which gushes from a boulder, believing this will give energy, good health and luck; old bottles are produced and filled to take home.

Beng Mealea

60km east of Siem Reap • Daily 7am–5.30pm • $5 • Beng Mealea is connected to Siem Reap by a good tarmac road, which continues to Koh Ker, meaning that a visit to both sites can be combined in a day-trip – it's about 1hr 30min from Siem Reap to Beng Mealea, and a further hour on to Koh Ker (count on about $35/55 by tuk-tuk/car, or $85 if you want to continue to Koh Ker (you'll need a car for this)

The largely unrestored temple of **BENG MEALEA** ("Lotus Pond") gives a good idea of what French archaeologists found when they first arrived at Angkor, with huge piles of mossy masonry tumbled amid huge trees and glimpses of intricate carvings peeping incongruously from between the jungle-smothered ruins. The whole site has been somewhat tidied up over recent years, with roped-off walkways and wooden staircases constructed to lead visitors safely through the various enclosures, but the complex as a whole retains much of its original lost-in-the-jungle atmosphere, eclipsing even the tree-studded shrines of Ta Prohm for wild appeal.

Exactly when or why the temple was built is unknown, although it occupies a strategic location roughly midway between Angkor and Koh Ker, and also marks the place where the roads to Koh Ker and Preah Khan divide (as well as being just a few kilometres from the Angkorian sandstone quarries of Phnom Kulen). The style of the temple suggests a construction date in mid-twelfth century, possibly by Suryavarman II, creator of Angkor Wat. Indeed basic layout of the two temples is remarkably similar and the plan of Angkor Wat on p.165 is almost identical with that of Beng Mealea – although you'll have to look at it upside down, since Beng Mealea is oriented to the east, and Angkor Wat to the west.

Whoever built it and for whatever reason, at just over a kilometre square and with a formidable 45m-wide moat, the site was clearly of some consequence. Constructed of sandstone from the nearby Phnom Kulen quarries, the temple is on a single level, divided into three enclosures. The main entrance nowadays is via the southern gate, over the customary causeway across the huge moat (now largely obscured by vegetation) to a second causeway flanked with naga balustrades (plus a fine pair of naga heads halfway down).

The southern gopura and adjacent cruciform terrace are now little more than an illegible jumble of stones, as is most of what lies beyond. Following the rope-walkways through the enclosures you'll see fine traces of carvings here on walls, lintels and pediments, along with the occasional apsara, and sections of surviving buildings (many of them now wrapped in tree roots). The overall plan is hard to discern, however, while

ANGKOR UNDERGROUND

Much of the beauty of Angkor is in its setting, with great temples standing in idyllic isolation, surrounded by nothing but jungle and paddy. That there was originally a city surrounding the now stranded temples has long been known, or at least conjectured, but the staggering size of ancient Angkor has only been fully realized in recent years thanks to two surveys (in 2012 and 2015) led by Australian archaeologist Damian Evans, using state-of-the-art **Lidar** (Light Detection and Ranging) technology which fires lasers at the ground from a helicopter, allowing researchers to literally see the hidden outlines of things buried beneath the soil and facilitating a string of ground-breaking discoveries without the need to move a single piece of earth.

Initial surveys using Lidar revealed the outlines of extensive residential areas and geometrical street grids surrounding major temples of "downtown" Angkor such as Angkor Wat, while further surveys revealed the layout of similarly huge but previously unsuspected cities surrounding the remote temples of Preah Khan, Koh Ker and, most dramatically, on top of Phnom Kulen – the last named, researchers believe, was once as large as modern Phnom Penh. The picture that emerges is of the world's largest urban settlement of pre-industrial times, covering an area equivalent to that of modern Berlin with a series of discrete urban centres spread over a huge area – more akin to a twenty-first-century urban conurbation than a traditional nuclear city. Full details of the project, plus some spectacular Lidar images, can be found at ⓦ angkorlidar.org.

FROM TOP BANTEAY SREI (P.188); APSARA DANCERS (P.154) >

the single central sanctuary tower is also now nothing more than a vast pile of rubble after being blown up by the Khmer Rouge while hunting for buried treasure.

Koh Ker

One of Cambodia's most remote Angkorian sites, 125km northeast of Siem Reap, **KOH KER** was briefly capital of the Khmer Empire in the tenth century, when Jayavarman IV – who was already ruler of his own state here when he ascended the imperial throne – decided not to relocate to Angkor but decreed instead that the court should come to him, ordering the construction of a road linking Koh Ker and Angkor, on which the temples of Beng Mealea and Banteay Samre were later built.

Now practically engulfed by jungle, the ruins of Koh Ker have been heavily looted and badly neglected, but plenty remains, including more than forty major monuments spread across eighty square kilometres – although only a small proportion are open to visitors, and much of the area has yet to be completely cleared of **mines** – on no account stray from well-trodden paths.

Prasat Thom

Koh Ker's major temple complex is **Prasat Thom**, consisting of three enclosures laid out in a row (as at Preah Vihear), with the sanctuary at the centre of the final courtyard. Entrance to the complex is from the east, past a distinctive red-brick **tower**, part of the temple's third enclosure and still showing flecks of its original white plaster.

Past the tower is a wide but now largely dried-up moat, crossed by a causeway flanked by collapsed naga balustrades, giving onto a narrow second enclosure, where long thin buildings almost form a gallery. A final gopura through a sandstone wall leads into the first enclosure, where a terrace supports nine small sanctuaries in two rows, five in front and four behind.

The Prang

Continue straight ahead, exiting Prasat Thom and crossing another causeway over the moat (with the scant remains of ruined naga balustrades) to reach Koh Ker's most memorable sight, the **Prang**, a 35m-high, seven-tiered sandstone ziggurat looking oddly like one of the great Mayan monuments of Central America and Mexico. This was meant to be Jayavarman IV's state-temple but was never completed. Instead of a sanctuary tower at the top there's just a pedestal, formerly topped with a gigantic 3.5m-high linga (one of the city's original names was Lingapura, "City of the Linga"). A modern wooden staircase hugs the north side of the ziggurat, with 160 steps leading to the summit and sweeping views over the surrounding sea of trees, and the mountains beyond.

Just as high as the Prang is the man-made hill beyond, known as **Pnoh Damrei Saw** (Tomb of the White Elephant), either the foundation of a second pyramid which never got built, or possibly the grave of Jayavarman IV himself, although it now looks simply like a natural jungle-smothered hill.

Outlying temples

Numerous further temples dot the surrounding area, many of them arranged around the **Rohal**, a 1km-long reservoir (now dry) hewn out of the rock at Jayavarman IV's behest. East of Prasat Thom, it's worth hunting out **Prasat Linga**, home to a massive metre-high stone linga and yoni, raised on a huge base supported by stone lions. Also worth a look is **Prasat Pram**, next to the western side of the main approach road around 3.5km south of Prasat Thom, with five (pram) beautiful towers (four of brick, one of laterite), two of which are being slowly strangled by fig trees, with photogenic results.

ARRIVAL AND INFORMATION   KOH KER

From Siem Reap Improved roads mean that Koh Ker is now easy to reach, although you'll need your own transport. The temple is usually (and most easily) visited from Siem Reap, from where it's a 125km (roughly 2hr 30min) journey. It's easily combined with a trip to Beng Mealea, from where it's a 65km (1hr) drive (55km to the Srayang turn-off, then 10km to Koh Ker itself). Various operators around Siem Reap offer this trip, or variants on it, for around $85.

Via Preah Vihear City (Tbeng Meanchey) The site can also be reached from the east via Preah Vihear City (70km; 1hr 30min) along a good surfaced road.

Opening hours Daily sunrise to sunset.

Admission $10.

Preah Khan (Kompong Thom)

Some 70km north of Kompong Thom, the temple enclosure of **PREAH KHAN (KOMPONG THOM)** is the largest in Cambodia, its central sanctuary featuring the earliest example of four huge faces looking to the cardinal directions, a motif that subsequently became almost synonymous with Cambodian temple architecture. Little is known about the temple's **history**. The earliest buildings are attributed to Suryavarman I, and it's believed that Jayavarman VII spent time here before moving to Angkor – the famous carved stone image of the king displayed in the National Museum in Phnom Penh (see p.65) was found on the site. In the 1870s Louis Delaporte carried off the temple's prize sculptures (they're now in the Guimet museum in Paris), while looters have also pillaged the complex in recent years, using pneumatic drills to remove statues – resulting in collapsed towers, crushed apsaras and the broken images that lie scattered on the ground.

The site

Four different temple groups and numerous prasats and buildings lie scattered around the extensive site over an area of several square kilometres. At the heart of Preah Khan, the **main temple group** dates from the twelfth century and was most likely built by Suryavarman II. Its well-preserved causeway, not dissimilar to those at Angkor Thom, is decorated with a frieze of swans (peer over the edge just before the steps up to the gopura). Making your way through the complex, via the elaborate east gopura and two sandstone galleries, you'll come to the central sanctuary, with its Bayon-style, four-faced tower.

East of the central sanctuary is the 3km-long **baray**, home to the remains of **Prasat Preah Thkol**, a cruciform sanctuary sat on an (inaccessible) island in the centre of the lake. At the west end of the *baray*, the elaborate eleventh-century **Prasat Preah Stung** boasts galleries, carvings of apsaras and a central sanctuary topped with four massive faces, the latter the hallmark of Jayavarman VII and found only in a few places outside Angkor. East of the *baray* is the small ninth-century temple, **Prasat Preah Damrei**, enclosed in a laterite wall and with its upper levels guarded by stone elephants, often draped in orange robes.

WHAT'S IN A NAME: PREAH KHAN

Note that we have followed the common practice of suffixing **Preah Khan** with the province name Kompong Thom in order to distinguish it from the temple of the same name at Angkor. It's also sometimes suffixed with the district name **Kompong Svay** and, just to add to the confusion, locals call it **Prasat Bakan**.

> ### THE VULTURE RESTAURANT
> In the depths of northern Cambodia, Preah Vihear Protected Forest is home to three critically endangered species of vulture – red-headed, slender-billed and white-rumped – protected by a project run by the Wildlife Conservation Society (❿wcs.org). Trips can be arranged through the Sam Veasna Centre (see p.146; Dec–May only), and involve camping overnight in the forest, followed by a morning watching the vultures breakfast on a dead cow.

ARRIVAL AND DEPARTURE PREAH KHAN (KOMPONG THOM)

Tours Preah Khan is one of the trickiest of the major temples to get to. The route to the temple **from Siem Reap** runs directly past Beng Mealea, although the last stretch of track beyond Beng Mealea is still unsurfaced – it's generally not too bad in the dry, but can become almost impassable in the wet. The temple can also be approached via the south **from Kompong Thom** – tours can be arranged through I.M. Sokhom (see p.204).
Admission $5.

Preah Vihear City (Tbeng Meanchey)

Ongoing road repairs have significantly improved access to the formerly remote provincial capital of **PREAH VIHEAR CITY** (in Khmer **Krong Preah Vihear**, and still sometimes referred to by its old name of **Tbeng Meanchey**), around 150km north of Kompong Thom along NR64 (and also now directly connected by tarmac road to Stung Treng in the country's far northeast). There's not much to the sprawling and largely featureless town itself, with wide, straight roads laid out on a simple grid, although it makes a useful place for an overnight stop en route to Preah Vihear temple, and is the best source of reliable accommodation within a day-trip of the site, which is around 100km (1hr 30min by car) distant. Koh Ker (60km; 1hr by car) is also within easy striking range if you have your own transport. You might also find yourself passing through if taking the cross-country shortcut from Stung Treng through to Siem Reap.

Weaves of Cambodia

250m east of the hospital • Mon–Sat 8am–5pm • ☎ 092 346415, ❿ weavescambodia.com

Originally a rehabilitation centre for local disabled people, the **Weaves of Cambodia** silk-weaving cooperative is now a prosperous concern, producing high-quality silk for overseas markets. Visitors are welcome to tour the sericulture chambers and the spinning and weaving workshops, and there's a selection of silk goods to buy.

Tmatboey

30km north of Preah Vihear City • Visits and homestays can be arranged through Sam Veasna Centre in Siem Reap (see p.146)

Of major interest to twitchers, **Tmatboey**, one of only two nesting sites of the **giant ibis** in Asia, is 30km north of Preah Vihear City from off the Preah Vihear road. White-shouldered ibis, greater adjutants and sarus cranes also frequent the area.

ARRIVAL AND INFORMATION PREAH VIHEAR CITY AND AROUND

Public transport to and from Preah Vihear City is sketchy. The only **bus** services are the twice-daily departures to Phnom Penh via Kompong Thom, and there are also a couple of daily **minibus** services to Stung Treng. To reach Siem Reap and other destinations you'll need to either change buses in Kompong Thom or catch a **shared taxi** from the transport stop, on the east side of the main road towards the northern end of town.

By bus There are currently two buses daily to Preah Vihear City from Phnom Penh (7hr) via Kompong Thom (3hr), one with Phnom Penh Sorya, the other with GST (both of whom have offices on the main road just south of the transport stop).
By minibus There are a couple of daily minibuses to Stung Treng (2hr 30min), run by Asia Van Transfer, originating in

Siem Reap and continuing to either Laos or Banlung.

Money The ATMs at the Acleda and Canadia banks (both on the main road towards the north end of town) accept foreign Visa and MasterCards.

GETTING AROUND

The town is very spread out – a couple of kilometres from top to bottom. Most accommodation and other services are strung out along the main road (Koh Ker St), running north to south through the town. **Motos** congregate around the transport stop, but **tuk-tuks** are few and far between. If you want to visit the temples of Preah Vihear, Koh Ker or Preah Khan, your best bet is to try hiring a **private taxi** either through your hotel or at the transport stop. Count on around $75 return (perhaps slightly less to Koh Ker).

ACCOMMODATION

Green Palace Hotel Main road, south end of town (1.2km south of the transport stop) ☎064 210757, ⓦgreenpalacehotel.com. Opened in 2015, this landmark new hotel is the biggest thing to have happened in Preah Vihear City for years, built using funds channelled via the Cambodian Red Cross by prime minister Hun Sen's wife for (it's alleged) assorted nefarious political and/or financial ends. The result is an upmarket (if utterly characterless) five-storey concrete cube with all the marble trimmings, the coolest lifts between Phnom Penh and Thailand, and 80-odd spacious rooms comfortably kitted out with lots of wooden furniture (plus nice views from higher floors). A rooftop restaurant and bar may have been finished by the time you read this, although there's no pool. BB $47
Home Vatthanak Guesthouse Town centre, St A14, 250m west of the main road (turn off just south of the Acleda Bank, around 350m south of the transport stop) ☎064 6363000. In a quiet side road close to the centre of town, this is more hotel than guesthouse. Rooms (all a/c) are smartly furnished with colourful fabrics and flatscreen

TVs, while more expensive deluxe options come with spectacularly mad wooden furniture and revolving chandeliers. $15
Ly Hout Guesthouse Main Road, south end of town (around 200m south of the Green Palace Hotel) ☎012 737116. Another hotel masquerading as a guesthouse for obscure tax reasons, with a foyer full of wooden carvings and a mix of fan (with cold water) and a/c (with hot) rooms – a bit dated, but perfectly comfortable and reasonably priced. More expensive deluxe rooms come with the obligatory (in Preah Vihear City) array of chintzy wooden furniture and fittings. Fan $10; a/c $16
★**Sokha Home** Main Road, south end of town (around 500m south of Green Palace Hotel) ☎077 600400, ⓦfacebook sokhahome. Excellent and very competitively priced guesthouse with smart modern rooms (all with hot water, plus a/c for $7 extra) nicely furnished with funky fabrics and equipped with big flatscreen TVs and kettles. There are fine views from the rooftop terrace, and the helpful and switched-on owner is a great source of local information. $10

EATING

Across from the transport stop, a couple of restaurants do fried noodle and rice dishes, plus coffee. There are also **food stalls** on the west side of the market.

Dara Reas Beside the Vishnu Circle about 200m west of the traffic circle and 1km south of the market. The name may be off-putting, but this is one of the town's few restaurants with an English-language menu and it actually serves up pretty good soups and stir-fries – shame about the inconvenient location.

Prasat Preah Vihear

Dedicated to Shiva in his manifestation as the mountain god Shikhareshavara, the magnificent temple of **PREAH VIHEAR** makes maximum use of its spectacular setting high up on the Dangkrek escarpment overlooking the plains of Cambodia and Thailand far below. The temple was built between the ninth and the twelfth centuries. Most of the work is attributed to Suryavarman I (r. 1011–50) who enlarged an old religious centre founded here by a son of Jayavarman II and installed one of three boundary linga defining the extent of his territory (the others were placed at Phnom Chisor and at the hitherto unidentified site of Ishanatirtha). Both Suryavarman II (r. 1113–50) and Jayavarman VII (r. 1181–1218) subsequently made further additions to the temple.

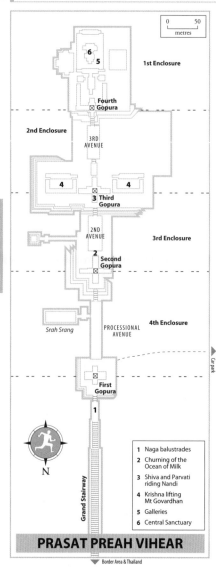

PRASAT PREAH VIHEAR

Map key:
1 Naga balustrades
2 Churning of the Ocean of Milk
3 Shiva and Parvati riding Nandi
4 Krishna lifting Mt Govardhan
5 Galleries
6 Central Sanctuary

Constructed entirely of sandstone, Preah Vihear has an unusual **layout** for a Khmer temple, with four enclosures laid out in a row, rather than concentrically, as is usually the case, each successive enclosure taking you higher and higher until you reach the summit, from where there are spectacular views along the jagged line of the **Dangkrek Mountains**.

The site

Note that large numbers of **land mines** (see opposite & p.305) were laid all around the temple right up until the end of the civil war in 1998, while further mines may have been laid during the subsequent Thai–Cambodia border dispute, although both sides deny it. Do not under any circumstances stray from well-marked paths. Note that the site can get busy with visiting Cambodians over the **weekend** – try to visit on a weekday if possible.

If you don't want to take a moto or truck up to the temple, the **Eastern Staircase** offers an alternative, but much more strenuous, approach to (or descent from) the site. More than two thousand steps lead through the forest using a mix of modern wooden steps and (in places) the old stone staircase itself. The bottom of the staircase is east of the ticket office, along a signposted dirt road.

The first and second gopuras

Walking from the car park brings you out to the top of the grand, 162-step entrance **stairway**, giving onto a narrow courtyard decorated with naga balustrades. The **first gopura**, in a ruinous state, is raised on a platform ahead. From here you get a terrific view along the **first avenue**, more than 200m long and boasting a monumental paved area lined with pillars originally used to support lanterns. To the east is a large stepped bathing pool, **Srah Srang**, guarded by a solitary stone lion.

At the end of the avenue, the steepness of the steps ahead means that the only thing that can be seen of the well-preserved **second gopura** is the entrance door and the impressive triangular pediment, outlined against the sky. Above the exterior of the south gopura's door (southern side) are two intricate and well-preserved **carvings** showing (on the lintel) Vishnu reclining and (on the pediment) a scene from the Churning of the Ocean of Milk (see p.168). Here Vishnu appears both as the tortoise

PRASAT PREAH VIHEAR: TEMPLE WARS

Much more than a simple archaeological site, **Prasat Preah Vihear** has been the subject of a bitter and often bloody tug-of-war between Thailand and Cambodia, as well as the setting for several landmark moments in the Cambodian civil war. Despite the fierce fighting that has regularly erupted around it, the temple itself has, almost miraculously, escaped relatively unscathed (although you might notice a few bullet holes here and there).

The roots of the Thai–Cambodian **border conflict** date back over a century. The area was under long-term Thai control until the intervention of the French authorities in Cambodia in 1907. Attempting to ratify the border between the two countries, the French produced a map claiming the temple for Cambodia, despite an agreement that the border should run along the watershed of the Dangrek Mountains – which would have placed the temple within Thai territory. Following the withdrawal of the French from Cambodia in 1954, Thai forces reoccupied the site in an attempt to assert their rights to the temple, forcing Prime Minister Sihanouk to take the matter to the International Court of Justice in The Hague which, in a fiercely contested ruling, finally awarded the site to Cambodia in 1962.

Thanks to its almost impregnable location, the temple played a surprisingly important role during the **civil war**. In 1975, Khmer Rouge forces drove out remnants of the Khmer National Armed Forces who had taken refuge in it – the last place in Cambodia to fall to them. In 1978, Vietnamese forces recaptured the site from the Khmer Rouge – who then reoccupied the site in 1993 and continued to control it before finally surrendering in 1998; their last major stand. The temple was also the scene (in 1979) of a particularly brutal repatriation of Cambodian refugees by the Thai military government during which more than forty thousand people were driven back over the border. As many as three thousand died after being forced over the cliff on which the temple stands and driven through the minefields below.

Following the end of the civil war, the old border dispute flared up again in 2008, when Prasat Preah Vihear was awarded **UNESCO Heritage** status – which Thailand felt further reinforced Cambodian claims to sole ownership of the temple, and which they continued to dispute. Rising tensions ensued, followed by a series of increasingly violent clashes, with dozens of military and civilian casualties on both sides, culminating in 2011 in an exchange of long-range artillery fire. The case was again returned to the International Court of Justice in The Hague, who (in November 2013) once again ruled in Cambodia's favour. Peace has subsequently returned to the temple following the new ruling, with access now open from both sides of the border, although the loss of the temple continues to rankle with many Thai nationalists and offers easy political capital for Bangkok politicians seeking a popular national cause, meaning that the possibility of future clashes cannot be ruled out entirely.

Kurma, with the churning stick on his back, and as Krishna on the stick itself, keeping a watchful eye on the surrounding activity. The serpent Vasuki, meanwhile, coils around the stick, serving as a rope, while gods and demons pull together.

The third gopura

Further uphill, beyond the 100m-long **second avenue**, the double vestibules of the cruciform **third gopura** form an imposing entrance to the **third avenue**. It was at this level that royal rooms were located for use by the king when he visited the temple; the two large buildings flanking the gopura were resting houses for ilgrims. Further fine carvings can be seen including (on the south side of the gopura) Krishna lifting Mount Govardhan and (on the north side) Shiva and Parvati riding upon the bull Nandi.

The main sanctuary

Past here, steep steps lead up to the **fourth gopura**, rising high above the third avenue to reach the **main sanctuary**, much of which has collapsed, leaving a jumbled heap of massive stones. In its day, the temple was a pioneering project, and the vaulted galleries that surround the enclosure are some of the earliest examples of their type in Angkorian architecture. Only the north gallery has windows facing out; the windows of the other galleries look in on the enclosure. You can climb through a small door in the western wall to get out onto the mountainside and enjoy the well-earned view.

ARRIVAL AND INFORMATION   PRASAT PREAH VIHEAR

Access to Prasat Preah Vihear is now much easier than it was, with good new **roads** from Siem Reap (roughly 210km and 4hr away, via either Koh Ker or Anlong Veng) and from Preah Vihear City (from where good roads run to Kompong Thom and Stung Treng). Due to the steepness of the road up, cars, buses and tuk-tuks can't go further than the bottom of the hill below the temple, where you'll need to transfer to a moto ($5 return) or the back of a pick-up truck ($25 return for the whole vehicle) for the 5km ride up the hill – a 10min trip with fantastic views. There is currently no direct access to the temple **from Thailand**.

By public transport From Sra Em you'll need to catch a moto (around $15 return, including waiting time), then another moto to the top of the hill ($5). Approaching the site from further afield you'll need your own transport.

Tours Given the difficulties of getting here by public transport, the vast majority of visitors to Prasat Preah Vihear come on organized tours. Longer tours to the temple can also be combined with other destinations en route such as Beng Mealea, Koh Ker, Anlong Veng and possibly Preah Khan (Kompong Thom) in numerous different ways – shop around tour operators in Siem Reap.

Opening hours Daily 7.30am–5pm.

Admission $10.

Sra Em

Around 30km by road south of Prasat Preah Vihear, the formerly modest village of **SRA EM** (or Sa Em) has experienced a massive boom over recent years as a result of military and tourist developments at Prasat Preah Vihear and it now provides a useful jumping-off point for visits to the temple. The village is located at the point where the road to the temple turns off from the main road between Anlong Veng and Preah Vihear City. Most guesthouses and other services are strung out along the turn-off to Prasat Preah Vihear, close to the roundabout where the two roads meet.

ARRIVAL AND DEPARTURE   SRA EM

There are once-daily **buses** (and shared taxis) to Preah Vihear City and Phnom Penh. For Siem Reap you'll need to catch a **shared taxi**. To reach Prasat Preah Vihear you'll either need to take a **moto** (around $20–25) or hire a **pick-up truck** (around $55 return, seating up to 6 people), if you can find one – try asking at your guesthouse or the Preah Vihear Boutique Hotel.

ACCOMMODATION

Chhouk Tep Guesthouse Preah Vihear road, 250m west of the main roundabout ☏097 5544447. Reliable and long-running option with dated but comfortable and well-maintained rooms (all with hot water, plus a/c for an extra $6). **$11**

Preah Vihear Boutique Hotel Preah Vihear road, 1.5km west of the main roundabout ☏071 9583333, ⓦpreahvihearhotel.com. This nice-looking resort-style hotel – with attractive Khmer-style buildings arranged around a fine pool – offers an amazing sign of the changing times in Preah Vihear province, although malfunctioning hot water, doors that won't lock, wi-fi that's constantly going off and staff who can't add up suggest that in fact things haven't actually changed as much as you'd think. Convenient for the temple, although given the hefty price, you might prefer to head elsewhere. BB **$100**

Thai Zavid Guesthouse Preah Vihear road, 600m west of the main roundabout ☏097 3048719. Sparkling new guesthouse on the edge of the town with bright and spacious fan and a/c rooms, all with hot water and small flatscreen TVs. Fan **$10**; a/c **$15**

EATING

Ly My Restaurant Preah Vihear road, 250m west of the main roundabout ☏097 2378111. Right in the middle of town, the Ly My (pronounced "lee mee") is signed in Khmer only but is easy enough to find (it's about ten doors west of the *Chhouk Tep Guesthouse* opposite the Neary Smart Stop) and has an English-language menu and a big selection of Khmer standards (mains $3–5), well prepared and served in generous portions. Daily 7am–9pm.

Anlong Veng

The sleepy little provincial town of **ANLONG VENG** would be utterly unremarkable save for its role as the last refuge of **Pol Pot** and several of the Khmer Rouge's other most notorious leaders, including the murderous **Ta Mok**, who fled here along with thousands of Khmer Rouge fighters still loyal to the cause following the collapse of the regime in 1979. Then little more than a remote village, Anlong Veng had the advantage of being far from the hostile government in Phnom Penh and close to Thailand, offering an easy escape route, if needed.

The view north of town is dominated by the dramatic escarpment of the **Dangrek Mountains**, some 9km distant, marking the border between Cambodia and Thailand and stretching away in an almost dead-straight line as far as you can see. It was up on this ridge that **Pol Pot** and several other fugitive Khmer Rouge leaders established themselves, and where Pol Pot was later put on trial by his own comrades, and subsequently died.

3

Ta Mok's house

Main road, about 300m north of the main roundabout · $2

The main sight in the town itself is **Ta Mok's House**, former residence of one of the most notorious Khmer Rouge leaders, known to his comrades as "Brother Number 5" and to the world at large as "The Butcher" for his role in ordering the murders of thousands of his compatriots. He was well respected in Anlong Veng itself, building roads, donating money and, in 1993, ordering the construction of a hospital and school. The house (which served as Ta Mok's main base from the fall of the Khmer Rouge in 1979 until he was forced to flee into the mountains following the death of Pol Pot in 1998) stands in the middle of a large wooded compound, its interior decorated with a couple of incongruous wall paintings of Angkor Wat and Prasat Preah Vihear. It's surrounded by a couple of other tall and rather bleak wooden and concrete buildings which would have provided accommodation for Ta Mok's colleagues and guards – thousands of Khmer Rouge cadres remained loyal to the movement and under Ta Mok's direction long after the fall of the regime in 1979. It's all oddly sylvan and peaceful nowadays, although a couple of reminders of former times stand in the grounds, including a battered old truck (looking rather like an armoured caravan) which formerly housed a Khmer Rouge mobile radio unit and a large wire "tiger cage" in which prisoners were once kept. Fifteen FUNCIPEC negotiators (see p.306) intercepted by Pol Pot's forces in 1994 were kept in such cages for five months. Only four emerged alive.

Lapping the grounds below the house and stretching eastwards around the edge of town for over two kilometres is the vast **lake** which Ta Mok also ordered to be constructed – either to provide water and food for his followers or (it's alleged) to prevent would-be attackers creeping up on him. It's now a beautiful but faintly eerie sight, with the stumps of hundreds of dead trees poking skeletally up out of the shallow waters. A local guide might also be able to point out remains of the small brick building east of Ta Mok's house which served as **Pol Pot's home** during his brief residence in Anlong Veng before an attack by government troops in 1994 forced him to flee up into the Dangrek Mountains.

Khmer Rouge sites in the Dangrek Mountains

9km from Anlong Veng: take the road towards the Thai border; around 500m short of the border turn right (signed) off the road, from where it's around 100m to the cremation site · $2.50

Determined travellers can see for themselves the meagre remains of the last days of the Khmer Rouge up on the ridge at the top of the **Dangrek Mountains** – the whole scenically spectacular but historically sombre area now incongruously overshadowed by the massive Sangam Casino built here for border-hopping Thai gamblers (gambling being illegal in Thailand). Several Khmer Rouge leaders, including Khieu Samphan, Nuon Chea and Pol Pot himself, established houses at the top of the hills here after Anlong Veng was briefly taken by government troops in 1994. Lesser commanders and those in disgrace (including Pot's one-time heir apparent Son Sen) lived further down the mountains in the so-called "middle houses".

It was Pol Pot's brutal murder of Son Sen in 1997 which precipitated a final reckoning. Alarmed by the killing, Ta Mok sent his own forces to capture Pol Pot. After a staged public trial, the former Khmer Rouge leader, already seriously ill with multiple medical conditions, was put under house arrest. He died nine months later of heart failure and was hastily cremated on a pile of furniture and old tyres.

The **cremation site** itself is indicated by a sign, although there's little to see beyond a few blackened rocks. Visiting Khmers still come here in the belief that the spirit of Pol Pot will reveal winning lottery numbers, heal the sick or provide auspicious luck in some other fashion from beyond the grave, and there's an impromptu shrine erected by one grateful winner standing nearby.

Beyond here, it's possible, with either a bit of persistence or a local guide, to follow a track (motorbike or 4WD only) along the ridgetop east for around 3km to reach the **mountain house** of the ubiquitous Ta Mok, now being developed as a new café and visitor centre. It's another 3km or so to the remains of the **house of Pol Pot** himself. There's little to see beyond a looted shell and an underground bunker, although the **views** are glorious.

ARRIVAL AND DEPARTURE   ANLONG VENG

There are a couple of early-morning **buses** from Anlong Veng to Siem Reap via Sisophon; otherwise transport is by shared taxi, with services leaving (mainly in the morning) from just south of the main roundabout. You can hire a **moto** for a day (around $25) to explore all the local sights. Occasional shared taxis run to **Prasat Preah Vihear** (1hr 30min); or you may be able to find a car for hire (around $40 return) – try asking at the *Bot Oudom Guest House*, whose helpful owner is one of the few English-speakers in town.

To/from Thailand It's just 12km from Anlong Veng to the Thai border crossing at Choam Sa Ngam (aka Chong Sa Ngam) – regular shared taxis run throughout the day, or catch a moto. Unfortunately there's no onward public transport on the Thai side – you'll need to hitch a ride or catch a songthaew to busy Highway 24 (around 40km distant) and then flag down one of the reasonably regular passing buses to the town of Si Saket, a further 65km on.

ACCOMMODATION

Bot Oudom Guest House Sra Em road, about 200m east of the main roundabout ☎012 779495. An unexpected find in dusty Anlong Veng, with a helpful and very clued-up English-speaking owner and surprisingly smart and spacious modern tiled rooms in the bright new orange accommodation block at the back (with hot water for an extra $2, or a/c and hot water for an extra $7.50).

Great views over the lake from upstairs rooms. **$7.50**
Monorom Guest House Main road, about 100m north of the main roundabout ☎065 6900468. Archetypal provincial Cambodian guesthouse offering neat, bright, old-fashioned rooms (all with hot water, plus a/c for an extra $8) plus attached restaurant, although not much (if any) English spoken. **$8**

Kompong Thom

KOMPONG THOM, 145km from Siem Reap (and slightly further from Phnom Penh), straggles along NR6 and the Stung Sen River. The town used to be known as *kompong pos thom*, "place of the big snake" – apparently the locals used to take offerings to a large snake that lived in a cave on the river, but this may be yet another Cambodian myth as no one now has a clue where the cave is. Most visitors stop over to visit the temples at **Sambor Prei Kuk**, 30km northeast, and the attractive **Phnom Santuk** religious complex; a couple of hours is quite enough to have a look around the town itself.

Kompong Thom is also a possible jumping-off point for the remote **Prasat Preah Vihear**, two days' journey to the north, though access is now easier from Siem Reap via Sra Em (see p.200). Closer, but even more of an adventure to reach, is the massive **Preah Khan (Kompong Thom)** – go now before the tour groups do.

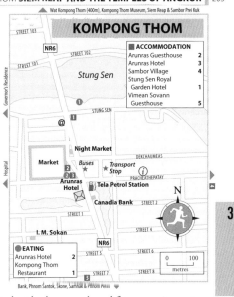

Central Kompong Thom

There's not a lot to central Kompong Thom, lined up along the NR6 and centred on the landmark *Arunras Hotel* and the nearby market. South of here a **double bridge** crosses over the Sen River – the rattling old original has been left in place alongside its modern replacement, which was built with Australian assistance (hence the kangaroos at each end). A pleasant riverfront promenade stretches west, dotted with playgrounds and fitness equipment. It's liveliest towards dusk, when the waterside becomes busy with impromptu aerobics classes and games of badminton and shuttlecock (*sey*). About 500m west of the bridge along the waterfront is the colonial **Governor's Residence**, next to a huge old tree that is home to a massive colony of **fruit bats**. They can be seen quietly hanging upside down from the branches by day, before flying off in search of food come dusk.

North of town

On the main road about 500m north of the river, it's difficult to miss the gaudy **Wat Kompong Thom**, its compound crammed with exuberant pagoda buildings and stupas. Around 2km further north along the NR6, Kompong Thom's modest **museum** (daily 7am–4pm; free) houses a small but interesting collection of objects from local archaeological sites, including the original lion statues from Sambor Prei Kuk and some beautiful Angkorian-era carvings and statues, although the inconvenient location means that it receives hardly any of the visitors it deserves.

ARRIVAL AND DEPARTURE   KOMPONG THOM

Arriving in Kompong Thom, most buses and minibuses set passengers down on the main road diagonally opposite the *Arunras Hotel* – make sure your driver knows you're getting off, or you might find yourself being whisked straight through town. **Leaving** Kompong Thom is generally a swift and painless experience. Dozens of buses, minibuses and shared taxis pass through en route along NR6 between Phnom Penh and Siem Reap (although few services actually begin here). Buy a ticket from one of the various ticket-sellers opposite the *Arunras Hotel* and they'll put you on the next available service – you shouldn't have to wait more than 15min. If you're heading to other destinations, note that scheduled services are run by Sorya Phnom Penh, whose office can also be found opposite the *Arunras Hotel*. A few minibuses and shared taxis stop at the **transport stop** just east of the main road. This is also where you'll need to come if heading north to Preah Vihear City (Tbeng Meanchey).

By bus Destinations Kompong Cham (4 daily; 3hr); Phnom Penh (every 10–15min; 5–6hr); Poipet (10 daily; 5–6hr); Siem Reap (every 10–15min; 3hr).
By minibus Destinations Kompong Cham (6 daily; 2hr

30min); Kratie (1 daily; 5hr 30min); Phnom Penh (12 daily; 4–5hr); Siem Reap (12 daily; 2hr 30min); Preah Vihear City (3 daily; 3hr).

ACCOMMODATION

KOMPONG THOM

Arunras Guesthouse NR6 ☎012 865935. Effectively an extension of the next-door *Arunras Hotel*, under the same management, in an almost identical (but smaller) building and with very similar fan rooms (plus optional a/c for $5), at fractionally lower prices. $̲7̲

Arunras Hotel NR6 ☎062 961294. Landmark seven-storey hotel right in the middle of town with small but very cosy and excellent-value rooms (optional a/c $7), including very cheap singles. Good restaurant, too (see below). $̲8̲

★**Sambor Village** 1km east of town along the river ☎062 961391, ⓦsamborvillage.asia. Delightful little hotel, surrounded by verdant gardens in a peaceful riverside setting, with nineteen cool and airy individually decorated bungalows (with a/c and hot water). There's also an inviting swimming pool, a good restaurant and bar, and free bikes for guests. BB $̲6̲0̲

Stung Sen Royal Garden Hotel NR6 ☎062 961228, ⓔstungsen_hotel@yahoo.com. A slightly more upmarket alternative to the *Arunras Hotel*, set in a shady garden overlooking the river with spacious and comfy modern rooms (all with a/c and hot water) at a very competitive price. $̲1̲3̲

Vimean Sovann Guesthouse St 7 ☎078 220333, ⓦvimeansovannguesthouse.com. Located in a quiet side street, a five-minute walk south of the centre, this friendly, efficiently run guesthouse offers bright, spacious, attractively furnished and spotlessly clean modern rooms (all with hot water) at giveaway rates, plus there are free bikes and a small restaurant. Fan $̲7̲; a/c $̲1̲2̲

AROUND KOMPONG THOM

Khmer Village Homestay Baray village, 50km southeast of Kompong Thom on NR6 to Kompong Cham ☎012 635718, ⓦkhmerhomestaybaray.com. Get involved in village life at this enjoyable homestay, with a range of activities including village tours, ox-cart rides and boat trips. Longer stays offering the chance to help out with local community projects can also be arranged. $̲2̲6̲ per person.

EATING AND DRINKING

Given the paucity of eating options you might prefer to head to the local **food stalls** which set up from late afternoon onwards along the main road north of the *Arunras Hotel*.

Arunras Hotel NR6 ☎062 961294. Lively hotel restaurant, busy with both locals and tourists, in a large mirror-walled dining room stuffed with wooden furniture. The menu features a large range of good Chinese and Khmer dishes (mains $3.50–4.50) served in large portions – although no Western options. Daily 7am–10pm.

Kompong Thom Restaurant Riverside ☎061 221081.

Upmarket but slightly moribund tourist restaurant overlooking the river and serving up a good selection of Khmer dishes (most mains around $5.50), plus a few more expensive Western options alongside assorted snacks, salads and sandwiches. Pricey for what you get, however, and you might find that half the stuff on the menu is unavailable at any given time. Daily 6.30am–9pm.

DIRECTORY

Bikes and motorbikes Bikes ($2/day) and motobikes ($8/day) can be hired from IM Sokhom (see below).
Money The Canadia Bank ATM accepts Visa and Mastercard.

Phones and post For international calls, go to the Camintel office which is inside the post office just south of the *Arunras Hotel*.

TOURS AROUND KOMPONG THOM

Kompong Thom's enthusiastic moto and tuk-tuk drivers will be all over you the moment you step off the bus, offering trips to Sambor Prei Kuk and Santuk – you might want to compare prices offered by different drivers before you agree to anything. Alternatively, local tour guide **IM Sokhom** (Street no.3 ☎012 691527, Eguideimsokhom@yahoo.com, ⓦfacebookIM .Sokhom) can arrange transport around Kompong Thom (including moto/tuk-tuk/car transport to Sambor Prei Kuk and Santok) plus a good range of tours. These include a rewarding day-trip combining Sambor Prei Kuk and Santuk along with a couple of other local temples (moto $15 per person, car $35 per person), cycling tours to Sambor Prei Kuk ($20 including guide) and day-trips to Preah Khan ($100 by car per group), as well as longer two- to three-day trips combining Preah Khan, Koh Ker and Beng Mealea (although the last two are easier to reach from Siem Reap).

Sambor Prei Kuk

30km north of Kompong Thom • $3; site guides available for around $7 for 3hr; food stalls near the ticket booth • The site is easily visited from Kompong Thom (return by moto $8–10, tuk-tuk $12–15; 1hr). If you're travelling independently, 5km north of Kompong Thom turn off north along NR64 for 10km and then take the wide dirt road (clearly signed) on the right for the last 15km – it can be slow going in the rainy season

One of Cambodia's most important pre-Angkorian monuments, the Chenla-era (see p.292) capital of **SAMBOR PREI KUK** once boasted hundreds of temples, although many of them have now been lost, smothered by the encroaching forest. Sixty or so temples remain, however, dotted among beautiful woodland, some of them now restored and sporting particularly fine brick carvings and decorated sandstone lintels and columns. It's all relatively modest compared to the great Angkorian sites, admittedly, although the sylvan woodland setting and almost total lack of visitors more than compensates.

The site

The temple divides into three main sections: the **north and south groups**, which date from the seventh century, and the **centre group**, a ninth-century addition. Separated from these by the access road are the ruined sanctuary tower of **Ashram Issey** and the single-towered **Prasat Bos Ram**, which has a lion's-head channel through which holy water flowed; it is now at ground level, but would originally have been more than 1m up the wall of the tower. Also just north of the entrance road is a small shrine, almost completely gobbled up by the roots of an enormous **strangler fig** which seems to sprout from the crumbling walls as if out of some enormous pot.

North group

The **north group**, sometimes called **Prasat Sambor Prei Kuk** after its central sanctuary tower, was extended and restored during the Angkorian era. As with most Angkorian temples, the main approach is from the east and the sanctuary's five towers are arranged in a quincunx pattern. Carved into the brick on several of the towers are bas-reliefs of **"flying palaces"**, believed to be home to the local spirits who look after the temples (several similar carvings can be found in the south group and at Ashram Issey). The carved sandstone lintels and columns on some of the towers also remain in reasonably good condition – look out for cute winged horses and tiny human faces – and there's a fine image of a voluptuous Durga in the northeastern tower. Though there were once numerous other towers here, all you'll be able to spot amid the ruins is the row of four on the west side. You'll also see a number of carved sandstone **pedestals** lying around, each about 1.5m square and designed to carry a linga.

Centre group

Of the **centre group**'s former buildings, only the main sanctuary tower, **Prasat Tao**, survives, although it's a particularly photogenic structure, with entrance steps flanked by reproduction lions and upper portions sprouting impressive quantities of weeds. The carving around a couple of the tower's doors is well preserved, including intricate foliage designs for which the Chenla period is famed.

Around 200m southwest of here, the crumbling **Prasat Trapeang Ropeak** stands almost lost in the woods, still sporting the remains of eroded friezes and an unusual triangular entrance that looks in imminent danger of collapse.

South group

The highlight of Sambor Prei Kuk is the so-called **south group**, built as the state-temple of Isanavarman I and also known as Prasat Yeay Poeun (or sometimes

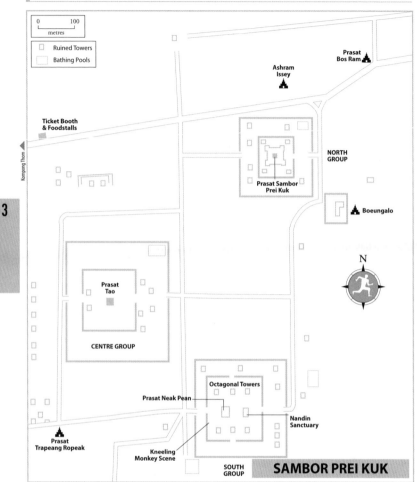

Prasat Neak Pean) after its central sanctuary tower. The main towers are located within two concentric walled enclosures: a ruined outer laterite wall plus a relatively intact inner wall built of brick. The west side of the inner wall still preserves some elaborate but eroded **reliefs** contained in a sequence of roundels among which you can just about make out a kneeling monkey and fragments of a fighting lion – only the mane remains.

The **central sanctuary tower** itself still boasts reasonably preserved carved lintels over three of its doors, while inside a battered but delicately decorated linga base stands beneath the tower's impressively high brick vault (minus its summit). The tower was originally linked to a smaller building opposite, housing a statue of Nandin. The statue is long gone (although you can still make out some of the carvings around the pedestal on which it would have stood), and all that can be seen of the raised causeway that connected the two structures are a few pillars.

A number of unusual octagonal towers are located in the enclosure, their walls decorated with large, circular medallion-like carvings and more flying palaces.

South of Kompong Thom

There are several interesting sights south of Kompong Thom, easily combined in a day-trip with Sambor Prei Kuk and including the stone-carving village of **Santok** and the colourful hilltop temple complex at **Phnom Santok**. Aficionados of Angkorian architecture might also consider a trip to the little-visited temple of **Wat Hat Nokor**.

Santok

15km southeast of Kompong Thom on NR6 • Around $8 by moto or $10 by tuk-tuk, or $15–20/$20–25 combined with Sambor Prei Kuk

Stretching for a couple of kilometres along NR6, the village of **SANTOK** (aka **Samnak** or **Kakaoh**) is instantly recognizable thanks to the long lines of stone carvings lined up along the roadside – ranging from huge Buddha heads fit for a temple to diminutive figurines which would fit comfortably on a small mantelpiece. Also in the village is **Santuk Silks** (Mon–Fri 7–11am & 1–5pm, Sat 7–11am; free), run by Vietnam veteran Bud Gibbons and his wife, where you can see silkworms munching on mulberry, watch spinners and weavers at work, and usually buy a scarf or two from the weavers (from around $20).

Phnom Santok

2km north of NR6, 17km southeast of Kompong Thom (the turn-off from NR6 is about 100m past Santuk Silks in Santuk village)

A couple of kilometres from Santok village, the jaunty modern hilltop temple of **Phnom Santok** sits atop a 180m-high hill, conspicuous in the pancake-flat countryside. The hilltop is a popular weekend destination, but quiet during the week when you can often have the place pretty much to yourself apart from the occasional monk.

From the car park at the bottom, 809 steps climb steeply up the wooded hillside (there's also a road to the top – too steep for tuk-tuks, although there might be a moto at the bottom to take you up for a dollar or two if you don't want to hike up the eight hundred-plus stairs). A pair of sweeping **naga balustrades** flank either side of the steps, with more than five hundred miniature figures on either side playing tug-of-war with a pair of giant snakes. The **summit** is topped with a colourful hotchpotch of mainly modern viharas, shrines and pavilions. Directly behind the central cluster of buildings, a rock overhang creates a natural shrine embellished with several small Buddhas carved into the rock face, although no one seems to know how old they are. Beyond here, a tiny path weaves across the hilltop past further small shrines and between large boulders (including two balanced precariously on top of one another), while to the west, a narrow path leads part of the way down the hill to a further collection of rock carvings, including an impressive reclining Buddha.

Wat Kua Hat Nokor

2km west of the village of Taing Kok, 70km from Kompong Thom • Donation • Public transport will drop you either in the village or at the turning for the temple, from where motos are readily available ($5 return including waiting time) – if you're using public transport on to Kompong Thom, you'll need to flag down a taxi or minibus, best done at Taing Kok's small market

The small, rural **Wat Kua Hat Nokor** (not to be confused with Wat Nokor just outside Kompong Cham – see p.218) is notable mainly for the eleventh-century **temple** built by Suryavarman I. The temple was never finished, and it's assumed that either the architect died or war intervened during its construction. A single gopura on the eastern side of the temple gives access to a courtyard enclosing a cruciform sanctuary, **Prasat Kuk Nokor**. The central section of the south wall has collapsed, but you can still see a chamber built into the wall, where the sick came to be cured with holy water that was blessed by flowing over the linga in the central sanctuary. The library in the southeast corner of the courtyard was formerly used as a prison by the Khmer Rouge.

Eastern Cambodia

MORNING MARKET, BANLUNG

Eastern Cambodia

The wide-open spaces of Cambodia's remote and sparsely populated east are a world away from the rest of the country, offering a quintessential slice of rural Khmer life largely unaffected by the modern world. Bounding the western side of the region, the mighty Mekong River forges its way south from Laos, dotted with river islands, dramatic stretches of flooded forest and the occasional floating village. Outside the main towns, much of the river remains largely off the tourist radar, although if you've got the time and energy there are myriad opportunities to explore the river and its rural hinterlands using a mix of boating, kayaking, cycling and walking.

East of the **Mekong** lie the distant highlands of **Rattanakiri** and **Mondulkiri** provinces. Rampant logging has taken a serious toll on these formerly pristine landscapes, although some jungle cover survives, providing a haven for wildlife – for the time being, at least. The highlands are also home to Cambodia's **chunchiet** population (see box, p.235) who have traditionally eked out a subsistence living cultivating crops and foraging in the jungle. This centuries-old way of life is now threatened by the encroachment of the modern world and the loss of forest on which they depend.

Gateway to the region is the laidback Mekong-side town of **Kompong Cham**, a quiet provincial capital that retains an air of faded colonial gentility. Further north along the Mekong, **Kratie** is another old French-era settlement, best known for the rare Irrawaddy dolphins that inhabit the nearby rapids at **Kampie**. There are more dolphins to be seen at **Stung Treng**, the most northerly town on Cambodia's stretch of the Mekong; this is also the starting point for rewarding tours of the beautiful surrounding countryside and for crossings into Laos. East of Stung Treng, **Banlung**, the capital of Rattanakiri province, is developing into a major centre for treks into the nearby highland jungles of the **Virachey National Park** and surrounding countryside. In the southeast of the region, tranquil **Sen Monorom**, the main town of Mondulkiri province, sees fewer visitors but offers further trekking and wildlife-spotting opportunities, including the chance to walk through the jungle with local elephants, plus visits to some of the spectacular waterfalls that dot the area.

GETTING AROUND
EASTERN CAMBODIA

Getting around eastern Cambodia is a time-consuming business, although ongoing infrastructure developments are steadily improving access. While the major gateway to the region is **Kompong Cham**, the construction of a new Mekong bridge near **Stung Treng**, linking up with NR64 to Preah Vihear City (Tbeng Meanchey) and on to Siem Reap, is already

YEAK LAOM

Highlights

❶ Kompong Cham Relaxed old colonial town with sweeping Mekong views and a lively selection of waterside restaurants and bars. **See p.213**

❷ Dolphin-watching Take a boat trip on the Mekong for a glimpse of rare Irrawaddy dolphins slaloming through the rapids at Kampie. **See p.221**

❸ Trekking in Rattanakiri Head out from Banlung for a day's or week's trekking through the jungle-clad highlands, with rare wildlife, bamboo river-rafting and encounters with the region's indigenous chunchiet en route. **See p.233**

❹ Yeak Laom Magical lake set in the crater of an extinct volcano surrounded by jungle just outside Banlung. **See p.234**

❺ Highland waterfalls Plunging more than 30m into a forested gorge, remote Bou Sraa is Cambodia's finest cascade, although the more accessible Chha Ong, near Banlung, makes a picturesque alternative. **See p.234**

❻ Walking with elephants Walk with elephants through the forests of Mondulkiri at one of Sen Monorom's various pachyderm projects. **See p.239**

HIGHLIGHTS ARE MARKED ON THE MAP ON P.212

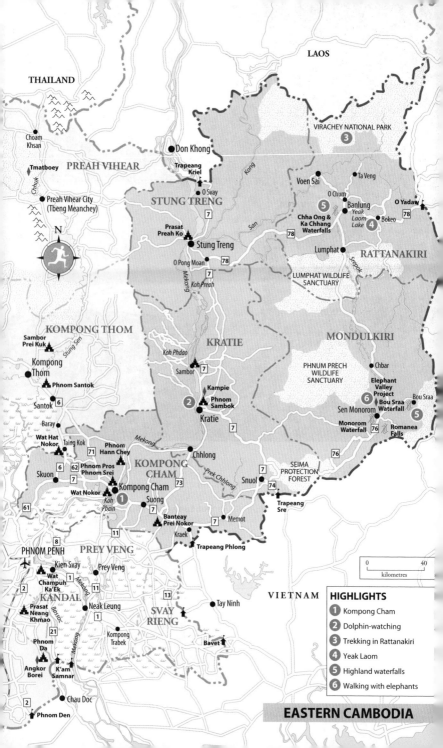

LAOS

THAILAND

Choam
Khsan

Tmatboey

PREAH VIHEAR

Chhuk

Preah Vihear City
(Tbeng Meanchey)

N

Don Khong

Trapeang
Kriel

O Svay

STUNG TRENG

Prasat
Preah Ko

7

Stung Treng

O Pong Moan

78

Koh Preah

Mekong

San

Kong

VIRACHEY NATIONAL PARK
3

Voen Sai

Ta Veng

O Chum

Chha Ong &
Ka Chhang
Waterfalls

5

Banlung

Yeak
Laom
Lake

4

O Yadaw

78

Bokeo

Lumphat

RATTANAKIRI

Srepok

LUMPHAT WILDLIFE
SANCTUARY

KOMPONG THOM

Sambor
Prei Kuk

Kompong
Thom

Phnom Santok

Santok

6

Baray

Stung Sen

KRATIE

Koh Phdao

7

Sambor

Kampie

Phnom
Sambok

2

Kratie

7

MONDULKIRI

PHNUM PRECH
WILDLIFE
SANCTUARY

Chbar

Elephant
Valley
Project

6

Bou Sraa
Waterfall

Bou Sraa

5

Sen Monorom

Monorom
Waterfall

76

Romanea
Falls

Wat Hat
Nokor

Taing Kok

71

Phnom
Hann Chey

6

62

Phnom Pros
Phnom Srei

7

Skuon

Wat Nokor

Koh
Pbain

Kompong Cham
1

Suong

7

KOMPONG
CHAM

Chhlong

Prek Chhlong

73

Snuol

7

74

Trapeang
Sre

SEIMA
PROTECTION
FOREST

76

61

Mekong

Banteay
Prei Nokor

Kraek

7

Memot

11

8

PHNOM PENH

Kien Svay

PREY VENG

Wat
Champuh
Ka'Ek

2

KANDAL

Prasat
Neang
Khmao

21

Phnom
Da

Angkor
Borei

K'am
Samnar

2

Chau Doc

Phnom Den

Prey Veng

Mekong

Bassac

11

Neak Leung

1

Kompong
Trabek

13

SVAY
RIENG

Tay Ninh

Trapeang Phlong

VIETNAM

Bavet

0   40
kilometres

HIGHLIGHTS

1 Kompong Cham

2 Dolphin-watching

3 Trekking in Rattanakiri

4 Yeak Laom

5 Highland waterfalls

6 Walking with elephants

EASTERN CAMBODIA

BORDER CROSSINGS IN THE EAST

Eastern Cambodia currently has four international border crossings: one with **Laos**, and three with **Vietnam**. All are open daily from 7am to 5pm. For entry into Laos and Cambodia, **visas** are issued on arrival (roughly $30–40 for a Lao visa, depending on your nationality; $20 for a Cambodian visa). Note that e-visas are not valid for entry into Cambodia at any of these crossings. Heading into Vietnam, you'll need to have acquired a visa in advance, since none are issued at the border.

TO LAOS

Trapeang Kriel (Dong Kralor)–Nong Nok Khiene Popular crossing 57km north of Stung Treng. Full details are given with our Stung Treng account (see p.226).

TO VIETNAM

O Yadaw–Le Thanh The most useful of the three border crossings into Vietnam, 70km east of Banlung along a good road. Guesthouses in Banlung sell through-bus tickets from Banlung to the town of Pleiku, in the central highlands of Vietnam (around a 4hr journey from Banlung).

Trapeang Phlong–Xa Mat Little-used (and tricky to reach) crossing around 70km east of Kompong Cham. Catch any bus travelling east from Kompong Cham towards Sen Monorom and alight at the town of Kraek (60km from Kompong Cham) from where you'll need to pick up a moto for the 14km trip to the border itself. From here you'll need another moto or taxi for the 45km journey to Tay Ninh, the first significant settlement on the Vietnamese side of the border.

Trapeang Sre–Loc Ninh Around 20km southeast of Snuol. This obscure crossing isn't of much practical use given the lack of public transport on both sides of the border and it's difficult to reach. Take a bus from Kratie or Kompong Cham to the large town of Snuol then a moto for the 18km trip to the border from where it's around 35km to Binh Long, the first town on the Vietnamese side.

4

opening up an alternative approach to Rattanakiri via central Cambodia – the Stung Treng account (see p.226) has more details. Beyond Kompong Cham, most transport (and all buses) follows the good, if circuitous, route along National Highway 7 via **Snuol** to **Kratie**, although there's also a more direct and slightly quicker route to Kratie along the river via **Chhlong** (currently served by shared taxi only). There's a good road north from Kratie to **Stung Treng** (and on into Laos) and **Banlung**. From Banlung it's possible to make a complete circuit of eastern Cambodia by continuing down the recently opened road to **Sen Monorom** and then returning directly to Kompong Cham.

Kompong Cham

Situated on the west bank of the Mekong, the mellow town of **KOMPONG CHAM** has little of the bustle that you'd expect of the biggest city in eastern Cambodia. Its small commercial port doesn't exactly hum with activity, and the riverfront, in the shadow of the massive Kizuna Bridge, is pretty quiet too since road improvements have led to the demise of most river transport. The town's attractive backwater somnolence belies its more energetic past. In the 1930s and 1940s, Kompong Cham – named after the sizeable population of local **Cham Muslims** (see box, p.217) – was a prosperous rubber and tobacco trading centre and the most cosmopolitan town in Cambodia. You can sense some evidence of its previous affluence in the wide, tree-lined streets and the faded shophouses and warehouses lining the waterfront.

Today's town has a distinct charm, and it's easy to while away a day meandering through the unhurried streets, taking in the faded colonial architecture (particularly around the market) and visiting the remains of the venerable **Wat Nokor** just outside town – as well as enjoying the convivial riverfront cafés, busy in the evenings with tourists stopping over on a slow journey through the country. In half a day you can follow the Mekong north to **Phnom Han Chey**, a quirky hilltop temple with fabulous views of the river, while a day-trip will get you to the pre-Angkorian site of **Banteay**

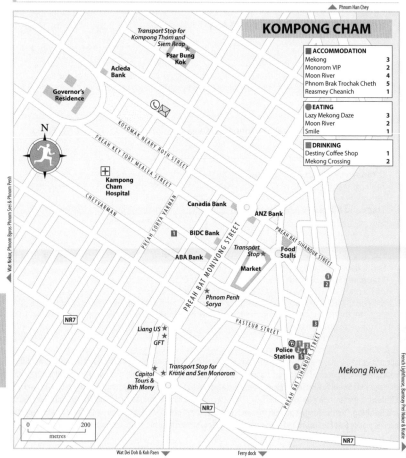

KOMPONG CHAM

■ ACCOMMODATION	
Mekong	3
Monorom VIP	2
Moon River	4
Phnom Brak Trochak Cheth	5
Reasmey Cheanich	1

● EATING	
Lazy Mekong Daze	3
Moon River	2
Smile	1

■ DRINKING	
Destiny Coffee Shop	1
Mekong Crossing	2

Prei Nokor, home to a few ruined towers surrounded by a massive earth embankment. Enjoyable **boat trips** can also be made to villages up and down the Mekong.

The riverside

Quiet by day, Kompong Cham's **riverside** really comes alive after dark, when locals come out to wander the waterside promenade and eat at the food stalls set up along its length, and the attractive string of Mekong-facing cafés fill up with crowds of tourists. Dominating the riverside is the great arc of the towering bridge, built with the help of a $65m grant from Japan and known as the **Spean Kizuna** after the Khmer word for bridge (*spean*) and the Japanese word *kizuna*, signifying a bond between nations. Completed in 2001, the 1.5km-long structure was the first Cambodian bridge over the Mekong (prior to its opening, crossing the river involved an hour-long ferry ride) and provides a strange contrast to the faded old warehouses and shophouses that you can still see along the waterfront.

Across the river close to the far side of the bridge is the salmon-pink French **lighthouse**, a three-tiered structure looking more like a church tower than a beacon for shipping. A very steep metal staircase inside leads to the summit, although you'll need a good head for heights to make it all the way to the top.

The market

Kompong Cham's neat little **market** doesn't get especially busy, which is just as well as the stalls are jammed together so tightly that inside there's hardly room to squeeze a cat, let along swing one. This is a good spot to pick up one of the **kramas** for which Kompong Cham province is famous, although you'll actually find a much wider choice of patterns and materials in Phnom Penh and Siem Reap.

Wat Dei Doh

Around 1km south of Kompong Cham centre, opposite the dry-season bamboo bridge to Koh Paen (see p.217) • Daily • Free

Just over 1km south of the centre of Kompong Cham, **Wat Dei Doh** is well worth a wander, though it's less than a hundred years old. In front of the complex is a huge standing Buddha, while the grounds are scattered with intriguing statues of people and animals, and a forest of miniature stupas.

ARRIVAL AND DEPARTURE

KOMPONG CHAM

By bus and minibus The majority of buses and scheduled minibuses (for Sen Monorom and Banlung) are run by Phnom Penh Sorya, arriving and departing from their office on Preah Bat Monivong St, a 10min walk (or less) from most of the hotels. Further services are provided by Rith Mony (which has more frequent departures to Siem Reap, plus services to Battambang), Capitol Tours, Liang US and GFT, whose various offices cluster along (or just off) the NR7 northwest of the centre. There are regular buses from Kompong Cham to Phnom Penh until late afternoon, although services to other destinations are much less frequent, and generally leave in the morning only.

Destinations Banlung (2 daily; 8hr); Kompong Thom (5 daily; 3hr); Kratie (3 daily; 3hr); Phnom Penh (12 daily; 4hr); Poipet (1 daily; 7–8hr); Sen Monorom (1 daily; 5hr); Siem Reap (5 daily; 6hr); Stung Treng (1 daily; 6hr).

By shared taxi Shared taxis and local minibuses to/from other destinations in the east arrive and depart from the Caltex petrol station on the roundabout just before the bridge. Services to/from Siem Reap via Kompong Thom use the Psar Bung Kok transport stop two blocks north of the post office. Transport to other destinations, including services to Phnom Penh, can be found on the northeast side of the market. Shared taxis also cover the more direct route (not covered by any buses) to Kratie via Chhlong.

GETTING AROUND

The centre is sufficiently compact to be easily explored on foot, although there are plenty of motos and tuk-tuks available if needed – English-speaking drivers hang out along the riverfront. The three Ms – *Mekong Crossing*, *Lazy Mekong Daze* and the *Moon River* restaurants – are the best places to enquire about tours, transport and to sort out bike ($1–2/day) or motorbike ($4–6/day) rental.

Boat trips *Mekong Crossing* can arrange three-hour afternoon/sunset boat trips along the Mekong for around

$5–7 per person, depending on numbers.

ACCOMMODATION

KOMPONG CHAM TOWN

Mekong Riverfront ☎ 042 941536. One of the town's

oldest hotels, showing its age but still a reasonable choice for its cheap and comfortable fan rooms (with hot water)

RIVER TRIPS AROUND KOMPONG CHAM

There are several interesting places within the vicinity of Kompong Cham that can be reached by boat and make for a rewarding day out if there are a few of you to share the cost – although note that most of these sites can also be reached more cheaply by moto or tuk-tuk. Possible destinations include **Wat Maha Leap** (about 20km south of Kompong Cham), an old wooden building with gilded teak columns; **Prei Chung Kran** village (just upstream from Maha Leap temple on the Tonle Tuok), where silk is woven on traditional hand looms; and **Wat Han Chey**, about 20km north of Kompong Cham, where there are fantastic river views from Chenla-era ruins and a modern temple. To find a boat, try asking around on the riverfront, at your guesthouse or at the *Mekong Crossing* restaurant.

HOMESTAYS IN EASTERN CAMBODIA

Increasing numbers of **homestays** can be found across eastern Cambodia, offering the chance to rub shoulders with locals and gain some absorbing insights into traditional village life. Good options can be found in Kompong Cham (see below), on Koh Trong island at Kratie (see p.224), on the Mekong river islands of Koh Preah near Stung Treng and Koh Phdao north of Kratie (contact CRDT in Kratie; see p.224), and at Preah Rumkel, close to the Lao border (see p.228). Village homestays can also be arranged as part of treks and tours around Banlung (see p.233) and Sen Monorom (see p.239).

despite the rather bleak and institutional atmosphere. The a/c rooms are drab and overpriced. Fan $8; a/c $15

★**Monorom VIP** Riverfront ☎092 777102, ⓦ monoromviphotel.com. Good-value mid-range option in a fine riverfront location, with a varied selection of big a/c rooms generously kitted out with wooden furniture, TV and fridge, plus spacious bathrooms with hot water. Cheaper rooms lack proper windows but more expensive ones have balconies with fine Mekong views. $15

Moon River Riverfront ☎016 788973, ⓔmoonriver mekong@gmail.com. Located above the attractive café of the same name, with a mix of fan rooms (optional a/c for $4 extra) of various sizes and standards. Not the best value in town, although the super-friendly service and attractive Mekong-facing balcony compensate. $11

Phnom Brak Trochak Cheth Riverfront ☎099 559418. Very basic guesthouse right in the thick of the riverfront action and with some of the cheapest beds in town. Rooms (fan only) are poky and slightly grubby, with tiny (or no) windows, although there's a small communal balcony overlooking the Mekong. $6

Reasmey Cheanich Off Preah Bat Monivong Street ☎012 358716, ⓔreasmeycheanich@gmail.com. Another good mid-range option if you don't mind being

slightly away from the waterfront, with neat bright white a/c rooms equipped with flatscreen TVs and tea- and coffee-making facilities – although the bathrooms are a bit poky. $15

AROUND KOMPONG CHAM

OBT Chiro Village Homestay East side of the Mekong, 6km from Kompong Cham ☎017 319194, ⓦ obtcambodia.org. Homestay programme run by the local OBT (Organization for Basic Training) NGO offering rooms in a couple of local houses, a pair of stilted cabanas and a traditional wooden house capable of sleeping six. Activities such as boat and fishing trips, ox-cart rides and village visits can also be arranged. Prices include meals. Rooms $6, cabanas $10, house $20

Rana 7km towards Kratie on NR7 ☎012 686240, ⓦrana-ruralhomestay-cambodia.webs.com or ⓦrana -cambodia.blogspot.co.uk. Enjoyable American-/Khmer-run homestay just outside Kratie which aims to give visitors a real insight into local rural life, with trips to nearby villages. Advance booking essential. Minimum two-night stay (one-person reservations are not accepted). Rates include all meals, tours, plus tea, coffee and bottled water. $25 per person (with discounts for children aged under 14).

EATING AND DRINKING

There's a good selection of restaurants and cafés along the waterfront. Food stalls can be found around the transport stop and market, while late in the afternoon further stalls set up along the riverfront. The tourist-oriented riverfront restaurants are usually fairly lively **after dark**, although most places usually shut up promptly at 10pm.

Destiny Coffee Shop Pasteur St, just off the riverfront. This chic café is more Phnom Penh than Kompong Cham, serving up good coffee and shakes plus snacks and light meals including all-day breakfasts, salads, sandwiches and a short selection of Western and Asian mains (around $4). Daily 7am–5pm, Fri & Sat until 8pm.

Lazy Mekong Daze Riverfront ☎011 624048. Simple and sleepy little café offers assorted pizzas plus a limited selection of other Western and Asian dishes (mains $4–6) and snacks. A decent place for a Mekong-facing breakfast or sundowner, although there's better food and atmosphere elsewhere. Daily 8am–10pm.

Mekong Crossing Riverfront ☎017 801788. Always lively, this bar-restaurant is the town's best place for a

drink, either in the cosy interior or lounging on a wicker chair on the terrace outside. Tipples include the biggest selection of beers in town plus a decent cocktail list, and there's the usual menu of Asian and Khmer staples (mains $2.50–3.50) plus pricier Western dishes. Daily 6am–10pm.

Moon River Riverfront ☎016 788973, ⓔmoonriver mekong@gmail.com. Smart riverfront restaurant with a good selection of Western and Asian cuisine including flavoursome Khmer fish, meat amoks and curries alongside distinctively sour and fragrant Cambodian-style soups like sngor ngam ngov (chicken and basil). Good coffee, too. Most mains around $3. Daily 6am–10pm.

★**Smile** Riverfront ☎017 997709. The top restaurant in

town, run as a training centre for orphans and vulnerable children and serving up excellent Khmer food, bursting with flavour, plus a decent range of Western dishes, salads, sandwiches and snacks. Popular with tour groups, so worth arriving early to beat the rush. Most mains around $4–5. Daily 6am–10pm.

DIRECTORY

Internet Almost all the hotels and restaurants reviewed here have free wi-fi.
Money Most banks are along Preah Bat Monivong St.

There are ATMs at the Canadia, ANZ and BIDC banks (all Visa and MasterCard) and the BIDC Bank (Visa only). The Canadia Bank also has a forex bureau.

Around Kompong Cham

Several low-key sights dot the area around Kompong Cham. Glimpses of traditional Mekong life can be had close to town on the idyllic **Koh Paen** river island, while it's worth making the short trip to the edge of town to visit **Wat Nokor**, a fine old temple with quirky modern additions, and the hilltop religious complex of **Phnom Pros Phnom Srei**.

Koh Paen

Around 1km southeast of Kompong Cham, the island of **Koh Paen** (or Koh Pen), in the middle of the Mekong, is perfect for an out-of-town jaunt, especially by bicycle. During the dry season it can be reached via a remarkable **bamboo bridge** ($1), rebuilt from scratch every year as the river waters subside. Come the rains you'll need to take the small **ferry** ($1, or $1.50 with bicycle), just big enough for a couple of motos and a few passengers.

The island itself is around 10km long, crisscrossed by tiny tracks and fringed with sand bars during the dry season – Kompong Cham's nearest equivalent to a beach. The primary crop here is tobacco – the tall, thin, mud-walled buildings are

THE CHAM

Originating from the kingdom of Champa, which formerly extended from Hue to Phan Thiet on the coast of present-day Vietnam, the **Cham** are the largest minority ethnic group in Cambodia, numbering in the region of 250,000 (estimates vary) and accounting for about a third of the country's non-Khmer population. They also represent Cambodia's largest minority religion, being Sunni Muslims who converted from Hinduism some time after the fourteenth century.

Historically, the Cham were frequently at war both with the Khmer, who bordered their kingdom to the west and south, and the Vietnamese, who occupied the territory to the north. In 1177, the Cham successfully raided Angkor, only to be defeated by the intervention of Jayavarman VII in a ferocious battle on the Tonle Sap – an event depicted in the bas-reliefs at the Bayon temple (see p.173). By the end of the seventeenth century, however, the gradual whittling away of its territory by the Vietnamese meant that Champa had effectively ceased to exist, and many Cham fled to Cambodia. The **traditional Cham** – who retain many of the old beliefs and rituals, but acknowledge non-Islamic gods – make up about two-thirds of Cambodia's Cham population. They settled around the Tonle Sap, along the central rivers, and in what is now Kompong Cham province. The **orthodox Cham**, who are more similar to Muslims in other Islamic countries, settled around Oudong, Kampot and Takeo. Establishing their own villages, they took up fishing, breeding water buffalo, silver-working and weaving – activities that the vast majority still practise today. Their villages can easily be identified by the presence of a mosque and Islamic school, and by the absence of pigs.

The Cham have generally coexisted peacefully alongside the Khmer throughout their history, despite speaking their own language (Cham) and maintaining separate traditions. Only under the Khmer Rouge did they suffer significant persecution: easily picked out thanks to their Islamic dress and distinctive features (they seldom marry outsiders), many Cham were either massacred or persecuted – often by being forced to eat pork – and their mosques destroyed.

4

drying-houses where the leaves are hung for several days before being packed into bamboo crates. The island also has a number of **Cham villages**. The men work mainly as fishermen, while in the dry season the women weave *hol* silk and cotton *kramas*, using looms set up under the stilt houses.

Wat Nokor

2km west of Kompong Cham • $2; ticket also valid for Phnom Pros Phnom Srei (see below) • Moto from Kompong Cham around $3 return, tuk-tuk $5 or around $12 combined with Phnom Pros Phnom Srei; if you're travelling independently, head out of Kompong Cham on NR7 until you reach the roundabout with four entwined golden cobras – the temple is down the small road on the left

Located in the grounds of a modern temple on the edge of Kompong Cham, the eleventh-century **Wat Nokor** (known locally as Nokor Bachey) is one of the few significant surviving ancient temples in Cambodia's east, built towards the end of the reign of the legendary Angkorian king **Jayavarman VII** (see p.294). The original shrine is enclosed within a laterite wall (painted black during the Khmer Rouge occupation) and decorated with finely executed and well-preserved carvings of apsaras, elaborate lintels and intricate panels covered in floral swirls.

The temple's main surprise is the central **sanctuary**, on top of whose eleventh-century remains a multicoloured vihara was rudely superimposed in the 1990s, complete with gaudy modern murals and fancy pillars. Notwithstanding the flagrant cultural vandalism involved, these quirky additions have proved a hit with Cambodians and ethnic Chinese. The latter closely identify with the temple's **legend**, which tells of a baby boy from Kompong Cham who was gobbled up by a large fish; the fish swam down the Mekong and on to the coast of China, where it was eventually caught and the child – still alive – discovered. The boy subsequently made his way back to Cambodia, bringing with him a retinue of Chinese, who all settled at Kompong Cham, which the locals say explains why so many Chinese live in the area, and possibly why there is a Chinese temple in the grounds.

Another modern building, just to the south of the temple complex, contains a **reclining Buddha**, decapitated during the Khmer Rouge era. The head was missing for years until a workman dreamed that it was buried close by; sure enough, the dream came true, and the head was soon dug up in the grounds and reunited with the body. Newlyweds use the temple as a backdrop for their photographs, and it's not unusual to find a group of women in the gopura helping a bride into each of her several wedding outfits.

Phnom Pros Phnom Srei

8km west of Kompong Cham off NR7 • $2; ticket also valid for Wat Nokor (see above) • Moto from Kompong Cham around $7 return, tuk-tuk $10, or around $12 combined with Wat Nokor

The twin hills of **Phnom Pros Phnom Srei** ("Man and Woman Hills") can be easily combined with a visit to Wat Nokor. The lower hill, **Phnom Pros** (or "Phnom Bros", as it's also transliterated), is topped by a collection of modern pagodas, the newest a grey cement structure with touches of ersatz Angkor Wat- and Banteay Srei-style decoration. It's possible to drive to the top of this hill, which is home to a colony of wild monkeys who hang around in the hope of being fed bananas sold at the refreshment stall. At the foot of the hill, on the way to Phnom Srei, is a collection of **stupas** built by relatives of the thousands of victims murdered by the Khmer Rouge in the surrounding fields; most of the remains were removed to Phnom Penh in 2000.

Phnom Srei is the higher of the two hills; leafy and less developed, it's reached by the track across fields beyond the stupas. From the base, a steep stairway goes straight to the top where, in addition to the view, you can take in the vihara's collection of Buddha statues dating back to the colonial period. The much-revered statue of Nandin in front of the altar just asks to be stroked, which is what you'll see many visitors doing.

WOMEN'S WORK

Phnom Pros Phnom Srei's unusual name derives from a popular local legend (curiously similar to the story attached to the Yeay Peau Temple, see p.101), dating back long ago when it was the custom for young women wishing to marry to propose to the man of their choice. Unhappy with this arrangement, the women offered the men a challenge: whoever could build the best temple by daybreak would win the right to be proposed to. The challenge was accepted and work commenced. Halfway through the night the women realized they were lagging behind and built a huge fire. The men, mistaking the fire for the rising sun, headed for bed while the women carried on building, producing a magnificent temple and winning the right to offer, rather than ask for, a hand in marriage.

Cheung Kok

Next to the entrance to Phnom Pros, **Cheung Kok** village (ⓦfacebook.com/cheungkok village) has been developed as a cultural tourism initiative offering visitors the chance to dip their toes into traditional Khmer rural life and meet local villagers. Drop-in visitors are welcome although it's more rewarding to call Ms Aline in advance on ☏069 555155 to arrange a tour. A one-day volunteer programme ($10) is also available, including a Khmer lesson and village tour plus lunch and dinner, with an afternoon spent helping teach local kids.

Phnom Han Chey

20km north of Kompong Cham • Moto from Kompong Cham around $12 return, tuk-tuk $15

For stunning views of the Mekong, **Phnom Han Chey**, on the west bank of the river, is hard to beat. The hill is also home to a modern temple complex in whose grounds you'll find a couple of brick-and-laterite prasats dating back to the Funan era (see p.291) cheek by jowl with wacky giant concrete fruits.

Kratie and around

Seventy kilometres north of Kompong Cham on the east bank of the Mekong, **KRATIE** (pronounced *Kra-cheh*) has become a popular tourist destination thanks to the rare **Irrawaddy dolphins** that inhabit the river upstream at nearby **Kampie**. Dolphin-watching trips can be easily combined with a visit to the lovely hilltop meditation centre of **Phnom Sambok** and the temple and turtle conservation project at **Sambor** further upriver, while the chance to explore nearby river islands, go kayaking or spend the night in a homestay on idyllic **Koh Trong** island may tempt you to linger longer.

Dolphins and other attractions aside, Kratie itself makes a pleasant spot to rest up for a night or two, with a decent clutch of hotels and some good restaurants lined up along the serene riverside. Parts of the town still retain vestiges of their old French colonial architecture, including the fine **Governor's Residence**, just south of the centre (now signed as the Provincial Council Kratie).

Koh Trong

Ferries shuttle roughly every 45min between Kratie and the island from the boat dock in the town centre (around 10min; 1000 riel)

Sitting directly opposite Kratie in the middle of the Mekong, the small island of **Koh Trong** provides a marvellous glimpse of rural river life within easy striking distance of the town centre. Sights include a couple of wats, a floating Vietnamese village (at the southwest of the island) and endangered freshwater Cantor's giant softshell **turtles** (*Pelochelys cantorii*) – although these are not the easiest creatures to spot, since they spend most of their time almost completely buried in sand or mud to escape predators.

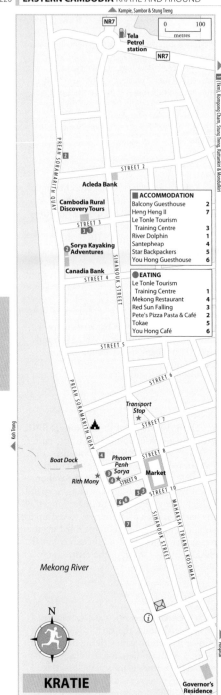

KRATIE

The best way to explore the island is by **bike**, available to hire for $1 on arrival at the ferry landing stage (you could bring your own bike over from Kratie, although manhandling it on and off the tiny ferry is not much fun), while you may also be able to organize an ox-cart ride here (or through one of the island's guesthouses; see p.224). A complete circuit of the island is around 10km.

Wat Roka Kandal

Chhlong Rd, on the riverfront around 2km south of the town centre

Dating from the late eighteenth/early nineteenth century, the pretty little temple of **Wat Roka Kandal** is among the oldest in Kratie province. The vihara, nondescript from the outside, conceals a beautiful interior with delicately painted, wooden hipped roof and pillars – it's usually kept locked, although you may be able to find someone to let you in if you ask around.

The road north from Kratie to Kampie

The road **north from Kratie** via Phnom Sambok to Kampie is one of the most magical in Cambodia, running for 15km along a seemingly endless avenue of majestic tropical trees flanked with a picture-perfect array of traditional Khmer wooden houses, raised on enormous stilts. Many are of considerable size, topped with hipped red-tiled roofs decorated with elaborate finials and linked to the road by long wooden walkways – it's particularly lovely in the rainy season when the road looks like a never-ending causeway between the encroaching waters.

Phnom Sambok

10km north of Kratie

Two-thirds of the way between Kratie and Kampie, the rustic hilltop temple complex at **Phnom Sambok** offers a tranquil slice of rural Cambodian Buddhism en route to the dolphins at Kampie. From the bottom of the hill, a steep staircase (361 steps in total), lined with life-size statues of Buddhist acolytes, leads up to the various monastic buildings scattered around the hillside above, split over three levels.

After 161 steps you reach the **first terrace**. To your left a scattering of meditation cells dot the hillside along with the living quarters of the temple's resident monks, arranged around a small **vihara**. Inside, the vihara (not always open) is decorated with cartoonish murals showing the gruesome punishments awaiting the unrighteous in the various Buddhist hells – gossips having their tongues pulled out, adulterers being impaled on a spiky tree, and so on. Some of the murals show Chinese and Japanese figures sporting bushy eyebrows and moustaches and wearing red shorts and turbans or bandanas, probably a hangover from the brief Japanese occupation during World War II.

Continuing on up, a further 73 steps bring you up to the small **second terrace** after which it's another 127 steps to reach the topmost terrace and a small vihara decorated with murals of the Buddha's life and enlightenment, with glimpses through the trees of the Mekong far below.

Kampie

15km north of Kratie • Boat trips $9/person, or $7/person in a group of three or more • The site is easily reached by motorbike or bicycle, or there is transport from Kratie (see box, p.224)

Cambodians traditionally believe that the **Irrawaddy dolphins** (*psout*) that live around the Mekong rapids at **KAMPIE** are part human and part fish, and they consequently do their best to look after them. Despite this, the dolphins' numbers have declined sharply due to the use of explosives and electric rods for fishing, and in 2004 the Irrawaddy dolphin was added to the IUCN Red List as a critically endangered species. There are currently around 22 dolphins at Kampie, out of a total Cambodian population of approximately eighty.

The **dolphin-watching site** is now run as an ecotourism project by the local community. Having purchased your ticket you'll be loaded into a boat for the trip (lasting roughly 1hr during the Nov–May dry season; closer to 1hr 30min during the wet season, when the dolphins travel further downriver). Once boats are out on the water in the vicinity of the dolphins the motor is cut and boatmen row their craft to create the minimum of disturbance. The dolphins are most active during the early morning and late afternoon, when they tend to feed, although sightings are pretty much guaranteed at any time. They're fairly easy to see (albeit almost impossible to photograph) and even easier to hear thanks to the characteristic noise they make (like the sound of someone taking a sudden deep breath through a large tube) when breaking the surface of the water to take in air.

4

IRRAWADDY DOLPHINS

Freshwater rivers, such as the Irrawaddy and Mekong in Southeast Asia, and the shallow tropical zones of the Indian and Pacific oceans, constitute the habitat of the **Irrawaddy dolphin** (*Orcaella brevirostris*). In the Mekong they now inhabit just a 190km stretch in the north of Cambodia, and can be spotted most easily at Kampie and north of Stung Treng near the Lao border, with occasional sightings elsewhere. In 2001, a pair were found just a few kilometres north of Phnom Penh.

Irrawaddy dolphins look more like porpoises than marine dolphins, with rounded heads and foreheads that protrude slightly over a straight mouth; noticeably, unlike their seagoing cousins, they have no beak. They're also more languid than marine dolphins, rarely leaping out of the water, chasing after boats or displaying any of the other skittish personality traits commonly identified with their species.

Irrawaddy dolphins reach maturity around the age of 5, when they can measure up to 2.75m in length and weigh up to 200kg. Family groups, or pods, usually consist of around six individuals, but larger groups are not unknown. In spite of good breeding rates, there is a high rate of calf mortality, which remains unexplained.

Sambor

Not much happens in the dusty riverside town of **SAMBOR**, 36km north of Kratie and accessible on various **tours** (see p.224) – for the time being, at any rate. The stretch of Mekong hereabouts has been earmarked for many years as the possible site of a huge dam and hydroelectric power station. This will be the largest in Cambodia, if it ever gets built, measuring up to 2km in length and forming a barrier across the entire river, although the project (along with a second, putative Mekong dam at Stung Treng) has now been mothballed until at least 2020.

Wat Tasar Moi Roi

For the time being, Sambor's most notable attraction is the modern **Wat Tasar Moi Roi** ("Pagoda of One Hundred Columns" – in fact there are 116 columns in total), built in 1986 with the express intention of beating the number of columns at any other wat in the country, although other pagodas have now surpassed this total. One of the columns originally belonged to a thatched temple that stood on the site and is believed to be four hundred years old. The oldest stupa in the grounds is the golden one to the north, which is claimed to house the ashes of a princess and a royal family; there's a less vague tale associated with the pagoda, depicted in a series of paintings in the pavilion near the vihara. The story tells how a woman turned herself into a crocodile for fun and gave a monk a ride – unfortunately an evil fellow-crocodile tipped the monk off her back and gobbled him up. The woman was eventually caught, in her crocodile form, at Banlung and brought back to the pagoda as a trophy – or perhaps to warn other monks against cavorting with crocodiles.

Mekong Turtle Conservation Centre

Behind Wat Tasar Moi Roi • Daily 8.30am–4.30pm • $4 • ⓦ mekongturtle.com

Tucked away at the back of Wat Tasar Moi Roi is the **Mekong Turtle Conservation Centre**, established by Conservation International with the aim of boosting the local population of endangered Cantor's giant softshell turtles (*Pelochelys cantorii*) in the Mekong. Local hatchlings are collected and kept in tanks here for ten months before being released back into the river, significantly increasing their chances of survival. You can also see a couple of adult Cantor's turtles here, along with a few other species.

Wat Preah Gouk

Now clad in concrete, the restored **Wat Preah Gouk**, about 500m beyond Wat Tasar Moi Roi, is interesting for the old timber-framed pagoda concealed within. The magnificent tree in the courtyard, with a trunk nearly 10m in circumference, is said by locals to be seven hundred years old.

Chhlong

Hugging the bank of the Mekong some 30km south of Kratie is the atmospheric little riverside town of **CHHLONG**, home to a sizeable community of Muslim Chams, whose fine mosque stands at the entrance to the town. Once an important colonial-era commercial centre, Chhlong is now an atmospheric monument to lost glory, with the remains of grandiose French-era buildings and early-twentieth-century shophouses, in varying degrees of dereliction, dotting the sleepy riverfront. These include the imposing former **Governor's Residence**, which subsequently served as a Khmer Rouge prison, and a fine orange-and-white mansion which until 2011 housed the beautiful little **Le Relais de Chhlong** hotel (rumours of whose reopening have circulated for several years now, although nothing has yet materialized).

Chhlong can be conveniently combined with a visit to Wat Roka Kandal in a longish half-day excursion; count on around $20 return by tuk-tuk or $15 by moto.

ARRIVAL AND DEPARTURE

Getting to Kratie **by bus** involves a roundabout inland journey via Snuol, although **shared taxis** and **minibuses** take the more direct route along the Mekong from Kompong Cham via Chhlong. **Shared taxis** arrive/depart from Kratie's transport stop, two blocks north of the market. There's a daily bus to Pakse in **Laos** leaving at midday and calling at Don Det and the 4000 Islands, and a daily minibus leaving at 7am.

By bus The main local operator is Phnom Penh Sorya, whose services pull up outside their office near the market. Destinations Banlung (1 daily; 5hr); Kampot (1 daily; 10hr); Kep (1 daily; 11hr); Kompong Cham (3 daily; 3hr); Kompong Thom (1 daily; 6hr); Phnom Penh (3 daily; 7hr); Siem Reap (1 daily; 9hr); Sihanoukville (1 daily; 11hr); Stung Treng (1 daily; 2hr 30min).

By minibus Seats on so-called "express" minibuses can be booked through most guesthouses in Kratie – although these are really just normal minibuses by any other name, and the "express" should be taken with a large pinch of salt. All services leave in the morning, usually at or before 7am. Destinations Banlung (2 daily; 5hr); Kampot (1 daily; 9hr); Kep (1 daily; 10hr); Kompong Cham (2 daily; 2hr 30min); Phnom Penh (6 daily; 6hr); Preah Vihear City (1 daily; 6hr); Sen Monorom (2 daily; 5hr); Siem Reap (1 daily; 8hr); Sihanoukville (1 daily; 10hr); Stung Treng (1 daily; 2hr 30min).

GETTING AROUND

Most restaurants (and a few places to stay) are clustered in the compact grid of streets around the market, with further accommodation options strung out north along the river. Count on $1–2 by tuk-tuk from the market to the Balcony or Le Tonle guesthouses. For trips further afield, **bikes** ($1/day), **mountain bikes** ($2/day) and **motorbikes** ($5–7/day) can be rented at the *You Hong* guesthouse and *Tokae* restaurant.

ACCOMMODATION

Kratie town is surprisingly lacking in good places to stay for such a popular destination, although there are a number of good options available on **Koh Trong island** just over the water.

KRATIE TOWN

Balcony Riverfront ☏ 097 7606393, ⊛ balconyguest house.net. Large and rather institutional concrete box of a guesthouse offering a mishmash of fan and a/c rooms (cold water only), most of which are bright and spacious but lacking in furniture and pricey for what you get. There's also a basic dorm ($5 per person) and a sunny river-facing balcony. Shared bathroom $10; en-suite $12; a/c $15

Heng Heng II Riverfront ☏ 012 929943. Right in the centre, this homely little hotel with a helpful English-speaking owner is Kratie town's best option – that is, if you can't snag a bed at *Le Tonle* (see below). The comfortable fan and slightly plusher a/c rooms (all with hot water) are kitted out with chinzy wooden furniture. Fan $7; ac $13

★ **Le Tonle Tourism Training Centre** Just off the riverfront north of the centre ☏ 072 210505, ⊛ letonl .org. Kratie's stand-out accommodation is run as a school training local youngsters in the dark arts of Western tourism. Accommodation is in a handful of attractive wood-panelled rooms (fan or a/c), all sharing a couple of immaculate bathrooms with solar-heated water. Ultra-attentive service and an excellent attached restaurant (see p.224) add further value. Fills up fast, so advance reservations generally essential. Fan $10; a/c $15

River Dolphin 2km northeast of the centre on the road

to Stung Treng ☏ 071 6586624, ⊛ riverdolphinhotel .com. A good choice if you don't mind being some way from the centre (although free tuk-tuk transfers are included), with bright, colourfully furnished modern a/c rooms at bargain prices (plus a few windowless economy rooms with fan for just $5). There's also a big pool plus good restaurant and bar. $15

Santepheap Riverfront ☏ 072 210210. The best of several decidedly knackered-looking hotels that dot the riverfront. If you don't mind the rather battered fixtures and dangling wires, the fan rooms (with cold water only) are at least cheap; a/c rooms (with hot water) are overpriced, although some have river views. Fan $5; a/c $13

Star Backpackers Street 10, opposite the market ☏ 097 3391285. Crammed into microscopic premises above the *Tokae* restaurant, this ultra-cheap accommodation is a very basic ten-bed dorm ($2.5 per person); it also has small and simple but inexpensive fan rooms. It's bang in the thick of the town centre action, with noise levels to match. $5

You Hong Guesthouse (also known as the U Hong Guesthouse) Riverfront ☏ 012 957003, ⊖ youhong _kratie@yahoo.com. Basic fan rooms above the popular travellers' café (see p.225). The cheery paintwork fails to camouflage the general drabness and pokiness (or the considerable noise from the street below), although rates are among the lowest in town. $6

4

4

TOURS AROUND KRATIE

Tours can be arranged through most guesthouses and hotels in Kratie. The dolphin-watching trip to Kampie costs around $5 by moto, $10 by tuk-tuk (not including boat ticket); you should also be able to include a visit to Phnom Sambok as part of the same trip for an extra $2. Combined visits to the dolphins, Sambor and Phnom Sambok cost around $15 by moto, $20 by tuk-tuk.

TOUR OPERATORS

Cambodian Pride Tours 088 8364758, cambodianpridetours.com. Good range of tours including 2-day motorbike or cycle trips around Kratie with an overnight village homestay, plus rewarding day-trips combining the dolphins at Kampie with other local attractions.

CRDT (Cambodian Rural Development Tours) Opposite Le Tonle Guesthouse 099 834353, crdtours.org. Excellent range of tours up and down the Mekong and elsewhere in eastern Cambodia, with several in and around Kratie and Stung Treng; featuring cycling, boat trips and homestays in the Mekong river-island villages of Koh Phdao and Koh Preah.

Sorya Kayaking Adventures Riverfront, north of the centre 090 241148, soryakayaking.com. Perfect half-day trips (morning and afternoon) kayaking 6km downriver past river islands and – when water levels aren't too high – through beautiful stretches of flooded Mekong River forest before finishing with a visit to the dolphins at Kampie (a quieter and more eco-friendly alternative to the tour boats). Trips start from $25/person, depending on group size, and include entrance to the dolphin pool at Kampie. When water levels are too high to visit the dolphins, alternative trips (from $17) run along the Te River (30km east of Kratie).

KOH TRONG ISLAND

★**Rajabori Villas** Northern end of the island 012 770150, rajabori-kratie.com. Drop-dead gorgeous little boutique resort looking like a very upscale traditional Cambodian village. Accommodation is in beautiful wooden villas arranged amid lush gardens around a superb pool at fiendishly competitive rates. **$55**

Arun Mekong Northern end of the island next to Rajabori Villas 017 663014, arunmekong .wordpress.com. Wonderfully peaceful boutique guesthouse in a fine traditional-style wooden house with five simple but attractive rooms (fan and cold water only)

in the main building plus two stilted bungalows in the garden behind. A great place to switch off – literally, since there's no electricity except in the evenings. Shared bathroom **$22**; en-suite **$27**; bungalow **$33**

Vorn Sovanny Community Tourism Homestay Northern end of the island, near Rajabori Villas 089 773020. The nicest of the two community homestays on Koh Trong, in a traditional stilted wooden house in a beautiful rural setting near the northern tip of the island. Opt either for a small private room with floor fan (and shared bathroom), or a mattress on the floor of the large communal living room for just $5. Rates include meals. **$10**

EATING AND DRINKING

Kratie's distinctive local speciality is **krolan**, a slightly bland but oddly more-ish concoction of sticky rice mixed with black beans and steamed with coconut milk inside a bamboo tube – you'll see hawkers selling bundles of the stuff all over town, particularly in the morning. Peel off the tube to get at the rice inside.

★**Le Tonle Tourism Training Centre** Just off the riverfront north of the centre 072 210505, letonle .org. Lovely open-air restaurant serving up quality Khmer and Western food (mains $3–4). Try the signature amok or pomelo salad. Good for breakfast too (the pancakes are a triumph) and the cocktails aren't too shabby either. Daily 6.30am–9.30pm.

Mekong Restaurant Riverfront. The very model of a respectable middle-class Cambodian restaurant, stuffed full of clunky wooden furniture and dishing up a huge selection of good, inexpensive Khmer standards (mains $2.50–4) plus Western and Chinese-style breakfasts. Daily 7am–9pm.

Red Sun Falling Riverfront 011 285806. This cosy café is a good place to either start or end your day, with attentive service and the best selection of Western breakfasts in town (carb-up with the "Super Full Monty", $6), good, very inexpensive Asian mains ($2–3) plus a few comforting Western favourites including chicken and chips, good salads and shakes. Daily 7am–9pm.

Pete's Pizza Pasta & Café (aka Sorya Café) Riverfront 090 241148, petescafekratie.com. Attractive café offering excellent pizza, pasta and salads (mains around $5) plus bakery items including the signature pumpkin bread. Daily 7am–9pm.

Tokae Street 10, opposite the market 097 3391285.

Charming little restaurant, romantically candlelit after dark, providing good breakfasts and a decent range of Asian dishes at below-average prices (most mains $2–3). Daily 6.30am–10pm.

You Hong Café Riverfront ☎ 085 885168. Spacious guesthouse café dishing up inexpensive Khmer and Western travellers' staples backed up by the biggest drinks list in town. Daily 6am–10pm.

DIRECTORY

Internet access The *You Hong Café* has a handful of rather aged terminals ($1/hr).

Money There are ATMs accepting Visa and MasterCards at the Canadia and Acleda banks.

Stung Treng

Situated on the Sekong River 140km north of Kratie (and a similar distance west of Banlung), the tranquil little town of **STUNG TRENG** is a bit of a backwater. For most visitors the town is simply a staging post en route to Laos, although the construction of a huge new Mekong bridge nearby, connecting with a new road to Preah Vihar City (Tbeng Meanchey) and then on to Siem Reap, may help revitalize the town's fortunes, opening up new routes between central Cambodia and the northeast, and establishing Stung Treng as an alternative gateway to the region.

There are various attractions in the countryside surrounding Stung Treng, while the town is also the jumping-off point for a splendid **river trip** along the Mekong to the Lao border, with glimpses of rare Irrawaddy dolphins and thundering waterfalls en route.

4

The riverfront

A statue of a *pasay* fish can be found on the **riverfront** (although it's now hemmed in by impromptu jewellery stalls, and easy to miss). The statue celebrates a prized delicacy which is caught locally in June and July near Stung Treng; although the statue is about the size of a dolphin, the real fish is quite modest, weighing 1–1.5kg.

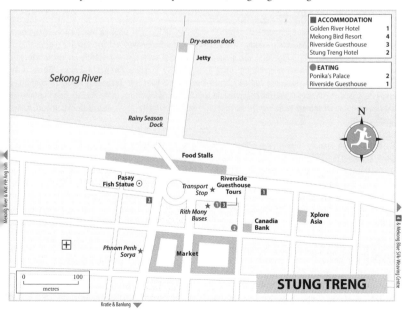

■ ACCOMMODATION	
Golden River Hotel	1
Mekong Bird Resort	4
Riverside Guesthouse	3
Stung Treng Hotel	2

● EATING	
Ponika's Palace	2
Riverside Guesthouse	1

Sekong River

Dry-season dock

Jetty

Rainy Season Dock

Food Stalls

N

Pasay Fish Statue ⊙

Transport Stop ★

Riverside Guesthouse Tours

Rith Mony Buses

Canadia Bank

Xplore Asia

Phnom Penh Sorya ★

Market

0   100
metres

STUNG TRENG

Mekong River & Wat Prei Aeg Loth

Kratie & Banlung ▼

& Mekong Blue Silk Weaving Centre

Further west along the riverfront is the attractive **Wat Pre Ang Tom**, reconstructed in 1992 after being destroyed by the Khmer Rouge. The central vihara, a glorious gold-and-pink confection, is so lusciously decorated it looks almost edible, while in the corner opposite stands an enormous bodhi tree, sheltering a cluster of pagoda-style shrines.

Mekong Blue silk-weaving centre

5km east of town along the river • Mon–Sat 7.30–11.30am & 2–5pm • Free • ⊕ mekongblue.com • Around $4 return by moto, $6 by tuk-tuk

One easy-to-reach destination is the **Mekong Blue silk-weaving centre**, established in 2001 and now one of a cluster of local projects run by the enterprising Stung Treng Women's Development Centre. Visitors are welcome to watch the weavers at work and visit the attached showroom, displaying some of the stylish scarves, accessories, bags and bedding created here (which you can also buy online).

Prasat Preah Ko

Head west of town to the Mekong bridge (around 4km; not to be confused with the older bridge over the Sekong which you can see from the town centre). Cross the bridge and continue north along the main road for around 5km, then head right along the side road to Thala Baravat village for around 2km to reach the temple

Across the Mekong from Stung Treng, the riverside village of Thala Barivat is home to the ruined **Prasat Preah Ko** Chenla-era temple, built in the seventh century during the reign of Jayavarman I and comprising six ruined brick towers arranged in two lines of three. Thai robbers stripped the stone statue of Shiva's bull, Nandin, of the gems with which it was once inlaid, but even stripped of its decoration it's still a splendid object. A unique annual **festival** is held here in late March or early April by the Jarai (see p.235), involving much loud drumming, men parading with fishing baskets over their heads and great quantities of rice wine being sprayed around.

ARRIVAL AND DEPARTURE   STUNG TRENG

Stung Treng is rather out on a limb when it comes to transport, all the more so given that services to and from Banlung bypass the town completely, meaning that you'll have to catch a minibus or shared taxi. The construction of a massive new 1.7km-long bridge over the Mekong just west of town has significantly improved transport connections with central Cambodia, linking Stung Treng directly to **Siem Reap via Preah Vihear City (Tbeng Meanchey)**. Cambodia's one and only border crossing into **Laos** is at **Trapeang Kriel**, 57km north of Stung Treng. Bus and minibus tickets can be booked through the *Riverside Guesthouse* and *Ponika's Palace* restaurant. The transport stop for **shared taxis** is in the north of town on the riverfront – given the paucity of transport, it pays to arrive early.

By bus The only local operator is Phnom Penh Sorya, whose office is in the centre of town close to the market.
Destinations Kompong Cham (1 daily; 6hr); Kratie (1 daily; 2hr 30min); Phnom Penh (1 daily; 9–10hr).
By minibus Banlung (2 daily; 2hr); Phnom Penh (2 daily; 9hr); Preah Vihear City (2 daily; 2hr 30min); Siem Reap (2 daily; 5hr).

TO LAOS
Leaving Cambodia The road from Stung Treng to the border at Trapeang Kriel is in good condition, with the journey taking just over 1hr. The border itself is open daily 7am–5pm; visas for Laos (roughly

$30–40 depending on nationality) are issued on the spot if you don't have one already. There's a once-daily Sorya Phnom Penh bus from Phnom Penh leaving at 6.45am and calling at Kompong Cham, Kratie and Stung Treng (at around 2pm) before continuing to Don Det and Pakse in Laos. A couple of minibuses also run daily between Stung Treng (leaving around midday) to Pakse via Don Det.

Entering Cambodia Visas are issued on arrival (roughly $30–40, depending on nationality); note that Cambodian e-visas are not valid at this crossing. If you're not arriving on a through-bus you'll have to take pot luck in terms of what onward transport is available at the border; arrive early if

TOURS AROUND STUNG TRENG

There are a number of attractions around Stung Treng: the widest range of local tours is run by Xplore Asia (see below), but there are other options available. Bikes (but not motorbikes) can be hired at *Ponika's Palace* and the *Riverside Guesthouse* for around $2/day, while Xplore Asia have quality mountain bikes for day hire or longer. CRDT (Cambodian Rural Development Tours; see p.224) in Kratie also run rewarding homestays and tours in the area focusing on the river island of Koh Preah, around 35km from Stung Treng.

TOUR OPERATORS

Riverside Guesthouse By the transport stop ✆012 257207, ✉ kimtysou@gmail.com. Full-day tours ($50 per person in a group of two) travelling by boat to the Anlong Chheuteal dolphin pool and on to Sopheak Mitt waterfall by tuk-tuk. They can also arrange shorter boat trips on the Sekong around Stung Treng ($15/hr).

Xplore Asia Just east of the centre on the riverfront; office open 8am–4pm, if the manager, Theara, isn't out on a tour – alternatively, call to meet up later ✆074 973456 or ✆011 433836, ⊛ xplore-cambodia .com and ⊛ cambodiamekongtrail.com. Excellent (if pricey) range of professionally run day-trips including a one-day trip combining kayaking, trekking and dolphin-watching at Anlong Chheuteal; a full-day trip kayaking from O Svay through a stretch of flooded forest before returning to Stung Treng by motorboat; and a third tour

that combines a boat trip to Anlong Chheuteal, a hike to Sopheak Mitt waterfall and a further boat trip to Don Kong Island at the southern end of the 4000 islands in Laos (with kayaking and a visit to the colonial-era Don Khon narrow-gauge railway). Trips are around $85 per person in a group of two but cheaper with more people. There's also an afternoon tour combining cycling and kayaking on the Sekong around Stung Treng ($35pp in a group of two) plus extended 3-day fishing trips. Good-quality mountain bikes ($5/day) are available for one-day hires around Stung Treng, while extended hires ($10/day) offer the possibility of doing longer rides such as the three-day ride along the Mekong Trail from Stung Treng to Kratie (dropping the bike off in Kratie although not vice versa); you could even cycle all the way to Siem Reap or Phnom Penh and drop off the bike there.

4

you don't want to spend the night in Stung Treng. Xplore Asia (see above) are planning to introduce a scheduled boat service from the Lao border to Stung Treng (Nov–April; 2hr; around $10 per person), possibly starting in late 2017. If the service materializes, it would provide the perfect way to arrive in Cambodia.

GETTING AROUND

Stung Treng is easily negotiated on foot; **motos** are readily available, although there aren't many **tuk-tuks** in town.

By bike and motorbike You can rent bicycles ($2/day) and motorbikes ($8–10/day) at the *Riverside Guesthouse* (see below) and *Ponika's Palace* (see p.228). The *Riverside* and Xplore Asia (see above) also have mountain bikes for $5/day and Xplore Asia offers a drop-off service whereby you can take one of their bikes for $10/day and deposit it in Kratie, Siem Reap or at their office in Phnom Penh.

ACCOMMODATION

Golden River Hotel Riverfront, just east of the transport stop ✆012 980678, ⊛ goldenriverhotel.com. Overlooking the Sekong River, this efficiently run hotel (the sign actually calls it "Gold River Hotel") is the town's smartest accommodation option, with neat and good-value a/c rooms with hot water; those with river views cost an extra $5. $15

Mekong Bird Resort 10km north of town ✆012 925182, ⊛ facebook.com/mekongbirdstungtreng. Back-to-nature Mekong-side retreat in the unspoilt countryside north of Stung Treng, with accommodation in basic wooden cabins and activities including kayaking and river tours. Fan $20; a/c $25

Riverside Guesthouse By the transport stop ✆012 257207, ✉ kimtysou@gmail.com. The epicentre of Stung Treng's very modest travellers' scene and a good place to find out about local transport and tours, particularly onward travel to Laos. Rooms (with cold water only) are basic and past their best, while the a/c rooms at the front overlook the noisy transport stop. The fan rooms (at the back) are OK for the price and there's a passable café downstairs (see p.228). Fan $6; a/c $12

Stung Treng Hotel On the main road, across from the market ✆012 916465. Downstairs it's a furniture showroom, stuffed to the gills with huge, floridly carved sofas, beds and chairs. Upstairs is a serviceable assortment of rooms of varying standards – some are quite nicely appointed; others are windowless boxes. A/c rooms come with hot water, fan rooms only with cold. Not much English spoken. Fan $7; a/c $12

EATING AND DRINKING

There are no culinary frills in Stung Treng, although you won't starve, and the two places listed below do a passable selection of Khmer and Western favourites. Alternatively, head to the long line of **food stalls** along the riverfront dishing up cheap meals, beer and fruit shakes from late afternoon until after dark.

Ponika's Palace Just northeast of the market ☎012 916441. There's nothing particularly palatial about this simple, family-run, tourist-oriented café, offering economical Khmer food (mains $3–4) alongside pizza, pasta and other Western and Asian standards – although the so-called Indian chicken masala bears a suspicious resemblance to Khmer chicken amok, but is very good all the same. Decent Western breakfasts too. Daily 6am–9pm.

Riverside Guesthouse By the transport stop ☎012 439454. Run-of-the-mill travellers' café dishing up a basic selection of Asian and Western staples (mains $2.50–3.50). The two street-side tables offer a nice perch from which to watch the world go by. Daily 6.30am–9.30pm.

DIRECTORY

Internet Internet PH, two blocks south of the market (2000 riel/hr; open 24hr).

Money The Canadia Bank ATM accepts Visa and MasterCard.

North along the Mekong: Stung Treng to Laos

4

The stretch of Mekong between Stung Treng and the Lao border (much of it now protected under the international Ramsar convention) is rich in ecotourism potential, most of it still largely untapped. River islands, waterfalls, rapids and impressive stretches of flooded forest dot the waters, culminating in the thundering **Sopheak Mitt waterfalls**, which block the route on into Laos. As at Kratie, pods of Irrawaddy dolphins are the major draw, and can be found at several spots along the river. Most visitors head for the so-called **Anlong Chheuteal dolphin pool** (admission $2), just south of the Lao border. There are just half a dozen or so dolphins here, although there's still around a ninety percent chance of spotting them.

Trips to the area can most easily be arranged through tour operators in Stung Treng (see box, p.227). It's also possible to arrange a homestay in the tiny village of **Preah Rumkel**, close to the dolphin pool, organized under the auspices of the Mlup Baitong NGO (⊕mlup-baitong.org) – contact Mr Mom Chantha (☎081 993693, ✉pcstmlup @gmail.com). Homestays cost $14.50 per person including all meals, and various activities can be arranged, such as boat trips, kayaking, fishing and village tours.

Rattanakiri province

Bordering Laos and Vietnam in the far northeast corner of Cambodia, the province of **Rattanakiri** used to abound in lush jungle. These days most of the region's ancient forests have been systematically logged (see box, p.236) of their valuable hardwoods and replanted with cash-crop plantations, mainly rubber, cashew and cassava, although the vistas of misty mountains and gushing waterfalls remain, if nothing else. As befits a province whose name means "gemstone mountain", traditional gem-mining also survives amid the hills, a difficult and dangerous activity, with miners dragging soil to the surface from deep holes where it is painstakingly sifted for the gems you see in every Cambodian market.

The town of **Banlung**, located pretty much in the centre of the province, is the region's one and only tourist centre and the place to come to organize treks and tours into the surrounding countryside. Notable attractions include the magical lake of

GEM-MINING IN RATTANAKIRI

Gem-mining is primitive and dangerous; miners dig a circular hole about 1m in diameter and as deep as 10m, without any internal supports or reinforcement, and with only candles for light. As the miner goes deeper, the earth is hauled to the surface in a wicker basket using a variety of low-tech winches made of bamboo and rope. A series of small steps are dug in the wall so that the miner can climb out. The main gemstone found in the area is semiprecious zircon, which looks like brown glass in its raw state but turns pale blue when heated. Also found in Rattanakiri are yellowish green peridot, pale purple amethyst, clear quartz and shiny black onyx.

Visits to gem mines can be arranged through most tour operators in Banlung and are sometimes included as part of day-trips to various attractions around town.

Yeak Laom, set in the crater of an extinct volcano just outside Banlung, along with a cluster of nearby **waterfalls**. North of Banlung, the small town of **Voen Sai** is the jumping-off point for visits to nearby Chinese, Lao and chunchiet villages and for treks into the vast **Virachey National Park**. South of Banlung, the surreal, bomb-scarred landscape at **Lumphat** offers another interestingly alternative sort of destination.

Banlung

Situated 588km from Phnom Penh by road, the small provincial capital of **BANLUNG** feels a long way from the rest of Cambodia – and indeed from anywhere else. The town sprang to prominence in 1979 when it was chosen as the new provincial capital of Rattanakiri, replacing Voen Sai (see p.236). Significant development followed (and continues to this day), although Banlung hasn't altogether shaken off its Wild West atmosphere. Most of what were formerly dirt tracks have now been roughly surfaced but are so indelibly stained with red dirt and mud as to resemble outback tracks, especially after rain, while the combination of local chunchiet descending on town to visit the lively market and marauding touts attempting to flog treks to the unwary all add to the place's slightly chaotic appeal. It's also notably cooler up here than down in the lowlands (for once, hot showers are more important than air conditioning), while the town experiences significantly more rainfall than most other places in the country.

Most people come to Banlung to **trek** (see box, p.233), and there are also a number of interesting day-trips in the surrounding countryside. The town itself is pretty much devoid of attractions, bar the lively local market and the tranquil lake of Boeung Kansaing.

Banlung market

Banlung market occupies a modern concrete building south of the Independence Monument. It's most colourful in the early morning, when local chunchiet women bus or trek into town, *khapas* laden with produce, to set up shop around the outside of the market, puffing on bamboo pipes or large cigars made from tobacco rolled up in leaves. The fruit and vegetables displayed neatly on the ground often include varieties you won't find in the lowlands, such as big red bananas, as well as outlandish-looking roots, herbs and flowers gathered from the forest.

Boeung Kansaing
1km north of the centre

Bounding the northern side of Banlung, the tranquil lake of **Boeung Kansaing** offers a complete change of pace and scenery from the slightly manic town centre. The lake is far from unspoilt, with increasing numbers of nondescript modern hotels mushrooming around its banks, but it remains a pleasant place for a wander at any time of day, particularly towards dusk, when a small cluster of food stalls set up around the lake's southern edge – a fun place to hang with the locals over a beer and watch the sun go down.

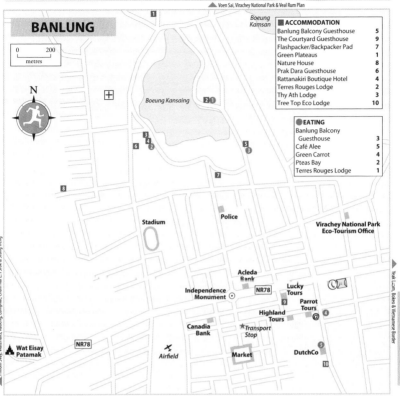

Phnom Svay

About 1km west of the airport crossroads off the Stung Treng road, from where a track runs behind Wat Eisay Patamak up to the hilltop

There are good views, especially at sunrise and sunset, from the modest hilltop at **Phnom Svay**, with panoramic vistas over the rolling countryside below and distant hills beyond. The path up heads through the pretty **Wat Eisay Patamak**, before reaching the top of the hill some 500m beyond, where an impressive reclining Buddha replaces one destroyed by the Khmer Rouge.

ARRIVAL AND DEPARTURE   BANLUNG

There's no quick way to get to Banlung, although the opening of the new road from Sen Monorom at least gives you a choice of approaches, and transport to the town is sketchy. If there's no scheduled transport available try catching a **shared taxi**; these can be found in the centre of the traffic circle on the main road near the market. Bus and minibus **tickets** can be bought through most guesthouses and tour operators. It's now possible to travel directly from Banlung via O Yadaw to the town of Pleiku in **Vietnam** without a change of vehicle. There are currently minibuses at 7am and noon, taking around 4hr to Pleiku. In order to travel from Banlung **to Laos** the most reliable option is to book a ticket through *Tree Top Eco Lodge*, changing vehicle at their sister guesthouse, the *Riverside* (see p.227), in Stung Treng.

By bus Kompong Cham (1 daily; 8hr); Kratie (1 daily; 5hr); Phnom Penh (1 daily; 10hr).
By minibus Kompong Cham (2 daily; 7hr); Kratie (2 daily; 4hr 30min); Sen Monorom (1 daily; 3hr);

Phnom Penh (1 daily; 9hr); Preah Vihear City (1 daily; 5hr); Siem Reap (2 daily; 7–8hr); Stung Treng (2 daily; 2hr).

WHAT'S IN A NAME? BANLUNG AND SEN MONOROM

Note that Cambodians habitually refer to **Banlung** as Rattanakiri and **Sen Monorom** as Mondulkiri, as many provincial capitals in Cambodia take their names from their respective provinces.

GETTING AROUND

By moto or tuk-tuk Banlung is quite spread out. Heading between the lake and town centre you might want to hop on one of the town's plentiful motos ($1–2) or grab a tuk-tuk ($2–3), although these can be hard to find.

By bike and motorbike Bikes ($1–2/day) and motorbikes ($5–6/day) can be rented from various places including Highland Tours (see opposite).

ACCOMMODATION

The nicest place to stay in Banlung is around the **lake**, which is also where you'll find most of the town's accommodation, including some of the best-value lodgings in the country, although it's a bit of a hike (or a short moto ride) from the centre and most of the town's tour operators.

Banlung Balcony Guesthouse Boeung Kansaing ☎ 097 8097 036, ⊛ balconyguesthouse.net. Large and rather institutional guesthouse in a peaceful location near the lake offering a range of spacious and good-value – if slightly knackered-looking – tiled rooms (fan only; some with shared bathroom) plus a handful of nicer wood-panelled rooms upstairs ($12, or $15 with a/c). Its plus points include a lovely big lake-facing veranda with hammocks and a good attached restaurant (see p.234). Shared bathroom $̄5̄; en-suite $̄8̄

The Courtyard Guesthouse Town centre ☎ 097 333 4626, ⊜ thecourtyardguesthouse@gmail.com. Cut-price, town-centre lodgings offering big, basic rooms (cold water only) and a small dorm ($2.50 per person). The helpful owners also run Lucky Tours (see opposite) and there's a small restaurant out the front. $̄5̄

Flashpacker/Backpacker Pad Boeung Kansaing ☎ 031 6665213. Two-in-one accommodation with neat, cosy and very good-value modern rooms (a/c $3 extra) in the main building and super-cheap mosquito-netted beds ($2 per person) in an airy seven-bed dorm in the building next door (with hot water, but no lockers). $̄8̄

Green Plateaus North of Boeung Kansaing ☎ 012 856 242, ⊛ greenplateauslodge.com. Lovely boutique guesthouse with traditional Khmer touches set amid spacious gardens in a beautifully tranquil rural location just north of the lake. The seven airy rooms come with cool wood-pannelled decor and svelte, vaguely colonial-style furnishings and there's a small restaurant attached. Fan $̄2̄5̄; a/c $̄4̄5̄

Nature House Edge of town, southwest of Boeung Kansaing ☎ 088 2045888, ⊜ sophann.ch@gmail.com. A virtuoso display of traditional Khmer-style wooden architecture set in peaceful semi-rural surroundings on the edge of town. The rustic accommodation consists of three huge stilted houses plus one large room (all with hot water) and to-die-for views over an endless sea of trees. Good value, and the helpful owner, Mr Sophann, is a great source of local info. $̄1̄0̄

Prak Dara Guesthouse Boeung Kansaing ☎ 012 614608. Modern hotel set high above the lake with neat tiled modern rooms (hot water for $2 extra, a/c and hot water for $6). A bargain at current rates – if you don't mind the almost total lack of atmosphere. $̄6̄

Rattanakiri Boutique Hotel Boeung Kansaing ☎ 097 3356044, ⊛ ratanakiri-boutiquehotel.com. This landmark new modern hotel is the biggest thing to have happened in Banlung for years. There's little ambience but it's great value for money, with crisp and attractively furnished white rooms currently at a price which might buy you a dorm bed in Europe. The slightly larger and plusher lake-facing rooms ($6 extra) are particularly nice, while the attached *Pteas Bay* restaurant (see p.234) adds further bang for your very modest number of bucks. $̄1̄6̄

★**Terres Rouges Lodge** Boeung Kansaing ☎ 012 660 902, ⊛ ratanakiri-lodge.com. Luxurious boutique hotel in lush gardens near the lake, offering an unexpected haven of designer chic in remote Banlung. The lodge's wooden buildings look a bit like a miniature Khmer village given a cool modern makeover, with beautifully designed colonial-style rooms in the main building, plus even more elegant suites in private bungalows arranged around the beautiful grounds. There's also a top-notch restaurant (see p.234) and a good-sized pool, plus small spa. Given the quality, rates are a steal. $̄6̄5̄

Thy Ath Lodge Boeung Kansaing ☎ 097 3155559, ⊜ thy.ath.lodge@gmail.com. Friendly, family guesthouse in a sparkling modern building close to the lake. Rooms (all a/c) are spacious, spotless and very comfortably furnished, while those upstairs ($5 extra) have good lake views too. Superb value at current rates. $̄1̄5̄

★**Tree Top Eco Lodge** Southeast of the centre ☎ 012 490333, ⊛ treetop-ecolodge.com. Banlung's oldest – and still its best – ecolodge, with accommodation in bungalows scattered across a thickly wooded hillside and

TOURS AND TREKKING AROUND BANLUNG

There's a bewildering variety of **trekking** options around Banlung a confusion, exacerbated by the wildly conflicting claims of rival operators, including some cowboy outfits that would give John Wayne a decent run for his money – the operators listed below are all reliable. Treks cost around $30–45 per person per day in a group of two, with per-person prices falling for larger groups.

Treks can be arranged both inside and outside **Virachey National Park**. The forest inside the park is generally wilder and less spoilt than that outside, offering a more authentic (and also more physically demanding) experience of hiking through dense tropical jungle. For longer treks (three days or more), going inside the park is probably your best option, since you'll have plenty of wilderness to yomp through as well as the chance of spotting elephants and other wildlife not found elsewhere. Note that all treks inside the park incur a $10 per person per day entrance fee. The best operators use indigenous guides wherever possible, and return part of their profits to local communities through various forms of assistance.

Treks outside the park are good for shorter one- or two-day hikes, and also offer easier terrain and cheaper prices, plus the chance to see local villages en route. Treks are organized in a number of places, including areas protected as "**community forests**" (each local tribe has their own preserved area). Popular areas include Kalai (with the possibility of spotting gibbons, although the jungle here is less impressive than elsewhere) and the Khoh Peak area, reached by boat from Voen Sai. Treks in the **Lumphat Wildlife Sanctuary** are another possibility. This is dry forest rather than Virachey's tropical jungle, so less scenically memorable, although the better visibility makes it a popular destination for birdwatching. Rafting is included in many tours.

The chance of spotting gibbons in the wild is a major attraction on some treks. The main area for gibbon-spotting is the Sai Siem Pang area, which offer an eighty to ninety percent chance of seeing both yellow-cheeked and black gibbons, as well as duc and silver langurs, and pink-tailed macaques. Other areas also boast resident gibbon populations, although the chances of seeing them are considerably lower.

Most operators (including Highland, Parrot and Lucky, listed below) offer a good range of day-tours combining visits to local villages, cemeteries, gem mines and assorted lakes and waterfalls (around $25–30 per person, with transport by moto).

TOUR OPERATORS

DutchCo Office next to Café Alee, east of the centre (although it's only sporadically manned, and you'd do better to make contact by phone or email first) ☏ 097 6792714, ⊛ trekkingcambodia.com. One of Banlung's longest-running operators, this reputable Dutch-run outfit organizes quality two- to five-day treks in the Tanop area of Virachey National Park.

Highland Tours ☏ 097 6583841, ⊛ highland.tour @yahoo.com. Efficient husband-and-wife operation offering a variety of treks in the Kalai Jungle (but not in Virachey National Park itself) including visits to a gibbon-rich area protected by the local community and to Koh Peak district. Choose between village homestays or overnight camping in the jungle.

Lucky Tours ☏ 097 3334626, ⊛ luckytours4u .blogspot.com. Switched-on operators offering a range of treks in and around Virachey of various lengths and difficulties. These include hikes in Kalai jungle and Koh Peak and visits to the Siem Pang Community Forest at the border of the park.

Parrot Tours ☏ 097 4035884, ⊛ jungletrek.wix.com /parrot-tours. One of Banlung's longest-established operators, offering rewarding treks, both short and long, inside Virachey National Park, including 5–7 night treks to the remote Veal Thom grassland and Ho Chi Minh Trail, and challenging 12-day treks to Chack Xous mountain on the Lao border in the far north of the park, where there's a good chance of seeing white elephants. The only operator offering rafting trips inside the park, they also arrange trekking in Kreung tribal areas outside the park and in and around Lumphat Wildlife Sanctuary (including boat trips on the Srepok River).

connected by a picturesque network of raised walkways. The bungalows themselves are surprisingly smart and comfortable, nicely furnished and with big French windows through which to enjoy the views, plus hammocks for lounging and quaint pebbled bathrooms (some with hot water for $3 extra). Small restaurant attached. $\overline{\$12}$

EATING AND DRINKING

In addition to the places listed below, a string of local cafés ring the northeast side of the Boeung Kansaing lake around Terres Rouges lodge – largely comatose during the day, but often enjoyably lively after dark.

Banlung Balcony Guesthouse Boeung Kansaing ☎097 8097036, ⓦbalconyguesthouse.net. A prime location overlooking the lake is the main draw at this attractive open-air restaurant, and the food's pretty good too, with a decent selection of Western mains ($5–7) including good burgers and an above-average choice of authentic Khmer food (mains $3–4) including good soups and stir-fries. Daily 7am–9pm, bar open until 11pm.

★**Café Alee** East of the centre ☎089 473767. This attractive wooden pavilion-style restaurant is one of the nicest places to eat in Banlung, with a wide-ranging menu stuffed with all the usual Western and Khmer favourites (mains $4–6) along with a truckload of other home-from-home comforts – anything from cookies and fruit bread to pancakes and popcorn, plus an interesting selection of local coffees. Daily 7am–10pm.

Green Carrot East of the centre ☎098 909453. Along with *Café Alee* (see above) this cosy little place is the best of the town-centre traveller cafés, with crisp service, cool music and good food ranging from Khmer favourites (mains $3–4) plus a smattering of slightly more Western

dishes including pizza and pasta. Veggies will appreciate the great range of Western and Asian-style salads and tofu dishes. Daily 9am–10pm.

Pteas Bay Boeung Kansaing ☎097 3356044. In an eye-catching traditional Khmer-style wooden pavilion next to the lake, this place specializes in quality Cambodian cooking (mains $5–6) including an excellent range of soups, stir-fries and curries, even if the menu translations ("fried bindweed of water" anyone?) don't always do them justice. Khmer-style venison dishes are a particular speciality, and there are also a few burgers, pasta dishes and other Western options. Daily 8am–10pm.

★**Terres Rouges Lodge** Boeung Kansaing ☎012 770650. The gorgeous restaurant at this stylish hotel (see p.232) is a great place for an upmarket meal, with its lovely wood-framed, open-air dining room and fine lake views. The menu offers a mix of Asian mains ($6–7) plus pizza and pasta alongside an extensive selection of French classics ($11–15) including coq au vin, boeuf bourguignon, andouillette sausages and duck confit. Reservations recommended. Daily 6.30am–10pm.

DIRECTORY

Internet There's a well-equipped (but nameless) internet café just around the corner from Parrot Tours (daily 7am–9pm; $1/hr).

Money The ATMs at the Canadia and Acleda banks accept foreign Visa and MasterCards.

Shopping A few dealers in and around the market sell cut and polished local gemstones (see p.230) either

loose or made up into jewellery. There's no evidence of fakes being passed off as genuine, although it's sensible not to pay a lot of money for a stone unless you have some knowledge of gemology and know what particular stones are worth.

Swimming Non-residents can use the pool at *Terres Rouges* for $5/day.

Yeak Laom lake

5km east of Banlung • Daily dawn–dusk • $2 • Head east out of Banlung and turn south at the Hill Tribe Monument roundabout; dropping down the hill you reach the lake after 1.5km; the return trip by moto costs around $5, or $10 by tuk-tuk, including waiting time

Surrounded by unspoilt forest, the clear turquoise waters of **Yeak Laom lake**, 800m across and up to 50m deep, are warm and inviting. There are wooden platforms for bathing, and the 3km track around the lake perimeter makes for a tranquil little hike. The setting is mesmerizing: stands of bamboo rim the lake, lush ferns sprout from fallen trees, the reflections of clouds skim across the lake's surface, and in the late afternoon an ethereal mist rises off the water. Watch out for your stuff though – there have been thefts from bags left on the bank while visitors are swimming.

The area is regarded as sacred by the Tampoun, who manage it for the benefit of their community. Chunchiet culture is showcased at the small and rather ramshackle **Cultural and Environment Centre** (300 riel), around 300m anticlockwise round the lake from the entrance steps, with a few dusty displays of chunchiet artefacts. The small craft stall next door sells locally produced textiles, the money from sales going directly to the community.

Waterfalls around Banlung

For Chha Ong head 2km west of Banlung along NR78 to reach the crossroads at the Lina petrol station, turning right immediately past the petrol station, then bearing left at the fork after about 1km and continuing through the small village of Chha Ong; for Katieng

THE CHUNCHIET

Cambodia's **chunchiet** (literally "nationality") or **Khmer Loeu** ("upland Khmer") are one of the ethnic minority groups found scattered throughout the hinterlands of Cambodia, Burma, Thailand, Laos, Vietnam and parts of southeastern China. The chunchiet live primarily in the remote villages of Rattanakiri and Mondulkiri provinces, although small communities also inhabit parts of Stung Treng and Kratie provinces, and a few live in the mountains of southwest Cambodia, near Koh Kong. It's estimated that the chunchiet make up one percent of Cambodia's population, although in the highlands of the east and northeast they have always been the majority, at least until the recent influx of Khmer from the rest of the country.

The chunchiet, like the Khmer, are regarded as **indigenous**. Smaller in stature and darker-skinned than the Khmer, they divide into more than thirty distinct tribes, ranging from comparatively large groups such as the Tampoun, Kreung-Brou, Jarai, Stieng and Phnong, all of which number in the thousands, to much smaller tribes, including the Kavat, Lun, Peahr and Meul, thought to number fewer than a hundred each. Every group has its own **language**, each with several dialects; additionally, none of the chunchiet tongues has a written form. Traditional garments are only used on ceremonial occasions, from which strangers are normally excluded. Indeed, relatively little is known about chunchiet rituals and ceremonies, though it is known that **animism** and **ancestor worship** are central to their belief system.

Unfortunately, the traditional way of life is now nearly extinct. Repeated attempts have been made to bring the tribes round to the Khmer way of life. The French recruited them to work in the rubber plantations and on road-building projects, while the Sihanouk government tried to restrict them to farming fixed plots. In the mid 1960s, government troops seeking the guerrilla Khmer Rouge – who had fled to the jungles of Rattanakiri – burned down chunchiet villages. Indeed, bombed by the US in the early 1970s and continually harassed by Lon Nol soldiers, the chunchiet were ripe for recruitment by the Khmer Rouge, although those who did join them were most likely siding against a common enemy rather than sharing their ideology.

Today, in theory, chunchiet lands are state-owned and cannot be purchased by private Cambodians. However, since 2001 tribal lands have been sold, sometimes by village headmen, to savvy Khmer who have cleared the land for farms. Latterly, the government has allowed economic land concessions (ELCs), which permit ground to be **cleared** for plantations. According to Cambodian law, ELCs can only be used to clear non-forested land, but regardless of this, vast swathes of forest have now disappeared to make way for plantations of rubber and cashew; according to a report by Global Witness this is a way of flouting the rules regarding illegal logging. The consequence for the chunchiet is that the forest on which they have long relied for their livelihood has been largely destroyed. Appeals for the return of their land have been to no avail. Some still manage to eke a living from the land, others have found work locally in tourism, while some have been forced to abandon their traditional way of life entirely.

Although many villagers have become accustomed to foreign visitors, they remain shy and modest – some may even see your presence as voyeuristic, so it's always better to visit in the company of a local guide. It's also worth noting that the chunchiet do not like having their pictures taken and are embarrassed by shows of public affection and by exposed flesh (bare legs, arms and so on).

turn left at the Lina petrol station, following the sign to Swift Rubber Factory/Rattanakiri Rubber Plantations, where you take a right turn immediately past the factory (unsigned, although the track is clear); for Ka Chhang continue straight on along the road past the rubber factory

There are a few modest but picturesque **waterfalls** within easy reach of Banlung, easily combined into a half-day trip along with a visit to Yeak Laom lake, or into day-trips with other assorted local attractions. The falls at **Chha Ong** (2000 riel entrance), around 8km northwest of Banlung, are the largest, the river flowing through lush jungle before plunging 30m into a gorge. The pool at the base is deep enough to swim in, and daring souls can climb onto a ledge behind the curtain of water.

Southwest of Banlung, hidden in a bamboo-clad valley, are the **Ka Chhang** falls (3000 riel entrance), just 10m high, but impressive after rain and with a pool for taking a dip. Nearby are the small and similar **Katieng** falls (2000 riel entrance).

ILLEGAL LOGGING

Between 2000 and 2005 Cambodia lost nearly thirty percent of its **tropical hardwood forest** cover, the third-highest rate of deforestation in the world at the time, surpassed only by Vietnam and Nigeria. Although deforestation rates have slowed slightly since then – as valuable timber becomes rarer and harder to extract – rampant illegal logging still continues to plague the country and travellers passing through the provinces of Pailin, Kompong Thom, Kratie, Rattanakiri or Mondulkiri will scarcely see any forest at all.

Most of the forest has been cleared to make way for **plantations** of rubber, cashew and cassava, a national scandal presided over by self-serving government officials and timber tycoons, many of them close to the prime minister, Hun Sen. At the same time, those fighting logging have been routinely harassed, including the murder in 2012 of leading activist Chut Wutty by military police.

In January 2016 the government announced new measures to crack down on the trade in illegal timber along the Vietnam border and shortly afterwards announced that it had largely succeeded in suppressing covert exports. However, according to American NGO Forest Trends, the measures have had little effect, with timber worth 12 million US dollars passing into Vietnam in February and March of that year alone.

One bright light amid the gloom has been the establishment since 2003 of a network of community forests, whereby areas of jungle are handed over to the protection of local communities to be sustainably managed. Over 400 such forests have now been established nationwide, although they still cover only one percent of the country's total land area, a small fraction of the forested areas devoted to commercial purposes.

Voen Sai

Stretching along the south side of the pretty **San River**, the former provincial capital of **VOEN SAI**, 35km northwest of Banlung and accessible by bus, is the largest village in the vicinity of Virachey National Park. From the centre of the village a **ferry** (1000 riel) runs to the far bank of the river, on which there are some Chinese and Lao villages, notably different in appearance to others in the area. The Chinese village a couple of kilometres to the west has a tidy school and a general store; the main street is flanked by neat bright-blue houses planted firmly on the ground rather than on stilts. **Boats** can be rented along the river for trips upstream to Kreung and Kraval villages (1hr; around $15 return) and further on to the Tampoun chunchiet cemetery (3hr; $50 return).

If you have your own transport you can make an interesting little diversion en route to Voen Sai at **Veal Rum Plan**, an ancient lava field of huge flat stones. To reach the lava field, head east at the O Chum crossroads, about 10km north of Banlung, and then continue straight down the road for around 4km.

Virachey National Park

Daily · $10/day · Treks into the park must be arranged through various tour operators in Banlung (see box, p.233)

Spreading north of Voen Sai, the **Virachey National Park** covers more than three thousand square kilometres of remote, mountainous countryside running north to the Lao border and east to Vietnam, comprising a mix of landscapes from dense jungle lowlands through to montane forests and rolling upland savannahs. It's also the largest "protected" area in Cambodia, although exactly what kind of protection it's currently receiving is a moot point – local reports suggest that as much as sixty percent of the park has already been earmarked for future logging.

Virachey's outstandingly rich **wildlife** is yet to be fully explored or understood. The world's largest population of rare northern yellow-cheeked **gibbons** in the **Veun Sai–Siem Pang Conservation Area** adjoining the park weren't discovered until as recently as 2010, while a couple of other entirely new species – the iridescent short-legged lizard and Walston's tube-nosed bat – have also recently been unearthed for the first time. Other forest inhabitants include elephants, pig-tailed macaques, douc langurs, sun bears, the rare giant ibis and clouded leopards. Rumours of tigers and Javan rhinos living deep inside the forest also occasionally surface, although the alleged sightings may contain rather more fiction than fact.

When **visiting the park** (see p.233), the traveller's most challenging and rewarding expedition is the week-long trek to the remote grassland wilderness of **Phnom Veal Thom**, with spectacular views over the mountainous hinterlands bordering Laos and Vietnam. Shorter treks include the overnight trek to Yark Koung Kreav mountain and the three-night trek to Yark Kea waterfall.

Lumphat

There's not much left of **LUMPHAT**, 35km south of Banlung. Capital of Rattanakiri until 1975, when the Khmer Rouge moved it to Voen Sai, the town sustained heavy bombing during the 1970s and still has a faintly postapocalyptic air. A few ruined shells of concrete buildings are all that survive from its days as provincial capital, along with patches of cratered wasteland caused by American B-52 bombing runs. There are no land mines here, but **unexploded ordnance** may still be a risk.

Lumphat is also the jumping-off point for trips into the **Lumphat Wildlife Sanctuary**. Some tour operators in Banlung (see box, p.233) offer treks, although as at Virachey National Park rampant logging is taking a steady toll on the natural environment.

Mondulkiri province

4

The country's largest but most sparsely populated province, mountainous **Mondulkiri** sees fewer travellers in a year than Rattanakiri does in a month, although improved access is gradually bringing Cambodia's "Wild East" into the tourist mainstream. As in neighbouring Rattanakiri, Mondulkiri's once wild landscape has suffered greatly from indiscriminate logging and other forms of development, including the creation of Chinese and Australian gold mines, although areas of impenetrable jungle survive, home to rare and endangered wildlife including elephants, Asian dogs and green peafowl. The compact provincial capital, **Sen Monorom**, makes a good base for local treks and visits to surrounding attractions, including the mighty **Bou Sraa** waterfall and the innovative **Elephant Valley Project**.

OPERATION MENU

Rattanakiri's proximity to Vietnam and inaccessible, jungle-covered terrain made it a favoured hide-out of North Vietnamese Army (PAVN) and National Liberation Front (NLF, aka "Viet Cong") fighters, who established bases here in the later 1960s with the covert approval of Prince Sihanouk's government in Phnom Penh. Along with their bases, the North Vietnamese also created an extensive network of supply routes, dubbed the **Sihanouk Trail**, which wound its way up from Sihanoukville into the Rattanakiri uplands and thence across the border, connecting with sections of the famous Ho Chi Minh Trail.

After repeated attempts to enlist Sihanouk's help in closing PAVN and NLF bases and the Sihanouk Trail, clandestine US military strikes were launched in March 1969 under the code-name **Operation Menu** (see p.300). Over a period of fourteen months, American B-52 bombers flew over 3500 sorties across the region, unloading in the region of 100,000 tons of ordnance in their attempts to destroy Vietnamese strongholds and in doing so more or less wipe the former provincial capital of Lumphat off the map. The campaign's military, political and, especially, human costs were nothing short of catastrophic. Thousands of innocents died in the bombings, while Vietnamese forces simply re-routed their supply chains and retreated deeper inside Cambodia. The devastation and terror of the bombing raids also provided an irresistible propaganda weapon for the fledgling Khmer Rouge, also entrenched in the region, in their efforts to rally further fighters and popular support to their cause.

Mondulkiri's main indigenous group are the **Bunong** (also known as the Phnong), who made up nearly eighty percent of the province's population until the 1990s, when they were joined by an influx of impoverished Khmer returning from the refugee camps in Thailand. The Khmer are still coming, though nowadays it's the rich who are buying land cheaply and then clearing it for farms and plantations.

Sen Monorom

The smallest of all Cambodia's provincial capitals, **SEN MONOROM** has transformed over the past few years into one of Asia's leading centres for **ethical elephant tourism**, inspired by the example of the pioneering Elephant Valley Project (see p.239), with a growing number of operators offering the chance to walk and interact with (but not ride) elephants in their natural forest environment. There's also some good **trekking**, as well as interesting indigenous villages in the surrounding countryside to explore.

Sen Monorom itself is still little more than a modest town set amid a landscape of rolling grass-covered hills dotted with copses of pine planted in the late 1960s at the king's behest. The two **lakes** on the northwest side of town are pleasant for an early morning or late afternoon stroll, while 2km northeast from town is the sacred mountain **Phnom DoKramom**, a small hill with a meditation pagoda, from where there are splendid views, particularly popular at sunset.

ARRIVAL AND DEPARTURE   SEN MONOROM

Transport to and from Sen Monorom is by minibus rather than bus – there's a cluster of operators in the centre of town, although it's usually easiest to find out timings and book **tickets** through your guesthouse. **Shared taxis** arrive and leave from the transport stop in the north of town, just uphill from the market.

By minibus Banlung (1 daily; 3hr); Kompong Cham (1 daily; 5hr); Kratie (2 daily; 4hr 30min); Phnom Penh (8 daily; 8hr); Siem Reap (4 daily; 10hr); Sihanoukville (2 daily; 12hr).

GETTING AROUND

The small town centre is easily manageable on foot. Motos are readily available for trips into the countryside (around $20–25/day), or you can rent a **motorbike** ($5–7/day) from several places around town.

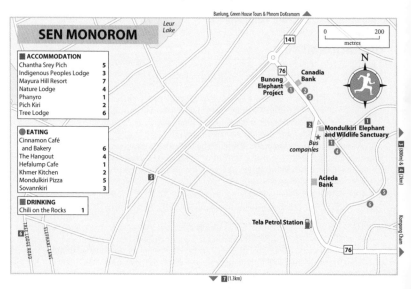

SEN MONOROM

ACCOMMODATION
Chantha Srey Pich	5
Indigenous Peoples Lodge	3
Mayura Hill Resort	7
Nature Lodge	4
Phanyro	1
Pich Kiri	2
Tree Lodge	6

EATING
Cinnamon Café and Bakery	6
The Hangout	4
Hefalump Cafe	1
Khmer Kitchen	2
Mondulkiri Pizza	5
Sovannkiri	3

DRINKING
Chili on the Rocks	1

Leur Lake

Banlung, Green House Tours & Phnom DoKramom

Canadia Bank

Bunong Elephant Project

Mondulkiri Elephant and Wildlife Sanctuary

Bus companies

Acleda Bank

Tela Petrol Station

TREE LODGE ROAD

ELEPHANT LANE

Kompong Cham

ELEPHANT TOURS AND TREKKING AROUND SEN MONOROM

Over the past few years Sen Monorom has emerged as a major centre for ethical elephant tourism, inspired by the pioneering Elephant Valley Project (see below) which has now spawned a string of copycat – although generally reputable – operations. Projects offer the complete antithesis of the usual tourist theme-park elephant interactions. There are no elephant rides here (something all the projects actively discourage), instead the focus is on walking with elephants as they wander through the forest and interacting with them in their natural environment. A number of operators also offer trekking in the town's wild forested hinterlands, as well as general tours of local waterfalls, villages and so on (which can also be arranged through most guesthouses).

Bunong Elephant Project Office on the Main Road, opposite the Canadia Bank ☎097 8162770. ⓦbunongelephantproject.org. Run by former Elephant Livelihood Initiative Environment (ELIE) volunteer Mr Torn, this operation offers one-day "elephant experiences" ($35) featuring elephant feeding, walking and bathing, with the option of combining these with an overnight village stay and jungle trek the following day ($65).

Elephant Community Project ☎072 676644 ⓦelephantcommunityproject.org. One-hundred percent, Cambodian-owned and -managed community project run by former WWF guide Sam Nang, offering one-day tours combining elephant interactions and a Bunong village visit ($35), and one-day treks in Seima Protected Forest ($50).

Elephant Valley Project Office at the Hefalump Café, Main Road ☎099 696041, ⓦelephant valleyproject.org. Sen Monorom's original elephant project, set up to create a haven for Cambodia's increasingly threatened pachyderm population. Visitors get the chance to shadow the project's two resident elephant families: walking with them through the jungle, observing them at leisure in their natural environment, and learning about them from their Khmer mahouts. Impeccable ethical credentials – they're still the only operation which doesn't include bathing with the elephants as part of their programme, believing that this is constricting for the animals (as well as potentially dangerous for visitors). Day-visits (Mon–Fri only) cost $85, or $55 with a half-day's volunteer work; longer visits (including seven-day volunteer programmes) are also available (see the website for details).

Green House Tours Banlung Rd, about 1km from the centre ☎097 362644, ⓦgreenhouse-tour .blogspot.co.uk. One of the town's longest-running tour operators offering a wide range of activities including combined elephant tours (in combination with the Elephant Community Project, see opposite) and visits to Bunong villages, local homestays ($65pp), jungle trekking (including treks in Seima Protected Forest; one-day $50pp, two days $120pp). Note that they're due to move in early 2017 out of the town centre offices on the main road next to Canadia Bank to new premises on the Banlung Road.

Mondulkiri Elephant and Wildlife Sanctuary Office on the main road, town centre ☎097 659 1101 ⓦmondulkirisanctuary.org. Run by the LEAF (Local Environmental Awareness Foundation) Cambodian conservation organization and offering one-day tours ($40) with the project's six elephants (with the option of a second day's jungle trekking). Also runs a volunteer programme, while profits support local community and reforestation projects as well as supporting a rescue and rehabilitation service for illegally captured local wildlife of all kinds.

Mondulkiri Project ☎097 7234177, ⓦmondulkiri project.org. One- and two-day tours ($50/$80 per person). Run by the aptly named Mr Tree and offering visitors the chance to feed, walk with and bathe the project's four elephants. The project is run in cooperation with Bunong indigenous elders and is fully Cambodian owned and managed – revenues help protect local forests and support Bunong communitites in the area and the ethos is on providing paid work for Mondulkiri's indigenous communities rather than volunteering opportunities for foreigners.

ACCOMMODATION

Sen Monorom is a bit cooler than most other parts of Cambodia and you can probably get away without a/c, although hot water is nice.

Chantha Srey Pich 500m west of the centre ☎011 550388. Good new cheapie with small, functional fan rooms (cold water only) – nothing much to look at but neat, comfortable, spotlessly clean and equipped with mosquito nets and TVs (although windows may be lacking). There's also a basic 13-bed dorm with very cheap beds ($2.50 per person), plus attached restaurant. §6

Indigenous Peoples Lodge 1km east of the centre 012 725375, indigenouspeopleslodge@gmail .com. Sen Monorom's most eye-catching and original place to stay looks like a miniature tribal village, with accommodation in a quirky range of bamboo-and-thatch buildings in various eye-catching indigenous designs. It's all pretty rustic, with mattresses on the floors rather than beds in most of the buildings and not much in the way of creature comforts, but for authentic Mondulkiri character it can't be beaten. Small restaurant attached. §10

Mayura Hill Resort 2km south of the centre 077 980 980, mayurahillresort.com. This intimate little boutique resort is currently Sen Monorom's most upmarket place to stay, with a cluster of chic, attractively furnished glass-fronted chalets scattered around lush grounds (although the battered kid's play area, miniature astroturf football pitch and piped muzak somewhat spoil the otherwise alluring effect). It's also enjoyably close to nature – expect to hear local wildlife bounding over your roof at night. There's also a small pool and passable restaurant. Nice, although a bit pricey. §100

★**Nature Lodge** 2km east of the centre 012 230272, naturelodgecambodia.com. Idyllic little ecolodge, tucked away in the countryside outside town, with accommodation in simple but comfortable stilted wooden cabins (with hot water) widely scattered around very spacious grounds that gently shelve down into a valley. Hammocks on the verandas encourage aimless idling, and there's also an attractively rustic little restaurant and bar. §15

Phanyro Town centre 017 770867. Attractive guesthouse with accommodation in a cluster of neat and cosy wooden chalets (with hot water and nice bathrooms) set around appealing leafy gardens on the edge of a hill (although no views). Excellent value. §8

Pich Kiri Main Road (NR76) 012 282370, pichkiri @gmail.com. One of Sen Monorom's best mid-range options, in a brilliantly central location and with spacious, good-value and very comfortable rooms kitted out with chintzy wooden furniture, big drape curtains and scalloped ceilings. Fan §10; a/c §15

Tree Lodge 1km west of the centre 097 7234177, treelodgecambodia.com. Reliable budget option offering a hint of jungle chic at a super-affordable price, with accommodation in a string of neat wooden cabanas (with enjoyably rustic bathrooms) plus lovely hill views from the little restaurant in the main building. Hot water available for a $2 supplement. §5

EATING AND DRINKING

Chili on the Rocks Town centre facebook.com /chiliontherocksbar. This lively little Swedish-owned hole-in-wall bar combines cheap beer with mellow music, and remains open long after most of Sen Monorom has gone to bed. Daily noon to midnight.

Cinnamon Café and Bakery (formerly Café Phka) South of the centre. Shoebox-sized coffee-shop-cum-bakery serving up a decent selection of coffees and juices alongside more-ish cakes and bakes plus assorted snacks, sandwiches and breakfasts ($2–5) – anything from all-day English through to Swedish meatballs with mash. Daily 8am–9pm.

The Hangout Town centre 088 7219991. Good all-round travellers caff run by a Khmer-Australian couple, with a decent selection of Khmer dishes (mains $3) and more expensive Western options ($4.50–6) including lots of comfort food like bangers and mash, chicken parmigiana, and fish and chips. There's also a burger selection (including veg, tofu and fish) plus salads, soups, baguettes and a good breakfast selection. Daily 7am–10pm.

Hefalump Cafe Main Road (NR76) 099 696041 facebook.com/hefalumpcafe and hefalumpcafe -tourismhub.com. Run by a quartet of conservation and development NGOs, this convivial little garden café serves as the nerve hub of Sen Monorom's expat and ecotourism scene and is also a great place for coffee, breakfasts and cake, including Mondulkiri's best lemon meringue pie. Mon–Fri 7am–6pm, Sat 11am–4pm, Sun noon–4pm.

Khmer Kitchen Main Road (NR76) 092 963243. Local restaurant given a makeover for the tourist trade with attractive wooden decor and wide-ranging menu (mains $3–4) of authentic Khmer staples including banana flower salad, *lok lak* and *samlor ktis*. Daily 6am–10pm.

Mondulkiri Pizza South of the centre 097 5222219. This rustic restaurant in a cute little bamboo pavilion offers a choice of 22 varieties of excellent thin-crust pizza (around $6) – the best Italian you could reasonably expect in the wilds of Mondulkiri. Daily 10am–9pm.

Sovannkiri Main Road (NR76). Tourist-friendly local restaurant with a distinctive decor of clunky wooden furniture and corrugated-iron architecture festooned with giant beer adverts. The menu (mains $3) features excellent food including stir-fries, curries and Khmer and Thai-style soups, all fresh and bursting with flavour, if a bit oily. Daily 6am–10pm.

DIRECTORY

Money The ATMs at the Acleda and Canadia banks accept Visa and MasterCard.

Yoga Sen Monorom Yoga with Lana (089 746931, senmonoromyoga@gmail.com) offers drop-in classes ($7) at its studios above the *Hefalump Cafe*.

Phnom Bai Chuw and the Sea Forest

7km northeast of Sen Monorom, along the road past Phnom Dosh Kramom

Northeast of Sen Monorom, an observation platform atop the grassy hill of **Phnom Bai Chuw** offers one of Mondulkiri's classic views, looking down over miles of jungle canopy as it sweeps and rolls over the hills below – the so-called "**Sea Forest**", as it's popularly known. Squint a little, and you really can almost believe you're looking at the supersized waves of some gigantic green ocean.

Waterfalls around Sen Monorom

To get to Bou Sraa or Romanea you'll need to rent a motorbike (see p.238) or a moto; you'll also need to pay a $2.50 toll to use the road; for Romanea take the main road back from Bou Sraa towards Snuol for about 10km, then fork left and left again; Monorom waterfall can be easily reached by moto (around $3–4 return) or on foot; tour operators in Sen Monorom (try Green House) can arrange the trip to Bou Sraa for around $15, or to all three falls plus the sea forest for $20 (see p.239).

Some 35km from Sen Monorom, towards the Vietnamese border, **Bou Sraa** is Cambodia's most dramatic cascade: a fabulous two-tiered waterfall formed as the river drops over 30m into a jungle gorge. For the ultimate view of the falls and the surrounding jungle canopy, buckle up for the new **Mayura Zipline** (Ⓦmondulkresort .com; $69), comprising a series of treetop ziplines and viewing platforms through the jungle canopy culminating in a spectacular 100m-zipline ride high over the falls themselves. En route to Bou Sraa, it's worth making a detour to take in the three-tier, but less dramatic, **Romanea falls**.

Closer to Sen Monorom is the 10m-high **Monorom waterfall** (also known as the Sihanouk falls), just 4km northwest of town. Along the way you'll pass the ruins of the (rarely used) royal residence, after which you should follow the left fork to the falls. You can swim in the pool at the base of the falls, even in the dry season.

Seima Protection Forest

Southwest of Sen Monorom, flanking the road to Snuol, is the **Seima Protection Forest (SPF)**. Established in 2009, the SPF is home to some of Cambodia's most spectacular wildlife, although the forest's daunting size and lack of infrastructure means that ecotourism here is still very much in its infancy. Resident animals include tigers, banteng and gaur, along with large numbers of wild elephants, more than 300 species of bird and some 2500 yellow-cheeked crested gibbons. The forest is also home to the world's largest population of **black-shanked douc** (*Pygathrix nigripes*), with an estimated 42,000 of these engaging blue-faced monkeys living here. Remarkably, their presence in the forest went completely unrecorded until a few years back – prior to their discovery the world's largest reported group of black-shanked doucs (in Vietnam) was a mere six hundred.

Visits can be arranged in Sen Monorom through Green House Tours and the Elephant Community Project (see p.239) or, more expensively, but with expert guides, through the local outpost of leading birdwatching and wildlife specialist the Sam Veasna Center (Ⓦsamveasna.org; day-trip $85 per person in a group of two, or $130 for two days), based at the *Hefalump Cafe*.

Mondulkiri Protected Forest

Beyond Sen Monorom, a great swathe of trees blankets the northern reaches of Mondulkiri province and onwards into Rattanakiri. Some of the most pristine forest can be found in the remote **Mondulkiri Protected Forest**, home to a superb range of endangered wildlife and avifauna including elephant, tiger, banteng, gaur, rare Sarus cranes and giant ibis. The tourism and homestay programme which formerly ran here is no longer operational, although it's possible that visits may restart at some future date – check locally for latest information.

Sihanoukville and the south

BEACH BAR, KOH RONG

5

Sihanoukville and the south

Cambodia's southern provinces form a rich mosaic – a near-iridescent green quilt of rice paddies, the looming crags of the Cardamom and Elephant mountain ranges, colonial towns of Kampot and Kep, lively Sihanoukville, tropical islands and a palm-fringed coastline stretching for more than 440km. The relative inaccessibility of much of the southwest around Koh Kong, thanks to heavy forest cover, mountains and lack of roads, only adds to its charm, although encroaching development, even within the region's pristine national parks, is a constant threat. Numerous islands dot the Gulf of Thailand, and although many are earmarked for resort development (with work underway on some), a castaway ambience still prevails.

Southeastern Cambodia – roughly comprising **Preah Sihanouk, Kampot** and **Takeo provinces** – is dotted with craggy karst formations that project starkly from the plains. This is one of the country's most productive agricultural regions; parts of Kampot province resemble a market garden, producing durian, watermelon and coconuts, while in Takeo province, rice paddies dominate. Salt, and more importantly, **pepper** (see box, p.282), are also key products. The former is extracted from coastal salt pans and plays an important part in the manufacture of the country's *prahok* (salted fermented fish paste); the latter is cultivated almost like hops, and was once *the* condiment of the colonial occupiers – at the time, no Parisian table worth its salt was without Kampot pepper.

Most visitors come to the south to hit the beach at **Sihanoukville** or to use the town as a jumping-off point for the **islands**, their white sands washed by warm, shallow waters. Sihanoukville sits on a peninsula jutting into the Gulf of Thailand, its coastline scalloped with gently shelving, tree-fringed, white-sand beaches, and hazy islands looming enticingly out at sea. While the town is attracting increasing numbers of party-animals, keen to live it up in the clubs by night and in the **Ochheuteal** beach bars by day, a short moto ride in either direction uncovers stretches of less developed shoreline. East of Sihanoukville is another area of outstanding natural beauty, **Ream National Park**, whose attractions include pristine mangrove forest, fine sandy beaches and the island of Koh Thmei.

Most itineraries feature the captivating riverside town of **Kampot**, its French quarter home to atmospheric bars, restaurants and hotels. Numerous places have sprung up in town and along the river, making it ideal for a few days relaxation. Nearby, **Bokor National Park** is worth visiting, its jungle-clad slopes home to an abandoned hill station, although private development threatens to diminish some of its unearthly appeal. East of Kampot is **Kep**, a sleepy seaside destination famed for its fresh crab, lively market and relaxing afternoons on Rabbit Island.

VILLAGE JETTY, REAM NATIONAL PARK

Highlights

❶ Sihanoukville Cambodia's premier coastal town mixes wild nightlife on Ochheuteal beach with the jungle vibe of Otres Village. **See p.247**

❷ Island hopping Swap the mainland crowds for tranquil, pristine beaches on the south coast's palm-fringed islands. **See p.259 & p.265**

❸ Koh Kong Southwest Cambodia's ecotourism hotspot offers waterfalls, jungle treks and enticing places to stay along the mangrove-lined Tatai River. **See p.266**

❹ Chi Phat An ecotourism initiative where you can sleep in a homestay and hike or bike through the Cardamom Mountains. **See p.270**

❺ Kirirom and Ream national parks From the cool jungle-clad hills and waterfalls of Kirirom to the stunning coastal scenery of Ream, the region's natural beauty is ripe for exploration. **See p.264 & p.271**

❻ Kampot A charming riverside town with a rich colonial history, it's an ideal base for exploring the caves, waterfalls and pepper farms in the surrounding countryside. **See p.274**

❼ Kep Enjoy crab feasts at the beachside market or sip a sundowner in sumptuous luxury at this 1960s seaside resort, now being restored to its former elegance. **See p.283**

HIGHLIGHTS ARE MARKED ON THE MAP ON P.246

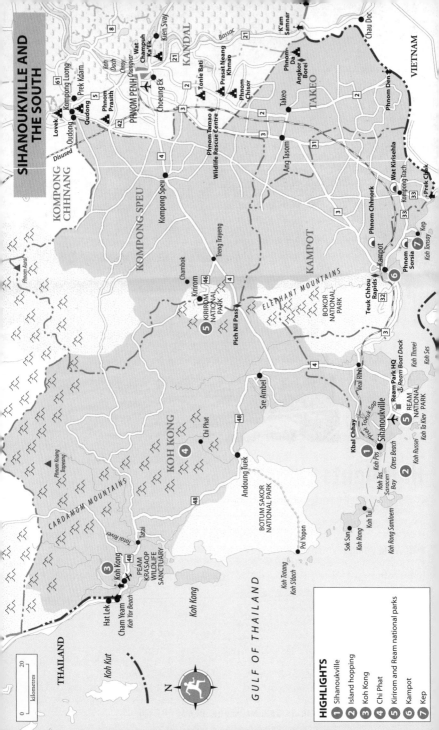

SIHANOUKVILLE AND THE SOUTH

HIGHLIGHTS

1. Sihanoukville
2. Island hopping
3. Koh Kong
4. Chi Phat
5. Kirirom and Ream national parks
6. Kampot
7. Kep

THAILAND

VIETNAM

GULF OF THAILAND

KOMPONG CHHNANG

KOMPONG SPEU

KANDAL

PHNOM PENH

TAKEO

KAMPOT

KOH KONG

CARDAMOM MOUNTAINS

ELEPHANT MOUNTAINS

BOKOR NATIONAL PARK

KIRIROM NATIONAL PARK

BOTUM SAKOR NATIONAL PARK

PEAM KRASAOP WILDLIFE SANCTUARY

REAM NATIONAL PARK

Koh Kut

Koh Kong

Koh Totang
Koh Sdach

Koh Rong

Koh Rong Samloem

Koh Tas
Koh Tui

Saracen Bay

Sok San

Koh Russei

Otres Beach

Koh Ta Kiev

Koh Thmei

Koh Ses

Koh Tonsay

Koh Duch
Chroy

Lovek
Oudong
Kompong Luong
Prek Kdam
Phnom Prasith

Kien Svay
Wat Champuh Ka'Ek
Choeung Ek

Tonle Bati
Prasat Neang Khmao
Phnom Chisor

Phnom Tamao Wildlife Rescue Centre

Ang Tasom
Takeo

K'am Samnar
Chau Doc
Phnom Da
Angkor Borei
Phnom Den

Wat Kirisehla
Kompong Tach
Prek Creuk

Kep
Phnom Sorsia

Kampot
Teuk Chhou Rapids

Pich Nil Pass

Chambok
Kirirom
Treng Trayeng

Kompong Speu

Veal Rinh
Kbal Chhay
Sihanoukville
Ream Park HQ & Ream Boat Dock

Sre Ambel
Chi Phat

Andoung Tuek

Pol Yopon

Tatai
Tatai River
Koh Kong
Cham Yeam
Koh Yor Beach
Hat Lek

Phnom Aural

Phnom Knang
Ta Bepong

Prek Tuek

Prek Toeuk Sap

N

0   kilometres   20

Bassac

Disused

Highways / routes: 8, 61, 5, 42, 21, 2, 3, 4, 46, 48, 32, 33, 31

East of Kep, you'll find the down-at-heel remains of the ancient Funan-era city of **Angkor Borei**, where a fascinating museum houses pre-Angkorian sculptures and interesting records found scattered around town during archaeological digs; together with the nearby hilltop temple of **Phnom Da**, it's easily visited by boat from **Takeo**, a shabby but compelling little town, far removed from the tourist trail, despite its proximity to Phnom Penh.

Southwestern Cambodia, namely **Koh Kong province**, is the region's rising star. Its hub is the sleepy border town of **Koh Kong**, slowly establishing its reputation as an ecotourism destination. Stay in town or along the serene **Tatai River**; attractions include **Koh Kong island**, **Peam Krasaop Wildlife Sanctuary**, waterfalls, isolated beaches and jungle treks into the **Cardamom Mountains**, a lush expanse of forested valleys, pristine jungle, and peaks rising to 1830m. Deeper in the mountains is **Chi Phat**, a community-based ecotourism project with opportunities for trekking and **homestays**. Back towards Phnom Penh in **Kompong Speu province** is **Kirirom National Park**, often overlooked, yet its towering pine trees are a unique sight in Cambodia, and the mountain air something of a relief during humid months.

Sihanoukville and the beaches

Cambodia's primary coastal town, **SIHANOUKVILLE** occupies a hilly headland rising above island-speckled waters and several gently shelving white-sand beaches. The sprawling centre, known as "**Downtown**", sits a little way inland and offers few attractions, but there's a relaxed atmosphere and it's where you'll find banks, markets and supermarkets.

The main hub is on and around **Serendipity Beach Road**, 4km south of Downtown – a lively strip of bars, restaurants and guesthouses with the beach bars of **Ochheuteal Beach** at the southern end. The main blight on the landscape, particularly around Serendipity Beach Road and nearby Victory Hill, is the number of concrete casino resorts, much loved by Chinese visitors. Consequently, the beaches of **Otres 1 and 2** – the town's furthest-flung beaches – have become increasingly popular for their relatively low-key, low-rise appeal. **Otres Village**, a kilometre inland, is even more laidback, while the sixty or so **islands** dotting the Gulf of Thailand offer further escapism, some easily accessible from Sihanoukville (see p.259). There are a couple of inland **waterfalls** to visit north of town, and a 40-min drive north along the coast brings you to pristine **Hun Sen Beach** and the traditional **fishing village** of Steung Hav.

Psar Leu

Psar Leu is a huge market that was given a facelift after being devastated by a fire in 2008. You can stock up here on everything from fishing lines to fruit and vegetables before heading out to the islands, and it's a great place to meander, especially the fish section with its sea urchins, octopus, huge coloured crabs and mighty sea creatures with fierce eyes and bristling whiskers.

Wat Leu and around

Wat Leu, on the summit of Phnom Sihanoukville, is one of five pagodas in town. Accessed by a track behind Cambrew (Angkor) Brewery, the temple atop this 132m hill – otherwise known as the "Upper Wat" – is the highest point in town and has fantastic panoramic views. It's easily visited in conjunction with **Wat Krom**, set on a boulder-strewn hillside off Santepheap Street, which is home to a sanctuary commemorating **Yeay Mao**, the "Black Grandmother" (see box, p.273).

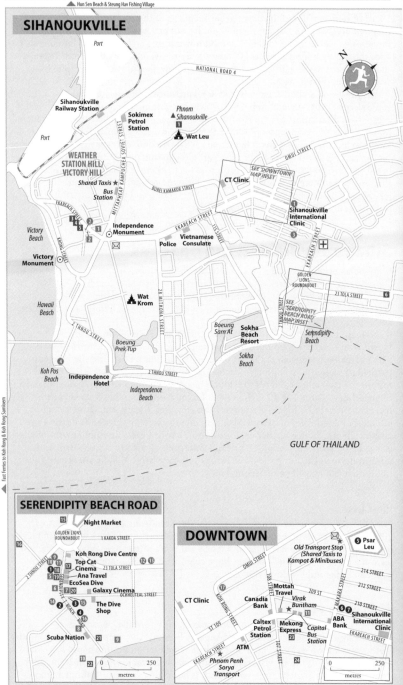

SIHANOUKVILLE

▲ Hun Sen Beach & Steung Hav Fishing Village

Port

NATIONAL ROAD 4

Sihanoukville Railway Station

Sokimex Petrol Station

Phnom
▲ Sihanoukville 1

♦ Wat Leu

DMUI STREET

Port

WEATHER STATION HILL/ VICTORY HILL

CT Clinic

SEE DOWNTOWN MAP INSET

Shared Taxis ★
Bus Station

BOREI KAMAKOR STREET

Sihanoukville International Clinic

3

Victory Beach

EKAREACH STREET

Independence Monument

EKAREACH STREET

Police

Vietnamese Consulate

Victory Monument

GOLDEN LIONS ROUNDABOUT

23 TOLA STREET

6

♦ Wat Krom

SEE 'SERENDIPITY BEACH ROAD' MAP INSET

Hawaii Beach

Boeung Sam At

Sokha Beach Resort

Serendipity Beach

Koh Pos Beach

4

2 THNOU STREET

Boeung Prek Tup

Independence Hotel

2 THNOU STREET

Sokha Beach

Independence Beach

GULF OF THAILAND

Fast Ferries to Koh Rong & Koh Rong Samloem

SERENDIPITY BEACH ROAD

15 Night Market

GOLDEN LIONS ROUNDABOUT

1 KAKDA STREET

16

Koh Rong Dive Centre

12 13

Top Cat Cinema

23 TOLA STREET

Ana Travel

EcoSea Dive

Galaxy Cinema

OCHHEUTEAL STREET

The Dive Shop

Scuba Nation

21 9

10 22

0   250
metres

DOWNTOWN

★ Psar Leu 5

Old Transport Stop (Shared Taxis to Kampot & Minibuses)

214 STREET

212 STREET

CT Clinic

DMUI STREET

108 STREET

Mottah Travel

Virak Buntham

209 ST

210 STREET

Canadia Bank

11

Caltex Petrol Station

Mekong Express

Capital Bus Station

ABA Bank

6 7

Sihanoukville International Clinic

EKAREACH STREET

ATM

Phnom Penh Sorya Transport

24

0   250
metres

5

Kbal Chhay Waterfalls

NATIONAL ROAD 4

MITTAPHEAP ROAD

POULOWAI STREET 300

ORES MARINA ROAD

Ochheuteal
Beach

Otres
Beach

DRINKING AND NIGHTLIFE

Above Us Only Sky	10
The Big Easy	6
Corner Bar	2
Dolphin Shack	9
Dune	4
G'Day Mate	11
Maybe Later	8
Mojo's	1
Monkey Republic	5
Otres Market	12
Straycats	13
Utopia	7
Wish You Were Here	3

SHOPPING

Casablanca Books	1
M'Lop Tapang	4
Psar Leu	5
Rogue iPod	2
Samudera	6
Sea Spirals	3
Starfish	7

ACCOMMODATION

Above Us Only Sky	22
Backpacker Heaven	3
Beach Road Hotel	17
Blue Sky Bungalows	28
BOHO	29
Chochi Garden	21
Divers Hotel	4
Don Bosco	2
Footprints	11
Geckozy	24
Hacienda	27
Makara Bungalows	6
Mama Clare's	25
Mealy Chenda	5
Mick & Craig's	18
Monkey Republic	19
One Stop Hostel	15
Otres Jungle Bungalows	30
Otres Marina	12
Pagoda Rocks	1
Patchouly Chill House	16
Pat Pat Guesthouse	8
Ren Resort	14
Sahaa Beach Resort	9
Sam's Beach Bungalows	13
Sea Garden	10
Sok Sabay Resort	26
The Small Hotel	23
Utopia	20
Wish You Were Here	7

Ou Treh Pagoda

Liberty
Ranch

ATM   ATM

Queenco
(watersports)

OTRES 1

SEE OTRES VILLAGE
MAP INSET

Golden River

ATM

Otres Beach
Resort
(watersports)

OTRES 2

Airport & Ream National Park

0 — 1
kilometres

EATING

Beach Club Resort	12
Carpe Diem	19
Delicious	14
Eno Café	15
Gelato Italiano	17
Happy Herb Pizza	13
Holy Cow	1
Karma Sutra	11
Ku–Kai	3
Marco Polo	10
Pacha Mama	18
Papa Pippo	6
Sandan	9
Sophary Restaurant	2
So	16
Secret Garden Otres	7
Sunshine Café	5
Tamu	8
Treasure Island Seafood	4

Liberty
Ranch

OTRES VILLAGE

Golden River

Lakeside Bar &
Fishing Lake

Koh Ta Kiev & Koh Rossei

0 — 250
metres

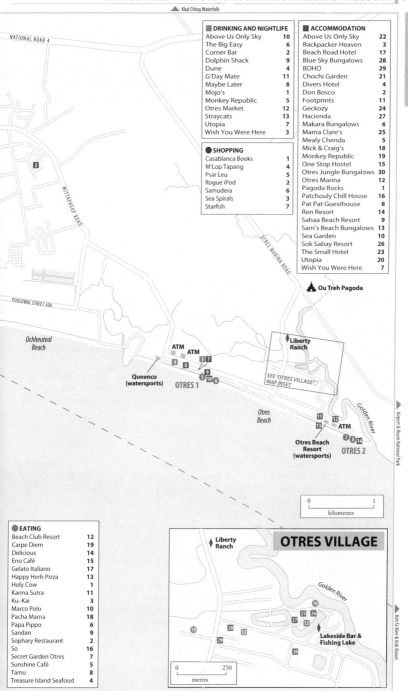

5

Ochheuteal Beach

South of the town centre, **Ochheuteal Beach**, the town's longest and busiest strand south of the main ferry pier, is a 3km stretch of sand lined with near-identical beach bars, separated from the beach by a walkway where vendors ply their trade, from pedicures to fried prawns-on-a-stick. By day, it's packed with Cambodian families and sun-soaking tourists; by night, BBQs are fired up and cocktails flow into the early hours. The roads behind have a good selection of bars, restaurants and guesthouses, and some of Sihanoukville's larger, mostly uninspiring, hotels.

Serendipity Beach

North of Ochheuteal Beach, on the other side of the pier, the short stretch known as **Serendipity Beach** is lined with bungalows that wind up the hill. There is no public sand here; the thin sliver, encased by rocks and boulders, is reserved for patrons of the bungalows. Fortunately, most of these have bars on the rocks just above beach level that make great spots for a sundowner. The most intensely packed patch of guesthouses, hotels, bars, restaurants and travel agents is along **Serendipity Beach Road,** between the pier and Golden Lions roundabout.

Otres Beach

A 6km moto or tuk-tuk ride southeast of the centre brings you to **Otres Beach**, Sihanoukville's whitest, widest stretch of casuarina-shaded sand, and your best bet for escaping the crowds and bustle of the town beaches.

In 2010, Otres Beach was split into two when 2km of beachfront was purged of resorts. The easterly strip of sand (**Otres 2**) is quieter and more intimate than **Otres 1**, a livelier, backpacker-orientated section, while the stretch in between, **Long Beach**, is the most tranquil.

In the absence of beach land, more options have sprung up in **Otres Village** along the river estuary, 1km inland. Home to numerous high-quality guesthouses, there is also a **Saturday night market** – an artsy space, with a wide range of stalls, that hosts regular live music events and parties that push on until dawn.

Victory Beach and around

Before 2012, when the action shifted to Ochheuteal and then Otres Beach, **Victory Hill** (or **Weather Station Hill**) was prime backpacker territory, densely packed with sunset-facing guesthouses and late-night hostess bars. It still has good budget options (if far too many casinos) and a nice local feel, although "girlie bar street" (as Victory Hill's Street 139 is commonly called) has a somewhat seedy, if unthreatening, reputation at night. However, **Victory Beach** nearby is a pleasant, family-friendly stretch, more relaxing than Ochheuteal, with a row of beach bars and a casino along the northern tip.

SIHANOUKVILLE BEACH LIFE

For the Khmer, a visit to Sihanoukville is often an excuse for an eating and drinking binge, with a dip in the sea as a fringe benefit. Their **conservative** nature, coupled with paranoia about maintaining whiteness, means **shade** is everything. Beaches have a plethora of parasols, and many Khmers swim fully clothed; and while most are used to seeing visitors in trunks or bikinis, going topless is a no-no.

You'll probably be offered countless **massages**, manicures and hair threading from women along the beaches; if you're not interested, smile and walk on. You should definitely avoid buying souvenirs from **children**, as it encourages them to stay out of school or work into the evening.

5

CRIME AND SAFETY IN SIHANOUKVILLE

As Sihanoukville flourishes, so does petty **crime**. It is rarely serious, and mostly opportunistic, and certainly not something that should put you off visiting, but it's a good idea to make the most of hotel safety-deposit boxes and keep an eye on your belongings when on the beach. Bag snatching, even from motos and tuk-tuks, is on the rise. As a rule, don't carry anything with you that you can't afford to lose.

Regarding personal **safety**, exercise the same caution as you would anywhere. Illegal **drugs** are widespread and there have been incidents of assault, usually where it's dark and unlit. As a rule, it is sensible to travel back to your accommodation by tuk-tuk, not on foot or by moto. Ultimately, the fun happens in the well-lit parts of town, so it shouldn't be hard to stick to those.

Sokha Beach

Just 200m of pretty **Sokha Beach** is fully accessible to the public. The rest is reserved for residents of the pricey and enormous (over 450 rooms) *Sokha Beach Resort*. Foreigners (but not Cambodians) can walk the length of the beach, but if you want to linger, you'll have to buy a day pass, which costs $20 (including use of pools). Rocky headlands at both ends offer great snorkelling, and it's wonderful at sunset when the islands of Koh Tre and Koh Dah Ghiel are thrown into silhouette.

Independence Beach

Independence Beach, over 1km long, is rather narrow, and best visited at low tide. Much of it is under development, but you can relax at the northern end. *The Small Hotel* (see p.255) runs a good (daytime) restaurant-bar, beyond which the pier marks the section reserved for guests of the historic *Independence Hotel*. Once a glamorous venue attracting celebrities such as Jackie Kennedy, it was abandoned at the onset of war and housed high-ranking Khmer Rouge officials from 1975 to 1979. It still oozes luxury, with its spa and glass elevator running down to a private beach. You can dine at the new *Sunset Restaurant*, and a beach club is set to open in 2017.

Hawaii Beach

Hawaii Beach is an under-rated, chilled-out stretch lined with beach shacks, one of the nicest being *White Rabbit*. The view is marred only by the enormous Techo Morakat Bridge stretching from the mainland to Koh Pos island, where another resort development is on the cards.

Kbal Chhay waterfalls

$1; Picnic platforms $1.25/day • Head east out of Sihanoukville on NR4, turning left after 7km at a sign for the falls, then continuing 8km north; moto/tuk-tuk return trips cost $8/$15

Popular with Khmer families, **Kbal Chhay waterfalls**, a series of cascades fed by the Prek Toeuk Sap River, gained recognition after appearing in Cambodia's post-civil war movie *Pos Keng Kong* (The Giant Snake); impressive in the rainy season, the falls aren't worth the trip in the dry. At weekends, the food stalls and huts get busy, but it's relatively peaceful otherwise.

ARRIVAL AND DEPARTURE   SIHANOUKVILLE AND THE BEACHES

BY BUS
Bus station The temporary bus park is behind Ekareach Street near the market in Downtown. It's about 5min by moto/tuk-tuk to Ochheuteal and Serendipity beaches and 15min to Otres. Several bus companies have offices nearby along Ekareach St, and a few pick up (and drop off) along Serendipity Beach Rd, especially at night. Prices and times change frequently;

5

local travel agents have the most up-to-date information.

Companies and routes Phnom Penh Sorya (☎012 631545, ⓦ ppsoryatransport.com.kh) and Capitol Tours (☎034 934042, ⓦ capitoltourscambodia.com) have offices along Ekareach St and operate direct buses to Phnom Penh, with numerous departures from early morning to afternoon. The best service with roomier buses (and a maximum speed limit) is Giant Ibis (☎089 999818, ⓦ giantibis.com) whose office is near Golden Lions roundabout on the road to Sokha Beach. Getting a seat is usually no problem, but it's best to book if it's a public holiday. Virak Buntham (☎016 754358, ⓦ virakbuntham .com) operates a daily bus to Koh Kong at 8.15am which continues across the Thai border (change of bus) and on to Bangkok or Trat for Ko Chang. They also operate night buses with beds to Phnom Penh, Battambang, Ho Chi Minh City, Poipet and Siem Reap. At the time of writing, Rith Mony and Angkor Express were best avoided for safety and punctuality reasons.

Destinations Bangkok (5 daily; 12–17hr); Battambang (2 daily; 11hr); HCMC via Ha Tien (6 daily; 10–12hr); Koh Kong (2 daily; 4–5hr); Phnom Penh (12 daily; 4–5hr); Siem Reap (6 daily; 10hr).

BY SHARED TAXI AND MINIBUS
Numerous routes operated by a bewildering array of companies leave throughout the day; most include hotel pick-up. Some guesthouses/travel agents will book shared taxis for destinations such as Koh Kong and Andoung Tuek (for the Koh S'dach archipelago), or you can negotiate with drivers at Psar Leu market. Mekong Express (☎012 787839,

ⓦ catmekongexpress.com) operate several minibuses to Phnom Penh, others travel to Battambang, Mondulkiri, Poipet, Phnom Penh and Siem Reap. Cambodia Post vans come particularly recommended. A few local companies serve Kampot and Kep ($5–6) and the Ha Tien border in Vietnam ($12), the first morning service connecting with Phu Quoc island.

Destinations Battambang (3–5 daily; 10hr); Ha Tien (5 daily; 5hr); Kampot (10 daily; 2hr); Kep (5 daily; 3–4hr); Koh Kong (4 daily; 4hr); Mondulkiri (1 daily, 9hr); Phnom Penh (20 daily; 4hr); Poipet (2–4 daily, 9hr); Siem Reap (6 daily; 10hr).

BY PLANE
Sihanoukville International Airport Off NR4, 23km from town; taxi $20, tuk-tuk $15, minibus $6. Cambodia Angkor Air (☎023 6666786, ⓦ cambodiaangkorair.com) operate daily scheduled flights to/from Siem Reap (1hr); Cambodia Bayon Airlines (☎078 2315553, ⓦ bayonairlines.com) and Sky Angkor Airlines (☎063 967300, ⓦ skyangkorair.com) run a charter service. Cambodia Angkor Air/Vietnam Airlines (☎023 990840, ⓦ vietnamairlines.com) also operate a joint route to Ho Chi Minh City.

BY TRAIN
A new route (see box, p.76) launched in 2016 operates between Sihanoukville and Phnom Penh via Takeo and Kampot on Fri–Sun, and on public holidays. Phnom Penh (7hr), Kampot (1hr 40min–2hr 40min), Takeo (5hr 30min); tickets $4–7. Tickets, available at the station, can usually be bought on the day (☎078 888582, ⓦ royal-railway.com).

INFORMATION AND TOURS

Tourist office The tourist offices on Ochheuteal Beach and halfway up Serendipity Beach Road are both friendly but have little useful information (daily 7am–10pm).

Visitor guides Three booklets, *Sihanoukville Visitors' Guide* (ⓦ canbypublications.com), *The Sihanoukville Advertiser* (ⓦ sihanoukvilleadvertiser.com) and *Coastal*

ON THE ROAD: SURVIVAL TIPS

Exploring Sihanoukville's coastline on the back of your own rented motorbike is certainly exhilarating, but be on your guard for prowling policemen looking for a **bribe**. There is currently no legal requirement for tourists to hold a licence, but that won't stop the police from coming up with reasons for pulling you over and taking your money. There are some measures you can take to keep them at bay.

The first, which we recommend regardless of police interference, is to wear a **helmet**; it's everyone for themselves on the road, so safety should be your number-one priority. Ensure that you have medical insurance and if you're an inexperienced rider, opt for semi-automatic mopeds. Riding without a shirt, number plate or mirrors can also get you pulled over and, bizarrely, so can driving with lights on during the day – allegedly, this is a privilege for travelling dignitaries only.

Being stopped usually results in being asked to hand over anything up to $100 but you can almost always barter this down to one or two. If you haven't done anything wrong, a useful deterrent is to insist on handling the situation at the police station.

5

(🖰 coastal-cambodia.com) stay up to date on new places to sleep, eat and drink, and are free in bars, restaurants and guesthouses.

Travel agents On Serendipity Beach Rd, Ana Travel next to *Beach Road Hotel* (📞 012 915301, 🖰 anatravelandtours.com)

and Cool Banana by *The Big Easy* (📞 012 941900, 🖰 coolbananatravel.com), and Mottah Travel opposite Canadia Bank/Caltex on Ekareach St (📞 012 996604, 🖰 mottah.com) are excellent for visas/extensions, boat/bus tickets, drivers, tours and flights.

GETTING AROUND

Sihanoukville's attractions are quite spread out, and as it's a little hilly, getting around on foot is hard work. You can walk from the beaches to Otres Village (30–45 mins).

By moto and tuk-tuk Motos and tuk-tuks are easy to find, especially around Serendipity Beach Rd, Ochheuteal Beach, Downtown, and most other tourist spots. A moto/tuk-tuk from Serendipity Beach to Downtown costs $2/$3 and to Otres, $3/$5. When picking up a moto or tuk-tuk on arrival, bear in mind that many drivers get commission from guesthouses, so be firm if there's somewhere particular you

want to stay (you may be regaled with stories about how your chosen hotel has closed or is full of prostitutes).

Motorbike rental Guesthouses/travel shops rent bikes from $5/day. See box, p.252 on how to avoid fines.

Car/driver hire Hotels, guesthouses and travel agents can arrange this from $40/day or negotiate with drivers at the transport hub by the market.

TOURS AND ACTIVITIES

Cookery courses Khmer cookery classes ($25) are offered by Sinuon on her rooftop (Road 1035, Victory Hill; 📞 078 942907, 🖰 bit.ly/sinuons) or book through the excellent Nyam Restaurant on Tola St (📞 092 995074, 🖰 bit.ly/nyamrestaurant).

Boat tours Sea Cambodia 📞 034 6666106, 🖰 seacambodia.com. A range of daytime party cruises to Koh Thas and Koh Rong Samloem (from $20) are provided by this outfit. Sun Tours (📞 016 396201, 🖰 suntours-cambodia.com) offer a great day-tour to Koh Rong

SIHANOUKVILLE DIVING

Diving Cambodia's uncharted waters is a colourful experience, with **visibility** up to 20m in some places. There's a wealth of islands to choose from, plus coral-rich reefs and a superabundance of marine life, including barracuda, pufferfish, moray eels, giant mussels and parrotfish. Closest to Sihanoukville is **Koh Rong Samloem** (see p.260); trips usually include a couple of dives, a lazy lunch and a spot of beachcombing on its gloriously white sands. You could also stay overnight. Further afield, more experienced divers might prefer overnight trips to Koh Tang and Koh Prins (a 5–7hr boat ride away), where there are reefs, coral bommies, a wreck or two and better visibility in their deeper waters.

DIVING OPERATORS

Cambodian Diving Group M'Pai Bai, Koh Rong Samloem 📞 096 2245474, 🖰 cambodiandiving group.com. From their base in this fishing village, this dive outfit arranges trips to Koh Rong, Koh Koun, and further afield to Koh Tang. Fun dives from $50, PADI Open Water $380, plus one-day dives ($80) and snorkelling ($25) trips from Sihanoukville.

The Dive Shop Ochheuteal Street, off Serendipity Beach Rd 📞 034 933664, 📧 diveshopcambodia.com. Friendly German-owned PADI five-star dive centre (HQ at *Happa Garden* on Sunset Beach, Koh Rong Samloem) offers two-dive day packages ($80), four-day Open Water ($380) including dorm accommodation, plus speciality courses.

EcoSea Dive Serendipity Beach Rd 📞 034 934631, 🖰 ecoseadive.com. Another experienced outfit running SSI and PADI courses, with fun dives from $60,

two certified dives for $80 and day-trips/overnighters in lovely bungalows or dorms at their M'Pai Bai base on Koh Rong Samloem.

Koh Rong Dive Centre Serendipity Beach Rd 📞 096 5607362, 🖰 kohrong-divecenter.com. This five-star centre offers intro dives ($95), two-dive packages ($80) and PADI courses from $380 around Koh Rong's reefs from their Koh Tui HQ by the island's ferry pier.

Scuba Nation Serendipity Beach Rd 📞 012 604680, 🖰 divecambodia.com. Renowned five-star PADI outfit, opposite Holiday Village Nataya, with highly qualified instructors and some of the most advanced courses in Cambodia; options include four-day Open Water courses ($445), day-trips ($85) and overnighters ($220–325) – including night dives – on their tailor-made boat; the pricier trips make for Koh Tang.

5

Samloem (10am–5pm; $25/person), including lunch and snorkelling at Koh Tas, while Romney Travel and Tours (☎016 861459, ✉romneytour@yahoo.com) offer an island-hopping tour to Koh Cha Lush, Koh Russei and Koh Tres ($15), as do On the Rocks (☎069 587586, ⓦontherockstours.com).

Flyboarding Ultimate Flyboard Experience, Queenco Palm Beach Resort, Otres 1 (☎070 467412, ⓦbit.ly /flyboardcambodia) Exhilirating hoverboard and flyboarding sessions ($55/15).

Fishing Arrange your trip at Otres Marina (☎067 210006, ⓦotresmarina.com) near Otres 2; In Otres Village, *Lakeside Bar* offers catch-and-release fishing (☎096 7334025).

Watersports Hurricane, Queenco Palm Beach Resort, Otres 1 (☎017 471604, ⓦbit.ly/hurricanewindsurf) Western-run outfit offering windsurfing, surfing and stand-up paddleboarding tuition (from $15/hr) plus gear rental. Kayaks are available for trips to nearby Koh Kteah Island and the mangrove river into Otres Village and there's a jet-ski rental next door ($30/15min). On Otres 2, Otres Beach Club, part of Otres Beach Resort (☎017 777545, ⓦbit.ly/otresbeachclub) rents kayaks ($4/hr); catamarans ($10/hr) and hobie cats ($12/hr).

Horseriding Liberty Ranch in Otres Village ☎097 2570187, ⓦlibertyranch-sihanoukville.com. There are one-hour rides ($25) to half-day trips ($65) on offer, that take you past wild beaches and through the Cambodian countryside.

Massage and spas Blind and sight-impaired masseurs work at *Seeing Hands* 3 Ekareach Street, near *Holy Cow* restaurant (daily 8am–9pm; $6/hr; ☎012 799016); you can also get an excellent massage at *Relax Massage*, Serendipity Beach Road (daily 10am–9.30pm; $10/hr; ☎085 352213, ⓦbit.ly/relaxmassagespa).

Off-road adventures Fun Buggies off Golden Lions roundabout ☎016 404807, ⓦbit.ly/funbuggy. See the sights in clutch/gear-free buggies and guided drives. *Stray Dog Adventures* (at Utopia, ☎017 668720, ⓦstraydogasia .com) also do guided tours (from $120/day) and dirt bike hire ($25/day).

Quad-biking Woody's All-Terrain Adventures ☎097 4037784, ⓦwoodys-quads-cambodia.com. Explore the Cambodian countryside on a guided- quad-bike safari from one-hour to all-day sessions.

Swimming The pool at Beach Road Hotel is available to non-residents if you buy a meal. Similarly, at Heart of Venice in Otres Village, it costs $2 or a drink. A day pass at Sokha Beach Resort costs $20.

Tennis There are floodlit tennis courts at *Sokha Beach Resort*.

ACCOMMODATION

From $2 bunks to $400 suites, Sihanoukville caters to all budgets. It can get very busy during public holidays and festivals, and it's best to **book** if you're set on a particular place, though you're unlikely ever to be completely stuck. During peak season (Nov–March) and major holidays (particularly Khmer New Year), hotels may hike prices, but it's always worth asking about discounts if you're staying for a few days. Pretty much everywhere offers free wi-fi and most places can organize travel and visas.

DOWNTOWN BEACHES

Most people head straight to Ochheuteal and Serendipity beaches for the widest range of budget and mid-range accommodation, with easy access to the bars, shops and restaurants along Serendipity Beach Rd. Just north, the beaches at Sokha and Independence are immaculate, but predominantly reserved for their respective namesake resorts. Otres beaches and Otres Village have a good choice of backpacker, boutique and bungalow resorts.

SERENDIPITY BEACH ROAD AND AROUND

Above Us Only Sky Serendipity Beach ☎089 822318, waboveusonlysky.net. These tastefully decorated a/c bungalows with private verandas are a favourite for their sea views and sunset cocktail bar (see p.258). Booking recommended as there are only five. $50

Beach Road Hotel Serendipity Beach Rd ☎017 827677, ⓦbeachroad-hotel.com. Despite its proximity to the wildest bars, and its own popular sports bar, the rooms and pool area are surprisingly quiet and refined.

Non-residents can lounge by the pool if they buy a meal. Breakfast from $2.75. Fan $20 a/c $27

★**Chochi Garden** Serendipity Beach Rd, near the pier ☎096 2747674, ✉chochiguesthouse@gmail.com. A haven along this busy road, its Japanese-Italian owners offer simple, stylish rooms extending back into a courtyard garden. Two stilted bungalows at the end are top pick, but rooms are inviting, and the streetfront restaurant is good. $20

Mick and Craig's Serendipity Beach Rd, next to Monkey Republic ☎017 322912, ⓦmickandcraigs .com. Good-value double, twin and triple fan rooms with cold-water bathrooms, and the on-site restaurant (daily 7am–11pm) hosts themed nights such as three-course Mexican for $6 plus Sunday roasts and barbecues. $12

Monkey Republic Serendipity Beach Rd ☎012 490290, ⓦmonkeyrepublic.info. This backpackers' favourite is a slick enterprise with a range of dorms, en-suite fan rooms sleeping four, newer a/c rooms with hot water, and an inviting pub-style restaurant. Dorms $5 Doubles $10

★One Stop Hostel Near Golden Lions roundabout ☎034 933433, ⓦonederz.com/sihanoukville. There are sparkling dorms, with separate male/female bathrooms, set around an open-air pool at this high-quality hostel. Sociable lounge area and cheap food; breakfast from $2. **$8**

Patchouly Chill House Off Golden Lions roundabout ☎098 832210, ⓦbit.ly/patchoulychillhouse. A six-room guesthouse offering stylish a/c rooms, hot-water showers, and an inviting pool in a tropical garden. Friendly owners serve up French-inspired dishes. **$40**

Utopia Serendipity Beach Rd ☎034 933586, ⓦutopia -cambodia.com. This 130-bed party hostel offers basic free dorms ($2 first night) as well as $3 a/c dorm and basic private rooms. *Utopia* is renowned for Saturday pool parties, 25 cents beer (happy hour 8–9pm), late-night bar-restaurant, and hot tub. Dorms **$2** Doubles **$8**

OCHHEUTEAL BEACH

Makara Bungalows Phumin St ☎034 933449, ⓦmakarabungalows.com. Located at the more peaceful, southern end of the beach, these clean, well-furnished a/c hot-water bungalows are always busy. There's a pool, restaurant and all tourist services, including motorbike rental. **$30**

VICTORY HILL/WEATHER STATION HILL

Once the backpackers' area, Victory Hill is now full of late-night girlie bars. While some guesthouses have closed down, many remain. By day, the area actually has more of a Cambodian vibe than the main Westernized beaches, and family-friendly Victory Beach is a short walk away.

Backpacker Heaven Ekareach St opposite Marina Hotel ☎010 237539, ⓦbit.ly/backpackerheaven. This clean and airy hostel in a converted villa has a lovely pool and sociable bar-restaurant with a huge menu. Spotless dorms, chill-out areas and travel desk. Dorms **$5**; doubles **$27**

Divers Hotel Opp Victory minimart ☎034 934725, ⓦhotel-divers.com. Formerly *Divers Inc*, it no longer has an on-site dive shop. While some rooms are a little dark, the a/c rooms are clean, bright and good value (some have balconies), and there's a pool and bar amid tropical gardens. **$35**

Mealy Chenda ☎096 8855445, ⓦmealychenda. com. A sprawling guesthouse occupying three buildings. Rooms in the newest block are bright, cheerful and en-suite, some with a/c and sea-view balconies. The cheaper, slightly dated rooms have shared bathrooms. Fan **$10**; a/c **$15**

DOWNTOWN

Downtown has a mix of budget and mid-range accommodation. Several sports bars (many of doubtful repute) also have rooms, but are best avoided by single women travellers or anyone who wants peace and quiet.

Geckozy Two blocks southeast of Caltex petrol station off Ekareach St ☎012 495825, ⓦbit.ly/geckozy. This little guesthouse ticks all the boxes with bright, well-equipped fan rooms (two with hot water, one has a fridge), friendly owner, lovely garden and hangout area. Only downside is that there is no food. **$7**

★The Small Hotel One block southeast of Caltex, off Ekareach St ☎034 6306161, ⓦthesmallhotel.info. A small place with a big reputation, thanks to its Swedish and Khmer owners who are authorities on the local area and run the guesthouse brilliantly. Rooms, with a/c, hot water, TVs, DVD players and safes, are superb value and there's an excellent library and restaurant-bar; they also have a little restaurant on Independence Beach. **$20**

OUT OF TOWN

Don Bosco 3km east of town ☎034 933765, ⓦdonboscohotelschool.com. Feel-good place which provides hospitality skills to young adults from poor backgrounds. Large, bright rooms all have a/c and are slightly more luxurious than you'd expect for the price; cheapest are cold-water only. Excellent student-run restaurant, garden, pool and free shuttle into town. **$25**

Pagoda Rocks Opposite Wat Leu ☎067 255545, ⓦpagodarocks.com. The pool with a view is the big draw at this hilltop boutique bungalow resort. The nine bungalows have ocean-view balconies, a/c, minibar and king-sized beds, and there's a good restaurant. **$65**

OTRES 1

Pat Pat Guesthouse Mid section ☎069 411574, ⓦpat-patguesthouse.com. Smart, comfortable rooms and an a/c 14-bed dorm with two en-suite hot-water bathrooms are all excellent value; extras include a pool, gym, boules and bar-restaurant. Dorms **$6**, doubles **$25**

Sahaa Beach Resort Eastern end ☎070 218607, ⓦsahaabeach.com. One of few boutique options on Otres 1, these 16 a/c bungalows with indoor/outdoor bathrooms are a real treat, set around a pool and gardens. There's a decent restaurant and the beach is just across the road. **$80**

Sea Garden Eastern end ☎096 2538131, ⓦbit.ly /seagardenotres. This laidback option is a great place to stay, or just hang out. The 11 fan-cooled bungalows (stilted ones are slightly breezier) share clean bathrooms and are footsteps from the ocean. The restaurant, scattered with cushioned chairs, is excellent value; offering filling breakfasts and dishes such as chicken with ginger ($3.75). **$15**

Wish You Were Here Mid section ☎097 2415884, ⓦbit.ly/wywh-otres. A backpacker-friendly hostel with a wide selection of dorms, rooms, some with hot water, plus bungalows. Tasty food too and a very long happy hour (4–10pm). Dorms **$6**, doubles **$16**

5

OTRES 2

Footprints Western end ☎097 2621598, ⊛otres footprints.tk. Currently the only backpacker hostel on Otres 2, it has wood-panelled dorms, whitewashed double and triple fan rooms and an open dorm above the beach bar. There's a TV area, restaurant, travel desk, and weekend parties. Dorms $\overline{\$5}$; doubles $\overline{\$20}$

Otres Marina Marina Rd, one back from the beach ☎067 210006, ⊛otresmarina.com. With a deck right on the river, these spotless, cosy bungalows have hot-water bathrooms and are only a short walk from the beach. Breakfast is included but there is no restaurant as such, although they do delicious Sunday roasts ($4.75). $\overline{\$22}$

Ren Resort Eastern end ☎066 292526, ⊛ren-resort .com. For a beachside treat, this is a good bet, with its wraparound pool, beach bar-restaurant and stylish rooms with large bathrooms. Friendly helpful staff too. $\overline{\$90}$

Sam's Beach Bungalows Western end, opposite Footprints ☎097 7055636, ⊛bit.ly/samsbeachbar. Five shared-bathroom bungalows are good value, as is the daily $5 BBQ which includes free beer and sides. Cocktails are $2 during happy hour (6–8pm). $\overline{\$10}$

OTRES VILLAGE

Blue Sky Bungalows Main road into the village ☎096 9945485, ⊛bit.ly/blueskybungalows. Ten bright-blue en-suite (cold-water) bungalows, with artwork and nice fabrics. Owners have cultivated a friendly vibe at the

bar-restaurant which does tasty build-your-own-breakfasts. A pool and sauna are planned. $\overline{\$30}$

★**BOHO** Just off Otres Village's main road ☎090 780993, ⊛bit.ly/otresboho. A beachy, boho vibe prevails at this new hostel with en-suite a/c and fan dorms. Rooftop terrace and friendly bar-restaurant with 75c beers at happy hour (6–9pm) and breakfast from $2.50. $\overline{\$6}$

Hacienda Otres Village, opposite Otres Market ☎070 814643, ⊛bit.ly/haciendaotres. Sociable set up with a ten-bed "freedom" dorm ($3 first night, free thereafter), garden bungalows, spacious bar-restaurant and cinema room. Dorm $\overline{\$3}$; doubles $\overline{\$12}$

Mama Clare's Past Otres Market ☎097 6902914, ⊛mamaclares.com. Stilted treehouse-style bungalows, some with shared bathroom, in a riverside garden. Londoner "Mama Clare" prepares home-made breakfasts and dinners served at a communal table. $\overline{\$20}$

Otres Jungle Bungalows Near the crossroads ☎071 7736844, ⊛bit.ly/otresjungle. Spotless, cosy bungalows, set within a lush garden. The lovely Italian owner has created a relaxing vibe; guests staying here can use the community kitchen. $\overline{\$14}$

★**Sok Sabay Resort** Past Otres Market by the water ☎016 406080, ⊛bit.ly/soksabay. One of the swankiest and most reasonably priced options in the Village, these riverside and poolside bungalows have terraces, TV, solar-powered showers and fridge. The open-sided waterside bar and restaurant serves up delicious dishes, from Khmer red curries to French galettes. The owner also runs *Chez Paou* restaurant on Otres 1. $\overline{\$45}$

EATING

Don't leave town without savouring the local **seafood**, priced by the kilogram and cheaper than anywhere else in the country. If you prefer something informal, flop in a deck chair on the beach and order what you fancy from passing hawkers, and the fabulous (and fabulously cheap) evening seafood **barbecues** on Ochheuteal Beach and in the many barbecue restaurants along the streets behind. For cheap eats the **night market** near Golden Lions roundabout opens up late afternoon, and street vendors flock around Psar Leu. Numerous **Western-oriented** places serve everything from fish and chips to wood-fired pizza and falafel, and there's a growing **food scene** at up-and-coming Otres Village.

THE BEACHES

SERENDIPITY BEACH ROAD AND AROUND

Delicious North Plaza ☎012 574603. This tiny café, just off Serendipity Beach Rd, feels like an extension of the charming owner's house, with one long table down the middle. The food is great, and cheap. Try the *roti canai* ($1.50), pizzas (from $3), amok ($2) and a breakfast eggburger ($1). Daily 7.30am–11pm.

Eno Café Mithona/Ochheuteal St ☎012 484603, ⊛bit .ly/enocafe. Coffee and wine enthusiasts will adore this café-cum-wine-bar, which serves big salads and home-made pizzas. Daily 7am–9pm.

Karma Sutra Serendipidty Beach Rd ☎097 9118539. Satisfy curry cravings at this excellent Indian café-style restaurant. Most dishes $4–5. Daily 7.30am–midnight.

Marco Polo Sokha Beach Rd, west of Golden Lions roundabout ☎092 920866, ⊛marcopolosihanoukville .com. There are delicious stone-baked pizzas (margherita $6.25) and big portions of Italian food (penne arrabbiata $5) at this friendly restaurant, which has a secluded garden out the back. Daily noon–10pm.

Sandan Sokha Beach Rd, west of Golden Lions roundabout ☎032 4524000, ⊛bit.ly/sandan restaurant. Staffed by former street children on M'Lop Tapang's vocational training programmes, *Sandan* serves creative Cambodian food (veggie amok $5.50, curry crab with lime $10) on a leafy pillared terrace. On Saturdays, catch a traditional dance show. Daily 11.30am–11pm.

★**So** Serendipity Beach Road ☎092 759753, ⊛bit.ly /sosihanoukville. This pretty courtyard restaurant is the

5

perfect place to treat yourself without breaking the bank, with filling breakfast and Mediterranean-inspired mains. Two courses for $5 (5–6.30pm) and cocktail deals. Mon–Sat 7am–4pm; 5–10pm. Closed Sun.

OCCHHEUTEAL BEACH
Beach Club Resort Tola St ☎ 034 933634, ⓦ beachcluburesortcambodia.com. The daily all-you-can-eat buffet breakfast ($5.50; 6.45–11am) is a favourite with expats, who also come for the burgers, sandwiches, steak, seafood and pasta. Decent rooms ($35) and a pool. Daily 6.45am–10pm.

Happy Herb Pizza Tola St ☎ 016 632198, ⓦ happyherbpizza.com. Consistently good pizzas, pastas and salads from $4.50 in this branch of the popular Phnom Penh pizzeria, plus all-day breakfasts, barbecues and 50c beer. Daily 7.30am–11pm.

BETWEEN WEATHER STATION HILL/ VICTORY HILL AND HAWAII BEACH
Sophary Restaurant Victory Hill ☎ 012 976107. Super-cheap breakfasts (pancakes/eggs $1, fruit salad $1.25) and mains $2–3 are on offer at this locally run restaurant which also has a travel desk. Daily 8am–9pm.

Treasure Island Seafood South of Hawaii Beach, Independence headland ☎ 012 830505. Located down the steps behind the decrepit *Koh Pos Hotel*, this beachside Chinese restaurant specializes in fish and seafood – the grilled squid is delicious ($5), and there's a lovely little beach to laze on. Go at lunchtime as the road is pitch-black at night. Daily 9am–9pm.

DOWNTOWN
Gelato Italiano Opposite the bus park near the market ☎ 015 919837, ⓔ gelatoitaliano@donbosco hotelschool.com. Ice-cream parlour dishing out delicious Italian-style ices made by students at the *Don Bosco* hotel school (see p.255); seasonal flavours, such as mango or jackfruit, are exceptional. Daily 7am–9pm.

★**Holy Cow** Ekareach St ☎ 012 478510, ⓦ bit.ly /holycowcambodia. Inexpensive Khmer and Western food (jacket potato with beef and beans $5.50) in a traditional wooden house back from the main road; laidback

atmosphere, eclectic music, local newspapers and 50c beer 4–7pm. Daily 8am–10.30pm.

Ku Kai 144 Makara St, off Ekareach St ☎ 012 593339. Dining in this atmospheric Japanese restaurant feels like you're a guest in someone's home. Food is authentic, and the nightly sashimi (a steal at $3) sells out early. Try the lightly seared beef ($2.75) or the fried pork with ginger sauce ($4.75). Tues–Sun 5–9pm. Closed Mon.

OTRES
Carpe Diem Otres Village, 400m back from Otres 2 ☎ 097 7011262, ⓦ carpediempreahsihanouk.com. The Italian couple who run this guesthouse, which has four bungalows ($30), also prepare home-cooked dishes at their teeny restaurant; try the penne puttanesca ($7), which is well worth the trek from the beach. Daily 7am–9pm.

★**Pacha Mama** Otres Village ☎ 097 8261402, ⓦ pacha mamacambodia.com. Enjoy truly creative and delicious vegan dishes – spinach wraps, healthy breakfasts and coconut milk lattes – at this wellness centre which offers bungalows, yoga and an eco-spa. Sun–Fri 8am–6pm. Closed Sat.

Papa Pippo Eastern end Otres 1 ☎ 010 359725, ⓦ papapippo.com. Try home-made pasta, gnocchi and pizza and home-baked cakes, pastries and tiramisu at this friendly joint. Themed nights include Trivia Tuesdays and live music on Thursdays. They also have decent bungalows. Daily 9am–11pm; late-night pizzas Sun–Thurs 9.30pm–2am.

Secret Garden Otres Otres 2 ☎ 097 6495131, ⓦ secretgardenotres.com. Rooms are pricey but the beach bar is fantastic, with 75c happy-hour beers, excellent food (salads $5, stuffed squid $7) and vegetarian options. Kitchen closes 9.30pm. Daily 7am–11.30pm.

Sunshine Café Otres 1 ☎ 012 828432, ⓦ bit.ly /sunshinecafe. Beach bar offering barbecues ($5), fried fish sandwiches ($4) and Khmer specialities including *ban chaev*; savoury pancakes ($3.50) are a favourite. Daily 8am–10pm.

Tamu Otres 2 ☎ 088 9017451, ⓦ tamucambodia.com. One of Otres' most upscale dining options, Tamu's beach restaurant is the place for fancier Asian and European dishes including salads and grilled fish. Also offers uber-stylish rooms. Daily 7am–11pm.

DRINKING AND NIGHTLIFE

Sihanoukville has some of Cambodia's best **nightlife**. With new favourites popping up and others closing constantly, check the listings guides for the latest hangouts. Wednesdays play host to the all-night Kerfuffle jungle rave (ⓦ bit.ly /kerfufflecambodia); Saturday it's the turn of Otres Market.

THE BEACHES
SERENDIPITY BEACH ROAD
The Big Easy Serendipity Beach Rd ☎ 017 827677 ⓦ thebigeasycambodia.com. Starting point for Friday's Sihanoukville Pub Crawl, live bands, party tunes

and good food (mac'n'cheese $3, Thai curry $3.25) make this hostel a favourite drinking spot. Daily 6.30am–midnight.

★**Maybe Later** ☎ 097 8695264 ⓦ bit.ly/maybe latercambodia. Come for the cocktails, or soak up the

5

tequilas and rums by grazing on the excellent menu of quesadillas, tacos ($3.50) and burritos ($5) right up until they close. Daily 11am–2am.

Monkey Republic ☎012 490290, ⓦmonkeyrepublic .info. A popular spot in the thick of the action, with a pool table and plenty of deals on shooters, spirits and beers (happy hour 6–9pm) including Jagermeister. Good food too. Daily 8am–midnight.

Utopia Serendipity Beach Rd ☎034 934319, ⓦutopia -cambodia.com. Possibly the busiest Western bar in town, with draught beer for 50c (9–10pm), $2.50 cocktails, fire dancers around the pool, a 25-person hot tub and parties every night from 10pm. Also serves cheap food. Daily 10am–late.

SERENDIPITY AND OCHHUTEAL BEACHES

Above Us Only Sky Serendipity Beach ☎089 822318, ⓦaboveusonlysky.net. Stunning sea views especially at sunset and delicious cocktails, best enjoyed from its green-cushioned loungers. Happy hour 5–8pm; all cocktails $2.50 and draught beer 75c. Daily 7am–midnight.

Dolphin Shack Ochheuteal Beach ☎068 55363, ⓦbit .ly/dolphinshack. Popular open-all-hours beach bar with DJs, vodka buckets, beer pong, fire shows and the odd mud-wrestling competition. Also runs booze cruises and full-moon parties. Daily 24hr.

WEATHER STATION HILL/VICTORY HILL

Corner Bar Cnr of Victory Hill ☎012 479395. Popular sports bar and restaurant serving sandwiches, pizzas and other Western dishes; hotdogs $1.50, toasties from $3. Daily 8am–late.

Mojo's Victory Hill ☎016 397704, ⓦbit.ly/mojosbar. This long-running, heavily muralled music-bar along Victory Hill's "drinking street" has parties every Mon night. Daily 11am–dawn.

DOWNTOWN

G'day Mate 163 Ekareach St. Expat bar and restaurant, with the usual Western and Asian dishes, plus a pool table and big-screen TV showing live sports including rugby, motor sports and Aussie rules football. Daily 24hr.

OTRES

Dune Otres 1 ☎031 2498014, ⓦbit.ly/duneotres. Beautiful chill-out lounge bar and restaurant, serving freshly prepared dishes such as seafood ceviche. Daily 8am–11pm.

Footprints Otres 2 ☎097 2621598, ⓦotresfootprints .tk. This hostel beach bar hosts weekend parties which go until dawn on otherwise quiet Otres 2. Daily 6.30am–late.

Otres Market Otres Village, opposite Hacienda ⓦbit .ly/otresmarket. Otres (Saturday) Market has crafts stalls, bars and food stands, with live music and parties that often go on until dawn. It operates during dry (high) season, usually from Nov–April at 4pm, although it doesn't tend to get going till 6pm. Sat 4pm–late.

★**Straycats** Otres Village ☎071 4762145, ⓦbit.ly /straycatsgh. Live music every night at this laidback bar. Food is good, particularly cold cuts and cheese platters. They also have bungalows from $10. Daily 8am–11pm.

Wish You Were Here Otres 1 ☎097 2415884, ⓦbit.ly /wywh-otres. The extensive happy hour (4–10pm), 75c draught beer and various events including Sunday Sessions makes this a popular spot on Otres 1. Daily 7am–late.

SHOPPING

Western groceries, toiletries and wines can be bought at numerous **supermarkets** and minimarts, while **boutiques** along Mithona/Ochheuteal St and Serendipity Beach Rd sell beach clothes and souvenirs. You can also pick up unusual crafts and jewellery at Saturday's Otres Market in Otres Village.

Casablanca Books Serendipity Beach Rd, inside Mick & Craig's. ☎034 6505000, ⓦbit.ly/casablancabooks. Sell, buy or swap used books, and check out their new ones. Daily 7am–11pm.

M'Lop Tapang Serendipity Beach Road & inside Sandan restaurant ☎010 297931, ⓦmloptapang.org. NGO-supported gift shops selling bags, scarves, phone covers and T-shirts made by parents of former street children. Daily 10am–8pm.

Psar Leu 7 Makara St. The local market (see p.247) is great for picking up fresh fruit and snacks, as well as cheap clothes and flip-flops. Daily 8am–5pm.

Rogue iPod Serendipity Beach Rd ☎016 591472, ⓦroguecambodia.com. A massive selection of iPod/MP3 tracks, TV series and films (75c each). They also sell cool beachwear in comfortable cottons. Daily 9am–9pm.

Sea Spirals Mithona/Ochheuteal St ☎096 3683380, ⓦbit.ly/seaspirals. Find sterling silver jewellery from Indonesia, Nepal, Tibet and Southeast Asia at this tiny shop, plus lovely bags, scarves and dream catchers. Daily 10am–10pm.

Samudera 7 Makara St, near Psar Leu ☎034 933441, ⓦsamuderamarket.com. This long-standing supermarket, popular with expats, is well stocked with meats, cheeses, drinks, canned goods, sweets and snacks. You can also change money here. Daily 7am–9.30pm.

Starfish Off 7 Makara St, behind Samudera supermarket, ☎012 952011, ⓦbit.ly/starfishbakery. Attached to Starfish bakery, the gift shop sells silks, recycled bags and clothing, plus Kampot pepper and Cambodian coffee and tea, with profits helping impoverished local families. Daily 8am–8pm.

DIRECTORY

Cinemas Galaxy Cinema (Mithona/Ochheuteal St ☎012 506549; $3) has over five thousand films and two private a/c lounges. Top Cat (Serendipity Beach Rd; ☎012 790630, ⓦbit.ly/topcatcinema; $4.50) has ten lounges, public screenings and over six thousand movies/TV series.

Consulate The Vietnamese consulate is on Ekareach St, west of the town centre (☎034 934039). Some nationalities can enter Vietnam for 15 days visa-free; no re-entry within 30 days of departure. A 30-day visa costs around $50; using a travel agent saves time.

Hospital Sihanoukville International Clinic, on Ekareach St (☎034 933911), has 24hr emergency service, English-speaking doctors, a pharmacy and accepts credit cards. CT Clinic, on Borei-Kamakor Rd, on the edge of Downtown

(☎081 886666), is another option; it accepts credit cards and has English-speaking doctors available (or on call) 24hr.

Money ATMs are plentiful along Serendipity Beach Rd. On Ekareach St, you'll find Canadia Bank, ANZ, Acleda and ABA. Otres 1 and 2 both have an ATM. Cash advances at Ana Travel and Mottah Travel (see p.253).

Police The main police station is at 316 Ekareach St between Independence Square and the town centre on the first hill. The Tourist Police (☎097 7780008) have a hub (often unmanned) next to the tourist office on Serendipity Beach Rd.

Post office The main post office, on Ekareach St near the Independence Monument, has all the usual services, including poste restante (Mon–Sat 7.30am–noon & 2–5.30pm).

Islands near Sihanoukville

Cambodia's coastal waters are peppered with tropical **offshore islands**, many of them an easy trip from Sihanoukville and a couple within Ream (see p.264). Lapped by clear seas and graced with **white-sand beaches**, they're peaceful and idyllic places to hole up for a few days – at least for now (see box below). There's plenty of accommodation, while snorkelling, sunbathing, gentle walks, lounging and early-evening swims are positively encouraged. The islands are also superb destinations for **diving** (see box, p.253). There are currently no ATMs and, Koh Rong aside, 24-hour electricity and wi-fi aren't a given, although increasingly common on Koh Rong Samloem.

Koh Rong

Offering the quintessential island experience, **Koh Rong** is Cambodia's second-largest island (after Koh Kong), with 43km of dazzling white casuarina-fringed beaches and a hilly, forested interior, ripe for trekking and home to wildlife and birds. Several fast ferry services from Sihanoukville have reduced travel time from over two hours to about 45 minutes, or 90 minutes on the slower ferry. Except in its southeastern corner

---

TROUBLE IN PARADISE

Although change doesn't come too quickly in Cambodia, many of the idyllic islands around Sihanoukville do have a shelf life. Since 2006, the government has leased several (it's hard to quantify) to international companies to develop **luxury hotels**, **casinos** and **golf courses**, and despite official coastal management plans these may wipe out fragile communities of wooden bungalows. In 2012, eco-luxury Song Saa Private Island opened near Koh Rong, and Six Senses Krabey Island and Alila Villas Koh Russei are scheduled for 2017.

A Russian company, which has leased Hawaii Beach and its off-island, Koh Pos (Snake Island), to be re-named Morakot Island ⓦmorakot-island.com), has already built a **bridge** between the two, which is juxtaposed grimly against the crystalline waters and the lush jungle on either side. Just beyond, Koh Dek Koul is already home to the luxury, Russian-owned Mirax Resort. While developments may provide **employment** for Cambodians, the downsides appear greater: the tourist dollars end up with overseas corporations, while the resorts themselves add to **conservation problems** such as water shortage, increased rubbish and reef damage.

For now, plenty of stalwart bungalows are weathering the developers' storm and some inactive developers have had their licences revoked. Even so, time is of the essence if you want to experience the islands before their tranquility is obliterated entirely.

5

at **KOH TUI** (the island's largest village, also known as Koh Touch), Koh Rong is largely undeveloped and it's easy to find peaceful bays and isolated accommodation. North of Koh Tui, westerly **Long Set Beach**, backed by cashew-nut groves, is one of the most beautiful, its turquoise water teeming with marine life and with decent snorkelling and diving to be had offshore.

Koh Tui is a favourite of young backpackers, with tiny-roomed guesthouses, cafés and bars crammed shoulder-to-shoulder beside a 300m stretch of beach, and a nightly diet of fire-dancers, barbecues and late-night music. Walk north and it's far quieter, with a couple of laidback beach bars along Long Set Beach. Alternatively, stay in **Sok San** village on west-facing **Long Beach**. If you do the trek between Koh Tui and Long Beach (1–2hr depending on fitness), take water and leave enough time to return.

Koh Rong's future is uncertain. It was leased in 2006 to the Royal Group with plans to build a $30million "eco" resort that includes marina, restaurants, reservoirs and golf course – even an airport. Amid reports of land grabs, only ten percent has been constructed so far and the project seems to have stalled. To check on their progress, see ⓦkohrong.com.kh.

Koh Rong Samloem

Koh Rong Samloem, 45 minutes by speedboat from Sihanoukville (90 minutes on the slower boat), has eight beaches and a rocky reef with good diving (see p.253). Low-key bungalow resorts are scattered all around the island, the largest concentration along the blinding white sands of shallow **Saracen Bay** to the east. On the west coast is **Lazy Beach** and the laidback resorts of **Sunset Beach** while the fishing village of **M'Pai Bai** (Village 23), on the northernmost tip, looks out to the small island of **Koh Koun** – great for snorkelling. The network of French roads have long since been swallowed up by jungle, although you can trek through the forested interior to the lighthouse on the southern tip, or east-to-west between Saracen Bay and Lazy Beach/Sunset Beach. **Wildlife** includes kingfishers, great hornbills and ospreys as well as macaques, black squirrels, lizards and snakes. In M'Pai Bai, Save Cambodian Marine Life/SCML (ⓣ010 354002, ⓦsavecambodianmarinelife.com) runs **marine conservation** dive programmes, ranging from two nights to several weeks.

Koh Ta Kiev

The white-sand beaches of **Koh Ta Kiev** and sprinkling of rustic thatched bungalows make this one of the most idyllic of Sihanoukville's islands, a real castaway experience. There are a handful of beaches to explore, trails to trek and decent **snorkelling offshore** with giant mussels to look out for to the north of the island. Sadly, the island has been leased to developers and a new eco-resort is already under construction, so who knows how long the current businesses (and mellow vibe) will be allowed to remain.

Koh Russei

Koh Russei (or Bamboo Island) is a common stop on island-hopping trips due to its glorious beaches, snorkelling and close proximity (under 1hr) to Sihanoukville. The last bungalows were cleared in 2013 to make way for a new resort development, Alila Villas Koh Russei, which opens in 2017.

Koh Tas

Koh Tas (1hr from Sihanoukville), is another popular stop-off, with gently shelving sandy beaches, great snorkelling and a good chance, if you take fishing tackle, of hooking a fish for the barbecue.

FROM TOP CHI PHAT (P.270); OCHHEUTEAL BEACH (P.250)>

5

Koh Tang and around

If you're a **diver** or have plenty of time, get out to deeper waters, such as those around **Koh Tang** and **Koh Prins** – between five and seven hours from Sihanoukville. Koh Tang's claim to fame is that it was the site of a major battle to free the *Mayaguez*, an American-owned container ship captured by the Khmer Rouge on May 13, 1975, in the early days of their regime. The US Navy and Air Force launched a mission to liberate the ship but met heavy resistance, and Ream naval base and Sihanoukville's industrial areas were bombed during the battle. Divers (see p.253) can check out two shipwrecks 40m down, northwest of Koh Prins.

ARRIVAL AND DEPARTURE   ISLANDS NEAR SIHANOUKVILLE

Times and routes for ferries and speedboats are prone to change so double-check, while some resorts (including all on Koh Ta Kiev) arrange their own boat transfers. For island-hopping trips, see Sihanoukville activities (see below).

By ferry At last count, there were five companies operating ferries/speedboats to the different bays on Koh Rong and Koh Rong Samloem, leaving from Serendipity Beach pier between 8am and 4.30pm (currently fixed $20 open return). The slower white ferry, often safer in rough weather, is Island Speed Ferry Cambodia, previously TBC (3 daily; 90min). Fast boat (approx 45min) services are offered by Koh Rong Dive Centre's yellow Speed Ferry Cambodia (3 daily), Buvasea

(7 daily), GTVC (4 daily) and Angkor Speed Ferry (3 daily). Supply boats, or "the backpacker ferry", are cheaper ($5 one-way) but take over two hours.

Inter-island travel There is usually at least one company operating any given route, although the more secluded bays are usually serviced by the accommodation's own boat. However, schedules change constantly so it's best to ask at the pier. The only other (expensive) option is to hire a longtail boat.

ACTIVITIES

Boat tours Adventure Adam (☎010 354002, ⓦadventureadam.org) offers interesting trips ($25) on Koh Rong, with visits to Prek Svay fishing village and deserted beaches. Most travel kiosks can book island-hopping tours and trips to swim with "glowing plankton".

Diving and snorkelling There are endless opportunities to explore the reefs on and around the islands. See box, p.253 for dive operators.

Guided hikes Stephanie Young who set up *The Wonderful Wildlife of Samloem* (☎097 5530819, ⓦbit.ly /wildlifesamloem) offers jungle tours (and snorkelling and SNUBA (snorkelling-diving hybrid) sessions on Koh Rong Samloem.

Ziplining High Point (☎016 839993, ⓦhigh-point.asia) on Koh Rong is an exhilarating ropes park with a 120-metre zipline and panoramic views.

ACCOMMODATION   KOH RONG

Much of Koh Rong's accommodation is squeezed into a small 300m stretch close to Koh Tui's piers. There are some good options, but with such a concentration – many with their own bars – don't expect a quiet night's sleep.

Happy Elephant Side street after third pier ☎096 9887476, ⓦbit.ly/happyelephantkohrong. Up a short slope – the views from the rooftop bar-restaurant are a big plus. Rooms are basic but clean, bungalows a nice treat. Doubles $25; bungalows $35

Lonely Beach North coast ☎081 343457, ⓦlonely -beach.com. Escapism doesn't get much better on Koh Rong's far northern tip. Bungalows enjoy sea views, there's an open-sided dorm and you can fish, trek or beachcomb to your heart's content. Boat transfers $20. Dorm $10; doubles $25

Monkey Island Koh Tui ☎081 830991, ⓦmonkeyisland -kohrong.com. Part of the Monkey Republic brand, these comfortable bungalows enjoy a quiet location set back from the beach yet only a few minutes from the action in Koh Tui. Also has a lively restaurant-bar (7am–11pm). $26

Prek Svay Homestay Northeast coast ⓦbit.ly /preksway. Stay with a local family in a fishing village homestay, run by local organizer Johnny. Transport from Sihanoukville can be arranged. On Koh Rong, contact Adventure Adam (☎010 354002, ⓦadventureadam.org) for a lift. All meals included. $17

Pura Vita Sonaya Beach ☎015 700083, ⓦpuravita resort.com. Its show-stopping location on Koh Rong's brilliant-white beach accounts for the higher-than-average rates for these timber bungalows. There's snorkelling nearby and free pick-up from the pier. $45

Thy Sok San Bungalows Sok San, Long Beach ⓦbit .ly/tsoksan. Simple bungalows over a lagoon near Sok San pier, with tasty local food available in the bar-restaurant (7am–10pm). $15

★ Treehouse Bungalows Between Koh Tui and Long

Set/4K T 010 758767, W treehouse-bungalows.com. On a small patch of beach, these atmospheric bungalows and treehouses have a great location – right between the best beach and the nightlife. Good pizzas too. Bungalows $30; treehouses $70

White Rose Guesthouse Koh Tui T 010 758767, E mengly007@gmail.com. Sociable, well-run guesthouse. Rooms are clean, have shared bathrooms and there's a relaxing hammock-strung deck with nice views. $10

EATING, DRINKING AND NIGHTLIFE — KOH RONG

Of all the islands, only Koh Rong has a stand-alone restaurant and bar scene, mostly in Koh Tui village (with a few in Sok San) plus cheap nightly beach barbecues.

3 Brothers Koh Tui, W bit.ly/3brotherskohrong. Free beer with dishes such as rice with chicken ($2) and amok curry ($3) make this exceptional value. Western food from $1.50. Daily 7am–9pm.

Dragon Den Pub Side street off main drag, Koh Tui W bit.ly/dragondenpub. Here at the island's first "pub"', the 50-plus beers include Five Men, brewed in Sihanoukville. There's also free popcorn and some creative shots such as chocolate rum. Daily 9.30am–2am.

★ **Eat Pray Love** Sok San, Long Beach T 090 451855, W bit.ly/eatpraylovesoksan. Three Italian friends serve up home-made pizzas and pastas from $5 and breakfasts from $3 on a relaxing hammock-strewn deck. Kitchen closes 10.30pm. Daily 7.30am–midnight.

Paradise Bungalows Koh Tui T 096 9548599, W paradise-bungalows.com. The stilted restaurant of this bungalow resort has wonderful sea views, and serves delicious food (Khmer curry $4, chicken wrapped in bacon $7.50). Daily 8am–10pm.

Rising Sun Koh Tui T 015 302413, W bit.ly/risingsunveg. Currently the island's only vegan and vegetarian restaurant, the menu includes couscous salads, wraps, dips and fresh shakes. Decent rooms ($10) upstairs. Daily 8am–10pm.

Sky Bar Up a side street by Rising Sun T 098 217090, W bit.ly/skybarkohrong. The views are worth the climb, and the food, cocktails (happy hour 6–8pm) and infused rums help. Nice bungalows ($25) too. Daily 8.30am–late.

The Moon Restaurant Sok San E yuk.chundy@gmail.com. Located near the pier, this beachfront restaurant serves excellent Cambodian and Thai dishes ($4–6) seafood, green curries and Asian salads. Daily 8am–10pm.

Vagabonds Koh Tui T 012 574603, W vagabondskohrong.com. Chilled-out late-night bar with an early happy hour till noon and another 7–9pm offering two-for-one cocktails. Daily 8am–2am.

ACCOMMODATION AND EATING — KOH RONG SAMLOEM

Accommodation is scattered all around the island, the largest concentration found along the idyllic, 3km-long eastern curve of Saracen Bay (where most boats disembark), but also at Sunset Beach and M'Pai Bai. No mains **electricity** but many places have 24-hour power via solar-charged batteries/generators. Apart from Saracen Bay, where there are several resorts, it's advisable to book ahead. Most resorts double up as restaurants, but for a late-night drink, go to *Octopussy Bar*, part of *Royal Retreats*, and Beach Park Resort's *Tree Bar* on Saracen Bay. In M'Pai Bai, *The Chill Inn*, *The Drift* and *Easy Tiger* are the best options.

Beach Island Resort Saracen Bay north of Orchid Pier T 077 765069, W thebeachresort.asia. The open, two-tier sea-view dorm is good-value on Saracen Bay. Mattresses can sleep two and come with a safe, charging point and mosquito net. There's a variety of bungalows to choose from and a well-priced menu. Dorms $10; bungalows $24

Big Moon Near the pier M'Pai Bai T 016 824211 W bigmooncambodia.com. Six lovely bungalows in a lush garden, five rooms with shared-bathroom plus a seafront restaurant serving fine Khmer and Western food. Doubles $20; bungalows $35

Dragonfly T 016 824211 W bit.ly/dragonflygh. New guesthouse with a scenic west-facing deck serving great food including cheese platters. Hammocks $5; dorms $6.50; doubles $17

★ **Fishing Hook** M'Pai Bai pier. The $6 all-you-can-eat buffet is a hit with vegans, vegetarians, meat-lovers and seafood fans. Daily 7am–10.30pm.

Green Blue Saracen Bay T 010 2614034, W greenblueresort.com. There are great-value seven-bed dorm and cosy bungalows at this friendly resort. Menu includes home-cooked Turkish dishes. Happy hour 4–6pm. Dorms $12; bungalows $70

Huba Huba Sunset Beach T 088 5545619, W huba-huba-cambodia.com. Sunset Beach's accommodation is all good, but these dorms, spacious tents and bungalows are particularly inviting. Excellent food with a French twist, and late-night beach bar. No wi-fi. Dorms $5; tents $20; bungalows $30

★ **Lazy Beach** Lazy Beach T 016 214211, W lazybeachcambodia.com. Eternally popular place with en-suite bungalows and comfy beds on a stretch of sand so fine it squeaks, and an atmospheric restaurant-bar. Boat $20 return. $65

5

Lime Beach Bungalows Saracen Bay ☎096 7922148, ⓦ bit.ly/limebeach. Good-value place with two ten-bed dorms and brightly coloured sea-view bungalows; the larger bungalows ($60) sleep four, all cold-water/fan. Good restaurant-bar (8am–late). Dorms $10; Bungalows $40

ACCOMMODATION AND EATING KOH TA KIEV

Koh Ta Tiev is the quietest of the three islands, and its unlit beach and jungle paths mean that most people eat at their accommodation, on the east/southeast coast.

★ **Crusoe Island** Top of Long Beach ☎093 549239, ⓦ crusoeisland.asia. Pick your own beachfront campsite (equipment provided), bag a hammock or kip down in a bungalow at this sociable, family-run place. Excellent food and they organize treks and boat trips. Boat transfer from Otres 1, $10 return. No wi-fi, electricity evenings only. Tent $3pp; dome tent $10; bungalow $15

The Last Point East coast ☎088 5026930, ⓦ lastpointisland.com. Solar power, private beach and hammocks aplenty. Sunrise views from the two-level dorm are sublime; they also have beachview bungalows and jungle "jungalows". A circular beach bar serves good food and wood-fired pizzas. Boat from Otres 1, $12 return. No wi-fi. Camping $2; dorms $5, bungalow $20

Nak's Shack South of Crusoe Island ☎097 9999367, ⓦ bit.ly/naksshack. Previously *KTK Bungalows*, this local place is run by friendly Nak and has a good restaurant. Cheaper bungalows have shared bathrooms; family bungalows ($25) have two doubles. A four-bed dorm ($5) is currently being built. $15

DIRECTORY

Medical services Koh Rong has a volunteer-staffed clinic (ⓦ bit.ly/kohrongclinic) in Koh Tui village, on a side street by *Rising Sun Guesthouse*. There's an emergency radio outside the clinic and also at most beachfront hostels.

Money At the time of writing, there were no ATMs on the islands and credit cards were not widely accepted. Cash advances can be pricey so arrive with enough money for your stay.

Ream National Park

Some 18km to the east of Sihanoukville, **Ream National Park** (also known as Preah Sihanouk National Park) is unique in Cambodia, covering 210 square kilometres of both terrestrial and marine habitat, including stunning coastal scenery, mangrove swamps, lowland evergreen forest and the **islands** of **Koh Thmei** and Koh Ses. However this hasn't prevented some sections being leased to overseas investors, with plans for a resort and even a port.

At least 155 species of **bird** have been recorded in the park, and for resident and visiting waders, the mangrove-lined **Prek Toeuk Sap River** is an important habitat. You can see the mangroves up close at a section called **Mangrove Island**, a popular stop on day-trips. Boats stop by the small jetty and a boardwalk leads to a viewpoint tower. Besides supporting a large population of fishing eagles, the river is also home to milky and adjutant storks, and kingfishers, regularly spotted on the river trips. Dolphins often put in an appearance between December and April. The list of **mammals** includes deer, wild pig and fishing cats, though these are all elusive and you're more likely to see monkeys. Most people visit on day-trips, but it's worth staying if you can. If exploring solo, a boat trip to Mangrove Island alone is underwhelming; either join a tour, or hire a boat and English-speaking guide for the day.

ARRIVAL AND INFORMATION   REAM NATIONAL PARK

DAY-TRIPS
Most visitors book day trips through cafés and guesthouses in Sihanoukville, with outfits including Romney Travel and Tours (see p.254), or through travel agents (see p.253). Around $25/person, a typical trip includes sailing down the Prek Toeuk Sap, guided jungle walk from/to Thmor Tom village, swimming and barbecue on Koh Sam Pouch's white-sand beach.

TRAVELLING INDEPENDENTLY
Park headquarters The park headquarters (daily 7.30–11am & 2–5pm; ☎016 767686) is in a green wooden building after Sihanoukville International Airport (see p.252). Arrive early or phone ahead to book a boat or guide.
By moto/tuk-tuk A moto/tuk-tuk from Sihanoukville to the park entrance costs about $10/$15; if you're

coming for the boat trips, ask to be dropped off at the ranger station, next to the bridge over the Prek Toeuk Sap on NR4.

Boat trips Boat trips cost $35 for up to five people ($8/person thereafter) for the 2-hr trip to Mangrove Island or $50/boat for a 4–5hr trip that continues to Thmor Tom

village and Koh Sam Pouch beach. Arrange via park headquarters or at the ranger station. You'll need to take food, water and sun protection.

Guided walks Treks along forested nature trails can be arranged at park headquarters ($8/person for a 2hr wander).

ACCOMMODATION AND EATING

Koh Thmei Resort ☎097 7370400, ⊚koh-thmei-resort.com. ⊚kavita@gmx.de. A secluded island resort within Ream (the only one on Koh Thmei) run by a friendly German couple who built the back-to-basics bungalows (cold-water showers) in 2010. A simple restaurant serves excellent Khmer and Western food; main dishes $5–8. Pass the time in a hammock, follow a jungle

path, or enjoy the solitude of the beach. No wi-fi. $45

★**Monkey Maya** Ream Beach ☎016 767686 ⊚monkeymayaream.com. Part of *Monkey Republic* hostels, *Monkey Maya* is the standout property. Perched idyllically above Ream Beach, the airy 16-bed dorm and sea-facing bungalows are excellent value. Lively staff and delicious food. Dorms $10; bungalows $45

Koh S'dach and the outlying islands

Lying in clear blue waters roughly halfway between Sihanoukville and Koh Kong, just off the coast of Koh Kong province, the small rocky island of **Koh S'dach** (King's Island) gets its name from the legend surrounding the **royal spring** behind the port, which is said to have gushed forth miraculously when a twelfth-century Khmer king and his army were desperate for drinking water as they battled Thai invaders. Supporting a population of a couple of thousand, Koh S'dach may not look too exciting at first glance, but is refreshingly authentic, has wonderful snorkelling and fishing, and is a good base for exploring the little-visited, largely undeveloped outlying islands. By fishing village standards, it is a prosperous community of some 700 families, thanks to the ice factory which supports the fishing fleet.

A couple of kilometres long and 1km wide, Koh S'dach has several small sandy **beaches** on its seaward side, reached by a path through the compound of the island's only pagoda. The beaches aren't brilliant, but the vivid coral and shoals of fish close to shore compensate.

The best of the nearby islands is dolphin-shaped **Koh Totang**, 2km off Koh S'dach, with a population of just seven (plus a few dogs); it almost doubles during dry season when *Nomad's Land*, the island's only accommodation, opens. The original owners, who built the bungalows, have recently added a massage pavilion and set up Koh S'dach Marine Adventures, which offers day and overnight fishing and snorkel trips. Otherwise, simply kick back and relax, or wander through the wooded interior and explore hidden beaches. **Koh S'mach**, 1km away, has some sandy beaches and Shark Island and Condor Reef are popular with divers and snorkellers. Rumours abound of plans to link some islands via a bridge for a so-called 'eco' resort with golf course, marina and heli-pad. For now, the archipelago remains intact.

KOH S'DACH BOAT TRIPS AND DIVING

To reach neighbouring islands or go fishing, you'll need to **hire a boat**; agree a schedule with the boatman beforehand and expect to pay upwards of $30/day. Alternatively, contact **Octopuses Garden** (☎011 384545, ⊚octopuscambodia.com) a diving outfit which can organize boats. They also offer introductory dives ($95), two-tank dives ($85) and PADI courses ($400) from their base on Koh S'dach, and can arrange overnight stays on remote islands. If you have more time (2–3 weeks minimum) you might be interested in **Projects Abroad** (☎023 881250 ⊚projects-abroad.net), which is based here. Volunteers receive dorm accommodation and take part in marine research and community activities.

Gone are the days of arriving by ferry; minibuses and motos ply the new paved, four-lane highway to Poi Yopon, the fishing village opposite the islands, off the NR48, a few kilometres west of Andoung Tuek. Sadly, this 64-km (40-mile) highway cuts a wide swathe through **Botum Sakor**, a supposedly protected national park, and is phase one of a sprawling, multi-billion, multi-resort Chinese hotel and gambling development which has already forced some fishing communities inland.

By bus and moto From Sihanoukville, take a Koh Kong-bound bus and alight at Andoung Tuek where minibuses (until 2pm; $7.50) and moto ($15) head to Poi Yopon. Alternatively, alight at *Café Sok Srei*, 6km after Andoung Tuek, and the owner will arrange transport. If you take the first bus (around 8am), you should arrive at the islands by 2pm. At Poi Yopon, speedboats whizz you over ($5), or Nomads Land or Octopuses Garden will send a boat.

By shared taxi Ask travel agents about shared taxis to Poi Yopon, as this is the most direct option ($10–15).

ACCOMMODATION AND EATING

KOH S'DACH

You can fill up on local food anywhere along the main drag. The grocery shop is well stocked with water, drinks, biscuits and general products.

May's Kitchen Main street, before the ice factory. No number or website but just ask anyone. Friendly owner May serves delicious Thai and Khmer food (papaya salad with squid $1.50, green curry $4, crab with tamarind sauce $7) in one of the island's few restaurants. She can also organize boat trips. Daily 7.30am–8.30pm.

Mean Chay Guest House On the west of the island ☎011 979797; no English spoken. Clean, concrete en-suite bungalows by the sea. Cheapest ones are smaller, the more expensive ($35) have a/c and sea views. **$15**

Octopuses Garden Near the pier ☎086 412432, ⓦoctopuscambodia.com. Well-organized dive centre run by a friendly Norwegian couple. They have their own boat and offer diving/snorkelling and PADI courses. Accommodation includes an open sea-view mezzanine

dorm and a bungalow, all with shared bathrooms. Breakfast is included, dinner $6. Dorms **$15** Bungalows **$35**

Yvonne On the west of the island ☎071 2454648. Known for its French, Khmer and Western food, particularly pizzas. The owner has built six colourful fan bungalows, with sea-view hammock terraces and shared bathrooms. Inexpensive food (breakfast $3.50, $2 rice/noodles and fish dinners $4.50). **$10**

KOH TOTANG

★**Nomad's Land** ☎011 916171, ⓦnomadsland cambodia.com. Five individually decorated bungalows, some open-sided and all with private terrace or beach, blend in with their glorious natural surroundings. Private bathrooms have bucket showers and compost lavatories. Owner Nicole and local staff serve delicious home-cooked meals and dinner is a communal affair; the vibe is irresistibly laidback and the lounge has games, books and comfy chairs. Book ahead. **$90**

Koh Kong and around

Once a prosperous little logging town, the provincial town of **KOH KONG** is something of a quiet backwater, part border town and part ecotourism hub. Laid out on a simple grid on the east bank of the Kah Bpow River, the town's wooden houses owe their style more to neighbouring Thailand than Cambodia. There's no colonial architecture and the sights, such as they are, are low-key; walk along the river, stop by the fish market and canal, and browse the local market, a few blocks back.

Many people come to Koh Kong just for the **border crossing** with Thailand at **Cham Yeam**, though eco-outfits in town are doing their best to change that. Outside town and across the province, stretching down as far as the northern tip of Sihanoukville, the Koh Kong Conservation Corridor is a fantastic destination for nature lovers and outdoor enthusiasts. The majestic **Cardamom mountain range**, over 1800m at its highest, is believed to contain some of the planet's rarest species, including the Asian elephant, clouded leopard, Siamese crocodile and, at one point, the Indochinese tiger – although the last official sighting was in the 1990s. Nowadays, you're more likely to see sun bear prints, hear the sound of gibbons, and spot wild pigs, macaque monkeys and lizards. There's plenty of wonderful **birdlife**, including hornbills, kingfishers and herons, and Irrawaddy dolphins can be seen playing in the saline waters of the extensive mangrove network along the coast, explorable in the **Peam Krasaop Wildlife Sanctuary**, 6km from town.

5

CHAM YEAM: THE BORDER WITH THAILAND

To get from Koh Kong to the border at **Cham Yeam** (daily 7am–8pm), a 20min trip, take a moto ($3), tuk-tuk ($6) or taxi ($10). Once across the border, take a minibus (20m beyond immigration, on the right-hand side; departs every 40min, 7am–5pm approx; 120 baht) to Trat where a/c buses leave regularly for Bangkok (300 baht; 6hr) and other destinations across Thailand.

Watch out for a couple of scams when entering Cambodia. One is an attempt to charge 1500 baht (around $40) or more for a visa with the excuse "This is a land crossing, it's different". It's not. A 30-day Cambodian tourist visa is $30 regardless of where or how you enter the country. If this happens, ask for a receipt; record the time, date and name of the border official (or note the number on his shoulder) and report it, as soon as possible to the Ministry of Tourism (☎023 884974, ✉info@tourismcambodia.org) and the Immigration Department (☎017 812763, ✉immigration@gov.kh). Other scams include a bogus "quarantine station" beyond Thai immigration (you don't need health forms for a visa) and touts offering to "facilitate" the visa process (anything from 100–300 baht); politely refuse as this is nothing you can't do yourself. You can also avoid these hassles, and save a passport page, by buying your visa online (🌐evisa.gov.kh).

The Cardamoms' virgin forests and secluded waterfalls are accessible on day-treks, while longer, multi-day adventures take you deep into the remote Areng Valley (see box, p.268). Alternatively, simply relax at one of the properties along the Tatai River, 20km from Koh Kong. Boat tours also depart for **Koh Kong island**, Cambodia's largest, where you can explore the coastline before a barbecue on one of the pristine beaches.

Wat Neang Kok

On the western bank of the river, across the bridge beyond the toll • Moto/tuk-tuk return from Koh Kong approx $3/$5

Wat Neang Kok, on the western banks of the river, is a Buddhist pagoda with a twist, where life-size statues by the rocks portray scenes of torture in hell. Inside the wat are tableaus depicting further gruesome images, some say of Khmer Rouge atrocities. It's presumed that these were painted recently, as this area was Khmer Rouge territory until around 1997.

Koh Yor Beach

7km west of town, across the bridge, after the toll • Moto/tuk-tuk return from Koh Kong $7/$15

Dotted with seafood shacks, **Koh Yor Beach** (also known as Bak Khlong Beach) is worth the short trip from town if you fancy a few hours of solitude (although the weekends can get busy). The soft white sand is good for shell collecting, and the best time to visit is late afternoon when you can sip a beer and feast on local fish and crab while watching the sun sink beneath the horizon.

Peam Krasaop Wildlife Sanctuary (PKWS)

6km south of Koh Kong • Daily 6.30am–6pm • 5000 riel • Moto/tuk-tuk from Koh Kong approx $5/$10

Koh Kong province has the country's largest area of mangrove forest, which forms a vast and intricate network of "islands", the foundations of a rich and varied saltwater ecosystem. From Koh Kong you can make an enjoyable excursion to the **Peam Krasaop Wildlife Sanctuary (PKWS)**, a 250-square-kilometre area of stunning mangrove forest, designated as a protected area in 1997. Ten thousand people, mainly fishermen, live in floating hamlets and make a living from the abundant marine life.

From the entrance, a 600m concrete walkway takes you through the eerie mangroves towards a rickety bridge and a 15m-high observation tower. Across the bridge, and at the entrance, you can hire a motorboat to take you through the waterways, past

5

mangrove islands and into local fishing villages (from $10). *Bang Kayak* café-restaurant, at the entrance, serves food (7am–5pm), and numerous stalls inside sell drinks, snacks and hot food.

ARRIVAL AND DEPARTURE   KOH KONG AND AROUND

By bus Buses drop off at the bus stop, northeast of town near Acleda Bank; it's a $1–2 moto ride into town. A few companies offer services to Phnom Penh (7.45am, 8.30am, 11.30am & 2pm) and Sihanoukville (8am, 8.30am, 11.30am & 2pm); note that for Sihanoukville, only Virak Bunthan's 8am service is "direct"; with others, you'll most likely alight at Sre Ambal to join a smaller minibus. Advertised routes also travel as far as Battambang, Siem Reap and Mondulkiri but all go via Phnom Penh.

Destinations Phnom Penh (4 daily; 6hr); Sihanoukville (4 daily; 4hr).
By minibus and shared taxi Several minibuses run to Phnom Penh ($7) and Sihanoukville ($6) from Koh Kong; shared taxis ($10) depart early near the bus station and the market. A few early-morning minibuses may go to Kampot and Kep ($10); check with your guesthouse or travel agent.
Destinations Kampot (2 daily; 6hr); Kep (2 daily; 7hr); Phnom Penh (6 daily; 6hr); Sihanoukville (4 daily; 4hr).

GETTING AROUND

Bike and motorbike rental Most guesthouses can arrange motorbike rental for around $5–6/day or a bicycle for $1/24hr.

Motos There are plenty of motos around; Mr Han (☎ 097 2800232) is reliable, and Ritthy (see box below) can also arrange moto/tuk-tuks.

ACCOMMODATION

Most accommodation is within a compact area, mainly along the river or along Hotel St (Chicken Farm Rd on maps). Alternatively, stay along the **Tatai River**. If arriving by public transport, ask to alight at Tatai Resort and Marina on Tatai Bridge (20km before Koh Kong); from Koh Kong, a moto or tuk-tuk costs around $6/$15. Boat transfers are organized by accommodations.

KOH KONG

Asian Hotel Riverfront ☎ 035 936667, ⓦ asiankohkong .com. Great value with friendly staff, this hotel has well-furnished en-suite a/c rooms with hot water, TVs and fridge. The more expensive ($20) have partial river views. The good *Baan Peakmai* restaurant is on site (see opposite). **$15**

Kaing Kaing Guesthouse Riverfront, near the old boat dock ☎ 089 836073. One of several good-value, friendly Khmer-run guesthouses in town, right on the river. The 18 fan or a/c rooms have TVs and smart bathrooms with hot water. Limited English spoken. **$20**
Koh Kong Bay Hotel Riverfront, 200m south of Koh Kong Bridge ☎ 077 555590, ⓦ kohkongbay.com.

KOH KONG TOURS AND ACTIVITIES

A few companies, restaurants and guesthouses offer excursions to **waterfalls** upstream or the **beaches** on nearby **Koh Kong island**, an hour away, although the choppy seas shouldn't be crossed between June and October. Guided treks and multi-day adventures into the Cardamoms are also easily arranged. As well as the operators listed below, staff at *Fat Sam's*, Oasis Resort and *Paddy's Bamboo Guesthouse* can also help.

TOUR OPERATORS

Koh Kong Wonders & Excursions Street 7, off the Riverfront ☎ 081 931392 ⓦ kkwonders.com. Newish, friendly French expat offers fishing, trekking, kayaking and waterfall trips.
Ritthy Koh Kong Eco Adventure Tours Riverfront, ☎ 012 707719, ⓦ kohkongecoadventure.com. The town's longest-running operator, Mr Ritthy provides a range of excursions such as day-trips to waterfalls and Koh Kong island, plus kayaking, dirt-biking, and camping overnighters in the Cardamoms.
Spice Roads ☎ 063 964323, ⓦ spiceroads.com.

Specializing in cycling and mountain biking, Spice Roads offers multi-day cycling trips around Koh Kong province and the Cardamom Mountains.
Wild KK Project ☎ 088 4439993, ⓦ wildkkproject .com. Working with local communities and grassroots movement Mother Nature, these adventurous small-group tours (from $65) explore the province and the pristine Areng Valley deep in the Cardamoms, home to rare Siamese crocs that are currently threatened by a proposed hydroelectric dam. Sleep in hammocks and go trekking, kayaking and cycling.

This 19-room hotel is the town's only boutique property, with clean white linen, wooden floors, a/c, hot water and TV plus a lovely riverside pool, bar and over-water restaurant. $3 cocktails during happy hour 5–7pm. $\underline{\$35}$

★**Oasis** 2km north of town ☎092 228342, ⓦoasisresort.netkhmer.com. This friendly resort has five simple, roomy, family bungalows with a/c, TVs, DVD players and mini fridges in an idyllic garden. There's also a nice pool (non-residents $4), restaurant and great mountain views. $\underline{\$35}$

Otto's Restaurant and Rooms Street 8, signposted 50m from the old boat dock ☎035 393927. This original backpacker guesthouse in a traditional stilt-house, set up in 1999, is still going strong. The eight rooms (2 with a/c and private bathroom) are a bit dated but clean, there's a good, inexpensive bar-restaurant and friendly Otto is full of tips. $\underline{\$8}$

Paddy's Bamboo Guesthouse Chicken Farm Rd, ☎015 533223, ⓦbit.ly/paddyskohkong. Probably the cheapest place in town, with hammocks, dorms and rooms, some with private bathrooms. Dorms are dark and hot; rooms are decent value. Extras include a sociable bar-restaurant, tour desk, pool table and small souvenir shop. Hammocks $\underline{\$2}$; dorm $\underline{\$8}$; doubles $\underline{\$6}$

Ritthy's Retreat Riverfront ☎012 707719, ⓦritthy .info@gmail.com. Inviting en-suite dorms and rooms with lovely wooden furniture plus shared and private bathrooms. The a/c room has hot water and a TV. Out front is a restaurant and travel desk, run by the same Ritthy of Ritthy's Eco Adventure Tours. Dorms $\underline{\$4}$; fan $\underline{\$7}$; a/c $\underline{\$14}$

Sunny Guesthouse Chicken Farm Rd ☎035 5005777. The pool (non-residents $2) makes this a particularly good deal. Rooms are clean, and have TVs and nice bathrooms. No restaurant, but plenty in the neighbourhood. Fan $\underline{\$8}$; a/c $\underline{\$11}$

TATAI RIVER

4 Rivers Ecolodge 20 mins downstream from Tatai Bridge ☎097 6434032, ⓦecolodges.asia. In a magnificent location on a bend in the river, these 12 luxury floating tents offer four-poster beds, DVD players and other mod cons, while neutralizing its carbon footprint with sustainable building materials and solar electricity. River- and land-based tours, including trips up to the thundering Tatai rapids, are available. Price includes breakfast, boat transfer and firefly boat trip. No wi-fi. $\underline{\$259}$

Neptune Tatai River, 10 mins upstream from Tatai Bridge ☎088 7770576, ⓦneptuneadventure -cambodia.com. This tranquil riverside guesthouse has four stilted bungalows in a garden of mango trees, coconut palms and tropical plants. Communal dinners (from $4) and $1.50 beers are enjoyed in the over-water dining area, and owner Thomas leads numerous river tours, including kayaking trips and boats to the fishing village, waterfall and nearby mangroves. No wi-fi. $\underline{\$25}$

★**Rainbow Lodge** Tatai River, 10 mins upstream from Tatai Bridge ☎012 1602585, ⓦrainbowlodgecambodia .com. Secluded, atmospheric ecolodge with seven stilted fan bungalows and an open-sided jungle-view restaurant. Eco initiatives include solar power and rainwater collection. They can organize treks to the Cardamoms as well as kayaking and waterfall trips. Rates are for two and include breakfast, lunch, three-course dinners, kayaks and boat transfer. $\underline{\$105}$

Thmorda Garden Riverside Resort 169 Neuk Kok Village, 6km northwest of town ☎035 690 0324, ⓦthmordagarden.com. Situated on the far side of the river, the en-suite a/c rooms here are well furnished and cosy. It's a good option en route to Thailand for those wishing to bypass the town. They offer free pick-ups from the border and Koh Kong bus station, if you book ahead. $\underline{\$25}$

EATING

KOH KONG

Baan Peakmai Riverfront ☎035 936667, ⓦasiankohkong.com. This smart a/c restaurant serves delicious Thai food, with good vegetarian options, at reasonable prices. The Thai green curry ($5) is particularly tasty. Daily 6.30–9.30am, 11am–2pm & 5–10pm.

Café Laurent Riverfront, north of the old boat dock ☎012 373737, ⓦcafelaurent.asia. A sumptuous plant-festooned over-water restaurant-bar with a huge menu of Khmer, Thai and Western dishes (fried squid $6, tom yam crab $12), plus home-made desserts and ice cream. Wed–Mon 10.30am–11pm.

Crab Shack Koh Yor Beach. For a good local feed or sunset beer, this family-run beach shack is a favourite with locals and visitors. Try fried crab with black pepper ($6) or ask for savoury Khmer pancakes ($3). Daily 8am–10pm.

Fat Sam's Chicken Farm Rd, near the roundabout ☎097 7370707. Jovial Welsh owner Sam is known for his hearty English breakfasts ($6), comfort food, and cheap beer. There's a pool table and staff also rent motorbikes and book excursions. Mon–Sat 9am–9.30pm, Sun 4–9.30pm.

Pizza Bar 23 Chicken Farm Rd, opposite Fat Sam's, ☎087 269620. Small, unassuming streetside terrace restaurant serving pizzas from $3.50, breakfasts from $1.75 and hearty favourites such as sausage and mash ($5). Daily 10am–10pm.

Thmorda Crab House 169 Neang Kok Village, 6km northwest of town ☎035 6901252, ⓦthmordagarden .com. Located on the water, this surprisingly stylish crab restaurant has good food and cocktails, plus kayaks, petanque and a pool table. It's part of the *Thmorda Garden Riverside* Resort. Daily 10am–10pm.

5

★**Wood House** Street 7, just south of roundabout ☎010 456061. French and Khmer-owned café-restaurant with outdoor patio, serving some of the best food in town; filling breakfasts, immense burgers ($6.25) and creative Khmer vegetarian dishes. Daily 8.30am–10.30pm.

DIRECTORY

Health Koh Kong Referral Hospital is said to have improved, but you're probably better off across the border at the better-equipped one at Trat. Pharmacie Jun Leap and Pharmacie Praseur near the market are helpful.

Phone calls International phone calls can be made from the phone shops near the market.

Money Baht, riel and dollars are all accepted. Baht can be exchanged at Ratha Exchange (7am–5pm) on Street 2 between the river and market. There are a few ATMs; Acleda by the bus station, Canadia Bank on the riverfront and Bank of Cambodia near the market.

Post office North of the hospital, on the same road (Mon–Fri 7.30am–11.30am & 2–5pm).

Chi Phat

A positive example of Cambodia's community-based ecotourism projects, **CHI PHAT** is a remote riverside settlement in the southern valleys of the Cardamom Mountains, accessible by moto or long-tail boat from Andoung Tuek some 20km away up the Preak Piphot River. Thanks to its isolation, Chi Phat is a good hike off the tourist trail and provides an excellent opportunity to enjoy the forest surroundings while supporting the local community. Established by the Wildlife Alliance in 2008 to protect forests from illegal logging and poaching, Chi Phat Community-based Ecotourism project (**CBET**) was set up in a four-village commune of around 550 families, with the aim of encouraging villagers to pursue more sustainable forms of income. Its members, many of them former poachers, are trained in nature awareness and earn their keep by guiding and opening up their homes to visitors.

There are scores of **guided activities** on offer; trips cost around $35/day including guide (some English-speaking), packed lunch and water. If you're travelling solo, email ahead with a wish list of tours, so you can join one with enough people on it.

An overnight stay gives you a flavour of Chi Phat, but a few days or a week is better if you want to hike or bike the huge network of **jungle trails**, or visit bat caves, ancient jar burial sites and waterfalls in secluded clearings. There are also sunrise **birdwatching** excursions (the silver oriole, the yellow-bellied warbler and great hornbill are highlights) and peaceful **river cruises** in traditional rowing boats.

From Chi Phat, you can visit the Wildlife Alliance's **Wildlife Release Station** (☎095 970175, ⓦbit.ly/wildliferelease), an animal sanctuary in the Cardamoms for injured, abandoned and trafficked animals. Three new bungalows allow a small number of guests to stay overnight; they also get to shadow the gamekeepers, take part in feeding animals and learn about Cambodia's fragile ecosystem. It's not cheap ($120 per person per night) but profits go to the project and it's a highly memorable experience. Activities, meals and transport (to/from Chi Phat or Andoung Tuek) are included.

ARRIVAL AND DEPARTURE   CHI PHAT

To reach Chi Phat, you need to get to the village of **Andoung Tuek**. From here, you can take a moto ($7; 45min) or a boat upriver. **CBET boats** ($10; 2hr) wait for the arrival of the Virak Buntham Phnom Penh–Koh Kong bus (around noon–1pm). However you're planning to arrive, book your boat place in advance (☎035 6756444, ⓦchi-phat.org). If you're on a morning bus from Sihanoukville (2hr 30min) or Koh Kong (2hr), you'll be there in plenty of time. From the bridge, you can also charter a **motorboat** ($30). Watch out for rogue motorboat owners claiming there's no scheduled boat, although if you miss the CBET boat it's a 24hr wait for the next one. Bring enough cash; there are no ATMs at Chi Phat.

ACCOMMODATION

This can be booked in advance with the CBET Visitor Centre or on arrival (☎035 6756444, ⓦchi-phat.org). The office is staffed 7.30am–11.30am and 2–5pm. You can book **homestays**, guesthouses or bungalows. Most, but not all, have electricity from at least sunset to 10pm. If you're heading off on a multi-day trek, hammocks or tents plus basic bedding are provided.

Cardamom Cottages 100 metres past CBET Visitor Centre ☎092 277313, ✉yanveasna@gmail.com, ⓦchiphatcardamomcottage.com. Book ahead for one of the seven spacious bungalows. There's also a good restaurant, Danatra Kitchen, and owners can arrange onward transport. $̄10

Chiva Guesthouse 100 metres past CBET Visitor Centre ☎092 277313, ✉yanveasna@gmail.com. With the same ownership as Cardamom, this nine-room guesthouse offers clean, simple rooms, some in the main house, others in the garden. Doubles $̄5

Homestays There are numerous homestays in Chi Phat. Hosts may speak limited English, but are wonderfully hospitable. They will have gone to great trouble to make your quarters spotless, but be prepared for outdoor loos, bucket showers and proximity to farm animals. Rates include dinner. One person $̄5; two people $̄7

Vanna Bungalow and Spa ☎016 733847, ✉vannaresort@gmail.com. These stilted bungalows with basic bathrooms enjoy a quiet location in the next village; owners are happy to taxi you to and fro, or you can rent a moto. Restaurant on site. $̄10

EATING

Food options are limited but more than adequate. You can buy $1 noodle dishes at the small market.

CBET restaurant CBET Visitor Centre. It's small but serves substantial meals made from local produce ($2.50 breakfast, $3.50 lunch/dinner) and is worth booking in advance. Good wi-fi at the centre and in the evenings, the bar is a sociable hangout, open till around 11pm. Daily 6–8.30am, 11am–1pm & 6–7.30pm.

Chi Phat Restaurant Next to CBET restaurant. Drop in

here for a change from the *CBET restaurant*. Hours vary.

Danatra Kitchen Cardamom Cottages. Delicious breakfasts include banana pancakes for $1 and it's $5 for a full spread. Dinners with the family cost $3; individual dishes around $3.50. They are sometimes closed at weekday lunchtimes. They also do cheap water refills and cooking classes ($10). Daily 6am–11pm.

Kirirom National Park

If you have time for a detour, you'll be well rewarded by a trip to the pine-clad hills of **Kirirom National Park**, an important wildlife sanctuary often ignored by travellers, but worth the effort for its alpine-like scenery, crisp air and mountain views. Whether approaching from Sihanoukville or Phnom Penh (it's actually closer to the capital), the NR4 winds through a typically Cambodian landscape of rice fields and sugar palms before the distant blue peaks of the Cardamom Mountains to the north and the Elephant Mountains to the south loom on the horizon.

Kirirom's rolling hills are zigzagged with well-trodden trails, some popular with mountain bikers, and scattered with abandoned villas, pagodas, waterfalls, lakes and wild plants. These slopes are still home, despite illegal logging, to **forests** of *Pinus merkusii*, a pine tree not found anywhere else in Cambodia. Although poaching has taken its toll, species of deer and wild ox (gaur and banteng) still inhabit the depths of the park; elephants and leopards less so. A 1995 survey found tiger tracks, but there's little hope they survive today; gibbons, eagles and double-beaked hornbills are more likely.

In the 1940s, a road was cut through the forest, and following a visit from King Norodom, who named the area Kirirom ("Happiness Mountain"), work began on building a **hill station**. Construction was hindered by the Khmer Issarak guerrilla troops who prowled the forests until the 1960s, and the completed resort was abandoned during the Khmer Rouge years. In the mid-1990s, it became accessible again as a holiday destination, including two royal residences, gaining national park status in 1993. Now entirely clear of land mines, the park is worth staying in for a few days for scenic waterfall treks and spectacular views of the Cardamoms from sheer-drop viewpoints such as **The Cliff** and **Phnom Dat Chivit** ("End of the World Mountain").

5

CAMBODIA'S CONSERVATION MUDDLE

With proper sustainable management, Cambodia's **forests** could be a valuable source of income, not just in terms of providing timber, but also as a focus for ecotourism. Regrettably, recent decades have seen the country's forest cover decline dramatically. The conservation organization Forest Trends (W forest-trends.org) recently reported that forest cover had decreased from 73 percent in 1993 to 55 percent in 2015. A 2014 survey by Open Development Cambodia put the figure even lower. Although five new protected areas were created in May 2016, experts suggest that there is insufficient manpower to police them. Illegal logging is the principal cause (timber is often repackaged and sold as "sustainably sourced") but also, more recently, forests have been cleared in vast swathes to make way for rubber plantations in Kompong Cham province and the illegal production of drugs in the Cardamom Mountains.

In 2001, the Cambodian government was forced by the World Bank to take action to reduce some of the most glaring environmental abuses. However, the government soon fell out with **Global Witness** (W globalwitness.org), the environmental watchdog appointed by the Bank to monitor Cambodia's forests, when its damning 2007 report named high-ranking government officials as using the country's resources for personal gain. The government's response was to call for sackings at Global Witness, but the watchdog has continued to publish its findings, including a 2013 report about illegal logging. In the meantime, the country's natural resources continue to diminish at an alarming rate. Cambodian human rights group LICADHO (W licadho-cambodia.org) estimates that half a million people have been negatively affected by over 200 state-linked land deals.

Cambodia's forests are home to a vast, diverse **wildlife** population, including globally threatened species such as the tiger and pangolin (scaly anteater). Ironically, the improvements in infrastructure that followed the establishment of the country's national parks in 1993 have sometimes made it easier for poachers to capture wild animals, subsequently sold in local markets for meat, or used in medicines and charms. It's relatively rare now but poachers still sell their bounty on the black market.

Despite its official stance, the government appears to lack the will to implement sound conservation policies, readily granting concessions to international companies for offshore exploration of oil and gas, and – after a change in the law – for bauxite, gold and copper in the protected areas of Mondulkiri, Rattanakiri and Kratie. Ecological organizations claim that this offers too many opportunities for personal profit – witness the current situations at Bokor (see box, p.280) and Botum Sakor (see p.266) national parks. Global Witness's 2009 report, *Country for Sale*, illustrates the extent of the problem. Unregulated sand dredging is another increasing concern. Environmental group Mother Nature (W mothernaturecambodia .org) recently found unrecorded sand being exported to Singapore. Meanwhile, a planned hydroelectric dam in the Cardamom Mountains threatens the ecosystem in the Areng Valley.

Exploring the park

From its entrance at the small town of Treng Trayeng, the road climbs steadily for 16km to a rolling forested **plateau**, where you'll find the majority of the park's attractions and its few facilities. About halfway up the hill, a signpost points down a narrow path to **Outasek waterfall**, a series of cascades a short hike off the main road. There's usually water for splashing about in, except during the very driest part of the year.

As you arrive on the plateau, you will see Kirirom Hillside Resort, and about 1km further on, the **park office**. After another 500m or so, you reach the only major road **junction** in the park, from where signs point towards various sights. The most appealing option (particularly in the rainy season) is the track north to a series of three **waterfalls**, I, II and III, numbered according to increasing size, and located roughly every 2km. Another road leads to a cluster of derelict buildings, including the newer of two **royal residences**. Further on, you can scramble through the overgrown garden of the older royal residence, the king's own house, for views over the forest and onto a magical lake, **Sras Srorng**, reached by heading downhill along a rough track from the

5

palace. A visitor centre by the palace displays several panels about the park's history. Abandoned villas and hillside getaways, built during the 1950s and 1960s, are scattered around the park.

Another option is to take the right fork from the entrance to **Chambok Eco Tourism Site** ($3) outside the main Kirirom area, which is home to a community-based ecotourism (CBET) programme as well as a 40-metre waterfall, bat caves and trails. They can organize homestays and activities such as Khmer dancing, village visits, treks and cooking classes.

For guided hikes, bicycle rental or transport around the park, hotels (see below) can arrange tours and guides. Tour company Spice Roads (☎063 964323, ⓦspiceroads .com) offers one- and two-day bike rides around Kirirom National Park and the Cardamom Mountains.

ARRIVAL AND DEPARTURE   KIRIROM NATIONAL PARK

By public transport Access to the park by public transport is difficult, as it's 24km from the NR4 turn-off to the upland plateau and Chambok. Take a Phnom Penh-bound bus from Sihanoukville or vice versa, alight at Treng Trayeng then ask a moto driver by the market/Sokimex petrol station to take you to the park ($5 one-way). State exactly where you're going before setting off. If you're overnighting, arrange for your driver to return, or ask your accommodation to call you a driver. Back in Treng Trayeng, numerous minibuses pass by for Phnom Penh and Sihanoukville

By motorbike or car The park is an easy day-trip from Sihanoukville or Phnom Penh; hire a car and driver (around $60) or rent a motorbike. The road to the top is sealed (if potholed in parts), so access is possible year-round.

INFORMATION

Entry fee Entry (daily 8am–5pm) costs $5 (for non-Khmers), payable at the small shack at the park entrance after *Kirirom Hillside Resort*.
Park office The park office has little visitor information although a notice board has a useful map and shots of various locations. Mr Mik, a former park employee, offers guided tours for $20 half-day (☎012 761526).
Temperature The temperature on the plateau averages 25˚C by day, dropping by 5–10˚C at night; long trousers and warm clothing are essential after dark.

ACCOMMODATION AND EATING

The most economical option is a **homestay** at Chambok with meals at their *Women's Restaurant*. Other places for **food** besides the hotels are the stalls beyond the park office (lunch only) and the food shacks by the waterfalls.

Chambok ☎012 500142, ⓦchambok.org. Community-based homestay project established in 2002, with over 50 homes enrolled. Homestays are basic but clean, with meals ($3–4) served at the *Women's Restaurant* at the eco-tourism centre by the entrance. Per person ̶$4
★**Kirirom Mountain Lodge** ☎097 6251124, ⓦkirirom.asia. Converted from two 1950s villas, the six rooms at this atmospheric lodge have comfortable beds, natural furnishings, hot-water showers and outdoor seating. A wide staircase leads to the second villa with magnificent views from the roof terrace and restaurant, where the friendly manager prepares generous portions of Khmer, Mediterranean and Moroccan dishes (around $8). Breakfast is included and there is in-room electricity

YEAY MAO: THE BLACK GRANDMOTHER

Regular traffic jams on NR4 south of Kirirom at the **Pich Nil pass** are due to Cambodian motorists breaking their journey to make offerings at the shrine of **Lok Yeay Mao**, or **Black Grandmother**, a powerful ancestor spirit believed to protect travellers and fishermen. One popular story has it that a sexually frustrated Yeay Mao boarded a ship to Thailand in search of her husband who had left her to fight at sea. The ensuing bad storms, thought by the captain to be caused by having a pregnant woman on board, prompted Yeay Mao to jump overboard. The crew survived and the myth of Yeay Mao as protector was born.

You can find her shrine by following the eye-watering haze of incense – a smoke-dimmed image can be found within, along with bananas and other phallic offerings. The rows of spirit houses are a bit of a scam by local stallholders, but most Khmer prefer to make an offering than risk offending the spirits.

5

mornings/evening; 24–7 electricity/wi-fi at the restaurant. $\underline{\$35}$
Kirirom Pine Resort ☏078 777284, ⓦvkirirom .com. This sprawling Japanese-designed resort offers tents, concrete pipe rooms, glamping and bungalows, across all budgets, and the *Pine View* restaurant

serves well-priced Khmer food ($3.50–8). There's a pool, and massage treatments are on offer, while other activities include stand-up paddleboarding, kayaking, pineapple picking and cycling. Free shuttle to/from Phnom Penh. Camping $\underline{\$20}$; Pipe room/hut $\underline{\$50}$; Glamping/bell tent $\underline{\$60}$

Kampot

Overlooked by the Elephant Mountain range, charming, compact **KAMPOT**, on the north bank of the Teuk Chhou River, enjoys one of the nicest settings in Cambodia, and has become a popular destination for tourists, weekending Khmer and expats from Phnom Penh. Once a bustling trading port, Kampot still has a Chinese population, their single-storey houses, built without stilts, contrasting with the Khmer stilt-houses and colonial shophouses that grace the town's streets behind the sun-kissed, tree-lined **riverfront**. Other attractions include the **Kampot Museum**, Psar Samaki – better known as **Kampot market** – and the distinctive **Durian roundabout**, where a larger-than-life durian fruit pays homage to the region's fruit production. Kampot is also an excellent base for exploring **Bokor National Park**, as well as **pepper plantations**, salt pans, fruit farms and fishing villages. A seaport, 10km away, is being planned for easier access to Phu Quoc, the Thai islands and Cambodian coast, but for now, Kampot's quiet charm remains.

The riverfront

Southwest of Kampot's central (Durian) roundabout is the colourful **French quarter**, where shophouses line the streets down to the **river** and flowers planted in cans and pots give the place an almost Mediterranean aura. Getting to the riverfront or onto

---

THE CHINESE IN CAMBODIA

There has been a **Chinese presence** in Cambodia since the very earliest times. Accounts written by Chinese traders and envoys from the third century onwards have played a major part in chronicling Cambodia's history, but it was only after the fifteenth century that the Chinese settled in significant numbers. Marrying into rich Khmer families and working as tax collectors, bankers, gold dealers and restaurateurs, ethnic Chinese soon established themselves as the country's most influential minority.

A flood of new immigrants arrived in the 1930s during China's economic crisis. In the main, the Chinese community continued to prosper until the 1970s, when they were **persecuted** first by the Lon Nol government – which resented their success – and then by the Khmer Rouge, who wanted them eliminated. Things became more complicated in 1979 when the Vietnamese liberation of Cambodia was followed by a short-lived Chinese invasion of Vietnam. This resulted in many Cambodian Chinese fleeing to Thailand; those Chinese who remained were subsequently permitted to resume limited business activities, but it wasn't until after the 1993 elections that they were properly able to reassert their influence on business – which they did wholeheartedly, capitalizing on their access to investment capital through their extensive overseas networks. Nowadays, the number of Chinese-owned businesses is clear to see from the Chinese signage on streets in any Cambodian town.

Cambodia's Chinese have managed to retain their own culture and language (most are **bilingual**) while at the same time integrating very well into Cambodian society. In towns such as Voen Sai and Kampot they are more visible by virtue of maintaining their own Chinese-language **schools**. And in Phnom Penh, although Chinese New Year is not an official holiday, it assumes a festive importance akin to the Khmer New Year, with energetic dragon dances performed in the streets.

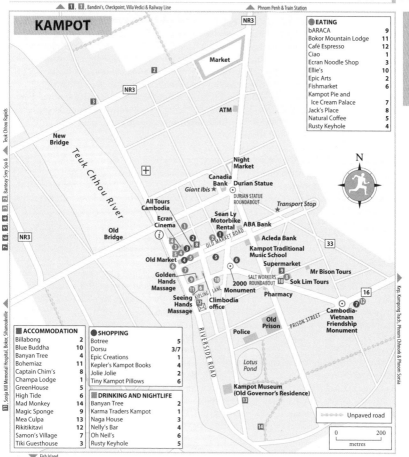

KAMPOT

▲ 1, 1, Bandini's, Checkpoint, Villa Vedici & Railway Line   ▲ Phnom Penh & Train Station

NR3

Market

NR3

ATM

New Bridge

Teuk Chhou River

Night Market

Canadia Bank

Durian Statue

Giant Ibis ★

DURIAN STATUE ROUNDABOUT

Transport Stop ★

All Tours Cambodia

Ecran Cinema

Sean Ly Motorbike Rental

ABA Bank

Old Bridge

OLD MARKET ROAD

Acleda Bank

Kampot Traditional Music School

Old Market

Supermarket

Mr Bison Tours

Golden Hands Massage

SALT WORKERS ROUNDABOUT

Sok Lim Tours

2000 Monument

Pharmacy

Seeing Hands Massage

KIPLING LANE

Climbodia office

Cambodia-Vietnam Friendship Monument

Old Prison

PRISON STREET

Police

RIVERSIDE ROAD

Lotus Pond

Kampot Museum (Old Governor's Residence)

Unpaved road

0 — 200
metres

▼ Fish Island

● EATING	
bARACA	9
Bokor Mountain Lodge	11
Café Espresso	12
Ciao	1
Ecran Noodle Shop	3
Ellie's	10
Epic Arts	2
Fishmarket	6
Kampot Pie and Ice Cream Palace	7
Jack's Place	8
Natural Coffee	5
Rusty Keyhole	4

■ ACCOMMODATION	
Billabong	2
Blue Buddha	10
Banyan Tree	4
Bohemiaz	11
Captain Chim's	8
Champa Lodge	1
GreenHouse	5
High Tide	6
Mad Monkey	14
Magic Sponge	9
Mea Culpa	13
Rikitikitavi	12
Samon's Village	7
Tiki Guesthouse	3

● SHOPPING	
Botree	5
Dorsu	3/7
Epic Creations	1
Kepler's Kampot Books	4
Jolie Jolie	2
Tiny Kampot Pillows	6

■ DRINKING AND NIGHTLIFE	
Banyan Tree	2
Karma Traders Kampot	1
Naga House	3
Nelly's Bar	4
Oh Neil's	6
Rusty Keyhole	5

Sonja Kill Memorial Hospital, Bokor, Sihanoukville

Banteay Srey Spa &

Teuk Chhou Rapids

Kep, Kampong Trach, Phnom Chhnork & Phnom Sorsia

a cruise boat in time for **sunset** is a must, as the night fishermen head out to sea in their brightly coloured boats.

The elongated **old market** – abandoned some years ago when a new market building was constructed – was restored in 2011 and now houses a burgeoning collection of bars, shops and cafés. Further along are the government offices, post office and the former Governor's Residence, restored to its original grandeur and now home to **Kampot Museum**.

For a pleasant stroll, follow the river from the old bridge to the disused **railway bridge** in the north. From there, cross the river on the rusty, pockmarked walkway, and return to town along the other bank; the docked riverboats are a good spot for a beer. In the other direction, follow the river south around the curve past Kampot Museum; dip behind it for the glorious **lotus pond** before continuing past the outdoor gym – heaving with Khmer families in the early evening – and on towards the small port and fishing village.

Kampot Museum

Riverfront Rd, after the post office • ⓦ kampotmuseum.org • Tues & Thurs 3–6pm, Sat & Sun 8–11am, 3–6pm • $2

It may take a couple of visits to get in, due to occasionally erratic opening hours, but it's worth it. The elegant colonial-era building of the former Governor's Residence has

5

been neatly transformed into the compact, informative **Kampot Museum**, aided by the expertise of local historian and anthropologist Jean-Michel Filippi.

Three rooms of information panels and photographs chart the history of Kampot, from its origins and period as Cambodia's second-largest city through to its various transformation during the French protectorate, the Sihanouk era and the Khmer Rouge years. It's an excellent, digestible introduction to the region and its various ethnic minorities. A room of evocative photos includes images of Bokor National Park and the oldest known photograph of Kampot – taken in 1886 by Adhémar Leclère, an ethnologist and the province's first French governor. Sculptures, some pre-Angkorian, are exhibited throughout.

Kampot Traditional Music School

Northeast of the old market, opposite Acleda bank • ⓦ kcdi-cambodia.org • Mon–Fri 6–9pm • Free, donations welcome

Kampot Traditional Music School teaches traditional music and dance to orphaned and disabled children. Visitors are welcome to watch the classes or attend one of the **performances**; a timetable is displayed outside.

ARRIVAL AND DEPARTURE   KAMPOT

Buses from Phnom Penh usually drop passengers off at the transport stop by Total petrol station, at the top of Old Market Street. Some shared taxis and minibuses also arrive here.

By bus Phnom Penh Sorya Transport, Capitol and Vibol run buses (3hr 30min–4hr) to and from Phnom Penh ($5), some via Kep (4hr 30min). Giant Ibis have comfortable, 22-seater minibuses to Phnom Penh ($9). Schedules change frequently; check with travel agents.
Destinations Kep (2 daily; 1hr); Phnom Penh (8 daily; 3hr 30min–5hr)
By shared taxi and minibus Shared transport departs from opposite the transport stop, although most minibuses do hotel pick-ups. Several companies, including Cambodia Post, serve Phnom Penh, Sihanoukville, Kep and Koh Kong,

and you can also get to Ha Tien, HCMC or Phu Quoc Island in Vietnam (often requiring a change of vehicle at the border), and Bangkok.
Destinations Bangkok (2 daily; 12hr); Ha Tien (3 daily; 2hr); HCMC (3 daily; 10hr); Kep (7 daily; 1hr); Koh Kong (1 daily; 5hr); Phnom Penh (10 daily; 3hr–3hr 30min); Sihanoukville (10 daily; 2hr 30min)
By train A new route launched in 2016 operates Fri, Sat, Sun and public holidays between Phnom Penh (4hr 30min; $6), Sihanoukville (1hr 40min–2hr 40min $4) and Takeo (3hr; $5). Tickets available at stations; you can usually buy on the day (☎078 888582, ⓦroyal-railway.com).

GETTING AROUND

Built on a grid system, Kampot is bordered on the west by the Teuk Chhou River with NR3 running northeast to Phnom Penh and southwest to Sihanoukville. The **town centre** is at the Durian roundabout, where roads converge from all directions, although the main area of interest is the French Quarter. Most places are easily reached on foot.

Car rental Cars with driver can be hired through hotels and guesthouses for around $40/day.
Motorbike rental Sean Ly rentals (daily 7am–9pm;

☎012 944687), opposite ABA bank has a good selection, and most travel agents and guesthouses can also arrange. A 125cc runabout costs $5/day, 250cc off-road bike $15.

INFORMATION AND TOURS

Tourist information centre Mr Pov and his team at the information centre on the waterfront by the old bridge offer good advice (daily 8am–1pm, 1.30–5.30pm; ☎012 462286, ✉kampottourismoffice@gmail.com). Free booklets Kampot Survival Guide (ⓦkampotsurvivalguide.com) and Coastal (ⓦcoastal-cambodia.com) have up-to-date listings.

Travel and tour operators Tried-and-trusted ones include All Tours Cambodia, Old Market St (north side), next to *Captain Chim's* (☎096 8777719), opposite the old market, and Sok Lim Tours (☎012 719872) and Bison Tours (☎012 442687, ⓦbit.ly/BisonTours) both on St 730 (Guesthouse St).

TOURS AND ACTIVITIES

Boat tours Bart the Boatman (☎092 174280; ✉boatmanbart@gmail.com) has been operating trips

around Kampot's brackish backwaters and mangroves for years (3–4hr; $20pp, minimum 2 people). Bjorn from *Love*

The River (☎016 627410) runs trips from the GreenHouse guesthouse (3 hrs; from $15pp).

Climbing Climbodia (☎095 581951, ⓦclimbodia.com) is a Belgian-run rock-climbing outfit using high-quality gear; programmes include beginner's half-day courses and full-day Via Ferratas. Caving and abseiling around the caves at Phnom Kbal Romeas, 5km outside Kampot, is also available.

Cooking classes *Jack's Place* (☎012 719872, ⓦbit.ly /kampotjack), opposite *Magic Sponge*, run cooking lessons for $20 including a market visit. *Ecran Noodles* offer hand-pulled noodle classes on Wednesdays (4pm, $15 per person, ☎016 627410). Outside Kampot by Secret Lake, Khmer Roots eco-farm (☎088 356016, ⓦkhmerrootscafe .com) has lessons for $20 including pick-up.

Massage Seeing Hands Massage, near *Bokor Mountain Lodge* on Riverside Rd (daily; 7am–11pm; $6/hr) plus Golden Hands around the corner (10am–11pm; $6/hr; ☎017 855200, ⓦbit.ly/spakampot) and Diamond Massage, next to Epic Creations (10am–11pm, $6/hr; ☎093 772577). You can also get a massage, scrub, mani or wax from JolieJolie, around the corner from *Captain Chim's* (daily 10.30am–7pm; ☎092 936067, ⓦjoliejolie-kampot .com). The women-only Banteay Srey Spa (☎012 276621,

ⓦbanteaysreyspa.com) on the west bank of the river, offers massages and yoga classes, plus veggie tapas and juices at roadside *Deva Café* (Wed–Mon 11am–7pm).

River activities *Checkpoint* (☎096 3134233; ⓦcheck point-kampot.com; 4km from town, east bank) have paddleboards, kayaks and a water trampoline. SUP Asia (☎093 980550; ⓦsupasia.org) provide stand-up paddleboarding lessons ($25). Cambodia Kiteboarding (☎089 290714; ⓦcambodiakiteboarding.com), operating from Villa Vedici, offer two-hour taster sessions $79, rental $30/hr.

Sightseeing Guesthouses, tourist office, *Captain Chim's* and many agents arrange trips, including to Bokor (from $10) and countryside/pepper plantation tours ($10–20). Jack at Sok Lim Tours (☎012 719872) and Mr Bison (☎012 442687, ⓦbit.ly/BisonTours), both on Guesthouse St, offer everything from multi-day jungle adventures to $5 sunset/firefly cruises. Butterfly Tour (butterflytour.asia: ☎093 775592) offer cycling and moto tours (3hr/17km backroads cycling tour $17; 26km guided moto to Bokor $33).

Swimming Purchase drink/food to use the pools at Villa Vedici and *Bohemiaz* out of town, and *Two Moons Hotel*, *Mad Monkey* and *Billabong* in town.

ACCOMMODATION

Accommodation in Kampot is plentiful, of generally high quality and includes some of the cheapest backpacker spots in the south. The most relaxing places are a few kilometres out of town, along both banks of the **Kampot River**.

IN TOWN

Billabong 250 metres west from the market ☎096 7672977 ⓦbillabongguesthouse.com. Renovated in 2016, the pool, swim-up bar and poolside restaurant are winning components, and Sunday live music sessions are popular. Accommodation consists of an en-suite, 10-bed fan dorm, fan/cold-water rooms and rooms with a/c and hot water. Dorms $̲5̲; fan $̲1̲2̲; a/c $̲1̲8̲

Blue Buddha Street 730 (Guesthouse St) ☎017 6372924, ⓦbluebuddhahotel.com. Excellent modern hotel with spacious rooms, super-comfy mattresses, powerful showers, a/c and TV. Family rooms ($38) sleep five. No bar/restaurant but on the cards. Knowledgeable owners and free use of bikes. $̲2̲4̲

Captain Chim's Old Market, north side ☎012 321043. Locally owned Kampot stalwart with fan and cold-water rooms, and a/c ones with hot water. They also offer free laundry, breakfast from $1.25 and travel services. Fan $̲7̲; a/c $̲1̲5̲

Mad Monkey Riverside Rd, near Kampot Museum ☎096 7390284, ⓦmadmonkeyhostels.com/kampot. This boutique-style hostel has a lovely pool, poolside bar-restaurant, social activities, and a variety of spotless rooms from female and mixed dorms to deluxe family rooms. A great menu includes all-day breakfasts, pizzas and Khmer

curries, with most dishes under $5. Dorms $̲7̲; fan $̲1̲5̲, a/c $̲2̲4̲

Magic Sponge Street 730 (Guesthouse St) ☎017 946428, ⓦmagicspongekampot.com. Recently revamped long-standing guesthouse in a refurbished villa. The six-bed "penthouse" dorm has padded mattresses, en-suite hot-water bathroom and a fabulous private balcony and five stylish private rooms with modern bathrooms and hot-water rainshowers. Mini-golf, happy hour noon–5pm and Western, Khmer and Indian food ($1 breakfast, veg thali $5). Regular events include jam sessions and a pub quiz. Dorms $̲5̲; fan $̲1̲2̲; a/c $̲1̲7̲

Mea Culpa A block back from the river, behind Kampot Museum ☎012 504769, ⓦmeaculpakampot.com. Clean, comfortable guesthouse with eleven bright bedrooms, all with TV, fridges and a/c. Great open-air restaurant; stone-baked pizzas (margherita $5.75) and "build-your-own-sandwiches" – ideal for day-trips. Free tea/coffee. $̲2̲0̲

★Rikitikitavi Riverside Rd, south of the old bridge ☎012 235102, ⓦrikitikitavi-kampot.com. Book ahead to secure one of the six beautifully decorated a/c rooms here. Upstairs, the restaurant and sunset bar is a popular spot, with two-for-one cocktails (5–7pm), and the food is some of the best in town. $̲4̲7̲

5

Tiki Guesthouse Riverside Rd, after the old bridge ☎ 096 7956409, ⓦ bit.ly/tikikampot. Brilliant backpacker option on the river with a sociable sunset bar that's open till late, cheap beer and tasty food ($2–6). Accommodation is dorms and rooms with shared/private bathrooms, and shared-bathroom bungalows. Dorms <u>$4</u>; doubles <u>$8</u>; bungalows <u>$8</u>

THE RIVER

Banyan Tree Teuk Chhou Road, 2km north of town ☎ 078 665094, ⓦ banyantreekampot.com. Formerly *Bodhi Villa*, this riverside guesthouse in a jungle garden is a favourite with backpackers for its clean dorms, bungalows and rooms (shared, cold-water bathrooms) and good-value restaurant. Friday nights are renowned for live music and parties. Dorms <u>$3</u> doubles <u>$6</u> bungalows <u>$8</u>

Champa Lodge Riverside Rd, 4km north of town ☎ 092 525835, ⓦ champalodge.com. Idyllic family-run riverside retreat offering three original stilted Khmer houses with fan-cooled rooms (but no TVs) and luxe bathrooms. The Boat Lodge ($65) is worth the splurge for its private balcony, and the two-bedroom Paddy Lodge ($60) is good value. A convivial restaurant-bar serves home-cooked food and Belgian beers. Kayaks are available for exploring the river. <u>$38</u>

★ **GreenHouse** Off Teuk Chhou Rd, 6km west of town ☎ 088 8863071, ⓦ greenhousekampot.com. Lovely rustic bungalows, some with river views, in a tropical garden. All have modern bathrooms and private terraces;

cheapest are cold-water, the rest (from $30) have hot water. The bar-restaurant is housed in a green timber structure, formerly a bar stilted over the Tonle Sap before being transported to the banks of the Kampot River. A French chef serves up excellent food, from galettes to Kampot pepper cuisine, best enjoyed on the river deck (for over-12s only, due to jetty). <u>$25</u>

High Tide Teuk Chhou Rd, 2km north of town ☎ 096 4169345, ⓦ bit.ly/hightidekampot. Previously *Blue Frog*, this riverfront guesthouse has cheap hammocks, a four-bed dorm, doubles and bungalows. Jump into the river from the jetty or hang out in the sociable bar-restaurant. Hammocks <u>$2</u>; dorms <u>$4</u> rooms <u>$7</u>; bungalows <u>$15</u>

Samon's Village Teuk Chhou Road, 3km north of town ☎ 096 4266663, ⓦ samonvillagekampot.com. Events, including Khmer music and dance, along with the river deck and small beach make *Samon's* a real favourite. The cheapest bungalows sleep up to four and have shared bathrooms; the more expensive ones ($15–25) are en-suite – some with river views. Good food and home-made rice wine. <u>$10</u>

OUT OF TOWN

Bohemiaz 4km out of town off NR3 ☎ 015 809005, ⓦ bohemiaz.com Get a sense of rural Kampot at this lovely spot, run by a father-and-daughter team. Great pool and restaurant, tasteful fan rooms with hot-water showers and flatscreen TV, plus bungalows and concrete "hobbit hole tents". Tents <u>$8</u>; doubles <u>$12</u>

EATING

Kampot has a dizzying array of fantastic restaurants, bars and cafés. You'll also find rice and noodle shops around Kampot market and the small **night market** by the Durian roundabout, while Khmer stalls selling fruit shakes and curries line streets 720 (opposite the old bridge, off Riverfront Rd) and 722, parallel to it.

★ **bARACA** Street 726, off Riverside Rd ☎ 011 290434 ⓦ baraca.org. The two Belgian owners produce delicious tapas and drinks; try creamy whisky mushrooms on toast ($4.50), Cava by the glass and inventive gin cocktails. They also have four lovely rooms upstairs ($12). Daily 5.30–10.30pm.

Bokor Mountain Lodge Riverside Road ☎ 017 712062, ⓦ bit.ly/bmlodge. Sunday roasts ($7.50), breakfasts, and Cambodian and Western classics remain popular at this long-standing hotel, bar and restaurant in a beautiful French colonial building. Happy hour 5–7pm and frequent live music. Daily 7am–11pm.

Ciao Street 722, off Riverside Rd. This Italian street-food stand has punters queuing for home-made pasta and pizza (from $3); get there early or be prepared to wait. Daily 6–10pm.

Ecran Noodles Riverside Road, opposite the old bridge ☎ 010 249411. Enjoy hand-pulled Chinese noodles and dumplings ($2.50) cooked streetside in this friendly café. Daily 11am–9pm. Closed Tues.

Fishmarket Riverside Rd, opposite Old Market ☎ 012 728884, ⓦ bit.ly/fishmarketkampot. As the name suggests, this was once Kampot's fish market. Now it's a nice river-view bar serving good breakfasts (from $3.50) and fusion cuisine, predominantly seafood (fish and chips/ fish amok $6.50, tofu salad $4). Half-price cocktails 5–7pm. Daily 7.30am–11pm.

Jack's Place Street 730 (Guesthouse St) ☎ 012 719872, ⓦ bit.ly/kampotjack. Popular, locally run joint serving good Khmer food (Kampot curry $2.50), filling Western breakfasts (pancakes $2) and the best soup in town. There's a sunset terrace bar upstairs, cookery lessons and $2.50 dorms next door. Daily 7am–10pm.

Rusty Keyhole Cnr Riverside Rd & Old Market St ☎ 012 679607, ⓦ bit.ly/rustykeyhole. This popular bar and restaurant has a prime position on the riverfront and is a top spot to relax over a beer or two (long happy hour 11am–7pm; 75c beer, $1.50 spirits), or try their much-talked-about spare ribs, comfort food and Sunday roasts. Daily 8.30am–11.30pm.

5

CAFÉS

There's a growing **café scene** in Kampot with several places to get a caffeine fix and home-baked snacks.

Ellie's Top of Street 726, near 2000 Monument ☎ 096 3092300, 🖥 bit.ly/ellieskampot. Good coffee and tempting cakes, salads, sandwiches and breakfasts from $2, and with a small outside patio. Wed–Mon 8am–3.30pm. Closed Tues.

Epic Arts Old Market St, north side ☎ 092 922069, 🖥 epicarts.org.uk. This friendly café employs people with and without disabilities, and supports various grassroots projects. Menu includes breakfast bruschetta at $3.50, scones for $2 and pesto chicken panini for $3.50. They also sell scarves, bags and other items both here and at their Epic Creations store a few doors along. Upstairs are displays of art by local students. Daily 7am–4pm.

★**Café Espresso** Cnr NR33 & Street 707 a 15min walk from river ☎ 092 388736, 🖥 bit.ly/espressokampot. If you

like your coffee, head to this café and roastery, which inside a converted salt-shed with a fabulous interior of murals, and shelves lined with ceramics, much of it discarded pottery from Kampot's river. Coffee from $1.50, breakfast muffins ($4) and a varied menu (fish tacos, falafel, chorizo burger from $4.50). Tues–Fri 8.15am–4pm, Sat & Sun 9am–4.30pm

Kampot Pie and Ice Cream Palace Riverfront Rd ☎ 099 657826, 🖥 bit.ly/kampotpie. There are ice creams and home-baked sweet and savoury pastries from $1 at this enduring spot. Daily 7am–11pm.

Natural Coffee Old Market St, north side ☎ 099 990898, 🖥 bit.ly/naturalcoffeekampot. Excellent breakfast spot, serving inexpensive coffee, bagels and omelettes plus Khmer dishes. Daily 7am–9pm.

DRINKING AND NIGHTLIFE

Nightlife is mellow but lively. Restaurants like *bARAKA*, *Rusty Keyhole* and *Fishmarket* double up as bars, as do many guesthouses including *Magic Sponge*, *Mad Monkey* and *GreenHouse*. There's also a growing live music scene. Community arts initiative, KAMA/Kampot Arts & Music Association (🖥 bit.ly/kampotkama) often hosts Khmer and international bands at its café near the 2000 Monument. In October, they open four nights a week and also host Kampot Writers & Readers Festival in November. The liveliest places are *Banyan Tree* on Fridays and *Naga House* on Saturdays.

Banyan Tree Teuk Chhou Road, 2km north of town ☎ 078 665094, 🖥 banyantreekampot.com. This jungle garden guesthouse is also popular for its river-view bar. There's live music on Fridays with Kampot Playboys and other local bands. Daily 7am–late.

Karma Traders Kampot Red Road, 400m after the railway line ☎ 016 556504, 🖥 bit.ly/karmatraders. This newcomer is both guesthouse and live music venue, with regular sets from talented musicians on its sunset rooftop bar. It also has a restaurant, dorms, private rooms and three-bedroom, en-suite villas. Daily 7am–late.

Naga House Teuk Chhou Road, 2km north of town ☎ 012 289916, 🖥 bit.ly/nagahouse. Best known for its DJ-led Saturday night parties, *Naga House's* lounge bar and

river deck is also perfect for chilled-out cocktails. Free boat pick-up from the old bridge on Saturdays; check for times. Daily 8am–late.

Nelly's Bar Cnr Street 722 & Riverside Rd ☎ 096 8639793, 🖥 bit.ly/nellysbar. Sit under a bougainvillea tree and sip a sunset beer or a late-night cocktail at this small but atmospheric streetside bar. Staff are friendly and there's usually a good crowd. Daily 2pm–late.

Oh Neil's Riverside Rd ☎ 015 207790, 🖥 ohneils.com. A favourite with both visitors and local expats, this small Irish bar gets livelier as the night goes on. Its sister property, *Oh Neil's Riverside Guesthouse*, near the fishing village, a half-hour walk east of town, has a good sunset rooftop bar. Daily 5pm–late.

SHOPPING

It's not a huge shopping scene, but it's generally good quality – even souvenir shops sell decent clothing and gifts, and Ecran Movie House sells cottonwear.

Botree Old Market St, south side ☎ 012 691379, 🖥 botree.asai. Quality Kampot pepper products from Botree farm, and a good wine selection. Daily 8am–8pm.

Dorsu Old Market St, north side ☎ 012 960225, 🖥 dorsu.org/store. Pretty dresses, *kramas* and other accessories in cool, comfortable fabrics produced by local women as part of an ethical social-enterprise initiative. A second store and sewing studio (daily 8am–5pm) is next to *Café Espresso*. Daily 10am–7pm.

Epic Creations Old Market St, near Epic Arts ☎ 033 55552201, 🖥 epicarts.org.uk. You'll find all sorts of souvenirs here, such as bags, scarves and clothes, with profits going to Epic Arts, which provides jobs for marginalized people. Daily 10am–5pm.

Kepler's Kampot Books Old Market St, north side ☎ 012 306410, 🖥 bit.ly/keplerskampot. A great selection of new and secondhand books, with a good range on Cambodia, as well as souvenirs and Kampot pepper products. Daily 8am–7pm.

5

JolieJolie Near Captain Chim's, off Old Market St ☎ 092 936867, ⓦ joliejolie-kampot.com. This beauty salon also sells one-off trinkets as well as cotton and silk clothing designed by the Khmer owner's French husband. Daily 10.30am–7pm.

Tiny Kampot Pillows East side of 2000 Monument junction ☎ 097 7666094, ⓦ tinykampotpillows.com. Lovely collection of locally made silk *kramas* (scarves), cushions and pillows, plus bags, placemats, photos and prints. Daily 10am–7pm.

DIRECTORY

Books In addition to Kepler's Kampot Books (above), *Bandini's* (☎ 087 923623, ⓦ bandiniskampot.com) guesthouse has a stash of 2500 books and does 2-for-1 swaps.

Cinema Ecran Movie House on Old Market St, north side (☎ 093 249411) has a big cinema room with regular screenings of Cambodian films and Hollywood flicks ($3). Alternatively, rent one of three a/c movie rooms ($3.50pp/per movie) and choose from 1700-plus films. Wed–Mon 11am–10pm. Closed Tues.

Hospital The Sonja Kill Memorial Hospital (ⓦ skmh.org), 7km west of town, is staffed by highly qualified Khmer- and English-speaking doctors. For medication, try Marany

Pharmacy, part of the guesthouse of the same name, on Salt Workers Roundabout.

Money There's an Acleda Bank near the Kampot Traditional Music School and an ABA bank one block south. Canadia Bank is by the Durian roundabout. There are money changers around the Old Market and an ATM opposite *Fish market bar*.

Post office The post office is on Riverside Rd, south of the old bridge, next to Rikitikitavi.

Supermarkets For toiletries and basic goods, Mittapheap Mart (daily 7am–9pm) by Salt Workers Roundabout and Darawin on St 724/Old Market (daily 7am–10pm). The Daily Meat on Old Market St sells locally made bread and imported cheeses.

Around Kampot

Kampot province is one of Cambodia's most picturesque, its landscape ranging from the cloud-topped mountains of **Bokor National Park**, an extraordinary deserted hill station that's fallen into the hands of developers, to salt flats and rural villages. Kampot is an ideal base for these nature-based attractions, including **rapids**, **temple caves**, the salt fields of **Fish Isle** and the region's famed **pepper plantations**.

Teuk Chhou Zoo

8km northeast of Kampot, on the west bank of the Teuk Chhou River

A long-standing campaign to close **Teuk Chhou Zoo** advises visitors not to support it, due to the appalling conditions provided for the animals, which include elephants, lemurs and gibbons. Check Ears Asia (ⓦ earsasia.org) for further developments.

BOKOR NATIONAL PARK

The story of **Bokor National Park**, 42km west of Kampot, is a fascinating but sad one. Wandering through the crumbling, chilling remnants of the 1920s **French colonial hill station**, often swathed in thick fog, remains a huge tourist attraction, even though in 2007 Hun Sen's government effectively sold the mountain in its entirety to the Sokimex Group for $100m. The Chinese conglomerate now owns a 99-year lease and has begun an extravagant development project that will see the refurbishment of the dilapidated hill station (which was also the scene of a dramatic showdown between the Khmer Rouge and the Vietnamese in 1979) and the construction of hotels (they've finished one already, as well as a neighbouring casino), numerous villas, golf courses, a cable car and water parks. Plans extend to the coast, where a major port is being built with a view to landing cruise ships before helicoptering guests to the plateau.

A 32km toll road carving a thick ribbon of tarmac into the steep hillside has been finished and development appears to be gaining pace. It's easy to avoid, for now, and well worth exploring the mountain's old relics, tea farm and two waterfalls before they become a thing of the past. Hire a moto with/without driver (it's too steep for tuk-tuks) or book a tour (see p.276).

FROM TOP CRAB FISHING, KEP (P.283); KAMPOT RIVER >

5

Teuk Chhou Rapids

8km northeast of Kampot, on the west bank of Teuk Chhou River • $2 for foreigners; $2 to cross the bridge • Moto from Kampot around $5

A couple of hundred metres upstream from the zoo, the river becomes more scenic, lined with durian plantations and racing down the valley and bubbling over the rocks in a series of gurgling **rapids**, the flow somewhat tamed by a Chinese-built hydroelectric dam 5km upstream. There are plenty of huts serving food and it can get rammed at weekends. Adventurous types might want to hike to **Wat Ey Sey** from here, an isolated, under-visited pagoda up a rocky, steep path.

Phnom Chhnork

12km northeast of Kampot • $1 for foreigners • Hiring a moto/tuk-tuk from Kampot to Phnom Chhnork and Phnom Sorsia (see below) costs $8/$10; organized "countryside tours" from $10 often include Phnom Chhnork. If you rent a motorbike ($4–6), take the road to Kep, turn left after about 6km, signposted through a portico, then head along a well-made but unsurfaced road to the hill (another 6km)

The Hindu cave temple of **Phnom Chhnork** is the closest cave system to Kampot. The entrance to the hill is through **Wat Ang Sdok**, where you can leave your motorbike with a local boy for a few hundred riel. From here it's a walk of around 1km or so through fields of well-tended vegetable plots to the foot of the hill. Intrepid types can explore a couple of poky holes before venturing up the rickety steps, passing a group of pagoda buildings, to the main caves. Child guides don't usually have much information, but for a dollar, they have torches and can help you navigate inside. Peering through the gloom, you will see a brick-built **pre-Angkor prasat**; the rock seems to be trying to claim the ruin, which is slowly being coated with limestone as water drips down. Wear sturdy shoes.

Phnom Sorsia

$1 • 16km southeast of Kampot • Hiring a moto/tuk-tuk from Kampot to here and Phnom Chhnork (see above) will cost $8/$10; If you rent your own motorbike ($4–6), take NR33 towards Kep for around 14km before turning left (signposted in blue and white) through another grand portico. A dirt track leads after 1km to the foot of the hill

The **Phnom Sorsia** caves sit within a hillside Buddhist complex; from the summit, panoramic views stretch across the province and the ocean towards the Vietnamese island of Phu Quoc.

From the pagoda, turn left at the top of the staircase and follow the rocky path for 50m to reach **Ruhng Dhumrey Saw** (White Elephant Cave), which has a seated Buddha

---

KAMPOT PEPPER

Until the 1960s, **Kampot pepper** was renowned worldwide. First documented in the 1200s by Chinese explorers, the native Indian vine was transported to Cambodia in the nineteenth century during the French protectorate. It flourished in the tropical climate and rich soil around Kampot, gaining a reputation for flavour and medicinal properties until the bruising civil war and Khmer Rouge years of the 1970s saw plantations abandoned.

It's now back in the game. Following the organic farming techniques of the Kampot Pepper Promotion Association, the region's plantations are again producing high-quality black, red and white peppers which are hand-harvested and sun-dried. However, it's the fresh green peppercorns, which can't be dried and must be consumed soon after picking, that are the regional speciality. In 2010, Kampot pepper became the first Cambodian product to gain PGI (Protected Geographical Indication) status and in 2016, the first to receive Protected Designation of Origin from the European Union. *La Plantation* (☎017 842505, ⓦkampotpepper.com) by Secret Lake and *Sothy's Farm* on the road to Kompong Trach (☎088 9513505, ⓦmykampotpepper.asia) both offer guided tours and have a shop and café. Take a tuk-tuk or visit on an organized countryside tour.

statue just inside the entrance. Head down the rickety steps into the cave proper where you'll see the large cream-and-grey rock formation, vaguely resembling an elephant's head, which gives the cave its name. Back at the main steps, take the path to the right, which, after about 150m, leads to the far side of the hill and **Leahng Bpodjioh** (Bat Cave) and the ear-splitting sound of squeaking bats. The stench of ammonia is overpowering – watch, you don't get guano in your eyes if you look up. This cave is smaller and darker than Ruhng Dhumrey Saw, although a few shafts of light highlight the tree roots poking down spookily from the roof of the chamber. Back outside, you may be able to spot the monkeys that live in the woods on the hillside, while from the top of the hill there's a good view over the rice paddies along the coast. Wear sturdy shoes and take a torch.

Kep

Back in the 1960s, when Sihanoukville was just a fishing village, **KEP**, 25km from Kampot, was an affluent seaside resort, known as Kep-Sur-Mer – a cool escape for the colonial French. Subsequent events before, during and after the Khmer Rouge years, were unkind to the town, but today, it's making a spirited comeback as both a day-trip destination from Kampot and a weekend getaway. The beach is decent, but that's not the biggest draw. Cambodians largely come for the **food**, particularly the offerings at Psar K'dam, the **crab market**, while foreigners linger to enjoy Kep's mellow atmosphere and explore the offshore Islands and beautiful countryside.

Traces of the town's sombre past remain. The region is dotted with the gutted shells of 1960s **colonial villas**, tragic evidence of both Khmer Rouge destruction and postwar ransacking for building materials. Until recently, most were smothered by prolific tropical vegetation and home to squatters; now some have been restored, with more likely to follow, although establishing ownership is challenging.

On a lighter note, Kep's distinct **monuments** are worth seeking out, from the White Horse, Yeay Mao and Vishnu statues located on roundabouts to the enormous "Welcome to Kep" crab structure jutting out of the sea.

Colonial villas

Between the Yeay Mao statue and Rabbit Island pier are several **colonial villas** that were deliberately wrecked by the Khmer Rouge and left to be swallowed up by the jungle. Dating back to Kep's golden era of the 1960s, many of these modern gems were inspired by the Swiss-French modernist architect Le Corbusier. You'll also see plenty of ostentatious government buildings and a vast hilltop mansion belonging to a government minister. If you only seek out one, make it the **Queen's Palace** opposite *Breezes* restaurant, which King Norodom Sihanouk built but never stayed in.

Kep National Park

On the hill behind Kep, you can get away from it all and enjoy fantastic views over the province and bay along an 8km track through **Kep National Park** ($1; access behind *Veranda Natural Resort*). The hike to the summit takes about an hour and a half, or you can go around the mountain in two to three hours; there are viewpoints and benches aplenty. The *Led Zep Café* (daily 10am–5pm), 300m inside the park, is a useful refreshment stop, serving delicious pancakes. The French owner is a long-time Kep resident, an authority on local wildlife and responsible for many of the park's trails and signs. Pick up his park map here plus information on other walks, including a hike to 182m-high Sunset Rock; take a torch for the return.

5

White Horse Monument & Kampot

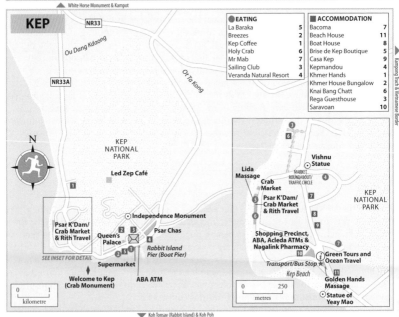

Koh Tonsay (Rabbit Island) & Koh Poh

ARRIVAL AND DEPARTURE

KEP

By moto/tuk-tuk A moto/tuk-tuk to Kampot costs $10/$15, or to the Vietnam border, $12/$18.

By bus Phnom Penh Sorya sometimes stop in Kep en route to Kampot but it's best to check schedules. There are plenty of motos by Kep Beach to take you to your guesthouse.
Destinations Kampot (5 daily; 1hr); Phnom Penh (7 daily; 3–4hr).

By minibus Several companies, including Cambodia Post and Rith Travel, operate from Kep to the Vietnam border, Kampot, Sihanoukville and Phnom Penh.
Destinations Ha Tien (daily; 2hr); Kampot (5 daily; 1hr); Phnom Penh (8 daily; 3hr); Sihanoukville (3 daily; 3hr).

By boat Crab Shuttle, a converted fishing boat, travels from Kampot ($9.50 one-way) and can include Rabbit Island (☎088 8296644, ⊛bit.ly/crabshuttle).

INFORMATION AND TOURS

Activities Kep Tours (☎071 8604528, ⊛bit.ly/keptours) and Kep Autrement (☎096 9903745, ✉kepautrement @gmail.com) offer motorbike countryside tours and boat trips. For watersports, visit The Sailing Club (☎078 737995, ⊛knaibangchatt.com/the-sailing-club), while Kep Plantation (☎097 8474960, ⊛kep-plantation.com) offers horseriding from $12 and ranch accommodation ($25).

Information The tourist office near Kep Beach isn't hugely informative. Of the many travel agents, Rith Travel (☎016 789994, ✉rithtravel@hotmail.com) is particularly helpful; others include Anny Travel (☎097 9061644, ✉annatours10@yahoo.com), Green Tours (☎036 6303666, ✉greentours2010@yahoo.com) and Ocean Travel (☎070 537272), most clustered around the shopping precinct at Kep Beach, a few at the crab market. Free listings booklet *Coastal* is also helpful.

Travel and tour operators Most operators offer similar things; countryside tours, fishing/snorkelling trips, Rabbit Island, transport to Phu Quoc/Vietnam border plus visa assistance.

ACCOMMODATION

Kep **accommodation** ranges from stunning converted villas to rustic guesthouses. Options are spread widely, near Kep Beach, along the road east of town, towards the national park and near the Rabbit Island pier.

Bacoma Road 33a, near Kep Beach ☎088 4112424, ⊛bacoma.weebly.com. Rooms, bungalows, huts and a Khmer house scattered within lush gardens. Round huts have shared bathrooms, the rest are en-suite. The lovely laidback bar and restaurant is where guests tend to congregate. $15

5

KEP ORIENTATION

Kep is a sprawling place. The road for town branches away from NR33 at the prominent **White Horse Monument**, from where it's 5 or 6km to the right turn to **Psar K'Dam**, the crab market. From here, the road runs along the seafront for about 1km to **Kep Beach**, where the narrow, dark-sand beach broadens out fractionally. Set back in a circular precinct is the transport stop, along with several hotels, restaurants, ATMS, local stores and the ubiquitous huts with mats and hammocks much-loved by Cambodians. To get back to the **crab market**, the one-way system dictates that you head north away from the beach and take the first left at the roundabout. East of Kep, the paved road runs past the local market towards Kompong Trach and the **Vietnamese border**, and the crossing at Prek Chak (for Ha Tien and Phu Quoc).

★**Beach House** Centre of Kep, near the beach ☎012 712750, ⓦbeachhousekep.com. Stylish, shabby-chic beach decor, smart a/c rooms, some with sea views, plus a pool and breakfast give this place a definite edge. There's also a jacuzzi, spa and excellent restaurant (salads $5, fish tartare $7.50) and $2 cocktails during happy hour (5–7pm). $15

Boat House Road 33a, a 7min walk from Kep Beach ☎077 430298, ⓦbit.ly/boathousekepbeach. Good option with pool, gardens and twelve lovely rooms (the cheapest have cold-water showers) plus rooms inside a traditional Khmer house. The friendly owner organizes barbecue night, and the regular food is good too. $10

Brise de Kep Boutique Near Rabbit Island pier ☎012 377460, ⓦbit.ly/brisedekep. Upmarket sister hotel to the *Brise de Kep* hotel-restaurant by Kep Beach; this one has lovely sea-facing a/c rooms, a sea-view restaurant and shaded day-beds on the beach. $25

★**Casa Kep** Road 33a, a 5min walk from Kep Beach ☎089 653593, ⓦbit.ly/casakep. There's a sociable feel at *Casa Kep*, run by Danny and Sara. The bungalow, family room and terrace room are nicely decorated and all have immaculate bathrooms. Meals aren't included but highly recommended – Danny is a trained chef. $25

Kepmandou Old Casino Road after Rabbit Island pier ☎097 7958723, ⓦbit.ly/kepmandou. Lively backpacker hangout with cheap beds including rooftop hammocks, mattress dorms and rooms including an en-suite ($15) with balcony. Plus pool table, movie room and late-night terrace bar; non-guests welcome. Hammocks $3; dorms $4, doubles $4

Khmer Hands Base of Kep National Park ☎088

2150011, ⓔinfo.khmerhands@gmail.com. Part-resort, part-hospitality training centre with thirteen wood, stone and grass bungalows, the cheapest have private (outside) bathrooms. An excellent craft shop sells products made by students and the sunset restaurant is very good. $10

★**Khmer House Bungalow** Northwest of Rabbit Island pier ☎097 3677745, ⓦbit.ly/khmerhouse. Family-run place with six en-suite Khmer-style bungalows with hot water and fan, all (except one) have balconies with a view of the mountain or the garden. An all-day restaurant and bar serves home-cooked Khmer and Western food (around $3) with ingredients from the organic garden. $10

Knai Bang Chatt On the coast down a track near the one-way system ☎078 888556, ⓦknaibangchatt.com. Three colonial villas have been converted into an exclusive resort with eleven boutique rooms, beautifully furnished in cool linen and polished stone. There's an inviting pool and bar, an acclaimed restaurant, and grounds that stretch down to the beach where there are shaded day-beds. Booking essential. $180

Rega Guesthouse A block south of the main road, close to Rabbit Island pier ☎097 3839064, ⓦkeprega .net. The thirteen en-suite rooms are well built, centred within a jungle garden with a good restaurant. The dorms and rooms (with shared bathroom) in a Khmer-style house are a recent addition. Dorms $5; doubles $8

Saravoan Kep Beach ☎036 6393909, ⓦsaravoanhotel -kep.com. This sixteen-room beachfront hotel is excellent value: rooms have warm stone and wicker features, a/c and hot-water showers, and there's a sea-view pool, sunset bar and café. $30

EATING, DRINKING & NIGHTLIFE

Kep doesn't really do **nightlife**. What there is mostly confined to Kepmandou's late-night bar, a couple of restaurant-bars by the crab market, and a new but promising live music rock bar by Kep Beach. It does have some good restaurants however, with **crab** the local speciality. Pick up barbecued seafood at the **crab market** or try one of many restaurants nearby. For basics, there's a supermarket by Rabbit Island pier.

La Baraka Crab market strip ☎097 4612543, ⓦbit.ly /labaraka. A little blue-lit respite from seafood, with good pizza (Margherita $7), great steaks and other Western food in a nicely decorated restaurant overlooking Bokor; it turns

into a decent little bar later in the evening. Daily 9.30am–10pm.

★**Breezes** Along the coast between Rock Royal Hotel and Rabbit Island pier ☎097 7243324,

5

ⓦ bit.ly/breezeskep. This excellent Swiss-run beachside restaurant serves fusion food – pork in caramel, Thai dumplings, and fish and seafood dishes such as tartare and ceviche. There's also a very good wine list. Daily noon–11pm.

Kep Coffee Café By Rabbit Island pier. ⊕ 089 612481 ⓦ bit.ly/kepcoffee. The best coffee in Kep ($1.50), and equally tasty sandwiches and home-made cakes. Menu also includes breakfasts, fajitas and tacos. Daily 7am–6pm. Closed Monday.

Holy Crab Crab market strip. ⊕ 086 366994, ⓦ bit.ly /holycrabkep. Atmospheric restaurant serving creative dishes such as crabmeat curry ($8) and crab in lemon cream sauce ($12.50). There's a lovely wooden bar to prop up, and a small shop selling Kampot pepper and jewellery made by the owner. Daily 8.30am–10.30pm.

Mr Mab Spring Valley Resort, below Kep National Park ⊕ 036 6666673, ⓦ springvalley-resort.com. The original Mr Mab (there are two more by the crab market) remains highly rated for fish. Two-for-one cocktails 5–7pm and a fun street-food event on Saturdays ($12 per person). Smart bungalows too ($45). Daily noon–3pm, 6pm–10pm.

★ **Sailing Club** Next to Knai Bang Chatt ⊕ 078 737995, ⓦ knaibangchatt.com/the-sailing-club. Make time for sunset happy-hour cocktails (5–7pm) at this stunning location by the sea. Food is good if pricey (Khmer curry $8.50, crab linguine $9) and there's a new cocktail lounge-bar (4pm–late). Daily 7am–10pm.

Veranda Natural Resort Kep Hillside Road ⊕ 097 3720185, ⓦ veranda-resort.asia. Even if you're not staying here (suites $70), have a beer in *The Secret* bar and restaurant which overlooks wild jungle fauna, dilapidated villas and across to Bokor. Relax in the Bookstore Lounge with coffee and cakes. The garden pool is $8 for non-guests. Daily 7am–9pm.

DIRECTORY

Massage Lida Khmer Massage by the crab market ($6/hr, 9am–10pm, ⊕ 012 347654, ⓦ bit.ly/kepmassage) offers a wide range of massage including traditional Khmer; Golden Hands Massage at Kep Beach is very good value ($5/hr, 10am–11pm, ⊕ 017 855200).

Money ABA and Acleda Banks have ATMs by Kep Beach and there's a Wing bank to change money. ABA ATMs at the crab market and by Rabbit Island pier.

Pharmacy Naga Pharmalink by Kep Beach.

Kep's offshore islands

The beaches in Kep aren't the most glorious, but the offshore islands are only a short boat ride away. Closest is **Koh Tonsay** (Rabbit Island), with three nice beaches; further out, **Koh Poh** (Coral Island) has white sands, turquoise water, coral reefs and great snorkelling. The huge island dominating the horizon is **Phu Quoc**, in Vietnamese waters; locals call it Koh Tral, dating back to when it belonged to Cambodia (although it's unclear when that was).

Koh Tonsay

A thirty-minute journey from the mainland, **Koh Tonsay**, or **Rabbit Island**, is a peaceful paradise of pale sand, clear waters and lofty palms, lined with massage pavilions, restaurants and rustic no-fan, no-electricity bungalows. Just 8km in circumference, it has stretches of beach around the southwestern side that take you further from the crowds. It's a good day out, but it's even lovelier after 4pm, when the final day-tripper boat has disappeared behind the peninsula and you're left behind with a few other shipwrecked souls, a cold beer and the sun heading gently for the horizon.

ARRIVAL AND INFORMATION   KEP'S OFFSHORE ISLANDS

Boats can be arranged through Kep's guesthouses or at Rabbit Island pier.

To Koh Tonsay The boat (30min) should cost no more than $8, including pick-up, and leaves around 9am, returning at 4pm – although you can pay a couple of dollars to leave earlier. Some operators offer lunch, guided walks and snorkelling, (the latter not that good), cheap restaurants are plentiful, and you can explore the island

yourself along the rocky path that circumnavigates it.
To Koh Poh and around The 2hr trip to Koh Poh is on a traditional fishing boat, *Les Copains d'Abord*, and costs around $50 (⊕ 097 623 6176, ⓦ lescopainsdabordkep .com). There's also a five-island tour from $25, which includes lunch.

Kompong Trach

5

East of Kep, amid stunning karst landscapes, lies the friendly, dusty town of
KOMPONG TRACH, 35km east of Kampot and 21km from Kep on NR33. The main
attraction is **Wat Kirisehla**, 5km outside town, home to a reclining Buddha in a
natural cavity in the limestone hills. However, if you have time en route, stop at
the beautifully empty stretch of **Angkoul Beach.** There's a small temple on the hill
behind the beach – you'll see the temple from the road and that's where you turn
right for the coast.

Kompong Trach itself offers a slice of local life and you can get food and drink at the
market and a couple of restaurants, all of which are opposite the main pagoda in the
middle of town.

Wat Kirisehla

$1 • From Kompong Trach, take the turning north off the main road, about 100m east of the market; the road passes the hospital/medical
centre before heading into rice fields, towards a large craggy hill

Before you reach **Wat Kirisehla**, you may well be approached by smiling children
offering guided tours, who are usually happy to be paid a dollar or so. They don't
have any real knowledge, but some have torches and can show you such dubious
relics as the blood of Buddha on the cave floor. If you're exploring alone, you'll need
a torch, as the 100m-long tunnel to the centre of the hill is rather dark. Many of the
formations have names; look out for the **elephant**, past the entrance, and a **tortoise**
just beyond it. There's also an eagle and snake – you may have to use your
imagination. The centre of the hill is an almost circular cavity, open to the elements
and ringed by high cliffs whose walls are eroded into caves. The large **reclining
Buddha** is a recent replacement for one destroyed by Khmer Rouge soldiers who
holed up here for years without being rumbled. It's all quite eye-catching but if water
levels are high, you may not get very far.

Takeo province

Much of **Takeo province** disappears in an annual inundation by the waters of the
Mekong and Bassac rivers, leaving **Takeo town** isolated on the shore of a vast inland
sea, with outlying villages transformed into islands. As the waters recede, an ancient
network of canals, which once linked the area to the trading port of Oc Eo (now a
ruined site across the Vietnam border), is revealed. These continue to be vital for local
communication and trade, and getting around the area is still easiest by boat – indeed,
for much of the year there is no alternative.

Takeo town

A key port on the trading route with Vietnam, the town of **TAKEO** (pronounced
ta-kow) consists of two separate hives of activity: to the south a dusty (or muddy,
depending on the season) town market and transport stop on NR2, and to the north
a more picturesque area around the **Rokha Khnong Lake**, canal and port. Most banks
and shops are located around the Independence Monument, a ten-minute walk
from the canal.

Takeo makes a good base from which to visit the only **Funanese** sites so far identified
in Cambodia, **Angkor Borei** and the nearby **Phnom Da**, which can be combined on a
boat trip from town; an informative museum at Angkor Borei displays artefacts and
statues unearthed at both sites. Since Takeo is only two hours from Phnom Penh, it's
possible to visit these sights on a day-trip.

5

Rokha Khnong Lake

Southwest of the canal, a park with views over the marshy, lily-covered **Rokha Khnong Lake** makes a pleasant spot for an early morning or sunset stroll. Occupying a beautiful spot in the middle of the lake is the home of former Khmer Rouge chief of staff, **Ta Mok**, nicknamed "The Butcher". Built in 1976 for seclusion and protection, until recently it was used as a police training facility; you can't enter the building, but you can cross the bridge and stroll in the grounds.

The port

At Takeo's **port** large wooden boats arrive from Vietnam laden with cheap terracotta tiles destined for Phnom Penh; the vessels are easily identified by the protective all-seeing eye painted on their bows. Takeo's colonial past is evident in the crumbling square behind the waterfront, and there's a small market, **Psar Nat**, which is busy in the early morning and late afternoon with local farmers and fisherfolk. The town's shophouses are sadly neglected, but still retain a discernible sense of French style.

ARRIVAL AND INFORMATION

TAKEO TOWN

By minibus or shared taxi There are few, if any, scheduled routes to Takeo now. A private taxi costs $30 from Phnom Penh; to see if any minibuses and shared taxis are heading there, ask at your guesthouse or travel agent, or go early to Phnom Penh's Central Market.

By train A train service (see box, p.76) now runs between Takeo and Phnom Penh (2hr), Kampot (3hr) and Sihanoukville (5hr 30min), on Fri, Sat, Sun and public holidays. Buy tickets ($4–7) at the station (📞078 888582, 🌐royal-railway.com).

Money ABA and Acleda banks by the Independence Monument and Canadia Bank with ATM after the new market Psar Chas, 3km from Takeo's centre.

Pharmacy Next to *Mittapheap Guesthouse* by the Independence Monument.

Tourist office By the town market (📞032 931323, 📧takeotourism007@gmail.com). It's not always open, but it does have some useful information. Mon–Fri 8–11am & 2.30–5.30pm.

ACCOMMODATION

7 Days In Hotel Between Independence Monument and Two Lions junction 📞087 997001, 🌐7daysinhotel .com. The smart a/c rooms come with fridge and flatscreen TV, and the modern bathrooms have hot-water rainshowers. Free steam and sauna are also provided. $15

Alice Villa Hotel Past boat dock road, after Daunkeo Guesthouse 📞032 210211, 🌐alicevilla.com. A surprising find in Takeo, with lovely rooms set around a pretty courtyard. The restaurant is also recommended (daily 7am–8pm) serving good coffee, breakfast and Khmer dishes for $3. $15

Daunkeo Guesthouse On canal near boat dock 📞032 210303, 📧info@daunkeo.com, 🌐daunkeo.com. Clean, no-frills fan rooms, some with a/c, all with hot water.

Decent restaurant and outdoor seating. Some English-speaking staff though it's easier to email. Fan $6; a/c $15

★ **Meas Family Homestay** Prey Theat, 2km from Ang Ta Som Market (intersection NR3 & NR33) 📞016 781415, 🌐cambodianhomestay.com. Absorb Takeo's rural ambience at Linda Meas' community-minded family-run homestay amid paddy fields. There are simple bungalows and rooms, pond-side hammocks, and free bikes. Meals are included and are communal, prepared by resident cook Paul who also organizes social enterprise projects such as weaving cooperatives. Guests can assist with teaching English or even the paddy harvest (June–Dec). Per person $18

EATING

Eating options are reasonably limited, but ample. For cheap eats, try the night market along the northern waterfront road, while the shacks along the lakeside promenade are good for seafood dishes and freshwater lobster (Aug–Nov).

Delikes Restaurant Near the market 📞032 4540345. Serving Western breakfasts, beef *lok lak* ($2) and pizzas ($4), plus $1 shakes and 50c ice cream. Daily 7am–7pm.

Le Petit Bistro Just past Daunkeo guesthouse 📞097 9911037 🌐chezfredrestaurantbartakeo.blog spot.com. This courtyard bistro, also known as Fred's, offers filling breakfasts for $3.50, French-style tapas from $4.50

and excellent wines. Work up an appetite with a game of petanque. Daily 8am–9pm.

Steung Takeo Street 9, boat dock road 📞016 404929. This huge, stilted Khmer restaurant serves various fish, meat and lobster dishes from $3 plus $2 vegetable noodles. It's a good spot for a beer overlooking the floodplains. The menu is in English but little is spoken. Daily 8am–9pm.

Angkor Borei and around

The leafy town of **ANGKOR BOREI**, some 25km from Takeo, sits on the banks of the Prek Angkor, a tributary of the Bassac. It's well known to scholars as the site where the earliest known example of written Khmer was discovered, and archaeological excavations have identified many features of the **pre-Angkorian town**, including a moat 22m wide, a section of high brick wall and numerous extensive water tanks. Unfortunately, there is now little to see of the site apart from the finds in the fine local **museum**.

Angkor Borei can be reached by boat when water levels permit, 20km up a canal and river, through **wetlands** that are home to a variety of waterbirds. The museum, in the grounds of an old pagoda, is the main draw, but you can also explore the excavated Funan-era archaeological sites here and at nearby **Phnom Da**.

Angkor Borei museum

Daily 10am–4.30pm; closed in the rainy season • $1

Boats pull up on the riverside near the bridge, just downstream from the terracotta colonial building surrounded by a large garden which houses the **Angkor Borei museum**. The collection isn't extensive (the best bits are in Phnom Penh's National Museum) but it's interesting, with a diverse collection of ceramics, Vishnu and Shiva sculptures and carved Funanese-era pediments. One highlight is a pediment relief removed from Phnom Da showing Vishnu reclining on a dragon. Aerial photos show the extent of the old settlement and identify many of the features being excavated. To the left of the museum is an old, crumbling, French-colonial building, once used as a residence for monks.

Phnom Da

$2

For a site that has given its name to a style of sculpture, the remains of the temple of **Phnom Da** are rather bare; everything of value now resides in the museums in Phnom Penh and Angkor Borei. However, the eleventh-century Angkorian-era towers, made of laterite, bricks and sandstone, are still pretty imposing. Constructed on top, of two 40m-high mounds, they protected the temple from rising waters. Experts differ on the date of the temple: some say it was built in the early sixth century, others think it was later.

Boats moor at the small village at the foot of Phnom Da or further out if water levels are low. Local children may offer to guide you up the meandering paths to the top passing three of the site's five caves en route – it's said that these were used as cremation sites by the Khmer Rouge. On the higher of the two mounds is the ancient **Prasat Phnom Da**, a single laterite sandstone tower dominating the landscape, with four doorways of ornate sandstone columns and pediments of carved naga heads.

On the lower hill, to the west, is a unique Hindu temple, **Ashram Maha Rose**, dedicated to Vishnu and built of basalt stone. Dating from the seventh or eighth century, the pre-Angkorian structure is a temple in miniature, the enclosing walls so close together that there's barely room to squeeze between them. Outside, a spout pokes through the wall from where holy water, blessed by flowing over the temple's linga, would once have poured.

ARRIVAL AND DEPARTURE   ANGKOR BOREI AND AROUND

Allow a full day to do justice to Angkor Borei and Phnom Da, though a half-day trip is sufficient to get a feel for them.

By boat The easiest way to get to both Angkor Borei and Phnom Da is to hire a boat from Takeo's jetty ($35; 40min; seats up to four). The boat from Angkor Borei to Phnom Da takes about 15min.

By moto In the dry season you can also usually reach them by moto. It's a 70km round-trip via Phnom Chisor.

Contexts

History

The study of Cambodia's history is hampered by a lack of records. During the time of Angkor, the texts that filled temple libraries were written on tanned skins or palm leaves, but unfortunately these were not copied by successive generations and none has survived; inscribed stone steles at temple sites usually recorded only aspects of temple life, and even this information ceased to be compiled with the demise of Angkor. But the steles, coupled with accounts by Chinese traders and envoys, have at least allowed historians to piece together something of Cambodia's story up until the late thirteenth century.

Though foreign traders and Western missionaries in Cambodia wrote various accounts after the sixteenth century, these leave substantial periods unaccounted for. More recently, the French documented their protectorate in some detail, but their records were largely destroyed by the Khmer Rouge. What is known of Cambodia's history is thus something of a hotchpotch, and though much has been deduced, even more remains obscure and will probably never be fully known.

Beginnings

The **earliest settlements** so far uncovered in Cambodia date from 6800 BC and were situated along the coast, where the risk of annual flooding was minor and there was a ready supply of food. Hunter-gatherers were living in the caves at Leang Spean, northwest of Battambang, by 4300 BC, cultivating dry-season rice and producing ceramics, which are similar in shape and decoration to those in use today. **Neolithic** settlements uncovered at **Samrong Sen**, in central Cambodia, indicate that by 2000 BC animals had been domesticated and slash-and-burn agriculture developed. Five hundred years later, Cambodia entered the **Bronze Age** when the art of smelting copper and tin was mastered, the ores probably originating from present-day Thailand. By 500 BC, a prosperous **Iron Age** civilization was in full swing: farming, implements and weapons were produced, and skills for working with ceramics, metal and glass were being refined. The population slowly divided: highland dwellers continued growing only rainy-season rice, while lowland settlers farmed the river valleys and coastal strips, where they learned to make use of the floods, conserving water for dry-season irrigation and prospering from the fertile soils deposited.

Funan

Cambodia's first large-scale civilization developed during the first century AD with the emergence of the kingdom of **Funan**, centred on the Mekong Delta and spreading across what is now southern Vietnam and southeastern Cambodia. Little is known about Funan – and much of what is known comes from the scant and perhaps

6800 BC	**2000 BC**	**1st century AD**
Earliest recorded evidence of human settlement in Cambodia	Neolithic settlements at Samrong Sen show evidence of primitive agriculture and domesticated livestock	Origins of the state of Funan, on the Gulf of Thailand, one of Southeast Asia's earliest large-scale civilizations

unreliable writings of Chinese merchants and travellers. It remains unclear whether Funan was a single unified kingdom or a collection of autonomous small states; where its capital was (if it had one); what language(s) its people spoke; or even what it was called (Funan is a Chinese rather than a Southeast Asian name). The ethnic identity of the Funanese is similarly mysterious, although they most likely comprised a mixture of **Mon** and **Khmer** peoples, the latter a dark-skinned tribe who had migrated from the north along the Mekong, and from whom Cambodians today trace their origins.

What is known is that Funan was an affluent and sophisticated society with major centres at Angkor Borei, Banteay Prei Nokor and Prey Veng (in Cambodia) and Óc Eo (in Vietnam). The Funanese maintained a powerful navy, constructed large-scale canals for irrigation and drainage, amassed extensive libraries of palm-leaf Sanskrit books and became skilful metalworkers in bronze and iron. They also exploited their location on trade routes between India and China, establishing wide-ranging commercial links, as shown by the Roman coins unearthed at various sites. The Funanese appear to have lived (like many modern Cambodians) in wooden stilt-houses, eating rice, fish and cultivated fruits. Cockfighting was a popular diversion, while the legal system involved trials-by-ordeal during which suspects were thrown into crocodile-infested canals and proved innocent only if they emerged unscathed.

Funan was also a heavily Indianized society, establishing a cultural pattern which would endure throughout the Angkorian period and beyond (the name "Cambodia", from Kambujadesa, is itself of Sanskrit origin). Indian traders brought Hinduism to the region, with many Funanese converting to the religion, probably blended with local folk beliefs and superstitions. Rich Funanese gained merit by financing temples and by the fifth century local rulers had begun to add the Indian suffix *-varman* to their name, meaning "protector". Funan appears to have fallen into decline by the seventh century AD, for reasons unknown, and by the eighth century much of the coast formerly under Funanese control had fallen to the sultans of Java, after which the centres of Khmer power moved steadily inland.

Chenla

Following the decline of Funan, Khmer power seems to have shifted during the late sixth century to the shadowy kingdom of **Chenla** (or "Zhenla"), although, as with Funan, Chenla was probably a loose confederation of small fiefdoms rather than a single unified state. Again, details are sparse – even the location of Chenla is disputed, although it most likely lay along the Mekong Valley and surrounding regions, from the coast around modern Kampot in the south up to the Tonle Sap, and perhaps even north into Laos. Indian influence remained strong, although there is also evidence of a growing Khmer identity, as suggested by the numerous stone inscriptions dating from the period (the earliest Khmer inscription dates only from 612 AD, during the latter days of Funan). Chenla's first notable ruler was **Bhavavarman I** (reigned c. 550–590), who may have launched an attack against Funan. His successor **Ishanavarman I** (reigned 610–625) founded **Ishanapura** (named in accordance with the Indian-derived custom of naming a capital by suffixing the king's name with *-pura* – the Sanskrit word for town), home to the imposing state-temple at **Sambor Prei Kuk**, the largest in Southeast Asia at that time. Chenla power appears to have reached its apogee under the great-grandson of

2nd–3rd century	Late 6th century
Increasing influence of Indian culture and religion on Funan, with many of the region's native Khmer converted to Hinduism. First temples built	The Khmer kingdom of Chenla asserts its independence from Funan. Bhavavarman establishes a new capital at Sambor Prei Kuk

Ishanavarman, **Jayavarman I** (reigned c. 657–690), who ruled over an area extending at least from modern Battambang to Prey Veng. When he was killed by invaders, probably from Java, the succession passed to his daughter, **Jayadevi**, one of only a handful of queens in Cambodian history, despite the fact that women were regarded as equals, and inheritance of property, slaves and lands passed through the female line.

The Angkor empire

Chenla appeared to have become increasingly fragmented during and after the reign of Jayadevi, entering almost a century of confusion and obscurity before the arrival of **Jayavarman II** (r. 802–835). Originally a noble or minor king from southeastern Cambodia, Jayavarman and his followers at some point left their homeland and began heading northwest across the country, subduing the old Funanese centres of Vyadhapura and Banteay Prei Nokor and forging alliances en route before eventually arriving in the Angkor region. It was at Phnom Kulen, near Angkor, in **802 AD** that Jayavarman proclaimed himself a **devaraja**, or "god king" (a tradition followed by all subsequent Angkorian monarchs). He then founded a new capital at Hariharalaya (aka Yasodharapura, in the area of present-day Roluos), the first city in the region which would later be known as **Angkor** (the name derives from the Sanskrit nagara, meaning simply "city").

Whatever the details, Jayavarman seemed to have succeeded in finally unifying the myriad Khmer micro-states into a coherent kingdom, known as Kambuja-desa. Angkor would go on to become Cambodia's first and only empire, a great multi-ethnic realm stretching from southern Vietnam and the South China Sea, across almost all of modern-day Thailand and into Myanmar and Laos. At its height, the sprawling city of Angkor was the wonder of its age, with a population of around a million people spread over an area of 1000 square kilometres or more.

Twenty-eight kings of Angkor succeeded Jayavarman over the next 600 years. All were regarded as living gods (but were regularly overthrown, even so). Successive rulers constructed great reservoirs and hydraulic systems, irrigating huge tracts of land and allowing the production of as many as four rice crops annually, creating a food surplus capable of supporting the empire's burgeoning numbers of nobles, priests and the thousands of labourers tasked with building its myriad temples. A network of well-maintained roads linked distant parts of the empire, built on stone causeways above floodplains, with travellers' rest houses en route, while an efficient army (supplemented by local peasants as need arose) enabled Angkor to keep their powerful Cham and, later, Thai neighbours largely at bay.

Angkor in the ascendant

Jayavarman II was succeeded by his son, **Jayavarman III** (r. 835–877), and then by **Indravarman I** (r. 877–889). The first of Angkor's great builders, Indravarman was responsible for the city's first great reservoir, the Indratataka *baray* (lake/reservoir) at Roluos and the great temples of Preah Ko and Bakong, both larger than any religious monument previously constructed in mainland Southeast Asia. Indravarman's son, **Yasovarman I** (r. 889–900) constructed the first state-temple in the Angkor area proper, on the hill of Phnom Bakheng, along with the massive East Baray reservoir, which was more than 7km long and almost 2km wide.

Early 7th century	**795**
Ishanavarman I (reigned 610–625) builds numerous temples at Sambor Prei Kuk, which develops into the greatest of Cambodia's pre-Angkorian capitals	Jayavarman II declares himself devaraja ("god king") and has himself consecrated in an elaborate ceremony at his new capital at Phnom Kulen

Angkor's imperial ambitions grew during the forceful reign of **Rajendravarman I** (r. 944–968), who waged war against the Cham (from the state of Champa in present-day central and southern Vietnam) and annexed neighbouring states, while his son **Jayavarman V** (r. 968–1001) succeeded in extending Angkorian territory into what is now northeast Thailand. **Suryavarman I** (r. 1011–50) oversaw further territorial expansion, reaching as far as Louvo (modern Lopburi) in present-day Thailand. He also left a substantial legacy including the temple of Preah Vihear and the massive West Baray reservoir, while his successor, **Udayadityavarman II** (r. 1050–66), added the huge Baphuon temple.

Brief turmoil followed the death of Udayadityavarman, with rival "kings" battling for control of Angkor before order was restored, ushering in the extended reign of **Suryavarman II** (1113–50), who commissioned the mighty Angkor Wat and oversaw one of the empire's golden periods, with control over lands stretching from Champa to the Gulf of Thailand.

Jayavarman VII and the triumph of Theravada

Jayavarman VII (r. 1181–1218) was arguably the most significant of all Khmer kings and the ruler under whom the Angkor Empire reached its pinnacle of power and extent – and perhaps revealed the first signs of fatally over-extending itself. Jayavarman seems to have seized the throne at a relatively advanced age following the brief chaos caused by two Cham invasions, the first by land in 1177 and the second by sea in 1178, during which Angkor itself was sacked.

Jayavarman eventually succeeded in defeating the Cham in 1181 and had himself crowned king. Inheriting the disorder following these attacks, Jayavarman put the empire onto an organized footing, under increasingly centralized control. Numerous public works were launched, including the construction of new roads and over a hundred hospitals employing perhaps as many as 80,000 people. Paradoxically, the cost of building and maintaining these vast schemes may actually have ending up impoverishing the very people they were intended to benefit. At the same time, Jayavarman embarked on the most spectacular of all Angkorian building sprees, with construction beginning on Ta Som, Preah Khan, Banteay Chhmar, Neak Pean and the Bayon. Jayavarman was also unusual among the mainly Hindu kings of Angkor in being a fervent Mahayana Buddhist, as attested by dozens of enigmatic faces of the bodhisattva Lokesvara which adorn his state-temple, the Bayon.

Signs of imperial decline began to emerge during the rule of Jayavarman VII's successor, **Indravarman II** (r. 1218–43), during whose reign the Khmer lost control both of Champa and of some of their Thai territories. Indravarman's rule may also have seen a revival of Hinduism as the state religion, a policy continued by **Jayavarman VIII** (r. 1243–95), who proceeded to destroy or rework many of Angkor's Buddhist images. Despite (or perhaps because of) his iconoclastic efforts, from the thirteenth century onwards Buddhism gained new impetus in the country, either as a result of the gradual decline in powers of the great Hindu god-kings of Angkor, or perhaps due to increasing contact with the Mon and Thai peoples who had been absorbed into the empire. The Thai and Mon's particular brand of **Theravada Buddhism** gained a ready audience and numerous converts, and by the mid-fourteeth century Cambodia had become the essentially Buddhist country it remains to this day.

Late 9th century	Early 11th century
At Roluos, Indratataka Lake and the Preah Ko and Bakong temples are created during the reign of Indravarman I (877–889). His son Yasovarman I (889–900) builds Phnom Bakheng temple and the great East Baray reservoir	Suryavarman I (1011–50) further consolidates the territory of the Angkor Empire, which now stretches as far as Lopburi in present-day Thailand. He also builds Preah Vihear and the West Baray reservoir

DAILY LIFE IN ANGKOR

Some 1200 stone inscriptions have been found in Angkor region written in Sanskrit, Khmer and (later) Pali, the classical language of Buddhism, while bas-reliefs at the Bayon provide vivid records of ordinary Khmer life. No books from the city have survived, however, and the only written account of Angkorian life is *The Customs of Cambodia* by Chinese traveller **Zhou Daguan**, who visited the city in 1295, during the later days of empire.

There was no caste system at Angkor, but society was rigorously stratified at all levels from slaves, peasants and farmers up to nobles, the priestly elite and kings. The city's temples employed vast numbers – some 80,000 worked in some capacity for Ta Prohm, for example, including over 2500 priests alone, plus singers, dancers and musicians. The city was also home to a vast population of slaves made up of debtors, tribespeople, prisoners of war and others. Zhou Daguan reported that "only the poorest peasant did not keep at least one slave", although given that the **Angkorian peasants** were also considered property of the king or local temple, there was not always a great distinction between free and bonded, and it appears that some slaves even owned slaves of their own.

The living conditions of the ancient Angkorians were perhaps not so very different from those of modern Cambodian peasants, surviving on a diet of rice, fish and fruit and living in simple stilted houses built from wood or bamboo and thatched with palm leaves – although higher officials and nobles were allowed to cover their roofs with tiles as a mark of status. Complicated sumptuary laws also defined permissible types of clothing, although most people wore simple loincloths or *sampot*-style skirts, with both sexes going naked from the waist up. Angkorians married during their teens but were allowed to sleep with others if their husband or wife was absent for more than ten days, while girls (rather bizarrely) were ritually deflowered by a priest using his hand during a major coming-of-age ceremony held at between seven and eleven years of age.

A harsh **legal system** applied, including widespread "trial-by-ordeal" – the accused sometimes had a hand thrust into boiling water and were deemed innocent only if their skin did not peel. Criminals (including runaway slaves) might expect to have lips, hands or limbs amputated as punishment or, for the worst felonies, to be buried alive, while human sacrifices may have been performed for religious purposes. All who transgressed could expect punishment in a hell, imagined by the ancient Khmer as a place of endless and eternal freezing cold.

The decline of Angkor

Following the high-water mark of Jayavarman VII's reign, Angkor fell into a gradual decline, with many of its dependencies in Thailand, including Sukothai and Louvo, reasserting their independence. Resurgent Thai forces subsequently launched a series of attacks, eventually capturing and sacking Angkor in **1431**, the traditional date given for the final collapse of the empire.

Easy as it is to blame the Thais for the demise of Angkor, the kingdom's actual decline was in fact probably a much more protracted affair, and the reasons for it more complicated than simple military defeat. The constant drain of money and manpower poured into temple building may have been a factor, as was the growing influence of the ascetic Theravada school of Buddhism, the very antithesis of the god-king cults which had shaped the city. The main reason for the city's eventual collapse, however, was probably ecological, with the ever-growing population eventually causing fatal deforestation, resulting in a loss of soil fertility and a silting up of the complex hydraulic system – whose increasingly stagnant canals and reservoirs then became a

Early to mid-12th century	1177
Suryavarman II (1113–50) commissions the building of Angkor Wat, along with numerous other works. The empire of Angkor now stretches from Burma to Vietnam	Cham invade Angkor and sack Angkor Thom

haven for malarial mosquitoes. At any rate, Angkor endured for some time, and visiting in 1570, Dominican friar Gabriel Quiroga de San Antonio found the city still busy and reasonably prosperous.

Lovek and Oudong

By then, however, Khmer power had long since shifted to a new location. Following the sack of Angkor in 1431, **King Ponhea Yat** left Angkor and set up a new capital in **Phnom Penh**. Thai records suggest that the capital may have returned briefly to Angkor around 1467, but by the early sixteenth century **Ang Chan** (1505/1516–56) had established his court at **Lovek**. While the Thais were busy fending off advances from invading Burmese, Ang Chan gathered an army and made a successful attack on the Thais, regaining control of towns such as Pursat and Battambang, which had been lost when Angkor was abandoned.

The sixteenth century saw the arrival of the first **Western** missionaries and explorers in Cambodia; though the former were utterly unsuccessful in gaining converts, some of the latter became influential within the Khmer establishment, such as the Spanish adventurers Blas Ruiz and Diogo Veloso, whose knowledge of firearms would eventually earn them marriages with Cambodian princesses and provincial governorships under **King Satha** (1575–94). Accounts of the time, by Spanish and Portuguese colonials from the Philippines and Malacca respectively, report multicultural trading settlements at Lovek and Phnom Penh, with quarters for Chinese, Arabs, Japanese, Spanish and Portuguese; the area around these two towns was the most prosperous in the country, trading in gold, animal skins and ivory, silk and precious stones.

The Khmer court continued to face threats from the **Thais**, however, forcing King Satha to ask the Spanish in the Philippines for help, although this aid never materialized and Satha fled to Laos (where he subsequently died), while Lovek was sacked by the Thais in 1594. The succession subsequently passed rapidly to a number of kings, including **Chey Chettha**, who established a new capital at **Oudong**, between Lovek and Phnom Penh, where it would remain for some two hundred years.

Towards the end of the seventeenth century, the **Vietnamese** began to move south into Champa and, before long, into the Mekong Delta. Cambodia was now squeezed between two powerful neighbours, and over the next century the royal family aggravated matters by splitting into pro-Vietnamese and pro-Thai factions, the crown changing hands frequently.

Events took a turn for the worse in 1767 when a Thai prince sought refuge in Cambodia, intending to set up a government in exile. This incensed the Thai general, Taksin, who launched an invasion, destroyed Phnom Penh and assumed control of Cambodia for several decades. The Thais put a 7-year-old prince, **Ang Eng** (r. 1779–97), on the throne under a Thai regent, and then reinforced their influence by taking him to Bangkok, where he stayed for four years. On his return, he installed himself at Oudong, where he died in 1797, leaving four sons and a lineage that lasts to this day.

The run-up to the French protectorate

Worsening to-ing and fro-ing between the Thais and Vietnamese ultimately led to the Cambodians appealing to France for protection. Ang Eng's eldest son and heir, **Ang Chan**, was only 6 at the time of his father's death and didn't assume the throne for nine

Late 12th–early 13th century	13th century
Jayavarman VII (r. 1181–1218) defeats Cham in a great naval battle on Tonle Sap, rebuilds Angkor Thom and embarks on a spree of construction works including Ta Prohm and the Bayon	Gradual decline of Angkor under Jayavarman VII's successors. Hinduism is once again in the ascendancy, with many Buddha images defaced or destroyed. Thai forces regain large swathes of territory formerly ruled from Angkor

years. Meanwhile, the Thais annexed the province of Battambang, which then stretched as far as Siem Reap, and which remained under Thai rule until 1907. By the time he was crowned monarch, Ang Chan (r. 1806–34) had become fervently anti-Thai and requested help from the Vietnamese – who then promptly annexed the whole of the Mekong Delta and took effective control of large parts of Cambodia, with the king reduced to a puppet ruler. In 1812, Ang Chan relocated the court to Phnom Penh, from where he proceeded to send secret emissaries to Bangkok, assuring them of his continued allegiance.

In 1832 the Thai king Rama III, seizing upon the opportunity provided by the death of the Vietnamese viceroy, sent in an army to oust the Vietnamese – who had already left by the time Thai troops arrived, taking Ang Chan with them. The Thais sought to install as king one of Ang Chan's two brothers who had been living in exile in Bangkok, but later abandoned the idea, unable to gain any popular support for either of them. The Vietnamese returned to Phnom Penh a couple of years later, while keeping Ang Chan under close supervision; he died shortly afterwards, leaving no male heir. They duly installed Chan's second daughter, **Mei**, as queen (r. 1835–41), thinking she would be malleable, and set about imposing Vietnamese culture and customs on the Cambodians. Their disregard for Theravada Buddhism and their attempts to enforce the use of the Vietnamese language sowed deep resentment, and anti-Vietnamese riots flared repeatedly from 1836.

Losing patience, the Vietnamese blamed Queen Mei for their own failure to install a disciplined Vietnamese-style administration, and arrested her in 1840. Though the Cambodians had not liked being forced to accept a Vietnamese-appointed queen, they now resented her detention and rioted again. Thai troops poised on the border marched in and forced the Vietnamese out, and despite sporadic skirmishes the Vietnamese never regained control and withdrew from the whole of Cambodia in 1847. The following year, Chan's brother, **Duang** (r. 1848–59), was crowned king at Oudong with full Buddhist ceremony.

Meanwhile, the **French** had arrived in Southeast Asia, but were rebuffed in their attempt to establish trading arrangements with Vietnam. On the pretext that French missionaries were being persecuted, they invaded the Mekong Delta, annexing the southern provinces of Vietnam. In Cambodia, Duang feared another Vietnamese invasion and asked the French for help; they eventually sent a diplomatic mission but it was turned back before it could reach him at Oudong, and Duang died before any discussions could be held, leaving it to **Norodom** (r. 1859–1904) to agree a treaty with the French in 1863.

The French protectorate

Norodom's **treaty** with France afforded Cambodia French protection in exchange for wide-ranging mineral and timber rights, along with freedom for the French to preach Christianity. Riots, however, began flaring in the provinces against Norodom and the French, who pressed for a new treaty allowing them to install administrative **residents** in all provincial centres – effectively taking over the day-to-day running of the country. Rebellion sprang up across the nation, which the French, even with the assistance of Vietnamese troops, had difficulty in quelling. Despite this resistance a new treaty was

1432	Early 16th century	1594
Thai forces sack Angkor. King Ponhea Yat abandons the ancient city and establishes a new capital at Phnom Penh	Ang Chan (r. 1505/1516 –56) establishes new court and capital at Lovek	Continuing Thai incursions culminate in the sack of Lovek. King Chey Chettha establishes a new capital at Oudong

signed in 1886, eroding much of Norodom's power and allowing the French to collect taxes and to have residents installed in ten provincial towns.

Towards the end of the century Norodom, already an opium addict, became ill, and the French *résident supérieur* was granted permission from Paris to assume executive authority. By the time Norodom died in 1904, France was effectively ruling Cambodia. Norodom's compliant half-brother **Sisowath** (r. 1904–27) was installed on the throne, the French having passed over Monivong, Norodom's son and natural heir.

The French did little to develop Cambodia's human resources but instead filled key clerical positions with Vietnamese, who also ran many of the small businesses and took labouring jobs. This neglect of the Khmer, and the crippling taxes levied by the French, bred resentment to which the French remained oblivious. They were shocked when revolts against taxation broke out in 1916, and doubly horrified when Félix Bardez – the French resident in Kompong Chhnang – was **beaten to death** by locals in 1925 while investigating resistance to tax payments in a provincial village.

World War II

The **Japanese invasion** of Southeast Asia in 1941–42 brought little change to the status quo in Indochina, where the Japanese allowed the (now Vichy) French to continue administering the day-to-day running of the country. The Thais, who were allies of the Japanese and who sensed a degree of vulnerability in the French position, took the opportunity to launch attacks across the border into Cambodia, with the aim of recovering the provinces of Battambang and Siem Reap, reluctantly given up to Cambodia earlier in the century. The French roundly defeated the Thai navy, however, forcing the Japanese to save Thai face by compelling the French administration to hand over the provinces for a nominal sum. **King Sisowath Monivong** (r. 1927–41) blamed the French for this loss of territory and refused to deal with them again – although this wasn't for long, as he died shortly afterwards. The Japanese allowed the next king to be chosen by the French who, seeking a compliant successor, passed over Monivong's son in favour of his youthful and inexperienced grandson, **Norodom Sihanouk**, who was crowned in September 1941.

Despite their hands-off approach in Indochina, the Japanese were supportive of anti-colonial feeling, partly to gain support for their own presence. The effect of these sentiments would become manifest after the Japanese surrender in August 1945, by which time they had dissolved the French administration.

Towards independence

Though the French had reinstated their officials by the end of 1945, the prewar status quo was never quite restored. The Thai government was now funding anti-Japanese and anti-French causes, and anti-royalist Cambodian groups in exile began to gather along the Thai border. A year later these factions had banded together to form the essentially left-wing **Khmer Issarak**, a band of fledgling idealists which grew into a powerful armed guerrilla movement that waged something approaching a war of independence against the French; between 1947 and 1950, the Khmer Issarak controlled fifty percent of the country.

The seeds of the movement had been sown back in the 1930s with the opening of Cambodia's first high school, the **Lycée Sisowath** in Phnom Penh, where students soon began to question the standing of educated Khmer in a country where Vietnamese

1767	1779
Thai general Taksin invades Cambodia, ransacks Phnom Penh and assumes control of the country	Ang Eng (r. 1779–97) is installed as king under Thai patronage, establishing a royal lineage which endures to this day

dominated the middle levels of the administration. When the first Khmer-language **newspaper**, *Nagara Vatta*, was launched (Khmer had hitherto been used only for the publication of religious texts), it was aimed at these newly educated Cambodians, propounding Khmer nationalist views. The editors were allied to the *sangka* (the Buddhist clergy), led by Phnom Penh's **Institut Bouddhique**, which had taken responsibility for most education until the opening of the *lycée*.

When Sihanouk requested Cambodia's independence late in 1945, the French reluctantly agreed to allow elections and the formation of a National Assembly, but refused to contemplate full independence. Thus, for the first time in Cambodian history, political parties were created, **elections** held (in 1946) and a new government formed. The election was won resoundingly by the democratic (and anti-royalist) party, Krom Pracheathipodei, which adopted a constitution along the lines of that of republican France; Sihanouk, although he retained his throne, was left virtually powerless. Late in 1949, Cambodia was granted **partial independence**, although the French continued to control the judiciary, customs and excise and foreign policy, and retained the right to maintain military bases in the country.

Frustrated by his lack of political power and the residual French grip on the country, in June 1952 Sihanouk staged a **coup**, dismissing the cabinet, suspending the constitution and appointing himself prime minister. In early 1953 he declared martial law, dissolved the National Assembly and travelled to Paris to lobby the French. With France fighting a losing battle in Vietnam against the communist Viet Minh, the French government eventually did an about-face, and on **November 9, 1953**, Cambodia duly celebrated full independence.

The Sihanouk era

Cambodians were ecstatic at achieving **independence**, and Sihanouk was feted as a national hero, although for the impoverished farmers who formed the majority of the population, independence made no change to their subsistence lifestyles. Sihanouk, meanwhile, was driven by an unquenchable need for public adulation and an unassailable belief that, having won independence for Cambodia, he should be the one to run it. When his attempts to manipulate the constitution to increase the power of the monarchy failed, he surprised everyone by **abdicating** in 1955 in favour of his father Norodom Suramarit, taking once again the title of prince.

Gambling on the continuation of his massive personal popularity, he set up his own political party, **Sangkum Reastr Niyum**, the Popular Socialist Community (Sangkum for short). The party managed to win all the seats in the National Assembly in the heavily rigged 1955 elections, and Sihanouk's dirty tactics ensured that Sangkum remained unchallenged at the next elections two years later. The monarchy was effectively dissolved in 1960 when King Suramarit died, whereupon Sihanouk became head of state once again – although he continued to be referred to as "Prince Sihanouk", rather than king. Sihanouk was both hard-working and creative – he even found time to produce a number of films that drew upon traditional Cambodian cultures and values – but his conceit and bullying made him difficult to work with. Many right-wing intellectuals, whom the prince perceived as competition, mysteriously disappeared; meanwhile, he toyed with socialism and often favoured the left.

Early 19th century	1812	1832
Thai forces seize Battambang, while the Vietnamese annexe the Mekong Delta, leaving the Cambodian monarch, Ang Chan (r. 1806–34), increasingly helpless	Ang Chan moves the royal court to Phnom Penh	Thai monarch Rama III sends an army into Cambodia to expel Vietnamese forces – who flee in advance of the invasion, taking Ang Chan with them

At the same time, in the schools and colleges, left-wing teachers and future Khmer Rouge leaders such as **Saloth Sar** (later known as Pol Pot) and **Ieng Sary** had become senior Communist Party figures by the early 1960s. In 1963, in yet another of Sihanouk's policy shifts, a government purge of known communists saw Saloth Sar flee Phnom Penh to take up the life of a full-time revolutionary. Along with many others in the Cambodian communist movement, he spent time in Vietnam and China, where he was trained and groomed by communist forces.

The slide towards war

In the late 1950s, with the knowledge of the US, plots had been hatched against Sihanouk by a paramilitary, right-wing, anti-Sihanouk group, the **Khmer Serei**, recruited and supported by the Thai and South Vietnamese governments. Although these events compounded his distrust of the pro-American Thais and South Vietnamese, Sihanouk continued to court the US and accept American military aid – while at the same time forming an alliance with China, who were anxious to prevent US dominance in the area. Subsequently, in another abrupt change of direction, in mid-1963 Sihanouk accused the US of supplying arms to the Khmer Serei, and later that year ordered all US aid stopped, as well as nationalizing banking, insurance and all import-export trade.

The economy was soon destabilized by the combination of Sihanouk's policies and shockwaves from the conflict between North and South Vietnam. Sihanouk was forced into a delicate **balancing act** to preserve some semblance of neutrality and avoid Cambodia being drawn into the Vietnamese conflict. In 1963, he broke off relations with South Vietnam (which was receiving financial and military support from the US), though US planes were allowed to fly over Cambodia on their way to bomb North Vietnam. Meanwhile Sihanouk had been unable to prevent North Vietnam sending men and arms via Cambodian territory to the communist **Viet Cong** guerrillas in South Vietnam, leaving him little option but to sign a secret agreement with the North Vietnamese in 1966, allowing them safe passage.

Meanwhile, in the northeast of the country, the CPK (Communist Party of Kampuchea) – or the **Khmer Rouge**, as Sihanouk dubbed them – comprising Cambodian communists who had been sheltering in North Vietnam, began a campaign of insurgency. Ironically, the Khmer Rouge probably owed their eventual victory to the US, who launched a vast, covert bombing programme, code-named **Operation Menu** (see p.237) over supposedly neutral Cambodia, aimed at destroying communist bases and supply lines in the southern provinces of Cambodia along the border with Vietnam. All in all, more than half a million tonnes of ordnance were dropped on the country in three thousand raids between March 1969 and January 1973, alienating provincial Cambodians and causing them to side with the CPK.

Lon Nol takes charge

Elected prime minister in 1966, **General Lon Nol** had been regarded as Sihanouk's man but began to shift his position in response to unrest among a military upset by a lack of equipment and supplies, and a middle class dissatisfied with the prince's economic policies. Plots continued to be hatched against Sihanouk, and in 1970, while he was out of the country, Lon Nol headed a coup, removing the prince as chief of state, abolishing the monarchy and renaming the country the **Khmer Republic**. Sihanouk

Mid-19th century	**1863**	**1904**
French forces invade the Mekong Delta and annexe southern Vietnam	King Norodom (r. 1859–1904) signs first treaty with French, securing French protection in return for wide-ranging concessions	Death of King Norodom. The French install his half-brother Sisowath (r. 1904–27), although the monarchy is increasingly reduced to a ceremonial figurehead

broadcast an impassioned plea from Beijing, begging his supporters to fight Lon Nol, but the Chinese persuaded him to join with the communists whom he had forced into exile in 1963 to form an alternative government.

At home, details of Sihanouk's secret treaty with the North Vietnamese surfaced, and the elimination of their supply trail from Cambodian soil became a national preoccupation. Thousands of Cambodians joined the army to help, but they were poorly trained and ill equipped (despite renewed US financial support, which served only to feed widespread corruption). In the event, the Cambodians were no match for the battle-hardened Vietnamese, and after tens of thousands of Cambodians died in fighting, Lon Nol called a halt to the offensive in 1971.

The **Khmer Rouge** meanwhile were battling towards Phnom Penh. In 1970 they already controlled an estimated twenty percent of Cambodia, primarily in the northeast and northwest; by the end of 1972, all but Phnom Penh and a few provincial capitals were under their control. Although heavy US bombing brought a momentary halt to their advance in 1973, they pushed steadily forward. By early 1975, Phnom Penh was surrounded, access to the rest of Cambodia was cut off and the US was flying in supplies to the besieged city. Endemic corruption and constant warfare had taken its toll on the people, and when the communists walked into Phnom Penh on April 17, 1975 they were greeted with relief. On April 30, the last Americans withdrew from Saigon, just ahead of North Vietnamese forces, and US military involvement in Indochina came to an end.

It's believed that more than 300,000 Cambodians were killed as a result of the four years of fighting against the Vietnamese and the Khmer Rouge, coupled with indiscriminate bombing by the US. Sihanouk's worst fears had been realized, but this was nothing compared to what was to come.

The Khmer Rouge era

The Khmer Rouge had its roots in the Khmer People's Revolutionary Party (**KPRP**), formed in the early 1950s. As well as appealing to anti-monarchist elements, the KPRP attracted young Cambodians who had been exposed to communist ideals while studying in France. Three of these rose to powerful positions in the Khmer Rouge: Saloth Sar – later known as **Pol Pot**; his contemporary, **Ieng Sary**, subsequently foreign minister of Democratic Kampuchea; and **Khieu Samphan**, the future party chairman.

When the Khmer Rouge arrived in Phnom Penh, they set out to achieve their ideal: a nation of **peasants** working in an agrarian society where family, wealth and status were irrelevant. Family groups were broken up, money was abolished and everyday life – down to the smallest detail – was dictated by **Angkar**, the secretive revolutionary organization behind the Khmer Rouge. Within hours of entering Phnom Penh, the Khmer Rouge had begun to clear the city; within a week the capital was deserted. In other towns around Cambodia (now renamed **Democratic Kampuchea**) the scenario was repeated, and practically the whole population of the country was displaced. **Forced labour** was deployed in the fields or on specific building projects supervised by party cadres. The regime was harsh and nutrition inadequate; hundreds of thousands perished in the fields, dying of simple illnesses and starvation. Almost immediately after seizing power, the Khmer Rouge began a

Early 20th century	1925	1945
Crippling taxes imposed by the French and extensive Vietnamese immigration and influence lead to widespread unrest	Félix Bardez, the French resident in Kompong Chhnang, is beaten to death by locals infuriated by French rule	End of World War II and Japanese surrender. The French attempt to reimpose their rule, but agree to allow national elections and the formation of a National Assembly

POL POT

The contemptible Pot was a lovely child.

Loth Suong, Pol Pot's older brother

The factors that turned **Pol Pot** from a sweet-natured child into a paranoid mass-murderer will probably never be fully understood. He was born **Saloth Sar** in 1928 at Prek Sbaur, near Kompong Thom, where his father was a prosperous farmer. Sent to live with his brother, Loth Suong, in Phnom Penh, at the age of 6, he had a relatively privileged upbringing – the family was well connected through a cousin, who was a dancer at the royal court. Academically, Saloth Sar was unremarkable, and it was probably thanks to the influence of his cousin rather than through aptitude that he was chosen to attend the newly opened Collège Norodom Sihanouk in Kompong Cham in 1942 – Sar subsequently left without passing a single exam. He went on to study at the Lycée Sisowath in Phnom Penh, and his academic performance must, at some point, have improved as, in 1949, he was among a hundred students chosen to study in France.

In Paris, Sar joined the French Communist Party (along with his friends Ieng Sary and Khieu Samphan) and was exposed to radical new ideas; he also met Khieu Ponnery, a highly educated Cambodian woman who was to become his first wife. Returning to Cambodia in 1952, Saloth Sar joined the Vietnamese-run Indochina Communist Party and set about campaigning for the socialist cause in Cambodia. Imperceptibly, he began veiling himself in secrecy, isolating himself from his family, keeping a low profile and beginning to use an alias, "Pol". An ardent member of the newly created **Cambodian Communist Party**, he appeared content to work in the lower ranks, giving seminars and recruiting for the cause through his job as a teacher. Those who met him at this time remarked that he was a kind-hearted and mild-mannered – albeit enigmatic – figure. Without ever seeming to promote himself, he rose steadily through the party ranks, from lowly assistant to Party Secretary.

By 1963, Sihanouk's support for the socialists had turned to persecution, and Saloth Sar, along with other key party members, was forced to flee the capital and seek refuge on the border with Vietnam. Moving frequently, the Cambodian communists were supported first by their North Vietnamese comrades, and later by the Chinese – whom "Pol" visited on several occasions and held in great esteem for the "success" of their Cultural Revolution. Isolated in the northeast by the escalating Vietnam War, "Pol" had ample time to develop his own plan for a better state, run on Marxist–Leninist principles. Living simply in the jungle he developed great admiration for the peasant's life, and by the time the revolutionaries – now dubbed the **Khmer Rouge** – had gained control of Cambodia in 1975, he was probably reasonably

programme of **mass execution**, though the twisted logic that lay behind this has never been made clear. Senior military commanders were among the first to die, but before long it was the turn of monks, the elite, the educated, those who spoke a foreign language, even those who wore glasses. Prince Sihanouk and his wife and family had returned to Phnom Penh from exile in Beijing in mid-1975; they lived out the rest of the Khmer Rouge years under virtual house arrest.

As time went on, the regime became increasingly paranoid and began to look inward, murdering its own cadres. It's estimated that between 2 and 2.5 million people, around **twenty percent of the population**, died under the Khmer Rouge, with the remains of almost 1.4 million bodies recovered from mass graves alone. Those who could escape fled to refugee camps in Thailand or to Vietnam, but the majority had no option but to

1946	1947–50	1952
The first elections in Cambodian history lead to the formation of a new government under Krom Pracheathipodei	The left-wing Khmer Issarak guerrilla movement launches attacks against French forces and gains control of large swathes of Cambodian territory	King Sihanouk stages a coup, dismissing the government and appointing himself prime minister

certain of his formula for returning to a basic agrarian society and the implementation of his (ultimately disastrous) "Four Year Plan".

Ever secretive, the Khmer Rouge leaders, rather than expose themselves as individuals, now hid behind a collective name, the mysterious "**Angkar**" – the central committee of the "Organization", as the leaders now referred to the party. This committee comprised thirteen members (eleven men and two women), its unchallenged head being Pol Pot, as Saloth Sar was now called (it isn't known why he chose this pseudonym, which has no meaning in Cambodian). He was also known as "Brother Pol" and, after his appointment as prime minister of Democratic Kampuchea (1976), as **Brother Number One**. Other leading members of Angkar were Pol Pot's long-standing comrade and second in command, Nuon Chea (Brother Number Two); and Pol Pot's friends from his student days, Ieng Sary (Brother Number Three) and Khieu Samphan, the party frontman.

Increasingly suspicious, the cadre was convinced that they were surrounded by traitors. The party was subsequently **purged** of "enemies", with around twenty thousand comrades and their families interrogated and murdered at the Toul Sleng torture prison (interrogation at Toul Sleng was reserved for those who were close to the leadership – in fact, most were loyal party members). While it's not clear whether Pol Pot directly ordered the interrogations and killings, it is certain that he was fully aware of, and probably supported, them. Whether or not he ever felt remorse isn't known, but he certainly refused to acknowledge responsibility – instead, when the atrocities were exposed by liberating Vietnamese forces in 1979, he accused the Vietnamese of being the perpetrators. Choosing to flee rather than face the Vietnamese army, he escaped to Thailand. He never doubted that the path he had chosen for Cambodia was the right one, believing instead that he had been betrayed by those whom he had trusted.

Sentenced to death by a Cambodian tribunal in absentia, Pol Pot lay low and remained at liberty in Thailand. In the mid-1980s, Khieu Ponnery went insane; Pol Pot divorced her in 1987 and married again, fathering his only child, a daughter called Malee. At some point, probably around 1993, Pol Pot crossed back into northern Cambodia where, surrounded by loyal supporters in the relative security of a Khmer Rouge enclave in the vicinity of Anlong Veng, he organized guerrilla attacks against the newly elected Cambodian government. Meanwhile, Ieng Sary, who had been waging a disruptive guerrilla war against the government from Pailin, defected in 1996, an event which signalled the end of the Khmer Rouge. Just a year later, an increasingly paranoid Pol Pot ordered the murder of his long-standing friend, Sun Sen and his family; for this murder, he was tried by his own people and sentenced to life imprisonment. Eleven months later he was dead – apparently in his sleep from natural causes – and his body was cremated a few days later on a pile of rubbish and old tyres.

endure the three years, eight months and twenty days – as any older Cambodian will still say today – of Khmer Rouge rule.

The Khmer Rouge's eventual **downfall** was orchestrated by their original mentors, the Vietnamese. Frequent border skirmishes initiated by the Khmer Rouge irritated the Vietnamese, who sent troops into Cambodia in 1977, though this incursion lasted just a few months. The final straw came when the Khmer Rouge attacked Vietnamese settlements along the border in early 1978 including a devastating attack on Ba Chúc in April 1978, during which they massacred all but two of the town's 3157 inhabitants.

On December 22, 1978, a **Vietnamese army** of more than 100,000 entered Cambodia, and within seventeen days had taken Phnom Penh. The leaders of the Khmer Rouge made their escape just ahead of the invading forces, Pol Pot by helicopter

1953	1963	1966
Cambodia achieves full independence from the French, now embroiled in fighting in Vietnam	Government-led communist purges lead to Saloth Sar and several other future Khmer Rouge leaders fleeing Phnom Penh to become full-time revolutionaries	Sihanouk signs secret agreement with Viet Cong guerrillas in South Vietnam allowing them access to Cambodian territory

to Thailand, the rest crowded onto the train north to Battambang. Following their leaders, Khmer Rouge troops and villagers loyal to them retreated to the jungles along the northwest border.

The Vietnamese era

Although opinions about the decade-long **Vietnamese era** are divided between those who call them liberators and those who call them occupiers, no one disputes that they were widely welcomed, their arrival saving countless Cambodian lives. The Vietnamese found Cambodia's infrastructure shattered and the country devastated – some 300,000 people starved to death during 1979–80 even after the Vietnamese arrival. Cambodia now became the **People's Republic of Kampuchea** (**PRK**) with the Vietnamese establishing a single-party socialist state headed by an interim government led by ex-Khmer Rouge divisional commander Heng Samrin. The foreign minister was another ex-Khmer Rouge member (and future Cambodian prime minister) **Hun Sen**, who had fled to Vietnam in 1977.

Although coverage of Cambodia's plight brought limited aid from the West, the havoc wrought by the Khmer Rouge was largely disregarded by the major powers, who refused to recognize the new PRK government, considering it a puppet regime (the USSR and India were notable exceptions). Safe in Thailand, Pol Pot was supported by the Thai, Chinese and US governments, all of whom were ardently opposed to the communist Vietnamese and who continued to recognize Pol Pot as leader of the legitimate government in exile, with the Khmer Rouge even retaining their seat in the UN. As news of Khmer Rouge atrocities surfaced, his supporters preferred to continue punishing the Vietnamese sponsored PRK. Bizarrely, the Thais and Chinese fed, clothed, trained and even rearmed Khmer Rouge soldiers and UN agencies were allowed to look after them in their camps, even while being prevented from helping the decimated population of Cambodia itself.

By 1980 the Vietnamese were largely in control of central and eastern Cambodia, although fighting still raged intermittently across parts of western Cambodia, with the Khmer Rouge continuing to harass the Vietnamese from their strongholds in Pailin and Anlong Veng, and from bases in Thailand.

A pattern was established which lasted through much of the 1980s, with Vietnamese and PRK government troops launching repeated major but largely unsuccessful offensives against the Khmer Rouge during the dry season, and Khmer Rouge guerrillas counter-attacking during the wet. Millions of explosives were also laid along much of the Thai border (and elsewhere in the west) by both sides – the start of the **land-mine scourge** which still plagues Cambodia to this day.

Meanwhile the arduous work of reconstructing the country continued, although severely hampered by a lack of international aid and the PRK's pariah status among much of the international community. Buddhist monasteries, schools and colleges were slowly rebuilt, cities repopulated, agriculture restored and a national administration painstakingly reassembled, despite the fact that most educated Cambodians had either been killed or had fled the country.

The Vietnamese withdrawal and its aftermath

Vietnam had never intended to occupy Cambodia permanently and by the end of the 1980s, following a drastic reduction in USSR aid to the PRK, the occupation became

1969–73	1970
The US launches massive, covert bombing raids over Cambodia in attempt to target Viet Cong, with huge civilian casualties. At the same time, the emerging Khmer Rouge begins a campaign of insurgency	Prime Minister Lon Nol stages coup against Sihanouk. Sihanouk forms a government-in-exile in Beijing

too expensive for the Vietnamese to sustain. By September 1989 they had withdrawn completely, ending their decade-long presence in the country.

Shortly afterwards, the PRK government renamed the country the **State of Cambodia (SOC)**, but despite the new name, it remained virtually bankrupt. Practically no aid was being received, electricity and fuel were in short supply, and even basic needs such as health care couldn't be provided. Corruption, although not on the scale of earlier regimes, was still rife: the nouveaux riches built spacious villas, drove smart cars and ate out in restaurants, while the majority of Cambodians could barely afford rice. On the borders, a black economy thrived, with gems and timber flowing out, and consumer goods coming in.

Meanwhile, the Khmer Rouge was stepping up its activities, capturing Pailin in 1989. During 1990 they consolidated their position along the Thai border and regularly encroached further into Cambodia, destroying bridges, mining roads and raiding villages; by the end of that year they controlled the jungle areas to the northwest and southwest, going so far as to threaten Sihanoukville and Kampot. In the middle of that year, however, first the US, then China, **withdrew support** from the Khmer Rouge, which was to prove something of a turning point: a ceasefire was declared in July 1991, and in October a conference was held in **Paris** to discuss the country's future.

LAND-MINE LEGACY

Land mines are supposed to maim rather than kill, but more than a quarter of Cambodians injured by mines die of shock and blood loss before reaching hospital. For those who survive – more than forty thousand Cambodians have become **amputees** as a direct result of land-mine injuries – the impact of an injury on their families is financially devastating, emotional consequences aside. To meet the costs of treatment, their families usually have to sell what few possessions they have, reducing them to an extreme poverty from which they seldom recover. For **young female** mine victims, the stigma is often unbearable: being disabled means that they are frequently unable to find a husband and have to remain with their families, where they may be reduced to the status of slaves. The more fortunate amputees have access to a **prosthetics** workshop where, once their injury has healed sufficiently, they can receive a false limb. However, even if they are subsequently able to get a place at a skills or crafts training centre, there's no guarantee of employment once they've completed their training, and without the capital to set up on their own, land-mine victims all too often find their prospects little improved.

In Cambodia, international and domestic **NGOs** are undertaking the painstaking task of mine clearance. Trained crews of Cambodians (many of whom are the widows of land-mine victims) work hard to inform rural communities in heavily contaminated areas of the **dangers** of mines, which are more subtle than might appear: during the rainy season, mines which are buried too deep to go off can move towards the surface as the land floods, rendering previously "safe" territory risky.

The actual process of mine clearance is slow and expensive. As yet, no mechanical system is available that is reliable enough to allow land to be declared as cleared. So, once a minefield has been identified, the site is sealed off and divided into lanes for trained **personnel**, lying on their stomachs, to **probe** every centimetre of ground systematically for buried objects, using a thin blade. The mines thus detected are carefully uncovered and destroyed, usually by blowing them up in situ. Given that as many as six million land mines (according to some estimates) have still to be removed, the scale of the problem is easily appreciated.

1975	1975–78	1978
The Khmer Rouge captures Phnom Penh and drives the capital's population out into the countryside	Khmer Rouge rules in Cambodia. Millions are executed or die as the result of starvation or disease	Vietnamese forces invade Cambodia, driving out the Khmer Rouge. Former Khmer Rouge commander Hun Sen assumes leadership under Vietnamese patronage

To the millennium

Thirteen years of war should have come to an end with the Paris conference, at which a number of agreements were reached. The central idea was to establish an interim coalition government for Cambodia, the **Supreme National Council**, pending UN-supervised elections. But the Khmer Rouge had other ideas and, still supported by Thailand, continued to create insurgency around the country, unsettling an already shaky peace.

UNTAC

The United Nations Transitional Authority in Cambodia, **UNTAC**, was created to stabilize the country and supervise the promised elections, though its forces didn't arrive in Cambodia until March 1992, and even then they were deployed slowly, allowing the Khmer Rouge to expand the area under its control. Refusing to lay down arms or be monitored, the Khmer Rouge continued its disruptive attacks, mining roads and railways, intimidating villagers and murdering ethnic Vietnamese; they also refused to stand in the elections. The return of refugees proceeded relatively peacefully, at least.

The UNTAC mission (costing $2 billion and numbering 22,000 military and civilian staff) was, at the time, the most expensive operation ever launched by the UN, though it's debatable just how successful it really was. The international forces (from around a dozen countries, including Indonesia, India, Ghana, Uruguay, Pakistan and Bangladesh) were ill-prepared for their role as peacekeepers – many were only trained for combat. Often criticized for insensitivity, many of the UNTAC forces – unaccustomed to the large salaries they were being paid – led high-rolling lifestyles, paying well over the odds for even basic services. At the time, business boomed, only to collapse when UNTAC withdrew; a fledgling tourist industry started up (albeit limited by the guerrilla tactics of the Khmer Rouge); and prostitution mushroomed – UNTAC did not test staff for HIV and, rightly or wrongly, is widely blamed for the AIDS epidemic now affecting Cambodia. Today, Cambodians' feelings about UNTAC remain ambivalent. Some say that it failed to restore peace – and created more problems than it solved. Others suggest that without UNTAC the country might well have fallen again into Khmer Rouge hands.

The return of constitutional monarchy

The elections of July 1993 saw a turnout of nearly ninety percent, despite being marred by intimidation and political killings. The **FUNCINPEC** party – headed by Sihanouk's son **Prince Ranariddh** – emerged with a majority, but the interim government, now led by former Khmer Rouge battalion commander **Hun Sen**, refused to cede the authority they had held since 1979. In the event, a government was formed which had two prime ministers, Prince Ranariddh and Hun Sen. A **constitutional monarchy** was reinstated, and Prince Sihanouk persuaded to resume the throne he had abdicated in 1955, although without being given any direct say in government.

Political infighting soon led to the government being dominated by the **Cambodian People's Party** (CPP) of Hun Sen, which had retained control of police, defence and provincial governments, and Prince Ranariddh became little more than a figurehead. The tensions between the two prime ministers grew until mid-1997, when fighting broke out on the streets of Phnom Penh, resulting in many deaths, and Prince Ranariddh, who had just left the country, was ousted by Hun Sen in the **coup of July**

Early 1980s	1989
Pol Pot takes refuge in Thailand, while enjoying the support of the US and Chinese governments suspicious of communist Vietnam's intentions	Vietnamese forces withdraw from Cambodia. The Khmer Rouge retakes Pailin and establishes itself in areas around the Thai border

1997. Foreseeing a bloody struggle, many foreign workers fled the country and investors hurriedly pulled out, leaving projects half-completed, bills unpaid and thousands out of work. The onset, more or less simultaneously, of the 1997 Asian financial crisis only exacerbated matters.

The **1998 elections** were the first to be held since before the Khmer Rouge era. In addition to the CPP and FUNCINPEC, the elections were contested by the **Sam Rainsy Party**, formed of ex-FUNCINPEC members (for all the proliferation of parties, there remains little real ideological difference between them, although FUNCINPEC is generally regarded as royalist, the CPP as "communist", and Sam Rainsy as "democratic"). The CPP won the majority of the seats in the Assembly, but failed to achieve the required two-thirds of the vote to form a government, and a tense few months ensued until another coalition was formed, with Hun Sen as prime minister and Prince Ranariddh as speaker of parliament.

The end of the Khmer Rouge

Outlawed in 1994, the Khmer Rouge started to suffer **defections** to the government almost immediately. Nevertheless, they retained control of the north and northwest of the country, where their leaders remained in hiding, amassing immense wealth from the proceeds of illegal logging and gem-mining. Their guerrillas continued to stage random attacks, kidnapping and murdering foreigners and Cambodians, while their presence prevented access to many parts of Cambodia and deterred tourists and investors alike.

The ultimate demise of the Khmer Rouge came a step closer in 1996 when, after striking a deal of immunity from prosecution, **Ieng Sary**, erstwhile Brother Number Three, and two thousand of his troops defected to the government side, leaving a last rebel enclave, led by Ta Mok and Pol Pot, isolated in the north around Anlong Veng and Preah Vihear. An internal feud led to Pol Pot being tried by a court of his comrades in July 1997 for the murder of fellow Khmer Rouge leader Son Sen. He was subsequently placed under house arrest, and within nine months had died of heart failure. Late in 1998, **Khieu Samphan** and **Nuon Chea** ("Brother Number Two") gave themselves up to the authorities. Anlong Veng was effectively returned to Cambodian jurisdiction the following year. **Ta Mok** (see p.201) was arrested attempting to cross to Thailand in March 1999, and finally, in May the same year, Kang Kek Leu, alias **Duch**, the notorious commandant of Toul Sleng torture prison, was tracked down and arrested.

The new millennium

The **elections** of 2003 were acknowledged as having been the most successful to date. Although they were won, unsurprisingly, by the CPP, opposition parties including the Sam Rainsy Party (SRP) – the nearest the country had to a liberal party – and FUNCINPEC were well represented.

In October 2004, just days before his 82nd birthday, Norodom Sihanouk surprised the country by abdicating on the grounds of age and ill-health. Prince Ranariddh had already ruled himself out of the succession (which is not hereditary in Cambodia) and the hurriedly assembled Throne Council quickly selected

1993	1996
Sihanouk's son Prince Ranariddh wins national elections – but is forced into a coalition with Hun Sen	Leading Khmer Rouge commander Ieng Sary defects to the government side, taking two thousand cadres with him

Norodom Sihamoni, the sole surviving son of Norodom Sihanouk and his wife Monineath – an uncontroversial choice.

National **elections** were held again in 2008. As expected, Hun Sen's CPP retained power with almost 60 percent of the vote, while Sam Rainsy finished in second place with just under 22 percent. Meanwhile, **tensions with Thailand** resurfaced in later 2008 as both countries moved troops into the disputed regions around **Preah Vihear** temple (see box, p.199), with soldiers on both sides being killed in exchanges of cross-border fire. In early 2009, **Duch**, the first of five prominent Khmer Rouge leaders arrested in 2007 (see box below), went on trial for war crimes.

The year **2012** was something of a watershed for Cambodia. In July, Thailand and Cambodia agreed to withdraw troops from around Preah Vihear, paving the way for a resolution of the conflict and the return of peace to this troubled area. More or less simultaneously, the three last surviving members of the Khmer Rouge hierarchy finally went on trial for war crimes, while in October Cambodia's self-proclaimed "King Father", Norodom Sihanouk, died in Beijing of a heart attack, just a few days before his 90th birthday, marking the end of an era in modern Cambodia.

The 2013 elections and after

The sense of a new chapter was reinforced by the **elections of July 2013** – the fifth and most controversial in the country's recent history. Results showed a massive swing against Hun Sen's ruling CPP, although they still secured a slender victory with 68 seats compared to runner-up Sam Rainsy, whose Cambodian National Rescue Party (CNRP)

THE KHMER ROUGE ON TRIAL

In 2001, after considerable procrastination, the Cambodian government reluctantly formed a tribunal to investigate former Khmer Rouge leaders for **war crimes** and **crimes against humanity**. Five of the regime's former supremos were eventually arrested in 2007, charged and held in detention pending trial. (A sixth leading Khmer Rouge potentate, **Ta Mok** , popularly known as "The Butcher", had already died, with exemplary timing, in 2006.)

Duch's trial began in March 2009 and lasted more than a year before he was found guilty and sentenced to 35 years (commuted to 19 years) imprisonment – subsequently extended in 2012 to life, following an ill-fated appeal. The long-awaited trial of the other defendants finally got under way in mid-2012. Of the four remaining accused, **Ieng Sary**, Pol Pot's brother-in-law, died in March 2013 before the end of the trial (his wife and fellow defendant **Ieng Thirith** had already been ruled mentally unfit to stand trial due to progressive Alzheimer's and was released in 2011). The trial of the two remaining commanders, **Nuon Chea**, Brother Number Two, and **Khieu Samphan**, the public face of the Khmer Rouge, finally concluded in October 2013, with both being sentenced to imprisonment for the remainder of their lives in August 2014. Both Chea and Samphan have expressed regret over the atrocities committed during the Khmer Rouge period, but both have continued to staunchly protest their innocence and lack of personal involvement in the crimes of which they have been convicted.

Charges were subsequently brought against a number of mid-ranking Khmer Rouge commanders – including former naval chief Meas Muth – during 2015, evidence of the tribunal's desire, having dealt with the leadership, to pursue those in the organisation's middle tier. The government, however, remains fiercely opposed to any further prosecutions, and none of the accused has yet been brought to trial.

1997	1998	2007
Hun Sen launches a coup against Prince Ranariddh; riots on the streets of Phnom Penh	Death of Pol Pot from heart failure in Anlong Veng	Several Khmer Rouge supremos including Ieng Sary, Duch, Ta Mok and Khieu Samphan arrested, pending trial

won all the remaining 55 seats. Widespread voting irregularities had been reported even before the elections were held, however, and given the closeness of the poll (48 versus 44 percent of the vote) Rainsy declared that he and his party were unable to accept the results. Hun Sen's CPP government, meanwhile, refused calls by both the CNRP and international community to address reports of electoral malpractice.

Mass demonstrations were held in late 2013 and early 2014 in Phnom Penh and elsewhere protesting the election results and other social concerns, with a number of protestors shot dead. Rainsy's CNRP, meanwhile, refused to take their seats in parliament, leading to a drawn-out political stand-off which was only finally resolved in July 2014 after Hun Sen and Rainsy thrashed out a new deal following further political horse-trading. Strained relations between the two parties unravelled once again in late 2015, with charges related to prostitution being brought against CNRP deputy leader Kem Sokha. In November Rainsy himself was charged with defamation and once again retreated into self-imposed exile (his fourth in two decades) in France rather than face the charges against him.

Further demonstrations followed in July 2016 with the killing in Phnom Penh of popular political commentator (and prominent Hun Sen critic) **Kem Ley**. Rainsy, from exile, accused the government of being behind the murder, and was once again promptly issued with charges for defamation in absentia. In October, with Rainsy still refusing to return to Cambodia, the CNRP resumed its parliamentary boycott.

The next **elections** are scheduled for July 2018. Even after 32 years in power, Hun Sen, now in his mid-60s, shows no sign of relinquishing the reins, while there is an increasing sense that Rainsy, three years his senior, is not the solution ("It's easy to be the authoritarian leader of a poor agricultural nation when your chief opponent lives in an apartment near the Eiffel Tower in Paris," as one commentator recently put it). Hun Sen, meanwhile, has increasingly attempted to soften his hard-man image, taking regularly to Facebook (where his page now has an astonishing 6.5 million "likes" – most of them, opponents allege, bought from overseas click-farms).

Modern Cambodia, meanwhile, faces many challenges. In spite of being supported by hundreds of millions of dollars of aid every year, improvements in basic living conditions have been slow in coming. Essentially an **agricultural** nation, Cambodia has never had much of a manufacturing base, although investors tempted by a plentiful supply of cheap labour have set up garment and shoe factories in Phnom Penh, Sihanoukville and Bavet. Many rural Cambodians still lack clean water, electricity, and adequate health care, while **land mines** continue to maim hundreds of villagers each year. Endemic **corruption** remains a fact of life, much of it closely connected to Hun Sen and his cronies, while the systematic destruction of the environment and uncontrolled **logging** (with proceeds going directly to the ruling elite) have already transformed large swathes of formerly beautiful and biodiverse countryside into a sterile monoculture of cash-crop plantations. The country's ever-expanding **tourism** industry remains one beacon of hope, offering increasing numbers of Cambodians the possibility of advancement, education and economic security thanks to the work of numerous socially enlightened hotels, restaurants, tour operators and NGOs. Such schemes are, necessarily, only a small solution to a wider problem, and to what extent the government of Hun Sen (or his possible successor) can succeed in providing a decent quality of life for Cambodia's long-suffering populace remains to be seen.

2009–11	August 2014	July 2016
Repeated clashes with Thailand in and around the disputed temple of Preah Vihear	Khmer Rouge leaders Nuon Chea and Khieu Samphan sentenced to life imprisonment	Killing of leading anti-government journalist Kem Ley

Religion and beliefs

Buddhism influences practically every aspect of Cambodian life, as is evident from the daily gifts of food made to barefoot, saffron-robed monks, and in the dedication shown in the preparations for major festivals, when pagodas take on a carnival air. However, it was Hinduism that predominated among the Khmer from the first until the early fourteenth century, and much temple art and architecture is influenced by Hindu cosmology.

Buddhism in Cambodia is noticeably less dogmatic and formal than in Thailand or Myanmar/Burma, and the age-old traditions of paying respects to **spirits** and deceased **ancestors** that survive are so woven into the fabric of Cambodian life that at times there is no clear line between them and local Buddhist practice. **Islam** is the most widespread of Cambodia's minority faiths, whereas **Christianity** has failed to make much impact.

Hinduism's historical role

Hinduism was introduced to the area by the Brahman priests who accompanied Indian traders to Funan (see p.291) around the first century, and was adopted by the majority of the pre-Angkorian and Angkorian kings. Even today, **Hindu influences** play an important cultural role in Cambodia: two Hindu epics, the *Ramayana* and (to a lesser extent) the *Mahabharata*, form the basis for classical dance and shadow-puppet performances and a subject for contemporary artists.

The Hindu creed is diverse, encompassing a belief in **reincarnation**, the notion of **karma** (the idea that deeds in one life can influence status in subsequent reincarnations), and a colourful **cosmology** – including a vast pantheon of gods. The three principal deities are **Brahma**, the creator and lord of all gods; **Vishnu**, the benevolent preserver who regulates fate; and **Shiva**, the destroyer, who is responsible for both death and rebirth. Shiva was especially worshipped in the form of a **linga**, a phallic stone pillar. These linga were frequently carved in three sections, the square base representing Brahma, the octagonal middle corresponding to Vishnu, and the circular top symbolizing Shiva. Just as linga were frequently a melding of the triad of gods, so the **Harihara**, a popular deity of the pre-Angkorian era, melded the characteristics of both Shiva (on the right-hand side of Harihara images) and Vishnu (on the left).

In the ninth century, Cambodian Hinduism was pervaded by the **devaraja cult** introduced by Jayavarman II: the idea was that, on ascending the throne, the king created an image (consecrated to Shiva or Vishnu) that was installed in the main sanctuary of his state-temple. On his death the king was believed to become one with the god and to be able to protect his kingdom from beyond the grave.

Buddhism

Buddhism has its origins in India, developing out of Hinduism around the sixth century BC, when the teachings of prince-turned-ascetic **Siddhartha Gautama** became popular. Born to a royal family in Lumbini, in present-day Nepal, around 560 BC, Gautama was protected from the sufferings of the outside world and knew nothing other than the comfortable life of the court, where he married and fathered a son. When he reached the age of 29, however, curiosity caused him to venture out of the palace, where he encountered an old man, a sick person, a funeral procession and a monk begging for alms.

Horrified by what he had seen, Gautama gave up his life as a prince, leaving the palace and living as a mendicant to see if he could discover a way to end suffering. Having sought out different religious instructors to no avail, he eventually adopted a programme of self-denial, fasting almost to the point of death, until he finally understood that this austerity only perpetuated the suffering he was trying to resolve. On three successive nights, while meditating under a bodhi tree, he received revelations leading to his **enlightenment**.

Rather than passing straight to **nirvana** – a state free of suffering – as was his right as one who had attained Buddhahood, he remained on earth to spread the **dharma**, the doctrine of the **Middle Way**, encompassing the Four Noble Truths (see below) and avoiding both the extremes of self-indulgence and self-denial. He preached his first sermon at Sarnath, near Varanasi in northern India, and spent the rest of his life travelling and teaching.

Mahayana and Theravada
Within a hundred years of the Buddha's death, two schools of Buddhism had developed, Theravada and Mahayana. **Mahayana Buddhism** propounds that nirvana is accessible to everyone, and not confined to a few ascetics. It also holds that nirvana can be attained with the help of **bodhisattvas** (literally "enlightened beings"), future Buddhas who, rather than entering nirvana, have chosen to remain in one of the various Buddhist heavens in order to assist other beings along the road to enlightenment. Such bodhisattvas are worshipped in their own right as compassionate deities. One example is Lokesvara (the local name for Avalokitesvara, as he's known in other countries), whose image appears on the towers of the Bayon and elsewhere.

In contrast, **Theravada Buddhism** (the dominant form of the religion in modern Cambodia, Thailand, Myanmar/Burma, Laos and Sri Lanka) rejects the concept of the bodhisattva and holds that enlightenment can only be attained by following a lengthy path of meditation, making nirvana practically unattainable even for monks, let alone lay people. Ancient Theravada Buddhist texts tell that seven Buddhas have already been to earth, the most important of whom was Gautama, with one left to come, though later texts say that nearly thirty Buddhas would appear (but only one per historic period).

Doctrine
Buddhism aims to release individuals from the endless cycle of birth, death and rebirth. Each life is affected by the actions of the previous life, and it is possible to be reborn at a higher or lower status depending on earlier actions. By right thoughts and deeds, individuals accrue **karma**, or merit, in this life towards the next world and the next reincarnation.

At the heart of Buddhist teachings are the **Four Noble Truths**, revealed to the Buddha under the bodhi tree. The first is that all of human life is suffering. The second that suffering results from desire (the need for possessions, company, food, even for rebirth) or ignorance (doing the right things, but in the wrong way). The third states that suffering can cease and that the cycle of reincarnation can be broken.

The fourth truth lays down the path by which suffering is removed, namely the **Eightfold Path**, comprising right knowledge (an understanding of the Four Noble Truths); right attitude (a quiet mind free from desire, envy and greed); right speech (truthful, thoughtful words); right action (good moral conduct); right occupation (one's way of life must not harm others); right effort (good actions develop good thoughts and deeds); right mindfulness (carefully considered actions, speech and mental attitude); and right composure (concentration and focus). The Eightfold Path fosters morality, spirituality and insight without austerity or indulgence; much store is set by meditation, putting away the dramas of everyday life to achieve a calm, untroubled mind.

WATS

A **wat** (often, if confusingly, described in English as a "pagoda") is essentially a temple-monastery, although the term is frequently used loosely to refer to any religious structure. Most wats are enclosed by four walls with entrances on each side. At its heart is the **vihara**, the main sanctuary, which contains the most important Buddha images. The vihara is used solely by the monks for their religious ceremonies, and is often kept locked. Separate buildings elsewhere in the wat will house the monks' living quarters and a hall in which meals and religious classes are taken and ceremonies for the laity performed. Also commonly found within pagodas are **crematoria**, reflecting the prevalence of cremation rather than burial, and numerous miniature **stupas** (also known as chedi) containing the ashes of the deceased. Buildings (especially the vihara) are often colourfully decorated with **murals and carvings** showing scenes from the life of the Buddha or from the various *Jataka* tales, a collection of stories recording the previous lives of the Buddha. Many are donated by rich Cambodians to earn religious merit.

There's no fixed programme of **worship** for Buddhist Cambodians, although many will visit on offering days or as and when they feel the need. Buddhists pay their respects to (rather than worship) images of the Buddha, placing their palms together in front of the chin and then raising them to the forehead while bowing slightly, an action which is repeated three times. It's also usual to light three sticks of incense; if asking for divine assistance, lotus buds are placed in vases near the altar. It is customary for worshippers to leave a donation of a few thousand riel.

Buddhism in Cambodia

In Cambodia, Mahayana Buddhism survived side by side with Hinduism from the days of Funan. Buddhism was not, however, widely adopted until the twelfth century when, under Jayavarman VII, it briefly replaced Hinduism as the state religion. With the passing of Jayavarman VII, Hinduism experienced a brief resurgence in the early thirteenth century, but thereafter it was **Theravada Buddhism** that gripped the population. **Monasteries** were founded, acting as schools and libraries, and serving as guardians of the national religion, language and moral code. They also provided other social services such as care for the elderly and sick.

In 1975, the Khmer Rouge banned all religion, destroying or desecrating temples, texts and statues, and persecuting Buddhist monks – fewer than three thousand out of an estimated 65,000 monks survived the regime. Buddhism was tolerated, if not encouraged, during the Vietnamese occupation, and reinstated as the national religion in 1989. Today, Buddhism is practised by some 95 percent of the country's population.

The sangha

Monks play an important role in Cambodian life, and it's not uncommon for Cambodian men to enter the **sangha**, or monkhood, for a period in their lives, often between the ages of 13 and 15 or upon the death of a parent (in the not so distant past this was seen as a right of passage, making men fit for marriage and raising a family). This ordination can be for quite short periods, perhaps a couple of months, or (reflecting modern times) even just a day. Novices are ordained in the rainy season, when their heads are shaved and they receive their saffron robes, comprising the *sampot ngout*, the undergarment; a *sbang*, covering the lower body; a *hang sac*, a garment with many pockets worn over one shoulder; and the *chipor*, a shawl that covers the upper body and is thrown across the shoulders (inside the pagoda, the right shoulder is left uncovered). **Women** are never ordained but can become lay nuns, undertaking various tasks around the pagoda, including looking after the senior monks; often this is a way for older women and widows with no family to be looked after.

Besides practising meditation and chanting, monks have to follow 227 precepts, and undertake daily study of Buddhist scriptures and philosophy. Life in the wat is governed by ten basic injunctions, including not eating after noon, abstaining from alcohol and sexual relations, not wearing personal adornments or sleeping on a luxurious bed.

The most evident aspect of the monkhood in Cambodia is the daily need to go out into the community to ask for **alms**. Begging monks go barefoot (the donor should also have bare feet). Donations of money go to support the wat or to pay for transport, while food is collected in bowls or bags, to be shared among all the monks. In return, the donors receive a simple blessing, helping them to gain merit.

Monks are often asked to bless couples who are to be married, and they also officiate at funerals, presiding over the cremation of the body and storage of the ashes at the pagoda. Monks also play a major role in private religious ceremonies, which may be held for reasons ranging from alleviation of bad luck to acquiring merit for the next life.

Islam and Christianity

Islam arrived with the **Cham**, who fled to Cambodia from Vietnam around the beginning of the eighteenth century; today, the Cham (see p.217) account for some two percent of the population. The most striking thing about Islam in Cambodia is the mixing of the standard precepts of Islam (the monotheistic worship of Allah, the requirement to pray five times a day and make the pilgrimage to Mecca, and so on) with elements of traditional animist worship – some Cambodian Muslims use charms to ward off evil spirits or consult sorcerers for magical cures. The Cham suffered badly at the hands of the Khmer Rouge; mosques were destroyed or desecrated, and forty thousand Muslims murdered in Kompong Cham alone. After the Khmer Rouge, the Cham were able to resume their religious practices, and Muslim numbers now exceed that of pre-1975.

In spite of the efforts of missionaries and a lengthy period under French rule, **Christianity** is followed by less than one percent of the population. Phnom Penh once had a Catholic cathedral but it was razed to the ground by the Khmer Rouge. More than a hundred Christian NGO and missionary groups operate in Cambodia today, although they have to seek approval before building churches and are banned from proselytizing as a result of reports of children being coerced with sweets and gifts into becoming Christian.

Animism, ancestor worship and superstitions

Offerings of incense, fruit, flowers and water are traditionally made at **spirit houses** to keep the spirits of the natural world happy, and to request good luck or give thanks, particularly before the rice harvest. Spirit houses can be found all over Cambodia (and often in the grounds of Buddhist wats), and consist of anything from simple wooden trays with a tin can filled with incense sticks through to elaborate, wooden or stone affairs resembling miniature temples. Offerings may also be seen laid out at particular trees, rocks and so forth which are considered particularly auspicious either for their beauty or their supposed magical or medicinal properties.

Respect for **ancestors** is important to most Cambodians. **Buddhists** celebrate their ancestors in the three-day festival of **Bonn Pchum Ben**, in September or October, when offerings are taken to pagodas. The homes of ethnic **Chinese** often have two spirit houses, one dedicated to the house spirit, the other to their ancestors; incense is burnt daily to assure good fortune.

Cambodians are highly **superstitious**, regularly consulting fortune-tellers, astrologers and psychics, and even making use of sacred **tattoos** for self-protection. Fortune-tellers are often found at the pagoda, where they give readings from numbered sticks drawn at random or a book of fortunes. Astrologers are key to arranging a marriage and are normally consulted early on to ensure that couples are compatible and to determine the best day for a wedding. The Cambodians also practise a form of *feng shui*, and practitioners are consulted to assess land before purchase and advise on the removal of trees and the construction of property.

Books

Until fairly recently books about Cambodia fell into two categories: dry, factual tomes about the temples of Angkor, and harrowing Khmer Rouge-era autobiographies. Coverage of culture and the rest of Cambodia's history was relatively sparse, and novels hardly existed. Now, however, there's an ample choice of contemporary books, but it's still worth seeking out older titles if you are interested in pre-Khmer Rouge history. Titles marked ★ are particularly recommended.

NOVELS, TRAVEL AND CULTURE

Liz Anderson *Red Lights and Green Lizards*. Moving account of early 1990s Cambodia through the eyes of a British doctor who volunteered in the riverside brothels of Phnom Penh and set up the city's first-ever clinic for prostitutes.

★**Robert Casey** *Four Faces of Siva*. Eminently readable 1920s travelogue, in which the author weaves fact and fantasy into his personal discovery of Cambodia's hidden cities. The compelling description of the author's foolhardy trek to explore the remote Preah Khan in Kompong Thom province still resonates today.

★**Karen J. Coates** *Cambodia Now: Life in the Wake of War*. Insightful, anecdotal tales from the time the author spent in Cambodia as a journalist on the *Cambodia Daily*, portraying the lives of ordinary Cambodians and showing how they survive in often distressing circumstances.

Amit Gilboa *Off the Rails in Phnom Penh*. Self-styled, voyeuristic "guns, girls and ganja" foray into the seedy side of Phnom Penh in the mid-1990s.

Gillian Green *Traditional Textiles of Cambodia: Cultural Threads and Material Heritage*. Full-colour study of Cambodian textiles; comprehensively researched and containing a wealth of information on why and how textiles are produced.

Christopher J. Koch *Highways to a War*. This novel embraces the war in both Cambodia and Vietnam; the conflict is given a human touch through the experiences of its intrepid, war-photographer hero.

Norman Lewis *A Dragon Apparent: Travels in Cambodia, Laos and Vietnam*. Though light on Cambodia content, what there is gives a fascinating, all-too-rare glimpse of the country around the time of independence; best of all are the observations of the people and everyday events.

Carol Livingstone *Gecko Tails: Journey Through Cambodia*. Light-hearted account of the life of a would-be foreign correspondent during Cambodia's free-rolling UNTAC era; a bit of politics, some history and a lot of human interest wrapped up in a sensitively told yarn.

Jeff Long *The Reckoning*. Novel with a supernatural bent: a missing-in-action team search the Cambodian countryside for lost comrades; while deep in the jungle a deserted temple gradually gives up the secrets of a disappeared GI patrol, but not without wreaking revenge on those who dare to venture there.

Walter Mason *Destination Cambodia: Adventures in the Kingdom*. Entertaining and insightful travelogue, set mainly in Phnom Penh and featuring an eclectic cast, from Vietnamese transsexuals to monks with dark pasts. A lot better than its lame title would suggest.

★**Henri Mouhot** *Travels in the Central Parts of Indo-China (Siam), Cambodia and Laos*. The first Cambodian travelogue, Mouhot's diary contains a fascinating account of the "discovery" of Angkor Wat in 1856 and was responsible for sparking off Cambodia-fever in nineteenth-century Europe.

R.K. Narayan *The Ramayana*. Condensed prose retelling of the great Indian epic by one of India's finest twentieth-century novelists.

Toni Samantha Phim and Ashley Thompson *Dance in Cambodia*. This compact guide crams in information on the history and styles of Cambodian dance, along with a pictorial glossary of traditional musical instruments.

Colin Poole and Eleanor Briggs *Tonle Sap: Heart of Cambodia's Natural Heritage*. Superb photographic record of life, people and nature on the Tonle Sap lake.

★**Geoff Ryman** *The King's Last Song*. Page-turner of a novel about the discovery of an ancient diary etched in gold. The story cleverly interweaves the intrigue of the twelfth-century Angkorian court with the lives of its present-day heroes, an ex-Khmer Rouge soldier and a young moto driver.

Lucretia Stewart *Tiger Balm: Travels in Laos, Vietnam and Cambodia*. A sizeable chunk of this book is taken up with a visit to the poverty-stricken and oppressed Cambodia of 1989, when only the bravest of travellers ventured there; the characters the author meets along the way make this a good read.

Jon Swain *River of Time*. Part love affair with Indochina and part eyewitness account of the fall of Phnom Penh, written by a respected war correspondent.

Connor Wall and Hans Kemp *Carrying Cambodia*. Delightful photographs of Cambodia's transport system in

all its amusing and colourful guises.

Camron Wright *The Rent Collector*. Unexpectedly life-affirming novel about Cambodia's urban poor, set in the vast Stung Meanchey municipal waste dump on the southern edge of Phnom Penh.

HISTORY AND POLITICS

Joel Brinkley *Cambodia's Curse*. Pulitzer Prize-winning journalist Brinkley's damning assessment of the present state of the Cambodian nation under the government of Hun Sen.

David Chandler *A History of Cambodia*. The leading scholarly history of Cambodia, although general readers will find John Tully's history (see below) a more readable and accessible introduction.

David Chandler *Voices from S-21*. This thought-provoking book delves into archive material from the interrogation and torture centre at Toul Sleng in an attempt to explain why such atrocities happened – often neither captive nor interrogator knew what crime had supposedly been committed.

★ **Chou Ta-Kuan** *The Customs of Cambodia* (o/p). The sole surviving record of thirteenth-century Cambodia, written by a visiting Chinese envoy Chou Ta-Kuan (Zhou Daguan), with graphic accounts of the customs of the time, the buildings and ceremonies at court.

Ian Harris *Cambodian Buddhism: History and Practice*. A readable, if slightly dry, account of the history and practice of Buddhism from its widespread adoption in the twelfth century to the present day.

Eva Mysliwiec *Punishing the Poor: The International Isolation of Kampuchea* (o/p). Dated but valuable chronicle of how the West ostracized Cambodia after the Vietnamese invasion.

William Shawcross *Sideshow: Kissinger, Nixon and the Destruction of Cambodia*. Starting with a single mission to destroy a North Vietnamese command base believed to be located in Cambodia, this book traces the unfolding of the United States' horrendous clandestine bombing campaign against the country and its subsequent cover-up – compulsive reading.

★ **John Tully** *A Short History of Cambodia: From Empire to Survival*. The best general history of Cambodia, offering a readable and insightful overview of the country from Funan to Hun Sen.

ANGKOR

Andrew Booth *The Angkor Guidebook*. The most up-to-date guide currently available, with contributions by leading authorities including Damian Evans (see p.192), beautiful historic illustrations, paintings and photographs, and ingenious overlay images simultaneously showing the temples now and as they would originally have appeared.

Bruno Dagens *Angkor, Heart of an Asian Empire*. The story of the rediscovery of Angkor Wat and the explorers who brought the magnificent temple to the attention of the Western world, illustrated with old photographs and detailed sketches.

Maurice Glaize *The Monuments of the Angkor Group* (o/p). Classic guide to the temples originally published in 1944, with detailed maps and photographs; read it online or download in full from ⓦ theangkorguide.com.

Geoffrey Gorer *Bali and Angkor: A 1930s Pleasure Trip Looking at Life and Death*. The acidic, condescending comments on everything from transport to temples make it hard to see why Gorer bothered to visit Angkor at all, but his off-the-wall interpretations of the rationale behind Khmer art certainly make for an alternative view to the accepted texts.

Charles Higham *Civilization of Angkor*. Useful overview of the history of Angkor including good coverage of the ancient kingdoms of Chenla and Funan from which the great empire eventually sprung.

★ **Claude Jacques and Michael Freeman** *Ancient Angkor*. Still the best and most comprehensive guide to the monuments of Angkor, full of absorbing detail and superb photographs, although changes to visitor access at some temples (and ongoing restoration at others) mean that some of the practical "visit" sections are now rather dated.

Claude Jacques and Michael Freeman *Angkor: Cities and Temples*. Stunning coffee-table volume featuring fabulous photographs and evocative descriptions of the temples.

Steve McCurry *Sanctuary: The Temples of Angkor*. Magical images of the temples from this renowned photographer.

Christopher Pym *The Ancient Civilization of Angkor* (o/p). Fascinating wander through the life and times of the ancient Khmer, exploring everything from how kingfishers were caught to the techniques used to move massive stone blocks for the building of temples.

Dawn Rooney *Angkor: Cambodia's Wondrous Khmer Temples*. Easy-to-use guide, with good background information and plans for each of the principal temples. Recently republished in a new, expanded sixth edition.

Vittorio Roveda *Sacred Angkor: The Carved Reliefs of Angkor Wat* (o/p). Perfect for temple buffs, this is a detailed study of the reliefs, offering alternative suggestions for their interpretation.

BIOGRAPHY AND MEMOIR

François Bizot *The Gate*. Gripping first-person account of being kidnapped by the Khmer Rouge for three months in 1971; the author's release was attributable to the rapport he built up with the notorious Duch, one of the regime's most murderous henchmen.

David Chandler *Brother Number One: A Political Biography of Pol Pot*. The original work on Pol Pot, this meticulously researched book reconstructs the life of this reclusive subject. The rather scant actual information about him is bolstered by juicy details about other Khmer Rouge leaders.

Nic Dunlop *The Lost Executioner: A Story of the Khmer Rouge*. Duch, the infamous commandant of the Khmer Rouge torture prison S-21, was found living in a remote area of Cambodia. This easy-to-read book reveals details of his life and ponders the rise of the Khmer Rouge, comparing their philosophy to those of Stalin and of the French Revolution.

Adam Fifield *A Blessing Over Ashes*. The author's candid account of growing up in 1980s America with Soeuth, his adopted Cambodian brother, seen from both sides of the cultural gap. Especially touching is the visit to Cambodia, where Soeuth discovers that his Khmer family is still alive.

Bree Lafreniere *Music through the Dark*. Musician Daran Kravanh only survived imprisonment by the Khmer Rouge because the cadre took a liking to his music, often calling him to play his accordion after a day toiling in the fields.

Harish C. Mehta and Julie B. Mehta *Hun Sen, Strongman of Cambodia*. Based on interviews with Hun Sen himself, his family and colleagues, this provides a frank portrait of the man, though the authors have undoubtedly chosen their words carefully.

Vann Nath *A Cambodian Prison Portrait: One Year in the Khmer Rouge's S-21*. A survivor's account of Toul Sleng. Nath, a trained artist, has since used his skills to create a pictorial document of the appalling practices once visited on inmates in the Toul Sleng Genocide Museum.

Haing S. Ngor and Roger Warner *Survival in the Killing Fields*. Harrowing account by a doctor who survived torture by the Khmer Rouge, but was unable to save his wife, who died in childbirth. Fleeing Cambodia, the author eventually reached America, where he won an Oscar for his role as Dith Pran in the film *The Killing Fields*. He was murdered in 1996 by muggers, eight years after this book was written.

Milton Osborne *Sihanouk, Prince of Light, Prince of Darkness*. No-nonsense behind-the-scenes look at the contradictory King-Father. He comes across as a likeable, all-too-human character, if often petulant and egotistical.

★ **U Sam Oeur** *Crossing Three Wildernesses*. Poet, scholar, engineer and politician, Oeur not only recounts his enthralling life story in this memoir, but also packs it with details of everyday Cambodian life, historic fact and political intrigue.

Philip Short *Pol Pot: The History of a Nightmare*. Definitive and gripping account of the life of Pol Pot and the rise and fall of the Khmer Rouge.

★ **Loung Ung** *First They Killed My Father*. The author pulls no punches in this heart-rending personal narrative of the destruction of her family under the Khmer Rouge. A sequel, *After They Killed Our Father: A Refugee from the Killing Fields Reunites with the Sister She Left Behind* completes the story.

Khmer

Khmer (pronounced "k'my") is the national language of Cambodia, and is also spoken in the Mekong Delta and pockets of northeast Thailand, as well as forming the basis of the language used at the Thai royal court. Many Khmer words have their origins in the two classical languages of India – Sanskrit and Pali – while Malay, Chinese, Vietnamese, Thai, French and English have also been absorbed over the centuries.

Although English is widely spoken in major towns and tourist centres, learning even a few words of Khmer will go a long way to endearing you to Cambodians; off the beaten track you'll find it especially helpful to know some basic Khmer phrases. Fortunately, it is a relatively easy language to get to grips with, being **non-tonal** and relatively simple in its grammar. Sentences follow the subject–verb–object pattern of English, although, as in French, adjectives are added after the noun. Khmer verbs don't conjugate, and tenses are indicated by the addition before the verb of a word indicating the time frame; *nung*, for instance, indicates an action taking place in the future. Articles and plurals aren't used in Khmer (quantity is indicated by stating the number or using general terms for "some" or "many").

Khmer **script** is an artistic mix of loops and swirls, comprising **33 consonants** and **23 vowels**; the vowels are written above and below the consonants and to either side. Capital forms of the letters exist, but are seldom used. In writing, words run left to right with no spaces in between; sentences end with a little symbol that looks a bit like the numeral "7", playing the role of a full stop. **Transliteration** into the Roman alphabet is not straightforward, and differences in approach account for many of the variations on maps and restaurant menus.

Pronunciation

Note that some sounds in Khmer have no English equivalent. Cambodians use intonation for emphasis – it's best to keep your speech somewhat monotonous in order to avoid causing misunderstanding. **Regional dialects** also present a challenge, as many words are quite different from the formally correct words spoken in Phnom Penh.

CONSONANTS

Most consonants in our transliteration scheme are pronounced as they would be in English, though note that consecutive consonants are pronounced individually. The "bp" and "dt" consonants given below are equivalent to a hard, unaspirated p and t – put your

---

LANGUAGE PRIMERS

The most widely available primer is the long-running *Colloquial Cambodian*, with book plus CD; alternatively, the interactive *Talk Now! Learn Khmer* CD-ROM is another good resource. The *Foreign Service Method Khmer Basic Course* (available at Ⓦ multilingualbooks.com) is for those wishing to delve deeper. In Phnom Penh, at Psar Thmei and Psar Toul Tom Poung, you can buy the excellent *Seam & Blake's English–Khmer* pocket dictionary, which lists words in Khmer script and in Roman transliteration.

A free **iPhone app** (also available as an iPod-compatible MP3 download) with a fifteen-minute Khmer language lesson and fifty introductory phrases is available at Ⓦ journals .worldnomads.com/language-guides. It's also worth searching for "learn Khmer" on **YouTube**, although the material available is pretty patchy.

hand in front of your mouth and try to say these letters without releasing the puff of air with which English speakers normally pronounce them.

bp sharp sound, between the English "b" and "p" (a hard, unaspirated "p").

dt sharp sound between the English "d" and "t" (a hard, unaspirated "t").

gk guttural sound between the English "g" and "k".

ng as in sing; often found at the beginning of words.

ny as in canyon.

VOWELS

a as in ago.

aa as in bar.

ai as in tie.

ao or **ou** as in cow.

ay as in pay.

e as in let.

ea as in ear.

ee as in see.

eu is similar to the French fleur.

i as in fin.

o as in long.

oa as in moan.

ohs as in pot (the **hs** is practically silent).

oo as in shoot.

OO as in look.

ow as in toe.

oy as in toy.

u as in fun.

Useful words and phrases

The polite **form of address** for men is "*loak*", for women "*loak srei*". In a formal situation Cambodians will often introduce themselves with one of these two terms, then give their full name with the family name first. Although you will be asked your name a lot as you travel around, Cambodians do not really use names in everyday situations, preferring to use a range of respectful forms of address. These terms can be either polite or familiar depending on the situation, and are used even when meeting someone for the first time. The choice of term depends not only on whether the person being spoken to is male or female, but also on whether they are older or younger than the speaker. An older person is often (both politely and familiarly) addressed as either *yeah* or *dah* (grandmother or grandfather), or *ming* or *boh* (auntie or uncle), depending on just how much older they are than the speaker. When speaking to someone younger, *kmoouy bprohs* or *kmoouy srei* (nephew or niece) can be used, or more familiarly, *bpohn bprohs* or *bpohn srei* (younger brother or sister). Take your lead from the Cambodians and listen to how they address you or other people.

GREETINGS AND CIVILITIES

hello (formal/informal)	chum ree-eu-bp soo-a/ soo-a s'day	**I'm well/fine**	k'nyom sok sa bai
welcome	swah-ghOOm	**goodbye (formal/ informal)**	chum ree-eu-bp lear/ lear haowee
good morning	a-roon soo-a s'day	**see you later**	chewubp kynear t'ngai keraowee
good afternoon	ti vea soo-a s'day		
good evening	sayorn soo-a s'day	**please**	som
good night	rea trey soo-a s'day	**if you please**	unchurn
how are you?	nee'ak sok sa bai gee-ar dtey?	**thank you**	or-kOOn
		excuse me/sorry	som dtohs

BASIC TERMS AND PHRASES

yes (spoken by a male/female)	baht/jahs	**come/go**	mow/dhow
no	dtay	**to have (also used for "there is/are")**	mee-un
large or big	tom	**sleep**	gayn
little or small	toight	**my name is…**	k'nyom chmoor

what is your name…?	chmoor eh?	I have one child/two children	k'nyom mee-un gk'cone moi/bpee
where do you come from?	nee'ak mau bpe pro-teh nar?	where are you staying?	nee'ak s'nak now ai nar?
I am from…	k'nyom mau bpe pro-teh…	can you speak English/ Cambodian?	nee'ak jehs nit-yaiy pia-sar onglai/k'mair roo dtay?
Britain	onglais	I know (can speak) a little	k'nyom jehs tick-tick
Ireland	ear-lond	I don't understand	k'nyom s'dabp men baan/k'nyom ot yull
US	amei-rik		
Canada	kana-daa	how old are you?	a'yup bpon-maan chnam?
Australia	orstra-lee	I don't know	k'nyom ot dung
New Zealand	nyew seelend	there aren't…/we don't have…	ot mee-un…
are you married?	nee'ak riep-ghar hauwee roo now?		
		none left/finished	ohs haowee
how many children do you have?	nee'ak mee-un gk'cone bpon maan nee'ak?	it can't be done	ot baarn
		no problem	ot banyaha
		not yet	ot toe-un
I don't have any children	k'nyom ot towan mee-un	just a minute/please wait a minute	som jam bon tick

GETTING AROUND

where are you going? (also used as a general greeting)	dtow nar?	minibus	laan dubp-bpee gonlaing
		motorbike taxi	motodubp/moto
I am going to a/an/the…	k'nyom dtow…	pick-up	laan nee-san/laan ch'noo-ul laan gk'bah
I want to go to a/an/the…	k'nyom chong dtow…		
where is the…?	…now ai nar?	taxi	dtak-see
airport	jom nort yoo-un hohs/ drang yoo-unhohs	express boat	karnowt lou-en
		slow boat	karnowt
bus station	seta-nee laan kerong	small boat	dtook
taxi stand	seta-nee laan dtak-see	where do I buy a ticket?	k'nyom trouw ting sambort now ai nar?
train station	seta-nee roteh pleung		
jetty	gkumpong bpai	how much to go to…?	dtow…bpon maan?
bank	t'nee-a-geer	will you go for…?	dtow…baan tday?
embassy (Thai/Lao/ Vietnamese)	sa-tarn-toot (tai/lao/ vietnam)	…per person	…moi nee'ak
		does this…go to?	laan neeh mee-an dtow…dtay?
guesthouse	pteah sumnat		
hotel	sontdakee-a/owhtel	when does the… depart?	…neeh je-ny dtow maung bpon maan?
market	psar		
money changer	gonlaing dt'loi	how long does it take to get to…?	doll…o'h bpon maan maung?
museum	sarat montee		
pharmacy	farmasee	is the…far away?	…che-ngai dtay?
police station	bpohs bpoli	it's (not) a long way	(ot) che-ngai
post office	bprey-sa-nee	do you agree to the price?	dumlai neeh baan dtay?
restaurant	porjarnee-a tarn/restoran		
shop	harng	is this seat vacant?	gonlaing neeh dohs dtey roo dtay?
go straight	dtow dtrong		
please stop here	som choap tee neeh	it's vacant	dohs dtey
(turn) left/right	(bot) ch'wayng/s'dam	it's taken	mee-un nee'ak
north	dteu khang jeung	what's wrong with the vehicle?	laan neeh koit dtay?
east	dteu khang kea-et		
south	dteu khang tb'ohng	toilet	bong koon
west	dteu khang leh'j	where's the toilet?	bong koon nell a naa?
bus	laan tom	I need to stop to go to the toilet	k'nyom som choap bong koon
cyclo	see-klo		

ACCOMMODATION

do you have any rooms?	nee'ak mee-un bontobp roo dtay?	a mosquito net	moohng
do you have a single room	bontobp sum-rab moi nee-ak	a telephone	toora-saap
room with two beds	bontobp graiy bpee	the room key	souw bontobp leik
with…	mee-un…	toilet paper	gro-dahs
air conditioning	maa-sin dtro-chey-at	a towel	gkon-saing
bathroom	bontobp dtuek	how many nights will you stay?	nee'ak s'nak now tee neeh bpon maan yoobp?
fan	dong harl	can you clean the room?	som sum-art bontobp neeh baan dtay?
hot water	dtuek g'daow		
toilet	bong-kgun	can I move to another room?	k'nyom som doa bon-tobp?
window	bong-ooit	this room is…	bontobp neeh…
how much is it per night?	moi yoobp bpon-maan?	full of mosquitoes	may-un moohs che-raan
can I see the room?	som merl baan dtay?	too noisy	telong payk
can you discount the price?	johs bon-tick baan dtay?	do you have a laundry service?	mee-un bauk cao-aow?
can I have…?	k'nyom som…?		
a blanket	bphooey	do you have a bicycle/ motorbike for rent?	mee-un kong/moto sum-rabp ch'ooel?

SHOPPING AND CHANGING MONEY

where do they sell…?	gay mee-unloo-uk …now ai nar?	too big	tome nah
do you have…?	may-un…?	too small	toight nah
cigarettes	baar-rai	very expensive!	t'lai nah!
medicine	t'nam	good	l'aw
mosquito coils	took dot	pretty	s'aat
silk	soort	colour	por
soap	saa-boo	different	sayn
souvenirs	kgar-dow/soo-ven-neer	what is your best price?	dait bpon maan?
toothpaste	t'nam doh t'meny	can you go down a bit?	johs bon tick baan dtay?
washing powder	saa-bo bowk cao-aow		
what is this?	ti neechee ahwy?	I only have riel/dollars	k'nyom may-un dtai riel/dol-lar
how much does it cost?	t'lai bpon maan?	I want to change money	k'nyom chong dow loi

EMERGENCIES AND HEALTH MATTERS

help!	choo-ee	I am not well	k'nyom men se-rooel kloo-un dtay
thief	jowl		
my passport has been stolen	brum-dain/pa'hport rebohs k'nyom gai lou'it	I need a doctor	k'nyom trauv ghar gkroo pay-et
I have lost my…	k'nyom bat lik-khet ch'long…	I have…	k'nyom mee-un…
		a fever	gkrun
my pack/suitcase is missing	gkar-borb/val-lee trauv bat	diarrhoea	rey'ak
		pain	choohs
there's been an accident	mee-un kroo-ah t'nak	where is the toilet?	mee-un bong-khun now ai nar?
please take me to hospital	som june k'nyom dtow mon-tee pey-et	are there any land mines here?	gon-laing neeh mee-un min dtay?
please call an ambulance	som hao laan pay-et	I'm lost	k'nyom vung-veing plaow

NUMBERS

zero	sohn	two	bpee
one	moi	three	bpai

four	bpoun	fifty	hahs-sep
five	bphrahm	sixty	hohk-sep
six	bphrahm-moi	seventy	jet-sep
seven	bphrahm-bpee/ bpel	eighty	bpaet-sep
		ninety	cow-sep
eight	bphrahm-bpai	one hundred, two hundred, etc	moi-roi, bpee-roi
nine	bphrahm-bpoun		
ten	dhop	one hundred and one	moi-roi moi
eleven, twelve, etc	dhop-moi, dhop-bpee	one thousand, two thousand, etc	moi-bpouhn, bpee-bpouhn
twenty	m'pay		
twenty-one, twenty-two, etc	m'pay-moi, m'pay-bpee	ten thousand	moi-meun
		one hundred thousand	dhop-meun
thirty	sam-sep	one million	moi-leuhn
forty	si-sep	first, second, etc	dte-moi, dte-bpee

TIMES AND DATES

The time is generally expressed by stating the word for hour, then the hour itself, then the number of minutes past the hour and the word for minute; thus 5.05 is rendered *maung bprahm, bprahm nee-ar tee*. Morning, afternoon or night are added to confirm the right time. In business the 24-hour clock is usually used, and months are referred to by number – thus October is *kai dhop*.

what's the time?	maung bpon maan?	Wednesday	t'ngai bot
hour	maung	Thursday	t'ngai brou-hohs
minute	nee-ar tee	Friday	t'ngai sok
morning	bpel p'ruk	Saturday	t'ngai sou
noon	t'ngai terong	Sunday	t'ngai ah-tet
afternoon	bpel rohsiel	last/next/this…	…mun/k'raowee/neeh
evening	bpel l'ngeit	week	ah tet
night	bpel yob	month	kai
day	t'ngai	year	chnam
today	t'ngai neeh	now	ailouw neeh
tomorrow	t'ngai sa-ait	later	bpel k'raowee
yesterday	m'sell-mine	not yet	ot t'w-an
Monday	t'ngai jarn	just now	a-bany mainy
Tuesday	t'ngai ong-keeya	already	hauwee

A food and drink glossary

As most Khmer dishes are ordered simply by stating what type of food you want to eat and how you'd like it prepared (thus stir-fried pork with ginger is *sait jerook cha khyay*), we've listed Khmer terms for various ingredients and standard cooking methods; a few specific dishes are also listed by name. To specify that a particular ingredient should *not* be added to your food, prefix the item in question with *ot dak* (without) – thus if you don't want sugar in your drink, say *ot dak skar*.

COOKING METHODS AND GENERAL TERMS

…cha	stir-fried…	nOOm-bpang	bread
…cha knyay	stir-fried…with ginger	pong	egg
		pong mowan	hen's egg
…jew aim	sweet-and-sour…	pong dteer	duck's egg
…ang	grilled…	be jaing/msow sobp	monosodium glutamate (MSG)
…dot	roasted…		
ma-horb	food (prepared)	m'rik	pepper

um-beul	salt	k'nyom poo ahs	I'm vegetarian
skar	sugar	ot bpah'aim	not sweet (useful when
bong ai'm	dessert		ordering drinks)

MEAT, POULTRY AND FISH

g'dam	crab	sait gow	beef
kongaib	frog	sait jerook	pork
ot yoh kroeng knong	offal, intestine or	sait mowan	chicken
	gizzard	trei	fish
sait dteer	duck	trei muk	squid

VEGETABLES (BON LAI)

bpenh pohs	tomato	pgar katnar	cauliflower
bpowrt sngaow	sweet corn	pset	mushroom
draw sok	cucumber	sal-lat	lettuce
dumlong barang	potato	spei	cabbage
gee	herbs	sun dike	beans
k'tum barang	onion	sun dike bon dohs	bean sprouts
k'tum	garlic	sundike day	peanuts
karot	carrot	tro-ab	aubergine/eggplant
mteahs	chilli	trokooen	morning glory
mteahs plouwk	capsicum		

SOME COMMON DISHES

amok trei	mild fish curry cooked in banana leaves	phnom pleung	thin slices of beef barbecued at the table over a charcoal burner
bai sait mowan/sait jeruk	rice topped with fried chicken/ pork		
		dumlong barang gee-yan	French fries
borbor	rice porridge	jay yior	spring rolls
cha bon lai cropmok	fried mixed vegetables	mowan dort	baked chicken
cha katnar chia moi pset	fried pak choy with mushrooms	somlar ngam ngau	lemon broth
		somlar khtiss jerooet	clear chicken or fish soup
kuy teav (sait...)	rice noodle soup (with...)	somlar troyoung jayk sait mowan	chicken with banana-flower soup (variations use fish or duck in place of chicken)
mee ganychop	instant noodles made up from a packet		
mee kilo	yellow noodles		
nom banh chok	flat white noodles served cold with a curry sauce		

FRUIT (PELAI CHER)

dum pay-yang bai jew	grape	pelai bporm	apples
jayk	banana	pelai burr	avocado
koulen	lychee	pelai seyree	pear
kroit chhmar	lime	pelai sroegar ne-yak	dragon fruit
kroit pursat	orange	sow maow	rambutan
kroit telong	pomelo	svai	mango
le-mot	sapodilla	tee-ab barang	soursop
lehong	papaya	tee-ab swut	custard apple
manoahs	pineapple	tooren	durian
meeyan	longan	troubike	guava
morkgoot	mangosteen	umpbel	tamarind
ohluck	watermelon		

SNACKS (JUM NEIGH AREHAR), CAKES (NOAM) AND ACCOMPANIMENTS

bok lehong/som tam	papaya salad	noam pong teeya/	cupcake
chook	lotus seed	noam barang	
krolan	sticky rice in bamboo	noam srooey	cookie
jayk ang	grilled bananas	pong dteer braiy	"thousand-year egg", a
jeruik	pickles		duck's egg preserved in
noam ensaum jayk	sticky rice cakes with		salt
	banana	pong dteer gowne	duck's egg containing
noam gdam	croissant (literally, crab		unhatched duckling
	cake)	prahok	fermented fish paste
noam pang patey	sandwich made with pâté	sait kreyuam	dried meat slices

DRINKS (PAY-SEJEYAT)

coca	Coca-Cola	kumpong	can
dorbp	bottle	siro	syrup
dtai gdouw	hot lemon tea	sraa bier	beer
kroit chhmar		tuk dhowng	juice of green coconut
dtai grolab	strong local tea	tuk duh	milk
dtai	tea	tuk kork	ice
dtai tuk kork	iced tea with lemon	tuk krolok dak kropmok	mixed fruit shake
kroit chhmar		tuk krolok	fruit shake
ka-fei	coffee	tuk sot	drinking water
kafei kmaow (tuk kork)	black (iced) coffee	tuk sun dike	soya milk
kafei tuk duh gow	white (iced) coffee	tuk tnaowt jew	sugar-palm beer
(tuk kork)		tuk umpow	sugar-cane juice

Glossary

Achar Learned lay-person at a pagoda.
Agni Hindu god of fire.
Amrita Elixir of immortality produced during the Churning of the Ocean of Milk.
APSARA Authority for the Protection and Management of Angkor and the Region of Siem Reap.
Apsara Celestial dancer of Hindu mythology, born of the Churning of the Ocean of Milk and commemorated in Cambodia's classical tradition of apsara dance (see box p.154).
ASEAN Association of Southeast Asian Nations.
Asura Demon (from Hindu mythology).
Avalokitesvara See "Lokesvara".
Avatar Incarnation of a Hindu deity.
Banteay Citadel or fortified enclosure.
Barang Slang term meaning French, and often applied to foreigners in general.
Baray Reservoir or Lake.
Bodhisattva One who has attained enlightenment but forgoes nirvana to help others.
Boeung lake.
Brahma Hindu god, often referred to as the Creator.
Brahman Hindu priest.
Buddha One who has achieved enlightenment.

Cham Major ethnic group living in Cambodia and Vietnam, and forming the majority of Muslims in both these countries.
Chedi See stupa.
Chunchiet Generic term for the minority hill-tribe groups.
Churning of the Ocean of Milk Hindu myth describing the creation by gods and demons of the elixir of immortality (see box p.168).
CPP Cambodian People's Party.
Cyclo Three-wheeled bicycle rickshaw.
Deva Male deity.
Devaraja Literally "god who would be king"; the Khmer king, according to the devaraja cult, would fuse with a deity upon his death.
Devata Female deity.
Dvarapala Temple guardians – usually carved figures found flanking entrances to shrines.
FUNCINPEC Front Uni National pour un Cambodge Indépendant, Neutre, Pacifique et Coopératif – the royalist political party.
Ganesh Elephant-headed Hindu god of good fortune and success.
Garuda Mythical creature associated with Vishnu, having the body of a man with the head and feet of a bird.

Gopura Entry pavilion/gatehouse to the sacred area of a temple.

Hamsa Sacred goose associated with Brahma.

Hanuman Monkey god and right-hand man (or, rather, monkey) to Krishna in the *Ramayana*.

Harihara God created from the union of Shiva and Vishnu.

Heng Mythical bird.

Hol Method of weaving; pattern of silk fabric.

Indochina Cambodia, Laos and Vietnam.

Indra Hindu god of the sky.

Jataka Tales recounting the past lives of the Buddha.

Kala Mythical creature with bulbous eyes, claws and no lower jaw.

Khapa Chunchiet basket with shoulder straps, worn on the back.

Khmer The principal indigenous people of Cambodia – the term is often used interchangeably with Cambodian – and also the name of their language.

Koh Island.

Kompong Village on a river or lake.

Krama Cambodian checked scarf.

Krishna The eighth incarnation (avatar) of Vishnu, often shown playing a flute.

Kurma Second incarnation (avatar) of Vishnu, when he appeared as a giant turtle to support Mount Mandara during the Churning of the Ocean of Milk.

Lakshmi Wife of Vishnu, and the goddess of good fortune and beauty.

Laterite Soft, porous rock that hardens in the sun to a hard, resilient stone.

Leahng Cave.

Linga Phallic-shaped stone representing Shiva.

Lokesvara Cambodian name for the bodhisattva Avalokitesvara, often called "the compassionate".

Mahabharata Hindu epic dealing with the rivalry between the Kaurava and Pandava families.

Mahayana One of the two principal schools of Buddhism, along with Theravada Buddhism.

Makara Mythical sea monster with the body of a crocodile and the trunk of an elephant.

Mandapa Antechamber attached to the central sanctuary tower of a Hindu temple.

Matsya The first incarnation (avatar) of Vishnu, during which he appeared as a giant fish.

Mount Meru Mountain home of the gods, at the centre of the universe in Hindu cosmology.

Mudra Traditional Buddhist poses, widely depicted in Buddhist art, and also in Cambodian classical dancing.

Naga Sacred multi-headed snake, seen as a protector and often depicted along staircases or across causeways.

Nandin Sacred bull, and mount of Shiva.

Narasimha Fourth incarnation (avatar) of Vishnu, as half man and half lion.

Nirvana A state in which desire ends and the cycle of birth, death and rebirth is broken.

NRP Norodom Ranariddh Party.

Pagoda Cambodian wat/temple.

Parvati Hindu goddess and wife of Shiva.

Phnom Mountain or hill.

Phum Village.

Pinpeat Cambodian "orchestra", usually comprising around ten instruments, mainly wind and percussion.

Prasat Sanctuary tower of a temple.

Preah A title of spiritual respect, used for gods and holy men; also means "sacred".

Psar Market.

Quincunx Arrangement of five objects with one at the centre and the others at each corner of a rectangle – like the five dots on the face of a die. Used to describe the placing of sanctuary towers in Cambodian architecture.

Rahu Demon with a monster's head and no body, usually depicted swallowing the sun and moon.

Rama Seventh avatar of Vishnu, hero of the *Ramayana*.

Ramayana Hindu epic tale describing the battle between Rama and the demon Ravana.

Ravana The great demon king of Lanka and Rama's principal antagonist in the *Ramayana*.

Reamker Cambodian version of the *Ramayana*.

Remorque Alternative name for Cambodian tuk-tuk.

Sampot Wraparound skirt; by extension, a length of fabric sufficient to make a skirt.

Shiva One of the three principal Hindu gods, often referred to as the Destroyer.

Sita Wife of Rama, who was kidnapped in the *Ramayana*.

Sompeyar Traditional Cambodian gesture of greeting, with hands placed together in a prayer-like gesture.

Spean Bridge.

Srah Pond, lake or reservoir.

SRP Sam Rainsy Party.

State-temple Principal temple built to house the god with whom the devaraja king was associated; a temple-mountain.

Stele Upright stone block inscribed with writing.

Stucco A type of plaster made with lime, and used for decoration, particularly of brick buildings.

Stung Medium-sized river, smaller than a tonle.

Stupa Structure in which cremated ashes are interred; also called a chedi.

Surya Hindu god of the sun.

Temple In the context of Cambodia, an ancient

building or collection of buildings, built by kings to honour ancestors, or to house the devaraja god.

Temple-mountain Temple constructed as a representation of Mount Meru.

Theravada One of the two main schools of Buddhism (along with Mahayana Buddhism) and the dominant form of the religion in Cambodia today.

Tonle Major river.

Toul Low mound.

Tuk-tuk Motorbike-drawn passenger carriage; sometimes called remorque.

UNESCO United Nations Educational, Scientific and Cultural Organization.

UNTAC United Nations Transitional Authority for Cambodia.

UXO Unexploded ordnance.

Valin Monkey king, killed by Rama in the *Ramayana*.

Vasuki The giant naga used to churn the Ocean of Milk.

Vihara Main sanctuary of a wat.

Vishnu One of three principal Hindu gods, the Preserver.

Wat Buddhist monastery and associated religious buildings; often translated into English as "pagoda".

Yaksha Male spirit, depicted with bulging eyes, fangs and a leer; serves as a temple guardian.

Yama God of the Underworld.

Yeak Giant.

Small print and index

Rough Guide credits

Editor: Joe Staines
Senior editor: Helen Abramson
Layout: Anita Singh
Cartography: Rajesh Chhibber
Picture editor: Aude Vauconsant
Proofreader: Susanne Hillen
Managing editor: Andy Turner

Assistant editor: Divya Grace Mathew
Production: Jimmy Lao
Cover photo research: Marta Bescos
Editorial assistant: Aimee White
Senior DTP coordinator: Dan May
Programme manager: Gareth Lowe
Publishing director: Georgina Dee

Publishing information

This sixth edition published September 2017 by
Rough Guides Ltd,
80 Strand, London WC2R 0RL
11, Community Centre, Panchsheel Park,
New Delhi 110017, India
Distributed by Penguin Random House
Penguin Books Ltd, 80 Strand, London WC2R 0RL
Penguin Group (USA), 345 Hudson Street, NY 10014, USA
Penguin Group (Australia), 250 Camberwell Road,
Camberwell, Victoria 3124, Australia
Penguin Group (NZ), 67 Apollo Drive, Mairangi Bay,
Auckland 1310, New Zealand
Penguin Group (South Africa), Block D, Rosebank Office
Park, 181 Jan Smuts Avenue, Parktown North, Gauteng,
South Africa 2193
Rough Guides is represented in Canada by DK Canada, 320
Front Street West, Suite 1400, Toronto, Ontario M5V 3B6
Printed in Singapore
© Rough Guides, 2017
Maps © Rough Guides

336pp includes index
A catalogue record for this book is available from the
British Library
ISBN: 978-0-24127-913-7
The publishers and authors have done their best to ensure
the accuracy and currency of all the information in **The
Rough Guide to Cambodia**, however, they can accept
no responsibility for any loss, injury, or inconvenience
sustained by any traveller as a result of information or
advice contained in the guide.
1 3 5 7 9 0 6 1 2

MIX
Paper from
responsible sources
FSC
www.fsc.org   FSC™ C018179

Help us update

We've gone to a lot of effort to ensure that the sixth
edition of **The Rough Guide to Cambodia** is accurate
and up-to-date. However, things change – places get
"discovered", opening hours are notoriously fickle,
restaurants and rooms raise prices or lower standards. If
you feel we've got it wrong or left something out, we'd like
to know, and if you can remember the address, the price,
the hours, the phone number, so much the better.

Please send your comments with the subject line
"**Rough Guide Cambodia Update**" to mail@uk
.roughguides.com. We'll credit all contributions and send a
copy of the next edition (or any other Rough Guide if you
prefer) for the very best emails.

A ROUGH GUIDE TO ROUGH GUIDES

Published in 1982, the first Rough Guide – to Greece – was a student scheme that became a
publishing phenomenon. Mark Ellingham, a recent graduate in English from Bristol University,
had been travelling in Greece the previous summer and couldn't find the right guidebook.
With a small group of friends he wrote his own guide, combining a contemporary, journalistic
style with a thoroughly practical approach to travellers' needs.

The immediate success of the book spawned a series that rapidly covered dozens of
destinations. And, in addition to impecunious backpackers, Rough Guides soon acquired a
much broader readership that relished the guides' wit and inquisitiveness as much as their
enthusiastic, critical approach and value-for-money ethos. These days, Rough Guides include
recommendations from budget to luxury and cover more than 120 destinations around the
globe, from Amsterdam to Zanzibar, all regularly updated by our team of roaming writers.

Browse all our latest guides, read inspirational features and book your trip at **roughguides.com**.

ABOUT THE AUTHORS

Meera Dattani is a freelance travel writer and editor for UK and international publications. In addition to the *Rough Guide to Cambodia*, she has also contributed to *Southeast Asia on a Budget* and writes for the Rough Guides website.

Gavin Thomas has spent most of his life trying to be somewhere else. A regular Rough Guide author for over fifteen years, he has written and contributed to numerous titles including the Rough Guides to *Myanmar*, *Sri Lanka*, *India*, *Rajasthan*, *Dubai* and *Oman*.

Acknowledgements

Meera Dattani In Phnom Penh, many thanks to Alexis de Suremain, Adi Jaya, Tola Thoeun and Bernard Cohen for assistance, Sheryl Paniec for showing me the nightlife and Muoy for her stories. Thanks also to Carla of *Showbox*, Amanda Bloom, Paul Mathew, Gevorg Babayan at *Envoy Hostel* and Warren at Mango Cambodia for their help. In Takeo, thank you Linda Meas, Paul Gill and Michael Sheppard, and in Kirirom, Bouchaib and Mr Mik. In Kampot and Kep, thanks to Jessica Rowe, Denise Ruygrok, Sara and Danny, John Black and John Watson for insightful chats, and to my drivers Ratha and Mr Blue. Massive thanks to Steve, Elliot and Gee at *Rainbow Lodge*, Anna at *4 Rivers* and Andrew at *Tatai Resort* for their hospitality, and Mr Rithy for Koh Kong advice. In Sihanoukville, my appreciation to Ana and Mick at Ana Travel and Soknay at Mottah Travel, Savin my driver, Henrik and Joel at *The Small Hotel* for local tips, Chantal at Relax Spa, and "Mama" Clare Shave. Thanks also to Adventure Adam on Koh Rong, Stephanie on Koh Rong Samloem, and Liam and family on Koh Ta Kiev. Finally, thanks to my co-author Gavin Thomas, editor Joe Staines, and everyone I met who made Cambodia so unforgettable.

Gavin Thomas In Cambodia, grateful thanks to: Ethan Crowley, Andrew Booth, Dany Toung, Mr Chhon, Bernard Cohen, and Robert and Morrison in Battambang. At Rough Guides, thanks to editor Joe Staines for stepping manfully into the breach, to Andy Turner and Helen Abramson for setting the ball rolling, and especially to fellow author (welcome to the fold) Meera Dattani for her enthusiasm, insights and assistance throughout. And of course to Allison, Laura, Jamie and Rosie for letting me wander, yet again, such a long way from home.

Readers' updates

Thanks to all the readers who have taken the time to write in with comments and suggestions (and apologies if we've inadvertently omitted or misspelt anyone's name):

Evgeny Bobrov; Frédéric De Rycke; John Garratt; Friedel Geeraert; Sarah Harris; Oliver Heard; Bronya James; Monica Mackaness; Jeff Waistell; Franziska Wellenzohn.

Photo credits

All photos © Rough Guides, except the following:
(Key: t-top; c-centre; b-bottom; l-left; r-right)

1 Alamy Stock Photo: Chris Bull
2 Getty Images: Pascal Deloche
4 Alamy Stock Photo: Gary Dublanko
6 AWL Images: Nigel Pavitt
8 Getty Images: Owen Franken
9 AWL Images: Hemis / Bertrand Gardel (t).
Dreamstime.com: Efired (b). **Getty Images:** imageBROKER RF / Guenter Fischer (c)
10 AWL Images: Ian Trower
11 123RF.com: Luciano Mortula (c). **Alamy Stock Photo:** Tom Vater (tl). **Getty Images:** Fairfax Media (b)
12 Alamy Stock Photo: Wendy Kay (tr). **Corbis:** Reuters / X01072 / Chor Sokunthea (tl). **Getty Images:** Grant Dixon (b)
13 Dreamstime.com: Toby Williams (t)
14 4 Rivers Floating Lodge: (t). **Alamy Stock Photo:** Kraig Lieb (b). **FLPA:** Thomas Marent (c)
15 Alamy Stock Photo: Michael Freeman (br); Hemis (bl). **Dreamstime.com:** Donyanedomam (tr)
16 Emma Boyle
18 Alamy Stock Photo: ADS
48–49 Getty Images: Pietro Scozzari
51 Robert Harding Picture Library: Matthew Williams-Ellis

73 123RF.com: jackmalipan (tl). **Getty Images:** Universal Images Group / JTB Photo (b). **SuperStock:** imageBROKER / Josef Beck (tr)
91 AWL Images: Travel Pix Collection (b). **Dreamstime.com:** Kelvintt (t)
107 Alamy Stock Photo: Neil Setchfield
121 Alamy Stock Photo: age fotostock (tr); Nick Ledger (b)
175 AWL Images: Shaun Egan (b).
iStockphoto.com: Mlenny (t)
229 Alamy Stock Photo: John Brown (b). **Corbis:** Kevin R. Morris (t)
242–243 Alamy Stock Photo: Jack Malipan Travel Photography
245 Dreamstime.com: Donyanedomam
261 Alamy Stock Photo: Pawel Bienkowski (t).
SuperStock: Bertrand Gardel (b)
281 Alamy Stock Photo: Jack Malipan Travel Photography (t). **Emma Boyle:** (b)
290 Latitude: TTL

Cover: *Monks at Bayon Temple, Angkor*
AWL Images: Matteo Colombo

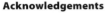

Index

Maps are marked in grey

Map symbols

The symbols below are used on maps throughout the book

✈ International airport	⊠ Gate/gopura	🐦 Nature reserve/biosphere	▩ Building
✗ Domestic airport	⛽ Fuel station	⬆ Border crossing	▢ Market
★ Transport stop	⊙ Statue/monument	🏠 Park HQ	⬭ Stadium
◆ Point of interest	⋀⋀ Mountain range	⚓ Dock	▢ Park
@ Internet access	▲ Mountain peak	⋯⋯ Road	▢ Beach
ⓘ Tourist information	◠ Cave	•=•=•= Unpaved road	▨ Swamp/ seasonally flooded area
⊠ Post office	🚿 Waterfall	▬▬▬ Railway	
🕐 Telephone office	⛩ Temple	═══ Disused railway	
⊞ Hospital	🏛 Monument	— — Ferry route	
⚲ Museum	🏯 Chinese temple	- - - Footpath	

Listings key

■ Accommodation

● Eating

■ Drinking and nightlife

● Shopping

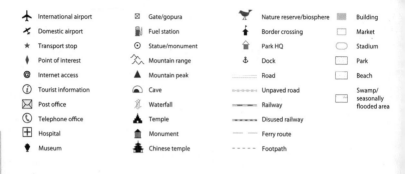